The History Of Malden, Massachusetts, 1633-1785

THE HISTORY OF MALDEN

THE

HISTORY OF MALDEN

𝔐𝔞𝔰𝔰𝔞𝔠𝔥𝔲𝔰𝔢𝔱𝔱𝔰

1633-1785

BY

DELORAINE PENDRE COREY

Lift we the twilight curtains of the Past,
And turning from familiar sight and sound,
Sadly and full of reverence let us cast
A glance upon Tradition's shadowy ground.
WHITTIER

MALDEN
PUBLISHED BY THE AUTHOR
1899

- Notice -

The foxing, or discoloration with age, characteristic of old books, sometimes shows through to some extent in reprints such as this, especially when the foxing is very severe in the original book. We feel that the contents of this book warrant its reissue despite these blemishes, and hope you will agree and read it with pleasure.

Copyright, 1898,
BY DELORAINE PENDRE COREY.

Facsimile Reprint

Published 1992 By

Heritage Books, Inc.
1540-E Pointer Ridge Place
Bowie, Maryland 20716
(301) 390-7709

ISBN 1-55613-562-9

University Press:
JOHN WILSON AND SON, CAMBRIDGE, U.S.A.

To My Wife

ISABELLA HOLDEN

AND TO

The Memory of our Son

ARTHUR DELORAINE COREY, Ph.D.

THESE PAGES ARE INSCRIBED

PREFACE.

THIS volume is the result of a careful collection and verification of facts and traditions extending over a period of more than forty-five years. It embraces the history of a New England town to the close of the Revolution — to a time when old customs and systems were disappearing and new forces in political, ecclesiastical, educational, and social affairs were springing into life. It is the story of an elder day and of a life in which much appears that is strange to a later age. If we read it aright we shall better understand our indebtedness to those generations whose labors and trials made possible the freedom and prosperity of the present; and we shall avoid that effusive worship of the fathers which is a fashion rather than the result of a knowledge of the true character of the past in its weaknesses and strength.

Materials for a history of the town during the succeeding period of transition and growth have been brought together and are abundant for the preparation of a companion volume, which, with a genealogical account of the old families of Malden, the present writer has in contemplation. In the meantime a regard to the uncertainties of life and a desire to place beyond the possibility of loss that which has been gathered of the earlier history have prompted the issue of the present volume.

I am especially indebted to the Massachusetts Historical Society and to the New England Historic Genealogical Society for the use of manuscript matter of much interest, particularly of material relating to the Wigglesworths.

Collections of papers made by the late James D. Green of Cambridge and the late Artemas Barrett of Melrose, the former of which is now in the library of the New England Historic Genealogical Society, have added much to my knowledge of important affairs, which would otherwise have been imperfect.

My acknowledgments are due to Albion H. Bicknell, Frank A. Bicknell, and Henry L. Moody for the pen-and-ink sketches of old houses and bits of scenery which are here reproduced.

I have indicated authorities with care, a practice the absence of which in most local, and many general, histories is to be deplored. Where the sources of information are obvious, as in extracts from the town and parish or church records, references have not been given.

The difference between Old Style and New Style is so generally understood that an explanation here is needless. The chronology followed is always that of the records, which is Old Style to September 13, 1752, inclusive.

It may be understood from a statement made on page 80 that a settlement on Mystic Side before the close of 1640 is conjectural. That is not correct, as John Greenland had " halfe built his house " during that year, and others appear with him. The statement should be made to apply before the beginning of the year and not before its close.

D. P. C.

October, 1898.

CONTENTS.

CHAPTER I.

OLD MALDON.

CHAPTER II.

DISCOVERERS AND INDIANS.

CHAPTER III.

ALLOTMENTS AND SETTLEMENT.

CHAPTER IV.

CHURCH AND TOWN.

CHAPTER X.

PIONEERS, SOLDIERS, AND WITCHCRAFT.

CHAPTER XI.

TOWN OFFICERS AND COMMON LANDS.

CHAPTER XII.

POVERTY AND SLAVERY.

CHAPTER XIII.

HIGHWAYS AND BRIDGES.

CHAPTER XIV.

DAVID PARSONS AND JOSEPH EMERSON.

CHAPTER XV.

CHARLESTOWN NEIGHBORS AND TROUBLE.

CHAPTER XVI.

THE SOUTH PRECINCT.

CHAPTER XVII.

THE SOUTH PRECINCT DECADENT.

CHAPTER XVIII.

THE TOWN SCHOOL.

CHAPTER XXIII.

MALDEN IN THE NAVY OF THE REVOLUTION.

CHAPTER XXIV.

SOLDIERS AND SAILORS.

APPENDIX.

ILLUSTRATIONS.

———•———

FACSIMILES OF TITLE PAGES.

AUTOGRAPHS.

CHAPTER I.

OLD MALDON.

O N the eastern coast of England, where the rivers Chelmer and Blackwater unite, a narrow inlet of the German Sea enters the land. In the early British days, along its shores was the land of the Trinobantes, now the modern county of Essex; and upon a pleasant sloping acclivity on its southern bank a British chief, called by the courtesy of history a king, had fixed his seat. The unfamiliar name of Cynobelin, son of Tenuantius, is only one in a roll of barbarian kings; but the life-giving touch of Shakspere has brightened it with eternal youth as Cymbeline, the father of Imogen.

The tide of the invasion of Julius Cæsar had left in its reflux, as drift upon the shore, many remains of the arts and manners of Latin civilization; and the use of coined money and the worship of the god Camulus — the Italian Mars — attested the enlightenment and progress of the British king. From this god the royal city of the Trinobantes took, in a Roman form, the name of Camalodunum — the hill of Camulus — which was modified in the British tongue to that of Camelot. How the blossoms and fragrance of poetry and romance gather around that name! All the tenderness, and bravery, and glory of the old Arthurian legends cling to it; for here, with all the state of one whose existence was half unreal and all romantic, King Arthur, in the unfixed and shadowy time of his realm, held his mystic court. The picture that we all know in our hearts so well, and which is all English, is as real to-day, though the many towers have passed away, as when Lancelot loved and Guinevere was fair.

> On either side the river lie
> Long fields of barley and of rye,
> That clothe the wold and meet the sky;
> And through the field the road runs by
>   To many-towered Camelot;
> And up and down the people go,
> Gazing where the lilies blow
> Round an island there below,
>   The island of Shalott.[1]

When Cymbeline had passed away, the Emperor Claudius in completing the reduction of Britain, which his generals had nearly achieved, placed a strong colony of his veterans in Camelot; and thenceforth the south-eastern portion of the island, dominated by the garrison of Camalodunum, became a province of the Roman empire.[2]

Less than ten years of prosperity, of fancied security, and of cruel tyranny over the Britons did the first and chief colony of Rome enjoy; for in the year A.D. 62,

The image of the Goddess of Victory at Camalodunum, without any visible cause, dropped down, and in the fall turned downward, as if it yielded to the enemy. Several women in ecstasies of frenzy foretold impending ruin. Strange noises were heard in the court; and a wild howling in the theatre, and a strange apparition in the arm of the sea,

---

[1] Tennyson, *Lady of Shalott.*   [2] Tacitus, *Annals,* xii. (32).

plainly signified the subversion of that colony. Moreover the sea looked bloody; and in the ebb dead men's bodies were left upon the shore.[3]

These signs were the precursors of evil; and in a short time after, the Britons under Boadicea, queen of the Iceni, who had in her own person endured the insults and cruelty of the Romans, fell upon the colony and routed with a great slaughter the ninth legion, which had come to its assistance. The town was destroyed and seventy thousand Romans and allies were killed in the general insurrection which followed.[4]

Although the place was rebuilt, its consequence was lost; and for a period of more than eight hundred years its name cannot be found. We only know that, passing from Camelot through its Roman form of Camalodunum, it came to be called, in the tongue of the Saxons, Maeldune, from a cross, say some, which stood upon the hill — *Mael*, a cross, and *dune*, a hill. Some writers, however, see in the new name only a Saxon shortening of the Latin word; as Camden, that rare old antiquary of the seventeenth century, who, taking away the first and last syllables of *Camalodunum*, found *Malodun* — Maeldune, Maldon, like the statue in the rough rock, waiting to spring into existence.

Near by, on the banks of the Blackwater, formerly the Panta and afterwards the Froshwell, stood the Saxon town of Ithancester, where in 653 Saint Ceada baptized the pagans of Essex into the religion of Christ. Not more completely than the town itself have saint and converts passed away. So utterly has it disappeared that an old writer supposed it to have been "swallowed up in the river Pant."[5]

Hitherto all is vague and uncertain that relates to the Maldon which now began to emerge from the obscurity of remote time. Even its existence as a British and Roman town has been denied; and to a rival colony, the modern Colchester, its honors have been transferred. However, good and true men, both of the elder and later generations of antiquaries, hold fast

---

[3] Tacitus, *Annals*, xiv. (32).
[4] Ibid.
[5] Ralph Niger, quoted in Camden, *Britannia* (1695), 344.

to the Camelot of the Britons and the Roman Camalodunum as the predecessors of the Saxon Maeldune and the Maldon of to-day. Henceforward, both among Saxons and Normans, it becomes a material thing; and, though romance and poetry may still cling to it, no veil of doubt can be thrown over its entity.

The first fact in the established history of Maldon is that Edward the Elder, while in the field against the Danes, who had subdued and occupied East Anglia and the surrounding districts, encamped there in 913, " whilst the fortress at Witham was wrought and built, and a good part of the people who were before under the dominion of the Danishmen submitted to him." [6] Four years later he rebuilt the town, and, raising a castle, furnished it with a garrison of soldiers.[7] In 918 the Danes besieged it, and Edward came again " and drove them from before that town, and slew many thousands of them as they fled." [8]

Once more did the spirit of poetry invest with its beauty the shores of Maldon; and the death of a Saxon hero gave birth to a contemporary poem which, imperfect and mutilated as it has come to us, is one of the pearls of Old English poetry. In this old song of *Byrhtnoth's Death* the story of the battle of Maldon and the defeat of the Saxons is told with great dramatic force and deep earnestness.

Under the brothers Justin and Guthmund the Northmen in 991 made another victorious descent upon the shores of East Anglia. This band, which appears to have been composed of followers of the celebrated Christian sea-king Olaf Tryggvesson of Norway, who seems to have accompanied them, attacked and destroyed Gipeswic (Ipswich) and overran the coast of Essex to Maldon. Here their ships lay in the river and their troops were gathered together on the promontory between the Blackwater and the Chelmer. Opposed to them upon the northern shore was the Earldorman Byrhtnoth with his East Saxons; and a bridge which crossed the river between them,

[6] *The Anglo-Saxon Chronicle, in loco.*   [8] Matthew of Westminster, *Flowers*
[7] Roger of Wendover, *Flowers of His-   of History* (Bohn), i. 464.
tory* (Bohn), i. 242.

the mediæval successor of which still remains, was defended by three Saxon champions, whose feat recalls the story of the Roman Horatius and his companions. "We will give you for tribute," shouted the old Earldorman, "our weapons for gifts, the poisoned points of our spears, our old swords, and the weight of our descending arms." He dared the vikings to meet the Saxons hand to hand, and gave them space upon the shore that they might cross the river and form without opposition. In the battle which followed, the Saxons were defeated with a great slaughter. As the old hero lay dying, surrounded by his hearth-company, who fought around him as the Greeks over the body of Patroklos, he prayed: "Thanks, Thou Ruler of Men, for the joys of the world and my life. Now need I, Maker of All, that Thou makest my spirit to pass to Thee, into Thy kingdom, O King of Souls." Said his old companion, Byrhtwold, as he fought above him: "My days have been many. By my Earl, the loved warrior, will I lay me down and go away no more."[9] Under the great tower of Ely, England's most stately cathedral, the headless body of Byrhtnoth rested nearly eight hundred years; and the loving hand of his wife Æthelflæd wrought the story of his death on a tapestry which rivalled the famous work of Queen Matilda at Bayeux.

In vain was the death of Byrhtnoth, and in vain did others like him stand against the arms of the Northmen. Retreating to their ships when hard pressed, the invaders quickly transferred themselves to unprotected points and soon overcame the eastern coasts. Æthelred the Unready sat in the seat of Ælfred and Edward; and a heavy tribute, paid by the advice of Sigeric, Archbishop of Canterbury, stayed for a while the course of the victorious vikings, and encouraged them to greater ravages a year or two later. From this unfortunate tribute sprang the Dane-geld, or Dane-money, a burdensome tax which oppressed the nation many years until it was finally abolished by Stephen in 1136, long after the Danes had retired or been absorbed into

[9] Cf. Ten Brink, *Early English Literature*, 93–96. The original Old-English text of the fragment which survives is printed in Thorpe, *Analecta Anglo-Saxonica*, 131; and a modern English translation is given in Conybeare, *Illustrations of Anglo-Saxon Poetry*, xc.

the English people. Near Maldon, on its western side, are
traces of a fortification or camp which has been considered as
Roman, Saxon, or Danish, as authorities differed. It covered
about twenty-two acres. In the middle of the last century
three sides were still visible; but already it had begun to be
defaced.[10] The traces which still exist are growing less distinct
and will finally be obliterated.

After so many varied seasons of peace and war under the
conflicting rule of the four nations which successively occupied
it, Maldon found a long period of repose; and its people built
churches and abbeys, founded a public library and schools,
lived by trade and the fisheries, which extended twenty miles
along the coast, and in their prosperity enjoyed their famous
Wallfleet oysters, which were found in profusion in the waters
of their bay.

Before the Norman Conquest the Saxon Ingelric, the father
of William the Conqueror's beautiful Ingelrica de Peverell,
founded Saint Mary's Church, now known from its situation as
the Lower Church. The building of the Saxons has disappeared, but much remains of that of the Normans in the
heavy buttresses and the chancel arch, which still keep their
places amid later work. The massive Norman tower fell in the
seventeenth century. It was rebuilt of red brick at a time when
from the neighborhood was taking place that removal which
carried the name of Maldon into the wilderness of New England. An hexagonal lantern which remains upon the tower was
for many years a beacon for sailors. The church itself was
restored in 1886 at a cost of about fifteen thousand dollars. Of
several ancient brasses and slabs which formerly existed in this
church, but one, that of John Fenne, 1486, now remains.

In 1056 — ten years before the coming of William the Conqueror, at which time Maldon contained " one hundred and
eighty houses, held by the Burgesses, and eighteen mansions
laid waste," [11] — was built the church of All Saints, with its
chancel, nave, and aisles, and a curious triangular tower. It

---

[10] Morant, *History of Essex* (1768).   [11] *Domesday*, cited by Camden, *Britannia* (1695), 349.

was carefully restored in 1867, and some recent additions have been made.[12] Time and the deeds of men have fallen heavily upon this church, which still shows many traces of its former beauty. It is said that a "lamentable destruction of monuments has taken place in this once magnificent church, since the beginning of the seventeenth century." Numerous ancient brasses have entirely disappeared; and of all the costly monuments which filled the spacious D'Arcy chapel but one remains.

In All Saints might formerly be read this inscription: "Hereunder lieth the Body of John Pratt, late one of the Aldermen of this Borough Town of Maldon. Ob. 30 July, 1619."[13] This has a familiar sound; and not only in name, but by the closer tie of relationship may this John Pratt of Essex have been connected with the Maldon in Massachusetts Bay; for Richard Pratt, who became an early settler at Mystic Side, was, it is said, the youngest son of John Pratt of Maldon, where he was baptized, June 29, 1615.[14]

Besides the churches named there was another — that of Saint Peter's, an ancient house, of which the tower alone

[12] Edward Bright, a shopkeeper, was buried in this church in 1750. His case was so remarkable that it was thought to deserve a place in the *Philosophical Transactions*, xlvii. 188; and a print was taken of him which may sometimes be found in the collections of antiquaries. "The body was drawn to the church in a carriage upon rollers, and lowered into the vault by means of a triangle and pulleys.

"He was a man so extremely fat, and of such an uncommon bulk and weight, that there are very few, if any, such instances to be found in any country or upon record in any books. At the age of 12 years and a half he weighed 10 stones and 4 pounds horseman's weight, i. e. 144 pounds. He increased in bulk as he grew up, so that in seven years more he weighed 336 pounds. He went on increasing, and probably in pretty near the same proportion: For the last time he was weighed, which was about thirteen months before he dyed, his neat weight was 41 stones and ten pounds, or 584 pounds. At the time of his death

as he was manifestly grown bigger since the last weighing, if we take the same proportion by which he had increased for many years upon an average, viz. of about 2 stones a year, and only allow four pounds addition for last year, on account of his moving about but very little, this will bring him to 44 stones or 616 pounds neat weight. — As to his measure he was 5 feet 9 inches and a half high. His body round the chest just under the arms measured 5 feet 6 inches, and round the belly 6 feet 11 inches. His arm in the middle of it was 2 feet 2 inches about, and his leg 2 feet 8 inches. After his death seven men were buttoned in his westcoat without breaking a stitch or straining a button. He dyed 10 November 1750, aged 29." Morant, *History of Essex*, i. 338.

[13] Salmon, *History of Essex*, 424.

[14] Savage, *Genealogical Dictionary*, iii. 475; Wyman, *Genealogies and Estates of Charlestown*, 770. The authority for this statement has as yet escaped my search.

remains. The building itself, being in a ruinous condition, was demolished many years ago. The parish once connected with it still exists, being joined with that of All Saints.

Near the town stood the Abbey of Belcigh, a foundation of the monks of the Premonstratensian Order. Of the house built by Robert Mantell in 1180 no traces remain; but a few rooms of a later house still exist in a picturesque cluster of mediæval buildings which stands upon the bank of the Chelmer, the only monument of its monks, who were suppressed, and whose lands were taken away at the dissolution of the monasteries in the sixteenth century. A portion of these remains is supposed to date from the first quarter of the thirteenth century.

South-west of the town was the Hospital of Saint Giles, a royal foundation for lepers of an ancient and obscure date. The materials of its building show traces of a Roman origin. In the last century, in common with many monuments of the olden time, it descended to base uses and became a barn, for the purposes of which it was still used in 1894, although it had become somewhat dilapidated. There was also in Maldon a Priory of Carmelite Friars, dating from 1292. The building has disappeared as utterly as its inmates; but the garden wall remained a few years ago — perhaps remains to-day. Of this convent the learned Thomas Maldon, a native of this town, who had been Professor of Divinity at Cambridge, was prior at the time of his death in 1404.

On the site of the fallen nave of Saint Peter's, Dr. Thomas Plume, a native of Maldon and a learned man, built a brick building just before his death in 1704, which he presented to the town for the purposes of a free grammar school. In this building, from which the school has been removed within a few years, is preserved his library, which he gave to the town at his death, with a fund for its support and enlargement.

Writing in the opening years of the seventeenth century, Camden, the father of antiquaries, says of Maldon: —

At present, for largeness and store of inhabitants, it is justly reckoned among the chief towns of this county, and is called by the lawyers the Borough of Maldon. It is a pretty convenient station, and for its bigness populous enough; being one long street, reaching for a mile together.[15]

It appears that the abbey was already in ruins, and Saint Peter's had disappeared by the middle of that century; for Dr. Holland, who visited Maldon about that time, and who seems to have taken a peevish dislike to the place, wrote as follows :

Upon the ridge of an hill answerable to the termination of Dunum, which signified an hilly and high situation, wherein I saw nothing memorable, unless I should mention two silly Churches, a desolate place of White-Friers, and a small pile of Brick, built not long since by R. Darcy, which name hath been respective hereabout.[16]

In its present aspect, Maldon retains many of the features which were familiar to that little band of pilgrims who, about the first of April, 1638, sailed down the river in an " Ipswich Hye." [17] Its single main street, running about a mile east and west, and now intersected by several cross streets, its venerable churches and halls, the ebbing and flowing river washing its ancient wharves, the green fields around, and all those kindly influences which have made Essex the garden of England, were often remembered by wistful hearts in New England.

Formerly the houses in Maldon were generally ancient; but in the early part of this century a considerable change in the appearance of the town was effected by the erection of many modern buildings; and the more recent growth of the place has tended still farther to destroy or hide the Maldon of the seventeenth century.

Besides the established churches already named, there are several places of worship belonging to Dissenters. The Maldon Congregational Church was founded in 1688, and had in 1894 a house with sittings for nine hundred and fifty persons. Beside this, there are chapels of Baptists, Brethren, Primitive Methodists, Wesleyan Methodists, and Catholics, a Society of Friends, and a meeting of Christadelphians.

---

[15] Camden, *Britannia* (ed. 1695), 349.

[16] Holland in additions to Camden, *Britannia* (1695), 349.

[17] "Transported from Malden in the County of Essex to London in an Ipsw^ch Hye." *Deposition* of Joseph Hills, Lechford, *Note Book*, 91. A hoy is a small sloop-rigged vessel used for carrying passengers and goods along the sea-coast.

Quite a growth in the population and trade of Maldon has taken place within the century, at the beginning of which the three parishes comprising the borough contained twenty-four hundred and twenty-eight persons. In 1881 the population had increased to fifty-four hundred and sixty-eight; but it has since shown a slight reduction to fifty-three hundred and eighty-three in 1894. The trade of Maldon is principally connected with its manufactures of crystallized salt, iron, bricks, and beer. There is a custom-house, and shipping is carried on to some extent. Eleven hundred and thirty-nine vessels, of sixty-seven thousand one hundred and sixty-one tons, entered the port in 1872.

Not far from All Saints is the ancient D'Arcy Tower, which was given to the town, in 1440, by Sir Robert D'Arcy for a Moot or Town Hall. Here has been the centre of the political life of the borough for more than four hundred and fifty years; and upon the walls of the Council Chamber hang the fourteen charters which remain to attest to the independence of the Borough of Maldon, the oldest of which — an Inspeximus — bears the date of 1290. The older charter of Henry the Second has disappeared, although it was in the chest of the corporation in 1816.

Maldon was a borough at the time of the Conquest and its corporate existence must have begun under Saxon rule; but it received its first recorded charter from Henry the Second, 1154–89. This charter was obtained by the petition of William de Mandeville, Earl of Essex, who owned lands at Maldon; and it confirmed, if it did not create, a free borough, free from all service except that of finding one ship for the royal use, when necessary, for the space of forty days. The burgesses were empowered to hold " for ever free and quiet with sac and soc, tol and team, nam and infangthef, graff, hamsoc and blowyte, fythwyte and grethbreg, ordell and orestall and flemenesfret, . . . by the service of free burgage; " and they were granted to " be quit of murder, of danegelt, of carriage, of summage, of scutage, of tallage, of stallage, of lastage and of all toll."

Queen Mary, of bloody memory, gave a second charter in

1553, which was forfeited in 1768; and the borough remained in abeyance until 1810, when the present charter was granted. The corporation now consists of a mayor, deputy mayor, four aldermen, and twelve councillors. The deputy mayor is a councillor.

The ancient and somewhat singular custom of Borough English, by which the youngest son — instead of the eldest as in other parts of England — inherits lands held in socage and other burghal rights at the death of the father, prevails here. Socage, or the holding of lands by certain and determinate service, was originally peculiar to the Anglo-Danish districts, but became the tenure by which realty is generally held in England.

Besides its municipal capacity as a borough, Maldon, with an additional area and an increased population from its immediate

vicinity, is a parliamentary borough, having from 1329 to 1867 returned two members to Parliament. In the latter year the representation was reduced to one; and in 1884, the borough, by a readjustment, was included for parliamentary purposes in the Eastern or Maldon Division of Essex. Formerly, the elections in this borough were hotly contested. That of 1826, it is said, lasted fifteen days, and nearly two hundred and fifty thousand dollars were expended by the opposing parties. My authority says: " In later days the elections have been shorter, often sharper, and hardly less expensive." [18]

The ancient shield of the borough — azure, three lions pas-

18 Fitch, *Maldon and the River* am indebted for several interesting *Blackwater*, 17. To this authority I particulars.

sant reguardant, or — appears upon the town and city seals of the Massachusetts Malden.

Out of this ancient Maldon came in 1638 Joseph Hills, a woollen-draper, and with him, or a little later, John Wayte, who married his daughter Mary. In the same year and in the same month of April came Thomas Ruck, going like Hills to London from Maldon in "an Ipswich Hye," but sailing to New England, where he arrived in July, in a different ship, — the "Castle." These men became early holders of land in the vicinity of Wayte's Mount on Mystic Side, and Richard Pratt settled in the vicinity of the South River. It is probable that they brought to New England the later name of the Camelot of the Britons. The misuse of many years, by substituting Malden for Maldon, has permanently fixed the incorrect form of the name which we now use.

CHAPTER II.

DISCOVERERS AND INDIANS.

ON June 24, 1497, John and Sebastian Cabot, Venetian adventurers holding a patent from Henry the Seventh of England, discovered the continent of America; and during the succeeding year the latter sailed along its shores from Labrador to Virginia. On this early discovery, the English government, in a vague way, founded its claim to the North American coast from the Gulf of Mexico to the icy cliffs of the northern sea, — although nearly a century elapsed before Sir Humphrey Gilbert asserted, at Newfoundland, its authority over a motley gathering of fishermen and adventurers of all nations. In the meanwhile, the French, Spanish, and Portuguese had explored, fished, and traded along the coast at many points, and the former had made actual settlements. After the early death of Gilbert, his half-brother, Sir Walter Ralegh, sought and obtained a patent from Elizabeth and established an unfortunate and short-lived colony upon the island of Roanoke.

At the beginning of the seventeenth century, with the exception of the fishing station at Newfoundland, which had now continued more than three-quarters of a century, "not a single
European family" existed north of the Spanish settlements in
Mexico;[1] and a recent writer remarks that "Colonization had
been virtually abandoned in despair."[2] A brief attempt at settlement, which deserved success, was soon after made at Cutty-
hunk, the westernmost of the Elizabeth Islands, by Bartholomew
Gosnold, with the approval of Ralegh and under the patronage
of Shakspere's friend, the Earl of Southampton; and though it
early proved a failure, it doubtless had a strong influence in
the formation of the London and Plymouth Companies, to
whom was granted, in 1606, the country between the thirty-
fourth and forty-fifth degrees of north latitude. To the latter
was allotted the northern portion of this territory from the
forty-first to the forty-fifth degrees, covering the coasts of New
England and Nova Scotia, with a right in common with its sister
company extending to the southern line of Maryland. While
the southern company met with some success upon the banks
of the James River, the operations of the Plymouth Company
produced no result of importance. A feeble colony on the
Kennebec merits little notice either from the character of its
members or the work which they accomplished; but its failure
retarded English colonization for more than twelve years.
Meanwhile, the French made fresh settlements upon the coast
of Nova Scotia and Maine and took formal possession of the
country, to which they gave the name of Acadie, from the
fortieth to the forty-sixth degrees of latitude; and the Dutch
founded the dynasty of the Knickerbockers at the mouth of the
Hudson. These rival settlements were hindrances and annoyances to the English for many years; and those of the French
were sources of almost ceaseless negotiations and a series of
disastrous wars which lasted more than one hundred and fifty
years.

At length, in 1620, the old charter having passed into desuetude, a new company was formed, of which the Earl of Warwick

---

[1] Holmes, *Annals of America*, i. 123.   [2] Haven, in *Early History of Massachusetts*, 140.

and Sir Ferdinando Gorges were the most prominent members. This company, which was styled "The Council established at Plymouth, in the County of Devon, for the planting, ruling, ordering, and governing of New England in America," was vested with absolute authority over the regions extending from Delaware Bay to Newfoundland and westward over unknown countries to the great South Sea. From beginning to end its efforts were a series of failures, and it finally disappeared in a cloud of obscurity. It made numerous grants of its lands, of which those only which relate to our own immediate territory need be mentioned here.

The first of these was made to Robert Gorges, son of Sir Ferdinando Gorges, and conveyed " All that part of the mainland commonly called Messachusiac, on the north-east side of the Bay known by the name of Massachuset, together with all the shores along the sea for ten English miles in a strait line towards the north-east, and thirty miles into the mainland through all the breadth aforesaid."[3] This grant revived the old feudal tenure of personal service; for, while the lands were held by the earlier company " in free and common soccage," they were now conveyed to be held by the sword, " per *Gladium Comitatus*, that is to say, by finding four able men, conveniently armed or arrayed for the wars, to attend upon the Governor for any service within fourteen days after warning."[4] The grantee came to Massachusetts Bay to take possession of his land and seated himself for a while where Thomas Weston had previously attempted a settlement, at Wessagusset (Weymouth). This was a good way out of his proper bounds, but in a location which probably suited him better at the time. The Gorges family, father and sons, were not over-scrupulous at any time in helping themselves in season and out; and had Robert lived his occupancy might have become the foundation of a claim as lasting as that of his illustrious father. While he had settled outside of the limits of his patent, he by no means abandoned his claim thereto, for he leased or granted to John Oldham and John Dorrell

---

[3] Gorges, *Briefe Narration*, in *Maine Historical Coll.*, ii. 46.

[4] Ibid., ii. 45.

All the lands wthin Mattachusetts Bay betweene Charles River and Abousett [Saugus] River, Contain^d in lengt by a streight lyne 5 Myles vp the said Charles River into the maine land north west from the border of the s^d Bay including all Creekes and points by the way and 3 Myles in length from the mouth of the foresaid river of Abousett vp into the maine land vpon a streight lyne S : W : including all Creeks and points, and all the land in bredth and length betweene the foresaid Rivers, wth all p^{r}rogatives Ryall Mynes excepted.

This grant covered the lands of Mystic Side and was held to be valid by Oldham in 1629. How his claim was finally quieted is not known; but Governor Cradock suggested that he might be " p^{r}vented " by " causing some to take possession of the cheife pt thereof." [5]

The settlement at Wessagusset was of short duration. Gorges returned to England, where he soon after died; and his territorial rights finally passed by purchase and descent into the hands of Mary Lenthall, who married " Mr. Levett of the Inner Temple." [5] Her claim was also, in time, brought forward and disappeared like that of Oldham. Some of the members of the company of Gorges returned with their leader to England; and others removed to better locations around Massachusetts Bay, where we shall meet them again.

Under the date of March 24, 162$\frac{7}{8}$, the Council for New England granted to a company of Dorsetshire gentlemen a patent, the origin of which, as well as the limits of the territory which it was intended to convey, is involved in some uncertainty. If the bounds recited in the later charter are to be considered as those of this grant it extended from three miles south " of any or every part " of Charles River to a line three miles north of the river " called Monomack alias Merrymack, or to the northward of any and every part thereof," and stretched from the Atlantic to the Pacific Ocean. It covered the land which had been granted to Robert Gorges, portions of which were evidently occupied by his assigns or by some of those who had been with him at Wessagusset. There are indications that

[5] *Suffolk Deeds,* i. xiii.
[6] This was in 1691, while the new charter was being prepared. Hutchin-

son, *History of Massachusetts-Bay,* i. 6. Ed. 1760.

some deception was used in this matter and that the Earl of Warwick, whose influence was nearly at an end in a council where most of its members were Royalists, was inclined to make the most of his position for the benefit of his friends. That the grant was the work of the Puritan element is evident, and its results were not accepted by the other side. A readjustment of the affairs of the Council took place several years later, and the control passed into the hands of the Royalists. They repudiated the grant of Massachusetts Bay; and, finding their charter defective, they decided, in 1634/5, to surrender it. They parted the lands which it conveyed among themselves in eight parcels and petitioned the king for separate patents in accordance with the division which they had made. In this assignment that portion which had then become occupied by the colonies of Plymouth and Massachusetts Bay, with all the country from the Narraganset to Salem, was allotted to the unfortunate Marquis of Hamilton; but the whole matter was frustrated, and the Great Council for New England itself disappeared in the political troubles and the civil war which supervened. The only patent which came out of this dissolution was that to Sir Ferdinando Gorges, which conveyed a strip of land sixty miles wide along the coast of Maine from the Piscataqua to the Kennebec. From the southern limits of this territory to Salem the country was claimed by Captain John Mason under a deed of the Council which never received the royal assent. Suits at law to establish these grants came down into the eighteenth century.

Hutchinson says, "The patent, from the Council of Plimouth, gave a good right to the soil, but no powers of government."[7] To remedy this defect, and perhaps to prevent complications which might arise from former grants, a royal charter was obtained, March 4, 162⅞, and the good offices of the Earl of Warwick were again apparent. This charter, which confirmed the rights of the new company "by the name of the Governor and Company of the Mattachusetts Bay in New England, one body politique and corporate in deed, fact, and name," gave

[7] Hutchinson, *History of Massachusetts-Bay*, i. 9. Ed. 1760.

2

authority and full powers of government within the limits
already described. The territory thus granted was, as has been
stated, liberal in its extent from east to west and exceedingly
indefinite in its northern and southern bounds; for lines drawn
at stated distances from streams whose courses are as irregular
as those of the Merrimac and Charles may be fruitful sources of
controversy; and the settlement of its borders perplexed the
General Court of Massachusetts Bay for many years.

Primarily the corporation of the Governor and Company of
Massachusetts Bay was formed to secure the enjoyment of
religious freedom, or rather the free enjoyment of the peculiar
principles and practices of those who were to control the affairs
of the new colony. But no allusion is made to spiritual matters
in the charter; and it seems likely that, foreseeing that an open
avowal of their wishes and intentions might be disastrous, the
fathers of Massachusetts exercised that worldly wisdom which
many times thereafter showed itself in their dealings, and veiled
their ultimate design under the disguise of a producing and
trading corporation such as those unfortunate companies which
preceded them had attempted to be. It was as a mercantile
company that its grant and charter were obtained. It was only
by degrees and with wariness that its true intent was allowed to
appear, until it grew into a mixed hierarchy — a government of
elders and magistrates, absolute and uncompromising in everything that pertained to freedom of thought and life; and such
it continued to be during the colonial period, growing weaker,
however, as the democratic spirit of the people worked upward
and through the body politic.

Under the authority of the grant from the Council for New
England, and while negotiations for the royal charter were in
progress, John Endicott, a gentleman of Dorsetshire and one of
the original grantees, sailed in the ship "Abigail," Gauden, master, from the little harbor of Weymouth, with a small company,
and arrived at Naumkeag, September 6, 1628. Others had preceded him and were seated along the shore from Cape Ann to
Scituate. Among these were Roger Conant, Peter Palfrey, John
Balch, and John Woodbury at Naumkeag, the Mavericks at

Noddle's Island and Winnisimmet, Thomas Walford at Mishawum, David Thompson at Neponset or Thompson's Island, William Blackstone at Shawmut, and John Bursley and William Jeffrey at Wessagusset. Some of these had been followers of Robert Gorges and had scattered in favorable trading places around the Bay; others were single adventurers or perhaps agents for those who claimed lands by former grants. Besides these, "the mad Bacchanalian," Thomas Morton, was still at Merry-Mount, and a gathering of fishermen and traders had become a permanent settlement at Nantasket.

During the next spring, six vessels with a large company of new adventurers sailed from England. As the "Talbot" passed the Land's End and the hills of Cornwall began to sink into the sea, Francis Higginson, one of their ministers who was destined to fill an early grave in the new world, called the passengers upon deck, "to take their last sight of England," saying, "Farewell, dear England! Farewell, the Church of God in England, and all the Christian friends there!"[8] Often were those words echoed by anxious, loving hearts as they entered upon the untried perils of that sea which would forever after separate them from the dear old home. Often were they recalled in the loneliness and discouragements of the new life.

The new settlers arrived at the little town, which had been planted at Naumkeag and named Salem, in the early summer of 1629. Among them, "coming at their own cost," were three brothers, — Ralph, Richard, and William Sprague, sons of Edward Sprague of Upway in Dorsetshire. They remained not long at Salem; but during the summer "with three or four more, by joint consent and approbation of Mr. John Endicott, Governor," they undertook a journey of exploration, and passing westward were the first white men who are known to have viewed the country on the northerly side of the Mystic River. Their probable course may be traced along the Salem path, which we may believe already existed as an Indian trail. Crossing the Abousett at a ford, it ran over the Saugus plains and entered the present bounds of Malden at Black Ann's cor-

[8] Mather, *Magnalia,* iii. (2), ch. 1.

ner, where, probably, another path, turning southerly, led to
the Indian villages around Sagamore Hill and Powder Horn.
Skirting the Scadan hills, the Salem path turned to the north-
west over the little section of old road which remains near the
junction of Salem Street and Broadway, where the Jenkins
house, which disappeared in 1882, stood more than two centuries,[9] and passed between the hills nearly in the line of the
present Forest Street.   Winding around the northern and
western base of Wayte's Mount, known to the first settlers as
Mount Prospect, it crossed the Three Mile Brook by a ford a
short distance above the falls at Black Rock; and, running
along the southern foot of the Middlesex Fells, it passed over
the Medford plain and sought the Mystic ford.   In the vicinity
of the Three Mile Brook, the present Clifton Street is the
modern representative of the old Indian trail, although that small
portion of the way east of the brook, only, has had a continuous
existence since the early days.

Passing along the southern bank of the Mystic, the travellers
entered the peninsula of Mishawum, where they found Thomas
Walford, a smith and an unauthorized pioneer, living in an
"English palisadoed and thatched house," whom, with his wife,
the distrustful magistrates ejected two years later.   There, by
the "free consent" of Wonohaquaham, the Sagamore John of
"a gentle and good disposition," the Spragues with others settled soon after and laid the foundations of Charlestown.

They found the country over which they passed, on the northerly, or easterly, side of the Mystic, "generally full of stately
timber," and "round about was an uncouth wilderness." Of the
general condition of the land we are not without good evidence;
for William Wood, who very likely accompanied the Spragues,
for he was in New England in 1629 and tells us that "the end
of his travel was *observation*," and Francis Higginson, who,
though a sick man and unable to travel through the woods,

---

[9] This old house, otherwise known as
the Rand house, was partially destroyed
by fire on the evening of November 14,
1882.   It had long been in a dilapidated
condition, and was soon after demolished.   It was popularly supposed to
have been older than the town, and to
have been used as a garrison house;
but it was probably built towards the
latter part of the seventeenth century.

doubtless talked with them on their return, wrote of the country soon after; and their accounts, although written under the influence of the glamour which a new country often casts over men's perceptions, enable us to see the New England of 1629.[10]

The general appearance of the country was not entirely that of " an uncouth wilderness ; " for a pleasant feature which struck the early comers was the extended and frequent areas of open lands around the margins of the marshes and meadows and upon the plains, — lands ready for the plough and tillage without much labor. Higginson says that in one place might be seen " thousands of acres of ground as good as need to be and not a tree in the same ; "[11] and Thomas Graves, who saw with the eye of an educated traveller, wrote to his friends in England : —

It is very beautifull in open lands, mixed with goodly woods, and again open plaines, in some places five hundred acres, some places more, some lesse, not much troublesome for to cleere for the plough to goe in, no place barren, but on the tops of the hils ; the grasse and weedes grow up to a man's face, in the lowlands and by fresh rivers aboundance of grasse and large meddowes without any tree or shrubbe to hinder the sith.[12]

These open lands and natural hay-grounds were also noticed by Wood, who wrote as follows : —

The Soyle is for the generall a warme kind of earth, there being little cold-spewing land, no Morish Fennes, no Quagmires, the lowest grounds be the Marshes, over which every full and change the Sea flowes : these Marshes be rich ground, and bring plenty of Hay, of which the Cattle feed and like, as if they were fed with the best up-land Hay in *New*

[10] The main authorities for the condition of the country around Massachusetts Bay at the first coming of the English are Higginson's *Journal* and *New Englands Plantation ;* Dudley's *Letter to the Countess of Lincoln ;* and Wood's *New-Englands Prospect.* Useful reprints of the works of Higginson and Dudley, and a portion of that of Wood may be found in Young, *Chronicles of Massachusetts Bay,* with other papers of value to the student and of interest to the general reader. The later portion of Hutchinson, *History of Massachusetts-Bay,* i. ch. 6, is compact with information. Morton, *New English*

Canaan ; Josselyn, *New England's Rarities* and *Two Voyages to New-England ;* and Smith, *Description of New-England* and *Advertisements for the Unexperienced Planters,* may be consulted with advantage, as may most of the early writers upon New England.

Of recent writers, Palfrey, *History of New England,* i. ch. 1, contains a good *résumé ;* and on all matters relating to the early history of the country his volumes are to be preferred.

[11] *New-Englands Plantation* in Young, *Chronicles of Massachusetts Bay,* 244.

[12] *Mass. Hist. Coll.,* i. 124.

England; of which likewise there is great store which growes commonly betweene the Marshes and the Woods. This Medow ground lies higher than the Marshes, whereby it is freed from the over-flowing of the Seas ; and besides this, in many places where the Tres grow thinne, there is good fodder to be got amongst the Woods. There be likewise in divers places neare the plantations great broad Medowes, wherein grow neither shrub nor Tree, lying low, in which Plaines growes as much grasse, as may be throwne out with a Sithe, thicke and long, as high as a mans middle ; some as high as the shoulders, so that a good mower may cut three loads in a day.[14]

Wood's estimation of the marshes was not higher than that of the farmers for many years. Their peculiar yield of salt-hay was esteemed beyond its real value and was carefully gathered and prepared. As English grasses were gradually brought into the uplands the marsh and meadow crops grew to be of less importance, and are now considered as of no great worth, compared with the finer upland grasses, except as they add variety to the usual feed of the stable and the barn.

Thomas Morton, in his *New English Canaan*, thus accounts for the existence of the open lands : —

The Salvages are accustomed to set fire of the Country in all .places where they come, and to burne it twize a yeare, viz : at the Spring, and the fall of the leafe. The reason that mooves them to doe so, is because it would other wise be so overgrowne with underweedes that it would be all a coppice wood, and the people would not be able in any wise to passe through the Country out of a beaten path. And this custome of firing the Country is the meanes to make it passable ; and by that meanes the trees growe here and there as in our parks : and makes the Country very beautifull and commodious.[15]

This custom is also mentioned by Wood; and it was followed in some measure by the English until the country was comparatively well cleared. It is very evident that the open lands were characteristic of Mystic Side, especially in the southwestern part along the borders of the marshes of the Mystic and the North River. The earliest land evidences, made at a time when the original forests could not have been cleared to any great extent, indicate the existence of natural lea-lands ; and it was

---

[13] Wood, *New-Englands Prospect*, 10.   [14] Morton, *New English Canaan*, 52,
Ed. 1634.   54.

upon such a tract that the first allotment of lands, in 1634, was laid out.

The country was well watered by frequent ponds and streams; and the early settlers at Mystic Side found several great springs whose waters have continued to gush forth unto the present day. The best known of these were the North and South springs, to both of which free passage and common use were carefully reserved and guarded. Public rights to the North Spring are supposed to have lapsed years ago in some unknown way; but the ownership of the South, or Waters's, Spring remained intact until 1881, when the Selectmen of Everett relinquished to a corporation of water vendors that which had been a public benefit for two centuries and a half.[16]

The first comers, looking upon the surface of things and seeing only the immediate returns of a virgin soil, were profuse in their descriptions of the richness of the land and the variety and quality of its products; but the expectations of the early settlers failed, and the next generation found that the rich woodland soil soon became exhausted, and that manures and careful tillage were as necessary in Massachusetts Bay as in Surrey or Essex.

[16] The North Spring is still in existence near the railroad station at West Everett. It formerly supplied the water used at Baldwin's Dye House, and is now utilized by the manufacturers who occupy the ground. It is a collection rather than a single spring, and has of late years been carefully excavated and surrounded by masonry. The adjacent lands contain several good natural springs, and one which is often overflowed by the brackish tide-water exists upon an island far out upon the marsh.

The South Spring is mentioned by that name as early as 1638, and was situated at the present junction of Chelsea and Ferry Streets in Everett. With its bubbling basin of gravel and its little brooklet flowing across the low land, forming an easy and roomy drinking-place for cattle, and its accompanying clumps of gigantic willows, it was a romantic and pleasant place in former years. But it lost its ancient character in 1852, when Chelsea Street was widened and straightened, the willows felled, and the cattle-place filled up. All the beauty of the spot vanished in a dead level of gravel grandiloquently called a square; and the bubbling spring developed into an awkward pump, whose creaking crank was the delight of small boys and a "baby-waker" for the neighborhood. Previous to its "improvement" the spring was said to give an average flow of about four hundred and fifty gallons per hour, and its temperature was uniformly about forty-eight degrees Fahrenheit.

In its new character the spring discharged thousands of gallons by the medium of a chain-pump, to the great benefit of thirsty travellers; and many hogsheads of pure water were carried to the neighboring city of Chelsea, by peddlers and others, until it ceased to supply the public needs and was applied to private uses.

Higginson, who endeavored, as he says, "by God's help, to report nothing but the naked truth," and "what I have partly seen with mine own eyes, and partly heard and inquired from the mouths of very honest and religious persons," remarks: — "All about Masathulets Bay, and at Charles river is as fat black earth as can be seen anywhere," and "the fertility of the soil is to be admired at." The open lands brought forth in abundance grains and herbs; and the country abounded "naturally with store of roots of great variety and good to eat." [16] Wood, in his enumeration of the products of the ground, says: —

The ground affoards very good kitchen Gardens, for Turneps, Parsnips, Carrots, Radises, and Pumpions, Muskmillions, Squonterquashes, Coucumbers, Onyons, and whatsoever growes well in *England*, growes as well there, many things being better and larger: there is likewise growing all manner of Hearbes for meate, and medicine, and that not onely in planted Gardens, but in the Woods, without eyther the art or the helpe of man. [17]

Higginson adds "plenty of single damask roses [sweet briar,] very sweet," and excellent vines "up and down in the woods; " [18] and Graves writes about "the biggest grapes that ever I saw, some I have seene foure inches about." [19]   With the grapes are mentioned "mulberries, plums, raspberries, currants, chestnuts, filberts, walnuts, small-nuts, hurtleberries, and haws of white-thorn; " [20] and in the summer the fields were filled with strawberries of "exceeding sweetness."

Nor was the animal life less abundant than the products of the vegetable kingdom. The bays and harbors teemed with fish which filled the streams at certain times of the year; and the shores and flats yielded excellent shell-fish of many kinds. In the woods and fields, deer were common, [21] and smaller game

---

[16] Higginson, *New-Englands Plantation*, in Young, *Chronicles of Massachusetts Bay*, 243–246.

[17] Wood, *New-Englands Prospect*, 13.

[18] *New-Englands Plantation*, 247.

[19] *Mass. Hist. Coll.*, i. 124.

[20] *New-Englands Plantation*, 247.

[21] Deer were common in this vicinity until the middle of the eighteenth century, and were frequently seen afterward. One was started by hunters in the Malden woods in 1773, and chased across the Chelsea marshes to the Saugus River, into which he plunged. Lewis, *History of Lynn*, 337. An act was passed in 1739, "for the better preservation of dear within this province," under which Deer-reeves were annually chosen in Malden until 1792.

in great variety afforded a plentiful sustenance to the earlier settlers when their scanty supplies had failed. Great flocks of pigeons at one time "flew over all the towns" for hours, obscuring the light and causing even the sober Dudley to fancy a portent in the unfamiliar sight.[22] Partridges "as big as our hens," and great turkeys, "exceeding fat, sweet, and fleshy," were to be had for the shooting. Geese, ducks, and other sea-fowl abounded in their season, so that during the scarcity of the first year it was said "that a great part of winter the planters have eaten nothing but roast meat of divers fowls which they have killed."[23]

Wood speaks of the "three great annoyances, of wolves, rattle-snakes, and mosquitoes." The former were nightly visitors among the unprotected herds and flocks. In the time of deep snows they hung around the settlements in great packs, and their fierce barking was a terror to man as well as beast. They infested the Saugus woods as late as 1753 and were not entirely extirpated until many years after. Bounties were offered for their scalps, and the grisly trophies were sometimes nailed on the meeting-houses. "For Beares," says Wood, "they be common being a great blacke kind of Beare, which be most feirce in Strawberry time."[24] They are said to have been seen in Malden woods within this century, and they yet prowl along sequestered roads in the traditions of old families.[25]

Among "creeping beasts or longe creeples" the rattlesnake was especially noticed by early observers. Higginson says that they "will not fly from a man as others will, but will fly upon him and sting him so mortally that he will die within a quarter of an hour after."[26] John Josselyn mentions

[22] Dudley, *Letter to the Countess of Lincoln,* in Young, *Chronicles of Massachusetts Bay,* 336.

[23] *New-Englands Plantation,* 253.

[24] *New-Englands Prospect,* 19.

[25] In a rock in the Middlesex Fells, near where the corners of Malden and Melrose touch the Medford line, is a deep rift in the rock called *Bears' Den,* where tradition says a bear was killed in the early days of the present century. Brooks, *History of Medford,* 484, relates how, in 1735, "Sampson, a negro slave, was sorely frightened by a wild bear and cub, which he met in the woods near Gov. Cradock's house."

[26] *New-Englands Plantation,* 255. Cf. Morton, *New English Canaan,* 82.

The *Rattle Snake*, who poysons with a Vapour that comes thorough two crooked Fangs in their Mouth ; the hollow of these Fangs are as black as Ink : The *Indians*, when weary with travelling, will take them up with their bare hands, laying hold with one hand behind their Head, with the other taking hold of their Tail, and with their teeth tear off the Skin of their backs, and feed upon them alive ; which they say refresheth them.[27]

Higginson speaks of the lesser annoyances mentioned by Wood, as the "little flies called mosquitoes" which "are troublesome in the night season;" and Wood adds, "Many that be bitten will fall a scratching, whereupon their faces and hands swell."[28]

The climate does not appear to have materially changed since the advent of the English. Great snows are mentioned; and extremes of heat and cold, and droughts and seasons of excessive moisture were as frequent as of late years. One who wrote at a later period says : —

In New England, the transitions from heat to cold are short and sudden, and the extremes of both very sensible. We are sometimes

[27] *New-Englands Rarities Discovered,* 38–39. The Indians' manner of holding the reptiles, as described in the text, was practised by one of their descendants. John Elisha, a colored man of mixed blood, who claimed descent from the Natick Indians, resided among the hills in the north-eastern part of Malden about the year 1820. He used to catch rattlesnakes, which then abounded in the crevices of the ledges and among the angular stones which the frost had detached from the cliffs and strewn at the bases of the hills. He carried the captives home in his hands, holding them fast just below their heads, their tails being wreathed about his arms. When their fangs became hooked in a piece of stout woolen cloth, which he held for them to bite at, he would pull them out by a sudden jerk and render them harmless. If they did not bite at the cloth, he would open their mouths with a stick, as he pressed them to the ground, while an assistant would entangle their fangs in the cloth, and so extract them. Sometimes he held them down with a forked stick, and removed the fangs with pincers. The "creeples" thus treated he exhibited in Boston and elsewhere, on public occasions, as tamed snakes, which he could handle and carry in his bosom with impunity, to the astonishment of the spectators.

Besides the "taming" of snakes, he and his family did quite a business in the preparation of rattlesnake oil, which was sold about the country as a specific for rheumatic complaints and diseases of the joints. Fifty cents for a small bottle was considered cheap by the purchaser, and amply repaid the seller. Mrs. William Hogans, who will be remembered by many old inhabitants, was an itinerant saleswoman in that line, and added to her stock skunk's fat, and roots and herbs, which she procured as ordered. (*Information of* William B. Shedd.)

In 1809 four "large Rattlesnakes taken on the Malden Turnpike, poisontooth extracted," were exhibited at the Columbian Museum in Boston. *Boston Patriot,* 1809.

[28] *New-Englands Plantation,* 255; *New-Englands Prospect,* 46.

frying, and at others freezing; and as men often die at their labor in the field, by heat, so some in winter are froze to death with the cold.[29]

But to the early writers the climate seemed perfect in the first flush of their new-found joys. Graves declared that all the bounties which Nature spread before them were "made good and pleasant through this maine blessing of God, the healthfulnesse of the countrie which far exceedeth all parts that ever I have beene in;"[30] and Higginson, speaking from his own experience, exceeds Graves in his commendations, and adds that oft-repeated line, "A sup of New England's air is better than a whole draught of Old England's ale."[31]

---

[29] Macsparren, *America Dissected*, 11.

[30] *Mass. Hist. Coll.*, i. 124.

[31] *New-Englands Plantation*, 252. Francis Higginson, to whose description of New England reference is made, was educated at Cambridge, receiving the degree of A. B. at Jesus, 1609, and that of A. M. at St. John's, 1613; although Mather says he was of Emanuel. Having committed himself to the Puritan party, he was excluded from his pulpit at Claybrooke, in Leicester, and was soon after invited by the Company of the Massachusetts Bay to go to their new plantation at Naumkeag, where he arrived early in the summer of 1629, and was ordained August 6 of that year. He lived but twelve months longer, and his case has much in common with many others which occurred in the early days of the settlements. He was both sickly and enthusiastic. That he was the latter, his exaggerated description of New England amply proves. That he had been troubled with long continued ails, he himself informs us. "I have for divers years past been very sickly," he tells us in his journal. Young, *Chronicles of Massachusetts Bay*, 236.

When he had passed but a few summer weeks in the new land, he wrote: "The temper of the air of New-England is one special thing that commends this place. Experience doth manifest that there is hardly a more healthful place to be found in the world that agreeth better with our English bodies. Many that have been weak and sickly in Old England, by coming hither have been thoroughly healed, and grown healthful and strong. For here is an extraordinary clear and dry air, that is of a most healing nature to all such as are of a cold, melancholy, phlegmatic, rheumatic temper of body. None can more truly speak hereof by their own experience than myself. My friends that knew me can well tell how very sickly I have been, and continually in physic, being much troubled with a tormenting pain through an extraordinary weakness of my stomach, and abundance of melancholic humors. But since I came hither on this voyage, I thank God I have had perfect health, and freed from pain and vomiting, having a stomach to digest the hardest and coarsest fare, who before could not eat finest meat; and whereas my stomach could only digest and did require such drink as was both strong and stale, now I can and do oftentimes drink New-England water very well. And I that have not gone without a cap for many years together, neither durst leave off the same, have now cast away my cap, and do wear none at all in the day time; and whereas beforetime I clothed myself with double clothes and thick waistcoats to keep me warm, even in the summer time, I do now go as thin clad as any, only wearing a light stuff cassock upon my shirt, and stuff breeches of one thickness without linings. . . . I think it is a wise course

It is not surprising that, with all these exaggerated excellencies of climate and soil, New England became to the English Puritans a veritable Canaan, a land overflowing with milk and honey, where they might rest secure in the shadow of their own vines and fig trees. And the political condition of England and the dangers which surrounded them there, were added incentives for removal. In 1637, eight years after the arrival of the Spragues, the English population of New England is supposed to have approached twelve thousand souls.

Thomas Dudley was of a less enthusiastic mind, or he saw with a clearer vision than did his companions; for he wrote to Bridget, Countess of Lincoln: "Honest men, out of a desire to draw over others to them, wrote somewhat hyperbolically of many things here." [32] A woman, who longed, I suspect, for the green hedges and old homes of England, wrote a few years later: —

When I remember the high commendations some have given of the place, and find it inferior to the reports, I have thought the reason thereof to be this, that they wrote surely in strawberry time. The air of the country is sharp, the rocks many, the trees innumerable, the grass little, the winter cold, the summer hot, the gnats in summer biting, the wolves at midnight howling. Look upon it, as it hath the means of grace, and, if you please, you may call it a Canaan.[33]

The exaggerations of the first comers, with other causes, added to the tide of immigration, which was very much

for all cold complexions to come to take physic in New-England." *New-Englands Plantation*, 251–252.

Poor fellow! he had experienced the bracing effects of a not unpleasant sea-voyage, and fondly thought that the "extraordinary clear and dry air" of New England had done in a few weeks that which came from the healthy air of the sea. He had yet to meet the untried rigors of an exceeding hard winter; and in the privations and severities of that season, amid the suffering, disease, and death which ensued, the delusive promise of health and strength departed, and "the hectic attacked him, which was to close his earthly career."

He lingered until August, 1630, when, in the words of Cotton Mather, "in the midst of many prayers, he fell asleep, in the forty-third year of his age."

He had seen the new world in a rosy light, and the messages which he sent back to England were colored by his desires and hopes. Sharp and bitter was the truth which to him and many who followed him came too late.

A memoir of Higginson, by the late Rev. Joseph B. Felt, is in *N. E. Hist. and Geneal. Register*, vi. 105–127.

[32] Dudley's letter, in Young, *Chronicles of Massachusetts Bay*, 324.

[33] Hutchinson, *History of Massachusetts-Bay*, i. 483. Ed. 1760.

increased in 1630, and Cambridge, Boston, Dorchester, and other places received their first inhabitants. The disappointments and sufferings of those who were not well prepared to meet the hardships and dangers of a pioneer's life were, no doubt, as strongly set forth to their friends in England as had been the attractions and advantages of the country before. As a consequence, in part, immigration nearly ceased, and some returned to England. But after a year or two ship after ship continued to arrive in the harbors of Salem and Boston; and growing communities of sturdy Puritans attested at once the troubles which had befallen the mother land, and the permanence of the refuge which Providence had opened upon the bleak shores of Massachusetts Bay. A new empire had been founded; and upon a narrow strip of country, between unknown forests and the barren sands and sombre rocks of an unkind coast, a handful of earnest men and women, in the language of the time, " chosen vessels " and " precious seed," began to work out that problem of freedom which forecasts the coming Glory of the Ages. From the green lanes and ancient towns of Essex, full of the traditions and associations of a thousand years, to the tangled forests and the wild shores of a new world; from the old English homes to the land which God had prepared for the chosen seed whose fruitage was to be a great nation, — these are to us of the nineteenth century but the turning of a leaf; but to the men and women of 1628 a stormy waste of waters and many weeks of anxiety and distress, of weeping and praying, lay between the homes of their childhood and the unknown land where they were to watch and work and lay their bones to rest.

In the year 1614 Captain John Smith, observing the shores of Massachusetts Bay, remarked that " the sea Coast as you passe shewes you all a long large Corne fields, and great troupes of well proportioned people." [31] It may be that the redoubtable champion and bearer of "three Turks heads, which with his sword, he did overcome, kill, and cut off," indulged somewhat in the exaggeration to which he was prone; but the

---

[31] Smith, *Generall Historie,* ii. 194. Ed. 1819.

corroborating testimony of other writers renders it certain that around the mouths of the Charles and the Mystic and along the shores and upon the islands of Boston harbor were gathered many villages of the aborigines.   Hubbard mentions this section as "the general rendezvous of all the Indians;"[85] and Hutchinson says, " That circle which now makes the harbors of Boston and Charlestown, round by Malden, Chelsea, Nantasket, Hingham, Weymouth, Braintree and Dorchester, was the capital of a great sachem, much reverenced by all the plantations of Indians round about."[86]   South of the Charles, among and around the Blue Hills, were the Massachusetts; and northward, extending to the Piscataqua and Penacook, were the Pawtuckets, an extensive and once powerful tribe, a portion of whose domain we occupy.

At the dawn of authentic history the latter tribe, or rather combination of tribes, for it included " the Pennakooks, (Concord Indians,) Agawomes, (at Ipswich) Naamkeeks, (at Salem) Pascatawayes, Accomintas (York) and others,"[87] was led by the Sachem Nanepashemet, who lived at Saugus on the border of the wide marsh which stretches from the easterly portion of Malden through Revere[88] to the sea.   Westward towards the Connecticut River, the Nipmucks owed him a rude allegiance. In 1615 the Tarratines, whom Mr. Lewis styled " the Goths and Vandals of aboriginal New England,"[89] in revenge for an

[85] Hubbard, *General History of New England,* 32.

[86] Hutchinson, *History of Massachusetts Bay,* i. 460.   Ed. 1760.

[87] Gookin, in *Mass. Hist. Coll.,* i. 149.

[88] Called by the English Rumney Marsh, which name it has retained to the present time.

Rumney Marsh, its English counterpart, from which it doubtless received its name, is an extensive tract of rich land in the county of Kent, which Camden called *the gift of the sea.*   It embraces more than forty-four thousand acres of land, which has been thrown up by the sea or left by the changes of the coast line and the courses of the small rivers which intersect it; and it is protected from the ocean by a strong earthen wall of a great antiquity.   Much has been added to its extent within the range of history.   It possesses a soil of great fertility, which nourishes numerous herds that are sent there to graze; and its reedy creeks and fens shelter large flocks of wild fowl.   Hardly a hedge or tree breaks its expanse, save a few near the villages, which are scattered here and there in convenient places.   Cf. Lewis, *Topographical Dictionary of England,* ii. 490; Camden, *Britannia,* 210.   Ed. 1695.   There is a map of the district in Harris, *History of Kent,* copied from Dugdale, *History of the Fens.*

[89] Lewis, *History of Lynn,* 33.   The Tarratines were a branch of the Aben-

injury, invaded the lands of the Pawtuckets and Massachusetts and overran the region from the Penobscot to the Charles. Gorges describes the slaughter as " horrible to be spoken of." [40] Nanepashemet retired from the banks of Rumney Marsh to a hill near the head-waters of the Mystic, where he built a fort which was seen by Edward Winslow of Plymouth in 1621.

About this time the natives attacked and burned a French trading vessel which was lying at anchor near Peddock's Island in Boston Harbor. The men were slain or distributed among the neighboring villages. One of these men, daring to rebuke the Indians for their wickedness, was told, " they were so many that God could not kill them." Thomas Morton of Merry Mount tells the result: —

In short time after the hand of God fell heavily upon them, with such a mortall stroake that they died on heapes as they lay in their houses; and the living, that were able to shift for themselves, would runne away and let them dy, and let there Carkases ly above the ground without buriall. For in a place where many inhabited, there hath been but one left a live, to tell what became of the rest; the livinge being (as it seemes) not able to bury the dead, they were left for Crowes, Kites, and vermin to pray upon. And the bones and skulls upon the severall places of their habitations made such a spectacle after my comming into those partes, that, as I travailed in that Forrest nere the Massachussets, it seemed to mee a new found Golgatha.[41]

Cotton Mather, in an apparent spirit of thankfulness, wrote: —

The *Indians* in these Parts had newly, even about a Year or Two before, been visited with such a prodigious Pestilence; as carried away not a *Tenth*, but *Nine Parts* of *Ten* (yea 't is said *Nineteen* of *Twenty*) among them: so that the *Woods* were almost cleared of those pernicious Creatures to make Room for a *better Growth.*[42]

This pestilence, which was described by various names, is supposed by recent writers to have been the small-pox, which

aquis nation and inhabited, if a people of their roaming habits may be said to have a fixed habitation, the region east of the Penobscot River. Williamson, *History of Maine,* i. 513, gives a specimen of their language. Nicholas John Crevay, who was killed at Spot Pond in

1813, by Samuel Angier and others of Malden, was probably a Tarratine.

[40] Gorges, *Briefe Narration,* in *Mass. Hist. Coll.,* xxvi. 90.

[41] Morton, *New English Canaan,* 23.

[42] Mather, *Magnalia,* i. ch. 2.

in later instances caused a great mortality among the Indians.[4]
Gookin, writing half a century later, says of this sickness: —

Doubtless it was some pestilential disease. I have conversed with
some old Indians, that were then youths; who say, that the bodies all
over were exceeding yellow, describing it by a yellow garment they
showed me, both before they died, and afterward.[44]

What the hatchet and the knife of the Tarratines had spared
of the nation of the Pawtuckets, the plague devoured, so that
but a feeble remnant remained to uphold the waning authority
of Nanepashemet. So great was the loss that, out of about
three thousand men which the united tribes could once muster,
" not above two hundred and fifty men, besides women and
children," remained when Gookin wrote.[45]

But the Sachem only escaped the plague to fall by the hands
of his old enemies, the Tarratines, who again swept over the
land and slew him in his fort near Mystic Pond in 1619. Two
years later, Edward Winslow passed along the banks of the
Mystic and thus recorded his observations in *A Relation of Ovr
Voyage to the Massachvsets :* —

On the morrow we went ashore, all but two men, and marched in
Armes vp in the Countrey. Hauing gone three myles, we came to a
place where Corne had beene newly gathered, a house pulled downe,
and the people gone. A myle from hence, *Nanepashemet* their King in
his life time had liued. His house was not like others, but a scaffold
was largely built, with pools and plancks some six foote from ground,
and the house vpon that, being situated on the top of a hill.

Not farre from hence in a bottome, wee came to a Fort built by
their deceased King, the manner thus; There were pools some thirtie
or fortie foote long, stucke in the ground as thicke as they could be set
one by another, and with these they inclosed a ring some forty or fifty
foote ouer. A trench breast high was digged on each side; one way
there was to goe into it with a bridge; in the midst of this Pallizado
stood the frame of an house, wherein being dead he lay buryed.

About a myle from hence, we came to such another, but seated on
the top of an hill: here Nanepashemet was killed, none dwelling in it
since the time of his death.[44]

---

[44] *Massachusetts and its Early History,*
261.

[44] *Mass. Hist. Coll.,* i. 148.

[45] Ibid., i. 149.

[44] Mourt *Relation,* 58. It was doubtless the burial place of Nanepashemet's
men, or of their ancestors, which was
disturbed in 1882, as related in the fol-

After the death of the Sachem and the retirement of the Tarratines his people again gathered around the Mystic and Rumney Marsh, where they dwelt, at the time of the settlement of the English, under the general government of the widow of Nanepashemet, the Squa Sachem, and the local rule of her sons, Wonohaquaham and Montowampate.[47]

The Squa Sachem appears to have had a large share of the masculine spirit in her character and to have been equal to the task of ruling the scattered bands of the roving Pawtuckets. She succeeded in establishing and maintaining authority over the domain of her deceased husband from Agamenticus to the Connecticut River. In 1621 Obbatinewat of Shawmut complained that she was his enemy.[48] In accordance with an Indian custom she married Webcowet, the powow or physician [49] of the

lowing extract, which, in its historical allusions, is as trustworthy as the average newspaper articles upon local history. Sagamore John died in 1633, among the English. They would hardly have taken the trouble to carry his body and those of his men from the lower Mystic and Rumney Marsh through the wilderness to Medford. The "Carkases" of Indians who had died of the small pox would have been more likely to be thrown into the nearest hole.

"A year ago last September, while workmen were engaged in excavating the earth for the large barn of Mr. Francis Brooks at West Medford, the skeletons of eighteen Indians were uncovered, found in sitting posture, together with implements of war, pipes, etc. These bones were preserved, and last week Mr. Brooks erected a monument to the memory of the red men, on a spot between his residence and that of Mr. Conant, his foreman, which is believed to have been the burial place of Sagamore John and those Mystic Indians who inhabited this region. It is about ten feet high, with a rough boulder weighing about one ton on the top, is rough throughout, with the exception of the panels, on which are the following inscriptions : 'In memory of Sagamore John and those Mystic Indians whose bones lie here; '1630-1884.'

Sagamore John, a friendly man, once saved a white settlement from a brutal massacre, by pitching his tent on the high rock on Mr. Edmund T. Hasting's premises to command the river, thus warning the people that the Indians were in ambush to slay them all. All the bones saved were put in a black box in a brick vault laid in cement, in which were also placed the different kinds of coins of this year, and copies of the Medford papers. The whole was covered with a large slab and firmly imbedded in cement." *Malden Mirror*, Aug. 2, 1884.

[47] "[December yᵉ 24, 1694.] The Testimony of John Devoreaux of Marblehead aged about Eighty years Testifieth & Saith yᵗ about yᵉ yeare of Our Lord One thousand Six hundred & Thirty J came ouer from old England to New England & yᵉ place of my abode and residence has been at Salem & Marblehead Euer Since & when J came hither here was an old Sqwah Called old Sqwaw Sachem yᵉ Sqwaw of yᵉ Decᵉᵈ Sachem Which had three reputed Sons viz John James & George whoe were yᵉ Reputed Sachems & Owners of all yᵉ Lands in these parts as Salem Marblehead Linn & as farr as Mistick." *Essex Co. Deeds*, xi. 132.

[48] Mourt, *Relation*, 57.

[49] *Powow*, priest, conjuror, or sorcerer.

tribe, of whom we know but little beyond the fact of his marriage. He subscribed to some papers, and he is mentioned as taking an interest in the efforts, which were being made, in 1647, to christianize the Indians.[50]

In 1639 the two signed a deed by which they conveyed to the inhabitants of Charlestown, with some reservations, all the lands which the Court had granted them, including the bounds of the present cities of Malden and Everett and the town of Melrose. This document is of interest to us as being the first and only conveyance of the aboriginal title in the territory which we occupy. The consideration, or "sattisfaction," proves how little the Indians valued their rights and how cheaply the settlers quieted their claims.

The 15th of the 2. m[o]. 1639

Wee Web Cowet & Squaw Sachem do sell vnto the Jnhabitants of the Towne of Charlestowne, all the land with in the lines granted them by the Court (excepting the farmes and the ground, on the West of the two great Ponds called misticke ponds, from the South side of m[r] Nowells lott, neere the vpp[r] end of the Ponds, vnto the little runnet that cometh from Cap[t] Cookes mills which the Squaw reserveth to their vse, for her life, for the Jndians to plant and hunt vpon, and the weare above the Ponds, they also reserve for the Jndians to fish at whiles the Squaw liveth, and after the death of Squaw Sachem shee doth leave all her lands from m[r] Mayhues house[51] to neere Salem to the present Governo[r], m[r] Jn[o] Winthrop Sen[r], m[r] Jncrease Nowell, m[r] Jn[o] Wilson, m[r] Edward Gibons to dispose of, and all Jndians to depart, and for

---

[50] Shattuck, *History of Concord*, 25.

[51] By "m[r] Mayhues house " is meant, I am convinced, the house built by Governor Cradock's people on the east bank of the Mystic, which is still standing and which was known in the early days as "Meadford house." I base my belief on the following affidavits in *Middlesex Court Files, in loco.*

"The testimony of Richard Beers, Benjamin Crispe and Garret Church, Testifieth and Saith that M[r] Thomas Mayhue lived at Mistick alias Meadford in y[e] yeare one thousand six hundred thirty and six. Charls-Towne the 17th of the 10th, 1662."

"I Joseph Hills aged about 60 yeares testify that about 1638, M[r] Davison lived at Meadford house, who shewed me the accomodations of the farme, being about to take y[e] said farme and stock of him and captaine Will. Ting: and I testify that M[r] Mayhew did not then dwell at Meadford house to y[e] best of my Knowledge. 17, 10. 1662."

Nicholas Davison was Cradock's agent and Mayhew had probably occupied the farm as tenant.

"1634, 14 May. M[r] Thomas Mayhewe is intreated by the Court to examine what hurt the swyne of Charlton hath done amongst the Indean barnes of corne, on the north side of Misticke, & accordingly the inhabitants of Charlton p[r]miseth to giue them satisfaction." *Mass. Colony Records,* i. 121.

sattisfaction from Charlestowne, wee acknowledge to have received in full sattisfaction twenty and one coates ninten fathom of Wampon, & three bushels of corne. Jn witnes whereof we have here vnto sett o' hands, the day and yeare above named. the marke of SQUA SACHEM. m.

the marke of WEB COWET. m.

Subscribed in the
p'senc' off
    J^N? HUMPHERY
    ROBERT FEAKE.[62]

This is to testifie that the aforenamed purchase was made at the charges of the Jnhabitants of Charlestowne, and to their vse, and for so much as lyeth with in their limitts, we do accordingly resigne, and yeld vp all our interest therein to the vse of the said towne, according to the trust reposed in vs. 10th m? 18th, 1639.

        J^N? WINTHROP *Gou'n'.*
        JNCREASE NOWELL.
        J^N? WILSON.

Entred & Recorded. 23th 8m? 1656.

      By THOMAS DANFORTH *Recorder.*[63]

In 1644 the Squa Sachem, with others, formally submitted to the colonial authority by subscribing an instrument in which the hand of the Indian is little apparent: —

Wossamegon, Nashowanon, Cutshamache, Mascanomet, & Squa Sachim did volentarily submit themselves to us, as appeareth by their covenant subscribed wth their own hands, hear following, & oth^r articles to wch they consented.

Wee have & by these presents do voluntarily, & wthout any constraint or perswasion, but of o' owne free motion, put o'selues, o' subiects, lands, & estates under the government & iurisdiction of the Massachusets, to bee governed & protected by them, according to their iust lawes & orders, so farr as wee shalbee made capable of understanding them ; & wee do promise for o'selues, & all o' subiects, & all o' posterity, to

---

[62] Frothingham, *History of Charlestown,* 67, makes this, Robert Heake — an unknown name. Robert Feake, the witness, was of Watertown, where he died February 1, 1663. Mount Feake in Waltham was named in his memory.

[63] *Middlesex Co. Deeds,* i. 190 (original vol.). It will be noticed that seventeen years elapsed before this deed was recorded. When it was finally put upon record the Squa Sachem had been dead five or six years, and Sagamore George had begun to "trouble" the English about his land. January 13, 16³⁹/4., the Squa Sachem and Webcowet, in consideration of "many kindnesses and benefites" and "for our tender loue & good respect" deeded to Jotham Gibbons the reversion of the lands around the Mystic ponds which had been reserved in the Charlestown deed. *Suffolk Co. Deeds,* i. 43; *Middlesex Co. Deeds,* i. 191.

bee true & faithfull to the said government, & ayding to the maintenance thereof, to o' best ability, & fro" time to time to give speedy
notice of any conspiracy, attempt, or evill intension of any which wee
shall know or heare of against the same ; & wee do promise to bee willing
fro" time to time to bee instructed in the knowledg & worship of God.
In witnes whereof wee have hereunto put o' hands the 8th of the first
m°, @ 1643–1644.

> CUTSHAMACHE,
> NASHOWANON,
> WOSSAMEGON,
> MASKANOMETT,
> SQUA SACHIM.[54]

Several questions relating to morals followed the signing of
this " volentary " submission, the answers to which are fully set
forth in the Colony Records.   Two of them would be regarded
as especially creditable to the Indian character, did we not
remember that the vices referred to are vices of civilized and
not of savage life.   They said " they know not w' swering is
among y"," and that it was their custom " to honor their
parents and their superiors."   At the close they gave the English twenty-six fathoms of wampum and received five coats of
red cloth and a potful of wine.

Little is known of the Squa Sachem beyond what has been
related.   With other Indians she had sold a large tract of land
at Concord, in 1637 ; and she had conveyed to Jotham Gibbons
the reversion of her lands which she had reserved in the Charlestown deed.   In 1640 the General Court ordered Cambridge " to
give Squa Sachem a coate every winter while shee liveth."   This
order apparently was not obeyed, for the next year " Cambridge
was enioned to give Squa Sachem so much corne as to make up
35 bushels, & 4 coates for the last year and this."[55]   Her needs

---

[54] *Mass. Colony Records*, ii. 55. Cutshamache was a sachem, or sagamore,
from near the Blue Hills; Nashowanon,
a Nipmuck from Wachuset; and Mas-
kanomett was that sagamore of Agawam
who is elsewhere called Mascononomo.
Drake, *History of the Indians*, 106, supposes Wossamegon to have been no
other than the great Wampanoag, or
Pokanoket, chief Massasoit, whose

friendship for the English formed so
great a contrast to the enmity of his
savage son, Metacomet, or Philip.

[55] It appears by these orders that she
had some special claim on the town of
Cambridge; and a clause in the deed to
Jotham Gibbons, *Suffolk Co. Deeds*, i.
43, indicates that she may have conveyed land there. Cambridge agreed,
April 10, 1643, " to pay to Squa Sachem

seemed not to require attention for a while; but in 1643, the Court granted her "haulfe a pound of gunpowder" and ordered "her peece to be mended;" and in the fall of the same year she was allowed to buy "1 lb of powder & 4 lb of shot."[56] After the submission and catechizing of 1644, she disappears from sight and nothing more is heard of her. A pathetic story is told of her as being old, blind, and worn-out; and with little reason it has been supposed that she was the "ould" blind Nipmuck squa who died in 1667 in consequence of ill treatment received from a party of Narragansetts; but the testimony of Richard Church, preserved in the Court files of Middlesex County, shows that she died about the year 1650.[57] Old she may have been, but there is no evidence that she was blind.

Wonohaquaham, or Sagamore John of Winnisimmet, " of gentle and good disposition,"[58] whom Thomas Dudley describes as " a handsome young man, conversant with us, affecting English apparel and houses, and speaking well of our God,"[59] dwelt "upon a creek which meets with the mouth of Charles River."[60] This is the creek, now known as Island-End River, or Chelsea Creek, which runs through the marshes between Powder-Horn Hill and Winnisimmet into the Mystic at Wormwood Point[61] in Everett. Here, on the south side of the creek, near its mouth, Samuel Maverick built a fortified house in 1625, which the savages attacked. They were so warmly received that they " never attempted it more," to their sincere regret in after years.[62] John gave Ralph Sprague and his brothers " free

8 bushels of Indian corn, after next harvest;" and again, November 11, 1643, "Agreed, that the cow-keepers shall pay six bushels of corn to Squa Sachem for the damage done to her corn, upon the Sabbath day, through the neglect of the keepers in the year 1642." Cf. Paige, *History of Cambridge*, 384.

[56] *Mass. Colony Records*, i. 292, 317; ii. 36, 44.

[57] Testimony of Richard Church, Jan. 15, 1659/60: "soone after Squaw Sachems Death wᶜʰ to the best of his remembrance was in the yeare 1650." *Middlesex Court Files, in loco.*

[58] *Charlestown Records*, in Young, *Chronicles of Massachusetts Bay*, 374.

[59] Young, *Chronicles of Massachusetts Bay*, 307.

[60] Hutchinson, *History of Massachusetts Bay*, i. 461. Ed. 1760.

[61] Sometimes corrupted to Wormall's Point; and at different times known as Sweetser's, Beacham's, and Van Voorhis's Point, from the owners of the adjacent lands.

[62] Maverick, *Briefe Discription of New England*, in *N. E. Hist. and Geneal. Register*, xxxix. 38.

consent" to settle at Mishawum, where they founded the town of Charlestown in 1629.[63]   His tendencies towards civilization did not prevent him from going with thirty men, in 1632, to the assistance of the celebrated Narragansett chief Canonicus, who was fighting the Pequots in Connecticut.[64]

Montowampate, called James by the English, was the saga-more of Saugus.   Compared with his brother Wonohaquaham he is said to have been " of a far worse disposition, yet repaireth often to us." [65]   In 1629 he married Wenuchus, daughter of the great Bashaba Passaconaway of Pennacook.[66]   There is a ro-mantic and somewhat amusing story of Indian stubbornness and fatherly dignity connected with this marriage, which the curious reader may find in Morton's *New English Canaan*,[67] and which Mr. Whittier has embalmed in his "Bridal of Pennacook," trans-ferring, however, with a poet's licence, the husband's place to his brother Wenepoykin and the time to a later generation.

In 1631 the Mystic Indians were terrified by another inroad of their old enemies, the Tarratines, "who they said would eat such Men as they caught alive, tying them to a Tree, and gnaw-ing their flesh by peece-meales off their Bones;" and many of them fled among the English for protection.[68]   During this in-road, both Wonohaquaham and Montowampate, who perhaps had gone to the assistance of their fellow sagamore, Mascono-nomo, were wounded at Agawam; and Wenuchus was carried away captive as far east as Pemaquid, where she was ransomed by Abraham Shurte.[69]   Tradition says that soon after Monto-wampate went to England in search of a man named Watts, who had "forced him" of twenty beaver skins.[70]

About the same Time the *Indians* began to be quarrelsome touching the Bounds of the Land which they had sold to the *English ;* but God ended the Controversy by sending the Small-pox amongst the

[63] *Charlestown Records*, in Young, *Chronicles of Massachusetts Bay*, 374.
[64] Winthrop, *History of New Eng-land*, i. 72.
[65] Dudley's Letter, in Young, *Chroni-cles of Massachusetts Bay*, 307.
[66] On the Merrimack, now Concord, N. H.

[67] Morton, *New English Canaan*, 38-40.
[68] Johnson, *Wonder-working Provi-dence*, 50.
[69] Hubbard, *History of New England*, 145; Winthrop, *History of New Eng-land*, i. 61.
[70] Cf. Winthrop, *History of New England*, i. 49.

Indians at *Saugust,* who were before that Time exceeding numerous. Whole Towns of them were swept away, in some of them not so much as one Soul escaping the Destruction. There are some old Planters surviving to this Day, who helped to bury the dead *Indians,* even whole Familyes of them all dead at once.[71]

Other writers attest the truth of this story. Edward Johnson writes : —

The mortality among them was very great, and increased among them daily more and more, insomuch that the poore Creatures being very timorous of death, would faine have fled from it, but could not tell how, unlesse they could have gone from themselves ; Relations were little regarded among them at this time, so that many, who were smitten with the Disease died helplesse unlesse they were neare, and known to the *English.*[72]

This disease spread among the Indians from the Connecticut to the Penobscot. Seven hundred of the Narragansett tribe, alone, are said to have perished. Many of the English took their lives in their hands and went among the sick and dying, administering relief and consolation. They "were very frequent among them for all the noysomenesse of their Disease, entring their *Wigwams,* and exhorting them in the Name of the Lord." Governor Winthrop records that Elias Maverick of Winnisimmet, who buried above thirty of Wonohaquaham's people in one day, " is worthy of a perpetual remembrance. Himself, his wife, and servants, went daily to them, ministered to their necessities, and buried their dead, and took home many of their children. So did other of the neighbours." [73]

Wonohaquaham, falling sick, was taken among the English at his own request, promising, " if he recovered, to live with them and serve their God." He died December 5, 1633, " in a persuasion that he should go to the Englishmen's God." His son, a child whom he gave to Rev. John Wilson of Boston, " to be brought up by him," probably died also, as we hear nothing more of him,[74] and but three of the children who were taken by

---

[71] Mather, *Early History of New England,* 110.

[72] Johnson, *Wonder-working Providence,* 51.

[73] Cf. Johnson, *Wonder-working Providence,* 51 ; Winthrop, *History of New England,* i. 120.

[74] Johnson says he had two sons, *Wonder-working Providence,* 52. Perhaps one died before the father.

the English were living three months later. One of them was living in the family of Governor Winthrop and "was called Know-God, (the Indians' usual answer being when they were put in mind of God, Me no know God)." [75]

By the death of Wonohaquaham and Montowampate, their brother Wenepoykin, then about seventeen years of age, became chief of the small band of Indians remaining in this vicinity.[76] He was known to the English as George Rumney-Marsh, from the place of his abode near Powder-Horn Hill; and he married Ahawayet, daughter of Poquanum, or Black William, who sold Nahant to Thomas Dexter for "a suite of Cloathes," and soon after resold it, together with Swampscott and Sagamore Hill, to William Witter "for two pestle stones." The latter sale appears to have been considered of importance by the Indians, as Montowampate, Wonohaquaham, Wenepoykin, Mascononomo of Agawam, and others were present.[77] The Indians had very limited ideas of the transfer of property, and there is no lack of proof that they were often outwitted in their transactions.

George Rumney-Marsh had a son, Manatooquis,[78] and three

---

[75] Winthrop, *History of New England,* i. 124.

[76] He had lived at Naumkeag, where he had a village, and came to the Mystic after the death of his brothers. The Rev. John Higginson, "Pastor of y⁰ Church at Salem," testified, December 25, 1694: —

"To y⁰ best of my Remembrance when J came Ouer with my father to this place in y⁰ yeare 1629 being then about 13 yeares old there was in these parts a Widow Woman Called Sqwaw Sachem who had 3 Sons Sagamore John kept at Mistick Sagamore James at Saugust & Sagamore George here at Naumkeke Whether he was an Actual Sachem here J Cannot Say for he was young then about my Age & J thinke there was an Elder man y⁰ was at least his Guardian but y⁰ Jndian Towne of wigwams was on y⁰ North Side of y⁰ North riuer not farre from Simondes & y⁰ both y⁰ North & South Side of that Riuer was together Called Naumkeke So that J remember Seuerall that

wrote ouer Then to Thier friends in England S⁴ y⁰ y⁰ Jndian name of y⁰ place where they were building a Towne Called Salem was Naumkeke." *Essex Co. Deeds,* xi. 132.

[77] *Essex Court Files,* April, 1657. This double sale did not prevent Wenepoykin himself from transferring the same territory at a later date; for, April 1, 1652, he mortgaged to Nicholas Davison, for twenty pounds "dew many yeeres since vnto mᵣ mathew Craddock deceased all that Tracke or necke of Land Comonly Called Nahant." *Suffolk Co. Deeds,* i. 205. This mortgage was to have been satisfied "within twenty dajes;" but no record of its discharge appears, and it was not recorded until May 21, 1652, some time after the twenty days had expired.

[78] Otherwise Samuel Manatooquis, or Manatahqua. This only son died before Sagamore George, leaving by his squa, Abigail, two sons, Nonupanohow, or David Kunkshamooshaw, and Samuel Wattanoh, who were living in

daughters, Petagunsk, Wattaquattinusk, and Petagoonaquah.
The unpoetic Puritans called one Cicely, Su George, or
Susanna, and to another gave the name of Sarah.[79] Ahawayet
was transformed to Joan, and Wenepoykin, himself, became in
after years "old Sagamore George No Nose," perhaps from a
facial peculiarity.   But little is known of Sagamore George until
after the death of his mother, the Squa Sachem, when he presented to the General Court the following petition and declaration: —

*To ye Rigt Wor^{ll} ye Go^r: the Wor^{ll} Dept Go^{r}no^r: & magistrates of
this hon^{ed} Courte.*

The humble Petticon of George Jndian, humbly Requesting Whereas
yor Peticon^r, hath often besought this hon^{ed} Courte to consider his
condicon, & weighing sure Grounds & euedenc as he hath produced
to declare & manifest his interest & Just Title to the Lands of his late
brother deceased, on mistick side, & conceiueing the hon^{ed} courte to
be soficiently informed & possessed with the truth & equitie of his
cause in and aboute the same That now at Last out of yor Great clemency & compastion towards yor poore Jndian & Petitioner, you will
bee pleased to vouchsafe him somme small parte parcell or proportion of his inheritance for himselfe & company to plant in, which he
only is bould to put you in Remembranc of as hertofore not doubt-

---

1686, and joined in the several deeds
which were given to the English in that
and the preceding year.

[79] Lewis, *History of Lynn,* 39, gives
these Indian girls three English names,
and affects to distinguish between them.
He says they were Cicely or Su George,
Sarah, and Susanna; but I cannot separate Cicely, Su George, and Susanna,
which appear to me as names of one
person in the three deeds of the Rumney Marsh, and Lynn and Reading lands
given in 1685 and 1686. As "Cisly and
Sarah two Surviving daughters of the
s^d Saggamore George" are mentioned,
and Thomas Poquanum, brother of
Ahawayet, testifies that "Sagamore
George left two daughters name Sicilye
and Sarah," it is evident that one of the
three had previously died. Su George
had a son John Tontohquon, who joined
in a deed with his mother in 1686. Wat-
tatinusk, wife of Peter Ephraim of Natick, appears in the same deed, and may
have been a daughter of Sarah Wattaquattinusk, who also appears at the
same time; but perhaps it is more
probable that she was daughter of Yawata, the sister of Wenepoykin.

Mr. Lewis further informs us that
the daughters of George were collec-
tively "called Wanapanaquin, or the
plumed ones." In the Indian deed of
Marblehead, Sarah is called by an evident change of spelling, "Sarah Wana-
panequin," being elsewhere in the same
paper referred to as "Sarah Wenepawweekin," and her sister as "Susannah
Wenepawweekin," both daughters of
"George Saggamore als Wenepawweekin." *Essex Co. Deeds,* vii. 1-2. Mr.
Lewis saw through a veil of romance
which was unfavorable to accuracy.

ing of his grante from yor Greate fauor toward him, whoe is willing to be now & euer

    An humble seru^t to this honnered courte & country

GEORGE JNDIAN.[80]

Quachamaquine saith : when George Jndians brother was sick of the pox before his death he spake to him & Egawam with him & said when I die I give all my wompam & coates & other things to my mother & all my ground to my owne brother meaning the Ground about powder horne hill, vnles his own sonne did liue but if his sonne dyed then none to haue the Ground but his brother George Jndian, and Egawam saith the same : & they both say that seauen dayes after this John Sagamore Georges Brother dyed.

    21 $\frac{1}{10}$, 1651. [81]

There is a touching simplicity in these documents. As we read them the whole story of injustice — an injustice perhaps unavoidable but not the less an injustice — is brought before us. The last chief of a once powerful tribe asks for "somme small parte" of his own inheritance of those who asked of his brother, the " gentle and good " Wonohaquaham, leave to settle in his lands. When the whites were weak they courted the red men's friendship. It was quite another thing when war and sickness had weakened the Indians and the Colony of the Massachusetts had become strong. There is also much simplicity in the answer by which the General Court showed its " Great clemency & compastion" towards the petitioner : —

    [1651 : 22 May.] George Indian, complayninge of land wrongfully detaynd from him on Misticke side, is referd to bringe his action agaynst any that withold it, in some inferior Court.[82]

There is worldly wisdom as well as simplicity in this advice; and its practical value — to the English — is proved by the fact that " George Jndian " was twice defeated in attempting to recover his own. The following petition is interesting as showing the extent of his claims and the position of the planters : —

---

[80] *Mass. Archives*, xxx. 19.   [82] *Mass. Colony Records*, iii. 233.
[81] Ibid.

To the Right wo John Endicot Gouv.* etc. The humble petition of John Newgate, John Coggine, Robert Keayne, Samuell Cole, Nicholas Parker, & other inhabitants of Rumne Marsh Showeth*

That whereas this Honored Court hath formerly giuen that necke of Land, caled by the Name of Rumne Marsh : diuers years since to Boston, for the accomodation of that Towne and the Townsmen thereof hath deuided the same to many of there Jnhabitants, Some whereof hath sould & passed ouer there Alotments to others, and many alsoe haue bought much of there Land there, and Layd out the greatest pt of there estates, in Buildinge, ffensinge, plantinge &c, and have inioyed the same peacably for these sixtene years & vpwards : as is the condition of most of yo' Petitione" : And yet now haue the Title of there Land called into Question by sagamore George and Indian, by some pretence of clayme that he makes thereto, and vpon that pretence (though he haue lyen quiet soe many years & neuer made any clayme thereto, yet Lately by the instigation of some discontented, or disaffected persons as we verely suppose, he hath bine full of molestation to yo' petitione". and hath by way of Petition brought vs twise into the Gene'¹ Court, who after strict inquire by committes chosen on purpose to examine it found no Just ground of clayme, & there vpon reiected his Petitions. yet after this. by Petition agayne, he brought vs before oure Honored Magistrates. at countie Court at Boston. who after hearinge all that he could aledge & some that pleaded for him, it was determined that they saw no right he had, nor any Just ground of his molestation, but that he ought to be quiet, w'ᵗʰ w'ᶜ we thought he had bine fully satisfied, and that we should neuer haue heard more of it, yet the Last country Court at Boston, he serued vs all agayne by way of question, wherafter we had attended all that Court, we at Last Nonsuted him, & had costs granted vs. And yet he still threttens vs w'ᵗʰ farther sutes.

Vpon all w'ᶜʰ grounds, as alsoe because this is not ou' case alone, but the case of many other Townes, & soe by consequence of the whole cuntrye : for if he can preuayle to draw vs to any composition, or to pt wth any of ou' Land. than he intends to doe the Like to Lyn &c as he hath threatned. And accordinge to his successe other Jndians wilbe incoraged to Lay clayme, not only to the ffarmes belonginge to other Townes, but to the Townes them selues, as some haue bine forward enough to expresse them selues that way.

Therefo' yo' petitiono" pray this Honored Court to take it into there wise consideration and to prouide some way by some Order of Court, that no Jndian shall make clayme nor any of the English shall tender composition, after soe many yea's quiet posession as some other Courts haue done, or how else you in yo' wisdomes shall judge best, that soe not only yo' Petitioners may haue Jndemnitie agaynst such continuall and vniust molestations (haueinge no other way to helpe ou' selues. for if we recoue' any thinge they haue nothinge to pay) but alsoe the whole cuntry may be cleared from such pretended Titles. wch if not timely preuented may proue of very bad consequenc And Yo' Petitione^rs shall euer pray. &c

> ROBERT KEAYNE
> JOHN COGAN
> JOHN NEWGATE
> JAMES PENN
> SAMUEL COLE
> GEORGE BURDEN.[83]

The answer to this petition is thus recorded: —

[1651: 14 October.] Capt Robt Keayne, Mr Joh Coggan, Mr Newgate, Mr Pen, Samuel Cole, & George Burden, preferinge a petition for releife in respect of vnjust molestation, as they conceiue, from Sagamore George, pretending a tytle to certayne land^s at or about Rumny Marsh, in answer to which this Courte doth order that their petition be graunted, provided that the petitiono^rs lay out twenty acors of good plantinge land in some convenient place, such as this Courte shall approue off, for Sagamor George to make vse off; but if Georg Sagamor sell it, the petition^rs are to haue the refusall of it. And it is also further ordred that if the petition^rs shall refuse to lay out twenty acors of good planting land, as is before exprest, that then the sd Sagamor is permitted the benefitt of the law to recouer what right he hath to the land.[84]

The democratic deputies, as appears elsewhere, would have increased this meagre allowance to forty acres; but the conservative magistrates refused to concur in so liberal a measure.[85] The " poore Jndian & Petitioner" was silenced for a time, if not satisfied, by this paltry grant, which appears not to have been laid out at once; for we have evidence that he again presented his " clajme," eighteen years later. Unfortunately the petition which he presented to the General Court is not in its place in the Massachusetts Archives, and we can only guess at its tenor; [86] but the answer which he received is before us, and

---

[83] *Mass. Archives*, xxx. 26.

[84] *Mass. Colony Records*, iii. 252.

[85] *Mass. Archives*, xxx. 26.

[86] It may be said that many documents are not in their *proper* places in that unfortunate disarrangement of papers which is a disgrace to the State and a cause of vexation to scholars. The paper in question has not been found. By the crude system of arrange-

shows how hopelessly closed, to the Indian, were the avenues which led to justice : —

[1669 : 19 May.] In ans' to the petition of Georg Sagamore, the Court declares that his clajme mentioned in his petition concernes not the Generall Court to determine, but leaue him to the proprieto's of the land to give him as they & he shall agree. [87]

It would be interesting to know if the parties were able to agree ; and we might find that the grant was located, if at all, in some eligible place where it would not be likely to interfere with the settlers. The strength of his friendship for the English thereafter does not appear to have been strong.

Having by the death of the Squa Sachem become the chief of the Pawtuckets and the nominal, if not the real, head of the Nipmucks, who occupied the land westward to the Connecticut River, he joined Philip in the bloody war of 1675–6. About the same time, the few remaining Rumney Marsh Indians left the banks of the Mystic and the Abousett and retired among their brethren, the Praying Indians, at Natick and at Wamesit, now Tewkesbury, near the Pawtucket Falls. There is evidence that, while some of the Christian Indians remained faithful to their pledges and performed important services for the English, there were many who resumed their savage habits and were far from being agreeable or safe neighbors. Accordingly, it was considered prudent to put them under restraint ; and it was ordered by the Court, October 13, 1675, " that all the Naticke Indians be forthwith sent for, & disposed of to Deare Island, as the place appointed for their present aboade." [88]

At the same time, those of Wamesit were " vehemently suspected to be actors & consentors to the burning of a haystacke at Chelmsford ; " [89] and two strangers, who were seized and sold as suspected spies, but who were really peaceable Indians who had come in from Wannalancet of Pennacook, were found among them. And so, " It is ordered, that the majo' generall

---

ment which prevails it should be under "Indians"; it may be classified with "Taverns," or hidden in the bulky volumes which are labelled "Miscellaneous."

[87] *Mass. Colony Records*, iv. (2), 428.
[88] Ibid., v. 57.
[89] Ibid.

forthwith take order to secure the Indians at Wamesicke, & about Chelmsford." [90]

It cannot be supposed that the condition of the Indians upon the bleak islands of Boston Harbor, where they were now placed, during a long winter, was particularly pleasant, or that they were supplied with many comforts beyond the mere necessities of life, although there were appointed "meet p'sons to vissit them from time to time," and the Treasurer was ordered to make provision, "so as to p'vent their perishing by any extremity that they may be put vnto for want of absolute necessaries." [91]   At the same time: —

It is *ordered*, that none of the sajd Indians shall presume to goe off the sajd islands voluntarily, vpon pajne of death; and it shallbe laufull for the English to destroy those that they shall finde stragling off from the sajd places of theire confinement, vnlesse taken of by order from authorjty, and vnder an English guard. [92]

There seems to have been a strong feeling against them in the community — a natural fear, perhaps, which was not without cause.   Out of eleven hundred and fifty Praying Indians, who were supposed to be in the towns just before the war, not over five hundred were ever confined upon the islands.   Some, like James Rumney Marsh and Thomas Quanapowitt, kinsmen of Wenepoykin, were with the English army or acting as scouts and spies in the Indian country; but many more were with the enemy upon the frontier or were skulking about the woods, singly or in small parties, thieving and murdering as opportunities appeared.   Some former teachers of the gospel were known to be with Philip.   That the English looked upon the prisoners in the harbor, poor and wretched though they were, with distrust was not unnatural : that some of the baser sort endeavored to compass their destruction was not strange.   There is good evidence of the latter fact.

15. 12. 75   Thomas Shepard of charlstown [Mystic Side] being exam.'! Saith y' y' last 6ᵗʰ day of y' week Abram Hill of Mauldon asked him if he would goe with him to Deare Jland.   His words were these.

⁹⁰ *Mass. Colony Records*, v. 58.   ⁹¹ Ibid., v. 64.   ⁹² Ibid.

Will you go with vs to Deare Jland to destroy ye Jndeans for ab^t 30 : of Linn men are intended to go thither ab^t ye work and wee are intended to get as many as wee can at Mauldon. & then go down thether. And the place of meeting is to be at Rumney marsh at Gm Muzzeys house.[96] or there ab^ts Hee did not speak as though they had come to an agree-m^t to meet there. but named y^t place as most fitting. & spake also of doing it in a moone light night.

THOMAS SHEPPARD.

This Exam^n taken vpon oath ye day & year above written

Before THOMAS DANFORTH *Assist.*

The Subtanc of y^s Abraham Hill owned before ye Council 15 febr 75.[94]

Meanwhile the poor Indians, among whom were Old Waban and Piamboho, who were the earliest to receive the teachings of the Apostle Eliot at Nonantum, were passing through a long winter; and their "want of absolute necessaries" was so well met that they were found to be in a suffering condition in the spring. The Court made a provision for them — on paper — as follows: —

[May 5, 1676] This Court, considering the p'sent distressed con-dition of the Indians at the island, they being ready to perrish for want of bread, & incapacitated to make provission for the future, doe *order*, that there be a man wth a boate provided, who, wth some of the Indians, shallbe imployed in catching of fish for theire supply, and that if any of the English tounes doe moove for some of them to imploy in scouting, labouring, or otherwise, with some of theire oune men, (the sajd tounes bearing the charge,) they shallbe accom^modated in that respect, the which improovement of them may tend much to theire supply, & much more to our security, and that the rest may be im-prooved in planting the island or islands where they now are.[96]

---

[96] Goodman Muzzey. This was Benjamin Muzzey, who was then in the occupation, as tenant, of the Keayne farm at Rumney Marsh. His house, the site of which is now marked by that of John P. Squire, was a convenient place for the proposed meeting, being on the only road which led from Lynn and Malden to Pullen Point and the shore opposite Deer Island.

[94] *Mass. Archives,* lxviii. 136. There appears to have been some provocation to this plan of destruction. Edward Page deposed [February 15, 167⅚,] in relation to a boat full of Indians, who acted strangely, coming to "Mannings Moone Jsland," where he was. He said, "J was affraide & durst not proseed in that J went aboute but hauing gunns & Amunition J went to strengthen the house." He further testified: "J haue inteligence that the indians haue sayd that when the spring comes they shalbe fetched of the Jsland by the other Jn-dians & that they will make Boston espe-sially the magistrates pay deare for euery houre they haue been kept theire." *Mass. Archives,* lxviii. 136.

[96] *Mass. Colony Records,* v. 84.

At the same session of the Court they were ordered to be removed " as neere as they may wth safety to their oune planting feilds;" and English garrisons, in which they were to lodge, "on pajne of death," were established for their protection or their intimidation. The Rumney Marsh Indians returned to Natick and to the banks of the Merrimac, and so the feeble remnant of the tribe of Nanepashemet was dispersed and finally disappeared.

What part Wenepoykin took in the massacres and burnings of those eventful years I know not; for he cannot be distinguished in the crowd of howling demons who drew a line of blood and flame around the frontier towns of New England. At the close of the war he again appears, and was sent, with hundreds of other prisoners, into West Indian slavery.[96] By some means he was finally enabled to return to Massachusetts Bay; and he died in or before 1681,[97] at Natick, in the house of his kinsman, Muminquash, who was otherwise known by the English as James Quanapowitt or James Rumney Marsh.[98]

[96] The following document may refer to the sale of Wenepoykin:

"To all people who shall see these presents or heare them read, greeting. Know yee that Lancelott Talbott and Joseph Smith have bought of the Tresurer of this Collony seaven Jndians, viz! George, William, Hawkins, Great David, Rouley, John Indian and Tommoquin, which Indians were sentanc'd to be sould for slaves : to which end the said Talbott and Smith may transport them to any place out of this continent. In testimony of the truth hereof, I have caused the publique seale of the Collony to be affixed hereunto, this 22 of 9[br] 1675, Ano'q. Regni Regis Coroli, secundi nunc Aug . . . . xxvii.

        "John Leverett, Gov[t]"

In *Boston Book of Possessions*, 145.

[97] Lewis, *History of Lynn*, 264, says, with admirable pretension to exactness, that he died in 1684, at the age of sixty-eight years, "sad and broken-hearted, . . . in a lone wigwam, in the forest of Natick, in the presence of his sister Yawata." Ahawayet and others, in consideration of " Six Indian Coats and other things,"

conveyed lands at Rumney Marsh and elsewhere to Thomas Savage of Boston, by a deed, December, 8, 1681, in which she is called " Jone Indian Relict of Sagamore George No-Nose dec[d]" *Suffolk Co. Deeds*, xiii. 190.

[98] Lewis, *History of Lynn*, 40, erroneously makes this James Rumney Marsh to have been a son of Yawata. Yawata, daughter of Nanepashemet, and sister of Wenepoykin, became the squa of John Awansamug, or Oonsumog, and was living in 1686. Her husband was living in 1682, when with Waban, Peter Ephraim, Piamboho, John Magus, Andrew Pittimee, and Great John, he sold lands in Sherborn to John Hull. *Suffolk Co. Deeds*, xil. 264. They appear to have had sons, John and Amos, who deeded land near Maspenock Pond in Mendon in 1692. *Suffolk Co. Deeds*, xxvii. 293.

James Quanophkownatt, or Quanapowitt, "alias James Rumney Marsh," was of Natick in 1686, and appears at all times as a near kinsman of old George No-Nose. His mother is mentioned as " Joanna Quanophkownatt, relict and widow of old John Quanophkownatt."

With him the line of the Pawtucket sachems came to an end. Members of his family were living sixty years later; but they went, long ago, into their nameless graves and are forgotten, save by the antiquary who pores with aching eyes over the faded and crumbling records of past generations.

Wenepoykin never abandoned his claim to the broad lands which he considered his own; and he died leaving his uncertain heritage in the lands from Naumkeag to the Mystic to James Rumney Marsh, who appears to have been a leader among his kinsmen.[99]

The Testimony of Daniel Tookuwompbait & Thomas Wauban Saith that Sagamore George when he came from Barbados he lived Sometime and dyed at y⁰ house of James Rumley Marsh y⁰ Said Daniel heard y⁰ Said Sagamore George Speake it & y⁰ Said Thomas Saith he heard his father Old Wabun Speak it that all that land that belonged to him that is from y⁰ Riuer of Salem alias Nahumkeke riuer: up to Malden mill brooke running from a pond called Spott pond that before his death he left all this land belonging to him vnto his kinsman James Rumley Marsh vpon y⁰ Condition that he would looke after it to procure it. This they offer to Testify vpon oath y⁰ 2ᵈ day of October 1686 as Witnis thier hands

DANIEL TOOKUWOMPBAIT

THOMAS WAUBAN

In the Indian deed of Salem she appears with " Yawataw relict Widow of Jn⁰ Oonsumoo." *Essex Co. Deeds,* vii. 126. At the same time, " Jsrael Quanoph- kownatt Son of sᵈ James" appears. The temptation to dwell on the story of In- dian kinship is not great and the liability of error is evident.

James Quanapowitt was employed by the English in 1675 as a spy among the Nipmucks; and his testimony was used against the old chief Matoonas who was shot to death by three Indians on Boston Common. He was a useful scout and forewarned the English of the assault on Lancaster. He had a brother, Thomas Rumney Marsh, who was a Christian Indian and did good service against Philip.

Indians bearing the surname of Rum- ney Marsh were frequently in the service during the early part of the last century; and the name of " James Rumlymarsh " is on a roll of those who joined the ex- pedition against the Spanish West Indies

in August, 1740. *Mass. Archives,* xci. 326. Thomas, son or grandson of Awan- samug and Yawata, owned a house lot in Natick in 1742. Barry, *History of Framingham,* 19. Widow " Rumne- marsh " was living in the same place in June, 1749. *Mass. Hist. Coll.* x. 135.

[99] He had given some portion of his claims to James Rumney Marsh, under conditions, before Philip's War.

" Georg Sagamore wᵗʰ: no nose ap- peared in y Court held at Natick among the Jndians y⁰ 15ᵗʰ of 6 month 1672 & also there appeared Jone Quanopoko- wait Kinsman to y⁰ sᵈ George they both agreed & declared in open Court yᵗ all y⁰ right of George Saggamore in the Lands of Marblehead of Antient tyme, George he Consents yᵗ: James shall have it, dispose of it & he will joyne wᵗʰ him to make y⁰ deed for it apon Condition yᵗ Georg Saggamore is to reseeve one moiety of y⁰ paye & y⁰ other Contrary to reseeve y⁰ other half." *Essex Co. Deeds,* vii. 9.

The Two persons above named Viz Daniel Tookuwompbait pastor of y⁰ Church at Natick aged about 36 yeares & Thomas Waban a member of y⁰ Church aged 25 yeares being Examined touching y⁰ Nature of an Oath they both made Oath before me this Second of October 1686, vnto y⁰ Truth of the above sᵈ Testimony as is Attested pʳ me.

DANIEL GOOKIN, *Justice*
of peac & Ruler of y⁰ Christian Jndians.[100]

While the settlers had but the Indians between them and the ownership of the soil, there was no difficulty in maintaining possession and little real attention was paid to their demands. What went into the courts seldom came out with advantage to the savage and a slight present quieted less pressing claims. But the political ruin which threatened the Colony during the reign of the last Stuart induced some appearance of tardy justice towards the former occupants of the land. Then the English, fearing the alienation of the lands which they had occupied for a half a century, began to seek a title older than that of the charter which had been annulled; and the claims of the Indians began to have a slight market value. Under the pressure of the times, several conveyances were obtained from those whom the English affected to recognize as the lawful heirs of Wenepoykin and others. Under these conditions and at this time, the peninsula of Boston, Deer Island, and the Rumney Marsh Lands were conveyed;[101] but no deed, save that of the

---

[100] *Essex Co. Deeds,* xi. 131. John Waabaquin, alias John Magus of Natick, "Susannah Potoghoomaquah," and others testified soon after in relation to the Indian claims. The testimony of Old Mahanton, then aged about ninety years, "Saith that y⁰ Land that is Testified about by Seuerall ancient Jndians that are Deceased which did belong to Sagamore George as is Expressed in y⁰ Euidence is y⁰ Truth & properly doth now belong to Dauid that is old Sagamore George his Grandchild & Scicily & Sarah y⁰ daughters of Sagamore George & y⁰ wife of John Owussumug now a widow Peter Ephraims wife & y⁰ wife of Appooquahamock thier daughter & old mahanton & James Rumney Marsh by right of his Mother a neer kinsman of Sagamore George in his life time." *Essex Co. Deeds,* xi. 131.

[101] An unrecorded deed of the Rumney Marsh lands, April 9, 1685, is printed by Chamberlain in his *Studies in Chelsea History* in *Chelsea Telegraph,* December 18, 1880; and others conveying neighboring lands are recorded in *Suffolk Co. Deeds,* xiii. 190, 281, 364. The deed of the territory of Lynn and Reading, September 4, 1686, is printed from *Essex Co. Deeds* in Lewis, *History of Lynn,* 51–54; and that of Salem, October 11, 1686, is in *Mass. Hist. Coll.* vi. 278–281, and Felt, *Annals of Salem,* i. 28–33. The deed of Marblehead lands, July 18, 1684, is earlier than those of Salem and Lynn, and is recorded in *Essex Co. Deeds,* vii. 1–2, 9. James Rumney Marsh and David

Squa Sachem and Webcowet of 1639, is known to have been given for the Mystic Side and Malden Lands.[102]

"As property is defined," says Judge Sullivan, "there may be a question, how far the savages had acquired one in the soil of this wilderness;"[103] and the practice of the settlers of New England indicates that they were of the same opinion and were inclined to take advantage of the doubt. They saw in the apparently aimless wanderings of the Indians no traces of that occupancy and subjugation of the earth which civilization has made a necessity and the Scripture enjoins as a duty.[104] The aborigines cleared no land, taking only for the temporary purposes of their rude agriculture such spots as might be found ready to their hands. They made no permanent enclosures; nor had they any clear idea of the nature of inheritance. Their occupancy had little more of fixity in it than that of the wild beasts that divided with them the scanty sustenance which nature, not their own exertions, afforded them. Notwithstanding the apparent solemnity and earnestness which attended their several treaties with the English, it is not difficult to see how imperfectly they understood the contracts which they made, and how much more important, to their minds, than the lands or privileges conveyed were the few necessities or useless trinkets which they were to receive. Nor did they appear to recognize in these formal contracts anything binding beyond the immediate future; for their claims were repeatedly renewed when the supplies which they had so easily secured were exhausted or a fresh band of unsatisfied kinsmen appeared.

On the other hand, there is too often an appearance of overreaching on the part of the grantees. Liberal and indefinite bounds were secured, and considerations, ridiculous in their

---

Kunkshamooshaw conveyed land lying in Lynn and the pan-handle of Boston, near Reading line, to Daniel Hitchens, July 28, 1686, *Essex Co. Deeds*, vii. 88. All these were given by heirs of George No Nose, and they are the sources of most of the information which has been gathered in relation to his family.

[102] In one of the Rumney Marsh deeds a small tract is described as "lyeing in Charlestowne and Mauldin Bounds." *Suffolk Co. Deeds*, xiii. 364.

[103] Sullivan, *History of Land Titles in Massachusetts*, 23.

[104] Gen. i. 28, ix. 1. In 1633 the Court measured the rights of the Indians by these references. *General Lawes and Libertyes*, 40. Ed. 1660.

scantiness, were rendered to the unsophisticated savages. Treaties and covenants were couched in language which it is impossible that the Indians could have understood. The handful of beads, the red coat, or the pot of wine was of more present consequence than the meaningless words which were read to them from the strip of paper on which they made their rude marks. There is no substantial evidence that the English themselves regarded the titles gained under such circumstances as of any great importance, except as they served to answer present purposes, until they sought them as a possible defence against the arbitrary measures of Andros. There is somewhat of grim justice in an incident which is related of that unpopular governor, who, on being shown " an Indian Deed for Land, said that their hand was no more worth than a scratch with a Bear's paw." [105]

The best that can be said of the Indians is, that they were often friends in need and that their virtues were those of simplicity and ignorance. The worst that can be said of them is, that they were savages and were true to their nature whether friends or foes. Their presence forms a romantic background in the history of New England; but it is a background blackened with terror and stained with blood. While the treatment which they received and the means employed in their removal were not always honorable to the settlers nor just to the Indians — sometimes wicked and cruel — humanity has not suffered by their disappearance. They were in the way of civilization, and, opposing it, they were doomed as surely as the wild beasts that infested the forests and have disappeared with them.

Tradition has preserved the memory of the red men in Malden, and still points with uncertain finger to the places of their former abode on the high lands and in the valleys in the vicinity of Powder Horn Hill; and, to enforce this vague testimony, the tool of the laborer has at times uncovered the bones of the lords of the forest. Near by, the name of Sagamore Hill, so called as early as 1641,[106] and now superseded by the some-

---

[105] *The Revolution in New-England Justified,* in *Andros Tracts,* ii. 92; also *Mass. Archives,* xxxv. 169.

[106] *Mass. Colony Records,* i. 340.

what inflated and less distinctive title of Mount Washington, recalls the memories of the old days; and traces of habitation around it and scattered implements and broken utensils, often found, are tangible proofs of the reality of the Indians' former presence.[107] On the old road to Winnisimmet there remained until within a few years the Nichols farm house, a well preserved relic of the seventeenth century, within whose walls the visitor might see the spot where household legend said the axe of the settler clove the head of an Indian and insured safety to the wife and child who were hidden from sight in the ample fireplace near by.[108]

Some remembrance or traditions of their former dwelling places may have lingered long in the Indian mind; for in the early part of this century a party from a distance visited Sagamore Hill and remained in its vicinity several months.[109]

[107] A skull and other portions of a skeleton were found on the Nichols farm in Everett in 1874; and skeletons were disinterred there about thirty years before. *Malden Tribune,* March 28, 1874. — A skeleton, with a pipe and other relics, was found in Revere twenty years ago. *Boston Journal,* March 23, 1878. — Remains of Indian habitations, with shell heaps and implements, have been found in the vicinity of Sagamore Hill and upon Powder Horn Hill in Chelsea. *Chelsea Telegraph,* December 11, 1880. — In 1888–90, burial places were found and interesting discoveries made at Winthrop on several occasions. *Boston Post,* April 30, 1888; August 23, 1888; February 21, 1889; April 4, 1890. — The *Malden Messenger,* March 19, 1859, contains a short article on the Indian works at Sagamore Hill, by the late William B. Shedd. — Indian bones and relics were found upon the Ballard farm at East Saugus in 1891. *Malden City Press,* December 26, 1891.

[108] This old house, which stood on the hill on the north side of the road, about half-way from Waters's Spring to Everett Avenue, was the homestead of John Nichols, who bought it of John Marble in 1746. It had been removed at some time from its original location at Moulton's Island, and then consisted only of the great chimney and the two or three rooms which leaned against its eastern side. About the year 1759, Nichols enlarged it upon the western side, employing therefor Benjamin Blaney, afterwards the Revolutionary captain, who had just completed his service as an apprentice. With its overhanging second story it was a most interesting example of a house of the colonial period; and it retained its peculiar characteristics until its removal, some time before 1879, to Central Avenue, near Hancock Street. It was then changed beyond recognition.

The tradition relating to the killing of the Indian is as briefly related in the text. The tribe to which he belonged is said to have lived in the vicinity, and to have exonerated the white man. No names are mentioned; but the story, which seems probable, must relate to events which took place at an early date at Moulton's Island.

[109] "Between the years 1806 and 1810, some Leominster Indians visited Sagamore Hill, and the late Mr. Robert Pratt's father let them occupy a house which stood near the residence of Dr. Cheever. Their chief man was named Comanche Brown." Chamberlain, in *Chelsea Telegraph,* December 11, 1880.

CHAPTER III.

ALLOTMENTS AND SETTLEMENT.

IT was not long after the Spragues passed over the land before the pleasant southern and western exposure of the uplands from Powder Horn Hill[1] to the head of the North River, with the open lands of the plains, and the natural hay-fields of the meadows and salt marshes, lying in close proximity, attracted the attention of the new-comers on the other side of the Mystic; and the "uncouth wilderness" began to be fitted for the uses of civilization. Governor Cradock's men had already crossed the river and built, west of Wilson's Point, the first house, probably a temporary one, upon its northern bank; and Governor Winthrop, with Increase Nowell, John Eliot, and others, viewing the country, February 7, 163½, had found

---

[1] So called by the earliest settlers.

"[Novembʳ 7ᵗʰ 1632] It is *ordered* that the necke of land betwixte Powder Horne Hill & Pullen Poynte shall belonge to Boston, to be enioyed by the inhabitants thereof for euer." *Mass. Colony Records*, i. 101.

The origin of the name is unknown. Its shape hardly suggests it; but it may have come from the winding creek in the marshes near by, which in 1640 was known as "pouder horne Creeke, parting betweene the land of Mʳ Bellinghame and Mʳ Nicholas Parker." *Boston Town Records*, i. 49. The neighboring hill was known as Sagamore Hill in 1641. The Chelsea hills in 1740, and long after, were covered with forests. Tuckerman, *Anniversary Sermon*, 8.

A very great pond, having in the midst an island of about one acre, and very thick with trees of pine and beech; and the pond had divers small rocks, standing up here and there in it, which they therefore called Spot Pond. They went all about it upon the ice. From thence (towards the N. W. about half a mile,) they came to the top of a very high rock, beneath which, (towards the N.) lies a goodly plain, part open land, and part woody, from whence there is a fair prospect, but it being then close and rainy, they could see but a small distance. This place they called Cheese Rock,[2] because, when they went to eat somewhat, they had only cheese, (the governour's man forgetting, for haste, to put up some bread).[3]

The territory thus passed over by John Winthrop and his companions, was the wildest and most picturesque which could be found in the country around; and Middlesex Fells still holds within its borders many traces of its old-time beauty. The exploring party had looked out upon the pleasant plain of Stoneham, and the hills above Mystic Side had met their view as their eyes ranged around the horizon to the glimpses of the distant sea; but they had not noticed the valley of the Three Mile Brook which was hidden by the forest and the hills. That was first to be settled.

1633
2 July.

It is *ordered* that the ground lyeing betwixt the North Ryv[r] & the creeke on the north side of M Mauacks, & soe vpp into the country, shall belonge to the inhabitants of Charlton.[4]

This order of the General Court confirmed to the Charlestown settlers the land between the Island End River and the North River, running northwardly to indefinite bounds. It may have been that some had already entered upon this land as settlers, but it is doubtful. Elias Maverick was seated at Winnisimmet, where he had been, perhaps, for several years, on the land now occupied by the United States Government. Of this place, Samuel Maverick, one of the "old planters," wrote in 1660: —

[1] This was Bear Hill in Stoneham, from which on a clear day they might have seen the distant Wachusett and Monadnock, lifting their heads from forests into whose depths no white man had entered.

[3] Winthrop, *New England*, i. 69.

[4] *Mass. Colony Records*, i. 106.

One house yet standing there which is the Antientest house in the Massachusetts Goverment. a house which in the yeare 1625 I fortified with a Pillizado and fflankers and gunnes both belowe and above in them which awed the Indians who at that time had a mind to Cutt off the English, They once faced it but receiveing a repulse never attempted it more although (as now they confesse) they repented it when about 2 yeares after they saw so many English come over.[5]

Opposite the Maverick plantation, upon the Malden side of the river, were good grounds upon Wormwood Point and Moulton's Island, which would be likely to be the earliest occupied of the Mystic Side lands.[6] Edward Johnson, writing of the arrival of Winthrop and his party in 1630, says : —

On the North side of *Charles* River, they landed neare a small Island, called *Noddells* Island, where one Mr. *Samuel Mavereck* then living, . . . had built a small Fort . . . to protect him from the *Indians*. About one mile distant upon the River ran a small creeke, taking its Name from Major Gen. *Edward Gibbons*, who dwelt there for some yeares after.[7]

This led Mr. Frothingham, and several writers after him, to declare that Gibbons had his house on the easterly bank of the Mystic in Malden. This would commend the old soldier to us as the earliest known settler of Mystic Side, did not a closer examination show that the river and the neck of Charlestown

[5] Maverick, *Briefe Discription of New England*, in *N. E. Hist. and Geneal. Register*, xxxix. 38.

[6] Wormwood Point has since been known as Sweetser's, Beacham's, or Van Voorhis's Point, as its ownership has changed. It was known as Wormwood Point as early as 164%. *Suffolk Co. Deeds*, i. 17. In a survey of the streets of Charlestown, 1713-14, the old name was preserved. *Charlestown Archives*, xxxiv. 265, 266. It was sometimes mentioned as Wormall's or Wormore's Point. *Malden Town Records*, 1738; March 5, 174¾.

Moulton's Island was that long, smooth hill in the marshes on the South River, of which a small section remained in 1898, most of the hill having disappeared before the shovels and carts of improvement. It received its name from Thomas Moulton, an early settler, who may have built near the landing there; and when, in the course of years, Moulton gave place to his son-in-law, Thomas Mitchell, its name was changed to Mitchell's Island. Latterly it has been known as the Island or Island End, and the river has become the Island End River. Island End must not be confounded with Island Hill, a rocky hill on the west side of Main Street, between Forest Street and Pine Banks Park, which in early days was surrounded by the meadows of Three Mile Brook. That, too, in 1898 is gradually crumbling before the steam drill and cartridge of restless improvement.

[7] Johnson, *Wonder-working Providence*, 37.

divided him from that honor. The Charlestown Records expressly declare that, with three others, he "went and built in the maine on the north-east side of the north-west creeke of this town."[8] This places him on the southerly side of Somerville, where Gibbons's River, as mentioned by Johnson, preserved his memory for many years.

West of the North River, and between that and the territory afterwards covered by the Cradock grant of 1634,[9] which became in time "a peculiar town" under the name of Medford, were the lands which soon became the subjects of the following grants: —

Apr. 1st. 1634. There is two hundred acres of land graunted to M[r] I. Nowell, lyeing & being on the west side of the North Ryv, otherwise called the Three Myle Brooke.

There is two hundred acres of land graunted to M[r] J[o]: Wilson, pastor of the church of Boston, lyeing nexte the land graunted to M[r] Nowell on the south, & next Meadford on the north.[10]

The Wilson farm included that promontory which juts into the marshes near the mouth of the North River, and which was formerly known as Wilson's Point, as Blanchard's Point, and now as Wellington. It extended from the Mystic to the little creek, which parts Medford and Malden, and from the North, or Malden, River, to the easterly line of the Cradock grant. A house was standing upon it in 1651, which I am led to believe was built before 1640, perhaps as early as the Cradock house. Traces of its cellar and chimney could be seen upon

---

[8] Frothingham, *History of Charlestown*, 59.

[9] The grant of 1634 appears to have merely confirmed to Cradock the territory of about twenty-five hundred acres which his men had already occupied. It did not include the Wellington farm, as Mr. Frothingham states, *History of Charlestown*, 90, as that was the tract granted to Mr. Wilson. This large grant, known as Medford, passed by purchase in 1652 into the hands of Edward Collins, who soon after sold sixteen hundred acres and the house, which still stands upon the bank of the Mystic, to Richard Russell. It was afterwards divided among the Wades, Tuftses, and others; and it gradually passed from its original form of a manor or plantation into that of a town, which it finally accomplished in 1684. This view, as stated by Mr. Frothingham, *History of Charlestown*, 89-93, is generally accepted, although a recent local historian has, with little success, attempted to disprove it. The original form of its name may have had a natural origin in its surroundings — Meadford, the ford in the meadow.

[10] *Mass. Colony Records*, i. 114.

the highest part of the Wellington farm in 1855.[11]   A landing-place was established on the North River, near by, which was reached by a way across the marsh.   Mr. Wilson retained pos-session of this grant until February 12, 1659½, when he sold it to Thomas Blanchard, of Braintree, for two hundred pounds.[12] After the death of Thomas Blanchard, in 1654, the house and lands were divided between two of his sons, George and Nathaniel; and the latter, in 1657, sold one-half of his land to their younger brother, Samuel, who was then building a second house on one acre of the land "called & known by the name of the flax ground, lying length ways betwixt the high way side, and some Swamp or waste ground."[13]   The lands gradually went out of the Blanchard family, by sale, and in 1795 the only house which was standing upon the point was owned and occupied by Captain Wymond Bradbury, a retired mariner.

The Nowell grant, which was situated north of the Wilson lands, covered the present Edgeworth ward and extended out upon the Medford plain to the Cradock farm.   On the north it was separated from the common lands by land which it was proposed, in 1635, to divide as hay-lots, and which Nowell described as "Joining [to] my ffarme bettweene [it] & the Salem Highway."[14]   For some reason the division was not made, and the intervening land became a portion of the seventh range of the allotment of 1638.   The two hundred acres were sold to Peter Tufts in 1663 by Parnell Nowell, as executrix,[15] and with large additions, gained by purchase from the Cradock farm, remained in the family of the purchaser many years.   A house was built upon the firm land jutting out towards the river, near where the property of the United States is now situated on Medford street.   Here in 1792 a bridge was built

[11] Brooks, *History of Medford*, 39. Mr. Brooks is in error in attributing the building of this house to Cradock's men. The Cradock grant, as I have before shown, did not extend so far east.   It was undoubtedly built by Wilson.   Drake, *History of Boston*, 176, and others have given the impression that this land was exchanged for a grant at Mount Wollas-ton; but Wilson received and retained the land at both places. *Boston Town Records*, i. 4.

[12] *Suffolk Co. Deeds*, i. 223.
[13] *Midd. Co. Deeds*, ii. 51, 96.
[14] *Charlestown Archives*, xx. 33.
[15] *Midd. Co. Deeds*, iii. 85.

across the river by Stephen Tufts, which, however, had disappeared before 1820. In 1823 this portion of the farm, comprising seventy-five acres, was sold by Joseph Warren Tufts to
Amos Newton,[16] and was occupied by the buyer and his son
until it became a part of the extensive purchases of the Edgeworth Company. The grants of Wilson and Nowell, forming a
part of Charlestown on Mystic Side, separated Malden and Medford until 1726, when they were annexed to the former town.

The order of 1633 having loosely defined the bounds of the
Charlestown lands north of the Mystic, that town appointed,
October 13, 1634, a committee, of which one member was
William Brackenbury, who was afterwards a selectman of the
town whose foundations were being laid, to divide the common
land in the territory which now was first known as Mystic Side
and Mystic Field. This division, which had been voted,
January 9, 163¾, gave ten acres to each inhabitant, but during
the next year twenty-nine of them "Willingly Surrendred for
the good of the Towne pᵗ of theire ground on mistick side."
The records may be understood to indicate that all finally
acquiesced, and that each alternate five-acre lot was reserved
for future settlers. The record of the completed allotment,
which was made two years later, shows seventy-five proprietors;
and although it is a list of Charlestown inhabitants, it is of
interest here as being the roll of the first white landholders of
the future town of Malden.

*The first Division of Lands one Mistick syde Ten Acres to A house:
wher of five were again resigned for the accommodatting of After
comers.*

No: of Lot	4:	Mʳ Increase Nowell	5
		pt. of Thō: Hubberd.	
	5:	Edward Jones	5
	6:	Thomas Moulten	5
	7:	William Learned	5
	8:	Thomas Squire	5
	9:	George Whitehand	5
	10:	Sam: Richeson	5

[16] *Midd. Co. Deeds,* cclxxii. 312.

No: of Lot 11 : William Baker 5
          12 : John Hodges 5
          13 : Peter Garland 5
          14 : Mr Zacha: Symes 5
          15 : Walter Palmer 5
          16 : Robert Hale 5
          17 : George Felch 5
          18 : Tho: Minor 5
          19 : John Greene 5
          20 : William Dade 5
          21 : Rice Cole 5
          22 : Nicho Stower 5
          23 :
          24 : Thō. James 5
          25 : Seth Switzer 5
          26 : Edwa: Gibbons 5
          27 : Edwa: Convers 5
          28 : M Andrews 5
          29 : Rich: Palgrave 5
          30 : M^n Higginson 5
          31 : John Haule 5
          32 : John Woolrych 5
          33 : Will: Brakenbury 5
          34 : Mr Eason of Hauks 5
          35 : Abrah: Palmer 5
          36 : James Browne 5
          37 : Tho: Squire : Tho: Ewer . . 5
                of Jos. Hubbe :
     38 : 39 : Mr Hough 20
          40 : Ralph Sprague 5
          41 : James Tomson 5
          42 : Abra: Palmer of m^r· Crow . . 5
          43 : Edwa: Burton 5
          44 : Tho: James 5
          45 : m^n· Eason 5
                Beniamine Hubbard 5
                Henry Lawrence 5
                William Johnson 5
                John Lewis 5
                Samuell Haule 5
                Michaell Bastowe 5
                Ezekiell Richeson 5
                James Pemberton 5
                Robert Longe 5

Robert Sedgwick	5
John Palmer	5
Widdowe Harwode	5
Widdowe Wilkins[on] . . . ⁓	5
Richard Kettell	5
Thomas Peirce	5
George Hepbourn	5
John Mowsall	5
William Nash	5
Ralph Mowsall	5
Thomas Richardson	5
Edward Sturgis	5
George Hutcheson	5
James Heyden	5
Edward Carrington	5
Thomas Ewer	5
Rice Morris	5
Thomas Knower	5
Thomas Lyne	5
Edward Mellowes	5
Richard Sprague	5
William Frothingham	5
Robert Rand	5
George Buncker	5
Abraham Mellows	5
Nicholas Davis	5 [17]

These lands, which were laid out in lots of ten poles wide by eighty poles long, began at the south-east corner of Mystic Side at a point near the westerly slope of Powder Horn Hill and upon the Boston line, which was soon after defined. The first lot was assigned to Thomas Hubbard, or Hobart, and soon transferred to Increase Nowell, who may be considered as the

[17] *Charlestown Archives.* xxxiv. 82. The record of this allotment was made, or probably copied from the committee's report, in 1637. which has led a recent editor to state that this first division of Mystic Side lands was made in that year. *Report of the* [*Boston*] *Record Commissioners*, iii. 73. Those lots which appear unnumbered in the record were made by dividing the original lots; and the order of the names in the numbered and unnumbered lists indicates very nearly the relative order of proprietorship. Thus Nowell and B. Hubbard would have occupied the two divisions of lot 4, and Jones and Lawrence those of lot 5; but by some arrangement or bargain, Jones and Hubbard exchanged places when the ownership was settled in the Book of Possessions. A few such changes are found in the final ordering of the division; but the sequence of the lists was generally followed.

first recorded land owner of Mystic Side east of the North
River. It was described in 1638, as

> ffive Acres of woodland scituate and lying in misticke feilde; butting
> to the south upon Rob. Long his meaddow, to the north upon
> Mr Simmes, bounded on the east by Boston line and on the west by
> [Edward Joanes.] [18]

From this the lots ran westerly along the edge of the salt
marshes of the South, or Island End, River to the neck of firm
land which runs down to Wormwood Point and the Mystic.
They then ran northerly, along the meadows and uplands,
towards the head of the North River and apparently beyond
Sandy Bank, where the burying ground was afterwards begun.[19]
Though these lots are described as woodlands, I am inclined to
believe that they were of light, open growth on the upper
portions and generally clear land towards the meadows.

On the inner or country side of the lots ran a land-way,
parting them from the reserved or common land; and on the
other side ran a drift-way or cattle-way along the marshes and
meadows. The present Chelsea Street in Everett, from the
Chelsea line to Everett Square, is certainly, from its position, a
portion of the old drift-way, although in a later record it is described, perhaps inadvertently, as running at the head of the five-
acre lots. It then turned to the south-west, and, running in the
line of School Street, met the way to the Mystic, where the
house of James Barrett stood as early as 1648.[20] This house,
or its successor, became known as the Call house, and was
razed not many years ago. The way to the Mystic formed the
eastern line of the lots running northerly, and ultimately
became the settled way to Reading. Bow Street in Everett and

[18] *Charlestown Archives*, xxxiv. 26.
This lot became a part of the farm of
Thomas Whittemore.

[19] At the head of the river was the
lot of Mrs. Easton, numbered 45 in the
list, which is often referred to as the
lot of Thomas Beecher, to whom it was
originally granted. Beecher was a sea-
captain who died before 1637. He had
married Christian Copper, a widow of
Wapping, near London, who, when the

allotment was recorded had married her
third husband, Nicholas Easton, afterwards President and Governor of the
colony of Rhode Island. This lot was
the most northerly of the ten-acre lots
of the earlier plan.

[20] This house stood on three acres of
land which Barrett bought of George
Felt in 1648. *Charlestown Archives*,
xxxiv. 121.

the portion of Broadway near Malden Bridge follow the ancient way. The drift-way on the westerly side, towards the North River, remains only in the form of ancient rights of way to the salt marshes.

It had been voted, April 2, 1634, "That the Hay Land bee Laid out as soone as convenient for wch 13 men were chosen to ord^r y^t bussines;" and, later, it was ordered, February 12, 163⅚, that "None [are] to have right to Hay ground y^t resigne not halfe theire 10 Acre Lotts at mistick side." Soon after "It was agreed y^t Ezek. Richeson, W^m ffrothingham, Tho: Peirce, Wm Baker, Edmo^d Hubberd Junio^r, and Thos: Squire, should goe & stake out the Hay ground, bettweene each stakes for two Cowes."[21] The allotment was agreed upon by the committee, February 9, 163⅚, and it divided among the inhabitants two hundred and seventy-seven lots, of varying size, of which by far the greater number were on Mystic Side, a few being at Menotomy, now Arlington, and others on the western bank of the lower Mystic. The lots upon Mystic Side, which are not as readily identified as the grants of arable and wood land, were in the marshes and meadows, which, as has been stated, produced a plentiful growth of native grasses, and ran between the rivers and the drift-way which formed the outer bound of the five-acre lots. Along the marshes of the North River, each lot generally ran from the upland to the river, although in some cases, where the bends of the river carried it far from the firm ground, intervening lots were granted with rights of passage over the adjacent marsh. Many of the larger lots have retained to the present day small pieces of hard land at their upper edges, or have prescriptive rights to land and cure hay upon the neighboring upland — a probable survival of the ancient drift-way and the privileges which it afforded. Besides the hay-lots along the five-acre lots, several were laid out in the meadows beyond Mount Prospect, now better known as Wayte's Mount.

While the arrangements were being made for the apportionment of the hay-lands, the following entry was made in the Charlestown records: —

---

[21] *Charlestown Archives, xx. in loco.*

[1635.] Edwd Convers, Wm Brackenbury & Mr Abrā. Palmer were desired to goe upp into the Country upon discovery 3 or 4 daies for wch we agreed they should bee sattisfied at the Charge of the Towne.[22]

A tradition in relation to this expedition has come down to us. It is said that a party, having been sent out into the country, "returned and reported, that, having reached a mountainous and rocky country, they deemed it best to come back, as there was little probability that the settlement would ever extend beyond these mountains."[23] They had seen the line of the Middlesex Fells or the hardly less wild range eastward of Wayte's Mount, bounding the Scadan woods.[24] However, the explorers saw something better than the dark forests which covered the rocky northern hills. They found the agreeable table lands which stretch from Powder Horn Hill to the head of the North River, and now form the most pleasant parts of Malden and Everett. Beyond the Great Swamp they saw the fair plain of Scadan, lying at the feet of its abrupt hills; and, farther west, was the fertile valley of Harvell's Brook, now in the centre of a growing city. Still farther west, they may have passed over the wide plain which lies beyond the Three Mile Brook and extends within the bounds of the Cradock grant.

[22] *Charlestown Archives,* xx. *in loco.*

[23] Rev. John G. Adams, D.D., in *Bi-Centennial Book of Malden,* 95.

[24] Scadan, the former name of the territory east of Faulkner. It is to be regretted that a tasteless affectation has in many instances destroyed the familiar names of earlier years. The sturdy sense which has preserved in London the titles of Rotten Row or Cheapside would have retained in Malden those of Scadan and Tyot. Certainly the elder names would have been as dignified as those of Maplewood and Linden, or Oak Grove.

I have sought diligently for the origin of *Scadan* without a great success. *Sceadan* in the old English, which our fathers may have brought here, was *separate* or *send away,* and it might have applied to the Great Swamp which separated the lands of Mystic Side, or sent the traveller away from a direct path into the crooked trail among the north-ern hills. Or, it may have been the spot which separated the sources of Harvell's Brook and the Pines River and sent away their waters on the one hand to the Mystic and on the other to the Abousett.

An Indian scholar, on being asked by the writer what Scadan should be, inquired if it were a locality, and said that it must be a low or swampy place near many great rocks. This certainly described the swamps and rocky hills of our Scadan, of which he had no knowledge. On the contrary, the eminent authority, the late James Hammond Trumbull, whose knowledge in the Indian tongues no man could equal, writes:—

"Scadan, as it stands, is not an Indian name, though it may be an abbreviation or a remnant of an Indian name. I can find in it no trace of the meaning you assign to it."

The report of the explorers, doubtless, prepared the way for a further division of the lands of Mystic Side.

Concerning which division of Lands it was Jointly Agreed

That yᵉ Lotts on Mistickside should be one hundred Pole in length each five Acres being eight Pole in breadth, to begin next Powder horne hill at & to goe by A Streight Line to A marked Tree at the end of Tho: Beecher's Lott at the head of the North River, & from thence to goe backe againe to Boston Bounds, & from thence againe to returne & to the end of the Plott toward the Written Tree : the othʳ Plott at the head of the North River to begin at Mʳ Nowell's ffarme whe. the formʳ is Laid out:

And it was farthʳ ordʳᵈ yᵗ where these Lands are so devided, convenient Highwaies shalbe allowed in the most convenient places through any such allottmˢ at the discretion of those who shalbe designed to Lay them out : And what Land is not found within the Plotts is to bee laid out after the Plotts in yᵉ most convenient places.

A reservation was then made by the following order : —

[1638. 20. 2ᵐᵒ·] It was ordʳᵈ yᵗ all the Land on Mistickside at the head of yᵉ 5 Acre Lotts to yᵉ straite Line from Powdʳ horne hill to the head of the North River shalbe reserved (togethʳ with so much as shall make it up 300 Acres above Mʳ Craddocks ffarme where it may bee convenient) in yᵉ hands of yᵉ Towne for yᵉ use of such desireable persons as shalbe received in with anothʳ officer, [*or minister.*] [26]

The reserved land embraced a tract nominally of two hundred acres, which was found upon measurement to amount to about two hundred and sixty acres, lying above the five-acre lots upon the plain in the vicinity of Corey and Bucknam Streets in Everett, and upon the highlands above it. Northward it extended beyond the line of Cross Street in Malden. We shall notice its final division hereafter. The portion reserved above the Cradock farm was not within the bounds of the future town of Malden.

The great allotment was made April 23, 1638, and divided the lands of Mystic Side and a larger tract above the Mystic Ponds in that part of Charlestown which soon became Woburn, to one hundred and fourteen inhabitants, of whom one hundred and seven received lots on Mystic Side. The record gives in three

---

[26] *Charlestown Archives,* xx. 18.

columns: — first, "ye number of Acres on Misticke side;" second, "the number of Acres above ye Ponds;" and third, "the five Acres y^t wee had in Possession Afforetime." The latter refers to the allotment of five-acre lots in 1633¾.

Land Laid out by Lot on Mistickside & above the Ponds the three & twentieth day of ye second month 1638

	M^r [Increase] Nowell	. . . .	60 –	135 –	5
	M^r [Zackary] Sims	. . . . .	40 –	100 –	5
	M^r [John] Greene	. . . .	45 –	50 –	5
	Ralph Mousall	. . . . . .	15 –	40 –	5
N° 2 :	Richd Miller	. . . . . .	5 –	15 –	5
N° 3 :	Sam^{ll} Cartar	. . . . . .	5 –	5 –	0
N° 4 :	Jno Goulde	. . . . .	10 –	25 –	0
N° 5 :	Thos Cartar	. . . . .	25 –	55 –	0
N° 6 :	Thos Wickes	. . . . . .	5 –	10 –	0
N° 7 :	Robt Blott	. . . . . .	15 –	35 –	0
N° 8 :	James Greene	. . . . . .	5 –	15 –	0
N° 9 :	John Martin	. . . . . .	10 –	20 –	0
N° 10 :	Edwd Convers	. . . . .	35 –	80 –	0
N° 11 :	Thos Moulton	. . . . .	10 –	30 –	5
N° 12 :	M^r [Jno] Crow	. . . . .	25 –	50 –	0
N° 13 :	Danl Shepherdson	. . . .	10 –	20 –	0
N° 14 :	Seth Switzer	. . . . .	10 –	30 –	5
N° 15 :	Edwd Gibbons	. . . . .	15 –	45 –	5
N° 16 :	Hen: Bullocke	. . . . .	5 –	25 –	0
N° 17 :	Jno Burrage	. . . . .	5 –	5 –	0
N° 18 :	Wm Smith . . . 5 – 5 – 0 ⎫ Jose: Ketchering . 5 – 15 – 0 ⎭		10 –	20 –	0
N° 19 :	Saml Haule	. . . . . .	20 –	40 –	5
N° 20 :	James Tomson	. . . . .	5 –	30 –	5
N° 21 :	Wm Powell	. . . . .	5 –	10 –	0
N° 22 :	Abra: Pratt	. . . . . .	10 –	20 –	0
N° 23 :	Isack Cole	. . . . . .	10 –	20 –	0
N° 24 :	Wm Batchelor	. . . . .	15 –	30 –	0
N° 25 :	Geo: Hutchinson	. . . .	5 –	30 –	5
N° 26 :	Thos Lynde	. . . . .	35 –	80 –	5
N° 27 :	Wm Brackenbury	. . . .	15 –	40 –	5
N° 28 :	James Pemberton	. . . .	5 –	30 –	5
N° 29 :	Peter Garland	. . . . .	5 –	15 –	5
N° 30 :	Robt Rand	. . . . . .	15 –	35 –	5
N° 31 :	Ezek^l Richeson	. . . . .	35 –	85 –	5
N° 32 :	John Hodges .	. . . . .	5 –	30 –	5

N.° 33 : Rice Cole . . . . 10 – 50 – 5
N.° 34 : M.ʳ Jn.° Harvard . . . . . . 60 – 120 – 0
N.° 35 : Rich.ᵈ Sprague . . . . . . 20 – 55 – 5
N.° 36 : Tho.ˢ Goble . . . . 15 – 35 – 0
N.° 37 : James Browne . . . . . . 15 – 40 – 5
N.° 38 : Robt Hawkins . . . . . . 10 – 20 – 0
N.° 39 : goo: Tho.ˢ Caule . . . . 5 – 15 – 0
N.° 40 : Jose: Coleman . . . . . . 5 – 15 – 0
N.° 41 : W.ᵐ Nash . . . . 5 – 30 – 5
N.° 42 : W.ᵐ ffrothingale . . . . . . 20 – 40 – 5
N.° 43 : M.ʳ Nicho.ˢ Trarice . . . . . 15 – 35 – 0
N.° 44 : Robt Shorthus . . . . . . 5 – 20 – 0
N.° 45 : Benia.ⁿ Hubberd . . . . . . 10 – 25 – 5
N.° 46 : Mrs. Ann Higginson . . . 20 – 45 – 5
N.° 47 : Nich.ˢ Davis . . . . ، . . 5 – 30 – 5
N.° 48 : Jn.° Haule . . . . 5 – 25 – 5
N.° 49 : Rich.ᵈ Kettle . . . . 5 – 20 – 5
N.° 50 : John Palmer . . . . 0 – 10 – 5
N.° 51 : W.ᵐ Dade . . . . 5 – 30 – 5
N.° 52 : Jn.° Lewis . . . . 0 – 15 – 5
N.° 53 : Jn.° Woolrich . . . . . . 5 – 25 – 5
N.° 54 : Wido: Wilkeson . . . . . . 5 – 15 – 5
N.° 55 : James Hubberd . . . . . . 5 – 10 – 0
N.° 56 : Tho.ˢ Pearce . . . . 15 – 50 – 5
N.° 57 : Rich.ᵈ Palgrave . . . . . . 20 – 50 – 5
N.° 58 : Edw.ᵈ Burton . . . . 0 – 10 – 5
N.° 59 : Tho.ˢ Richeson . . . . . . 0 – 15 – 5
       Abra: Hill . . . . . . } 5
N.° 60 : John Mousall . . . . . . } 20 – 45 – 5
N.° 61 : Geo: Hebourne . . . . . . 5 – 30 – 5
N.° 62 : James Mathews . . . . . . 10 – 20 – 0
N.° 63 : Abra: Palmer . . . . 20 – 55 – 0
N.° 64 : M.ʳ [W.ᵐ] Witherall . . . . 15 – 30 – 0
N.° 65 : Walter Palmer . . . . . . 30 – 65 – 5
N.° 66 : Geo: Buncker . . . . . . 75 – 180 – 5
N.° 67 : Geo: Knore . . . . 5 – 10 – 0
N.° 68 : Edw.ᵈ Carrington . . . . 5 – 15 – 5
N.° 69 : Jn.° Brimsmead . . . . . . 5 – 15 – 0
N.° 70 : Phillip Drincker . . . . . . 10 – 20 – 0
N.° 71 : Geo: ffelch . . . . 5 – 20 – 5
N.° 72 : Edw.ᵈ Sturges . . . . 0 – 5 – 5
N.° 73 : Rice Morris . . . . 5 – 15 – 5
N.° 74 : Joshua Tedd . . . . 5 – 15 – 0

Nº 75 : Mᵣˢ [Widow Katherⁿ] Coitemore   20 –   40 – 0
Nº 76 : John Sibley . . . . 10 –   20 – 0
Nº 77 : Edwᵈ Johnson . . . . . . 40 –   80 – 0
Nº 78 : Hen: Lawrance . . . . . . 0 –   15 – 5
Nº 79 : Wᵐ Johnson . . . . 5 –   30 – 5
Nº 80 : James Hayden . . . . . . 5 –   15 – 5
Nº 81 : Thoˢ Knore . . . . 5 –   20 – 5
Nº 82 : ffra: Norton . . . . 25 –   45 – 0
Nº 83 : Robt Long . . . . 30 –   65 – 5
Nº 84 : Robt Cutler . . . . 10 –   25 – 0
Nº 85 : Nichoˢ Stowers . . . . . . 25 –   60 – 5
Nº 86 : John Tedd . . . . 10 –   20 – 0
Nº 87 : Wᵐ Baker . . . . 5 –   20 – 5
Nº 88 : Geo: Whitehand . . . . . 10 –   30 – 5
Nº 89 : Robt Leach . . . . 5 –   10 – 0
Nº 90 : Robt Hale . . . . 15 –   40 – 5
Nº 91 : Thoˢ Brigden . . . . 15 –   25 – 0
Nº 92 : Mathʷ Smith . . . . 5 –   15 – 0
Nº 93 : Abra: Mellowes . .   10. 35. 5 }
         Edwᵈ Mellowes . .   25. 60. 0 } 35 – 95 – 5
Nº 94 : Widow Harwood . . . . . 0 –   15 – 5
Nº 95 : Wᵐ Lerned . . . . 15 –   40 – 5
Nº 96 : Samˡˡ Richerdson . . . . . 15 –   40 – 5
Nº 97 : Michˡˡ Barstow . . . . . . 10 –   25 – 5
Nº 98 : Stephⁿ fforsditch . . . . . 20 –   40 – 0
Nº 99 : ffaintnot Winds . . . . . . 5 –   10 – 0
Nº 100 : Captⁿ Robt Sedgwick . . . 35 – 160 – 5
Nº 101 : Theophiˢ Higginson . . . . 5 –   10 – 0
Nº 102 : Thoˢ Ewer . . . . 25 –   60 – 5
Nº 103 : Ralph Sprague . . . . . 35 –   90 – 5
Nº 104 : James Garrett . . . . . . 10 –   30 – 0
Nº 105 : Thoˢ Squire . . . . 5 –   20 – 5
Nº 106 : Edwᵈ Jones . . . . 5 –   25 – 5
Nº 107 : Wᵐ Quicke . . . . 5 –   10 – 0
Nº 108 : Thoˢ Coitmore . . . . . . 35 –   70 – 0 [26]

[26] *Charlestown Archives*, xx. *in loco.* Of Nowell, Symmes, and Greene, the first three in the list, it is said, "These were agreed to have the first without Lott." Forty-five acres were allotted to Greene, the ruling elder of the church, but in the *Book of Possessions* he is credited with fifteen only. James Hayden (No. 80) received ten acres in his lot.

It will be seen that Richard Sprague (35) and Ralph Sprague (103) received, according to the allotment, fifty-five and ninety acres respectively in the land "Above the Ponds." In the *Book of Possessions* they are given sixty and ninety acres, adjoining, in "Pond feilde," southwest of Ell Pond; and there is nothing to correspond with the allot-

The lots on Mystic Side, *east* of the North River, were north of a line drawn from Powder Horn Hill to the head of the river, and ran in six ranges, each one hundred poles in width, northwest from the Boston line. Northerly, they were limited by the rocky hills of Scadan, and by the Long Meadow — the marshes at the head of the North River and along the banks of Pemberton's or Harvell's Brook. On and beyond those hills, too wild and rocky for immediate use, were the commons, which were not divided until 1695.[27]

The first lot of the lower range was the forty acres of the Rev. Zechariah Symmes, the greater part of which became a portion of the farm of Thomas Whittemore and his descendants and so remained until 1845, when it was sold to Nathaniel Sands of New York, and became the subject of an unfortunate speculation which involved a large tract of land in that vicinity. Sagamore Hill, named by a tasteless generation Mount Washington, was within or near its bounds. Next was the unnumbered portion of Increase Nowell, which being sold to Robert Burden, the progenitor of the Burditt family, was a part of his possessions in 1667, when he died. In the same range was the lot, numbered twelve, of John Crow. Fifteen acres of this lot were sold by William Roberts to Rowland Lahorne in 1648. Six years

ments about the Mystic Ponds. This may be explained by the following entry : —

"[18. 12ᵐ 1638.] Inasmuch as it appᵗˢ yᵗ the Land in the great Lotts yᵗ was laid out to Thomas Line & Richᵈ Sprague prooves altogethᵗ unusefull being nothing but Rockes wᶜʰ was wholly besides oᵗ intent, & only through oversight of the Surveyoᵗˢ wee Judge it to bee Just & equall yᵗ they have allowance elswhere to theire sattisfaction they leaveing the afforesᵈ Rocks to lye Common." *Charlestown Archives*, xx. *in loco.* Cf. note 35, this chapter.

²⁷ The completion of the great allotment was marked by the compilation of the *Charlestown Book of Possessions*, now preserved as *Charlestown Archives*, xxxiv., which is fully described in the following extract from the *Charlestown Town Records.*

" 1638.

"On the 28th day of the X month was taken A True Record of all such houses & Lands as are Possessed by the Inhabitaⁿˢ of Charlstown, whethᵗ by purchase, by gift from the Towne, or by allottments as they were devided amongst them by A Joynt Consent aftᵗ the Genⁱⁱ Court had setled theire Bounds, by granting eight miles from the old Meeting house into the Contry Northwest Northrly, &c. the bounds of the sᵈ Towne Lying or being bettwixt Cambridge *alias* New Towne, on the West South west, & Boston Land on the East as it appᵗˢ upon Record by the severⁱⁱ grants of Genⁱⁱ Courts to all the afforesᵈ Bounds."

This volume, which has been printed in the *Third Report of the [Boston] Record Commissioners*, is the Domesday Book of Mystic Side.

later Lahorne transferred his purchase, with a house, to Thomas Skinner, "victualer;" but it is soon found in the occupancy of Thomas Call, as a grantee or tenant of Skinner. The marriage of Skinner with Call's widow, Lydia, after 1678, returned the house and land to their earlier possessor. The later history of this house, which stood near the corner of Cross and Walnut Streets, is given in another place.[28] Farther north, the lot nineteen bordered the Long Meadow, and its twenty acres, forming a sharp angle to the north-east, closed the first and began the second range.

In the second range, lot thirty-one had the Great Swamp near it upon the east; and lot thirty-four, passing through several hands, became the "westermost" of the farms of Job Lane. Here in 1652 were Turkey Hill, afterwards known as Burden's or Burditt's Hill, and a path, the former of which remained almost unscarred by the works of man until 1892, when it began to be built upon. In the latter, perhaps, we may trace the origin of the present Elm Street in Everett. This land was for forty years the home of the Mudges, then of the Chittendens. Lastly, it was the farm of Leavitt Corbett, who will be remembered by many. It is now a portion of the Woodlawn Cemetery Company's lands. Lot forty, a triangle of five acres, met the Boston line and closed the second range.

In the third range, the first three lots, forty-one to forty-three, having been acquired by Nicholas Parker, were sold to Job Lane in 1656 and formed, with some adjoining lands, the "eastermost" of his farms. Before 1688 it was occupied by John Scolley and John Ross, [29] and in that year it was improved by Thomas Wayte, who purchased it in 1704 of the Lane heirs. It was the home of the Waytes for nearly a century, when, the last male of the name in that branch having passed away, it was sold, in 1787, to Captain Naler Hatch of Revolutionary fame.[30] The "Mansion" which was probably built by Job Lane, who was himself a house-carpenter, stood near the present gate of the Woodlawn Cemetery and was demolished by the Cemetery

[28] *Vide* chap. xiii. note 11.
[29] John Scolley had been a ferryman. His wife was Hannah, daughter of James Barrett. John Ross was his brother-in-law, having married Mary Barrett.
[30] *Midd. Co. Deeds,* xlv. 14; xcv. 210.

Company. The farm itself is rapidly becoming a city of the dead.

Next to the lots just mentioned, on the Boston line in the fourth range was a triangle of six acres which was accounted as a part of the twenty-five acres of Francis Norton, the remainder of his allotment forming the first lot in the fifth range, bounded likewise by the Boston line. This land, which in time became the property of the Sayes women and after them of James Millinor, is elsewhere noticed.[31]

Across the centre of these ranges ran the Great Swamp, some remnants of which still remain east of Cross and Ferry streets. Fifty years ago, in its extent and dense growth, it was worthy of the ancient name which it still bore. Slight attention appears to have been paid to its disadvantages, unless some of the lots may have been made larger in consequence; and there are one or two indications of an allowance for waste land.

A seventh range, beginning above the Nowell grant, *west* of the North River, ran eastward to the vicinity of the Three Mile, or Spot Pond, Brook, embracing the territory through which afterwards ran the Medford road, our present Pleasant Street. Above it was the common, and once a highway is mentioned as running along its northern side. This was the Indian trail, known as the Salem Path, which Nowell noted as running north of his farm in 1635. This range comprised five acres of number ninety-seven [32] and the remaining lots of the division, all of which were west of the Three Mile Brook, except that of Thomas Coytmore, whose thirty-five acres were on the eastern side, and the two lots of Edward Jones and William Quick, which covered the piece of upland between the marshes of the two brooks in the vicinity of Middlesex and Centre Streets.

The lot numbered one hundred was transferred to Joseph Hills and, passing from his possession, formed, with the adjoining lot of Faintnot Wines, Samuel Eldred's farm of forty acres,

---

[31] *Vide* chap. xi. note 48.

[32] Lot 97 was the ten-acre portion of Michael Barstow, of which the five acres here mentioned were at the extreme western limit of the future town of Malden, while the remaining five acres formed a triangular piece at the end of the sixth range of the larger division, far east on the Boston line, at or near the present Black Ann's Corner.

which was taken in 1660 on an execution in favor of Edward
Lane.[38]   It was afterwards occupied by the blacksmith, George
Durand.   Richard Dexter purchased this with other lands in
1663 and it remained in the Dexter family without division
until the present generation.   On the adjoining land, allotted
to Stephen Fosdick, the almshouse was built in 1821.   The
allotment of Richard Sprague, descending to his heirs, ultimately absorbed all the range east of the Dexter land, including
a portion of the Coytmore lot east of Three Mile Brook.   On
the northern end of his farm in the vicinity of Clifton Street,
between Washington and Summer streets, Richard Sprague
settled very early.   Summer Street, and perhaps a portion of
Pleasant Street, was a lane leading from Sprague's house to a
landing-place — Sprague's Bank, on the river at the lower extremity of his lot.

How far east the lot of Thomas Coytmore, on the easterly
side of Three Mile Brook, extended cannot now be ascertained.
Certainly it was bounded on the south by the meadows of
Pemberton's Brook, and on the north, as at first granted, it ran
not far beyond the falls, near the bridge by which Mountain
Avenue now crosses the brook.   On the east it reached the
vicinity of Sprague Street, for the easterly line of the High

---

[38] *Suffolk Co. Deeds*, iii. 375; *Midd.
Co. Deeds*, iii. 132.   How Eldred got the
land from Joseph Hills, or who built
the house, which was standing upon it
in 1663, I do not know.   The old house
stood near the south-easterly corner of
the present Dexter and Rockland Streets,
where a few years ago its ancient foundation was found and the depression
which marked its site was filled.   The
Salem Path ran upon the northerly side
of the rocky hill near by, nearly in the
line of Clifton Street.   West of the
Village Lane, now Summer Street, fifty
years ago, bars in the walls and traces
of an old way across the fields remained
to show the location of the Indian trail.
Still farther westward, evidences of several ways were visible in 1890, by one
of which the old path sought the Medford plains.

Towards the end of the seventeenth

century, a second house was built farther
south under the great elm which still
remains.   Tradition says that this tree,
which in its later years has been known
as the Washington Elm, and which
spreads its branches over a hundred
feet, was a large one even at that time.
With a girth of twenty-seven feet in
its largest part, it is still vigorous and
shows few signs of decay.   It is the
only relic of the primal forest which
once covered the town.

Some of the material of the first was
used in the second house, which in its
later days was an interesting example
of the domestic architecture of the colonial period.   It was demolished in 1848
and the present house was built upon
its site by Richard and Samuel G.
Dexter, in whose possession and occupancy it still remains.   *Information of
Samuel G. Dexter.*

School land, which represents the limit of the Coytmore allotment in that direction, is one of the few ancient boundaries
which can still be recognized with almost absolute certainty.
However it may have been bounded at first, it was after a few
years limited to the narrow strip of land west of Main Street by
unrecorded transfers to Joseph Hills on the northerly side of
Salem Street, and to Abraham Hill on the southerly side.
Before its diminution, however, it was enlarged on its northerly
side by the following grants : —

[May 29, 1640] Mr Thos Coitmore was granted the end of his Lott
bettwixt ye Mount Prospect & the River for his p^{r}per use in case he
goe on with building the Mill wch if hee doe not hee is then to Leave
4 Acres to the use of such as shall have Liberty to build ye Mill to bee
sett out by such as shall be appointed.[34]

[Feb^r 15, 1649½.] Mr Tho: Coitmore was granted the ground
above his Lott over the Mount Prospect to the Land Laid out to Tho:
Line to runne upon A Streight Line from ye parting line bettwixt him
& m^r Jose: Hills.[35]

Beyond the line of the Coytmore land and extending to the
hills and swamps toward Scadan was a plain, on which are now
located the populous sections of the fifth ward and Faulkner,
which was not covered by the grants of the great allotment,

[34] *Charlestown Archives,* xx. *in loco.*

[35] Ibid. In 1638, Thomas Lynde
owned three acres of meadow " on the
north side of mount prospect," which
he had evidently received in the division
of hay-lots. The eighty acres which
were assigned him "above ye Ponds "
in the great allotment, proving "alto-
geth^r unusefull being nothing but
Rockes," it was agreed, August 26, 1639,
" ye Tho: Line shall have some Land
by the Mount Prospect, if upon view it
may bee had by his Hay ground."
Charlestown Archives, xx. *in loco.* This
land, which was laid out, as proposed,
on the north side of Wayte's Mount,
was a part of the large property which
Thomas Lynde and his descendants
afterwards held. Here, as the Lynde
family increased, several houses were
built, the oldest of which was probably
built by Thomas, the grantee, on the
site of the brick-end house now standing
near the entrance of the cemetery on
Forest Street. The old house, with
about forty acres of land on both sides
of the road, was sold, in 1753, by Jacob
Lynde to Ebenezer Harnden, and by
the latter, in 1761, to Thomas Pratt,
whose son John, to make room for the
present house, demolished it about 1830.
The older part of the house, known as
the Joseph Lynde house, now standing
at the corner of Main Street and Good-
year Avenue, was built about 1720. The
view of this house which is given in
the text was taken in 1873. In the
cellar of this house there was formerly
"an oak log, a little larger and taller
than a barrel, scooped out like a mortar,
with an iron hoop around the top; the
pestle is gone. In this the corn was
pounded and ground." Goss, *Historical
Address,* 11.

except on its easterly side, where a portion, at least, of the lot of Walter Palmer appears to have passed into the hands of George Bunker.[86] The unappropriated portion remained not long in its primitive condition; and the entry which records the grant introduces us to one who became prominent and "helpful" to both church and state.

[July 30, 1638.] M: Joseph Hill [*Hills*] was admitted A Townsman, & is granted 25 Acres of Land on mistickside by M: Coitmores Lott, & 50 more aft: the great Lotts are finished.[87]

The twenty-five acres were located east of the Coytmore land. Farther east were twenty acres of the Palmer land, which,

---

[86] This was No. 65 of the allotment, which covered the westerly ends of the third and fourth ranges of the first division. Of this lot, seventeen acres were north and thirteen acres south of Long Meadow, or Harvell's Brook; and both divisions were evidently east and south of the present Cross Street.

[87] *Charlestown Archives*, xx. *in loco.* The fifty acres were probably laid out on the south side of Smith's Pond. Mr. Hills sold his sixty-acre lot at that place to Henry Evans in 1660. *Midd. Co. Deeds*, ii. 131.

before the end of the year, George Bunker sold to Thomas Ruck, and which in time became a part of the possessions of Joseph Hills. On its eastern side was afterwards laid out that way " between Mr Hils & Mr Bunkars farmes," which, known for many years as Harvell's Brook Lane, became in time a part of the present Cross Street. These three lots were covered by the forest, and the whole territory was bounded by the Three Mile Brook, by the common which contained Mount Prospect, or Wayte's Mount, and the Faulkner hills, by the Scadan swamps, and by the meadows of Pemberton's Brook between Salem Street and Eastern Avenue. In the Charlestown Book of Possessions [1638] these lots are described as follows: —

[COYTMORE.] Thirtie and five acres of woodland, scituate and lying in mistik feilde, N° 108,   length, and   in breadth, butting to the south upon the meaddow, to the north upon the common, bounded on the west by the fresh riverett, and on the east by Mr Hiles.

[HILLS.] Twentie and ffive acres of woodland, more or lesse, scituate in mistick feilde, butting south upon long meaddow, north upon the com̃on; bounded on the west by Thō Coytemore and on the east by Thō Ruck.

[RUCK.] Twentie acres of land, more or lesse, scituate in mistick feilde, bounded on the north by the common, on the west by Josseph Hiles, and on the south east by a swamp and meade.[38]

The unappropriated land between the five-acre lots and the lots of the great allotment, as has been seen, was reserved for such as might be received with another minister, that is for the use of those new comers who should bring the strength necessary for the formation of a new church; but the town having called Thomas Allen, " a studyent" from England, to fill the office left by the deceased John Harvard, and new settlers having come in, it was divided as follows: —

[The 28 day of ye viij month 1640.] Abram Palmer & Robt Hale were appointed to Lay out the 200 Acres of Land on mistick side to the men appointed in wch they are first to accomodate Mr Serieant, Tho: Martin then Mr Tho: Allen and ye rest by Lott.

[38] *Charlestown Archives,* xxxiv. 9, 28,   co. Essex, in England, or its vicinity. 61. Thomas Ruck was from Maldon,   Lechford, *Note-Book,* 78, 91.

[*In the margin.*] This is p^t of ye 300 Acres reserv^d ye 6 of ye ij^d month 1638 call^d heere but 200 Acres at Mistickside, tho at measuring it held out 260 Acres there, laid out to m^r Tho: Allen (now called to the office of Teacher of this Church) and to the rest heere imediatly aft^r mentiond.

A devission of the Land lying bettweene the five Acre Lotts at the head of them allotted out as heereafter exprest.

Names of Persons	Acres	Names of Persons	Acres
Mr Thomas Allen	25	Bro: Robinson	3
M^r [W^m] Seargeant	20	Tho: Gould	4
Tho: Martin	10	Wm Stitson [Stilson]	20
Abra: Hill	2½	Jno Pentecost	3
Robt Leech	2½	Edwd Wood	5
Walter Popes Child	5	Goo: [Tho:] ffrench	2½
Gaudy James	2½	Goo: [W^m] Smith Tailor	2½
Tho: Weilder	2½	Jno Seer	2½
Alexand^r ffield	2½	Richd Lowden	3
goo. [Jno] Whitman	2½	Tho: Graves	20
M^r [Robt] Cooke	10	John Allen	20
Ralph Woorie	6	Manus Jackson	4
Micha^l Long	4	John Martin	4
Wm Phillips	10	Isack Cole	4
Bro: [Jno] Baker, ye Tailor	3	Robt Nash	4
		goo: [Jno] March	4
		M^r [Rich^d] Russell	20
		ffra: Willoughby	20
		goo: Edwd Larkin	3
		Augustine Walker	4 [20]

Several lots of this division may be identified. The most northerly was the twenty acres of John Allen, which, being sold to John Lewis, who died in 1657, passed into the hands of the Greens and others. Out of it came the six and one-half acres of the Rev. Michael Wigglesworth, which in 1657 was bounded on the north by the common field in the vicinity of the present Newhall Street, west by the ministry land, and south by the highway which is now Cross Street. The corner of High and Ashland Streets is upon this lot.

South of the Allen lot was the land of Thomas Graves, which, being purchased by James Green of Richard Harrington in 1656, remained in the possession of the Greens until 1765, when it was sold by Darius Green to Joseph Perkins of Danvers and continued with the descendants of the latter another century. South of this lot was that of Robert Cooke.

The great lot of Francis Willoughby was farther south. It was sold to William Bucknam in 1649 and formed a part of that farm, the memory of which is preserved in the name of Bucknam Street in Everett.[40] South of this was the allotment of the Rev. Thomas Allen, which was sold to William Johnson, the brickmaker, in 1651. Eight acres of the easterly portion· of this lot were purchased by William Sargeant in 1654; and the remainder, accounted as fourteen acres, was sold to Joses Bucknam in 1677, when it was bounded, north-west, west, and south, by the highway at the head of the five-acre lots — the present Norwood Street. This land, which was known as " Johnson's Playn," may still be recognized by its bounds opposite the head of Corey Street. A part was for many years in the possession of the late Captain Solomon Corey, whose land on the south side of Norwood Street was apparently within the limits of the five-acre lots.

North of the Willoughby lot was that of William Phillips; and on the west was the twenty-acre lot of Richard Russell, which was sold to William Stilson. The latter occupied the level land west of Bucknam Street and the slope of the woodland towards the marshes; while still farther west lay the four acres of Augustine Walker, which were sold to Edward Carring-

[40] Upon the Bucknam farm was the interesting old house, known in its latter years as the Swan house, which was demolished in 1875. A portion, being the northwest corner, was the first house built upon the land. Around or against it a later construction was raised in the early part of the eighteenth century. A highly imaginative article, which was reprinted from the *Boston Herald* in the *Malden Mirror*, August 14. 1875, gives the early date of 1630 to its erection; but there was evidently no house standing there in 1649. It was not upon the Willoughby lot that William Bucknam, who was himself a carpenter, built, but upon an adjoining and later purchase. At his death, March 28, 1679, the house, which was in Malden very near the Charlestown line, standing upon four acres, is mentioned with the Willoughby lot of twenty acres. When his son Joses died, August 24, 1694, he left to his son Samuel the house with its four acres and the twenty-acre lot, with six acres adjoining " buting To the homsteed so as it may Reach to the Spring for yᵉ benifit of watring." Lieutenant Samuel probably built the addition above mentioned, and he lived in the house until his death, July, 1751. His descendant, Joseph Swan, who resides upon the site of the old house, has family papers to which I am indebted for information of interest. A view of the old house is given in *Everett Souvenir*, 9.

ton in 1652, being bounded on the west by the "highway bordering on John Upham," or the way to Penny Ferry. North of Walker was the lot of John March, and on the south was that of John Martin. Beyond Willoughby's land, on the east, was the allotment of William Sargeant, occupying the brow of that highland above Everett Square, on the line of Broadway, which was long known as Sargeant's Hill.

The bounds between Boston and Charlestown were not definitely fixed by the order of 1633, but two years later the following order and report were entered upon the Colony Records: —

1635 6 May.   It is referd to M! Holgraue, M! Colbran, & S'ieant Sprage, to sett out the bounds of land betwixte Boston & Charlton on the nore-east of Misticke Ryver.

1635: 8 July   The bounds betweene Boston & Charlestowne are from the creeke along the creeke vpward in the same till wee come to a little neck of land that come from the east side of the same neck : there the first stake stands a little on the east side of it, & from thence to a m'ked tree at the foote of the marsh agreed vpon of all sides, & from that tree to another that lye right opposite over a hill, & from thence to a high, tall pine, that stands vpon a point of rock, on the side of the high way to Mistick [upon the] other side of Rumney Marsh, & from outside to outside by a straight line.

p! IOHN HOLGRAVE.[41]

The line between the towns, in its remoter course, was settled by the following agreement: —

The 28th day of the first moneth, 1636.

Agreed by vs, whose names are vnder written, that the bounds betweene Boston & Charles Towne, on the nor east syde Misticke Ryver, shall run from the m'ked tree vpon the rocky hill above Rumney Marshe, neere the written tree nore-nore west vpon a straight lyne by a meridean compass vpp into the countrie.

ABRAHAM PALMER,
WILL" CHEESEBOROUGH,
WILL" SPENCER.[42]

In the meantime the Court settled the extent of the territory of Charlestown on the north by the following order: —

---

[41] *Mass. Colony Records,* i. 148, 150.   [42] Ibid., i. 162.

163⅚
3 March. *Ordered,* that Charles Towne bounds shall run eight myles into the country from their meeteing howse, if noe other bounds intercept, reserueing the p'prietie of ffermes graunted to John Wintrop, Esq', M' Nowell, M' Cradocke, & M' Wilson, to the owners thereof, as also ffree ingreese & egresse for the serv's & cattell of the said gent', & common for their cattell, on the backeside of M' Cradocks fferme.[48]

The limit of eight miles from the meeting house carried the Charlestown line nearly to Smith's Pond, where it met the indefinite line of the Saugus (Lynn) plantation. By a liberal allowance of distance, it finally fixed itself at the northeast corner of the pond, at a point which may be readily ascertained by an extension of the north-easterly line of Melrose. Within this bound was included that part of the present town of Wakefield now known as Greenwood. At the extreme northern point, bounded by the pond, was a lot of sixty acres belonging to Joseph Hills, which was probably the grant of fifty acres, which he was appointed to have after the great allotments were settled.

In 1639 the Court appointed a committee "to settle the bounds betweene Charlestowne, Boston, & Lin;" but I have not found a report of the result. A document written by Captain Thomas Brattle is extant, which gives the line as run between Malden and Rumney Marsh in 1678.

We whose names are underwritten being Appointed by the Selectmen of the Towne of Boston to be perambulators to runn the line betwixt the town of Maulden and this towne, we accordingly did goe to Leivtenants Smiths house where wee meeting some of Maulden men appointed for that service being on the 15⁰ day of Aprill 1678 Captaine Weight and Leivtenant Sprague being tow of the men for Maulden wee began the line at the Corner of A stone Wall next unto Aaron Wayes house save one and Contined it over the Corne field to an Oak tree at the Corner of the same fence from thence to A stake nere unto the house called Job Lanes house where augment to the heap of stones about the saide Stake, and from thence to A pine tree on the side of A rocky hill over Against the Way yt goeth from Winnesimmet into Salem path from Malden and from thence to A heape of stones, and from thence on A North north West lyne to A tree to the westward

of   his house which we marked M × B and laide stones to the
root of it, from thence renewing sevrall marks untill we came to A
greate oak yt was felled which had m & B on it and its stub A great
heap of stones the which we renewed, and from thence to A forked
oake on A playne with A stone in the Cratch of it the line goeing A
litle Westerly of it and from thence to A small Oake marked M × B
with A heape of stones at the roote of it on the top of hill before we
came to doctor Waldrons house and from thence leaving Doctor
Waldrons house on the right hand to An Oake standing on the top
of A hill by the saide Waldron house marked M × B and so to A
heape of stones in Malden line where Redding and Boston head line
meett

these bounds were runn by Capt hutchinson Cap. fairweather Leift
Smith & my Self for this Towne & Cap.t waite Leift Sprague & Corporall Green the 15.th day of April 1678 and agreed vpon Coppy in the
towne house.[44]

The line fixed as the easterly bound of Charlestown in 1636
has never been changed and still marks the eastern limits of
Everett, Malden, and Melrose. The "point of rock on the side
of the high way to Mistick"—the Salem Path, may still be
recognized and is a prominent feature near Black Ann's Corner;
but the "high, tall pine" which crowned it, after having been a
landmark for more than a century, came to be, in 1738, "an
old Pitchpine tree marked B. M." Twenty-one years later it
was only "an old pitch pine stump with an heap of stones about
it," and so it disappears from our view.

The eastern boundary being settled, the Court ordered: —

1640   M.r Tynge, M.r Samu: Sheopard, & Goodm. Edward
7 October.   Converse are to set out the bounds betweene Charlestowne
& M.r Cradocks farme, on the north side of Mistick Ryver.[45]

This completed the settlement of the bounds of Mystic Side.
By the close of 1640 all the larger grants of the lands south of
the Scadan hills and the rocky edge of the western fells had
been made; but the more rocky and remote portions north of
these lines remained common land until 1695. That some
settlers may have entered upon their allotments or purchases is
possible, perhaps probable, but an assertion to that effect can

---

[44] *Mass. Archives*, cxii. 246.   [45] *Mass. Colony Records*, i. 304.

only rest upon conjecture. In 1638, when the compilation of the Charlestown Book of Possessions, by Abraham Palmer, gives an opportunity to ascertain with a great degree of certainty the location of most of the allotted lands, no house is mentioned.

The first hint of a settlement is found in the following petition; but whether the petitioner or his neighbors, Moulton and the widow Wilkinson, first built, I cannot determine. That a settlement was first made at Sweetser's Point or Moulton's Island, where the river afforded a convenient means of communication with Charlestown and Boston, I am convinced. That Thomas Moulton [46] settled at an early day upon the island which bore his name is probable; but, however it may be, we have here the first notice of actual settlers at Mystic Side.

JOHN GREENLAND *carpenter petitions the Court*

That yo[r] petitioner hath bin an inhabitant in Charlestowne by the space of two yeares last past and all that while sojourned in other mens houses because he had none of his owne at length he spake to some of the Townesmen to entreate them to be a meanes to the rest that he might have a house lott given him whereon he might build an house but he received answere that the Towne had no house lott to give & therefore the said Townesmen wished him to buy one Whereupon yo[r] petioner hath bought of Samuel Richardson of Charlestowne five acres of land within Charlestowne bounds on Misticke syde near to Thomas Moulton & the widdow Wilkins [47] and hath begun & halfe built his house upon it as yo[r] petitioner conceiveth it was lawfull for him to do seeing that he hath built on five acres of ground. Notwithstanding some of

[46] Thomas Moulton was an inhabitant of Charlestown in 1631. His early settlement at Island End, or Moulton's Island, while a matter of conjecture, is one of great probability. He shared in the allotments and afterwards purchased of Walter Palmer the five-acre lot in number eleven which had been assigned to William Baker. This lot was between those on which George Felt and James Pemberton built; but no house was upon it in 1646, when it was sold to Richard Dexter. He died, December 24, 1657.

[47] Widow Prudence Wilkinson was in Charlestown in 1630, having been, perhaps, a passenger in the Winthrop fleet. She received her portions in the two allotments, and apparently built upon her five-acre lot somewhere to the eastward of the way to the Mystic and near the marshes of the South River. A slight clue to its location may exist in the fact that Wilkinson's Creek was that stream which, running into the South River, received, itself, on its easterly side the waters which came down from the South Spring. Its early name long since passed out of use and is unknown to those now dwelling in its vicinity. Widow Wilkinson died in 1655, leaving her homestead to her only son, John. Other land was left to her grandson, John Bucknam, whose troubles are elsewhere mentioned

6

the said Towne have given forth words to discourage yo[r] petitioner to goe on to plant there w[ch] may turne to his great hinderance if he should be now caused to remove. Yo[r] petitioner humbly prayeth this wor[d] Cort to be pleased in consideration of the premises to confirme yo[r] petitioners said planting on misticke syde in the place aforesaid. And yo[r] petitioner shall pray for this Cort, &c.[48]

This petition, which remains in the note-book of Thomas Lechford, who wrote it, has disappeared from the colonial archives; but ample evidence of its presentation and consideration exists in the answer which it received.

1640: 7 October.   John Greenland is granted his petition, w[c] is to plant upon a five acre lot in Charles Towne bounds on Mistick side.[49]

We can easily identify the spot on which John Greenland "halfe built his house." The portion of Samuel Richardson comprised the westerly five acres of the lot numbered ten in the allotment of 1634. In 1638 it was described among his possessions as follows: —

ffive Acres of woodland in misticke feilde N[o]. 10, butting to south upon the highway toward Cap. Robert Sedgwicke his meaddow ; and to the north upon the misticke feilde, bounded on the west by the high way and upo the East by Micheall Bastow, 80 pole in length and tenn pole in bredth.[50]

The subsequent conveyances of this land are very clear, and unlike those which attach to many ancient titles, they form an unbroken line of evidence to the present time. The highway towards Captain Sedgwick's meadow was that part of Chelsea Street in Everett which is east of the South Spring; and the highway upon the west was the narrow way leading into the great allotments, which in time became Ferry Street. Greenland, who afterwards acquired the adjoining five acres of Barstow, lived here, continuing a resident within the bounds of Charlestown, until his death, in 169¾.[51]

---

[48] Lechford, *Note-Book*, 178.
[49] *Mass. Colony Records*, i. 309.
[50] *Charlestown Archives*, xxxiv. 10.
[51] Greenland received an additional grant from the town :

"[10. 11[mo] 1641] Jn[o] Greenland was

graunted the West ground bettweene him & Geo: ffelt, to begin A Pole above Geo: ffelts house from the South Spring upwards to the head of the 5 Acre Lotts." *Charlestown Archives*, xx. *in loco.*

He left his housing and lands on

To the three settlers who had planted upon the allotments were soon added others, who before the close of the year 1640 had built in the vicinity of the South Spring. It is difficult to understand why the older settlers at Mishawum opposed the settlement of Mystic Side; but it is certain that the troubles which Greenland encountered continued after the action of the Court in his favor. I have found no evidence that the following petition was ever presented to the authorities. Like that of Greenland, it was written by Lechford and is preserved in his note-book. It is probable that the grievances of which the petitioners complained ceased without the intervention of the General Court.

To the right wor *the Governor Council & Assistants*

The humble petition of James Pemberton Prudence Wilkinson widdowe Lewis Hulett George Felt George Knowe John Greenland and Thomas Whittimore

Mystic Side to his only surviving son, John, with the use of the house to his widow, Lydia, during her natural life. What time the son, Deacon John Greenland, removed into the bounds of Malden is uncertain; but it was probably about the time of his marriage with Lydia Sprague in 1670, and it is sure that he was here in 1673. He built upon a piece of rising land in the woodland west of the Great Swamp, where his father, in 1655, had acquired a portion of the lot numbered thirty-one in the great allotment. His farm, which he left by will to his grandson, John Shute, the long-lived deacon and town clerk, was that which, lying east of Ferry Street, became in later years the property of Captain Henry Rich, and more recently of George A. Sammet.

How long the widow lived to enjoy her rights in the Mystic Side house is unknown; but apparently it was not long. In January, 1688, it was sold with its ten acres, and other lands, to John Ridgeway, mariner, who already occupied it. Ridgeway died of the small-pox in 1721; and his son John, having purchased the rights of his brothers and sisters, sold it to Ebenezer Pratt, boatman, in 1725. Whether the house which was then transferred was, wholly or in part, that which

was built by Greenland in 1640 is uncertain; but it is sure that the house in which the younger Ebenezer Pratt was born in 1725, was that which remained unto the present generation. With the exception of about two years, when it was in the hands of Samuel Waite, it was owned and occupied by the Ebenezers, father and son, who were large holders of land in that vicinity, until it was purchased, in 1782, by the Revolutionary captain, Isaac Smith.

After the death of Captain Smith, the house, with a large tract of adjoining lands which he had acquired, passed by purchase into the possession of Nathan Nichols, who had married his daughter Dorcas. A portion of these lands, which occupied the extensive tract now known as Nichols's Hill, was sold by the heirs of Captain Nichols to a party of operators who formed the Nichols Land Association. The old house stood until May 18, 1874, when, with the exception of a modern addition, it was burned. Recent improvements have nearly obliterated the old landmarks. *Midd. Co. Deeds, in loco; Information of* the late John Smith Nichols. A view of the house is in *Everett Souvenir*, 12.

The petitioners shewe that whereas they having bin heretofore in-habitants in Charlestowne and could not there have accommodation to live comfortably they were forced to crave leave of the Cort to build and plant upon Mysticke syde wch they did by the leave of the Court afores^d and have expended a great parte of their estates therein, Some of the Towne endeavoring to straighten the petitioners and to hinder others from comming to them as they say have procured divers orders to be made in the Towne meeting wch to the petitioners are very pre-judiciall and they thinke unreasonable vizt that any of the petitioners shall pay for every swine taken in the marsh 2^s 6^d a tyme besides the dammage, whereas the orders for the towne are but to yoake & ring the swine or els to pay double dammage. 2^ly whereas yor petitioners cannot live to pay rates to Towne & Country except they have some convenient common allotted them to keepe some cattel about them, their said opponents have procured a towne order to be made for the making of a common fence a great way from yor petitioners houses wch will not keepe out swine and yet would have the petitioners con-tribute and afford wood to the said common fence wch yet tends to their undoing, whereas the fence is made for the present only to defend the Townesmens medow ground wch the petitioners were willing to joyne wth them so they would only have fenced in the medow and left the petitioners convenient common. These things yor petitioners humbly desire the Court in their wisdome to consider and to order that they may have a convenient common allowed them and may have equall remedie in their said greivances. And they shall as their duty bindes them pray for yor wor^pps.[52]

---

[52] Lechford, *Note-Book*, 203. James Pemberton received the easterly half of the ten-acre lot, No. 12 in the first allot-ment, on which he evidently built a house, which in 1717 was occupied by Isaac Wheeler. This was the third five-acre lot west of the way which is now known as Ferry Street in Everett. The intervening lots on Chelsea Street were those of George Felt and Thomas Moulton, which are elsewhere noticed. Pemberton is supposed to have been a passenger in the fleet of Winthrop in 1630. In 1647 he was at Hull; and afterwards he removed to Rumney Marsh, where he lived upon the farm of Robert Keayne, being mentioned in the will of Captain Keayne in 1653, which gave " Vnto James Pemerton, & his wife, sometimes my Servant, now partner with me at my ffarme, forty shillings."

The sometime servant was his second wife, Margaret, who outlived him. After the death of Keayne in 1656, he became an inhabitant of Malden, where he had a house, standing on a lot of ten acres, and land in the Great Swamp and in the salt marsh. He died here, Feb-ruary 5, 166½, leaving his Mystic Side house to Edmund Barlow, the husband of his daughter Mary, and his Malden property to his widow and his son John. Pemberton's Island in Boston Harbor, upon which stands Fort Warren, bears in its name the record of his early and disputed ownership; and Pemberton's Brook preserved his memory in Malden until it was superseded by the later name of Harvell.

Of Lewis Hulett little is known and that little is not creditable. He was in Charlestown in 1636, and afterwards

It is evident that the allotments in other parts of Mystic Side, as well as those around the South Spring, were beginning to receive inhabitants and that occasions to pass and repass the Mystic were frequent; for the inhabitants of Charlestown voted, April 2, 1640, that Philip Drinker should keep "a ferry at the Neck of Land with a sufficient boat." For his service he was to have two pence for one person and a penny each "when there goe any more." This was the beginning of the Penny Ferry which served the inhabitants of Malden and the upper towns until 1787, when it was superseded by the Malden Bridge.[63]

appears as the reputed owner of a lot on the west of the Mill Hill; but his possessions are not specifically noted.

"[December 3, 1639.] Lewes Hewlet, for his extortion, was fined 20 sh⁵, & was bound over in 10l to the first month for his contemptuous speaches." *Mass. Colony Records*, i. 284.

"[March 3, 16⅜.] Lewes Hewlet, not appearing, forfected his recognisance of 10l." Ibid., i. 286.

Besides this, I have met nothing relating to him. He evidently was not long at Mystic Side.

George Knower received no land in the allotments and he may have come as a tenant rather than as a landowner. He died in Malden, February 13, 167⅘; and his lands and those of his descendants were within the limits of this town, near the Boston line, north of Sagamore and Turkey Hills.

Thomas Whittemore did not participate in the allotments, but he purchased the five-acre lot of Increase Nowell and other lands around it and above it at Sagamore Hill. His homestead, which was bounded upon the east by the Boston line, continued in the possession of his descendants until it was sold in 1845, as has been stated. A house, which was doubtless that built by Thomas Whittemore, stood upon the premises until 1806, when a second house was built in its place, or near, by Joseph Whittemore, which remained until destroyed by fire in 1866. In 1898, the site was still marked by a cellar hole and an old cherry tree on the northerly side of Chelsea Street, a short distance west of Everett Avenue.

[63] Drinker, who died June 23, 1647, was succeeded a few months before his death by Peter Tufts, who afterwards became a large landholder on Mystic Side and in Malden, and the owner of the Nowell grant. He was assisted by his brother-in-law, William Bridge. In 1651 it was voted to let the ferry for one year to John Harris; but for some reason the vote was not carried out, and the ferry was soon after granted to Philip Knight, a cooper, who agreed "to attend the ferry carefully, and not to neglect it, that there be no just complaint." Frothingham, *History of Charlestown*, 147. Little Island, by some supposed to be that since known as White Island, over which the railroad now passes, but more probably an island in the marsh afterward known as the Ferry Island, on the southerly side of which the ferry-ways were built, was granted to the ferry, which continued to be maintained by the town of Charlestown, and at a later period produced a small income. The causeway over the marsh and some traces of the ways remained upon the easterly side of present street until its widening covered them. A few years earlier, remains of piles might be seen in the mud of the river. The position of ferryman was far from being a permanent one and its holders were often changed. Paul Wilson, who is noted in many records as a sinner and a roysterer, appears in 1664, but soon left it to "keep the cows in the stinted Pasture." Many names appear until 1726, when the ferry was leased for twenty-five years to Joseph Frost of Charlestown and Samuel

That settlers were beginning to gather in the fields and woods of Mystic Side is still more plainly evinced by the building of a corn mill by Thomas Coytmore, whose grant for that purpose, in 1640, has been noticed. It is certain that he built a dam at Black Rock at once, for the next year the town passed the following vote : —

[27. 6ᵐᵒ 1641.] It was granted yᵗ Thos: Coitmore should have one daies worke throughout the whole Towne, to helpe to breadthen A Damm (at the 3 mile brooke) to A convenient highway for horse & Cart ; & yᵗ : hee shall have Liberty to appoint what number hee shall thincke ffitt for A day : proceeding accordᵉ to the Liste of the Surveyoᵗ for the Highway.[64]

The "convenient highway for horse & Cart" has continued to the present time to be a travelled way, and Mountain Avenue, formerly Mill Street, is laid over the dam which was "breadthened" by the men of 1641. Although the dam was built in the place where it continued to furnish power until recent years, the original mill stood far away, near the present Middlesex Court, between Pleasant Street and the river. For this purpose, Coytmore appears to have acquired the lot of Thomas Squire on the westerly side of the brook, and perhaps that of James Garrett ; and he also apparently purchased those of Edward Jones and William Quick on the south side. When the dye works of Benjamin W. Dodge were being built, about 1835, charred timbers were found in the ground ; and an old lady was living in the neighborhood who remembered to have heard that the old mill stood there and was burned. Afterwards traces of the water-way, leading down from the dam, were found on the side of the hill near Barrett's Lane, now Dartmouth Street.[65]   In

Sweetser of Malden, each paying five shillings a year. The former assumed control of the southerly side and the latter that of the northerly ; and each agreed to maintain good ways to low water and to keep good boats for the accommodation of the public. It was settled by the Court "yᵗ the fair for every person be stated at two pence for each person, & Seven pence for man & Horse." *Midd. Court Records — General Sessions,* July 12, 1726. Frost does not appear to have long followed the craft of ferryman ; but Sweetser continued therein, and was followed by his son Stephen, who is supposed to have used the oars until the bridge was built.

[64] *Charlestown Archives,* xx. *in loco.*
[65] *Information of* Charles Hill, 1888.

this connection the testimony of the Hills, given about 1731, is of interest.

Isaac Hill of malden Aged about 63 yeeres and Abraham hill about 61 Testifieth and saith y⁺ their fathar Abraham Hill was tennent and keeper of yᵉ corn-mill jn malden formerly belonging to mʳ Thomas Coitmore at yᵉ time of mʳ John Coggains marrige with yᵉ widdow wintrope formerly yᵉ widdow Coitmore And y⁺ after said Coggins marria: wᵗʰ sᵈ wido: he yᵉ sd Abraham Hill continued Tennant in possession of said mill : In right of said Coggan for sundrey yeeres — and paid yᵉ rent to said Coggan : but yᵉ mill-pond in Malden beeing neer half a mile distance from yᵉ mill and considering yᵉ grate charge in maintaining of troues and frams to bare yᵉ troues over a thurt yᵉ Streeme to carry yᵉ water ouer yᵉ land doun to yᵉ sᵈ mill : The sᵈ Coggain Altred and Remoued yᵉ said mill further up yᵉ streeme neere to yᵉ sᵈ mill-pond. And after sᵈ mill was remoued The same was still Jmproued and possessed by said Coggan : and his sucessers. . . . and y⁺ yᵉ mill possessed by Edward Sprague stands upon yᵉ same streeme and watter cours neer to yᵉ place whare mʳ Coggans Mill stood, &c.[66]

From its first building the mill, descending by purchase or by inheritance through the hands of John Coggan, of Job Lane, and the Spragues, became an important factor in the life of the new and growing community; and the power which supplied it became the centre of years of strife and the cause of lawsuits not a few, which continued even to the present generation.

In an entry relating to highways made in January, 164¾, and hereafter given, the house of William Luddington is mentioned; and it is soon after again noted in a grant of upland made to Edward Mellowes. Luddington had bought the five-acre lot which had been laid out to William Dade, and I am led to believe that here he built his house. If so, it was situated near the marshes of the South River and not far from Sweetser's Point, as it " butted " upon that river, and the highway to the Mystic was not far away.

The next indication of actual settlement is shown in a petition of Thomas Call, which is redolent of piety and in a measure of good cheer and proves the existence of a community of settlers in the country above.

[66] Original MS. in the possession of Artemas Barrett.

To the honora^b^ Cort assembed at Boston the humble petition of Thomas Caule Whereas yo' petitioner Dwelleth by the water, at the fferry place on mistick side, many people haveing accasion to come that way, & when they cannot have passage are necessitated to stay at yo' petitioners (many of o' owne towne, & of other townes have moved yo' petition' to desire leave to sell them some thing; for their refreshing) now yo' petition' Doth humbly request leave to sell bread, beare & other victualling for the refreshing of such, as have occasion to stay, & yo' petition' shall humbly pray the lord to bless, guide, & counsell yo^u in all yo weightye affaires, & so I rest yo' humble suppliant

THOMAS CAULE.[57]

This petition, in which twenty-two others joined, is undated, and in the exasperating disarrangement of the Massachusetts Archives the original document has been defaced by a supposititious date; but the time and the reply are readily ascertained.

1645: Thomas Caule is alowed to keepe victualing in his house for
14 May. strang's.[56]

There now began to be mentioned cattle and swine upon Mystic Side; and rails were built to keep out the wolves, and pens were made for the sheep and swine. In 1645 the selectmen were given

the letting and disposing of all the common ground on mistike syde eyther w^th^in or w^th^out the rayles: By letting it out to them that will hire it for 21 years: at the price of 6 shillings an Acre by the year. . . . It was then ordered that all the cattell and swine w^th^in the field on mistike syde w^th^in the fence shalbe kept out by the midst of the first Moneth.

At a meeting of the "Seven men," January 12, 1645 6, Robert Wilder was appointed as "officer to see to Trespasses;" and

Hee is alsoe to see that all the front fences on mistike syde bee made vpp ag^st^ the midell of the first moneth ensuing and to see that they after be kept sufficient.

At a later meeting in the same month, Rowland Lahorne was chosen to keep the "Dry heard," for twelve shillings a week, and "to burn the woods in the fittest season, and to help about the pen." That Lahorne was a faithful herdsman was shown at the end of the season, when it was recorded: —

[57] *Mass. Archives*, cxi. 6.   [56] *Mass. Colony Records*, ii. 98.

[7. 10. 1646.] Royland Layhorn had out 100 dry cattell and brought them all well home but one.⁵⁹

A year later, the selectmen passed the following order: —

[25. 11ᵐ 1647.] It was *ord'ᵈ* yᵗ noe man is to keepe any Cattle within any enclosed ground on Misticksd aftᵉ the first Month 1648 upon forfeit of 6ᵈ each beast so found, & 6ᵈ each time any beast is so found in any enclosed field.⁶⁰

In the meanwhile, the town made special grants of land or renewed and laid out old ones. In 1647 a committee was appointed to lay out Major Robert Sedgwick's two hundred acres by Reading bounds. This grant had been made by the Court in 1639, and it is described in the Book of Possessions as

Eight score acres of land by estimation, more or lesse, scituate at the northeast point of the towne bounds, bounded on the east by Boston line, and on the north by Lynne villiage ;

but I cannot discover that it was laid out in the place prescribed; and it does not otherwise appear that Sedgwick ever owned land at the head-line of Malden. Soon after, January 3, 164⅞, " John Wait was granted to have the 8 Akers more or less that lies next to Tho Lines farme on mistik syde ; " and a little later a committee was chosen to " lay out yong Thomas Coitmores twoo lotts by Ell pond." ⁶¹

With the clearing of fields and the building of homes came the necessity of roads ; and we have already seen how the Indian trails, followed perhaps for centuries, gave the first comers ways through the forests and brushwood of Mystic Side. Of these the great trail known as the Salem Path and its branch, leading

---

⁵⁹ *Charlestown Archives*, xix. *in loco.* Burning the woods in the spring and fall was the continuance of an Indian custom, which is elsewhere mentioned.

⁶⁰ *Charlestown Archives*, xx. *in loco.*

⁶¹ Ibid., xix. *in loco.* Wayte's land was laid out in the meadows above Mount Prospect. Captain Thomas Coytmore was lost on the coast of Spain in 1644, and his unlocated land was laid out to his young son, Thomas, who died in his minority. Widow Martha (Rainsborough) Coytmore mar-ried Governor John Winthrop, and after his death, John Coggan, and inherited the Coytmore lands. After the death of Coggan, although the widow of three husbands and the mother of six children, she became "discontented that she had no suitours," and "encouraged her Farmer, a meane man." If we may believe report, "she grew discontented, despaired, and tooke a great quantity of ratts bane, and so died." *Mass. Hist. Coll.*, xxx. 45.

southward from Black Ann's Corner to the Indian villages near
Powder Horn, were the principal, and were at once adopted by
the settlers. The former is first mentioned in 1635 [62] and appears
several times in the Book of Possessions. Its course from the
Abousett to the Mystic, through Malden, is elsewhere traced.
In the great allotment little or no attention appears to have
been given to highways, although it was provided that "convenient Highwaies shalbe allowed;" but such ways as were
most direct or practicable, through the woods and across the
meadows, were taken by the earlier comers without much regard
to private bounds. From this cause, in part, arose the custom
of placing gates across the roads near farm boundaries. It was
not long, however, before the convenience of settled ways which
could be permanently maintained became apparent. Especially
were they desirable in difficult places, as around hills or over
meadows, and the earliest orders appear to have reference to
such cases. Thus, the first order after the allotment was designed to settle a way across the Long Meadow — apparently
that part of the present Main Street which lies between the City
Hall and Bailey's Hill.

[30. v. 1638.] Edw.ᵈ Convers & Ezek.ⁿ Richeson were desired to lay
out A highway in yᵉ most convenient place over the Meadow at yᵉ head
of the North River allowing the owners of yᵉ Ground sufficient for theire
pportions allotted them, or els to make them allowance elsewhere.[63]

The land-way and the drift-way along the five-acre lots ended
at the head of the North River, where the lot of Christian Easton
closed the range in that direction, until the new way across the
meadow extended the united ways northward. A still further
extension was soon made; and in the following order we may
find the origin of that part of Salem Street which was long
known as Baptist Row.

[24. 8ᵐ 1640.] It was ord.ᵈ that Ralph Sprague, Tho: Line &
Abra. Palmer should determine the bounds bettwixt M.ʳ Hills fferm, &
the Medow & to sett out the Highway for Cattle from the five Acre
Lotts to yᵉ common.[64]

---

[62] *Charlestown Archives*, xx. 33.   [63] Ibid., xx. *in loco.*   [64] Ibid.

This way at that time probably extended no farther eastward than the hills at Faulkner. Here the road long known as Barnes's Lane, and later as Jacob Pratt's Path,[65] led northward into the woods of the common, and by a circuitous route, along the swampy depths of Green's Hole, gave a rough and dismal way to the Salem Path by the Round World.[66] Later, a path

[65] Jacob Pratt's Path was one of the most delightful forest roads to be found in the vicinity. In 1897, I found a few traces of it, between Spruce and Marshall Streets; but they appeared likely to be soon "improved" from the face of the earth. It cannot but be regretted that the destruction or the degradation of our most charming natural scenery has attended the growth of the city. In many instances an absence of taste, or an undue haste to build cheap houses has inflicted injuries which cannot be repaired.

On this path, in a pleasant valley west of Green's Hole, was the home of Thomas Barnes, and later that of his son-in-law, Jacob Pratt. Here were two houses, the elder of which was used as a pest-house during the Revolution. The other, which is supposed to have been built soon after the Revolution, was demolished about thirty years ago. The view represents it in its latter days.

[66] The Round World was that tract west of Lebanon Street which was formerly known as John Pratt's Plain. In 1662 Joseph Hills sold to Samuel

was developed between the western Scadan hills and the Great Swamp to the Salem Path, which in a few years became a travelled way and completed the line of Salem Street to the vicinity of Maplewood Square. Eastwardly it was still unsettled, passing the Scadan plain far north of its present course.

The next entry in relation to highways on Mystic Side is as follows, and evidently refers to a way leading to the landing place on the South River at Island End, which then appears to have been known as Whitehand's Island, its later names of Moulton's and Mitchell's Island being as yet unborn: —

[9 : ij^d mo. 1641.] Ralph Mousall & W^m: Stilson appointed to lay out ye highway on Mistickside to ye South river by Whitehands Ileand & about Luddingtons.[67]

Later in the same year, the Indian trail leading southward from the Salem Path at the point of rocks [Black Ann's Corner], being a country way, was defined by an august committee composed of the governor, the deputy governor, John Winthrop, and others. Two years before, the town of Boston had been fined twenty shillings for its defects.[68] A committee was soon after appointed " to set out the nearest, cheapest, safest, & most convenient way ; "[69] and a bridge was ordered " to be donne with all speede."[70] This way, changed somewhat in later years, as other ground was found more favorable, was the country way from Lynn to Winnisimmet. In Malden, it is that portion of Lynn Street which runs from Black Ann's Corner to Linden; and in Revere and Chelsea it is known as Washington Avenue. For a short distance it formed a part of the eastern boundary of Charlestown, as it still bounds a portion of Everett.[71] The

Haward about forty acres, which had been the lots of Edward Jones and Thomas Squire, "and are comonly called by the name of the round O." This land was bounded by the rocks and a little swamp and "Mr Bunkers farme house & land." *Midd. Co. Deeds,* iii. 125. The little swamp, or Green's Hole, was a famous locality for snakes. The way mentioned in the text passed along the foot of the rocky hill on the northerly side of the swamp.

[67] *Charlestown Archives,* xx., *in loco.*
[68] *Mass. Colony Records,* i. 285.
[69] Ibid., i. 289.
[70] *Boston Town Records,* i. 48.
[71] The following order, which was passed by the General Court, indicates an early change in the travelled way.
"[May 27, 1670.] Whereas the country highway ouer some part of Rumny marsh was Layd out long since from a point of upland to the written tree and tho s^d way was never made

written tree was at the point of rocks above Black Ann's Corner. The "new bridge" was that over Pines River and it was long known as the County Bridge. It was covered with logs or plank until about the year 1830, when it was carried away by a high tide and was rebuilt of stone.[72]

[7 Oct. 1641.] *The Order for the High Way fro^m the Written Tree to Winnet semet.*

Wee, whose names are hearunder written, being appointed by the Co't to lay out the country high way fro Winnet semet towards Linne, have agreed that it shall go, as formerly, from the water side to the foote of Powder Horne Hill, & from thence about the west end of the said hill, & over the east end of Sagamore Hill, & thence to turne up above the swamps to the line of partition between Charlstowne & Boston, ruñing along thereby conveniently near to the great swamp, turning downe by the south side thereof to M Keaynes cart way over the said swamp, & so along in the said cart way over the brooke neare unto the ould bridge, & thence in the most convenient way to the New bridge

RICHARD BELLINGHAM, *Go:*,
JOHN ENDECOT, *Dep:*,
JOHN WINTHROPE,
& INCREASE NOWELL.[73]

The next year a committee was appointed " to view A percell of ground to in lieu for allow for consideracõn of A Highway for John Grover by the North Spring; " and grants were made to Increase Nowell and Robert Haile for land taken — for the way by Whiteland's Island, as I suspect. Later in the same year, Edward Mellows was granted " A percell of ground in lieu of A Hig way that is made over his Meadow;" and Joseph Hills was chosen surveyor of highways for Mystic Side.[74]

Passing over one or two orders relating to minor or indefinite ways, we find the following: —

[Jan. 12, 1643¾] M' Hill and Lieften! Sprague are appointed to settle y⁰ Highway y! comes out of the Woods to y⁰ Water side y! is by

passable, but instead thereof a Causey & bridg hath beene made in another place which hath beene made use of but is now & hath beene often out of repaire Jt is *ordered* that the select men of Boston shal take speedy care to make & maintaine a sufficient Causey & bridge ouer the marsh & creeke where the way was layd out first or to see & cause the Causey & bridge that is already made to be sufficiently repaired & so kept from time to time." *Mass. Archives*, cxxi. 53.

[72] *Chelsea Pioneer*, February 4, 1882.
[73] *Mass. Colony Records*, i 340.
[74] *Charlestown Archives*, xx., *in loco.*

M.ʳ Palmers Lott, & likewise the way to the Mill from Goo: Luddingtons house.⁷⁵

The house of William Luddington and its probable location
in the vicinity of the South River have been elsewhere mentioned.   If there was a mill at that early period on the arm of
the South River since known as the Mill Creek, the latter portion of this entry may refer to a short way leading down to it;
but I use a Yankee privilege and am inclined to the opinion
that it contemplated a settlement of the landway which led
northward to Coytmore's mill on the Three Mile Brook — the
unsettled and indefinite way which after many changes became
the present Main Street.   The way first mentioned in the order
was soon after laid out; and the following entry was made upon
the records: —

[1644.]   The Highway from yᵉ Lotts of yᵉ reserved Land, of yᵉ
200 Acres on Mistickside is to bee laid through yᵗ Lands of M.ʳ Abra:
Palmer to runne downe to the landing place over ꝑgᵗ M.ʳ Nowells
ffarme, & the s.ᵈ Highway is to bee laid out two Pole wide, & m.ʳ Palmer
to have yᵉ Ancient Highway in liew of the oth.ʳ ⁷⁶

I cannot determine with satisfaction the location of this new
way.   The lands of Abraham Palmer soon became a part of the
farm of James Green and the landing place was that at Sandy
Bank.   If the way was not that which passed along the southern
side of Bell Rock, where the meeting house was soon after built,
it must have been a long-forgotten way which crossed the
brow of Green's Hill or ran even farther south.   That such a
way existed I have long believed, but the records which hint of
it are insufficient and vague.

In the same year authority was given to lay out a way from
the river at Lewis's Bridge, by Wayte's Mount, into the heart
of the commons beyond Ell Pond.   This is definite, and a part
of the way we still travel; but north of the Mount it ran far
eastward of the present course of Main Street.   Its track may
still be traced, and will soon be noticed.

[24. 12. 1644⅚.]   It is agreed yᵗ Tho: Line, Robt Hale & Tho:
Pearce should lay out A convenient Highway on Mistickside from

⁷⁵ *Charlestown Archives*, xx., *in loco*.   ⁷⁶ Ibid.

y⁴ Woods to the head of the North River & to allow for yᵉ Highway & to bound the Meadows from y⁴ Mount to Ell Pond, & to allow them y⁴ Highway in bounding yᵉ Meadow."⁷⁷

At the session in May, 1647, the Court, seeing the great importance of convenient and permanent highways, appointed Ralph Sprague of Mystic Side and Francis Smith of Reading "to lay out yᵉ way froᵐ Winnetsemet to Reading." ⁷⁸ This was a part of a general plan by which a continuous highway was opened to the settlements in New Hampshire, passing through Reading, Andover, and Haverhill; and its survey brought forth the first of that long series of humble petitions in which are preserved much of the history of Mystic Side and Malden.

[16 : 3 : 48]   *To the Hon'd Court.   The Humble petīcon of sev'll the Jnhabitants of Mestick side & others Jn Charles towne.*   May jt please you to vnd'stand, that there hath beene Lately Layd out A highway from Winesemet to Redding by Appointment of the gen'll court, whose orders in all things, wee most willingly as dutie binds vs submit vnto, Assuring ourselues that their principall Ayme is the publ. good : wᶜʰ vnder fauor we concᵣ is not consistent wᵗʰ the Lying of that way as now it is done : for that it thwarts neere twentie small lotts & Allso many other lotts : wᶜʰ if by means thereof, the owners be forced to fence out the way A great pᵗ of the land must be sould to make the fence, the owners being many of them pore & not able to beare the charge thereof. some of them hauing foure fences All readie Against comon & high way ground.   Wherefore oᵣ humble request is that the said Act may be recalled & that the way vnto wenesemet from Redding may be in the highway leading toward the penie ferrie, vnto the house of James Barritt & so by the towneway leading directly vnto winesemet, lying on the head of the fiue Acre lotts, by the South spring, wᶜʰ is Allso A playne, firm trodd way & but litle about.   the wᶜʰ they now stand charged to fence Against & cannot secure their planting wᵗʰout it.   So shall wee be bound to pray as wee desire dayly to doe for yᵣ pᵣsptie & peace temporall & Eternall.

J⁰. GREENELAND
RICH. DEXTER
FRANCIS WHEELER
GEORGE FFELT
*Jnth name of the rest.*⁷⁹

---

⁷⁷ *Charlestown Archives,* xx., *in loco.*
⁷⁸ *Mass. Colony Records,* ii. 192.   ⁷⁹ *Mass. Archives,* cxxi. 21.

This petition indicates that portions of the land-ways and drift-ways of the allotment of 1634 had become the highways to Penny Ferry and Winnisimmet. The petitioners, one of whom, Frances Wheeler, was a widow, were inhabitants or landowners in the southern section, where the new way "thwarted" the grants above the five-acre lots by cutting across the angles made by the highways already in use. In answer to this petition the Court added to the committee the names of two inhabitants of the more northerly portion of Mystic Side in the following order, upon which the report of the committee was endorsed:—

Vpon the petition of mistick side men Jt is ordered that thomas Line Junior & m' Joseph Hills shall be added to the former Comittee to take a newe survey of the most convenient place for the way from Reding to wennetsemet, & to make certificate of their apprehensions there about.   *by the gen'all Co'te*
                                        JNCREASE NOWELL *Sec*.
Dated the 8th m° 1648.

Vpon S'uey for A way w^{th}in menčoned. wee App'hend it most con-uenient Jn All points to Lay it in the wonted roade from Redding to thomas Lines cornefeild & so ouer some p' of the sayd feild 2 pole broad on firm ground Aboue his house & so in the highway by the meeting house on Mestick Side Leading toward Charlestown unto the southerly side of Richard Adams Land : & so to the head of the fiue Acre lott' & vpon the head of the sayd lott' unto m' Pygraues [*Palgrave's*] lott, & then by A southeast line on the left hand 3 rodds from the new fence ouer A corner of Will: Jonsons playne two rods broad & over John Palmors & Richard Dexters land on the southside of A treble marked walnut by the corner of Richard Cookes feild & so in the high way to the lower end of the rayle betwixt m' Bellinghams & Tho' Whittamors land. 10th 2m° 1649:

                                        RALPH SPRAGUE
                                        FFRANCIS SMITH
                                        JOSEPH HILLS
                                        THO.' LINE.[90]

As three of the committee were Mystic Side men and no less subject to the weaknesses of humanity than those who compose like committees of the present day, it may be that some "private int'est," or at least a regard for the "conveniency" of their fellow inhabitants, may have influenced them. That the Court so conceived is evident, for the only action taken upon the report is indicated in the following order: —

[May 2, 1649.] Seeing it concernes this Co'te to p'vide the best high wayes to be layd out fro^m towne to towne for publike use, wch concerne all the posterity as well as o'selves, & therefore that no private int'est should hind' it, & forasmuch as the way fro^m Reding to Winnetsemet last layd out is thought to be lesse behoofull for the country then the form' way layd out by ord' of this Co'te, M' Robt Clements, John Osgood, & Franc^ᵇ Smith are hereby authorished & appointed to lay out the way, as men most indiff'ent to lay out the same.⁸¹

As these men were of Haverhill, Andover, and Reading, in the order of their names, they were in the meaning of the record " indifferent " men, and so they really proved; for in 1651, when Osgood and Smith died, the way was still unsettled. In the meantime Malden had become a town and its corporate history had begun; but before we turn to that we may with propriety continue the story of the " great country road " to the time when it became a well-defined and settled way. Nothing having been done, the Court passed the following order, and the road was laid out in accordance: —

[May 27, 1652.] Whereas this Court did long since appoynt sundry p'sons to lay out the way from Reding to Winesemett, which is not yet determined, & some of the p'sons mentioned in the sd order are dead, and forasmuch as it was ordred by Cambridge Court, that it should forthwith be done by the townes of Redding & Malden, it is now ordred by this Court, that the laying out of the sd highway shalbe done by the townes of Redding & Maldon, according to the law in that case provided, any act of this Court to the contrary notw^thstanding.⁸²

[September 10, 1653.] Thomas Marshall, John Smyth, & John Sprague, beinge chosen to lay out the country high way betweene Reddinge & Winnesemett, do lay it out as followes: from Reddinge towne, through Maldon bounds, betwixt the pond & John Smyths land, & so by the east side of M' Joseph Hills land, to New Hockley Hole, & so in the old way by the Cow Pen, & thence along on the east side of Thomas Coytmores lott, by Ele Pond, in the old way, to Thomas Lynds land, then through the first feild, & so by the feild by his howse, from thence, on the old way, by Maldon meeting howse, through the

⁸¹ *Mass. Colony Records*, ii. 271. ⁸² Ibid., iii. 274.

7

stony swampe, from the road there vpp betwixt Richard Addams &
John Vphams lottes, into Charlstowne bounds, through Wm Johnsons &
Richard Dexters land into ye way by the South Springe, & so on the
south side of Tho Whitamores howse into Mr Bellinghams land, into the
way that goeth to the fferry : the sd way to be fower pole broade, in
good ground, & six or eight where need requires.[88]

This highway, although many of its landmarks have long
been forgotten, may still be traced. From Lewis's Bridge to
Wayte's Mount, passing in a still older way, it was Main Street
as it now exists, except that it was narrower and more crooked.
On the hillside by the First Baptist Church it has been widened
towards the brook by a broad terrace, and many eccentric elbows
have disappeared. Beyond Wayte's Mount, it turned to the
eastward, to avoid the meadows, and followed in the Salem Path
to a point represented on the map of 1885 by the line between
the land of O. W. Ennis and Forest Dale Cemetery. Here it
left the Salem Path and ran northerly until it came to the still
unsettled and rocky hills which cover that section, through which
it ran with many windings as the ground presented more or less
difficulties. Here, until they were obliterated by the laying out
of the cemetery, the traces of the old way were very distinct.
Although disused for more than a century and a half, its marks
were seemingly those of yesterday, and the curious pedestrian
might cross a little brook on a rude stone bridge which served
the men of 1653. It could be followed with certainty to the
south-west corner of Wyoming Cemetery; and it reappeared on
the north side of Sylvan Street, opposite the north-east entrance
of the cemetery. Here, in 1894, it was still clearly defined,
winding around the eastern side of Boston Rock, where there
remained a low rough wall laid on the lower side of the road to
keep the way from washing out. A little farther on it unites
with a modern street, which occupies the ancient way and is
known as Linwood Avenue — an unmeaning and pretentious
title like many others, beneath which are buried older and better
names. From Linwood Avenue it passed easterly over a portion
of Lynde Street to Louisburg Square, where the John Lynde

house, a relic of the eighteenth century, long stood beneath its magnificent elm. South of this point, Lebanon Street is a modern road,[84] but northerly it is the old way to its junction with Green Street at Ell Pond, where a common watering and flaxing place long remained until by some means it became private property. Beyond Ell Pond, the great road followed the present Green Street by a circuitous route, perhaps to pass " along on the east side of Thomas Coytmore's lott," to a point near its northerly junction with Main Street; thence it followed the direction of that street, running mostly east of it until it came into Reading bounds.

South of Pemberton's Brook, the course of the old way is not so clear. Whether at first it went directly over Lewis's, or Bailey's, Hill to the meeting house at Bell Rock, or passed around it, in the old way to the landing-place at Sandy Bank, is uncertain;[85] although I am quite sure that a way over the hill was in use a few years later. Leaving Bell Rock, it traversed the ministry land and passed over the line of the present Cross Street near the corner of High Street; from whence it ran up the hill to the house of James Green, a portion of which still exists, though concealed by a later structure, in the Perkins house on Appleton Street. Here some traces of the old way were to be seen as lately as 1850. South of the Perkins house was the Stony Swamp, a tract of land which has been reclaimed, but which formerly showed many traces of its early condition, around which the road ran to Bucknam Street at the point where it is crossed by Bradford Street. The latter street for a short distance eastward is laid over the old way; and on the higher land near by could be seen, forty years ago, an old cellar which was once covered by an early home of the Dexters.[86] That part of Bucknam Street which lies south of Bradford Street, and

[84] Lebanon Street, from Forest Street to Upham Street, was laid out as a town way, "from Isaac Upham's house to John Pratt's house," in 1839. When the streets were named in 1846, the whole way from Salem Street was called Back Street.

[85] The old way to Sandy Bank was afterwards known as Poor House Lane; Burying Ground Lane; Marsh Street, 1846; and Madison Street.

[86] This house is said to have been the birthplace of the eccentric Lord Timothy Dexter. He was son of Nathan and Esther (Brintnall) Dexter, and was born January 22, 174⁴⁄₅.

was once known as Bucknam's Lane, has nothing of the rural beauty which it formerly possessed. From a narrow, winding, country way, lined with wild roses and berry bushes, it has become a broad and straight suburban street; but it is, nevertheless, the old way of 1653, which, passing into Norwood Street, found, in Everett Square, once known as Oakes's Corner, the "firm trodd way" from James Barrett's house to the South Spring. Onward it is all the old way by the South Spring, now hidden, and the site of Thomas Whittemore's house until it crosses the old Boston line and passing along the lower edge of Powder Horn loses itself "into the way that goeth to the fferry."

It appears that the new way was not entirely satisfactory in its northern part; and in 1655 the General Court "suspended from being made vse of for present" a portion of the "Highway by Maulden" until "this Court shall take further order, that so . . . present contentions and sujtes of lawe may be prevented."[87] Sixteen years later some part of the way near Boston Rock became unsettled and was defined by order of the County Court.

This 19 September 71.

In Order to what the County Court held at Charlestown the   of June 1671 who hath Chosen and impowered James greue Josias Conuers and Jonathan Poole to state the hyway now Jn question towards Redding nere Ensigne Thomas linds being in his grounds : : we Whos names are aboue mentioned do therefore Se Cause to remoue the hywaye from where Jt did former ly that Js to say through the Oald feld to the place vnder the rocks where the waye now lyes. Witness our hands.

JAMES GRENE
JOSIAS CONUARS
JONATHAN POOLE[88]

---

[87] *Mass. Colony Records*, iv. (i.) 237.   [88] *Midd. Court Files*, October, 1671.

CHAPTER IV.

CHURCH AND TOWN.

A LL the elements out of which an independent community could be made might be found in 1648 on Mystic Side. From landowners, merely, men had become planters; and their rude houses, rough and of a temporary character as many of them undoubtedly were, might now be found scattered along the plains and upon the uplands of the rivers from Moulton's Island and the Mystic to the forests around Wayte's Mount and Boston Rock. I do not think that settlers had advanced beyond the house of Thomas Lynde, above Wayte's Mount, although one or two may have gone beyond Ell Pond towards the headline, where Thomas Green soon after planted and founded the little forest-bound neighborhood of the Greens of the Woods. If so, they had met the tide of civilization coming from Lynn and settling around the ponds in Reading. There is reason to believe that Joseph Hills had built his house, if he had not found it already built by Coytmore, at the corner of Salem and Main Streets, where his well-known well yielded its cooling draughts to man and beast until 1894. His son-in-

law, John Wayte, who soon after added to his grant of eight
acres portions of the Coytmore lands, may have built his house
farther north, where he died, at the foot of the rock which bears
his name.

On the highland, since known as Bailey's Hill, John Lewis
had settled on his five-acre lot " in y⁰ common field," and given
his name to the bridge at its foot, which it retained until within
a few years, when the brook lost its ancient character and the
passage beneath the street became a culvert. Not far from
Lewis, in the vicinity of Bell Rock or farther south, beyond the
meadow, on Green's Hill, was William Brackenbury, a prominent man, who is
supposed to have
been one of the
earliest to plant on the banks of the North River. The improbable tradition " that he occupied what is known as the Russell
[Nowell] farm," [1] owes its origin, perhaps, to his ownership of
land adjoining the Wilson grant.

On the highlands near Sandy Bank, where land was reserved
for a landing place and a burying ground, a few families had
settled, the first of those who advanced into the country towards
the head of the North River. Traces of habitation might be
found there within my memory, and a few hardy flowers, first
planted by hands that were long ago folded and forgotten, still
lingered around the hollows that alone remained of those early
homes. Farther east on Green's Hill, James Green had built
on the Graves lot the house of which a portion, as has been
mentioned, is still standing on Appleton Street. Far south of
Sandy Bank in the easterly vicinity of the North Spring, we may
place Rowland Lahorne and his Sabbath-breaking wife, Flora,
with their " House having a cubbord and Bedstead in it; " [2]
and near by was Philip Atwood's house and garden. The
Bucknams had not yet settled near Willoughby's lot in Johnson's Plain; but Edward Carrington had apparently built on
his land near by, which, having received additions, he afterwards
described as " all that is mine or that may be called mine on

---

[1] *Bi-Centennial Book of Malden,* 239.   [2] *Midd. Court Files,* xi. 10.

Mistick side from the Pennie ferry to Lewises Bridge."[3] This land, descending to his son-in-law, Stephen Paine, was long known as the Paine farm, more recently as the Simon Tufts farm. Of the two ancient houses formerly standing upon this farm, one of which has recently been demolished, that which may still be seen beneath the hill by the side of Main Street, south of Winthrop Street, in Everett, was the elder, and was probably built by Edward Carrington. The other house, upon the hill above it, was built by the Paines.

William Sargeant, a haberdasher and a preacher, who is de-scribed by Edward Johnson as a "godly Christian," was upon the pleasant highland in Everett which long bore his name, but which has since been known as Nelson's Hill from a later resident, the Rev. Ebenezer Nelson of the First Baptist Church; and James Barrett, with his house at the present corner of Main and School Streets, has been mentioned. At Moulton's Island and upon the highlands above we have seen Thomas Moulton and his neighbors, John Greenland and George

---

[3] Carrington's Will, 1684, *Midd. Probate Files, in loco.* Views of the two houses mentioned in the text are given in this chapter. In that of the Paine-Tufts house, the roof of the other is seen over the hill.

Felt, and the other petitioners of 1640; and it is very probable that Seth Sweetser had early crossed the Mystic as a settler, landing at Wormwood Point, which became his place of habitation and received his name. Others may be located as inhabitants of Mystic Side with a degree of certainty, and of others the presence as sojourners can only be ascertained.

It has been seen that the land which was reserved for those who came with another minister had been diverted from its original purpose; but it is probable that it was intended from the first that a church should be formed on Mystic Side when it had received a sufficient number of inhabitants.

Meanwhile, the settlers had formed a part of the church of Charlestown, from which they received the ordinances and to which they carried their infants for baptism. The distance and the difficulties which lay between their homes and the meeting-house across the wide river were great, and in the winter season must have been all but insurmountable, save to the strongest. What time the new church was formed and the circumstances which attended it are alike uncertain. It was a small gathering and in some respects a most forlorn one; for while the fathers may have been rich in spiritual gifts, in material means they were poor indeed. Religious services may have been held on Mystic Side and some steps taken towards a church organization in 1648, under which date John Josselyn wrote, "A Church gathered at *Malden* Mr. *Sarjant* pastor;"[4] and Edward Johnson says: —

About this time the Town of Malden had his first foundation stones laid by certain persons, who issued out of Charles-Town, and indeed had her whole structure within the bounds of this more elder Town, being severed by the broad ipreading river of Mistick the one from the other, whose troublesome passage caused the people on the North side of the river to plead for Town-priviledges within themselves, which accordingly was granted them ; the soyl is very firtile, but they are much straitned in their bounds, yet their neerness to the chief Market Towns, makes it the more comfortable for habitation, the people gathered into a Church some distance of time before they could attain to any Church-Officer to administer the Seals unto them, yet in the

---

[4] Josselyn, *Two Voyages to New England*, 264.

mean time at their Sabbath assemblies they had a godly Christian named M. *Sarjant,* who did preach the Word unto them, and afterwards they were supplied at times with some young Students from the Colledg.[5]

That the gathering of the church was not accomplished without difficulties and, perhaps, some irregularities, is indicated by events which will be considered elsewhere. That they " treated " with several clergymen without success is known. Michael Wigglesworth wrote in 1658: —

Consider how long y* hand of y* Almighty hath been stretched out . . . frustrating yo* endeavo's after one, crossing & disappointing yo* hopes in anoth*, & it may be in a third, keeping you with in a forlorn condition, & altogeth without a minister, or at an uncertain pass with. out an officer; so y* it was long before you enjoyed Christ in all his ordinaces.[6]

The M. Sarjant of Johnson was William Sargeant, who has already been mentioned, a lay preacher and a ruling elder of the church, who led in religious services and exhortation, but was not allowed by ordination to perform the rite of baptism and to administer the sacramental bread and wine.[7] Joseph Hills is also mentioned as a ruling elder soon after.[8]

[5] Johnson, *Wonder-working Providence,* 211.

[6] *Mass. Hist. So. Proc.,* May, 1871, 94.

[7] "[November 14, 1639.] William Sergeant late of Northampton haberdasher of Hatts and now of Charlestown in New England planter & Sarah his wife late the wife of William Minshall of Whitchurch in the County of Salop gent. Deceased, are both blessed be God in full life & good health at the time of the making hereof." Lechford, *Note-Book,* 137.

Extensive researches of John S. Sargent of Chicago, the results of which were generously placed in my hands for use long ago, and which have since been given in full in Sargent, *Sargent Genealogy,* show the social position and descent of this "godly Christian." Hugh Sargeant, of Courtenhall, Northamptonshire, gent., was born about 1535 and died February 23, 1595⁄6. His wife was

Margaret Gyfford. Their son, Roger, maried Ellen Marcharmes of Finedon, January 3, 15⁸⁹⁄90. He was a linendraper and mercer at Northampton and was mayor of that city in 1626. His wife was buried, October 21, 1645; and he was buried, July 16, 1649. William was the seventh child of Roger and Ellen, and was baptized at Northampton, June 20, 1602. He became a freeman and married, (1) Hannah; (2) Marie; (3) Sarah, widow of William Minshall. He came to New England in 1638 and was admitted to the church at Charlestown, March 10, 163⁸⁄9.

Elder Sargeant removed to Barnstable in, or prior to, 1658, being made a freeman of Plymouth Colony in that year. He died, December 16, 1682, leaving his Malden lands to his eldest son John, who became the ancestor of a numerous progeny.

[8] *Midd. Court Files,* ii. 16¼.

The gathering of the church was the beginning of political
life, for in it lay the roots of all secular as well as ecclesiastical
authority. Out of it came the town and the state; and on its
usages were based the usages and forms of primary assemblies,
elections, and courts. Church members were the only freemen
of the Colony. As early as 1631 the Court ordered:—

To the end the body of the commons may be p'serued of honest and
good men, it was . . . ordered and agreed that for time to come noe
man shalbe admitted to the freedome of this body polliticke, but such as
are members of some of the churches within the lymitts of the same.[9]

They alone could vote in town and colony affairs and hold
office. Nor could they avoid the privileges which were con-
ferred upon them; for it was ordered, "concerning members
that refuse to take their freedom, the churches should bee writ
unto, to deale wth them."[10] They who had taken the residents'
oath might hold lands and become members of "any trayned
band;" but, although they might vote for such officers, they
could not become "captaines, or other inferio^r officers . . . for
it is the intent & order of the Court that no person shall hence-
fourth bee chosen to any office in the commonwealth but such
as is a freeman."[11]

Having then the beginnings of municipal existence, measures
of separation were soon taken by the freemen of Mystic Side.
An apparently misplaced leaf in the Charlestown Records bears
an agreement, which must have been written in 1648. It contains the first intimation of a division; although it is not clear
that the intention was not to settle the bounds as between two
churches for the purpose of laying ministerial rates rather than
to found a new town. The names of the signers, as they are
the first to appear in this connection, may be considered as
those of the fathers of Malden.

Wee whose names are heer vnder written weighing wth our selus
what may most promote the glory of God, and conduce to the increase
of brotherly Love and Peace: wee according to the Churches aduice
are willing to Suspend o^r gathering till next third day a month certaine
in which tyme we alsoe promise to apply our selus to the setling of the

---

[9] *Mass. Colony Records,* i. 87.   [10] Ibid., ii. 38.   [11] Ibid., i. 188.

bounds betwixt the town and vs: and if wee and their Agents cannot agree it, we agree to chuse twoo or three men for each partie to doe it

JOSEPH HILL[S]	JAMES GREENE
RALPH SPRAGUE	ABRAHAM HILL
EDWARD CARRINGTON	THOMAS OSBORNE
THOMAS SQUIRE	JOHN LEWIS
JOHN WAITE	THOMAS CAULE[12]

It is probable that this document contains the names of all, or nearly all, the male members of the infant church. How long a delay occurred cannot be ascertained; but on the first day of January, 164⅚, the inhabitants of Charlestown chose a committee

to meet with the 3 chosen brethren on Mistike Syde . . . to confer with them about the bounds of the land and division therof between vs and them and all particular cases pertaining theretoo, And to give report therof vnto the Generall towne at the next publike meeting of the towne.[18]

There are two copies of the result of the work of the committees; one in the Charlestown Records; and a second in the Middlesex Registry of Deeds, put upon record, January 4, 169½, from a defaced original, which was apparently the copy of the agreement which was retained by the Malden committee. I print the preamble to the Malden copy and the whole of the Charlestown copy that both may be preserved.

Charlestowne & Mistickside. Agreement respect their Bounds Viz! Richd Sprague Ralph Mousall Wm Stilson & Robert Halle were Deputed and Authorized by & on ye behalfe of the Jnhabitants of Charlestowne on ye one part as by a certain writing bearing date ye 26 day of ye first m^o: 1649, agreed in a publick Town meeting doth appear, And Willm Sergeant. Jo^s Hills Ralph Sprague & Edward Carrington were likewise Deputed and authorized by and on ye behalfe of the Jnhabitants of Mistick Side on ye other part as also by a writing dated ye last of ye 1st m^o 49 : agreed at a publick meeting of theire said Jnhabitants [as] doth also appear to agree and settle the bounds both of Jmpropriate and Common Ground betwixt ye Jnhabitants of Charlestowne and ye Jnhabitants of Mistickside. Jt is agreed and Concluded by ye Commissioners for both parts as followeth That in Consideration the brethren on Mistick side are by the Providence of God shortly to go into a

---

[12] *Charlestown Archives*, xix. 23. [18] Ibid., *in loco*.

Church Estate by them selues, and for y⁰ more Comfortable proceeding, and Carrying on of that worke of Christ amongst them Jt is granted and hereby agreed, that all y⁰ Land both Allottments and Common on y⁰ north side of the High way from y⁰ written tree, &c.

A True Coppy of the Propositions concluded bettweene us the Jnhabitants of Charlestowne who were appointed Commission⁹ heerein by y⁰ whole Towne : And o⁹ brethren on Mistickside (or Maulden) who were appointed Commissio⁹ by theire whole Towne heerein the seaventeenth day of the second month, (or Aprill) 1649.

To y⁰ end the Worke of Christ, & the ᵗhings of his house there in hand may bee the more Comfortably carryed on. It is agreed as followeth.

1ˢᵗ That all the Land both Allottments & Common on y⁰ North East side of y⁰ Highway from [*the*] Written Tree to the Bound Marke bettwixt Mʳ Nowells & M⁹ Cradducks ffarmes, & so besides Meadford ffarme & Wobourne, & thence to Readding [*to Charlestowne*] head Line & [*so*] to the written Tree are to bee measured at the Joynt charge of both parties, after the allowances made to [*some*] Wobourne men [*as y' Committee in that thing shall determine*] & [*also to*] Meadford ffarme, as the Court shall determine. then the rest to be equally devided ; bettwixt the Towne & mistickside y⁰ Bounds to beginn at [*Stephen*] ffosdicks Southwest Corner.[14]

2ly :   That all the Timber & Wood behind Leiftenᵐ [*Ralph*] Spragues Lott & the rest of y⁰ Lotts within Spott Pond Brooke runing to the Mill shalbee & remaine to the use of Charlestowne over & above all y⁰ within theire Line [*of Common, Excepting*] & [*alwaies reserved*] for the use of the [*Mistick side*] Inhabitᵃⁿ⁰ within [*y' Compass of*] y⁰ sᵈ Brook & no other [*from such time as y' partition aforesaid is settled.*]

3ly :   That M⁹ Joseph Hills sixty Acre Lott, & M⁹ [*William*] Serieants forty Acre Lott to bee deducted also out of Mistickside's p'portion of Common, & y⁰ for Partition of Townes [*touching Jmpropriated Lands,*] the Line shall runne from the uttmost head Corner of Thomas Whittamores five Acre Lott (some time M⁹ Nowells) on the head of the five Acre Lotts, to M⁹ [*William*] Serieants garden, & along by his fence till it comes on A straite Line with Richᵈ Pratts Northside Line, & so upon the same Line to y⁰ North River.

---

[14] Fosdick's lot was the last but one in the allotment towards the common between Cradock's grant, or Medford, and the lands of Mystic Side. As has been stated, it was afterwards occupied by the Malden Alms House. The highway from the written-tree, at Black Ann's Corner, to the mark between Nowell and Cradock was the Salem Path ; and a division of the lands north of it to Reading line, as provided in this article, fixed the western line of Malden through the Middlesex Fells to Smith's Pond.

4ly : That the Inhabit^{nts} without the [*said*] Line shall have Liberty to water theire Cattle at the North Spring after Havest time p'vided they damage no mans Meadow or Corne [*notwithstanding any fence that may be erected.*]

5ly : That Mr Wilsons & Mr Nowells ffarmes shall remaine to Charlstown.

6ly : That the Inhabit^{nts} on Mistickside shall beare A p'portion of ye Charges imposed on Charlstowne touching ye Castle as form'ly they have done, dureing the p'sent engagem^t

7ly : That the Inhabit^{nts} of Mistickeside shall beare theire p'portion of all Towne charges propper to the Towne in gen^{ll} to this day.

8^{ly} That the Inhabit^{nts} of Mistickside shall beare A p'portion of ye Charge of the Battery in Charlstowne as formerly forever, unlesse the Towne see cause to slight it :

9^{ly} All the Inhabit^{nts} on Mistickside now resident to Common theire Cattle with them, but if any oth^r shall settle henceforth wth in the Towne Line they are heereby exempted Commonage with them on Mistickside.

10^{ly} ffor farth^r Incouragem^t of ye worke affores^d wee acquitt the Inhabit^{nts} within the Line of Charlstowne from Church charges, for three yeares next ensueing & noe more.

11^{ly} for the Common ground on Mistickside bettwixt the fferry and the Mill Bridge, after Sufficient Landing places at sandy Banck, & A burying place also there [*Excepted:*] Also it shalbee at the disposeing of Charlstowne to sattisfy Highwaies, & answ^r Just engagem^{ts} bettwixt the fferry & the Mill Bridge.

12^{ly} And if Charlstowne p'portion of Commons shall need High-waies & Landing places out of ye Proportion of Mistickside it is heereby granted them, & concluded on : wittness o^r hands the day & yeare aboves^d

The Comissioⁿ names for Charlstowne were	The Comissioⁿ for Mistickside were
RICH^D RUSSELL	W^M SERIEANT
FFRA^S WILLOUGHBY	JOSEPH HILL[S]
RICH^D SPRAGUE	RALPH SPRAGUE
RALPH MOUSALL	EDW^D CARRINGTON
W^M STILSON	
ROBT HALE	

Memorand it was agreed by the Committe within mentioned before the signement by the whol Committe in referrence to the sixth [11th] Article y^t the two landing places at Sandy Banck shalbe divided in this man-ner namely the uper banck at the Tree formerly apportioned & marked by Ralph Mousall, Robert Hale & Joseph Hills. The lower in the middle of the Land by A just measure betwixt William Brankenbury and the marsh ground. And that the halfe part next William Bracken-bury[a] & y[e] part above the Tree at the uper place shalbe and remain in proprietie unto the towne of Maldon for ever; And the other two parts shalbe & remaine in proprietie unto the use of Charlestowne for ever provided that no part of the Land behinde the said Landing places, namely bounded by the said Ralph Mousell, Robert Hale and Joseph Hills be no time disposed to any other use but for landing & laying of Wood, Timber, fframe[s] of house[s], hay & other things, nor to hinder highwaye[s] for the use of each Towne : Also to the Seventh [9th] Article it is Agreed y[t] it be understood & intended to give interest in the Common of Maldon for Timber, Wood & Cattle to the Inhabitants now resident and to their naturall Children y[t] Shall hereafter live in any of the house[s] of the present Inhabitants or upon the land belonging to them provided the number of dwelling house[s] be no time more than are now extant there.

And for a cleer determination of the Eight [6th] Article touching the Castle it is agreed y[t] the proportion for Maldon shall be A ninth part of the charge thereof dureing the present Engagement as is expressed.

Also to the Eleventh [12th] Article it is agreed that the Commons of Charlestown shall have need full highwaye[s] through proprietie[s] as well as the common ground in Maldon. Also it is agreed y[t] where ever the word Mistickside is mentioned for distinction from Charlestown it is intended & shall henceforth be understood to denominate the town of Maldon. Witness our hands the fourth of the fourth month, one Thousand Six hundred ffifty one.

JOSEPH HILLS   In the presence of
WILLIAM SERGEANT   JAMES GARETT
JOHN WAYTE being chosen   JOHN UPPAME
   in the Roome of Lieut Sprague
EDWARD CARRINGTON

Touching the Alowance for Meadford farme mentioned in the first Article. It is agreed & concluded by the Commissi[n] here under written that there shalbe deducted out of y[e] tract of land mentioned in the said Article. One hundred twenty five Acre[s] of Land before y[e] line of divission betwixt the two Towne[s] Common[s].

Stephen Pain aged fifty Eight years or thereabouts doth testifie and say that this Jnstrument here produced was seen by y[e] abouesaid p[r]son w[th] the names of the Committee men to it, before they were defaced, and that they were Subscribed by y[e] Clerk of a True Coppie, w[th] y[e] priviledged Hous[e]n that belongs to Maldin common for Timber, Wood &

Cattle, namely Edward Carrington & Thomas Molton, James Pemmerton, Richard Dexter, John Greenland, James Barrett, and severall other ffamilies, that he can & doth Attest to :

> Xb' : 29 : 1691 : Charlestowne :
> At y° Adjournm' of y° Court
> Sworn Jn Court by STEPHEN PAIN
> Att* SAM^LL. PHIPPS *Cler*

John Pratt aged 35 years or thereabouts testifieth and said, that these articles concerning y° p'viledge housen on mistick side, that haue p'viledge in Maldon common, for Timber wood and Cattle, wth y° names of severall houses, as Edward Carrington, Richard Dexter, James Barrett, and severall others, this was brought to me to convince me that J had no priviledge in maldon common, because J was a Tennant, and not an heire of that J lived on & further saith not :

> [*Sworn to as above.*][15]

Having made a definite and, apparently, an amicable agreement with their Charlestown brethren, the men of Mystic Side now carried their petition to the Court; and the following entries on the records of the Colony, indicating the action of the Council and the consent of the Deputies, form the simple act of incorporation under which the town of Malden existed for two hundred and thirty-three years.

[1649:]
[2 May.]
M.don

Upon the petition of Mistick side men, they are granted to be a distinct towne, & the name thereof to be called Mauldon.

[1649:]
[11 May.]
Misticke
named
Maulden.

In answer to the petition of seu'll inhabitants of Misticke side, their request is graunted, viz., to be a distinct toune of themselves, & the name thereof to be Maulden.[16]

---

[15] The first part of this document, to "A True Coppy of the Propositions," is from the Malden copy, *Midd. Co. Deeds*, xi. 83. The second part, to "Memorand it was agreed," is from the Charlestown copy, *Charlestown Archives*, xx. 151, 153, with additions, in italics, from the Malden copy. The "Memorand," following the names of the commissioners, is from *Charlestown Records*, v. 5. The affidavits of Paine and Pratt are recorded with the Malden copy, *Midd. Co. Deeds*, xi. 83. William Mellins, "aged 21 years or there about," testified to the same effect. This collation must give the full agree-

ment as it was understood by the inhabitants of the two sections.

[16] *Mass. Colony Records*, ii. 274; iii. 162. The next year the town was granted a brand mark.

"[1650 23 May.] Maldons marke. Vppon the request of the inhabitants of Maldon, the Court hath appoynted that: M.: shalbe the brand-marke for theire towne." *Mass. Colony Records*, iii. 188.

It will be observed that in the record of the Council the new town is given its proper name of Maldon, which it does not receive in the Deputies' record. Its

The financial settlement between the towns is the subject of at least two entries in the Charlestown Records:—

That wch o.^r Brethren of Maulden are to allow theire p'portion of to this Towne for Debts oweing when they went from us: vizt oweing to the Cap^{tn} of the Castle when or brethren

went away	22: 2: 11
To Mr Long for diett	5: 6: 4
To Mr Mellows	15: 0: 0
To Wido: Rand	10: 8: 0
To Mr Nowell for a man at Castle	2: 10: 0
To Laurance Dowce	6: 0: 0
To goo: Tedd	6: 4: 0
To ffoxes & Wolves	9: 0: 0
To Mr Norton for charge about ye Castle	6: 0: 0
To A Petition about Meadford	0: 10: 0
To o.^r Eld.^{rs} allowances	4: 0: 0
To the Trayning place	20: 0: 0
To Cap^{tn} Davenpord from the 9: month 1648 to the ffifte moneth 1650	31: 4: 0

The bills wch are paid to Charlstowne by o.^r brethr: of Malden since the 10: of the X: month 1653 when was due to Charls Towne from ye Towne of Maulden thirty five Pounds thirteene shillings

	li	*s*	*d*
Imprimis paid to bro: Pentecost	0:	19:	0
paid by A bill to bro: Stilson	1:	0:	11
paid by A bill to Rowse & Morley 12 Cord of Wood . .	2:	14:	0
paid to Welch 12 Cord of Wood & in A bill	4:	1:	7
paid 16 bush.^{ls} of Turneps at 16^d	1:	1:	4
paid by knower 39½ bush.^{ls} of Indian Corne	4:	10:	5
paid by knower in Tobacco	0:	12:	4
paid to Robt Hale in Cord Wood	10:	12:	6
	25:	12:	1

The 14: of ye xj: 1655 [17]

origin in the name of the English town has been noticed. Although the form, Malden, was used and perhaps generally so, from the beginning, the usage of many of the best informed and more careful people favored Maldon. Deacon John Shute, who was town clerk for thirty-six years, and who was one of the most careful of scribes, employed the incorrect form in the earlier portion of his term; but in 1743 he adopted the other and invariably used it thereafter in his records. When he closed his books and his term at the annual town meeting, March 6, 1769, Maldon departed from the records. The propriety of placing it, *in memoriam,* upon the town seal was once considered, but the proposition met with little favor and no success.

[17] *Charlestown Archives,* xx. 180, 186.

The line between the two towns, on the southerly side of Malden, ran from the head of the five-acre lots near Powder Horn Hill north-westerly to the North River, which it appears to have met near Sandy Bank. This division left to Charlestown the territory now occupied by the south-western portion of Everett, which retained the old name of Mystic Side, and its inhabitants were known as "our Charlestown neighbors." Practically, they were a part of the new town, having their religious and social privileges with its inhabitants, and burying their dead in its graveyard at Sandy Bank.

Not unlike the people of Mystic Side, in relation to Malden, were the planters in that section of Charlestown which lay along the western banks of the North River and Three Mile Brook, separating Malden from Medford for many years, and many of those who had settled at Winnisimmet and Rumney Marsh and on that narrow and peculiar strip of six hundred acres which began at Bride's Brook, near Black Ann's Corner, and ran along the eastern side of Malden to the Reading line. These, like the Charlestown neighbors of Mystic Side, worshipped, married, and were buried with the Malden people. So intimate were their relations that it is sometimes difficult to separate them from their Malden neighbors; and the names of Floyd, Breeden, Boardman, Blanchard, and Tufts, although the names of settlers beyond the proper bounds of Malden and Mystic Side, may become as familiar to the Malden antiquary as those of Wayte and Hill, or Upham and Green. Some of the few inhabitants of Medford, who were without a meeting house until 1696, were also members of the Malden congregation, if not of the church.

A vivid impression of the scattered condition of the population of Middlesex and a part of Suffolk in 1649 may be gained if it can be realized that the little church of Malden, with hardly more than a score of members, stood alone in the midst of the "uncouth wilderness," which stretched from the Mystic to Reading and Woburn, and from the Abousett and the sea to the frontier settlement and church at Concord.[18]

[18] The year 1649 was rendered memorable in the annals of early New England by the deaths of John Winthrop and Thomas Shepard, and by "innumerable

8

There are no records of the town before 1678. A "first town book" was in existence in 1701, but no member of the living generations ever saw it.[19] In its absence the perplexed antiquary must gather from widely scattered sources the story of the birth of the town and its early years of growth. The authorities are documents and records, often indefinite and unsatisfactory — papers made for a purpose soon past, and not intended to convey information to a distant age; but in the vagueness and uncertainty of the light which they shed we may see a sparse and sturdy population, ever working and praying amid discouragements and fears, overcoming a wilderness and laying deep the foundations of the institutions we enjoy.

Of the acts of the town in its first essays at self-government we know but little. Joseph Hills, who had already served as Speaker of the House of Deputies, was chosen deputy, or representative to the General Court at the first election. John Wayte appears as clerk of the writs, filling the place of a town clerk at a time when that office did not exist by name;[20] and Thomas Squire, John Upham, William Brackenbury, John Wayte, and Thomas Call, appear in 1651 as the first board of Selectmen of which we have knowledge. At the same time, Richard Adams filled the not unimportant office of constable.

If the record of the early years of the town could be read, we would find that those were the days of small things. But small as they might seem to us, these things were of the utmost importance to our fathers. Regulations for the fencing of common lands against private grounds, the adjustment of indefinite bounds, the settling of highways and townways, the care of the flocks and herds by public shepherds or herdsmen,

hosts of catterpillars, which destroyed the fruits of the earth, in divers places, and did eat off the leaves of trees, so as they looked as bare as if it had been winter; and in some places did eat the leaves from off the pease straw, and did not eat the pease." This was followed the next year by a great mortality among children, and by "new diseases the fruits of new sins." Morton, *New-England's Memorial*, [1826] 144, 146.

[19] It is mentioned as "yᵉ first Town book " in the report of a committee on "yᵉ Country Rhoads," recorded in the Town records in 1701. The missing volume was advertised in 1862 and a liberal reward offered for its recovery.

[20] The duties of a clerk of the writs and the gradual merging of the office in that of the town clerk are noticed in the chapter on town officers. Captain John Wayte held the office from 1649 to 1684.

the hanging of gates across public ways, and like matters were the staples which formed the fabric of town business. Mixed with it all was the care which maintained church privileges and fostered the school, that through ignorance the cause of religion might not decline.[21]

Having a church and a town government, the people of Malden waited not long for another accompaniment of English populations, as is shown in the following petition: —

To the hon'd Cort for the counti of Midlesex Wee whose names are herunder written doe well App'ue Thomas Skinner for Keeping An ordinary for the Accomodation of Travellers & such like accasions : humbly desiring he may by you be licenced herunto for our Town of Maldon 22 : 1 : m? 1651 :

THOMAS SQUIRE	
JO. VPPAM	
WILL BRAKENBURY	*Selectmen*
JO. WAYTE	
THO. CALL	RICHARD ADAMS *Const.*[22]

John Hathorne, however, who had come to Malden from Salem, and whose action as a witness in the Matthews troubles apparently gained him the favor of the authorities as well as the displeasure of his neighbors, received the appointment from the General Court to which he had petitioned.

[1651 : 23 May.] In ans' to the petition of John Hawthorne, this Courte judgeth it meete to encourage and appointe him, the sajd John Hawthorne, to goe on and keepe the ordjnary at Malden.[23]

It may be presumed that the ire of the Malden people was visited upon their offending townsman, for his business does not seem to have prospered and he remained here but a short time. As early as during the succeeding November he removed to Lynn, where he was guilty of practices which received the atten-

---

[21] A Puritanic reason, but a good and righteous one. Said the law-givers : —
" *It being one chief project of Sathan to keep Men from the knowledg of the Scripture, as in former times keeping them in unknown tongues, so in these Latter times by perswading from the use of tongues that so at least the true sence and meaning of the Originall might be Clouded and Corrupted with false closses of deceivers, to the end therefore that learning may not be Buried in the graves of our forefathers in Church & Commonwealth, the Lord attesting our endeavours.* It is therefore Ordered etc." *Lawes and Libertyes,* [1660] 70.

[22] *Midd. Court Files,* i. 11.

[23] *Mass. Colony Records,* 4 (i.) 47.

tion of the General Court.[24] The next year the following record appears: —

[1652: 26 May.] In ans^r to the petition of the inhabitants of Malden, the Courte doth graunt libertje and licence to Thomas Skinner to keepe an ordinary there, in the roome and stead of John Hawthorne, who was formerly licensed there.[25]

Later the selectmen asked and received a broader license for "our Bro^r," as is shown in the following petition and reply: —

To the hon^d Court

Wee whose Names are vnderwritten, Desyre that our Bro^r Thomas Skinner, may be lycenced to sell Strong waters And Wine to Supplie the necessitys of the Towne, and Travellers, paying the Accustomed fees.

Malden 30th. of ye 10th mo 1653

JOHN VPPAM
WILL BRAKENBURY
THO^S. GREEN
JOH SPRAGUE
JOH. WAYTE
} *selectmen.*[26]

[3. (11) 1653.] Vpon the request of the Select Men of Mauldon, This Court doth grant Licence vnto Tho: Skinner to retale strong waters in there Towne.[27]

As Thomas Call was the first beer seller of Mystic Side, so to Thomas Skinner belongs the doubtful honor of being the first recorded dealer in "strong waters" in Malden. Although the latter remained in life and in Malden until 1704, he appears to have soon retired from the "Ordjnarie" business. The following petition lies in the Court files: —

To the honoured Court at Charlet^e. 16. 4th. m^e. 1657: The Town of Maldon being destitute of An Ordinarie keeper for Accomodating the Town and Countrie. Jt is the desire of the Selectmen of the sayd Town: that A Bro^r of the Church there: namely Abraham Hill may by this Court be licenced to keep an Ordinarie there. As Allso to draw wine for the better Accomodating both the Church and Countrie

The Court consents hereto 23. 4. 1657.
THO: DANFORTH *Record^r.*

JOH WAYTE
JOHN SPRAGUE
JOHN VPHAME
WILL BRAKENBURY[28]

---

[24] He was a brother of Major William Hathorne of Salem, whose abilities and services rendered him prominent in the infant state. For the offences of the Malden inn-holder at Lynn, see *Mass. Colony Records*, iii. 299; iv. (i.) 134.

[25] *Mass. Colony Records*, iv. (i.) 89.
[26] *Midd. Court Files*, i. 15.
[27] *Midd. Court Records*, i. 48.
[28] *Midd. Court Files*, vi. 27. Abraham Hill was "tennent and keeper of ye corn-mill" on the Coytmore property;

A similar petition, made two years later, is worthy of reproduction for the information which it may give us in its final clause.

Jt is the Request of the Select men of Maldon to the hon'd Court at Cambridge that Abr. Hill may be lycenced to sell strong liquo's in the s^d Towne for the necessary supply of Travelle's as allso for the Jnhabitants that p'sons may be p'vented from keeping such quantities in their priuate Houses, the abuse whereof haue proued of uery euill consequence.

5th 2mo 1659 :

> JOHN VPPAM
> WILLM BRAKENBURIE
> JOHN SPRAGUE
> THO^s GREEN
> JOHN WAYTE [20]

The house of Abraham Hill was on the easterly side of the Great Road, near its junction with the Medford Road, which, at first, was merely the way to the mill. The bridge by which the latter road crossed the Three Mile Brook, the Mill Bridge of 1649, was early known as Hill's Bridge and so remained until recent years. After the death of Abraham Hill, his widow, Sarah — herself the daughter of an innkeeper, Robert Long of Charlestown — kept the ordinary until 1679, when she was succeeded by her son Jacob.

It has been seen that the early innkeepers were licensed to sell wine and strong drinks. The evils of license were not long in appearing. Drunkenness was of frequent occurrence and many sins which drunkenness might often incite were not unknown. As a remedy the County Court passed the following order: —

and his house stood on that portion of the Coytmore land which had come into his possession by some unrecorded purchase. All the land west of the easterly line of the High School land, between Salem and Main Streets and the brook at the railroad, was included in this parcel, and remained many years in the possession of the Hill family. The house which became the tavern in 1657 was not that house on the site of the City Hall which was later known as Hill'- Tavern. The early house must have been farther south, I think, somewhere between the present Irving Street and Harvell's Brook.

[20] *Midd. Court Files*, viii. 2. Licenses were granted for one year only by the County Court, upon the "Approbation of the Selected Townsmen." *Lawes and Libertyes*, [1660.] 43, 46.

[October 4, 1659.] This Court doth *order* y[t] all y[e] inkeepers within the limitts of this Coun. shall henceforth be p'hibited selling of strong waters by retaile.[20]

I think this prohibition must have been soon withdrawn, or, like many Court orders, it fell into disuse. Licensed sales of spirits and the milder forms of intoxicating drinks were allowed by the colonial law, but they were strictly guarded. Samuel Sprague of Malden was fined twenty shillings and costs, in 1672, for " retayleing cider without license, & at vnreasonable times enterteyneing persons in his family." [31]

Our forebears in their early essays at government showed at times a disregard of their civil obligations that gained the attention of the County Court. It was a grievous neglect of duty that caused the following entry in the records of the Court : — " 4. 8[mo] 1653 : Mauldon for deffect in stocks is fined five shillings." [32] Nor was that much less in 1655, when the town was presented for the lack of scales and weights.[33] In 1658 defective ways called the selectmen to answer to the Court, and in due time the offence was condoned. Whether it may have been from inability to meet the requirements of the law or a thoughtless neglect, many times did the selectmen, or a special committee, have to wend their weary ways to Cambridge or to Charlestown to appease the wrath of the Court, escaping sometimes by a confession of guilt and a promise of better care ; meeting sometimes a fine, the burden of which must have been harder to bear than threats or reprimands.

Nor were these shortcomings confined to the people in their corporate capacity ; for their social and private matters furnished a plentiful harvest of suits and " small causes," which must have kept the little town in a fever of excitement from one year's end to another. Breaches of morals and minor lapses from duty or rectitude were not infrequent. While these things are sometimes whimsical, seen through the quaintness of the records which have preserved them, they are sometimes of a darker nature. Whether whimsical or sad, they prove, always,

---

[20] *Midd. Court Records*, i. 191.
[31] Ibid., iii. 34.
[32] Ibid., i. 45.
[33] *Midd. Court Files*, x. 2.

that the much lauded virtue of those early days was in its weaker moments no better than its sister of to-day. A few cases may be cited.

If Robert Burden, whose surname became Burditt, and Sarah the wife of William Bucknam, with whom Burditt boarded, had not drawn upon themselves the admonition of the Court, " for severall imodest and suspitious cariages in their familiarity together," in 1652,[34] much evil might have been prevented; for, aside from the wicked tendencies of their actions, they set the neighborhood by the ears. The list of those who testified in this case is nearly a roll of the men and women of Mystic Side. A suit by Bucknam against his neighbor William Marble, otherwise Mirable, appears to have had some connection with this affair; but a more important case was that of Joseph Hills. Mr. Hills, in his capacity of general adviser and man of business for the neighborhood, unfortunately pleaded the cause of the indiscreet wife before the Court. To this Thomas Squire referred as "the base buissines of Bucknam's wife." Mr. Hills was a ruling elder; but that did not hinder the disrespectful Squire, passing from the affairs of his neighbors to his own, from calling him, " Alexander the Copper Smith who hath done me much harm." He said that

Mʳ Hills at his daughter Harris her wedding, in the hearing of Mʳ Sims, Brother Line Leiutenant Wayte & others: did say that his wife must be his Master and that since that speech of mʳ Hills & by means thereof he neuer had quiet day with his wife.

" Upon seuerall Lords days in the publique Assembly in the meeting-house in Maldon," he uttered " his euil and reuiling speeches against the Elders and especially against mʳ Hills." Among other things he said : —

That his wife had stollen his goods and that mʳ Hills children had receiued them, and farther Sayd what shee had giuen to mʳ Hill hee knew not.

That mʳ Hill was not fit to be Rouling Elder for hee took part with A theif . . . .

That mʳ Hill is one day in the desck and the next day pleading

---

[34] *Midd. Court Records,* i. 31.

baudie buissines in the Court.   will you say that hee is an honest man?
doe you think that hee is an honest man? or words to that effect.

is hee fitt to sit in the place of A ruling Elder that will plead the
cause of rogues.[36]

Of course a suit for slander followed.   In the meantime,
Bridget, the wife of Squire, went to the Court, complaining of
bad treatment.   She had lived twenty years with her husband
and was now aged and weak and in fear of becoming a burden
upon the town or the church.   This was bad enough, but Thomas
Squire, with William Marble, had filled the measure of iniquity
by defaming the government in the person of Richard Bellingham, the deputy governor.[30]   How he was punished and how
the wisdom of those days furnished a means of working off a
fine, when money was wanting or the culprit was not sensitive,
appears in the record of the Court: —

[3 (11) 1653] m^r Joseph Hill, Plant against Thomas Squire Deff. in
an action of Deffamation, the Jury findes for the plaintiffe Damage Ten
pounds, and costs of Cort. one pound 17^s 6^d Provided in Case the
Defft shall at Mauldon meeting house, upon their Last Lecture day in
march next, make such an acknowledgment of his offence, before the
publique assembly after Lecture, as shall in the Judgment of Mr Edward
Collines, Tho: Goold, Edw. Winship and Tho: Wilder, be a sattis-
factory acknowledgment of those Slanderous Speeches and imputations
witnessed in Cort agst the Deff. concerning the plaintiffe, then the
Deff. to be abated fiue pound of the aforesaid 10.^ll [37]

Henry Swillaway was the unfortunate servant of Peter Tufts,
who " beate his man with the greate end of A goade Sticke,"
and " said that he would tie him to a tre and beat him for he
was his moneie."   Under such provocations, it is not strange
that the servant began to retaliate and " abused " his master
and " his dame in blose and words."   Thomas Mudge saw him
" strike his master upon the brest with his hand ; " and Mary
Mudge testified : —

that she being at Goodman Torfs of an arand : Gudie Torfe and
she hereing the Dine in the yard, we went out of the dore, and his
man had got vp a great stone and held it vp to thro at his master, as

        [36] *Midd. Court Files,* li.   [36] Ibid.   [37] *Midd. Court Records,* i. 46.

I conseved, but when he se me he threwe it doune; I further Testifie I herd him cal his master base Rouge.[38]

It may be supposed that neither Goodman Tufts nor the rebellious Swillaway could desire to keep close company for a long time, and accordingly the latter became servant to John Bunker. He was soon after brought before the Court by his late master for his miscarriages; but, in the end, the master got more justice than he liked. James Barrett, his neighbor, said: —

J James Barot aged about 40 yeres or ther aboutes J doth heare testifie that J herd goodman tufes sai that he had not Justis before the Debeti Gove: in the cas betwen him and his man and for his man was wrong out of his hand   Therefor he wod make it apear at this corte: [39]

Thus was government, in the person of Richard Bellingham, again defamed as it had been aforetime by Thomas Squire. Peter Tufts was speedily convicted and humbly acknowledged his sin, with the wish that it might

not only be a warneing to myselfe for the future, unto a greater watchfulnes over all my words & wayes, but also a meanes to detere all others that either have or may heare here of, from all offenses of this or the like nature.[40]

Well would it have been for the goodman if " Gudie Torfe " had profited by the experience of her husband; but her woman's nature could not control her tongue, which soon brought her to grief. James Barrett and William Luddington had been witnesses in the Swillaway case, and it was for slander against them that she was found guilty. The penalty was

damages ten shillings apeece, & an acknowledgm[t] to be made by the deff[t] at Mauldon, vpon the Lords day in the after noone, within the space of thirty dayes next ensueing, and to be made after the publicke exe'cise is ended, before the congregation depart in mann' following. viz[t] in these words. That whereas J Mary Tufts am legally convicted of slandering & wronging James Barrat, & William Luddington, or any other whom my words might reflect vpon, by speaking Rashly, irregularly, & sinfully, J am heartily sorry, & doe desire to be humbled for the same, & in case of non observance to doe as above p'mised either to pay y[e] said ten shill. apeece, or makeing such acknowledgm⸪ both for mann⸳ & time : the Jury do find that y⸳ deff⸳ shall pay vnto y⸳ pts fifty shill apeece, & costs of Court, thirty one shill & two pence.[41]

When George Knower " P⸳phaned the Sabbath " and struck " James Barratt on the Sabbath day," he forced Barrett to become a " Coacter " to the extent that he " fetched bloud on Knower." For this companionship, they were fined thirty shillings and twenty shillings respectively, with costs of Court.[42] This was a neighborly broil, which appears to have been not uncommon. Of a like nature was the case of Thomas Shepherd, who called Samuel Sprague " a bays uilliane," and said " when euer I see you mye spirit Rises at you & Whereuer I meet with you I shall Remember you." A boy, Thomas Mudge, " did heare Thomas Shepherd: strike Samuel: Sprague two blows." To the credit of Sprague, he struck not back, but said " what dost thou meane to playe the foole: I: am Resolved: I: will: not strike: " although the other dared him with many " Reuiling Speaches."[43]

John Pemberton of Malden was found drunk in the street in Boston and was put into the stocks; but he took a drunkard's revenge in beating his wife.[44] For the latter offence, he was presented by the grand jury; nor was he without companionship, for at the same Court James Fosdick was fined ten shillings and costs, " for rude cariage with some others in the night time, at Mauldon, & for contempt."[45] Of a different class, but more fruitful of evil results, was the offence of Thomas Dickerman.

[December 19, 1676.] Thomas Dickerman appearing before y⸳ Court to answ⸳ the p⸳sentm⸳ of y⸳ Grand Jury for neglect of family goverm⸳ made answ⸳ that he bound out his daughter, whose miscariage was the cause of y⸳ compl⸳ & was discharged.[46]

Well would it have been for the daughter had the discharge of the father released her from the effects of his negligence.

[41] *Midd. Court Records,* i. 200. [1660.]
[42] Ibid., i. 147.
[43] *Midd. Court Files,* xvii.
[44] Ibid., xxii. 7. [1671.]
[45] *Midd. Court Records,* iii. 12.
[46] Ibid., 160. The fact that Elizabeth Dickerman, the mother, died May 10, 1671, may go far to excuse the father; for paternal government has often failed, since the world began, to fill the place of maternal love.

She appears to have borne in her character the results of the paternal fault, for which she sorely suffered, if the cruel sentence in the following record was executed.

[April 2, 1678.] Elizab: Dickerman serv⁺ unto Jnᵒ Starky appearing before yᵉ Court, & convicted of setting her masters house on fire, & of meditating & contriveing to put copperas into yᵉ victuals of one of her fellow servᵗˢ Shee is sentenced to be severely whipt twenty stripes at Cambr. & within one month to haue twenty more inflicted upon her at Mauldon.⁴⁷

There was one Paul Wilson, a rollicking blade, whose evil propensities brought him often to the notice of the Court. After a real estate transaction, which eventually involved the Rev. Michael Wigglesworth in law and losses, he appears to us as a drunkard. Being, by his own confession, convicted of excessive drinking, he was fined.⁴⁸ Two years later he was convicted of "disorderly carriage" at Charlestown, where on the evening of a day of public thanksgiving there was gathering into companies, fences were pulled down and burned, and a house was tumbled into the river. For his participation in this frolic, he was sentenced to pay a fine of thirty shillings and the costs of Court, or to receive five stripes.⁴⁹

Priscilla, the daughter of Deacon John Upham, was, in 1658, about sixteen years old, while Paul Wilson was about nine years her senior. It is evident that the suitor was not held in high esteem by the watchful father; but in spite of the paternal frowns, the claims of love were pushed with ardor. John Martin, a cousin of Priscilla, said that Wilson told his uncle, "that if he could get or had gotten the Affections of a maid and he could as for the maid he would haue her do al her ffreindes or all the men in new england what they can."⁵⁰ As a natural consequence, Deacon Upham entered a complaint against the lover, "for violent soliciting his daughter against his will; " and the offender was duly admonished at the County Court. At the same time, he was bound in ten pounds, "yᵗ he will no more frequent the Company of Priscilla Vpham, nor by no

⁴⁷ *Midd. Court Records*, iii. 218.   ⁴⁹ Ibid., i. 274.
⁴⁸ Ibid., i. 206. [1660.]   ⁵⁰ *Midd. Court Files*, vii. 6.

means whether direct or indirect, make any more adresses vnto her without her fathers leave first orderly had & obteined." [51]

In connection with this case is the story of a serenade, which is both quaint and diverting, as told by the brother of Priscilla, Phineas Upham, whom we shall hereafter know as the gallant soldier who fell in Philip's War. He had recently married Ruth Wood.

Upon the last day of April [1658.] in the night at too of the cloke after midnight; There was a noise heard by Phinehas Vpham and his Wife At the side of the house; by which they ware awakned out of their sleepe his wife being awakned first was strucke with agreat feare: Wee heard musicke and dansing which was no smal disturbance to us: And they came harkeing unto our window where wee lay; which they did three times; between which times they danced and played with their musicke: with much laughter.

Three days after this affair, Paul Wilson went to the house of Phineas Upham and acknowledged that he was one of the revellers, when

It was farther demanded of him what musicke they had among them; whether it was not a kit, or a Jewsharpe; who answered no, Jt was a Smal Vial; Ading also you could not know us by our Voices, for wee said at our departure nothing, but two of the cloke and a faire morning.[52]

Paul Wilson, becoming an inhabitant of Charlestown, married after a number of years, had a large family and died at a good old age; while the fair Priscilla married Thomas Crosswell of Charlestown and brought him a family of twelve children.

While we may deplore the weaknesses which marred the Arcadian simplicity of those early days, we are indebted to them for the records that give to us many a vivid picture of colonial life. Witnesses, in quaint, archaic terms, have left us unnumbered items of family history, of local description, or of lively neighborhood gossip, that would not otherwise have been preserved. Thus, even the follies and wrangles of our fathers become of interest to us of the latter times and enliven or illumine the history of the little town which had now taken its place in the

[51] *Midd. Court Records,* l. 156, 157.　　　[52] *Midd. Court Files,* vii. 6.

sisterhood of towns that made the Colony of the Massachusetts Bay. It was not these cases alone which made up the daily life of the settlers at Mystic Side and Malden. These were of minor importance in the general life of the community; for around and above them was a life of busy work creating out of hard conditions the humble homes in which were nourished industry and virtue. Under the influences of this daily life, the wilderness gave place to cleared fields, on which the yearly harvests smiled; while the beasts and game of the forest retired before the flocks and herds of civilization.

At this period, one who had known the story of the settlement and the town from the day when the first comers crossed the Mystic, who had looked across the South River to the pleasant shores of Sweetser's Point before the Spragues had followed the Indian trail from Salem through the forests of Scadan — Samuel Maverick, who had fortified the house at Winnisimmet in 1625, wrote: —

MAULDON. — Two miles above Winnisime Westward stands a small Country Towne called Mauldon, who imploy themselves much in flurnishing the Towne of Boston and Charles Towne with wood, Timber and other Materials to build withall.[53]

[53] *Briefe Discription of New England,* in *N. E. Hist. and Geneal. Register,* xxxix. 38. This was undoubtedly written by Samuel Maverick, in 1660, and was discovered in the British Museum by Henry F. Waters, in 1884.

CHAPTER V.

MARMADUKE MATTHEWS.

HARDLY had the men and women of Malden begun to enjoy their new privileges before troubles came from the blessings for which they had labored. So characteristic of the times and the people were these troubles, and so important were they in their progress and results, that no apology need be made for the minuteness with which I shall record the first instance of resistance to the constituted authorities by the people of Malden.

We have seen that the new town came out of a wish for an enlargement of religious privileges, as the Colony itself was the accomplishment of a similar desire. Cotton Mather says: —

Briefly, The God of Heaven served as it were a *Summons* upon the *Spirits* of His People in the English Nation; stirring up the Spirits of Thousands which never saw the *Faces* of each other, with a most Unanimous Inclination to leave all the Pleasant Accommodations of their Native Country, and go over a Terrible *Ocean*, into a more Terrible *Desart*, for the *pure Enjoyment of all His Ordinances.*[1]

We shall see how the religious element made all others subordinate to itself; how it colored and influenced all the thoughts and actions of the people; so that it cannot be separated from the history of this, or any other, New England town, until within a recent period. It was an essential part of the Puritan life and mind. In themselves a protest against the excesses of the established church, the founders of the Colony of Massachusetts Bay carried to the extreme the beliefs and practices which made them a peculiar people. Coming out of a church which was dominated by the state, they sought to found a state which should itself be circled and guarded by the church.[2]

[1] Mather, *Magnalia*, i. (4).
[2] "In Winthrop's Reply to Vane's Answer to his Defence of an order of Court, 1637, forbidding habitation without allowance of the magistrates, occurs a most remarkable sentence, giving us a

Naturally, although disregarding time and place, they built upon the model which God had before prepared for a people in whom they saw a similitude of themselves and whose experiences they often compared to their own. Their laws, their customs, and their manners were animated and limited by the teachings of the Scriptures; more by the harsher laws of the Old Testament, literally understood, as the exponent of a material hierarchy, than by the milder precepts of Jesus Christ, whose kingdom is a spiritual dominion of peace and love. In their statutes the code of Moses, with its strict and merciless justice, left no room for laws tempered with Christian forgiveness and brotherly care. Their new commonwealth was of the Lord and they were a new Israel, a chosen people, for whose inheritance the hand of God had prepared a new Canaan in the land of the heathen.

No such a scheme of government had existed since the days of Samuel the Prophet Judge; in some respects no such a government had ever existed. It was the embodiment of Theocracy without its purity; a government of God, evolved from the minds and pervaded by the prejudices of men. A philosophic mind might have foretold no long life for such a system; and, in fact, with all the sincerity and earnestness of its founders and supporters, it remained in its integrity not many years. It was already in its decline when the church of Malden was gathered. It remained a shadow many years; but the gradual strengthening of the state apart from the church, the adoption of the half-way covenant, the intrusion of the Baptists and other antagonistic sects, the decline of clerical authority, and the many adverse influences by which dogmatism and con-

key to the singular ecclesiastical policy of the Puritans. The sentence would appear to have been incidentally written, but it is of emphatic importance. '*Whereas the way of God hath alwayes beene to gather churches out of the world, now the world, or civill state, must be raised out of the churches.*' This explains everything to us in the religious institutions of our ancestors. The English Magna Charta restricted the right of suffrage in the choice of their own representatives in the Commons to *freeholders*. Puritanism restricted the right of suffrage to *Christians*. It tried to evolve a state out of a church. There have been many more fanciful, many less inspiring aims than this, proposed in the great schemes of men." The Rev. Geo. E. Ellis in *North American Review*, lxxxiv. 453.

servatism may be surrounded, limited its operation and numbered its days.

Its mistakes were many; but all was not weakness and error in the Puritanic system and in the institutions and laws which grew out of it.   There were in it arteries of healthy life, which remain to-day as pure as when they first flowed full of the faith and liberty of Puritan hearts.   It was a life filled with the spirit of a people who, emancipating themselves from the spiritual authority of the state in the old world, in a new world came at last to throw off the political authority of the church; and who, through trials and dangers, building, perhaps, better than they knew, in pain laid deep and sure the foundations on which we rest.

There are those who affect to believe that the works of our fathers were stable from the beginning and that the religious polity and civil condition of New England were steady growths from firm and far-reaching roots.   No historical belief can be more false; for during the colonial period, at least, both the ecclesiastical and the political records show a long series of experiments and mistakes — a blind groping.   The glory of those days is that there was a constant approach toward better things. One by one, after many weary and disheartening conflicts of tongue and pen, old prejudices and errors were laid aside. There was a sturdy element of conscience and common sense in the body of the people, which, in the end, proved stronger than courts and synods or magistrates and ministers. We owe nothing to the errors of those who came before us, nor to their institutions which time has destroyed; but to the freedom of thought, to the free will, and the ability to work and watch and wait, we owe all that makes the present full of good and the future promising.   Out of the hearts and thoughts of the Puritans, and not out of the imperfect works which they or their children rejected, came the good seed and the plentiful fruitage.

By the year 1650 the state had gradually strengthened its authority over the churches; and the churches, on the other hand, were perfecting that system of councils which, as a conservator and lawgiver in ecclesiastical polity, has come down to the present day. Besides the civil power and that of the councils, or the combined churches, there was another interest which was anxiously watching its rights. That interest was composed of those who recognized the individual right of the churches to govern their own affairs, as in the settlement of ministers and in cases of discipline.

The early churches were self-formed — democratic and independent.[3] They formed their own compacts and rules and settled pastors of their own choosing, sometimes, even, ordaining by means of some of their own laymen, as at Woburn in 1642.[4] After a little while, as a new church was formed, or grew out of another, it became the custom to ask the advice and presence of the elder churches at the gathering and their assistance in the ordination and settlement of ministers; but a jealous care was taken to protect the interests and independence of the individual church; and its identity as a free agent was not lost in the convention or council which assembled. But in 1636 the General Court began the exercise of that authority which in time it was to wield with a master hand, by the passage of the following act: —

[163⅚: 3 March.] Forasmuch as it hath bene found by sad experience, that much trouble and disturbance hath happened both to the church & civill state by the officers & members of some churches, wᶜʰ have bene gathered with in the limitts of this jurisdiction in a vndue

---

[3] It was settled that a church ought not to be of a greater number than could conveniently meet in one place, nor so few as to hinder church work. Cf. *Platform of Church Discipline*, iii. (4). The earlier church covenants contained no declarations of doctrine — a strong contrast to the practice of later years when points of doctrine were considered to be all-important. A simple promise "to walk in all oʳ wayes according to the Rules of the Gospell, — and in all sinceer conformity to his holy ordinances: and in mutuall Love and Respect each to other: so near as God shall give us grace," bound them together as brethren "into one congregation or church, under oʳ Lord Jesus Christ our Head." Cf. Emerson, *First Church in Boston*, 11;

Frothingham, *History of Charlestown*, 70; *N. E. Hist. and Geneal. Reg.*, xxiii. 190; Upham, *Second Century Lecture* (Salem), 67; Robbins, *Second Church in Boston*, 209.; Sewall, *History of Woburn*, 21. The General Court declared in 1646, in allusion to the church covenants of the Colony: — "What ever the severall expressions may be, this sufficeth us (which we conceive to be intended by them all) that in this covenant we professe our engagement of relation to God, and one to another, in all the duties which belong to the publick worship of God, and edification one of another, according to the rule of the gospell." Hutchinson, *Collection of Papers*, 215.

[4] Johnson, *Wonder-working Providence*, 179.

manner, & not with such publique approbation as were meete, it is
therefore ordered that all persons are to take notice that this Court
doeth not, nor will hereafter, approue of any such companyes of men
as shall henceforthe ioyne in any pretended way of church fellowshipp,
without they shall first acquainte the magistrates, & the elders of the
great' parte of the churches in this jurisdiction, with their intentions, &
have their approbation herein. And ffurther, it is ordered, that noe
person, being a member of any churche which shall hereafter be
gathered without the approbation of the magistrates, & the greater
parte of the said churches, shalbe admitted to the freedom of this
commonwealth.[5]

This law, which might have been styled an act to ensure
Uniformity, was considered by many as containing the " seeds
of usurpation on the liberties of the Gospel."[6] That it aimed
at the destruction of Independency is evident : it accomplished
more ; for the " seeds of usurpation " germinated and became
both healthy root and vigorous branch. In a few years the
Court dominated the Church and discussed discipline as well as
morals, while it ordered councils to compose breaches and dis-
cords and procure peace and quietness for the churches.[7]

There was a twofold aspect to the trouble which came upon
the Malden church ; or rather, there were two cases which antiquaries have confounded as one. There was an offending
clergyman, who had essayed to exercise free thought ; and
there was an offending church, which had settled a pastor without the approbation of " the magistrates, & the elders of the
great' parte of the churches." To understand these cases it
will be necessary to remember that, at the time when the
Malden church was gathered, the civil power was exercising
paramount authority over the churches ; that the combined
churches, or their ministers, were striving to regain their
authority and enforce uniformity by means of councils ; and
that individual churches, with the ancient Puritanic traditions of

---

[5] *Mass. Colony Records,* i. 168. *Also:*
" [1631, 18 May] To the end the body
of the commons may be p'serued of honest & good men, it was likewise ordered
and agreed that for time to come noe
man shalbe admitted to the freedome of
this body polliticke, but such as are
members of some of the churches within
the lymitts of the same." Ibid., i. 87.

[6] Cf. Clarke, *Congregational Churches
in Mass.,* 21.

[7] *Mass. Colony Records,* iv. (1), 225.

Independency, were seeking to maintain freedom of choice and action.

In the midst of this confusion of civil and ecclesiastical affairs, by the providence of God, the brethren of Mystic Side went into a church estate. It has been shown that there were difficulties in the way of procuring a pastor or teacher, and that for some time the seals were administered by a layman and by students from the college. It appears that at least nine clergymen and church officers were called without favorable results; that the Roxbury brethren interposed between the Malden church and Mr. John Wilson,[8] who went to Dorchester as colleague with the Rev. Richard Mather; and that the members were denied the ordinance of baptism by a neighboring church. These facts might be taken to show that something was wrong at the beginning; and a remark by Hutchinson indicates that the church was "gathered without the allowance of the magistrates."[9] Beyond these indications, however, there is no proof that any unusual occurrence was connected with the matter; and the causes of the coolness which seems to have held the elder churches apart from their younger sister are hidden from us.

An American antiquary making a pilgrimage of love to the Old England of his fathers, more than half a century ago, found the following entry in the matriculation books of Oxford University: —

Colleg. Omnium animarum 20 Feb. 1623 Marmadukus Mathews Glamorgan. fil. Mathæi Mathews de Swansey in Com. pred. pleb. an. nat. 18.[10]

Of the youth and early life of this son of Matthew Matthews of Swansea in Wales, who entered All Souls College at the age of eighteen, nothing is known, until at the age of thirty-three he arrived, with a company of west-country people, in a ship of Barnstaple, at Boston, September 21, 1638.[11] His wife, Katherine, came with him, or followed soon after, and joined

---

[8] Son of the Rev. John Wilson of the First Church in Boston.

[9] Hutchinson, *History of Massachusetts-Bay*, i. 423.

[10] Savage, *Mass. Hist. Coll.*, xxviii. 250.

[11] Winthrop, *History of New England*, i. 273.

with the Boston church in the following February. In the same month, he "tooke the ooath of allegiance to the King, and of fidelitie to the gou[nt]" of Plymouth Colony; and during the next year, he is found among those "that are p[r]posed to take vp their freedome at Yarmouth."[12]

To the latter place he went among the earliest settlers, and became their first minister. He was admitted as a freeman of the Colony, September 7, 1641.[18] It is said, with no authority, that he was a schoolmaster, "but exercised the ministerial functions;"[14] and Baylies, with as little authority, says that he "had some learning but was weak and eccentric."[15] On the contrary, he was commended by those who were able to speak of him with knowledge. Governor Winthrop calls him "a godly minister;"[16] and Nathaniel Morton names him in a list of the "specialest" of those whom he nominates as "worthy instruments," and of whom he says: —

About these times the Lord was pleased of His great goodness, richly to accomplish and adorn the colony of Plymouth (as well as other colonies in New-England) with a considerable number of godly and able gospel-preachers, who then being dispersed and disposed of to the several churches and congregations thereof gave light in a glorious and resplendent manner as burning and shining lights.[17]

When Matthews left Yarmouth is not known; but, probably, it was not before 1648, as his successor, Mr. Miller, had not left Rowley in that year, or, perhaps, a few months later.[18] From Yarmouth he went to Hull, which was then a thriving settlement

---

[12] *Plymouth Colony Records*, i. 107–108.

[18] Ibid., ii. 23.

[14] Freeman, *History of Cape Cod*, ii. 180.

[15] Baylies, *Historical Memoir of New Plymouth*, i. 315. This writer may have seen the following: "[7 October, 1639.] Edward Morrell, being sworne, deposeth & sayth, that W[m] Chase (at his return hoame from the Court when M[r] Mathewes & hee were here together) did report that M[r] Mathewes had nothing to say for himself, & that he marvailed how any durst joyne w[th] him in the fast, & further said that some being then in

p[r]sence w[th] the ma[trats], did hold vp his hand, & cyed, Fye, fye! for shame!" *Plymouth Colony Records*, i. 135.

[16] Winthrop, *History of New England*, i. 273.

[17] Morton, *New-England's Memorial* (Ed. 1826) 131, under the date of 1642.

[18] I am of the opinion that trouble preceded his departure from Yarmouth. Michael Wigglesworth, writing in 1658, at a time when the facts were well known, speaks of him as one who "had been excommunicated at one place, disliked & discarded at anoth place, once (if not oftener) censured in y[e] court." *Mass. Hist. So. Proc.* May, 1871, 95.

of traders and fishermen, where he "continued preaching, till he lost the approbation of some able understanding men, among both Magistrates and Ministers, by weak and unsafe expressions in his teaching."[19]

Besides losing "the approbation of some able understanding men," it appears that he ran a greater risk — that of banishment. George Bishop, the Quaker, writing before 1661, tells the story : —

And it's like Governour *John Wintrope*, Senior (who was an honest Man, and had some Hand in this, being drawn to it by your Priests) was made sensible of it on his Death-Bed, when old *Dudly*, a Man of Blood, and the rest of you sent to the said *John Wintrope*, to set his Hand to a Paper, for the Banishment of one *Matthews*, a *Welch*-man, a Priest; which he refused, telling them, *He had had his Hand too much in such things already.*[20]

Hutchinson also narrates this incident, mentioning "an heterodox person" in the place of Mr. Matthews.[21] The story seems worthy of belief; and that neither Hubbard nor Mather, the fullest chroniclers of that period, speak of it may be attributed to the wish to represent the wisest of the magistrates of Massachusetts Bay as a stanch supporter of that political and ecclesiastical condition which Mather, at least, labored to uphold and perpetuate. As John Winthrop died March 26, 1649, this must apply to Mr. Matthews before his settlement at Malden; and to prove that he left Hull perforce, we find that the inhabitants of that place, desiring his return, petitioned the Court "for the encouraging Mr Mathews to goe to them & preach amongst them."[22]

The result of this petition was twofold; for after "a publicke hearing in the meeting howse" in Boston, the granting of the request was denied and Mr. Matthews was personally brought into trouble. The record is worthy of perusal as an introduction to the arbitrary transactions which are to be related and as showing how closely the civil power was watching the spiritual condition of the church.

[19] Johnson, *Wonder-working Providence*, 211.

[20] Bishop, *New-England Judged by the Spirit of the Lord* (Ed. 1703), 226.

[21] Hutchinson, *History of Massachusetts-Bay*, i. 151.

[22] Cf. *Mass. Colony Records*, ii. 276; iii. 153.

[1649: 9 May.]   In answer to the petition of the inhabitants of Hull, concerning Mr Mathewes, the 15th day of this instant was appointed for a publicke hearing of the case, wch was attended in the meeting howse.   The Dep^ts, considering of what they had heard in the case, *voted,*

1. That they would not enquier into the matters of chardge or answers, as respecting error conce^r Mr Mathews.

2. Notw^thstanding this vote, the house, by vote, judged it meete to consider whether Mr Mathews, in respect of inconvenient and weake exp^rssions, was not worthy of some censure.

3. The whole Courte agreed by vote, that Mr Mathewes should not retourne to Hull, nor reside wth them.

Voted, That wee will proceed no further at present wth Mr Mathewes then to an admonition.

The Courte, for seuerall considerations, judge it not meete at present to dilate all the p^ticular chardges and ans^rs of Mr Mathewes, yett, notw^thstanding, doe declare that they finde seueral erroneous exp^rssions, others weake, inconvenient, and vnsafe exp^rssions, for which they judge it meete to order, that the said Mr Mathewes should be admonished by the Gou^rno^r in the name of the Courte.[23]

There are indications that the aristocratic branch of the Court, or the Assistants, who in this case, as in many others, represented the most arbitrary portion of the State, brought about this result; and that the democratic deputies, who came directly from the body of the people and often showed themselves to be possessed of the leaven of liberty and progress, which in due season leavened the whole body politic, would at least have forborne to question Mr. Matthews.   As the prudent and liberal Winthrop was dead and the austere and bigoted Endicott was in the chair of the Governor, it may be supposed that the admonition was given with due severity.   That it was given is clear, for it was afterwards said of Mr. Matthews that " he had his sentence & ffulfild it."

Where he now went does not appear; but, the next year, he was in Boston and was granted leave to " give satisfaction," or to retract, which was probably intended.

[1650: 19 June.]   This Courte, beinge willinge that Mr Mathews should haue an op^rtunitie to giue satisfaction for what he formerly deliuered as eronious, weake, &c, which is his owne desire also, doe

---

[23] *Mass. Colony Records,* lii. 159; cf. ii. 276.

order, that he shall haue oppertunitie soe to doe the 28[th] of this instant moneth, at Boston, at M[r] Phillips his howse, by eight of the clocke in the morning, to giue satisfaction for the same, if he can, to the elders·of Boston, Charlstowne, Roxbury, & Dorchester, with such of the magis[ts] as shall please to be p[r]sent there.[24]

It may be that this occasion for righting himself before the authorities was sought by Mr. Matthews while the question of his settlement in Malden was pending. What the result of this meeting at " eight of the clocke in the morning " was, or whether the meeting was held, is not known; as no other mention of it has been found. Evidently, nothing favorable to the accused minister came out of it, if we may judge by the events which followed. Some detached notes of accusations and answers may belong to this period; but in spirit and form, they are a part of later evidence, with which I shall consider them.

About this time, or soon after, Mr. Matthews was brought into relations with the Malden brethren. When it was known that steps were being taken preliminary to his ordination, there was a more general desire evinced to hinder the settlement of the new church than to promote its welfare. The church of Roxbury, which had interfered in the business with Mr. Wilson, wrote " to fforbeare ordination; " but when asked " to discover to vs Any sin either in m[r]. Mathews or the Church which might be a ground of fforbea[r]g," it remained silent. The mother church of Charlestown, following the spirit of that of Roxbury, proposed " a brotherly conference," which was accepted. It remained for the elder church to appoint a time and place, but no more was heard from that quarter. Several of the magistrates also wrote letters of " advice," which seem to have been composed in the spirit, if not in the form, of mandates; but when explanations were asked of " eurie one of them before ordination," none replied but Increase Nowell.[25]

Unless we assume that some irregularities, of which the church was still unpurged, had attended its formation, it is difficult to understand these proceedings; and even if the church had committed an offence, neither the justice nor the propriety

[24] *Mass. Colony Records,* iii. 203.   [25] Cf. *Mass. Archives,* x. 31, 80.

of this method of dealing can be affirmed. Under the circumstances, but one course ought to have been taken; and that course, with a foreshadowing of the spirit of later days, the Malden brethren pursued. They ordained Mr. Matthews as their minister; and as they stood alone among the churches, it is very probable that they resorted to the elder practice of lay-ordination. Nor were they without sufficient authority for their action; for as recently as 1646 the General Court had declared the following as the first "Fundamentall of the Massachusetts": —

All persons orthodoxe in judgment and not scandalous in life, may gather into a church estate according to the rules of the gospell of Jesus Christ. Such may choose and ordaine theire owne officers, and exercise all the Ordinances of Christ, without any injunction in doctrine, worship or discipline.[26]

It does not appear that any immediate notice of this offence was taken. Johnson, writing at this time, says that "some neighbour-churches were unsatisfied therewith, for it is the manner of all the Churches of Christ here hitherto, to have the approbation of their Sister-churches, and the civil Government also in the proceedings of this nature, by the which means Communion of Churches is continued, peace preserved, and the truths of Christ sincerely acknowledged;"[27] but he does not indicate that Mr. Matthews was not in the peaceable possession of the Malden pulpit. He "minds him in the following Meeter," which blends admonition with exhortation, and must have been a source of disquiet to Mr. Matthews, especially if he was possessed of any literary taste: —

> *Mathews!* thou must build gold and silver on
>   That precious stone, Christ cannot trash indure,
> Unstable straw and stubble must be gone,
>   When Christ by fire doth purge his building pure.
> In seemly and in modest terms do thou
>   Christs precious truths unto thy folk unfold,
> And mix not error with the truth, lest thou
>   Soon leave out sense to make the truth to hold:
> Compleating of Christs Churches is at hand,
>   *Mathews* stand up, and blow a certain sound,
> Warriours are wanting Babel to withstand,
>   Christs truths maintain, 'twill bring thee honors crown'd.[28]

[26] Hutchinson, *Collection of Papers,* 203. Cf. *Mass. Hist. Coll.,* xxviii. 234.   [27] Johnson, *Wonder-working Providence,* 211.   [28] Ibid., 212.

And so, for a brief time, Mr. Matthews and the church were untroubled. There is reason to believe that he preached with freedom, according to his faith, and to the edification of the church, and that his way was honorable to himself and helpful to his little flock. But the "former miscarriages" were not forgotten; and a sermon preached from the suggestive text, *Behold, I lay before Joshua a stone with seven eyes,*[29] became a copious source of trouble to the unfortunate minister. There was a watchful and traitorous element in that rural congregation in the little hut of a meeting house at Bell Rock, which, represented by John Hathorne and Thomas Lynde, the latter, at least, a member of the church, while the former was a tavern-keeper, who, removing to Lynn, was two years later found guilty of forgery on his own confession, reported and "proved on oath" many heterodox or heretical teachings. Out of that sermon, and some others, they culled more "weak and inconvenient expressions" — inconvenient they certainly were for Mr. Mathews. Some of these "vnsafe expressions" have been preserved for us.

Christ is gone up to heaven to prepare mansions for us, for as ye sin of Adam did shutt paradise soe ye Ascension of X^t doth open paradise againe

To think we can have any conviction before we have X^t is a very delusion.

Y^e saints have more varietyes of righteousnes than X^t, for X^t hath only a double righteousnes, & ye saints have a trebble.

When ye body of X^t was lifted up on ye crosse his soule was in hell what in hell : yea in hell, in y^t hell where ye devill rules and raignes.[30]

Here were offences gross and monstrous for churches and councils to consider; but there is no indication that any power save that of the state was called into action, at the outset, in this purely theological and doctrinal matter. Mr. Matthews was summoned to appear by the General Court, May 7, 1651, in the following order : —

---

[29] So stated, *Mass. Archives,* x. 75. For behold the stone that I have laid before Joshua ; upon one stone *shall be* seven eyes : behold, I will engrave the graving thereof, saith the Lord of hosts, and I will remove the iniquity of that land in one day. *Zech.* iii. 9. The sermon was "about ye foundation of iustifying faith."

[30] *Mass. Archives,* x. 75, 77.

It is *ordered*, that Mr Marmaduke Mathews shallbe warned & summoned to appeare before this Courte on the fifth day next in the
morning, being the 15th of this instant May, to make answer to a bill
p^{r}sented to the Magis^{ts}, wch concernes former and latter miscarrjages of
his, before the Court goes on to any hearing thereabouts.[81]

He appeared before the Court at the appointed time, when

there was declared to him seuerall passages which he deliuered in his
sermons at Malden, w^{ch}, though he owned not, was prooved on oath by
John Hauthorne and Tho Line, about wch offence had binn taken, to
wch he gave in his answer to the Courte, the chardge and answer
remajning on the file.[82]

The "chardge" has, unfortunately, disappeared; but the
answer still "remajns" in the archives of the state. This document, which is dated May 16, 1651, was written by Mr. Matthews,
himself, and begins in a tone of meekness, which, I think, must
have been characteristic of the man and which is in strange contrast to his apparent independence of thought and action.

Jn his name & presence whose J am & whom J desire to serve (&
y^t wth childlike feare) as also for evermore to reioyce in, & y^t wth christian trembling, J ye sayd accused M. M. thinke good thus to answer.[88]

He proceeds to carry out his answers into all the divisions
and subdivisions of which the theology of that day was capable.
He complains that his words are placed out of order in the
accusations; and his endeavor is plainly to make more clear his
" offensive " teachings, instead of explaining them in a retractive
way. Of the twenty-two, or more, accusations which were then,
or finally, presented, he replied at this time to but four; and, as
if to disprove the testimony of John Hathorne and Thomas
Lynde, five of the most prominent men of the town filed this
affidavit on the following day: —

> *To the Hono^{r}d Court.*
>
>   wee whose naimes are hereunder written
> haveing Seriously Considered the Answe's y^t our Rev^{r}nd Pastor m^r Mar-
> maduke Mathews Hath given into the Court in Relation to Severall
> p^{r}ticulars charged uppon him & wittnessed against him by Jo: Haw-

---

[81] *Mass. Colony Records*, iv. 42.   [82] Ibid., iv. (1), 42.   [88] *Mass. Archives*, x. 75.

thorne & Tho Lynd : we Affirme those Answers are the Substance off
what was Publiqly Delivered by him and are the truth & nothing but
the truth.

16. 3. *mo.*	EDWARD CARRINGTON	*Deposed the 17th of the*

<table>
<tr><td></td><td>EDWARD CARRINGTON</td><td>*Deposed the 17th of the*</td></tr>
<tr><td>16. 3. *mo.*</td><td>JOHN VPPAME</td><td>*3d m: 1651 by these*</td></tr>
<tr><td>1651</td><td>JOHᴺ WAYTE</td><td>*5 p'sons before me*</td></tr>
<tr><td></td><td>THOMAS SQUIRE</td><td>JNCREASE</td></tr>
<tr><td></td><td>ABRAHAM HILL</td><td>NOWELL [84]</td></tr>
</table>

The examination was satisfactory to the Court, inasmuch as
the answers of the accused were found to be "vnsafe" and
"offensive" in point of doctrine and gave grounds for a further
and more comprehensive examination; and the record proceeds,
giving what may be called, in the language of those days, his
presentment as follows: —

After a full hearing & examining the same, the Courte declared,
that, whereas Mr Marmaduke Mathewes hath, formerly and latterly,
given offence to magistrates and elders, and many bretheren in some
vnsafe, if not vnsound expressions in his publicke teachings, and as it
hath binn manifested to this Courte, hath not yett given satisfaction to
those magistrates and elders that were appointed to receave sattisfaction
from him, since which tjme there have binn deliuered in his publicke
ministry other vnsafe and offensive expressions by him, whereby both
magis^{ts}, ministers and churches were occasioned to write to the church
of Malden to advise them not to proceed to the ordination of Mr Mathewes, which offences taken against him were also made knowne to the
sajd Mr Mathewes, yett, contrary to all advice, and the rule of Gods
word, as also the peace of the churches, the church of Malden hath
proceeded to the ordination of Mr Mathewes, — this Courte, therefore,
taking into consideration the premisses and the daingerous conse-
quences and effects that may follow such proceedings, doth order,
that both the former and latter offences touching doctrjnall points be
first duely considered by Mr Sjmon Bradstreete, Mr Sjmons, Capt W^m
Hauthorne, Capt Edward Johnson, Mr John Glouer, Capt Eleazer
Lusher, Capt Daniell Gookin, Mr Richard Browne, and Capt Humphry
Atherton, on the eleventh of June next, at the Shipp in Boston ; and
in case of difficulty the committee hath liberty to call in for helpe and
advise from such of the reuerend elders as they shall judge meete, and
make retourne of their offence against him, or sattisfaction from him be
retourned to this Court at the next session thereof.[85]

[84] *Mass. Archives,* x. 78.   [85] *Mass. Colony Records,* iv. (1), 42.

Fifteen of the deputies were entered as " contradicentes " against the passage of this order.   At their head were William Hathorne of Salem, a member of the committee, and John Leverett of Boston, who was afterwards Governor.   Joseph Hills, of course, favored the minister whom he elsewhere sustained; and it is noticeable that, save William Cowdrey of Reading, no member of a neighbor church opposed the prosecution.

So the General Court rested from its labors with Mr. Matthews until the next session; but before they rested they had another matter to settle with him.   This settlement required but little time and the record indicates no great desire for concession on either side.

As concerning M[r] Mathewes suffering himself to be ordajned, contrary to the rules of Gods word, which should not have so proceeded, to the offence of magistrates, reuerend elders, and some churches, y[e] Courte doth order that the sajd M[r] Mathewes shall give sattisfaction to this session of this Court by an humble acknowledging his sinne for his so proceeding, which if he refuse to doe, to pay the some of tenn pounds within one month.

M[r] Mathewes appearing, and not giving sattisfaction by an humble acknowledging of his sinne, &c, itt was ordered, that the secretary should within one month, give warrant to the marshall to levy on the goods of M[r] Mathewes the some of tenn pounds, as his fine, according to the order of this Courte.[86]

In June, as appointed, the committee, composed of leading men — " shining lights " and " godly timber," — in the Colony, convened " at the Shipp in Boston," that tavern at the corner of Ann and Clark streets, which, afterwards known as Noah's Ark, was destined to outlive the Colony and the Province, to see two revolutions and the downfall of many shams and superstitions, and to remain until the second half of the nineteenth century before it should be " improved " from the face of the earth.   If the spirits of old houses remain, that of " the Ship in Ann street " must be a rare and wise old ghost.

At this meeting, Mr. Matthews presented his defence in a document which is noteworthy for its chirography if for nothing else.[87]

[86] *Mass. Colony Records*, iv. (1), 43.   [87] *Mass. Archives*, x. 77.   On this

In the space of two small pages he compressed matter which comprises eleven pages of the work of a modern copyist. He deserved to be fined for his manuscript if not for his theology. At the same time, he offered an appeal in the form of a letter, in which submission and a natural independence are intimately blended, and in which we can see, between the lines as it were, a flashing eye, betraying a feeling of inward wrath and grief combined.

To y Honored Comittee of y* Generall Court appointed to examine some doctrinall points delivered att Hull and since y* time at Maldon by M. M.*

Honored of God and of his people

Haveing given you an Account of my sence & of my faith in ye conclusions wch were accused before you, J thought good to acquaint you, y^t if any among you (or others) should count that faith a fansie, & y^t sence to be non-sence J desire y^t god may forgive them : I doe, conceaving y^t such doe not yet soe well know what they doe, as they shall know hereafter

Yet in case y^t this should reach any satisfaction to such as are (yett) vnsatisfied wth my expressions for to know y^t J doe acknowledge y^t there be sundrie defects in sundry points y^t I have delivered, J doe hereby signifie y^t throw mercy J cannot but see & also ingenuously confesse y^t some of my sayings are nor safe nor sound in the superlative degree, to wit, they are not most safe ; nor yett eyther sound or safe in a comparative degree, for J easily yeald y^t not onely wiser men probably would, but also J my self possiblie mought have made out X's mynd & my owne meaning in termes more sound & more safe than J have done had not J beene too much wanting both to his sacred majesty whose vnworthy messinger I was, & also to my hearers & to my self, for wch J desire to be humbled & of wch J desire to be healed by ye author of both. as I doe not doubt but y^t conscientious & charitable-harted christians (whose property and practise it is to put uppon doubtfull positions not ye worst construction but ye best) will discerne, as J doe, y^t there is a degree of soundness in what J doe owne, tho but a positive degree.

However it is & (I trust) for ever shallbe my care to be more circumspect than J have hitherto been in avoyding all appearances y^t way for ye tjme to come, y^t soe I may ye better approve my self throw

paper the following is endorsed : "here is the substance of what was publiqly delivd: by m^r mathes Pasto^r of the Church of christ at Maldon wittness : Edw carrington. Tho. Squir^s. Jo. Wayte. Tho. Call. Tho. Ozban. Abr. Hill : Tho. Hett. Jam^s Greene: John vppam. only Jo. vppam not the : 6th."

yᵉ grace of christ and to yᵉ glory of god such a workman as need not be ashamed. in yᵉ interim J remayne amongst his vnworthy servants yᵉ most vnworthy, &

> Your Accused & condemned
> fellow-creature to comand
> in yᵉ things of christ
> MARMADUKE MATTHEWES.

Boston this 13ᵗ of yᵉ 4 month
1651.[38]

The result showed that the "conscientious & charitable-harted christians" to whom he appealed were not in the committee which tried him. Besides the papers already mentioned, there is extant one evidently written by a member of the committee, which contains several charges and answers briefly stated.[89] From these papers we may gather the peculiar beliefs and manner of expression of Mr. Matthews. Dr. McClure says "that he was both an ingenious and learned preacher, soundly orthodox and sincerely pious," and that his expressions were "over-strong rather than 'weak' and, as some would say, *too* orthodox."[40] There is a slight tincture of the Antinomian heresy which had so troubled the Colony fourteen years before and had been silenced by scriptural arguments and the power of the Court; and, in general, his words give evidence of a spiritual theology, which in its subtile distinctions would not appeal to the popular mind of that time. He was in advance of his age, though still within its influence. He might have been a transcendentalist in later days; but I think he would have been orthodox still, although his theology might have been modified by Arminianism and a doubt of the reality of the Trinity. One, at least, of his "vnsafe expressions" foreshadows a belief which afterwards became far from uncommon in the churches. "The Gospell of grace & yᵉ Sacred Scriptures ar a false foundation of ffaith to build our Justification vpon." In explication he said, "The Scripturs ar the foundation of Dogmatticall & historicall faith but not of saueing faith."[41]

The answer now presented is carried into divisions and sub-

---

[38] *Mass. Archives,* x. 78.   [40] *Bi-Centennial Book of Malden,* 136.
[39] Ibid., ccxlii. 184.   [41] *Mass. Archives,* ccxli. 184.

divisions as the other; and there is visible the same intent to explain and make clear rather than to retract. What passed during the examination of this answer and its author there is no present means of knowing. On the seventeenth day of the month Mr. Matthews laid before the committee, as his "last deliberate answer," another paper containing replies to five of the charges which seem to have been retained as most material to the case. This document has never been printed. It may perhaps be of more interest to the antiquary than to the general reader; but it is of importance as containing that which was considered as final by both parties.

To y[e] 1 charge here mentioned.

J doe beleeve & profess y[t] all sins of all persons both vnder y[e] law & vnder y[e] gospell are to be reproved both in vnbeleevers & others

And if any words att any tyme in any place among any persons have falne from my lipps or penne wch in y[e] iudgment of any seeme to sound otherwise, J doe not owne them as my iudgment

To y 2 charge heere

Jf y[e] workes of y[e] law could be performed according to y[e] true meaning of y[e] law, they would not be damning evills, but wayes of life; but y[e] contempt or dependance of or vppon y[e] workes of y[e] law or of y[e] gospell for Justification J doe beleeve are to be accounted damning evills. if any words of myne sound otherwise, J approve them not.

To y[e] 3 charge, concerning loveing y[e] thgs y[t] are in y[e] world

when J sayd y[t] there is noe loue due to y[e] things of y[e] world, J spake from y[e] words of John 1 Jo. 2. 15. Where J conceave y[e] spirit of god doth meane the honours pleasures & profitts of y[e] world & y[t] he doth noe where forbydd any to love persons according to y[e] relations wherein they may stand to them eyther coniugall, parentall, filiall fraternall or christian.

To y[e] 4 charge heere mentioned

The Apostle sayth y[t] noe other foundation canne any man lay than Jesus christ (that is to say for iustification or Salvation) 1 cor: 3: 11. And as for y[e] Scriptures, J acknowledge noe X[t] but such a one as is revealed in the scriptures.

And as for beleeving vnto Justification J acknowledge noe other faith (in men of yeares) than such as resteth on X[t] declared in a word of grace by y[e] scriptures.

when we read y y[e] churches are built uppon y[e] foundations of y[e] prophets & Apostles J doe conceave (vnder favour) y[t] they are calld foundations in y[t] they layd christ for y[e] foundation if any word of myne may seeme to sound otherwise J would be vnderstood according to these expressions

To y[t] last charge, concerning variety of righteousnes

when J sayd y[t] saints have more variety of righteousnesses than X[t] hath I was in y[e] explication of y[e] word in esay 45. 24 wch in y[e] originall is in y[e] plurall number righteousnesses, surely Jn y[e] Lord have J righteousnesses & strength ; not y[t] they have more variety of righteousnes than he hath to give : but because they have from him beside inherent righteousness & morall righteousness, imputative righteousness alsoe wch he needed not for himself.

Such are y[e] conceptions & confessions of

MARMADUKE MATTHEWES.

On the back of this "deliberate answer" is endorsed the report of the committee.

Boston.   17th 4th m 1651.

Upon serious consideration of the charges brought against M[r]. Mathewes togeather wth the answers to them by himselfe gyven, as also upon conference wth himselfe concerning the same. Wee the Comittee yet remayne much unsatisfyed, fynding seuall pticul's weake, unsafe & unsound, & not retracted by him some whereof are conteyned in this pap wth his last deliberate answer thereunto.

SIMON BRADSTREET,   W[M] HATHORNE,
RICHARD BROWN,   EDW: JOHNSON,
JOHN GLOUER,   ELEAZER LUSHER,
          HUMPHRAY ATHARTON.

15th 8th 51

Being by p'vidence absent when the Comittee examined m[r] mathews case being p'sonally p'sent before them J cannot speake but onely to what appeareth by the writings And having wth the comittee p'vsed them J Doe fully agree wth what they have returned to the Court

SAMUEL SYMONDS.[42]

So the committee, having heard and considered the replies of the heretical preacher, found themselves, in the end, where they had begun; and Mr. Matthews was neither justified nor silenced. In the meantime the case had begun to assume that dual aspect which has deluded antiquaries; for the Court had ordered, in May, as follows : —

[42] *Mass. Archives,* ccxli. 183.

And touching the church of Malden for offence in ordajning him, (notwithstanding all advice formerly,) itt is *ordered*, that they answer their offence the next sessions of this Courte.[43]

Here are now two distinct cases moving together awhile as one. The one is an offence of " weake and vnsafe expressions," or an assertion of individual thought and speech; the other is a contempt of authority, or an assertion of the freedom of the Church against a usurping power.

It may be assumed without direct proof that the magistrates and deputies were far from being satisfied with the report of the committee. Nor could they have been more pleased with the outcome of the fine of ten pounds, which they laid upon Mr. Matthews for allowing himself to be ordained; for the afflicted minister was as poor in worldly goods as he was rich in grace, and the marshal found no available property. The Court was obliged to order that " the execution thereof shalbe respited till other goodes appeare besides bookes." [44]

At the October session a day was assigned for the consideration of " Mr Mathewes his offence retourned by the committee, as also the offence of the church of Malden; " and notice was given to the offending parties.

Att the tjme appointed, Mr Marmaduke Mathewes appeard; so did Mr Joseph Hills, Edward Carrington, and John Waite, wth seuerall others of the church of Malden, & on the churches behalfe appeared to answer their offence, &c, according to the order of the last Gennerall Courte.[45]

In behalf of Mr. Matthews, whose case first received attention, a petition was presented, which is one of the most interesting of the many which relate to the history of the town. It is especially valuable in this case as showing the esteem in which the Malden minister was held by his congregation; but it is more noteworthy because it bears the names of thirty-six of the wives and mothers of that early day and is the first known petition of Malden women.

---

[43] *Mass. Colony Records,* iv. (1), 43.   [44] Ibid., iii. 257.   [45] Ibid., iv. (1), 70.

To the Hono d Court

The petition of Many Jnhabitants of Maldon & Charlstowne on Mestickside Humblie sheweth

That y⁰ Allmighty God in great mercie to ou' souls as we trust hath Affter many prayers Jndeavoⁿ & long Wayting Brought m' Mathews Among vs & putt him into the worke of the Ministrie. By whose pious life & labo's the lord hath Afforded vs Many Saving Convictions directions and Consolations whose Continuance in y' Service of christ if it were y⁰ good pleasu' of god wee much desy', And it is ou' humble Request to this Hono'd Court y' you would please to pass by Some personall & perticul' ffaylings (which may as we humbly conseaue be yo' Glory & no greife of heart to you in tyme to come) And to p'mitt him to Jmploy thos tallents god God hath ffurnishd him wᵗʰ all.   so Shall we yo' humble petionⁿˢ wᵗʰ many others be Bound to pray &c.

28. 8. 51

Mᴿˢ Sergeant	Sarah Bucknam	Eliz. Mirrable
Joan Sprague	Thankslord Sheppᴿᴰ	Sarah Osburn
Jane Learned	ffran. Cooke	An Hett
Eliz. Carrington	Eliz. Knoher	Mary Pratt
Bridget Squiᴷᴱ	Bridget Dexter	Eliz. Green
Mary Wayte	Lyda Greenland	Joan Chadwick
Sarah Hills	Margᴿt Pemᴿton	Margᴿt Green
An: Bibble	Han. Whittamore	Hellen Luddington
Eliz. Green	Eliz. Green	Susan Wilkinson
wid: Blancher	Mary Rust	Joana Call
Eliz. Addams	Eliz. Grover	Rachel Attwood
	Han. Barret	Margᵀ Welding
		Rebec: Hills

The magistrates conceaue the answer to this petition wilbe the result of the Magistrates & deputies agreemᵗ of Mʳ Mathewes censure :

Edward Rawson *Secrᵒ*

The deput consent & agree hereto

William Torrey *Cleric* ⁴⁶

At the same time, a letter was given to the Court, which seems to have been written for the purpose by some other than Mr. Matthews, for the signature only is his. It is submissive and humble, and shows that the accused had lost some part of his original independence, or that he had become wearied in the contest and had submitted to the advice of more tractable friends.

⁴⁶ *Mass. Archives,* x. 79.

To the Hono'd Court

Marmaduke Mathews Humblie sheweth That through mercie J am in some measure sensible of my Great Jnsufficiencie to declare the counsell of God vnto his people (as J ought to doe) And how (through the darkness & Jgnoranc that is in mee) J am verie Apt to lett ffall some expressions y⁺ are weake & Jnconvenient; & J doe Acknowledge y⁺ in severall of those expressions reffered to the examination of the Hon'd Comittee, J might (had the lord seen it so good) haue expressed & deliu'd my selfe in Termes more free ffrom exception. And it is my desyre (the lord strengthning) as much as in me lyeth to Avoyd all appearances of euill therin ffor Tyme to Come, as in all other respects whatsoeur, wᶜh y⁺ J may doe, J humbly desyre yoʳ hearty prayers to God ffor me, & in speciall that J may take heed to the Ministrie comitted to me y⁺ J may ffulfill it to the prays of God & p'ffitt of his people.
28 : 8. 1651   yoʳ Humble S'vant in long
                                        Service of christ
                                MARMADUKE MATTHEWES.[47]

The petition of the women of Malden or the " humble shewing" of Mr. Matthews — perhaps both — so influenced the austere minds of the members of the General Court that, judging that " it doeth stand wᵗʰ wisdome to haue the Churches to act before themselues," they concluded to end, as they should have begun, by referring the matter to the ecclesiastical authorities. They, therefore, thought meet to

appoint the Church of Maldon speedilie to consider of the erro's Mʳ Mathewes stands charged wᵗʰ in Court, and in case vpon the Churches dealing wᵗʰ him hee doeth acknowledge his errors & vnsafe expressions & giue satisfaction vnder his hand, so as the Secretarie being certified thereof, doe acquaint the Counsell therewᵗʰ wᵗʰin six weekes the matter at present may so rest. Else the Secretarie shall giue notice vnto the Churches of Cambridge, Charlestowne Lyn & Redding to send their messengers in way of counsell & advice vnto the Church of Maldon & not excluding any other Churches wᵗʰ them to debate the doctrines there deliuered by Mʳ Mathewes now in question That by this meanes the trueth may the better appeare. And that they prosecute the same to effect according to the rule of Christ, ffor the Conviction of the said Mʳ Mathewes & helpefulnes of the Church of maldon.[48]

[47] *Mass. Archives*, ccxli. 185.   [48] Ibid., x. 79.

There was some little difficulty here, for the democratic deputies were disposed to withhold their consent to this measure; but it was finally voted by the whole Court in conference.

So Mr. Matthews, being turned over to the only authority which ought ever to have considered his " offences," the church of Malden, stood in the way of judgment. That church, far from submitting, appeared before the Court, as already has been seen, in the persons of three of its most prominent men, Joseph Hills, then a deputy and four years before the Speaker of the House, Edward Carrington, and John Wayte. They gave in writing an answer to the charge against them, dated October 26; and, some dissatisfaction having been expressed, Joseph Hills presented a second and additional answer, dated five days later. In these papers may be found a statement of the early condition of the Malden church, its troubles in finding a pastor, and the circumstances under which Mr. Matthews was settled. They are strong and earnest pleas for the right of free action in the election and ordination of church officers, asking consideration both from moral and legal points. They seek rather to justify than to excuse their authors; and they assert in plain terms the liberty of the churches and the absence of any "law of Christ or the Countrie " to the contrary.

The Church of Maldon J:1 Answ[r] to the offence by the Hono[r] Gen-e[r]all Court charged vpon them in Ordayning m[r] Mathews Notwithstanding all advice which we acknowledge was of some of the Hono'd Magistrats & two of the neigbo[r] churches, namely Roxbury & charlstow͞ desyre humblie to Express themselves as followeth

ffirst. that the other vnsafe & offensive expressions recited in the beginning of the order to be deliu'd in his public ministry at Maldon, were not before the ordination so much as Charged vppon him by the Court. & so it was (vnder ffavour) as we conceiue onely the busines at hull on which all advice was grounded for which offences he had his sentence & ffulfild it & so stood cleare in law [To the punishm[t].

2. we humbly tender to Consideration of the Hono'd Court whether we should not haue been dealt & p'ceeded with in a Church way in case we had swerved ffrom any Rule of X[t] or been so Apprhended ffor we both owne & Honour Church Comunion.

we also putt the churches y[t] wrote to vs to fforbeare ordination, to discover to vs Any sin either in m[r] Mathews or the Church which might be a ground of fforbea'g but they Jnstanced none

3. we humblie present to consideration y' we wrote & sent to Roxburie Church before wee proceeded. since which we heard no more ffrom them. also we sent to Charlstow̄ Church beffore ordination & since & theire last to vs was ffor a brothrly conference to which we assented & expected them to call on it. And had those Churches conceived sin in o' p'ceedings their way was open & our Church readie to Attend conviction therin.

4. be pleased to Consider what those hono'd Magistrats wrote to vs, & what our Adresses were to them & eurie [one] of them before ordination ffrom whom we received no returne saue only from m' Nowel

5. Wee p'ffess it was a greife of heart to vs, & is, that we should seem to wave or vnd'value the advice of any Magistrate or Church, but considering the libertys of the Churches alowe by law to chuse their owne officers, & Apprehending him to be both pious able & orthodox as the law provides we p'ceeded.

Lastly wee humbly plead to the words of the Charge which are (And touching the Church of Maldon her offence in ordayning him Notwithstanding all Advice form'ly Jtt is ordered that they Answ' their offence the next sessions of this Court)

Our plea is that we know no law of X' or the Countrie that binds Any Church of Christ not to ordayne their owne officers without Advice of Magistrats, & churches. Wee frely Acknowledge ou'selues Jngaged to any that in loue afford Any advice vnto vs. but we conceaue a Church is not bound to such Advice ffarther than god comends it to their vnd'standing & conscience. And if a Church Act contrary to such advice wee see not how or by what Rule they are Bound to take offence against A Church of Christ in y' respect namly ffor not Attending y' advice, or y' a Church of christ so doeing should be concluded offendors in any Court of Justice & so p'sent'd. our laws allow eurie Church ffree libertie of all the ordinances of god according to the rule of the scriptur, Eccl Sect 3. 4. 6. & perticular ffree libertie of ellection & ordination of all their officers ffrom tyme to tyme p'vided they be pious able & orthodox. And y' no Jnjunction shall be put vpon Any Church officer or member in point of doctrine or discipline whether ffor substance or circumstance besides the Jnstitutions of the lord.

Thus to our abillitie with hearty desyre of satisfaction. hauing given our humble Apprehensions ffor our p'ceedings in the ordination affors'd (vnwilling to occassion more trouble,) we shall Add no more, onely ou' humble Acknowledgem' y' wee haue not walked so safely so prudently so Jnoffensively in y' point of ordination as wee might haue done, & had the Order Title eccles. 8. 12. ffor Elders & bret'n meeting to discuss points of doc'm & dissipline been attended the breach might haue been healed & this troubl p'vented. wee humblie Reffer our selues And answers to yo' most wise & godly consideration as the lord shall direct ffor the glory of Christ and good of his poor Church & Towne of Maldon

26. 8. 1651.   yʳ humble seruants
                                      Jos: Hills :
                                      Ed: Carington, } *in yʳ name of*
                                      Johⁿ Wayte   } *yᵉ chuʳch.*[•]

To the Hon'd Court

Vnd'standing that the answʳ of the Ch'ch of Maldon in reference to their Ordination of mʳ Mathewˢ is not satisfactory on the behalf of the Ch'ch of Maldon Joseph Hills humbly craueth that this Hon'd Court, will please as an Addition to our former Acknowledgment to consider the many motions Jndeauours & humbl Addresses of the sayd Church to diuers Orthodox App'ued men before we moued or had thought of mʳ Maˢ for beside our request at the first to Charlstᵒ Chʰ to help us in p'curing one we gaue Solemn Jnuitation to theis vnd'written.

m'r Miller then at Rowle

m'r Blinman   wherby it may Evidently
m'r Jᵒ Wilson   appʳ we affect not any
m'r Samuel Mader   thing tending to disturb
m'r Ezekiel Cheeuer   or distast, Either Magistˢ
m'. Lyon   Eldˢ or Ch'ch of Christ therfor one of Wat'tᵒ officers   in & so the necessitie of
one of Charls Chʰ officers   the Ch'ch to attend yᵉ guid-
m'r John Brock   ence of God for supply as
                                      they could.

2 the Ch'ch of Maldon app'hended themselues to haue manifest wrong about mʳ John Wilson & in speciall by Roxburie wᶜʰ we shold not haue mentioned, onely to manifest, our non acting wᵗʰ mʳ Ma. had we not by their means been bereaued of mʳ Jᵒ Wilson

3 be pleased to considʳ that we were denyed yᵉ ordinance of Baptism at a neighbour Ch'ch before the aduise about Ordination, although it was desired in the name of the Church (& so signified in writing) as the Platform of discipline doth direct.

Lastly be pleased to considʳ that, that wᶜʰ came from the Hon'd Magistˢ & Churches of Charlstᵒ & Roxbury was onely in way of advice & had we sind agˢ the ch'ches, we app'hendᵉᵈ & allso Exspected them to follow the rules of Discipline warranted by Gods word & described in the Plattforme in such a case

and had we vnd'stood yᵉ Hon'd Magist. that wrote to us had intended other or more in their lʳ to us, then matters of aduice, we shold haue demurred & disposed oʳ selues otherwise & not haue Exposed ourselues to so much displeasure as we haue incurred from such p'sons &

Relations, whom we so much honour & acknowledge ourselues so transcendently vnder God Jngaged vnto for that pious & peaceable Gou'nment, wch by their means we haue Jnioyed for so long a time & hope farther to Jnioy if the lord will.

31· 8· (51.)   Y^r Humbl seruant

                                                      Jos: Hills: [50]

Under the circumstances there could have been but one reply to the justification contained in these papers, and that the Court was ready enough to give. Nine of the troublesome deputies, eight of whom, including William Hathorne of the committee and John Leverett, were found among the former " contradicentes," dissented from the action of the Court, and Richard Bellingham, the deputy-governor, joined with them from the magistrates ; but the efforts of so small a minority resulted only in their names being written in the margin of the record for honor or disgrace as posterity may agree.[51] The Court declared that they " hauinge p^rvsed an answer of the church of Maldon, touchinge those thinges wherein they had giuen offence, are not satisfied therewith," and fined the members of the church fifty pounds, to ensure the payment of which it was levied on the estates of Joseph Hills, Edward Carrington, and John Wayte,[52] who began to find that to stand before the Great and General Court as the representatives of a contumacious church implied something more than distinction. They were empowered to " make proportion of the sajd some on the rest of the members of the church," excepting, however, " any person that hath given this Courte sattisfactjon, and that consented not to Mr Mathewes ordjnatjon."[53] This exception reduced the number of those who were to bear the material burden of the Court's displeasure to " ten or eleven brethren."

There must have been both chagrin and grief, and a touch of wrath, in the little church at Bell Rock that winter. There are indications that Mr. Matthews continued to preach, probably with more circumspection while a fine and the displeasure of the Colony were still hanging over him. In the meantime, as

[50] *Mass. Archives*, x. 80.
[51] Ibid., 32.
[52] *Mass. Colony Records*, iii. 250.
[53] Ibid., iv. (1), 71.

ordered by the authorities, the church made a show of dealing with him, with perhaps more of apparent than real zeal. Meanwhile, also, the members of the church showed how their inclinations turned by giving their offending brother, Thomas Lynde, what was not inaptly termed in Malden in later days " a church-hauling; " and regardless of the " tenderness and caution " with which he was said to have given his testimony, they proceeded so far that excommunication seemed likely to follow censure.[54]

But the civil authority interposed at this juncture. At a session of the Council, held at Boston, March 4, 165½, the unsatisfactory condition of affairs at Malden and the immediate danger of the government's witness were made known ; and in consonance with the earnest request of Thomas Lynde, a letter was written to the " Christian freinds & bretheren " at Malden. At the same time the matter of dealing with Mr. Matthews, in which the church had failed, was considered and referred to a council of neighboring churches, as had been ordered by the General Court in October. The record is worthy of perusal as showing how completely the civil power had usurped authority in ecclesiastical matters at that time. The disclaimer, which is printed in italics, is strangely at variance with the actual state of things, and may have been the sugar-coating which the magistrates thought might render the pill less bitter to the palates of the Malden brethren.

[54] The innkeeper, John Hathorne, appears to have received his due measure of the indignation of the inhabitants. The selectman, with Richard Adams, constable, preferred a request for Thomas Skinner to keep an ordinary or inn; but the General Court soon after passed the following vote: "[1651: 23 May.] In ans^r to the petition of John Hawthorne, this Court judgeth it meete to encourage and appointe him, the sajd John Hawthorne, to goe on and keepe the ordjnary at Malden." *Mass. Colony Records*, iv. (1), 47. He was under the protection of the Court just then; but although that authority might "encourage and appointe," it could not force an unwilling public to visit his house. As a natural consequence, he removed the next year to the neighboring settlement of Lynn, where he succeeded Joseph Armitage, and committed the forgery which he confessed. The people of Malden had their will in this case, if not in that of Thomas Lynde; for the following was soon passed: "[1652: 26 May.] In ans^t to the petition of the inhabitants of Malden, the Courte doth graunt libertje and licence to Thomas Skinner to keepe an ordinary there, in the roome and stead of John Hawthorne, who was formerly licensed there." *Mass. Colony Records*, iv. (1), 89.

Att a Councill held At Boston 4ᵗʰ march 1651 :

A letteʳ being pʳsented & Comunicated to the Counsell by the secretary that was directed to him from mʳ Joseph Hills signifying the sattisfaction which the church of Malden had receaved from mʳ marmaduke mathewes in relation to an order of the last session of the Generall Courte the Counsell not taking satisfaction therein did order as followeth.

Whereas Jtt was ordered by the Generall Courte in the last session thereof in Octobeʳ last, mʳ mathewes having formerly bene dealt withall for publishing divers erronjous vnsound & vnsafe opinions & being called to give sattisfaction to the Courte for the sajd Errors, which he did not Accordingly doe, the Courte therefore did thinke meete to Appointe [*here follows the order of the Court which has been already given.*] That by this meanes the trueth may the better Appeare : since which the church of maulden have sent their retourne of the pʳmisses together with something written with mʳ mathewes name to it but not as wee are credibly Jnformed signed with mʳ mathewes owne hand the Copie whereof is heerewith sent you ; Jn all which wee are not sattisfjed mʳ mathewes not expressing any sorrow for his opinions nor promising for time to come to forbeare such vnsafe & vnsound expressions and therefore according to the order of the generall Courte aforesaid This Courte does Order that the Secretary shall give notice to the churches of Cambridge Charles Towne Lynne and Redding to send their messengers in way of Counsell and Advice to the church of malden as aforesajd not excluding any other churches for the ends afore specifjed, Desiring them to deale effectually therein betweene this & the nexᵗ Generall Courte & to send in a retourne to the sajd Courte what effect their Advice doth take & what sattisfaction they doe receave.

The Counsell being Jnformed of the church of maldens Jntention to pʳoceed to Censure Thomas Line for what evidence he gave into the Generall Courte against mʳ marmaduke mathewes did order that the secretary should write to the church of malden in their names as followeth

Christian freinds & bretheren

wee being Credibly Jnformed of some purpose of yoʳs to pʳoceed further to censure Tho. Ljne for the Testimony he gave in Court agᵗ mʳ mathewes & that to excomunication knowing ourselves with what tenderness & caution he gave his aforesajd testimony and wᵗ disturbance yoʳ pʳceeding may probably occasion both in the churches & Civill government we thought it no lesse than our duty (in a Case of this Concernment) *yett without any Jntention or desier in the least to Jnfringe the libeʳty the lord Jesus christ hath purchased for his churches* doe desire you to take the Counsell and advice of 3 or 4 of youʳ next

neighboring churches in the Case aforesajd before you proceede to
further censure; Jt being also Tho Lynes earnest request as wee are
Jnformed so that if the Case shall appeare cleare to others as it may
seeme to doe to you you may then proceede with more peace & Comfort and be more fully convinced if then he should Continew obstinate
but in case it should appeare otherwayes to other churches then it doth
to you the rule of Gods word may be further attended therein for the
p'servation of true love & peace which we desire you will joynctly
endeavor to promote with ou'selves So we rest

your loving freinds:

By order from the Counsell:

EDWARD RAWSON *Secrty* [44]

The six weeks allowed by the Court in October had length-
ened to more than four months, and over two months more
elapsed before the council of churches was convened. At this
council, the churches of Charlestown, Cambridge, Lynn, and
Reading appeared as ordered; and the First Church of Boston sent its pastor and teacher, the learned and orthodox John
Wilson and John Cotton, and two brethren,

at the request of y⁻ Church of Malden to be Assistant to them in y⁻
agitation of such matters as y⁻ cause would require by reason yᵗ foure
other churches were sent by y⁻ Governor and Counsell, to deale wᵗʰ yᵗ
church vppon some offence Conceived they had given. [44]

The examination of Mr. Matthews was as unsatisfactory to the
ecclesiastical council as the former answers had been obnoxious
to the magistrates and deputies; for although the messengers
hoped " by what he expresseth, that in the general he doth indeed see cause more than formerly to bewail the use of any
such unsound expressions in time past, and to forbear the use
of them for time to come," they regretted that he did " too
much labor to put too fair a gloss upon his former expressions,
which in themselves are very unsavory and ungrounded upon
Scripture pattern."

The preacher was evidently still bent upon justification rather
than upon retraction, and was unwilling to allow that truth did
not lie at the bottom of his "weak and inconvenient expres-

---

[44] *Council Records, in loco.*
[44] *First Church* (Boston) *Records, in* *loco.* A MS. copy of these records is
in the library of the Mass. Hist. So.

sions." The messengers reported to the deputies, May 27, 1652, and their "retourne" was as unsatisfactory to the latter as the result of the council had been to the former. But the Court had evidently got tired of Mr. Matthews; for though they had humbled him and made him much trouble, they had not broken him, and he was as ready as ever to "gloss" his "former expressions;" and so they came to this conclusion: —

The Courte, having pervsed M⟨r⟩ Mathewes confession, and considering the sattisfaction tendered by him, and finding it not to be such and so full as might be expected, yett are willing to accept of it at present as to passe it by.[87]

They were more ready to pass by the doctrinal than the financial points of the case; and they put their unwillingness upon record as follows: —

For the remittment of the churches and pastors fines, they see no cawse to graunt their request therein, the countrje being putt to so great trouble, chardges, and expenses in the hearing of the cawse.[88]

As has been before noticed, there was among the deputies a tendency to be more liberal and progressive than the magistrates, — to be in advance of the times. It was the living spark which in due season, fanned into flame, burned away all the old hindrances to political and religious life and freedom. It was the flame of two revolutions; and it has never died out in New England. In June they endeavored to do something like justice to Mr. Matthews and originated the following bill: —

Forasmuch as it appears to this Court, wheras m⟨r⟩ Marmaduke Mathews of Mauldon about y⟨e⟩ defectiueness of his ordination was by y⟨e⟩ Court fined Tenn pounds sinc wch Jt appears to this Court y⟨t⟩ ye church of mauldon doe take y⟨e⟩ whole blame therof on ym, and m⟨r⟩ Mathews haueing vsed some Jndeuers to remoue offence of diuers spirrits, referring to sundry greuances & his Condition being but Lowe in estate, y⟨e⟩ Deputyes see Cawse to remitt y⟨e⟩ fine aforesayd Desiring y⟨e⟩ Consent of our honnored magistrts heerin: 9 : 4 : 52.

WILLIAM TORREY *Cleric.*[89]

But the other branch of the civil power was not yet ready to recede from the position which the Court had taken, and the

---

[87] *Mass. Colony Records,* iv. (1), 90.   [88] Ibid.   [89] *Mass. Archives,* x. 81.

conservative magistrates silenced the bill by adding these words:
" The magists Cannot Consent heereto." On the twenty-third
day of October, however,

M' Joseph Hills p'ferring a petition for the remittment of fines imposed on the chh of Maldon & theire pasto', receiued this answer: that
M' Mathewes fine should be remitted, & ten pounds remitted of the
chches censure.[60]

The magistrates concurred with the deputies in this vote three
days later. This was a most lame and impotent conclusion so
far as the actions against Mr. Matthews and the Malden church
were concerned; but in respect to the Colony at large, the immediate influence of these cases was in favor of the principles
which the Court sought to establish. Though many had been
found to uphold the oppressed church in some measure, or at
least to sympathize with it, practically, it stood alone in the
contest. Grave offences had been committed, and in answering
them the fathers of Malden had the honor of standing foremost
in the struggle between the church and the state. Their glory
and offence was that they defended the independence of the
church in the election of its officers and in its internal government — an independence which had already been defined by
the Body of Liberties and the Cambridge Platform. Moreover,
with their pastor they asserted the right of free thought and expression, limited only by God's word and individual conscience
— a right which, with the liberty of the church, had, above all
others, been stoutly upheld by the Puritans in England. They
showed a spirit of self-reliance and strength which proved them
worthy champions of freedom; and the principles which they
maintained, though for a season defeated, were triumphant in
the end and are to-day a crowning glory of New England.

Twice at least had the General Court assailed the rights of
the churches before; and now the authority of the civil power
in matters of ecclesiastical government and discipline was established. The next year the Court endeavored to make the work
more strong and enduring by the passage of an act entitled

[60] *Mass. Colony Records*, iii. 294.

None to preach w'^*out approbation, &c.*

Whereas by the providence of God, the noumber of our plantations are increased, diuerse of which, especially in their beginning, are destitute of persons fitly qualifjed to vndertake the worke of the ministrje, whereby they are necessitated to make vse of such helpe as they haue to exercise and preach publicquely amongst them, by occasion whereof persons of bolder spiritts and erronious principles may take advantage to vent theire errors, to the infection of their hearers and the disturbance of the peace of the countrje, for the prevention whereof, itt is *ordered* by this Court, that no person shall vndertake any constant course of publicque preaching or prophesying w^th^in this jurisdiction without the approbation of the elders of the fower next neighboring churches, or of the County Court to which the place belongs. And if any person shall, after publication of this order, continew such a practize, the next magistrate, or magistrates, who shall be informed thereof, shall forbid such person; who if he shall not forbeare, he shall binde him ouer to the Courte of Asistants, who shall proceed wth such person according to the merit of the fact.[61]

This was pressing too strongly the authority which had been assumed and was " dissatisfactory to diuers of the inhabitants whom the Court hath cawse to respect and tender; "[62] and it called forth fervent remonstrances from the people. The Salem church declared that : —

It entrencheth much vpon ye liberties of ye several churches, who have power (as is confessed by all ye Orthodoxe) to choose and sett vp over y^m^, whom they please for theyr edification & comfort w^th^out depending on any other power.[63]

The church and town of Woburn were more pointed in their memorial, saying : —

This we cannot but conceive to be a taking the free course of church liberty into the hand of civil authority and whom they shall be pleased to bestow it upon, . . . we cannot but conceive it to be a crossing the lines of their authority and a coming in to intermeddle before Christ call them hereunto.[64]

The Court saw its mistake and hastened to retrace its steps, " that all jealowsies may be remooved," although declaring " the sajd order, rightly vnderstood, to be safe and much conducing to the preservation of peace and truth amongst vs." The obnox-

[61] *Mass. Colony Records*, iv. (1), 122.
[62] Ibid., 151.
[63] *Mass. Archives*, x. 84.
[64] *Mass. Hist. Coll.*, xxi. 41.

ious order was repealed in a little more than three months after its passage.[65] The Court, however, abated no part of its acquired authority, although it was transferred ostensibly to the consideration of individual errors of doctrine; for the act which repealed the former order contained a provision that

> Euery person that shall publish and majntajne any hœthrodoxe and erronjous doctrjne shallbe ljable to be quæstioned and censured by the County Court where he liveth, according to the merrit of his offence.[66]

The question was settled for a time; and henceforth, for many years, the civil magistrate ordered the things of God.

How long Mr. Matthews remained at Malden is not known; but apparently he had removed in 1654. It is said, on doubtful authority, that he preached awhile in Lynn. He returned to England in 1655, and several of the Malden church went with him. Of these returning pilgrims I can recognize the widow Margaret Wheldon, who left a law-suit over the estate of her deceased husband, Gabriel;[67] and with them, perhaps, was William Marble, otherwise called Mirable.

But little is known of the family of Mr. Matthews. His wife, Katherine, who came with him from England, was a witness of the will of Gabriel Wheldon in 1653, as was Michaiah Matthews,

[65] It is worthy of remark that the prudent Court so clearly felt the force of public dissatisfaction that the execution of this order was immediately suspended until the next session, when, as stated in the text, it was repealed. Cf. *Mass. Archives*, x. 81.

[66] *Mass. Colony Records*, iv. (1), 151.

[67] Gabriel Wheldon, or Welding, who appears to have been a personal friend of Mr. Matthews, was with that minister at Yarmouth, and took the oath of fidelity with him. He came here with Mr. Matthews, and in his will calls himself "of the Towne and church of Mauldon." With his youngest son, John, he sold to William Crofts, of Lynn, four parcels of land in Arnold, county Nottingham. *Essex Deeds*, i. 24. This forbids the conclusion that he was a fellow countryman of Mr. Matthews; but from the apparently close connection of the parties, I am inclined to believe that his wife, Margaret, was from Wales, and perhaps owned a relationship with the pastor.

He died in Malden in January, 165½; and his will contains the first intimation of a burial at Sandy Bank, now known as the Bell Rock Cemetery. He says:—
"I give my body to be layd asleepe in the bed of the grave in the Common burying place for the Inhabitants of this Towne."

With the exception of a legacy of ten shillings to the Malden church, his estate, valued at £40, 11, 8, was left to his wife; but the claims of his elder children caused a contention, as stated in the text. The widow, who may have been a second wife, returned to England; but descendants of Gabriel Wheldon, bearing the name in its several forms, may still be found on Cape Cod and in other portions of New England.

who may have been his son. Mordecai Matthews was one of
the two who were graduated at Harvard College in the class of
1655. At the same time another Matthews, apparently his
brother, was in a lower class. College charges against each end
June 8, 1655; and as nothing more is known of them, it is supposed that they were sons of the Malden preacher and returned
to England with their father in that year. One Mordecai Matthews was minister at Roinolston in Glamorganshire. The
younger student may have been that Manasseh who was baptized at Barnstable, January 24, 1641, or the Michaiah of the
Wheldon will.[68]

The experience of Mr. Matthews in New England had not
been of the kindliest, nor was his future to be brighter at home;
for after a few years of comfort and peace, he was again to be
brought into trouble for the sake of conscience. He returned to
Glamorganshire and became vicar of St. John's in Swansea, his
native town. Here, in a good living, he remained until the
Restoration and the enforcement of the Act of Uniformity —
that act by which on St. Bartholomew's Day, August 24, 1662,
as Macaulay says, "about two thousand ministers of religion,
whose conscience did not suffer them to conform, were driven
from their benefices in one day."[69] In Calamy's story of his
subsequent life we may see a vivid picture of the condition of
the many unbeneficed clergymen who remained in England.
Godly and suffering men were they, saints to their friends and a
derision to their enemies. They were learned and able in their
day and generation; and in their distresses they were no less
martyrs in the cause of religion and liberty than those whose
lives went out in flame and blood.

He had been in New England. He left a good living when he had
nothing else to subsist upon. He afterwards preached, by the conni-
vance of the magistrates in a little chapel at the end of the town. He
was a very pious and zealous man, who went about to instruct people
from house to house. All his discourse, in a manner, was about spiritual matters. He made no visits but such as were religious and minis-

---

[68] Sibley, *Harvard Graduates*, i. 403;
Savage, *Genealogical Dictionary*, iii.
177.

[69] Macaulay, *History of England*,
chap. ii. Cf. Palmer, *Calamy's Nonconformist's Memorial*, 33.

terial, and received none but in a religious manner. When any came to visit him, after common salutations, he would soon enter into some discourse about their souls; and when any thing was brought for them to drink, it was his custom to take the glass into his hand, give solemn thanks to God for it, and drink to his friend, telling him he was heartily welcome. He would often go out on market-days to the country people, and speak to them about spiritual matters, some of whom received him with respect, and others with contempt and scorn. He lived above the world, and depended wholly upon Providence for the support of himself and his family. He had no estate, but subsisted by the piety of his children, (of whom two or three were sober Conformists) and by the kindness of relations and friends; which made him sometimes pleasantly say, he was comfortably maintained by the children of God, his own children, and the children of this world. His way of preaching and catechizing had some peculiarities, which became him, and were of advantage unto many. He lived to a good old age, and continued useful to the last. He died about 1683.[70]

At the time of the departure of Mr. Matthews, the church, or rather the offending portion of it, had not satisfied the fine of forty pounds which had been laid upon Joseph Hills, Edward Carrington, and John Wayte to collect of the other brethren. This sum was apportioned to three classes; and Edward Carrington complained afterwards that his associates had "reserved to theire proportion such brethren of the Church as are able to pay," and had left him "to Gather vp that proportion that belongs to me to take vp of the poorer sort of brethren."[71] A fairer explanation seems to be that his particular class was formed among "our Charlestown neighbours," of whom he was one, who were either less able or more unwilling to pay than the Malden members of the church.

At the session of the General Court in May, 1655, Joseph Hills, Abraham Hill, John Wayte, John Sprague, Ralph Shephard, John Upham, James Green, and Thomas Call presented a petition, "in wch they humbly acknowledg the offenc they gaue to the Court & seuerall churches about the ordjnation of Mr Mathewes," asking that the church might be cleared of the whole fine or that Joseph Hills and John Wayte "may be for-

[70] Palmer, *Calamy's Nonconformist's Memorial,* ii. 627.   [71] *Mass. Archives,* x. 47.

giuen their offence, & discharged of the two p^{rts} of the fowre [*three*] charged on them." [72] The petitioners were unsuccessful in respect to the fine; but their acknowledgments, about which they probably cared the least, were accepted. Their answer was as follows: —

> The Court doth well approue & accept of the petitio^n acknowledg-ments of their iregular actings in those times, but vnderstanding y^t much, if not most, of the fine being payd for, & y^t the rest is secured, & should long since haue been payd in, the Court doth not thinke meet to graunt the petitiono^{rs} request herein. [73]

Poverty or unwillingness, or both together, caused the money to come slowly from the pockets of the Malden farmers; and though two parts of the three had been " gathered in," or secured by the fall of 1658, it is not clear that anything had been paid to the authorities, unless the portion of Joseph Hills had been paid before May, 1655. Edward Carrington, who was the last to " humblie acknowledge " his shortcomings, addressed the Court in a petition dated October 28, 1658, in which he expressed his " Greife " and the poverty of his neighbors.

The humble Petition of Edward Carington humbly Shewth,

That wheras this Hono^{rd} Court was pleased some time sinc to Jmpose & Lay a fine vppon the Church of maulden of the sume of fortie pounds, for ordeining m^r Mathews Pastor w^{th}out or Against the counsell & Advice of the hono^{rd} magistrats and Rev^{nd} Elders (The Euill of wch the Lord hath convinced yor Petition^r of being on of them and is made Realy sensible of the great dishon^r don to god, and disturbanc to the Churches peace therby, to the Greife of his heart which he is Redie to Confess on all occations & to take the shame there^f; yor Petion^r being allso Appoynted to be one of the three for the Gathering and paying the said ffine, the other two haueing a fitter opertunitie haue gathered in, and Reserued to theire proportion such brethren of the Church as are able to pay wherby they may discharge theire dutie, but haue left to yor petition^r such persons to receiue his proportion of which some are gone for England, some are remoued to other Townes, and the rest not able to pay whereby yor Petition^r is made vtterly vncapeable of discharging that iniunction Laid vppon him Except to the great wrong of himselfe & family he should pay it out of his owne estate which he presumeth is not the minde of this hono^{rd} Court, wherfore

---

[72] *Mass. Colony Records,* iv. (1), 236.   [73] Ibid., iii. 389.

he humbly requesteth yo[r] fauo[rs] That either, that part of the whole sume inioyned yo[r] petitioner to gather & pay may be remitted to yo[r] petition[r] and the rest of the poore vnable and abscent brethren as aforesaid to the vallue of 13[li] : 6[s] : 8[d] : w[ch] is ⅓ pt of y[e] 40[li], or otherwise that yo[r] petition[r] may only pay his proportion allotted for him to pay (being only one single p[r]son in that offenc, which the lord hath giuen him to see the euel of, and humbled him for) and that some other more meet p[r]son or persons be put in the Roome & sted of yo[r] Petition[r] to Rec & pay w[t] remaineth of those other brethren as afores[d]. And yo[r] Petition[r] shall euer pray for the prosperitie of this hono[rd] Court and abide

Yo[r] humble & Devoted Serv[t]
EDWARD CARINGTON.[74]

To this petition and request the magistrates consented " that the petitioner payinge his part of the fine the remainder shall be remitted & giuen to the towne for towne stocke." But the deputies refused to concur, feeling, perhaps, that, though the fine ought not to have been laid at all, justice required that if two parts had been " gathered in " the third should be paid also, or else all be forgiven and returned.

Nineteen months now elapsed and nothing appears to have been done towards settling the debt. The condition of Edward Carrington's neighbors, — " the poorer sort of brethren," — remained the same. At a session of the General Court, May 30, 1660, the petition was renewed, and the whole matter was referred to the County Court of Middlesex for consideration and such settlement " as in theire wisdomes they shall thinke meete." [75] The Malden committee now joined in a memorial which contains some items of interest.

To the Hono'd Court at Charlstowne this 19. 4. 1660. May it please you to consider that the fine Jmposed on vs respecting m[r] Mathews ordination, was by the gen[r]ll Court charged onely on the church, Exempting allso some of the Brethren by means whereof it fell heavie vppon the rest, being but 10 or 11 Brethren wher of one Dyed before Any paym[t] made to the Treasu[r], & his wife since gone to England with m[r] Mathews. Allso some Breth[r]n of whom we expected help are Removed out of Towne Tho: Hett, Tho: Ozban. and another we conceiue is unable to beare it (viz) Tho: Skin[r], as Jndeed we all are, And it presses hard vppon vs. Wherfore ou[r] Humble Request to this Hono'd Court to whom power as we hope is seasonablie now deriued

[74] *Mass. Archives*, x. 47.   [75] *Midd. Court Files, in loco.*

to releiue vs that not only this third part be remitted, but the other Returned we now hauing a new Meeting-house in Building which will Cost
vs aboue 150ᵈ: and our Teachⁿ great and long continued weaknes
calls for more than ordinarie from vs.

your verie humble Seruants
JOSEPH HILLS,
EDWARD CARINGTON,
JOHN WAYTE,[76]

By the County Court the petitioners were ordered to " give a
clear accᵗ of all their pʳceedings therein, vnto Leift. Ri: Sprague,
Edw. Oakes, & Ephraim Child, or any two of them, who are by
this Court appoynted & impowred to examine the matter, &
make report of wᵗ they find therein vnto yᵉ next Court at
Cambridge." [77]

This committee considered the matter nearly two years before
they reported that they had received and approved the account
of the petitioners, and that " the some of twentie fower pound
six shillings two pence " had been paid; and, " hauing taken
notice of there pouertie, and some other reasons that doe moue
vs thearvnto," they became " bould " to request that the remainder be abated.[78]

On the first day of April, 1662, ten years and five months
after the fine had been laid, Edward Carrington was " abated ten
pounds of the fine imposed on Him to gather at Mauldon by the
authority of the genʳall Court; " and the Malden church was
finally purged of its offences.[79]

That the offending members of the church ever seriously
repented of the support which they gave Mr. Matthews is very
doubtful. That their actions were the root of much trouble in
after years seems very probable. Michael Wigglesworth wrote
a letter to be read " vnto the Church," in 1658, in which he
strongly reviewed their proceedings and exhorted them to
repentance and a renewal of brotherly love. In referring to Mr.
Matthews he wrote as follows: —

I besesch you first to considʳ seriously & sadly of yᵉ manner & circumstances of yoʳ calling Mʳ Mathews unto office in this place. A man

---

[76] *Midd. Court Files, in loco.*
[77] *Midd. Court Records,* i. 212; also
Midd. Court Files, in loco.
[78] *Midd. Court Files, in loco.*
[79] *Midd. Court Records,* i. 252.

known & often prov^d to be of an unsound judgem^t, unsavory and unsafe in expression, stiff & unmoveable as a rock in what ever he asserted, who for these th^ngs had been excommunicated at one place, disliked & discarded at anoth place, once (if not oftener) censured in ye court; This man (such was then yor p^rcipitancy & wilfulnes) you would haue against ye counsel of magistrates, elders, & other godly neighbors although it were to ye grief of ye spirit of God in the hearts of his people, to ye endangering and endamaging of yor ow^n soules, to ye justifying of his erro^rs, at least in appearance (for yor action hold forth no less then a justifying of him from erro^r w^rof he had been convicted) if not also to a real closing with them for a time; finally, tho it were to ye hazzarding of yor peace love & communion with other churches. Brethn I fear this sin had not yet been sufficiently seen, felt, bewailed, repented off, confessed to God, & men upon occasion, that ye anger of God for it might be turn^d away. And I fear it ye rath. 1. Becaus I could never discern any signs of sorrow for it in any, except one or two. 2^ly Bec. o^r punishmt seems to point at ye sin, being in ye same kind. The Lord open yor eyes to see if this be not one cause & a leading cause of y^e Lords contending with you to this day; and I believ it wil be so until y^e Lord make you feel it to be an evil & a bitter thing.

[80] *Mass. Hist. So. Proc.*, May, 1871, 95.

CHAPTER VI.

JOSEPH HILLS AND JOHN WAYTE.

OF the early settlers of Malden, two men, above all others,
filled prominent positions in the local affairs of the town
and took no mean part in the civil and religious concerns of
the Colony. Closely united by family ties, they were no less intimate in their public lives; and the stories of their careers
will be found to have much in common, both in what they
performed and in the honors which they received. They
earliest bore the responsibilities and honors of the highest
offices in the gift of their fellows; and for a period of thirty-
four years, from the incorporation of the town until the elder
had removed and the younger had been stricken with blindness,
they were the only representatives of the town at the General
Court — the Congress of the young Colony. Each in his time
was Speaker of the House of Deputies, an office which no other
citizen of Malden has taken to the present time. Both are

nearly forgotten in the town where their busy lives were passed, and which owes them much for what they did in its earlier days. Nothing remains of one, save the memory of the old town well at the corner of Main and Salem Streets, — Joseph Hills's well. Of the younger, we have a thick old English slatestone in the " burying place near Sandy Bank," and an ever present memo-rial in the sturdy form and honest name of Wayte's Mount.

Joseph Hills was an inhabitant of Maldon, a town in the county of Essex in England, where, with his wife Rose, he lived, it is said, as " a woollen draper, having large transactions at London." [1] Whatever his calling may have been at that time, his apparent skill in legal matters and his career in New Eng-land justify the assertion that if he was not a lawyer by pro-fession he was so by his tendencies and habits and perhaps by education. We have his own testimony, given in 1639, in which, calling himself "of Charlestowne in New England, Woollen-draper, aged about 36 yeares," he tells of the transpor-tation of goods from Maldon to London " in an Jpsw^{ch} Hye," which he cleared at the custom house " in the ship called the Susan & Ellen of London, whereof was Master Mr Edward Payne," in which he arrived in Massachusetts Bay, July 17, 1638.[2]

About the same time, or perhaps with him, came John Wayte, a son of Samuel Wayte of Wethersfield, a town about eighteen miles from Maldon. His mother, Mary, was an aunt, or a

[1] Savage, *Genealogical Dictionary*, ii. 417. The statement in Coffin, *History of Newbury*, 393, that he was from Shrewsbury, although, perhaps, tradi-tionary, is an evident error. Savage's supposition that Rose Hills was a sister of President Dunster has been accepted as a genealogical fact by most writers; but there was no ground for the suppo-sition at first. Dunster's will, which was written in 1658, mentions " my sister Mrs. Hills of Mauldon," and appoints Joseph Hills an overseer. If the Mrs. Hills of that date was his sister, it was not Rose, who had been dead eight years. The living wife was Helen, or Eleanor, Atkinson; and the title may have been used as a recognition of

friendship or of sisterhood in the church. Still, I think that the words as twice used and the provisions of the will im-ply a relationship; and I venture to suggest that Elizabeth, the second wife of Henry Dunster and the mother of his children, was a sister of Helen Atkinson. The will may be found in Chaplin, *Life of Henry Dunster*, 303-308.

[2] Lechford, *Note-Book*, 91. Mr. Hills appears to have been received as a person of some importance among the new comers; as thirteen days after his arrival, he was admitted as a townsman and received the grant of land at Mystic Side which is elsewhere noticed.

sister,[3] of the celebrated Rev. Nathaniel Ward of Ipswich, whose *Simple Cobler of Aggavvam in America* and his services in compiling the *Body of Liberties* have given him an undying name among the fathers of New England. John Wayte, who was in 1638 about twenty years of age, soon married, if he had not already done so in England, Mary, the young daughter of Joseph Hills, and following into the forests of Mystic Side he seated himself near his father-in-law, on the south-west side of Mount Prospect, which took from him its later names of Captain's Hill and Wayte's Mount.[4]

The coming of Joseph Hills as an undertaker in the ship which brought him to New England gave him, perhaps, some distinction over humbler adventurers; and his abilities soon brought him into notice and employment. He was received

---

[3] Probably a sister. For the information compiled from the Candler and Tanner manuscripts in the British Museum and Bodleian Library see the pedigrees in Dean, *Memoir of the Rev. Nathaniel Ward*, 129, and *N. E. Hist. and Geneal. Register*, xli. 282.

[4] John Wayte had received a grant of eight acres in the vicinity of Wayte's Mount from the town of Charlestown in 1647. In 1654 he bought of John Coggan, who had married the widow Coytmore after the death of her second husband, Governor John Winthrop, several parcels of the Coytmore land, one of which was bounded on the west by the brook "below the falls and by the Pond above the falls," and on the east, by the common and other land of John Wayte. Over this land ran "a cart way of Two rods wide from the falls streight forth into the Country way;" in which may be found the origin of an old way over which Mountain Avenue now passes from Main Street to the brook or, more likely, that of the way long known as Barrett's or Dye House Lane and now as Barrett Street. In this parcel was included Mount Prospect, which was to be defended against "the Towne of Mauldon wch is vallued at five pounds." *Midd. Co. Deeds*, ii. 18.

The house, which he built and where he died, stood on the easterly side of Main Street, north of Mountain Avenue, on land which, in 1885, was owned by the heirs of Otis Tufts. *Atlas of Malden*, 1885, plate xvi. On this site, in a house which probably contained a portion of the old building, if it was not that structure itself, died in 1797 Edward Newhall, to whom it had come by an unbroken descent in the fifth generation. It was afterwards owned and occupied by the late Joseph Warren Tufts.

In the division of the estate of Captain John Wayte, his house and lands near Wayte's Mount became possessed by his third son, Samuel; and, at the death of the latter in 1720, they passed to his younger children, Edward and Jabez. Edward retained the old house and land east of the Reading road, which passed at his death to the Newhall family. Jabez took his share in the westerly land and built the house which recently stood at the corner of Main and Clifton Streets. This house, occupied successively by the son and grandson of its builder, was known from them as the Micah or Peter Waite house. In its later days, it passed through the descending conditions of dilapidation and ruin, until at last, no longer habitable, it was burned, October 10, 1893.

into the church of Charlestown, with his wife, soon after his arrival; and, although he was not admitted as a freeman until 1645, he was chosen a selectman of the town in 1644. Although he appears in the Book of Posses-sions as the owner of a house " in the middle row," near the market place, it is probable that he soon removed to the land which was granted him at Mystic Side.[5]   He represented the town of Charlestown in the House of Deputies during the years 1646 and 1647, and was chosen Speaker in the latter year.   It was during these

---

[5] The grant of land to Joseph Hills and his early purchase of the twenty acres of Thomas Ruck and a portion of the lot of Thomas Coytmore have been elsewhere noticed. The land embraced in these parcels lay on each side of the Salem Path, and was described, in 1638, as woodland. That on the northern side extended from the way now known as Main Street to the rocks at Faulkner. On the southern side, it began at the present easterly line of the High School land and ran to the swamp which began at the ancient path now called Cross Street. Southerly, it was bounded by Pemberton's Brook; but, later, Mr. Hills became possessed of all the land south of the brook and north of Cross Street to its junction with Ferry Street.

Whether Coytmore had built upon his land at the present corner of Salem and Main Streets and dug the well, which for nearly two centuries and a half yielded its cooling waters for the use of man and beast is unknown; but there is reason for believing that Joseph Hills was in the enjoyment of both house and well as early as 1650. To this house he refers late in life as his "lesser house and ground," he having built another house upon the Salem Path near the present Sprague Street, to which he may have removed and which he sold in 1681, with sixty acres of land, to Thomas Newhall of Lynn, who had married his granddaughter, Rebecca Green. This farm was bounded on the north by Mount Prospect, or

Wayte's Mount, and on the south by the water course, or Pemberton's Brook. Thomas Newhall removed to Malden and became the ancestor of that branch of the Newhall family which still remains here.

Two years before the sale to Thomas Newhall, Joseph Hills had sold to Joseph Wilson, for eighty-five pounds, the house, with eight acres of land, at the corner of the Salem and Reading roads. Wilson was a blacksmith; and his shop was one of the public places of the town where notices were posted. It may have been upon the westerly side of Main Street, as tradition says that the rubbish of a forge was found there while excavating many years ago. To the land bought of Joseph Hills, Wilson added, in 1699, six acres of the Wayte land, which gave him a strip of fourteen acres from the Salem road to Wayte's Mount. This land, with other lots in various parts of the town, he owned at the time of his death in 1705.

After the death of their father, John, in 1741, Elizabeth and Tabitha Wilson, spinsters and granddaughters of Joseph Wilson, were joint owners and occu-pants of the house. Tabitha married Benjamin Parker in 1768; and nine years later, Elizabeth, at the age of sixty-five years, became the third wife of James Kettell, who is variously styled baker, tavern-keeper, deputy-sheriff, and jail-keeper. It was he who transformed the house of Joseph Hills into a tavern, the succeeding history of which will be considered in its place. *Vide*, chap. xix.

years that he became "active for to bring the Lawes of the
County in order."[6] This service, which was fully recognized
at the time, was forgotten in the course of years. In 1867
the honors which he had earned by a series of faithful labors
were appropriated for another; and Edward Johnson, of
Woburn, the author of the *VVonder-working Providence of
Sions Saviour*, passed into written history as the compiler of
the Massachusetts Laws of 1648.[7] This error, originating in
a work of importance and ability, has been repeated by later
writers with an air of authority, which might effectually stifle
all doubts were not the records extant in which the whole story
is clearly related.

The able editor of the *Wonder-working Providence* gives his
author a prominent part in the labor and honor of the compilation of the Laws, although he does not claim that he was the
chief compiler. He declares, however, that, "when Captain
Johnson was on the committee, then, and only then, efficient
progress was made in the work." That Mr. Poole had overlooked a more important person than Lieutenant Johnson was
promptly shown by a writer in the *Historical Magazine*[8] and
soon after by the present writer in the *Malden Messenger.*[9]
What the latter, with its limited local circulation, did not
accomplish, the former, then the leading historical publication in America, also failed to effect; and the truth in
relation to the real compiler remained comparatively unknown. Nine years later the claim of Edward Johnson was
reasserted in a report of the Council of the American Anti-
quarian Society,[10] with an appearance of certain knowledge
which can hardly fail to ensnare the unwary reader; but it remained for a writer in the *Winchester Record* to perfect the
work.

After a reference to a strife which he assumes took place
between the magistrates and the deputies over the laws, the
latter writer says: —

[6] Johnson, *Wonder-working Providence*, 110.

[7] Poole, Introduction to *Wonder-
working Providence*, ciii. *et seq.*

[8] Moore in *Historical Magazine*, xiii.85.

[9] *Malden Messenger*, May 16, 1868.

[10] *American Antiq. So. Proc.*, April,
1877, 29, 30.

Committee after committee had been appointed, whose work was frustrated, until Captain Johnson was put upon such a committee in 1648, when the work was speedily done.   He devotes a chapter in his book to exultation that the thing so long desired was at length accomplished, yet he does not speak of *what every one else knew,* his own agency in the matter.[11]

Considering the insufficiency of the foundation of the claim in its original form, this exaggerated statement is an eminent example of how theories, growing by transmission, appear at last as facts and take the place of authentic history in the minds of those who write without investigation.

The three writers here considered intimate that the work of the committees was purposely delayed or their purposes frustrated, except when Johnson was present.   A more eminent authority, writing in 1860, says: —

There is no reason to suppose that they who now had the business in charge desired to frustrate it; but it was not of a nature to be, at the same time, well and hastily done.[12]

Referring to the late Francis Calley Gray, whose well-known article is still the best that has been written on the early history of our laws,[13] it is said that " it is remarkable that Mr. Gray should have failed to connect Johnson with the original publication of these laws."[14]   Mr. Gray's article is clear in its statement of facts and polished in their presentation.   It is the work of a scholar and careful investigator; and it would have been remarkable had its author anticipated the later error and given Edward Johnson a place to which he had no right.   He did mention, in several extracts from the Colony Records, the name of " the leading man; " and Johnson, himself, speaks of Joseph Hills as " active for to bring the Lawes of the County in order."[15]

The facts which Mr. Gray did not recognize as important, and on which is based the undeserved distinction of Lieutenant Johnson, are that he was a member of the committee at times;

[11] *Winchester Record,* i. 45, 46.
[12] Palfrey, *History of New England,* ii. 261.
[13] *Mass. Hist. Coll.,* xxviii. 191.
[14] *American Antiq. So. Proc.,* April, 1877, 30.
[15] *Wonder-working Providence,* 110.

that, in 1648, he was "pressed wth many urgent occasions; " and that he mentioned with apparent pleasure the completion of the laws.   Not a very firm foundation is this on which to build the reputation of " a wise and energetic legislator."

It is not the purpose of this chapter to tarnish the merited fame of Edward Johnson but to restore to one who deserves them the honors which time has obscured.

In the year 1641 the Colony of Massachusetts Bay adopted for a trial of three years the first code of laws in New England. This was the famous *Liberties of the Massachusets Colonie in New England*, better known as the *Body of Liberties*, of Nathaniel Ward, which, after remaining in manuscript two hundred years, was found by the late Francis C. Gray and printed in 1843.[16]   These laws being proved by experience during the allotted period, the necessity of the establishment of a permanent code, in which the fundamental laws that Ward had presented should be revised and enlarged, became apparent. Several orders, anticipating such a work, had been passed since the presentation of the Liberties.   It has been said that little was accomplished under these orders by " the Magistrates, who did nothing, and whose interest was to do nothing; "[17] but I infer that the magistrates wisely desired to test the code by its operations and a careful consideration, as its tentative adoption allowed, rather than to hazard the permanent acceptance of laws which might be adverse to the interests of the Colony and unsuited to the temper and habits of the people.   When the appointed time was fully expired, the following order was passed.

[1645: 1 July.]   Itt is *o'dered*, y^t seuerall p'sons out of each county shall be chosen to drawe vp a body of lawes, & p'sent them to ye consideration of ye Genne'all Cou'te, at their next sitting.[18]

Under this order, committees of six persons from each of the three counties of the Colony were appointed.   At the next session of the Court, in October, some changes were made in the formation of these committees, and they were desired

---

[16] *Mass. Hist. Coll.*, xxviii. 216, *et seq.*   [18] *Mass. Colony Records*, iii. 26.
[17] Introduction to *Wonder-working Providence*, ciii.

To appoint their owne meetings for the accomplishment of the end so desired, & to make their returne of what they shall do herein to the next siting of y⁰ Generall Court.[19]

The committee from Middlesex was composed of Herbert Pelham of Cambridge, Increase Nowell of Charlestown, the Rev. Thomas Shepard of Cambridge, the Rev. John Knowles of Watertown, Joseph Hills of Charlestown, and Lieutenant Edward Johnson of Woburn. It is worthy of notice, as an evidence of some peculiar fitness in the person chosen, that while the committees, except in this instance, consisted of magistrates, ministers, and deputies, Joseph Hills, who was neither, was placed upon the Middlesex commission. He was not appointed upon the commission as it was first constituted; but upon the resignation of Captain George Cooke of Cambridge, who was Speaker of the House that year, he was put [20] " in Capt. Cookes roome, at his request." Johnson and Knowles appear to have taken no part in the deliberations of the Middlesex committee.[21]

It does not appear that the work of the committees, which was simply preparatory, was not fully and promptly performed; and there is reason for believing that a code drawn by Joseph Hills from the statutes of England and other sources was accepted by the Middlesex committee as the result of their labors, which, with the reports of the other committees, was before the General Court at the session in May, 1646. The book of Mr. Hills was afterwards lost; and "although it were in harvest time," he made another copy for the use of the committee which was appointed by the Court in the following order.

[May 6, 1646.] This Cou'te thankefully accep^ts y⁰ labo^rs of y⁰ seue-e'all committees of y⁰ seuerall shieres as they are retou'ned by them, & being very vnwilling y^t such p'etious labo's should fall to y⁰ ground wth out y^t good successe as is genne'ally hoped for, have though^t it meete to desier Richard Bellinghm, Esqr, & Left Duncan, Mr Nowell & Lef^t Johnson, Mr Symonds & Mr Warde, to cawse each committees re-tou'ne about a body of lawes to be transcribed, so as each committee

[19] *Mass. Colony Records*, ii. 128.
[20] Ibid.
[21] This is to be noted, as it was in the labors of this committee that "the working-man," Edward Johnson, is claimed to have been most serviceable. *Vide* Introduction to *Wonder-working Providence*, ciii. civ.

have the sight of ye othe's labo's; & y^t ye p'sons mentioned in this o'der be pleased to meete together at or before the tenth of August next, at Salem or Ipswich, & on ye p'vsing & examining ye whole labor^s of all the committees wth ye abreviation of ye lawes in force, wch Mr Bellinghm tooke great store of paynes, & to good pu'pose, in & vpon ye whole doe make retourne to ye next session of ye Courte at wch time ye Courte entends, by ye favo^r & blessing of God, to p'ceed to ye establishing of so many of them as shallbe thought most fitt for a body of lawes amongst vs.[22]

There was not a great advance in the work during the months which intervened between this and the succeeding session of the Court. There were the codes of the shire committees to be brought into unity and to be compared with the existing laws; and the lost compilation of Mr. Hills was to be restored. There were also other affairs which could not be passed by; and it was not strange that the committee could not present a completed code at the appointed time. That they did not is evident from the action of the Court, although, misled by confidence in Lieutenant Johnson's presence, it is said that "the committee completed their labors."[23] In the order of the Court thereupon, the failure of the committee to perfect its work is recognized. There is no indication of dissatisfaction at the result nor is a censure implied in the action which was taken; but a full sense of the importance of the labor and the necessity of care in its performance is expressed. It may be observed that Mr. Hills, whose labor had forwarded the work, was now given a place, by name, upon the committee and that Lieutenant Johnson was not reappointed.

[November 4, 1646.] The Co'te, being deeply sensible of ye earnest expectation of the country in gen'all for this Co'ts compleating of a body of lawes for ye bett^r & more ord'ly weilding all ye affaires of this common wealth, wiling also to their utmost to answere their honest & harty desires therein, unexpectedly p'vented by multitude of oth^r pressing occasions, thinke fit & necessary y^t this Co'te make choyce of two or three of o^r hono'ed magistrats, wth as many of ye deputies, to p'use, examine, compare, transcribe, correct, & compose in good order all ye liberties, lawes, & orders extant wth us, & furth^r to p'use & p'fect all such

[22] *Mass. Colony Records,* iii. 74, 75.　　[23] Introduction to *Wonder-working Providence,* ciii.

oth's as are drawne up, & to p'sent such of them as they find necessary for us, as also to suggest what they deeme needful to be aded, as also to consider & contriue some good methode & order, titles, & tables for compiling y⁶ whole, so as we may have ready recourse to any of them upon all occasions, whereby we may manifest o' utt' disaffection, to arbitrary goverm', & so all relations be safely & sweetly directed & p'fected in all their iust rights & priviledges, desireing thereby to make way for printing o' lawes for more publike & p'fitable use of us & o' successo's.   O' hono'ed Gov'n', M' Bellingham, M' Hibbens, M' Hill, & M' Duncan, as a committee for y⁶ busines above mentioned, or any three of them meeting, y⁶ oth' haveing notice thereof, shalbe sufficient to carry on y⁶ worke.²⁴

There is no evidence that the work of compilation and comparison was not diligently followed, although the writer before quoted sees that, as the "working man" had been removed, "little or nothing was done."²⁵ Care and deliberation, no doubt, retarded a labor which it would have been unwise to hurry or imperfectly perform. At the next Court, the inadequacy of the time was admitted; but it is apparent that the new code was so far advanced that a limit could be placed for its completion. Lieutenant Johnson was now restored to the committee.

[May 26, 1647.] The Co'te, und'standing y' y⁶ committee for p'fecting y⁶ lawes appointed by y⁶ last Gen'all Co'te, through streights of time & oth' things intervening, have not attained what they expected, & on all hands so much desired, touching a body of lawes, thinke meete & necessary y' o' hono'ed Gov'n', M' Bellingham, M' Hibbens, y⁶ Audito' Gen'all, Leift Johnson, & M' Hills be chosen as a committee of this Co'te to do y⁶ same, according to y⁶ aforesaid ord', against y⁶ next sessions in y⁶ 8ᵗʰ m°. or y⁶ next Gen'all Co'te.²⁶

The connection of Lieutenant Johnson with the committee may not have delayed its action. There is no evidence that it hastened what was already near completion. The work of the committee at large now appears to have been one of criticism or approval. The weightier labor of preparation and arrangement had been left to Mr. Hills; and that it had been left in careful and skilful hands the code of 1648, as it has been preserved in

²⁴ *Mass. Colony Records*, ii. 168, 169.   ²⁵ *Mass. Colony Records*, ii. 196.
²⁶ Introduction to *Wonder-working Providence*, civ.

that of 1660, bears ample proofs. At the next session of the Court the results were evident. "Five Books or Rowls," prepared by Joseph Hills, were presented and the transcription of a perfect copy for the press was authorized. This action was taken in two orders, the latter of which was passed towards the close of the session. Edward Johnson, whose presence upon the committee had been intermittent, was again dropped and appeared no more in connection with the compilation of the early laws.[27]

[November 11, 1647.] The lawes being to be put in print, it is meete y' they should be conveniently penned ; y'fore it is desired y' y' committee for drawing up y' lawes wilbe carefull y'in, & to y' purpose they have lib'ty to make some change of forme, to put in apt words, as occasion shall require, p'vided y' sence & meaning in any law, or p't thereof be not changed.[28]

[November 11, 1647.] The lawes now being in a mann' agreed upon, & y' Co'te drawing to an end, it is time to take ord' : 1. How all alt'ations of form' lawes may be, w'hout mistaking, compared & fair written ; 2. Y' all ould lawes not altered be also written in y' same coppy ; 3. Y' y' be a committee chosen for y' busines, to be made ready ag't y' first day of y' first m° next, so as y' Co'te of Assistants, if they see cause, may advise for a Gen'all Co'te, to p'pare y' for y' presse.

4. Y' y' be larg margents left at both sides of y' leafe, & y' heads of each law written on y' two outsides y'of, & upon y' oth' margent any references, scriptures, or y' like ; 5. Y' these be written coppy wise. The Gov'n', M' Bellingham, M' Hill, M' Auditor, & M' Ting are ioyned in y' committee, to act according as in y' pap' is expressed.[29]

The new code, being completed and approved, although there is no record of its formal acceptance, was now in the hands of the committee for its final examination. Two copies were made for the press, one, perhaps, by Mr. Hills himself, the other, certainly, by his son-in-law, John Wayte. The following orders

[27] "[March, 164¾.] Leift Johnson, upon his request, (being pressed w'th many urgent occasions,) is dismissed fro' any furth' attendance on y' service of y' Co'te." *Mass. Colony Records,* ii. 231. This extract is of little interest, except that it may be noted as forming the corner stone of the Johnson theory. " What was this urgent business ?" asks his biographer. " It is highly probable that he was wholly absorbed during the spring, summer, and fall in revising and printing the Massachusetts Laws of 1648." Introduction to *Wonder-working Providence,* cv., cvi.

[28] *Mass. Colony Records,* ii. 209.

[29] Ibid., 217, 218.

contain the action of the Court concerning the two copies; and it was by the authority of the second order that the new laws were sent to the press.

[March, 164⅞.] The Co'te doth conceive it meete that John Wayte of Charlestowne Village, shall be alowed out of the next country rate, for his writing one booke of the lawes, & for finding paper for both bookes, 4ˡ 18 shˢ.[90]

[March, 164⅞.] The Co'te doth desire that Mʳ Rawson & Mʳ Hill compare yᵉ amendments of the bookes of lawes passed, & make them as one; & one of them to remaine in yᵉ hands of yᵉ committee for yᵉ speedy committing of them to the presse, & yᵉ othʳ to remaine in yᵉ hands of yᵉ Secretary, sealed up, till yᵉ next Co'te.[81]

In the May following the new code was at the press, and it seems probable that the printing was completed during the year, although, perhaps, not until after the adjournment of the Court in the fall.[82] It may be remarked that the Auditor-General, Nathaniel Duncan, and Joseph Hills, are the only persons who are mentioned in connection with the work of printing.

[May 13, 1648.] It is *ordred*, that the coppie of lawes in the two roles, which were by order of Court sealed vp, with intent that, if hereafter any question should arise about the coppie now at the presse, it might be examined by this, wherby the faythfullnes of the committee might be tried, & that the other coppie, now remayning with Mʳ Hill, should forthwith be sent for, for the vse of the Court.[83]

[May 13, 1648.] Its *ordred*, that the auditoʳ gen: & Mʳ Joseph Hill shall examine the lawes now at the presse, & to see if any materiall law be not put in or mentioned in the table as beinge of force, & to make suply of them.[84]

[October 27, 1648.] It is *ordred* by the Court, that the booke of lawes, now at the presse, may be sould in quires at 3ˢ the booke;

---

[90] *Mass. Colony Records*, ii. 227.

[81] Ibid., 230.

[82] I prefer to call the first publication of the Laws the *Massachusetts Laws of 1648*, although Whitmore, in his introduction to the *Colonial Laws of Massachusetts, 1660*, 79, prefers the date of 1649. It seems evident from the extracts given in the text that the book was so far towards completion in Octo-ber, 1648, that a price could be set upon it; and if it was not presented to the Court until May, 1649, it was because the Court did not meet between the close of the October session and that time. Johnson says, "in the year 1648 they were printed."

[83] *Mass. Colony Records*, iii. 125.

[84] Ibid., 130.

p'vided, that every member of this Court shall haue one without price, & the audito' generall, & M' Joseph Hills, for which there shall be fifty in all taken vpp, to be so disposed of by the appoyntment of this Court.[35]

So the *Lawes and Libertyes of Massachusetts Bay*,[36] the first printed code of enacted laws in New England, was given to the world, in the words of Edward Johnson, who would have been surprised at the claim which a later generation has made for him,

To be seen of all men, to the end that none may plead ignorance, and that all who intend to transport themselves hither, may know this is no place of licentious liberty, nor will this people suffer any to trample down this Vineyard of the Lord.[37]

This book, which was printed by Stephen Daye at the press in Cambridge, was probably issued in an edition of six hundred copies. Mr. Whitmore has shown, by the traces which are left in the Laws of 1660, that it contained about fifty-six pages of text; and other matter may have filled out the sixty-eight pages of the seventeen sheets which appear to have been used.[38] It was carried to each town in the Colony, and was in the hands of all the leading men. It was carried out of Massachusetts, and left its impress upon the laws of at least two colonies. Yet it has utterly disappeared. In less than ten years no copies were " to be had for the supply of the Country." [39] How long stray copies may have remained may not now be known; but

---

[36] *Mass. Colony Records*, iii. 144. It is significant that Johnson, who was not a member of the Court in that year, was not considered in the distribution.

[36] If the title of the Laws of 1648 is preserved in that of the edition of 1660 it was, *The | Book of the General | LAWES AND LIBERTYES | concerning the Inhabitants of the | Massachusets, collected out of the Records of | the General Court, for the several years | wherin they were made and | established.* A similar title, with extracts from the book itself, is preserved in Thorowgood, *Jewes in America*, published in 1650. *Vide N. E. Hist. and Geneal. Register*, xliv. 129.

[37] *Wonder-working Providence*, 206.

[38] Introduction to *Colonial Laws of*

Massachusetts, 1660, 86, 95. *American Antiq. So. Proc.*, April, 1888, 299, 300.

[39] Address "to our beloved Brethren and Neighbors," prefixed to the Massachusetts Laws of 1660. The laws of Massachusetts and the codes of Connecticut and New Haven may be compared in Whitmore, *Colonial Laws of Massachusetts*, 1660; Trumbull, *Public Records of the Colony of Connecticut*, i. 509, 563; Hoadly, *Records of the Colony of New Haven*, ii. 571, 616. The code of New Haven was first printed at London, in 1656; and the reader is advised that "they have made use of the Lawes published by the Honourable Colony of the Massachusets."

none have been found in the old collections which were being gathered when such copies might well have been in existence. For half a century antiquaries and scholars have looked in vain for the one copy which, if found, would be one of the most precious books known in American bibliography. It is worthy of note that, while a supplement to the laws was published in 1651, and others, perhaps, in 1654 and in 1657, not a leaf or scrap has been recognized as belonging to them. Nevertheless, the work of Joseph Hills has not wholly passed away; for as the code of 1672 contains the form of that of 1660, so the latter has preserved for us its predecessor of 1648; and the careful student, by the help of its marginal references, may reconstruct, in part, the pages of the earlier book.

At the session of the General Court in May, 1649, when the printed code was presented as a finished work and may have received its final approbation, the services of Mr. Hills were recognized in the following vote : —

[May 11, 1649.] Mʳ Joseph Hill is graunted, as a gratuity, tenn pounds, to be paid him out of the treasury, for his paines about the printed lawes.[40]

At the same Court, with Richard Bellingham, the Secretary, Increase Nowell, and Edward Rawson, Mr. Hills was appointed to examine and put in fitting order the public papers received from the late Governor, John Winthrop;[41] and in the fall of the same year, the Court, by the following order, showed its appreciation of the printed laws and its approval of the labors of Joseph Hills.

[October 18, 1649.] The Courte, finding by experience the great benefitt that doth redound to the country by putting of the lawes into printe, doe judge it very requisite that those lawes also that have past the consent of the Gennerall Courte since the booke of lawes were printed should be forthwᵗʰ committed to the presse, and therefore have appointed Richard Bellingham, Esqʳ, Mʳ Increase Nowell, Mʳ Nathaniell Duncan, Capt Robᵗ Keajne, and Mʳ Joseph Hill, or any three of them, a committee to pʳvse and prepare them, wᵗʰ those lawes also referred to in the end of the printed lawes, wᵗʰ a suitable table, making their retourne to the next Courte of Election, that they may be printed.[42]

[40] *Mass. Colony Records,* iii. 162.   [41] Ibid., 164.   [42] Ibid., 173.

The work thus ordered was apparently performed with care, and was not completed until a year had passed, when the result was presented to the Court and approved by its action.

[October 18, 1650.] Itt is *ordered,* that Richard Bellingham, Esquier, the secretary, and M⁏ Hills, or any two of them, are appointed a committee to take order for the printing the lawes agreed vppon to be printed, to determine of all things in reference therevnto, agreeing with the præsident ffor the printing of them withall expedition, and to allow the title if there be cawse.[42]

This book, which was printed by Samuel Green, the successor of Daye, at the Cambridge press, contained some laws which had been left out of the former code and all others to the close of the year 1650; and it is referred to as Liber 2 in the margins of the laws of 1660 and 1672.

Joseph Hills was afterwards placed upon several committees for the examination of new laws; and in 1654, when the printing of a second code appears to have been contemplated, it was ordered : —

[May 3, 1654.] That M⁏ Samuel Symonds, Majo⁏ Denison, & M⁏ Joseph Hills shall examine, compare, reconcile, & place together in good order all former lawes, both printed & written, & make fitt titles & tables for ready recourse to any p⁏ticuler contayned in them, & to p⁏sent the same to the next Court of Election to be considered of, that so order may be taken for the printing of the same in one booke, whereby they may be more usefull then now they are or can be.[44]

In 1661, the laws having been reprinted in the edition of 1660, Joseph Hills was joined to a committee with the deputy-governor, Richard Bellingham, and others " to pervse such lawes as are vnprinted & vnrepealed, & committ them to the presse, so farr as they shall judge convenient." [45]

That the services of Mr. Hills in the preparation and codification of the laws should have been forgotten is somewhat remarkable in view of the distinctness with which he appears in the records which I have cited. More remarkable still is it that, after more than two centuries had passed, another, who receives but a meagre mention in connection with the trans-

---

[42] *Mass. Colony Records,* iv. (1), 35.   [44] Ibid., iii. 342.   [45] Ibid., iv. (2), 5.

action, should have been brought forward to claim his hardly earned honors. However, Joseph Hills, unconscious that he was writing his defence against a far-off generation, twice put upon record, while his story, if false or overstated, could have been disproved, such full and distinct statements of his labors that no room is left for doubt; and those statements were admitted by those who had an intimate knowledge of his life and services. The first of these was that petition which he addressed to the General Court in 1653.

To the Honnor[d] Court

Jn as much as it hath pleased the Gen'all Court to engage me in sundry great and weighty services in refference to all the generall laws here established & now in print ffor publiq good, Jn Considera[n]: whereof as J conceive a Gratuity of Ten pounds was Appointed me by the Treasu[r]: which as it holds forth the good acceptance of the Hono'd Court, J thankfully acknowledge, as duty binds me Yet App[r]hending that my Great care paynes & studies in these difficult Jmployments was not truly Jnformed or vnd[r]stood, J desire briefly to tender you an Account thereof as ffollows :

1. ffirst it pleased the Gen'all Court to jmploy me in a sheir Committe to draw vpp a Body of Laws in which J tooke vnwearied payns, p[r]using all the Stat. Laws of Engl. in Pulton att Large out of which J took all such as J conceiued sutable to the condition of this commonw[lth] which with such others as in my observation Experiences & Serious Studies J thought needful, all w[ch] J drew vpp in a Booke close written Consisting of 24. pages of pap[r] Jn folio. which uppon the Committees p[r]usal. viz. M[r] Noel. M[r] Pelham M[r] Tho: Shepp'd & my self. J was Appointed to draw upp for the vse of the Gen[rll] Court. which Book was by some means lost & could not be ffound. ffor further Jmprovement by anoth[r]. committe of the gen[rll] court viz. m[r] Bellingham, m[r] Nat. Ward. &c. whereuppon m[r] Bellingham spake to me to help them to Anoth[r] coppie of the Afores[d] Booke which jn tender Respect to publiq good, to the Hon[rd] Court & Committee, J did fforthwith Again Transcribe out of my ffirst coppie although it were in haruest time.

2. Affter that it pleased the Gen[rll] Court Againe to Jngage me in the p[r]using all the laws in the Books of Records to Consider, Compare, Compose and Transcribe all laws of publiq Conc[r]nment, coppie-wise all which J did draw vpp together. and Drew vpp in five Books or Rowls, which done were examined by the Committe & presented to the Gen[rll] Court :

3. Thereuppon. J was Ordered by the Court to Transcribe the five

Books affores^d with some other new laws. all which (save onely a few the Audit^r did) J with Great care & vigilancie p'fformed & ffrequented the press & otherwise took care to Examine them during the Jmprinting the same.

4. Since which it pleased the Gen^{rll} Court to Appoint me wth. some others to Compose & Transcribe the Second Booke of Laws Coppiewise. which J Allso did ; which Affter Examination by the Committee was allso p'sented to the Gen^{rll} Court : who were pleased ffurther to Jmploy another Committe ; whereof J was one, to ffitt them ffor the press. · Jn all which Services jn reference to publiq good J putt fforth my selfe to the vttermost to the Great Neglect of my p'sonall & p'ticul^r occasions Devoting my selfe there vnto ffor the most p^t of Two years tyme (as neer as J can rememb^r) the benefit wherof doth J hope verie manifestly Redound both to court & Country who doubtless vppon a right vnderstanding will not be unwilling to Afford such Due encouragement & Recompense as services of such Jmportance & Advantage to the Countrie doth Require

Your Humble Servant,

Jos. HILLS.

The Magistrates Referr the consideration of the Petition to theire brethren the Deputies :

EDWARD RAWSON, *Secre*!

27 : may 1653

The Deputies think meete to allow Mr Hills ten pounds out of the next County rate in reference to what is herein exprest if the honord magistrates please to Consent thereto

WILLIAM TORREY, *Cleric.*

Consented to by the magists hereto

EDWARD RAWSON, *Secre*! ⁴⁶

The connection of Joseph Hills with public affairs was not confined to his labors on the laws. Having been elected a representative of Charlestown in 1646 and 1647, he was in the latter year Speaker of the House of Deputies; and upon the formation of the town of Malden he became its first representative and continued in that office until the close of the year 1656. For some reason the town was not represented at the General Court from the beginning of the year 1657 until December, 1660, when Joseph Hills again appeared as its representative and so continued until the end of 1664. In the following March he married, as his fourth wife, Ann, the widow

⁴⁶ *Mass. Archives,* xlvii. 19. Cf. *Mass. Colony Records,* iii. 308.

of Henry Lunt of Newbury,[47] and he is supposed to have re-moved, soon after, to the home of his wife, where he lived until his death.

He was deputy from Newbury in 1667 and 1669, after which he appears to have retired to private life, perhaps in view of the increasing infirmities which burdened his latter days. During all the years of his public life he is often found upon important committees and serving in various trusts; and the records of the Colony and of the county of Middlesex show, in their many references, how busy was his life in the performance of the manifold duties which came to him.

Besides that for the labor upon the laws, he appears to have had claims upon the Colony for money contributed as adven-turers, both by himself and Edward Mellowes, the first husband of his second wife. In the record of a grant of land made to William Parke in 1653, mention is made of "the land lately graunted to Mr Joseph Hills, at a place called Nanacanacus." [48] Three years later this grant was confirmed, or perhaps an addi-tional grant was made, which was afterwards laid out in accord-ance with the following votes: —

[May 22, 1656.] This Court doth graunt vnto Mr Joseph Hills fiue hundred acors of land neere Northwootucke, where Mr Bradstreet & others haue graunts; & it is in consideration of an adventure of 33^{li} 6^s 8^d, & for seu^{r}all services to the country.[49]

---

[47] Rose, the first wife, died March 24, 164^2/$_{40}$; and Mr. Hills married, June 24, 1651, Hannah (Smith), the widow of Edward Mellowes of Charlestown. His third wife was Helen, or Eleanor, Atkin-son, daughter of Hugh Atkinson, of Kendall, co. Westmoreland, whom he married January, 165%. She was living January 8, 166%, but died before Novem-ber 10, 1662. With this marriage a curious incident was connected, which resulted in the censure of Mr. Hills for breach of a law in the code which had been prepared by himself.

"[April 1, 1656.] Mr Joseph Hills of Mauldon being p^{r}sented by the Grand Jury for marrying of himself. contrary to the Law of this Collony page. 38 in ye old Booke. Hee freely acknowledged his offence therein, and his misvnder-standing the grounds whereon he went wch he now confesseth to be vnwarrant-able, And was Admonished by the Court." Midd. Court Records, i. 95. In this he had followed the example of his associate, Governor Bellingham, who married himself, in 1641, to Penelope Pelham, and escaped censure by his position upon the bench as a magis-trate. Winthrop, History of New Eng-land, ii. 43. Mr. Hills married Ann Lunt at Newbury, March 8, 166%.

[48] Mass. Colony Records, iii. 300; iv. (1), 134.

[49] Ibid., iii. 415.

[May 31, 1660.] In ans' to the petition of M' Joseph Hills, the Court judged meete to graunt that M' Jonathan Danforth & Jn° or James Parker be impowred to lay out vnto M' Hill the fiue hundred acres formerly, in 1656, graunted him in any place not formerly graunted.[50]

Norwottocke or Nanotuck is now Northampton; but the grant was probably laid out at Dunstable, where he owned five hundred acres at the time of his death. Once more he appears upon the records of the Colony in a pathetic petition, in which he again recites in detail the story of his former public service.

To the hon'ed Generall Court holden at Boston 24. *May*, 1682

The petition of Joseph Hills, humbly shewing, How it hath pleased the righteous God to lay vpon y petitioner, a smart hand of visitation in the later part of his pilgrimage totally bereaving him of the sight of his eyes, for more than 4 yeares now past, (besides sundry yeares dimness before) by meanes whereof he hath been utterly uncapable, of getting or saving any thing towards his necessary subsistence, being now also more than 80 yeares of age besides other infirmities of body, which long have, and are like to accompany him to his grave, your petitioner hath not been backward to his ability to be serviceable with his person & estate to the commonwealth : for besides other ordinary services, it pleased y° court to make him one of the county committy to draw vp some orders necessary for y° country, in which service J went ouer all y° Statutes in Pulton at large, collected such as J deemed just & necessary, drew them up in a small book in folio, and transmitted them according to order to the grand committy at boston (viz) M' Winthrop, M' Ward & others, after this it pleased the Court to appoint a committy to draw vp a body of lawes for the Colony (viz) M' Winthrop & sundry others whereof your petitioner was one, to examine all y° court records, from y° first to that time, which for avoyding of far greater charge it being the worke but of one fell to my lot to be active in, in which J went ouer y° 2 old bookes of recordes, y° book of libertyes, & y° great booke then & since in y° hands of M' Rawson, which lawes J brought together under theyr proper heades coppy-wise with exact markes of y° severall emendations one way or other made therein which (after examination & approbation of y° court) J was ordered to prepare for the presse, which J did, putting them together under theyr proper heads with y° dates of y° sundry lawes in the foot thereof, in the year 1648 in an alphabetical order, with an apt table for y° more ready recourse to each law :

[50] *Mass. Colony Records,* iv. (1), 430.

for which last service it pleased the court to make me some allowance, which was to my Satisfaction, though short of the elaborate care, paines and time spent therein (these things J should not have touched upon, but that there are few of yᵉ Court as now constituted that had yᵉ opertunity to have yᵉ cognizance thereof. The premises considered my petition is that J may be freed from all publick assessments to yᵉ country, County, (and secular thinges for yᵉ towne if it may be) for my infirme person and little estate now left, during the remaining part of my pilgrimage in this vale of teares. So with my dayly prayers to god only wise Just, & mercifull to guide you in all your momentous concernments J crave leave to subscribe myselfe

Your very humble servant
JOSEPH HILLS

Jn answer to this petition the Mags: Judge meet that yᵉ petitioner bee freed from Country & County rates during his life. their Bᵖ the Deputyes hereto consenting.

June : 1 : 82 :   P. BULKELEY ꝑ order

Consented to by the Deputs.

WILLIAM TORREY Cleric.[51]

A little longer he lingered in the darkness and the infirmities of age, dying at Newbury, February 5, 168⅞, at the age of eighty-five years.[52]

In the year of the removal of Joseph Hills to Newbury the town was not represented at the General Court; but the next year, John Wayte, who had followed his father-in-law as captain of the trainband, was elected as his successor in the office of town representative. For an unbroken series of nineteen years he filled this office, an honorable service, the duration of which is unparalleled by that of any other representative in the history of the town. Like his predecessor, he filled many places of trust and importance in the Colony, the county, and the town. In 1680 he was appointed upon a com-

---

[51] *Mass. Archives*, c. 282.

[52] The will of Joseph Hills, dated Sept. 14, 1687, *Suffolk Co. Wills*, x. 248, is printed in *N. E. Hist. and Geneal. Register*, viii. 309. His connection with President Dunster points to him as the benefactor to the library of Harvard College mentioned by John Dunton in

1686. "The library of this College is very considerable, being well furnished with books, and mathematical instruments. Sir Kenelm Digby, Sir John Maynard, Mr. Baxter, and Mr. Joseph Hill, were benefactors to it." *Mass. Hist. Coll.*, xii. 108.

mittee to revise the laws, a duty with which his labor in 1647 and his long experience as a legislator had doubtless made him familiar; and in 1683 he received the honor of a nomination to the magistracy or Court of Assistants.[58]

At this time the strife between the people of New England and the mother country, as represented by its rulers, had begun. On the one hand spies and informers were busy, and the ground was being prepared for the short and tyrannical rule of Andros. On the other side stood the party of liberty, at times with petitions to the king, at others with prayers to the Ruler of nations, but always with an unflinching hold upon their duties and their rights. Arbitrary orders were openly disobeyed or silently disregarded. Captain Wayte was identified with the popular party, and his name is on the roll of honor in the " Articles of high misdemeanour exhibited against a faction in the generall court," in which Edward Randolph denounced to the British government the eight magistrates and fifteen delegates who defended their chartered rights.[54]

In 1684 he was chosen Speaker of the House of Deputies. In the quaint language of a document relating to him, he soon after became " dark " and ended his public life when most honored. The petition in which he related his misfortune and asked relief from his military duties is elsewhere given. He died September 26, 1693, at the age of seventy-five years.

[58] Hutchinson, *Collection of Papers*, 541. [54] Ibid., 527.

CHAPTER VII.

A TEACHER AND A NEW MEETING HOUSE.

AFTER the departure of Mr. Matthews, "this poor church," as it was afterwards, not unfitly, styled, came again to be "in a forlorn condition, & altogeth' without a minister, or at an uncertain pass without an officer."[1] William Sargeant and Joseph Hills appear as ruling elders;[2] but otherwise the peo-

[1] Wigglesworth's letter, *Mass. Hist. So. Proc.*, May, 1871, 94.

[2] The office of ruling elder in the New England churches was instituted apart from those of pastor and teacher as assistant to those superior offices in executive matters. The elders had a supervision in matters of admission, excommunication, and restoration. They reviewed affairs carried before them in private, that grievances might be speedily ended or that the labor of the church in public might be lessened. They admonished the wavering and visited the sick. They were the watchmen of the church. "Unworthy the name of a Ruling Elder is hee," says Johnson, "who loses his Lyon-like courage, when the sound and

ple " were without y⁰ seales of y⁰ covenant," unless they were
administered by such transient supplies as had been furnished
before the time of Mr. Matthews by " young Students from the
Colledg" and others.[3]

It seems very likely that Nathaniel Upham, a son of John
Upham, who had removed from Weymouth to Malden a few
years before, may have preached here a short time at this period.
He had probably been educated in England, had been made a
freeman in 1653, and was certainly here in 1654. He died in
Cambridge, March 20, 166½, at the early age of thirty years,
having married Elizabeth, daughter of John Stedman of that
town, only fifteen days before.[4] The Rev. Samuel Danforth
speaks of him, in the Roxbury Church Records, as " m⁰ Vpham
who sometime preached at Malden." [5] Considering his age and
known presence in Malden in 1653 and 1654, I must place the
time of his brief ministration here after the departure of Mr.
Matthews, rather than before his coming, as did the editor of
the Bi-Centennial Book, who made an error of eleven years in
the date of his death.

Besides the " forlorn condition" into which the people had
fallen, there are indications that the Matthews case had left embers of discontent and " private burnings," which were not likely
to be conducive to great spiritual peace, and which appear to
have been the prolific cause of strife for many years. It was
while in such an unpromising condition that Malden received a
minister who was destined to spend a long life with her people
and whose name became a household word throughout the
English colonies.

---

wholesome Doctrines delivered by Pastor or Teacher are spoken against by
any." *Wonder-working Providence,* 5.
Cf. Mather, *Magnalia,* Book 5 (2), chap.
vii. For some reason the office of ruling
elder fell into disrepute, although in some
churches it was retained into the eighteenth century. Perhaps an explanation
may be found in the words of Edward
Randolph. "The clergy," he wrote to
the Privy Council, "are for the most part
very civill and inclining to his Majesties

government, being held in subjection by
the ruling elders, who govern all affairs
of the church." Hutchinson, *Collection
of Papers,* 500.

[3] Johnson, *Wonder-working Providence,* 211.

[4] She married (2), April 27, 1669,
Henry Thompson of Cambridge and
Boston, and (3) John Sharp of Cam-
bridge. She died March 9, 1688, aged 58.

[5] *Report of the [Boston] Record Commissioners,* vi. 199.

This was Michael Wigglesworth, who at the time of his call was about twenty-four years of age, having been born in England, October 18, 1631. The place of his birth was undoubtedly in Yorkshire; and he tells us that it was "an ungodly Place," which "was consumed wth fire in a great part of it, after God had brought" his parents out of it.[6] He was the only son of Edward Wigglesworth and his wife,[7] "Godly Parents, that feared ye Lord greatly, even from their youth," who "meeting with opposition & persecution for Religion, because they went from their own Parish Church to hear ye word & Receiv ye L^s supper, &c., took up resolutions to pluck vp their stakes & remove themselves to New England." Landing at Charlestown in the early fall of 1638, they soon removed by sea to New Haven, where, "Winter approaching, we dwelt in a Cellar partly under ground covered with earth the first winter."

The next summer the boy Michael, being then in his ninth year, was sent to Ezekiel Cheever, afterwards the celebrated pedagogue of New England, who passed from the teacher's bench to the new life at the advanced age of ninety-four years, so long was he master of the rod and the rudiments, who "at that time taught school in his own house."[8] Here the child

---

[6] *Autobiography of M. Wigglesworth.* The full paper may be found in the *Christian Register,* June 29, 1850; *New Eng. Hist. and Geneal. Register,* xvii. 137-139; Dean, *Memoir of Rev. M. Wigglesworth,* 136-139; *Day of Doom,* Ed. 1867, 10-12.

[7] Edward Wigglesworth lived "under great & sore affliction for ye space of 13 yeers a pattern of faith, patience, humility, & heavenlymindedness," (Wigglesworth, *Autobiography*); and died at New Haven, October 1, 1653. He left a widow, Esther, and two children, Michael and Abigail. The latter is supposed to have been wife (1) of Benjamin Sweetser of Mystic Side, a forward Baptist, and (2) of the Rev. Ellis Callender of the First Baptist Church of Boston. Cf. Dean, *Memoir of Wigglesworth,* 47, and Wyman, *Charlestown,* 921.

[8] Ezekiel Cheever, the famous pedagogue of New England, was born at Lon-don, January 25, 161⅘. He was the son of Ezekiel and Margaret Cheever and was educated at Cambridge. He came to Boston in 1637. The next year he went to New Haven, where he married his first wife, Mary ——, who died January 20, 1649. At New Haven he taught school and preached occasionally, being at one time sought as a pastor for the Malden church. An interesting account of his trial before the church at New Haven, in which he displayed much fearlessness and self-reliance, and which resulted in his being "cast out of the body, till the proud flesh be destroyed, and he be brought into a more member-like frame," is preserved in *Coll. Conn. Hist. So.* i. 22-51.

From New Haven he went to Ipswich, becoming the first master of the Grammar School there, and marrying, November 18, 1652, his second wife, Ellen Lathrop of Beverly, who became the

"began to make Latin & to get forward apace." Necessitated, however, by an ever increasing paralysis of the limbs and body which attacked his father after an injury to the spine, he was obliged to leave school for other employments until he had lost all that he had "gained in the Latine Tongue."

When he had attained his fourteenth year, he was again sent to school, apparently somewhat against his will, for he afterwards wrote: "At that time I had little or no disposition to it." In a little time he recovered what he had lost and so improved his time that in less than three years he finished his preparatory studies, and went to Cambridge, where the infant college, which President Dunster had begun to invigorate with lasting life, received him as a member of its eighth class. A remark of Increase Mather leads me to infer that it was not altogether his father's wish that he should enter college. He speaks of him as "being favored with a learned education after his father had designed otherwise concerning him;"[9] but Mr. Wigglesworth, himself, says: "My Father I suppose was not wel satisfied in

mother of the future pastor of Malden and Rumney Marsh. In 1661 he removed to Charlestown, "where he Laboured Nine Years. From *Charlstown*, he came over to *Boston, Jan.* 6. 1670. where his Labours were continued for Eight & Thirty Years," being master of the "Free Schoole," now the Latin School, until his death. His school house of one story stood on the northerly side of School Street and its site is now covered by the easterly wall of King's Chapel. It was removed in 1748.

" He Died," says Cotton Mather, "on Saturday morning, Aug. 21, 1708. In the Ninety Fourth Year of his Age; After he had been a Skilful, Painful, Faithful *School-master* for *Seventy* Years; And had the Singular Favour of Heaven, that tho' he had Usefully spent his Life among *Children*, yet he was not become *Twice a Child;* but held his Abilities, with his Usefulness, in an unusual Degree to the very last." Sewall says: ".A rare Instance of Piety, Health, Strength, Serviceableness. The Wellfare of the Province was much upon his Spirit. He abominated Perriwigs."

His *Latin Accidence* was used in the schools of this country for nearly one hundred and fifty years and passed through at least twenty-one editions. Samuel Walker, an eminent instructor, says: "The Latin Accidence, which was the favorite little book of our youthful days, has probably done more to inspire young minds with the love of the study of the Latin language, than any other work of the kind, since the first settlement of this country. I have had it in constant use for my pupils, whenever it could be obtained, for more than fifty years; and have found it to be the best book, for beginners in the study of Latin, that has ever come within my knowledge; and no work of the kind have I ever known, that contains so much useful matter in so small a compass."

He was also author of *Scripture Prophecies Explained*, which was published in 1747. Cf. Mather, *Corderius Americanus;* Barnard, *Ezekiel Cheever;* Hassam, *Ezekiel Cheever.*

[9] Introduction to C. Mather, *A Faithful Man Described and Rewarded.*

keeping me from Learning whereto I had been designed from
my infancy."

Of himself and his college life he wrote: —

God in his mercy & pitty kept me from scandalous sins before I
came thither & after I came there, but alas I had a naughty vile heart
and was acted by corrupt nature & therefore could propound no Right
& noble ends to myself, but acted from self and for self. I was indeed
studious & strove to outdoe my compeers, but it was for hono' & ap-
plause & preferm' & such poor Beggarly ends.

Giving the glory to God, in a manner which was characteristic
of him through life, he records that he grew "in Knowledge
both in y* Tongues & Inferior Arts & also in Divinity." At
first he had "thoughts of applying himself to y* study &
Practise of Physick;" but when he had been in college
"about 3 yeers and a half," he experienced "a great change
both in heart & Life, and from that Time forward learnt to
study with God & for God." He put aside his former desires
and resolved to "serve Christ in y* work of y* ministry if he
would please to fit him for it & to accept of his service in that
great work."

He was graduated, August 12, 1651; and his name stands at
the head of a class of ten, placed there, I think, by his scholar-
ship and not by his social rank as had been the prevailing custom of the college.[10] A copy of his Commencement part in
his own handwriting is preserved. It is headed "*August 12,
1651 : Omnis Natura inconstans est porosa.*"

He was soon chosen a fellow of the college and entered its
service in the capacity of a tutor. This station he is said to have
adorned "with a rare *Faithfulness,*" taking every occasion "to
make his *Pupils* not only good *Scholars,* but also good *Christians,* and instil into them those things, which might render them
rich Blessings unto the *Churches* of God," and bearing within
himself "a flaming zeal to make them worthy men."[11] So self-
accusing and sensitive was his conscience that he was afraid,

---

[10] Pierce, *History of Harvard University,* 190, says "from the rank of his
family;" but Dean. *Wigglesworth,* 33–35,
differs. Cf. *Mass. Hist. So. Proc.,* October, 1864, 32–37; July, 1866, 253; Sibley,
Harvard Graduates, i. 259, 260.

[11] Mather, *A Faithful Man,* 23.

says Cotton Mather, " Lest his cares for their Good, and his affection to them, should so drink up his very Spirit, as to steal away his Heart from God." [12]

His diary shows a zealous mind transfused by a spirit of great tenderness and humility, but, unhappily, so pervaded by a morbidness, which might indicate a mind as diseased as his body came to be, that we involuntarily feel an emotion of pity rather than of admiration. Especially was this morbidness shown in many "cases of conscience," as when he prayed for pardon after having " Neglected to go & reprove some carnal mirth in ye lowest Chamber til it was too late." Seeing " a stable door of Mr Mitchells beat to & fro wth ye wind," he was sorely tried and " distressed in conscience," not knowing his duty and fearing lest his " wil should blind reason." On a like occasion, he records.

The wise god who knoweth how to tame & take down proud & wanton hearts, sufferth me to be sorely buffeted wth ye like temptation as formerly about seeing some dore^s blow to & fro wth ye wind in some danger to break, as I think ; I cannot tel whether it were my duty to giue y^m some hint y^t owe them. W^n I think 'tis a common thing & that 'tis impossible but y^t ye owners should haue oft seen them in y^t case, & heard them blow to & fro, & y^t it is but a trivial matter, & y^t I haue given a hint to one y^t dwels in ye hous, & he maketh light of it ; & y^t it would rather be a seeming to check oths mindlesness of y^r own affairs, & lastly y^t y^{re} may be special reasons for it y^t I know not ; why ye case seemeth clear y^t 'tis not my duty.[13]

[12] *A Faithful Man*, 23. In his journal Wigglesworth writes : " September 5, 6: [1653.] Too much bent of sp^{r}t to my studys & pupils, & affectio^s dying tow^d god."

[13] Wigglesworth's *MS. Diary, in loco.* The diary, or rather commonplace-book, of Mr. Wigglesworth, covering the period, 1653⅔–1657, is now in the library of the Massachusetts Historical Society, and is the most interesting of the series. A later volume, 1658–1687, is in the possession of the New England Historic Genealogical Society, and is the source of our information respecting the circumstances attending the writing of his books. After the completion of *Meat*

out of the Eater, there was nothing entered by him worthy of note. There is a page of shorthand under the date of April 3, 1670, and nothing more until November 27, 1687, when he records his thoughts upon serving " At ye Lords Table" that day. In the meantime there had been stirring events in church and state and troubles in his own town, a brief notice of which by his hand would have been worth all the meditations and complaints which he ever penned. With the latter entry his work as a diarist ceased ; and the book was afterwards used by his son Edward for similar purposes.

Of these volumes I have had free

But it was not alone from without that temptations and incentives to spiritual fears and abasement came; for from within they poured forth as a scorching blast of pestilential winds. Under their baleful influence his spirit sat in the dust all the day long and his nights were as those of the Psalmist: — "All the night make I my bed to swim: I water my couch with my tears." He seems never to have felt the hopefulness of youth and never to have experienced its elasticity of spirit. While yet upon the threshold of life he wrote: —

[165⅔.] Now y^t J am to goe out into ye world J am affraid, nay J know J shall lose my heart & my affectio^s. J can do nothing for god receiv noth. fro^m him but tis a snare unto me. . . . . . J took a good deal of time y^s day to look thorowly into ye vileness of ye sin of pride & see y^t w^c might make me go mourn all my dayes, yet J can find little heart breaking for it, nor pow agst it.

How much influence the weight of physical ills and the weakness of a distempered body may have had in inducing this spiritual condition of Mr. Wigglesworth cannot now be known; but it is probable that they were not without effect. The disease which made of him " a weary wight " and life a bitter cup, which he drank to the dregs, had already fastened upon him. In the winter of 165⅔ he wrote: —

J have found more sensible weakn: of body & pressure by ye sple^n & flatulent humo^{r}s y^s week y^n for so oft together y^s winter before. god still crosses outwardly, & J meet wth vexation & rebuke, yet pride & vain thoughts are too hard for me, & J find my self too weak to make resistance. oh ! Lord hast to my help : be thou my defe^{n}ce & ye stay of my soul, for all oth^{r}s fail me.

At another time he writes: —

On ye 2^d day at night in my sleep I dream'd of ye approach of y^t great & dreadf. day of judgem^t ; & was y^{r}by exceedingly awakned in sp^t (as I thought) to follow god wth teares & crys until he gave me some hopes of his graci^{os} good wil toward me.

use, by the courtesy of their custodians, and have made liberal quotations in this and the succeeding chapter. The latter was used by Mr. Dean in the preparation of his *Memoir of Wigglesworth ;* and both were in the hands of Mr. Sibley, who has given copious extracts in his *Harvard Graduates,* i. 259–286.

There are three other volumes of the series in the library of the New England Historic Genealogical Society, containing shorthand notes of sermons, Latin and English theses and orations and other memoranda, written while he was at Cambridge, 1649–1653.

This dream, which must have startled his sensitive nature, may have given the first impulse to write that sombre poem which was the result alike of a sick body and of a mind which sympathized with its weakness.

Of such web and woof did he weave a diary which rarely shows a brilliant or enlivening thread, so crowded is it with woes of mind and body combined. Little of value beyond things merely personal to the writer can be found therein, and it took no hues from the everyday lives of the men and women around him. Mr. Sibley says of him: —

He was free from cant, conscientious even to morbidness, perpetually praying and struggling against pride and what he regarded as his besetting sins, aspiring after a religious state altogether unattainable, ever faithful to the extent of his strength and capacity, and fearful lest his interest in his pupils and others should steal away his heart from God, in whom his trust was so strong as to appear almost ridiculous to men who regard the Almighty as quite indifferent to their fortunes.[14]

While performing the service of a tutor with faithfulness and honor, he continued his theological studies; and in March, 165⅔, he writes: "J haue sin'd J fear in ye salem business, ag^st god & man, in not coming clear wth Cambridge first in saying J was not ingaged to any others." I suspect this "business" was a call as a secular teacher. That it was not a call to preach seems probable; for later in the same month he records: "I preacht my *first* sermon at Pequit [Pequot — New London]," while on a journey to his father at New Haven. On his return by water he was detained at Martha's Vineyard "6 dayes by a strong Northeast wind," and preached there with one day's preparation.[15] A call to settle at Hartford followed his visit and was a sore trouble to him. He seems to have had no power to decide for himself, whether the occasion were trivial or weighty; and at this time

---

[14] *Harvard Graduates*, i. 283.

[15] This was his second sermon. One of his commonplace-books contains a sermon which is headed: "The 2^d sermon y^t ev^r was p^rched by my self at Martins Vineyr^d may. 1653." The text is from Psalms, lxxxi. 12, "Israel would none of me, so J gaue y^m up unto their owne hearts lust &c."

a half-formed wish to return to England added to his natural indecision.[16]

About this time he appears to have had an unusual exaltation of spirit, produced by thoughts of his " good estate," which was soon destroyed by his rising conscience.   He writes: —

[September, 1653.] J felt fears & misgivings about my good Estate. yet much pride got head in me ; & p'sently y° Lord let loos upon me some scruples of conscience w° put me in fear least J went cross to gods. will, & this to abase me.

The business with the Hartford church, hindered by its teacher, the Rev. Samuel Stone, whose latitudinarian tendencies soon set the churches of two colonies by the ears, came to naught; [17] and Mr. Wigglesworth in November, and afterwards, preached at Roxbury, Cambridge, and Charlestown. Of the latter place, whose teacher, the Rev. Thomas Allen, had returned to England in 1651, he writes: " The church sent to me after Sermon, & J could not get off without engaging to preach once a month til march equinox."

During the succeeding year he continued at the college, exercised by temptations of the spirit and fears, troubled doubtless by his increasing disease, and preaching at times. It is not improbable that he may have preached at Malden sometime during this period, but no indications of his having done so. appear until July, 1655, when he writes: —

J got a sev' cold by preaching at mauldon. . . . my strength is. well recov'd again now J thank god this p'sent. 10 of. July.   But these ilnesses, colds rhewms & keeping y° hous so much have made me so tender y' J cannot preach but catch a grievous cold. yea these continued colds disable me to any service eith in family or in publick. And thro: a light & frothy heart J cannot hono' god w'h y° little remaynder of strength w° J have y° (God knowes) is my daly grief.

Soon after he mentions the " maldon Jnvitation; " and later he writes: " J went into y° Bay Aug. y° 4th & preacht at maldon

---

[16] He writes: "[September, 1653.] J am at a strait concern. my answer to Hartford motion; J am indifferent to engage or not to look toward England or not, if J could be clear in gods call. ffriends advice cannot satisfy my con-science. who but God can now be my counseller?"

[17] "From the *Fire of the Altar*, there issued *Thundrings* and *Lightnings*, and *Earthquakes*, through the Colony." Mather, *Magnalia*, Book iii. (2), ch. xvi.

twice on y⁰ Sabbath." He had then left Cambridge and was living at Rowley, the home of his cousin, Mary Reyner, whom he had recently married.

The course of his treating with the Malden people was marked by many doubts and fears, — " by importunities," writes Mr. Sibley, " on the part of this small society, and by extreme vacillations on his part because of his health."[18] His own account of his feelings and actions is characteristic, and throws much light upon his condition at that time and the nature of the disease which afflicted him.

[August, 1655.] When J was at maldon; J told them that J thought it would be te^{m}pting of p^{r}vide^{a}ce to accept of their Jnvitation for 1. J found p^{r}ching v^{r}y hazzards at p^{r}se^{n}t in y^t it exposed to such da^{n}gers coulds. 2. Jt was feared y^t my stre^{n}gth would never sute with double work

after y⁰ debating this matter too & fro they left me to consider more of it a while. Howe^r upon furth consideration : J could not satisfy my self in y⁰ force of my former argument : becaus the harm J found by preaching was principally (if not onely) in y⁰ time of y⁰ g^{n}ral visitation by colds; since, all y^t J haue found hath bee^n onely some little returns of a sore throat, y^t hath soon gone away again. Yea J found no great harm by my Sabbath dayes work at Maldon, tho: y⁰ weth was very cold & wet. And for y⁰ 2^d Argument. double work in so small a co^{n}grega-tion is not much more the^n single work in a great one ; & if it be more yet y^r are oth. things to balla^{n}ce it : these th^s considered made me p^{r}mis to delib^{r}ate more about it anoth fourt'night. J asked m^r Alcocks advice, who told me he thought neith of these plea's of such weight as to ground a refusal of this Jnvitation upon them. He thought J might hope to be better in a settled way ; & hoped wel jt would be better wth me hereafter; And to help y⁰ double work, J might preach y⁰ less while. off y⁰ same mind was my uncle Reyner.

[September, 1655.] At my next being in y⁰ Bay J found less incouragem^t to yield unto Maldons invitation. ffor having taken it into consid^{r}ation a fourtnight longer & finding my self wors, it seemed a burr put in by p^{r}vidence to stop furth p^{r}ceedings. So according to advice of friends J wholy putt by y⁰ motion upo^n y⁰ onely ground of p^{r}sent unfitness for any co^{n}stant service. y⁰ wil of y⁰ Lord be done. . . . Since J beg earnestly his blessing upon y⁰ cours of physick J am about, knowing y^t if He say y⁰ word they shal do me good, not els. To y⁰ end J haue beggd y⁰ prayers of divers this being a season of fayth & prayer.

[18] *Harvard Graduates,* i. 269.

[September 10, 1655.] Jt is a time of more y^n ordinary trouble bec: J am yet unsettled winter approaching & know not what to doe about it because my weaknes & colds stil co^ntinue & J fear in cold weth it should be wors wth me. . . . my moth & sister are come to me fro N $Have^n$, & J haue no hous to put my ow^n head in much less room for y^m w^c is discouraging unto y^m w^m J haue brought fro^m another to an unsettled state. . . . Christ hims. my Lord had not a hole to put his head in.

[September 16, 1655,] About $maldo^n$ business with some furth inclinations to it upo^n y^c grounds above specify'd where J found y^m y^t J spake withall still earnest in y^r desires after me and y^t they needed not y^t J should begin it afresh. J defer'd any $conclusio^n$ till m^r Hill come up to Jpswich to y^c g^nrall training.

[October 7, 1655.] After many and earnest prayers unto God ffor $guida^n$ce in y^e weighty business of settlemt, J haue determined to go to maldon about a 14:n. hence. J issued y^e business wth y^e messengers sent fro^m Maldon church upon y^e g^nrall training day being $Octob^r$ 4th.

[October 12, 1655.] when J feel my ow^n p^rsent weakn. to be such, J am apt to be affraid lest J should be unserviceable at Maldon by y^e coldn. of winter and live upo^n $expe^n$ces unprofitably. Yet J do desire not to giue way to $discourageme^n$t ffor J am in Gods way to remove thith & cast myself upo^n Gods $p^r$$vide^n$ce to see w^t he will do for me & by me.

Cotton Mather, in a strain of that delightful fustian which has made him famous, thus records his coming to Malden: —

From *Cambridge*, the Star made his Remove, till he comes to dispense his Sweet Influences, upon thee, O *Maldon!* And he was thy *Faithful* One, for about a *Jubilee* of years together.[19]

He was dismissed by the Cambridge church to the church at Malden,[20] August 25, 1656, by the following letter: —

To the Church of Christ at Maldon, Grace and Peace from God our father, and from ye Lord Jesus Christ.

Whereas, the good hand of Divine Providence hath so disposed that our beloved and highly esteemed brother, Mr. Wigglesworth, hath his residence and is employed in the good work of ye Lord amongst you, and hath seen cause to desire of us Letters Dismissive to your Church,

---

[19] *A Faithful Man*, 23.

[20] "There is a seasonable care taken that, if the candidate were a member of some other church, he have his dismission (his relation declared to be transferred); that, as near as may be, according to the primitive direction, they may choose from among themselves." Mather, *Ratio Disciplinæ*, 22.

in order to his joining as a member with you. We, therefore, of the Church of Christ at Cambridge, have consented to his Desires herein, and if you shall accordingly proceed to receive him, we do hereby re-signe and dismiss him to your holy fellowship, withall certifying that as he was formerly admitted among us with much approbation, so during his abode with us, his conversation was such as did become the gospell, not doubting but that through the grace of Christ, it hath been and will be no otherwise amongst you ; and that he will be enabled to approve himself to you in y* Lord as becometh saints.

Further desiring of the Father of mercies that he may become a chosen and special blessing to you, and you also againe unto him through Christ Jesus.

We commit him and you all, with ourselves, to him who is our Lord and yours.

In whom we are,

Your loving brethren,

JONATHAN MITCHELL
RICHARD CHAMPNEY,
EDMUND FROST.

With y* consent of y* brethren of y* Church at Cambridge.

Cambridge 25 of y* 6ᵗʰ m. 1656.[21]

The time of his ordination is a matter of uncertainty ; for it may have been about the time of his admission to the Malden church, September 7, 1656, or after May 19, 1657,[22] when he wrote : — "This day is appointed for an issue about my set-tlemᵗ. Lord J look up to thee for wisdoᵐ & guidaⁿce in so sollemn a business." I am inclined to fix it after the later date, ascribing the delay to sickness and uncertainty. I am strength-ened in this belief by the fact that the benefit of the parsonage, although it had been built several years before, was not con-firmed to the use of the ministry by record until December 29, 1657. A letter, which he afterwards wrote to the church, places

[21] *Christian Register*, June 29, 1850; Dean, *Wigglesworth*, 50-52.

[22] Savage, *Genealogical Dict.* iv. 541, with his not uncommon habit of jumping at conclusions, antedates the time of Mr. Wigglesworth's ordination by not less than two years, placing it in 1654, when he had not yet been called to Malden.

Often has the antiquary or genealo-gist reason to mourn over hours of lost time and vexatious errors caused by the many shortcomings of the *Genealogical Dictionary*. Let it not be supposed that the great labor of its compiler or the value of his work are overlooked by those who have serious grounds for criticism; but it may not be amiss to warn the young seeker against blindly accepting its statements or taking for granted that which may not be war-ranted by a closer investigation.

the time of his acceptance in the early summer of 1657. He says: —

> Since y⁰ Lord inclined yor hearts to invite me hither, it pleased him to hold me und^r weaknes & you under suspence at uncertaintys half a yeer almost ere I durst adventure to come to you; and after I did come, above a year & a half it was before I could see God clearing my way to accept of yor call to office.

It is not improbable that he may have contemplated a return to England during the delay; for a letter written by a relative of his wife, dated April 6, 1657, indicates that correspondence looking towards such a result had taken place. This friend writes: —

> Ma. Boyes thinks our climate would better agree with yor constitution than New England doth and promises to mee or rather seems confident that you would not want a call now, a comfortable maintainence even in these parts of Yorkshire about Leeds if you would come.[23]

Cotton Mather printed from the "reserved papers" of Mr. Wigglesworth some passages, written "after he was invited unto Maldon, and then was taken off by Long Sickness;"[24] and it is certain that he had already become a confirmed invalid from the effects of the "sickly constitution" which had shown itself before he left Cambridge.[25]

His own account of the trials which beset him in the "Maldon business" is not without interest, and shows how "great afflictions" came to the sensitive nature of the young man out of the smallest things.

> [May 19, 1657.] J haue all along been exercised with disco'agem^ts since J came hith. 1. with m^r Hills marrying of himself w^c J und'stood to be very ridiculous in ye opinion of ye country w^r it was noised. 2. with the co^ntestations between the Tow^n & the Treasurers

---

[23] *Lane Family Papers*, 12; or *New Eng. Hist. and Geneal. Register*, xi. 110. The original is in the *Ewer MSS.*, i. 5, in the library of the New England Historic Genealogical Society.

[24] *A Faithful Man*, 40.

[25] Mr. Wigglesworth, himself, gives testimony as to the early appearance of his malady. Writing in 1662 he says in the address prefixed to the *Day of Doom*: —

> "Let God be magnify'd,
> Whose everlasting strength
> Upholds me under sufferings
> Of more than ten years length."

This places the beginning of his bodily troubles as early as 1652; and an entry in his diary, already quoted, indicates that he was suffering from it in the winter of 1652⅗.

slownes in Keeping their seasons of bringing in, & making good their engagem^ts. 4. with ye returns of my nightly diste^mp occasion^d by study about ch. Goverm! & my wa t of insight thereinto, or of stre^ngth to attain it. 5. with fears of m^r Hills judgem^t about baptism; he being an elder elect. now finding him staggering or unsound J hold it altogether unsafe to let his ordination p^rceed, so J used means to bring out his opinio^n & p^rvent ye oth. The Lord hath in some measure removed all these, qua^d discouragements, so far & J find my self inclinable to ye place & peop. & work of chr. am. them. There is yet another afflicting thing; And that is a multitude of great black buggs w^c do swarm all ov^r ye hous no room nor place free, no cupboard, pot, &c. like Pharaohs froggs, & they eat all kind of food & we apprehend they haue eate^n some cloathes also. J am loath to make this a disco^ragem^t (tho a great affliction) bec. J hope it may be removed in some measure by plaistring the chimneys & stopping their holes or els by building new chimneys of brick or if there be no remedy by building a hous in anoth place. There seems to be a clear call of god unto office work. ffor, 1. Here is a poor desolate peop. always without an officer til they got a bad one & were glad to be rid of him. but now brought low^r then ever. 2 This peop importunate, consta^nt in desiring me. 3 The neighbo^rs also resorting much unto us. 4 Gods marvelous work in carrying me (so weak) thro: ye difficulty of ye work in this place. his p^rse^nce wth me hath here been such as this seems to be the place. 5. J apprehend this place both in resp. of nearn. to ye bay & many oth ways most sutable to my weaknes. 6 The co^nsta^nt inclination of my ow^n spt unto it notw^thstand: all discouragemts, & not to any oth; tho: J haue not been w^thout some sollicitatio^ns.

Mr. Wigglesworth apparently came to Malden not as a pastor but as a teacher, a distinction which was recognized by the Cambridge Platform and the common usage of the churches. Mr. Matthews had been pastor of the church, and so were two of the colleagues of Mr. Wigglesworth, Benjamin Bunker and Thomas Cheever; but it does not appear that he ever assumed the title, while he may have performed its offices, although it was applied to him by others after his death.[26] I feel certain,

<hr />

[26] "The distinction between the duties of the pastor and teacher, is thus defined in the Cambridge Platform: 'The pastor's special work is, to attend to exhortation, and therein to administer a word of wisdom; the teacher is to attend to doctrine, and therein to administer a word of knowledge.' Both

adopting the supposition of his biographer, that his bodily weakness prevailed upon him to take upon himself the lighter duties of the lesser office. Mr. Dean says: —

> Perhaps Mr. Wigglesworth may have thought himself not well fitted for the active duties of parochial life, and may have chosen the office of teacher to indicate the service he was best able to render to his parish. Precedents are not wanting where the only minister of a church was settled as its teacher.[27]

Mr. Wigglesworth brought a young wife to his new home. He had married, May 18, 1655, after considerable deliberation and seeking of advice,[28] Mary, daughter of Humphrey Reyner of Rowley; and their only child, Mercy, was born in Malden, February 21, 1655⁄6.

He found here a house prepared for him, which had probably been built during the pastorate of Mr. Matthews and had perhaps been occupied by " that much afflicted and persecuted man of God." The deed which was given in this connection was signed by the selectmen and witnessed by the elders of the

---

are empowered to dispense the sacraments, to execute church-censures, and to preach the Word, as to which duties, 'they are alike charged withal.' The pastor on whom chiefly devolved the care of the flock when out of the pulpit, was expected to spend his strength mostly in exhortation, persuading and rousing the church to a wise diligence in the Christian calling. The teacher was to indoctrinate the church and labor to increase the amount of religious knowledge. His workshop was the study; while the pastor toiled in the open field." McClure, *Life of John Cotton*, 115. Cf. *American Quarterly Register*, xiii. 37; and *Congregational Quarterly*, v. 182–183.

[27] *Memoir of Wigglesworth*, 54.

[28] It was the cruel fate of Mr. Wigglesworth to be unable to approach anything without doubts and fears. Especially did the subject of his contemplated marriage press upon his mind and conscience in the winter of 1654⁄5. His bodily condition and the faint promise which it gave of comfort and usefulness in this life, and the relationship of his intended wife, his cousin, were fruitful causes of trouble to his sensitive mind. In February he writes: —

" Now yᵉ spring approaching, J addrest my self to write for advice to mʳ winthrop, mʳ Alcock mʳ Rogʳ. Jn writing yᵉ Lord helpt me to do it wᵗʰ plainess & simplicity, declaring yᵉ difficultyes truly on both sides; & he helpt me to do it wᵗʰ out disquieting trouble. J also writ to my cousin dealing plainly wᵗʰ her in yᵉ business, wᵗ daⁿger J apprehended wishing her to be advised & take couⁿsel, yᵗ she may know wᵐ she matches with & have no caus to repeⁿt her."

As late as the early part of the month in which he was married, he still had doubts about marrying with a kinswoman; but in the end he says: "yᵉ Lord gaue me coᵐfortable satisfaction in yᵉ point also, that my scruple was invalid."

After his marriage he intimates that he followed God, "by fayth," in this matter.

church; and it was put upon record, December 29, 1657, as if to reaffirm the grant, soon after the probable date of the ordination of the new teacher.

Maldon gift   Know all men by these p'snts that the Jnhabitants
   to y   of the Towne of mauldon Have given & granted to the
Ministry.   vse of a p'sent preaching Elder & his next successo^{rs},
and so from time to time to his successors foure acc^{rs} of ground purchased of James Greene for that end, and a house built therevppon, at the charge of all the Jnhabitants by a Towne rate pportionably made the 22th of the 10th m^{o}. 1651. Witness the hands of these vnder written in the name of the Jnhabitants, 6. m^{o}. 55: also a rate in 52.

JOSEPH HILLS	*Selectmen.*	JN^{o}. VPHAM
W^{m}. SERGEANT.		W^{m}. BRACKENBURY
		THOMAS CALL
		JN^{o}. WAYTE.[29]

The " foure acc^{rs} of ground purchased of James Greene " were the beginning of the parsonage estate, which for nearly two hundred years, to the close of the pastorate of the Rev. Sylvanus Cobb in 1837, was the home of the ministers of the First Parish. In 1674 the town made an exchange with Henry Swillaway, by which, for six pounds in money and five acres of common or town land on the northerly side of " the highway to Sandy Bank," this estate received an addition of three acres, which had formerly formed a portion of the land of William Brackenbury.[30] A further addition on the same side was obtained, March 4, 167⁸⁄₉, by a deed of Benjamin Blakeman con-

[29] *Midd. Co. Deeds,* ii. 43. Joseph Hills and William Sargeant were elders of the church.

[30] This land, bounded, s. ministry land; e. Mr. Wigglesworth; N. widow Mary Bunker; w. the country highway, was deeded by Samuel Brackenbury, in consideration of eight pounds and five shillings paid by his father-in-law, Michael Wigglesworth, to Henry Swillaway, December 10, 1674, and soon after, deeded by Swillaway to the town. The deed of the selectmen was not made, however, until March 25, 1679; but as both deeds were acknowledged at about the same time in May, 1682, the long pending transaction appears to have been carried out as at first designed, *Midd. Co. Deeds,* ix. 398, 404; x. 572.

The lot conveyed to Swillaway on the northerly side of the highway, afterwards known as Burying Ground Lane, Marsh Street, and now Madison Street, was next to "the burying-place." It was, apparently, a portion of the common land which had been reserved as a landing place for the inhabitants of Charlestown. It was finally quitclaimed by John Cutler in behalf of Charlestown, December 30, 1695: *Midd. Co. Deeds,* xii. 329. It was then bounded — N. e. the fence or stone wall of John Green; s. e. a common highway leading to Sandy Bank; s. w. the burying-place; N. w. common land.

veying seven acres, which in some unrecorded way had come into his possession from the estate of Mr. Bunker.[31] The lot thus purchased of Mr. Blakeman was afterwards claimed by John Bunker of Cambridge, nephew of Mr. Bunker and only surviving son of his brother John, who had died in Malden, September 10, 1672. I cannot trace the grounds of his claim.[32] At a town meeting, September 2, 1695, it was

uoted That thare be a Commity Chosen to agree with John Bunker Consarning the towns land he laies Clame to

uoted Deken John Green Deken John Greenland Henery Green Thomas Newhall John Green are Chosen a Commity to agree with John Bunker if thay Cane one Resenaibel termes and the towne to pay the Charge : if not to Stand Sute and the towne to bere the Charges

The committee obtained what they probably considered " Resenaibel termes ; " and eight days after the town meeting, John Bunker executed a deed of release in consideration of eight pounds, the original purchase money having been one hundred and twenty-five pounds, including, however, whatever value may have been put upon the interest of Mr. Blakeman " to or in the dwelling house for the ministry in the s[d] Towne or any of the lands thereto adjoyning." [33]

These lands, lying together upon the easterly side of " the Country road leading to Penny Ferry," otherwise called " the Great Road," formed the house or home land of the parsonage, and so remained, with little or no change, until the estate was sold to George W. Wilson in 1845, when it contained about sixteen acres lying around the house. Besides this, a portion of the Bell Rock pasture, upon the westerly side of the road, was

---

[31] Seven acres, s. land of the town of Malden ; e. Mr. Wigglesworth ; n. Thomas Lynde ; w. the country highway. *Midd. Co. Deeds*, x. 574.

[32] Widow Mary Bunker released all her right in the estate of " M[r] Bunker late of Mauldon " to his brother Jonathan of Charlestown, January 12, 167⅚, for forty shillings per year during her life. *Midd. Co. Deeds*, v. 338. Jonathan Bunker died of small-pox, June 2, 1678 ; but his youngest son, Benjamin, was liv-

ing, and another son, Jonathan, had but recently died at Newfoundland, when John Bunker made the claim, which he was apparently able to enforce, upon the lands which were formerly the estate of his uncle.

[33] This deed, dated September 10, 1695, was never recorded. It remained in the possession of Deacon John Green and his descendants, and is now with the *Green MSS.* in the library of the New England Historic Genealogical Society.

appropriated to the use of the ministry after the removal of the meeting house in 1730. The whole estate at the time of its sale comprised eighteen and three-quarters acres and twenty-nine poles.

Upon the original purchase of four acres the "ministry house" was built on a knoll, now removed, eight or ten rods south of the present house.[84] To this house the teacher brought his little family; and in it, filled with despondency and worn with bodily weaknesses, he passed the most discouraging portion of his life.

Mr. Wigglesworth preached at his first coming in the building in which Mr. Matthews had uttered his "inconvenient" words and in which the church was probably originally gathered. It had been built as early as April, 1649; for, in the report of the committee appointed to survey a way from Reading to Winnisimmet, it was then mentioned as "the meeting house on Mestick Side." It stood on the southerly slope of Bailey's Hill, perhaps a little to the westward of Bell Rock, where indications of a former

[84] Frequent entries appear upon the town records relating to the care and preservation of the "ministry house" and its lands. August 16, 1699, it was voted "yt there shall be a Lento erected to on ye backsid of ye parsonag-hous The wholl length of ye house: ten foots wide: And deuided jnto three parts: one for a citching with a chimne: and ouen: one for abuttere: one for a Logging roome: all suficantly finished." John Greenland, Phineas Upham, and Samuel Sprague were chosen "to prescribe a Rule how ye bulding of the lento shall be carried on: and to agree with a workman: for yt end." Deacon John Green was added to the committee a few weeks later. The building of the leanto was not hurried. April 19, 1700, Samuel Green, Senr., Capt. John Green, and Joseph Lynde were "chose and jmpoured as a committie To see aftar ye carrying on ye finishing of ye lento latly erected To ye parsonag house."

October 24, 1701, twenty shillings of the money that was raised to shingle part of the meeting house were diverted to "parches meterials To Repair ye parsonag hous." In 1705 it was voted, "That mr Wigglesworth hath liberty to Remoue ye parsonage barn neerar to ye dweling house: to ye north side of ye paire tree behind ye dweling-house."

July 29, 1706, after Mr. Wigglesworth's death, it was "*Voted* yt Mrs Wigglesworth shall be paid for whatt Mr Wigglesworth hath erected to ye parsonag: Thatt shall be juged benificall to the towne—And ye selectmen are apointed to take a vew of all Those things and jug: what ye are worth and make Report thereof to ye town. The Select men Refuse to exept." The next year it was proposed to sell "the parsenag;" but "the uot passed on the negitife." In December, 1711, the town raised ten pounds to repair the house: but in 1718 there was less liberality; for in October of that year, "It was put to vote whether ye Town will Repaire ye well yt belongs To ye parsonag hous by Taking up ye stons and jndeuor to Get watar and jt past in ye negitiue." Perhaps the dissatisfaction which then existed in relation to the pastor, Mr. Parsons, may have influenced the town in this vote.

occupancy of the land were still visible a quarter of a century ago. It could not have been a building of any pretensions even for those days; and it is not unlikely that it was built for some other purpose and utilized as a temporary place of meeting. Whatever its character may have been, it soon became unfit for church purposes; and the town, in the midst of its "distractions and discouragements," voted to build a new house. The selectmen, November 9, 1658, concluded a contract with Job Lane, which, as showing the peculiarities of building at that early day and the manner of house in which the little church of Malden gathered for seventy years, is worthy of being reproduced.

Articles of agreement made and concluded y.ᵉ 11ᵗʰ day of yᵉ ninth mᵒ, 1658, betweene Job Lane of Malden on the one partie, carpenter, and William Brackenbury, Lieut. John Wayte, Ensigne J. Sprague, and Thomas Green, Senior, Selectmen of Malden, on the behalf of the towne on the other partie, as followeth:

Imprimis: The said Job Lane doth hereby covenant, promiss and agree to build, erect and finish upp a good strong, Artificial meeting House of Thirty-three foot Square, sixteen foot stud between joints, with dores, windows, pullpitt, seats, and all other things whatsoever in all respects belonging thereto as hereafter is expressed.

1. That all the sells, girts, mayne posts, plates, Beames and all other principal Timbers shall be of good and sound white or Black oake.

2. That all the walls be made upp on the outside with good clapboards, well dressed lapped and nayled. And the inside to be lathed all over and well struck with clay, and uppon it with lime and hard up to the wall plate, and also the beame fellings as need shalbe.

3. The roofe to be covered with boards and short shinglings with a territt on the topp about six foot squar, to hang the bell in with rayles about it: the floor to be made tite with planks.

4. The bell to be fitted upp in all respects and Hanged therein fitt for use.

5. Thre dores in such places as the sayd Selectmen shal direct, viz: east, west and south.

6. Six windows below the girt on thre sids, namely: east, west and south; to contayne sixteen foot of glass in a window, with Leaves, and two windows on the south side above the girt on each side of the deske, to contayne six foot of glass A piece, and two windows under each plate on the east, west and north sides fitt [to] conteine eight foote of glass a peece.

7. The pullpitt and cover to be of wainscott to conteyne ffive or six persons.

8. The deacons seat allso of wainscott with door, and a table joyned to it to fall downe, for the Lords Supper.

9. The ffloer to be of strong Boards throughout and well nayled.

10. The House to be fitted with seats throughout, made with good planks, with rayles on the topps, boards at the Backs, and timbers at the ends.

11. The underpining to be of stone or bricks, and pointed with lyme on the outside.

12. The Allyes to be one from the deacons seat, through the middle of the house to the north end, and another cross the house ffrom east to west sides, and one before the deacons seat ; as is drawne on the back side of this paper.

13. And the said Job to provide all boards, Timber, nayles, Iron work, glass, shingles, lime, hayre, laths, clapbords, bolts, locks and all other things whatsoever needful and belonging to the finyshing of the said house and to rayse and finish it up in all respects before the twentie of September next ensuing, they allowing help to rayse it.

And the s^d Selectmen for themselves on behalfe of the town in Consideracōn of the said meeting house so finished, doe hereby covenant, promise and agre to pay unto the s^d Job Lane or his Assigns the sume of one hundred and ffiffty pounds in corne, cord wood and provisions, sound and merchantable att price currant and fatt catle, on valuacōn by Indifferent men unless themselves agree the prices.

In manner following, that is to say, ffiffty pound befor ye first of ye second m^o, which shall be in the year sixteen hundred 59 and other fiffty pounds before the first of ye second m^o which shall be in the year one thousand six hundred and sixtie. And it is further Agreed that when the s^d house is finished, in case the s^d Job shall find and judgeth to be worth ten pounds more, that it shall be referred to Indifferent workmen to determine unless the sayd Selectmen shall se just cause to pay the s^d ten pounds without such valuacōn.

In witness whereof the partys to these presents have Interchangeably put their hands the day and year above written.

WILLIAM BRACKENBURY.

Witness,   JOHN SPRAGUE.

    JOSEPH HILLS :   JOH. WAYTE.[85]

and GERSHOM HILLS.

[85] The original document, which was in the hands of the compilers of the *Bi-Centennial Book* in 1849, cannot now be found ; and I am obliged to follow their apparently modernized copy. It will be noticed that the signatures of Job Lane and one of the selectmen do not appear. It is likely that the original had become mutilated, or that the signatures were illegible from some cause.

This " Artificial meeting House" stood upon the side of the hill a little below and south of the well known Bell Rock.[86] Although it was to be finished in September of the next year, it was still uncompleted in June, 1660, when it was stated that " a new Meeting-house is Building will Cost vs aboue 150.^{li} "

A "territt to hang the bell in" was specified in the contract; but for some reason it was not built and the bell was hung in a frame upon the rock, which thus received the name by which it is still known.[87] It was not until more than thirty years had passed that it was voted in a town meeting, March 21, 1693, " That ye bell shall be Hanged one the top of ye Metinghous." At the same time it was ordered, " That the Select men shall Take care for to agree with a workman for the hanging of the bell one ye Top of ye meeting hous." The building of this turret was not hurried. It was voted, November 29, 1694,

[86] While the meeting house was being built, the town of Charlestown granted or quitclaimed a parcel of land, which appears to have been land in which the mother town held reserved rights of commonage.

"Att a metting of the selectt men the 23 the 11: 1659, was granted and Confirmed unto the Towne of Malden a parsill of land, more or les, which pasill of land is bowndid on the west by m^r Joseph hills medow, and on the north by the land of michell Smith, and so joying to the high way, And william Brankenbury on the northeast. This pesill of land Aforsaid is given to the towne of Maldon in Consideration of ther buldin a meeting house: that this is ther Reall Actt and Deed, witnis in the name of the selectt men.

SAM ADAMS,
Reco."

Charlestown Archives, xxxiv. 104.

I am sure that this was not the lot on which the meeting house was built; but it was near Sandy Bank and the burying ground, probably near the Swillaway five acres, which Charlestown likewise quitclaimed in 1695. *Midd. Deeds,* xii. 329.

[87] It was found "at a meeting at Jsak hills of the Selectmen and commissioner," August 30, 1684, that "expenses about the bell taking downe and hanging vp 2 shillings and 4 pence," had been incurred. This doubtless refers to some necessary repairs, or the building of a new bell-frame.

The old bell was apparently removed to its proper place when the new meeting house was built in 1730, and it hung there during the Revolution; but sometime during the parish troubles it had been taken down to prevent the precinct people from abstracting it, as they had threatened. It lay hidden in the parsonage well for many years. When the third meeting house was demolished in 1802, it was again removed and placed upon the school house on Baptist Row, the town having received a new bell for the meeting house from the eccentric "Lord" Timothy Dexter, of Newburyport. In 1822 it was placed upon the new brick school house on Pleasant Street. Here the bell which had called Wigglesworth and the people of his charge, and had warned the townsmen on the morning of the Lexington Alarm, tolled the incomings and outgoings of the Malden youth for more than twenty-five years, when it fell from its turret, in the conflagration which partially destroyed the school house in 1848, and became silent forever. It was soon after sent to the melting pot.

" that Isaac Wilkeson shall Haue Two accres of Land In y° Common neere his house for bulding y° Tarrat one y° meting-hous and y° laddar; " and six months later, May 8, 1695, it is recorded, " that the town will alowe Samuel Stoures aighteene shillings with what he hath had all Ready for the finesing of the teret and hanging the bell."

The contract shows that the new house was square and probably of the " tunnel " type, as the meeting house of Lynn, which was built in 1682 and demolished in 1827, and that at Hingham which is still standing. From the specifications and the well known manner of building at that time its appearance can be described with a great deal of certainty. Within, aisles or " alleys " crossed the floor, dividing the seats or benches with which the house was furnished into four unequal divisions. The pulpit stood on the south side of the room, with a small door near by; but it was removed to the " north east side " when the house was enlarged. The deacons sat before the pulpit facing the congregation. The windows, " few and small, on account of the great expense of them, were [probably] constructed with diamond panes in leaden sashes, according to the fashion of the times." [88]

Although the floor was " fitted with seats throughout, made with good planks," pews were afterwards allowed to be set up, apparently without regard to appearance, the taste and means of the owner being the limitations. These pews, unlike their degenerate successors, the slips of our modern churches, were those large and square structures which of yore were irreverently called "sheep-pens." The first person who is known to have enjoyed this privilege was Colonel Nicholas Paige,[39] in relation to whom is found the following record: — [March 14, 169½] *Voted* that corronall page hath liberty to build a pue

[88] *Bi-Centennial Book*, 125.
[39] This was a man to be favored, for

he was of no mean note in the Colony. By marriage with Widow Anna Lane,

and it is left to the select men to order it and in case corronall page leave the seat it shall returne to the towne." Later
it was voted [January 28, 169½] "That Collonall paige hes Liberty
to Remove his pewe jnto That corner of yᵉ meeting hous by
yᵉ litell dore," and " Deken Green and Iohn Greenland are chosen
to goe and Treate with collonall paige jn order to yᵉ Removing
of his pew." The "litell dore" was that at the southerly side
of the house, by the pulpit, the larger eastern and western doors
being the main entrances to the building. On the enlargement
of the house in 1703, another vote was taken in relation to this
important pew. "[November 5, 1703] *Vot* yᵗ Collonall paigs
pew shall be finished up jn yᵉ place whare jt stands yᵉ wholl
length of yᵉ platform : excepting about one foott shortned at
yᵉ end next yᵉ dore." December 6, 1717, Colonel Paige having
died a short time before and Nathaniel Oliver having married
Martha Hobbs, the heiress of the Keayne estate, which Colonel
Paige had enjoyed in the right of his wife, the unfortunate and
ill-famed Anna Keayne, the younger, the following vote, which
closes the history of the Paige pew, was passed : "*vot.* that
Capᵗ Nathaniel Oliuer shall haue yᵉ same priuilidg in yᵉ pue
that was Collonall paiges as Collonall paige had in his Life
time in maldon meeting hous on yᵉ wast side."

Colonel Paige's pew, standing in its aristocratic solitariness
in the corner of the Malden meeting house, must have been an
object of admiration, perhaps of covert envy, to the brethren of
the congregation ; and some might have been found among

he became possessed of the great farms
of her grandfather, Robert Keayne,
comprising nearly one thousand acres
on the easterly line of Malden, in Rumney Marsh, where he apparently resided
a portion of the year, when he and his
family became hearers of the Word at
the Malden meeting house. His wife
was a niece of Governor Joseph Dudley,
and inherited the "wickedness" of her
mother, who had led a scandalous life;
but although her first husband, Edward
Lane, separated from her at one time,
Colonel Paige appears to have had no
great trouble with her. She died June

30, 1704. He commanded a company
of horse in Philip's war; afterwards became colonel of the Second Suffolk
Regiment; and was actively engaged in
the deposition of Sir Edmund Andros
in 1689. In 1695 he became commander of the Ancient and Honorable Artillery Co. He died November 22, 1717,
aged about eighty years, leaving no children. A pair of silver chalices, bearing
this inscription : "*The Gift of Col: nichᵗ:
Page / to the Church in malden / 1701,*"
are still preserved, and are used in the
service of the First Church.

their wives and sisters who would gladly have changed places with Mistress Anna Paige, despite her tarnished reputation.

There is no indication of pew-rights being granted to others until after the alteration of the house, when [November 5, 1703,] Samuel Sprague, Jr., John Dexter, and John Sprague had " liberty to finish up y^t vacant place between Colonal paiges pew and ye stayres: flush out with colonal paigs pew: and jt shall be for them and there wifes conueneanc." If they removed, the pew was to become the property of the town. At the same meeting, Samuel Wayte, John Tufts, and Joseph Sargeant were given leave " to finish up y^t vacant place: behind ye decons wifes pew." The next year, Samuel Stower of Mystic Side and his sister, Widow Elizabeth Sprague, had " liberty to buld a pew on ye East side of ye south dore ; " and it was provided " y^t when either of these parsons dye or Remoue from this meting: y^t there pew shall Return to ye town." At the same time, it was " *voted* y^t Joshua blanchard shall haue liberty to Remoue ye south doore to ye west side of ye post y^t jt shuts Against: upon his one charg and y^t ye said Joshua blanchard and his wife shall haue ye Roome to beuld a pew whare ye dore now hangs And after ther death or Remoues y^t there pew shall Return to ye town Again." To each of these votes was added, " ye alley to be left 3 foots wide."

At a meeting held April 2, 1708, it was "*uoted* That thare may Be pues erected from the dore to the stares in the metting house one the sam termes that the other pues are erected to such parsions as the town shall Graint liberty to; " and it was further "*uoted* That Deacon Greenland hath Liberty to erect a pue in the uacand place Be hinde the dore in the meting house on the west side." Soon after John Green, Sen., was allowed to " erect a pue in the hinder part of the meting hous next to deacon Greenland pue; " and Samuel Wayte, Jr., and John Lynde, Jr. had the same liberty respecting " a pue in the hinder part of the meting house next the stares."

The occupants of the pews must have formed an aristocracy in the congregation; and they doubtless enjoyed more ease in their seats and chairs, during the long services which were characteristic of the early days, than did they who sat upon the plank benches on which the more common people passed the two or three hours of spiritual delectation and bodily discomfort. But there were degrees among the occupants of the benches, even after the men and women were parted to opposite sides of the house. The higher seats, or those nearest the pulpit, were occupied by the most worthy, the test of worthiness being " the Minestars Reate : with Consideration of age : and dignity." The committees which were appointed to adjust this delicate matter must have encountered many "discouragements; " for human nature has been very sensitive on points of honor since the world began. That impartial justice might be done, it was voted, January 2, 1694/5: "that yᵉ Two Deakens shall seate those commitis that is appointed to seate yᵉ meting hous." A special vote, January 6, 1695/6, provided "That Charlestown men that are Constant hearers and constant Contributers amoungst us [are] to be seated in the meting house." An instance of the purchase of dignity occurred in 1708, when it was "*uoted* That if james Baret will make up the twenty aight Shillings which the town is in detted to him for worke at the meting hous forty Shillings then he Shall haue as conueneant a seat in the meting hous as his naberas haue." James Barrett was a " Charlestown neighbor."

The churchgoers of the better class found need of a shelter for their beasts from the scorching sun and the inclement storms, during the long hours of Sabbath service, while the more careless or less merciful stabled their horses to the most convenient tree or fence. In 1698 Tryal Newberry, Simon Grover, and Samuel Bucknam, of the extreme eastern and southerly portions of the town, William Paine and James Barrett, of Mystic Side, with John Greenland, who lived at a distance from the meeting house on his farm, since known as the Richard Shute or Henry Rich farm in Glendale, had the privilege of a piece of land near the southwest corner of the parsonage garden for a stable. This gave four feet in width to each horse, but it must be remembered that the saddle and pillion were almost exclusively used in those days, and that carriages, even of the two-wheeled variety, were extremely rare even in the larger and richer towns. Four feet were considered a liberal allowance, and, later, the space was limited to three and one-half feet for each horse. In January, 169⅚, Deacon John Green and seven others were allowed to set two stables near the meeting house.[40] This supply of shed room seemed to be sufficient for twelve years; but in March, 17¹⁰⁄₁₁, John Pratt, John Upham, Phineas Upham, Jr., James Upham, Nathaniel Upham, Jr., Samuel Sprague, Edward Sprague, Phineas Sprague, Jonathan Barrett, Samuel Green, Jr., Ebenezer Harnden, John Brintnall, Thomas Wayte, Jonathan Sprague, Samuel Green, miller, Thomas Wayte, tailor, and Daniel Floyd had "liberty graunted Them to set up Stabls: on yᵉ Towns Land sumwhare neer yᵉ meting hous: To Sheltar ther horses on Sabath days And To be set out whare and so much as the Select men shall se cause prouided no man shall haue more than Three foots and half jn breadth for on hors." The next month Colonel Paige proved his superiority, or his greater needs, by getting "liberty To erect or set up a stable for 3 or 4 horses upon yᵉ Towns land sum whare neer yᵉ meting-hous and yᵉ select men to say whare or set out yᵉ place whar yᵉ sᵈ stable shall stand." At the end of another year the town's land had become crowded or the horses had become smaller; for Hugh Floyd of Rumney Marsh, and Deacon Phineas Upham, Nathaniel Upham, Benjamin Hills, Jonathan Sargeant, John Lynde, Thomas Lynde, Samuel Newhall, and Joseph Lynde, of Malden, in building their stable "by yᵉ fence nere yᵉ bell Rock,"

[40] Deacon John Green, Samuel Sprague, Jr., Jonathan Haward, Isaac Wilkinson, Mr. Sweetser, John Sprague, Sen., Samuel Sprague, Sen., and Samuel Sweetser. He who was distinguished by the title of Mr. must have been Benjamin Sweetser of Mystic Side, a fervent Baptist in 1668, when he was severely fined for circulating a "scandalous and reproachful" petition in favor of his imprisoned brethren, Thomas Gould, William Turner, and John Farnum. If, as is probable, he married Abigail, the sister of the Malden teacher, his respect for his brother-in-law, which led him to give the name of Wigglesworth to his youngest son, may have brought him to visit the meeting house, although he appears to have retained his Baptist principles. He died July 22, 1718, at the age of eighty-five years, and left legacies to ministers of the unpopular faith. It may well be claimed for him that he was the first inhabitant of the northerly bank of the Mystic who openly professed the doctrine which denies the validity of infant baptism.

were each limited to " Rome to set Two horses and 3 foots jn bredth for each hors." In 171$\frac{6}{7}$ the names of Benjamin Sweetser of Mystic Side, and John Mudge, whose farm in the south-easterly part of the town, formerly belonging to Job Lane, is now a portion of the Woodlawn Cemetery lands, were added to the list of proprietors of stables, the latter having room for two horses.

In the course of twenty years the congregation became straitened for room; but at a meeting held December 4, 1682, the town refused to enlarge the meeting house, although a vote was passed, " That the Meeting house be repaired to keep out the weather & save the sells from rotting."[41]   In 1701 may be found an item of five pounds in the town charges " for shingles and nails to couer one half of ye roof of ye meting hous." Two pounds of this sum were, however, diverted towards the expense of a committee " concerning Worster farm," and twenty shillings were used to " parches meterials To Repair ye parsonag hous." In 1702 the need of a larger house had so increased that a more earnest attempt was made to " jnlarg ye Meting hous ; " and a vote was passed, —

[April 14, 1702.] That wharas jt hath ben agreead on by this town y^t ye Meting-hous shall be jnlarged and Repaired : by a free Contribution : and Jf ther can be a suficant sum of money Gathared in this town and Amongst our naighbours of Charlestown to finish ye work acording as jt js agreead on : Then those our Charlestown naighbours They and ther haires Shall haue free liberty to com jnto ye s^d meting hous To heare ye word of god.

Deacons Phineas Upham and John Greenland were chosen to see what money might be gathered for this purpose.   A month later it was voted : —

[May 15. 1702.] y^t ye meeting-hous shall be cut jn two neer ye midle and carry of one end 14 foots : and close both parts again : with a new bulding by a free contribution : and jf our Charlestown naighbours doe aford towards ye said bulding : acording to ye list they haue showen which js 30 pounds and upwards then they shall be seated jn ye s^d meting-hous As ye maiger part of this town shall se cause.

[41] It was afterwards voted: " That phinias Sprague and Joses Bucknam are to Joyne with the Townes men in repairing of the meeting house the 28 June 86."

The plan of a "free contribution" failed; and it was voted, June 15, 1702, to make the addition of fourteen feet upon the southerly side of the house and to defray the charges by a town rate. The Charlestown neighbors might contribute as proposed; but in case of their refusal or neglect to do so, "then we will only Repaire our old meting-hous and will Rais money for y^t end." Four days later John Sprague, William Paine, John Tufts, and James Barrett appeared in behalf of "all ye Jnhabitants of mistickside: y^t are our Charlestown naightbours," and promised to pay thirty pounds "prouided this meting will pas a uote to Remoue ye pulpitt to ye west side and y^t ye s^d charlestown naightbours they and their haires shall haue a right Jn ye s^d meting-hous and y^t ye Shall be seated jn ye meting-hous by ye same Rules as this town do atend jn seating their own Jnhabitants." The town agreed to these conditions, and voted to raise twenty pounds. This sum was afterwards increased to forty pounds, and a committee of three was chosen " to se aftar and take care y^t ye meting-hous be Repaired."

A new committee, consisting of Lieutenant John Lynde, John Greenland, Phineas Upham, Jonathan Sprague, Joseph Lamson, Edward Sprague, and Samuel Wayte, was chosen the next day; and the alterations were thereafter carried on with all the slowness which usually attended such matters. The forty pounds which had been voted proved all too small, and, June 4, 1703, forty pounds more were raised "to carry on ye finishing of ye meting-hous: and to pay what js due: for what js alredy don for ye meting-hous." That not much had been done towards "jnlarging ye hous" at this time is indicated by a vote passed soon after.

[June 14, 1703.] All Those y^t haue a Right jn ye meting-hous: In Those seats y^t must be defaced or Remoued doth Giue up there Right to ye town: jn order for ye more conuenant Inlarging of ye meting-hous namly Capt John Line: Leu^t Henery Green: John Sprague Senr: Samuell Sprague juner: In behalf of his mothar brown:[43] deacon Green. John Greenland, Jonathan Sargeant: beniamin Whitemore jn behalf of

[43] Rebecca (Crawford), widow of Lieutenant Samuel Sprague, who died October 3, 1696, aged 65, married, June 24, 1697, Captain John Brown, of Reading.

his son ben : Samuell Sprague Senr In behalf of his mother Sprague : Nathaniell waitt Joses bucknam Sam^ll Stower Sam^ll sweetcer : And jt js uoted with This prouizo y^t jf euer this town seeath Cause To purches aney other seats or pues jn ye meting-hous : Thos parsons That ther names are heerunto subscribed shall be freead from aney charg therunto.

A general town meeting was held, July 6, 1703, for the special and only purpose of considering the question of the location of the pulpit. It had been agreed with the Charlestown neighbors that it should stand on the west side of the house; but the record of this meeting relates that "Considering the jnconuenences and damig : acurring to ye pulpitt on y^t side : by Reson of ye extreem heate : at sum time of ye yeere : Therfor haue voted and ordered that The pulpitt shall be placed on ye north-east side of ye meting hous." The alterations now proceeded apace; and in February, 170¾, Joshua Blanchard was paid thirty-eight pounds and one shilling in full for "Timbar : shingls : clobards and Glaze." It was voted, October 20, 1704, "y^t Those Gen^t y^t contribated to ye jnlarging of The meting-hous : y^t they are welcom to com to heare ye word with us;" and a list of names, which was entered upon the records soon after, proves that the people of Mystic Side had fulfilled their pledges.

The names of our Charlestown naightbours with there summs that haue contributed Towards ye Inlarging and Repairing of malden meting house:

Wm Pain	2	5	0	Danl Whittemore	1	10	0
John Tufts	3	3	0	John Whittemore	1	0	0
Joses Bucknam	2			John Mitchell	1	0	0
Sam Stower	2			John Sprague	3	0	0
Thos Shepard	1	10		Isaac Wheelar	1	0	0
Joshua Blanchard	2	10		Abraham Blanchard	1	4	0
Sam Townzen		16		Mothar Tufts [48]		12	
Thos Mitchel	1	0					
John Rigeway	2			[Total £29. 10. 0.]			
Jos Sargeant	2						
John Marble	1						

[48] The Blanchards lived on Wilson's Point, or Blanchard's side, now Wellington, in Medford, which was then a portion of Charlestown. "Mothar Tufts" was probably Mary, the widow of Peter Tufts the elder. She died before the recording of this list, January 10, 170¾.

The free-will ofering of Seuerall Gen^t and frends Towards the Inlarging of Malding meting house

Colanal paig	6	0	0		Jonathan Tufts	2	0	0	
Capt Tufts	1	0	0		daniel Huchens		10	0	
Ensigne Center	1	0	0		M's Wigglesworth	1	0	0	
Thos pratt	2	0	0		['Total £13. 10. 0.] ^{44}				

There were no galleries specified in the contract of Job Lane; but they were added on three sides, either while the house was being built or at some time prior to 1684. At a meeting, March 8, 170¾, as the repairs were being completed, it was voted, " That ther shall be a new stack of stayrse erected jn ye norwest-corner of the meting-hous and ye other stayres jn ye northerly end taken down." Several seats were taken away in consequence, and the town clerk carefully recorded ample compensation for the removal. A fourth gallery was added in 1713, when Benjamin Hills, Ezekiel Jenkins, John Mudge, Thomas Burditt, Samuel Newhall, and Nathaniel Upham had liberty granted " y^m To buld a gallery between ye Two grat bames ouer ye front Gallery."

The meeting house was again becoming too small for the increasing congregation; and, March 3, 171¾, Samuel Green, John Wilson, and William Sargeant were chosen " to treat with our charlestown naighbors consarning ye jnlarging of Roome jn ye meting hous." At an adjourned meeting, a fortnight later, it was " *voted* That There shall be new Gallires bult jn ye meting-hous: That js to say Ther shall be Two seats erected ouer each Gallire Round; " and John Griffin, a young housewright of

---

44 This list of "Gen^t and frends" shows how widely scattered were the members of the Malden congregation. Colonel Paige has already been the subject of a note. Jonathan Tufts was a son of the first Peter, and married Rebecca, daughter of Captain John Wayte. He occupied a moiety of the Nowell farm, which intervened between Malden and Medford. Captain Tufts was his eldest brother Peter, of Medford, who lived upon a portion of the three hundred and fifty acres of the original Cradock farm, which his father had bought of Richard Russell's estate in 1677. Ensign John Center was of Rumney Marsh, or Winnisimmet; and it is supposed that he may have occupied that land near Powder Horn Hill since known as the Carter Farm. Chamberlain, in the *Chelsea Telegraph*, April 28, 1883.

Daniel Hutchens, or Hitchens, was an inhabitant of the "pan-handle" of Boston, near the Reading and Lynn lines. Thomas Pratt lived in the neighborhood of Sagamore Hill, where a little village springing up around his former dwelling place perpetuates his memory and that of his descendants. Mrs. Wigglesworth will become better known to us.

Charlestown, who had recently married a daughter of Deacon Phineas Upham, "apeering in s^d meting," agreed to find the material and do the work within three months for twenty-five pounds. "On ye 16: of August 1714 nathaniell upham Senr Resaiued Ten shillings money which js a Gift of Jonathan Tufts Towards ye bulding of ye new Gallery jn ye meting-hous and js to be jmproued for y^t end."

The new gallery did not long answer the demand for room; and it was finally voted : —

[March 6, 1727.] That this Town will Build A new meetinghouse upon the Towns land neare ye place whear the Old meetinghouse now Stands.

This new meeting house, which was the third house occupied by the Malden church, was the source of much strife and division among the people of the town.

CHAPTER VIII.

MICHAEL WIGGLESWORTH.

THERE are many indications that the settlement of Mr.
Wigglesworth was not altogether satisfactory to some of
the leading members of the Malden church and that their un-
friendliness caused him much uneasiness. He had come among
them, as a young man, to fill the place of one who had been
endeared to them in the mutual endurance of trials and difficulties, of one around whom they had gathered with an unflinching devotion, which must have strengthened the bonds which
seem to have existed between the pastor and the people from
the first. He came to stand in the room of one in whose behalf
and defence they had suffered, and in whose cause they were
still under the displeasure of the Court and, perhaps, of their
sister churches. Nor could they have heartily sympathized
with the spirit of the religious views of Mr. Wigglesworth,
opposed as they were in their sombre conformity to the established creed with the more spiritual and unfettered teachings of
Mr. Matthews. If they admired the Antinomian tendencies of
the one, they must have secretly disliked the uncompromising
Orthodoxy of the other. Mr. Dean well remarks: —

As Mr. Wigglesworth's opinions seem to have called forth no protest
from the opponents of his predecessor, we may infer that they were
satisfactory to them. Under such circumstances, it would not be surprising if the ardent friends of Mr. Matthews should manifest a coolness towards the person whom they were forced to hear.[1]

The increasing ill health of Mr. Wigglesworth could not have
failed to excite increased dissatisfaction rather than sympathy:
the more so that his bodily troubles were not always apparent
to the careless observer, but were hidden and deceptive. A

failure to appear in the pulpit, or any omission of pastoral work
when suffering, was apparently misinterpreted and made a fresh
cause of complaint and a conserver of discontent; and his sickness came to be looked upon as a case of that trouble which
was popularly known as " hypo," or " hyp." The evidence of
Mr. Wigglesworth, himself, is conclusive upon this point. In
the address prefixed to the *Day of Doom* he says : —

Yet some (*I know*) do judge,
Mine inability,
To come abroad and do Christ's Work,
To be Melancholly;
And that I'm not so weak,
As I my self conceit,
But who in other things have found
Me so conceited yet ?

My prisoned thoughts break forth,
When open'd is the door,
With greater force and violence,
And strain my voice the more.
But vainly do they tell,
That I am growing stronger
Who hear me speak in half an hour,
Till I can speak no longer.

Or who of all my Friends,
That have my trials seen,
Can tell the time in seven years,
When I have dumpish been?
Some think my voice is strong,
Most times when I do Preach :
But ten days after what I feel
And suffer, few can reach.

Some for, because they see not
My chearfulness to fail,
Nor that I am disconsolate,
Do think I nothing ail.
If they had born my griefs,
Their courage might have fail'd them,
And all the Town (perhaps) have known
(Once and again) what ail'd them.

This dissatisfaction was, perhaps, openly expressed at first,
and may have been a cause of the hesitancy of Mr. Wigglesworth in accepting the office, even after he had removed to
Malden. It might well have been one of the " disco^{r}agem^{ts} " by
which he was exercised in his earlier dealings with the church.

Nor was the temper of the people of such sort as to offer
much encouragement to spiritual life. A spirit of ill-will and
strife seemed to pervade the whole community. Slanders,
assaults, domestic broils, and other evils kept the people in a
state of unrest; and the files and records of the County Court
show a plentiful harvest of resulting cases and suits. In a long
letter, which is extant and on which Joseph Hills wrote " dd
vnto me from Mr Wigglsworth the 19 day of the 4th M 1658:
Signifying his desire to haue it read tomorrow vnto the
Church," the teacher, who appears then to have been afflicted
by " lingring weaknes & long restraint," wrote : —

consid[r] whith there be no havock made of Brotherly love amongst you. For Brethn to be like two flints that they can never meet but they must strike fire togeth, becaus neith part wil yield a little or condescend y[t] they might gain upon each oths infirmity by a sp't of meeknes ! for Brethn to be so estranged y[t] they know not how to fast & pray togeth for common mercys; for Brethn to interpre[te] every word & action of one anoth to y[e] worst sence, to make mountains of mole hils & think evry smal greevance intollerable ! for Brethn to intrmeddle with strife y[t] belongs not to them, as if there were not jarrs enough already ! for Brethn to censure one another for their private communications & actings w[ch] they y[t] censure cannot be privy too, & out of a spirit of jelousy to conclude y[t] such was their carriage in such a private or secret p[r]ceeding, because it use to be such at oth times ! for Brethn to giue one anoth y[e] ly & provoke one anoth in their speeches as becometh not men, much less christians ! for Brethn to be so incesed agst each oth that they cannot liue togeth in a Town ! For Brethn whilest y[e] Lord hath some und[r] y[e] rod and all [under] his frown ! to be quarrelling at such a time . . . Brethn you add affiction to y[e] afflicted by such things; you need not ask then what keeps me weak so long.[2]

A little more than a year later, his troubles had so increased that he had " thoughts of a jo[r]ney to Rowley . . . to advise about my own health & laying down my work." Difficulties from within and without thickened around the poor teacher. The quakings of conscience matched the weakness and pain of his body; a sick wife added to his cares, and the troubles of the church increased.

That an antagonism existed between Mr. Wigglesworth and Joseph Hills is apparent. Its probable cause was in the Matthews troubles; and the course of the teacher, whatever may have been his motives, seems not to have been such as to cause it to pass away. Unfavorable allusions to Mr. Matthews fell upon sensitive ears. The " fears of m[r] Hills judgem[t] about baptism," which had beset the preacher in 1657, were not forgotten nor allowed to fall asleep. At length, in November or December, 1659, Mr. Hills was indicted by the grand jury for his false beliefs. There is still preserved a paper, written by Mr. Wigglesworth, in which the substance of the offence of Mr. Hills is clearly stated. Little cause may be found therein, to-

[2] *Mass. Hist. So. Proc.* May, 1871, 96.

day, for the teacher's fears. Perhaps little would he have found had a healthier body or a less distempered mind been found among his possessions. Mr. Hills may have held to some of the unfortunate teachings of Marmaduke Matthews: that he was tinctured with some of the peculiar doctrines of his friend Henry Dunster, the former President of Harvard College, is very clear. The charges, as written by Mr. Wigglesworth, are interesting as showing how little could offend "a shining light and faithful pillar" of the colonial church.

The perticulars : as my memory prompd them to my pen.

1. That all Baptized persons, are already ch: members, as being vnder the badge of the cov^t & the free donation thereof. (or to y^t effect)

2. That such are to be called upon to renew there Cov^t wth God, & so doeing to be admitted to all ch: priviledges; except they be of a scandalous life. (or to y^{is} effect)

3. That such being scandalous (openly) the ch: should deale with y^m & censure them, if obstinate

4. That they professing they haue sinned ; or saying it Repent them : promising reformation, & renuing there Cov^t : this should in charity suffice for there Reacceptance. (or to y^t effect)

5. That the Gathering or Constituting of churches is Humane. (or to the same effect.)

6. That the Declaration, or Relation of the worke of Grace (as is required of them, that desire Admission) is not requisite : (or to ye same effect)

7. That Baptized persons, as who are vnder the badge of the cov^t doe clayme there right in ch: priviledges. (or to y^{is} effect)

[And some such, haue ben, either directly or indirectly stirred up by him, so to doe. (as J am enformed.)]

8. That members of one church, are members of an other church & ought not to be debarred the priviledges of members. (w^h hee expounds, according to the largest size of the congregational way, as to my vnderstanding)

9. That L^n of Recpmmendation, & there renuing of Cov^t (to use his owne phrase) is all that in poynt of order, need be required. (or to y^{is} effect.)

10. That we cannot expect good times, till there be a Reformation of the Churches : & tis to be desired, the Magistrate did promote it. (or to the same effect)[8]

---

[8] *Midd. Court Files*, December, 1659. He was one of the overseers of Dunster's The connection of Joseph Hills with will. President Dunster is elsewhere noticed.

In the time of these outward difficulties and in the midst of mental uncertainties and bodily weaknesses he records in his diary: —

Dec. 21, [1659,] about 2 of ye clock in ye morning I received word y^t my wife was dead. Oh its a heart-cutting & astonishing stroke in itself. Lord help me to bear it patiently & to p^rfit by it, help me to hono^r thee now in ye fiers, by maintaining good thoughts of thee, & speaking good & submissive words concern. thee. and oh teach me to dy every day. fit me for y^t sweet society she is gone unto, w^r solitarines shal no more affright or afflict me. Oh Lord make up in thyself w^t is gone in ye creature. I believe y^u canst & wilt do it: but oh help my unbelief.

After this his bodily weaknesses, the nature of which is imperfectly known, increased;[4] and there are evidences that the few faint signs of the " presence of God's spirit " in the church and among the people disappeared. He had written in 1658: —

How long, Lord, wilt thou be angry wth us? What? for ever! oh what will y^u do with this poor sinful afflicted people? what meaneth ye heat of this great indignation? where is thy zeal & thy strength; ye sounding of thy bowels (Lord!) are they restrained? oh Return for

---

[4] Dr. McClure, who, perhaps, had some papers relating to Wigglesworth on which to base his assertion, says he was troubled "apparently by some pulmonary complaint, perhaps the asthma." Mr. Dean gathered together "the various notices of his disease and his feelings," and submitted them to several physicians. Samuel A. Green, M.D., of Boston, says : " I am sorry that I cannot make out a *diagnosis,* as physicians call it. I have shown your case to several, all of whom agree that the data are not sufficient to warrant an accurate conclusion." Ebenezer Alden, M.D., of Randolph, "thinks it evident that he had the asthma; but says, that the asthma will not account for all his symptoms." Cf. Dean, *Wigglesworth,* 61–62; *Bi-Centennial Book,* 153.

The data, however, which Mr. Dean submitted to these authorities were gathered from the later volume of the diaries. Mr. Wigglesworth, himself, refers more definitely to his condition in the earlier volume in the library of the Massachusetts Historical Society. The extracts which I have already given show that a great susceptibility to colds and their consequent evils was a prominent feature in his case. He frequently complains of being troubled by the spleen; and his almost continual melancholy favors the surmise that he may have suffered from *hypochondriasis,* induced perhaps by dyspepsia or some similar evil. As early as 1653⁄, as we have seen, he found a "weakn: of body & pressure by ye sple^n & flatulent humo^rs." In February, 1654⁄, while troubled about the illness of his wife, he writes : "The next day ye spleen much enfeebled me, & setting in wth grief took away my strength, my heart was smitte^n w^th^in me, & as sleep dep^rted fro^m myne eyes so my stomach abhorred meat. J was brought very low."

thy servants sake, the people of thy holynes have possessed these ordinances, these priviledges but a little while.[5]

In December, 1661, there appears to have been a wish among
some of his people that he should " lay down " his office.   An
entry made in his Diary at this time seems as a wail drawn from
the very depths of a heart discouraged and broken.

The Breth[n] are now below consid'ing & consulting about a future supply & a constant help in y[e] ministry ; as also wheth I am call'd to lay
down my place or not. ffath I leav my self & all my concernm[ts] with
thee ; I h. neith way of subsistence, nor house to put my head in if
turnd out here, but Lord I desire to be at thy disposing. Let thy
fathly care app[r] tow'ds me in these my straits, as hith'to it hath done, O
my God : ffor oth[r] friend or helper besides thee I have none.   Lord I
beleev ; help my unbeleif."

A few weeks later he wrote : —

y[e] world seem now to account me a burden (I mean divers of o[r]
chief ones) w[t] ever their words p'tend to y[e] contrary. Lord be thou my
habitation & hiding place ; for oth I have none.   Do thou stand my
friend, w[n] all oth friends fail me, as they are now like to do.   I will not
torm' my self wth feares concern. y[e] future ; for I know thou art alsuffi-
cient, & canst eith p'vide for me in my weakn. or recov[r] me out of my
weakness by a word after all means used to no purpose, or els thou
canst make me welcome in Heaven w[n] y[e] world is weary of me.   Lord
und'take for me for mine eys are unto thee.   Tibi Domine &c.

As Mr. Wigglesworth continued in Malden, it seems likely
that some help and " a future supply" was the result of the con-
sultation of the brethren.   That he was obliged to forego his
pulpit duties in a great measure is evident, although he may
have preached at times.   It was now, as " David's affliction
bred us many a Psalm," that the Malden teacher's " Affliction
turn'd his Pen to Poetry ; "[6] and he began to write as a means
by which he might, as he expressed it, " serv my Lord christ
who is my best & onely friend & supporter."   Cotton Mather
says of him at this time : —

---

[5] *Mass. Hist. So. Proc.* May, 1871,
94.   A year later he records in his
diary : "June 15, [1659] This being a
day of humiliation ; we are to consider
seriously & labo[r] to find out y[e] causes
of gods contending wth us."

[6] J. Mitchel in lines prefixed to the
Day of Doom.

That he might yet more *Faithfully* set himself to Do Good, when he could not *Preach*, he *Wrote* several Composures, wherein he proposed the Edification of such Readers, as are for Truth's dressed up in a *Plain Meeter.*[1]

The Day of Doom:

OR, A

DESCRIPTION

Of the Great and Laſt

Judgment.

WITH

A SHORT DISCOURSE

ABOUT

ETERNITY.

Ecclef. 12. 14.

*Por God ſhall bring every work into Judgment,
with every ſecret thing, whether it be good,
or whether it be evil.*

LONDON,

Printed by *W.G.* for *John Sims*, at the *Kings*
Head at *Sweetings Alley-end* in *Cornhill*,
next Houſe to the *Royal-Exchange*, 1673.

His first published work was the dismal and celebrated *Day of Doom*, that "grim utterance of the past," which has passed through at least ten editions and which gained an instant and

[1] *A Faithful Man*, 24.

long enduring popularity, unequalled by any book published in America before 1800. If we except the *Latin Accidence* of Wigglesworth's master, the famous Ezekiel Cheever, and the *New England Primer*, no volume from the colonial press attained so great a circulation. Professor Tyler cites the fact of the rapid sale of the first edition of eighteen hundred copies " within a single year, which implies the purchase of a copy of the *Day of Doom* by at least every thirty-fifth person then in New England, — an example of the commercial success of a book never afterward equalled in this country."[8]

Of the time of the preparation of the *Day of Doom* and its first appearance, we are not without evidence. The Diary or Commonplace-book, of the author indicates that it was begun as early as January, 166½, and it must have been published during the following summer; for he tells us that "there were scarce any unsold (or but few) at yᵉ yeers end, so that I was a gainer by them, & not a loser; " and it appears that "yᵉ first impression " was sold before September 23, 1663. "About 4 yeers after," he writes, " they were reprinted wᵗʰ my consent, & I gave them the proofs & Margin. notes to affix." Of these editions, the first and second, no perfect copy is known to exist; but there is in the library of the New England Historic Genealogical Society a fragment, which is proved by a peculiarity of certain letters and the absence of " proofs & Margin. notes " to be of the first edition. From this unique copy, so far as it affords them, I have made the quotations in the present chapter.[9]

Of the great popularity of this " Composure," mention has been made. It was " hawked about the country printed on sheets like common ballads." Cotton Mather said that it " may perhaps find our Children, till the *Day* itself arrive."[10]   Fran-

---

[8] *History of American Literature*, ii. 34.

[9] This fragment contains the entire poem from the sixty-third verse, and the first twenty-one verses of the *Short Discourse on Eternity*. A perfect copy of the third (London, 1673) edition is in " *the* New-England-*Library*," of the Rev. Thomas Prince, now deposited in the

Boston Public Library. Dean, *Wigglesworth*, 140–148, gives notices and collations of the several editions, of which the last is that of William Henry Burr, New York, 1867; and Dr. Samuel A. Green has a bibliographical notice of the first five editions in *Mass. Hist. So. Proc.* January, 1895, 269–275.

[10] *A Faithful Man*, 24.

cis Jenks, writing in 1828, informs us that aged persons of his acquaintance could still repeat its verses which had been taught them with their catechisms.[11]

Of the estimation in which it was held, both by the learned and unlearned of colonial and provincial New England, there is no lack of proof. The secret of its power was not in musical versification nor pleasing rhyme; for it is rude and rugged to the extreme, and is but seldom relieved by smoother or more melodious strains. It is quaint and grim, and uncompromising in its directness and logical strength. And yet, with all its roughness and crudities, in spite of its cheap and clattering rhymes, there come forth at times images and thoughts which prove its author, with all his limitations, to have been at the bottom a poet whose Muse under circumstances more favorable and with taste and thoughts refined by a larger companionship with the great singers who had preceded him, of whom he appears to have known little, might have sung in fitting strains words and thoughts of beauty, which would have had a place in the world's mind forever. A recent writer has said: "There was in him the genius of a true poet; his imagination had an epic strength, — it was courageous, piercing, creative; his pages are strewn with many unwrought ingots of poetry." *But*, " he was himself forever incapable of giving utterance to his genius — except in a dialect that was unworthy of it." [12]

His biographer says:

There are passages in his writings which are truly poetical, both in thought and expression, and which show that he was capable of attaining a higher position as a poet than can now be claimed for him. The roughness of his verses was surely not owing to carelessness nor to indolence, for neither of them were characteristic of the man. The true explanation may be that he sacrificed his poetic taste to his theology, and that for the sake of inculcating sound doctrine he was willing to write in halting numbers.[13]

As for the poem itself, which was Mr. Wigglesworth's masterpiece, it is the true embodiment of all that was terrible in the

[11] *Christian Examiner*, vi. 537. [13] Dean, *Wigglesworth*, 131.
[12] Tyler, *History of American Literature*, ii. 23.

theology of the seventeenth century.   Its subject and its
earnestness place it far above the region of the grotesque;
and he who reads it aright can approach it with neither sarcasm
nor ridicule. It is a horrible nightmare, which we of the present,
with more generous views of the relationship between God and
man, can hardly understand.   There is no attempt to gloss the
description of that which the author felt to be true, and the
simple directness and force of its awful realism must have made
naked sinners quake with fear.   The late Joseph T. Bucking-
ham relates that in his youth certain passages caused him
" many an hour of intense mental agony." [14]   In this complete
utterance of the belief and fears of Puritanic New England lies
the secret of the great popularity of the *Day of Doom*.

There is a perfect calm and a sense of security in the opening
of the " Composure."

> Still was the night, Serene and bright,
>   when all Men sleeping lay;
> Calm was the season, and carnal reason
>   thought so 'twould last for ay.
> Soul, take thine ease, let sorrow cease,
>   much good thou hast in store:
> This was their Song, their Cups among,
>   the Evening before.

But suddenly the whole world is awakened by " the sudden-
ness, Majesty, and Terror of Christ's appearing."

> For at midnight brake forth a Light
>   which turn'd the night to day,
> And speedily an hideous cry
>   doth all the World dismay.
> Sinners awake, their hearts do ake,
>   trembling their loynes surprizeth;
> Amaz'd with fear, by what they hear,
>   each one of them ariseth.
>
> They rush from Beds with giddy heads,
>   and to their windows run,
> Viewing this light which shines more bright
>   than doth the Noon-day Sun.
> Straightway appears (they see 't with tears)
>   the Son of God most dread;
> Who with his Train comes on amain
>   to Judge both Quick and Dead.

[14] *Personal Memoirs*, i. 19.

Then is there great fear and confusion. "The Mountains smoak, the Hills are shooke, the Earth is rent and torn;" and "The Judge draws nigh, exalted high upon a lofty Throne;" while

> His brightness damps heav'ns glorious lamps,
> and makes them hide their heads,
> As if afraid, and quite dismay'd,
> they quite their wonted steads.

In the midst of this great brightness and woe, the last Trump sounds and the dead are raised; while all the living, becoming immortal, "are made to dy no moe."

> His winged Hosts flie through all Coasts,
> together gathering
> Both good and bad, both quick and dead,
> and all to Judgement bring.
> Out of their holes those creeping Moles,
> that hid themselves for fear,
> By force they take, and quickly make
> before the Judge appear.

Then takes place the last great and terrible Day of Judgment, when the sheep and the goats are separated and stand "before the Throne of Christ the Judge." It is not upon the happy state of the blessed that the author lavishes his choicest work, but upon the terrors and punishments of the damned.

> With dismall chains and strongest reins,
> like Prisoners of Hell,
> They're held in place before Christ's face,
> till He their Doom shall tell.
> These void of tears, but fill'd with fears,
> and dreadful expectation
> Of endless pains, and scalding flames,
> stand waiting for Damnation.

Sinners of all grades and conditions — civil, honest men, ignorant men, fearful men, as well as hypocrites and transgressors of a deeper dye — make up the crowds of the wicked who "are brought to the Bar, like guilty Malefactors."

> Of wicked Men, none are so mean
> as there to be neglected:
> Nor none so high in dignity,
> as there to be respected.

Of these trembling sinners "At this sad season, Christ asks a Reason (with just Austerity),"

Why still Hell-ward, without regard,
    they boldly ventured,
And chose Damnation before Salvation
    when it was offered?
Why sinful pleasures and earthly treasures
    like fools they prized more
Then heav'nly wealth Eternal health
    and all Christ's Royal store?

The hypocrites characteristically appear foremost to "plead for themselves"; and their unfortunate companions of all degrees follow their example. But in vain are all glosses and extenuating pleas; for "The Judge replyeth," and they are cut short by a relentless logic, before which their pleadings become as cobwebs and are rent in twain.

Thus all mens Plea's the Judge with ease
    doth answer and confute,   -
Untill that all, both great and small,
    are silenced and mute.
Vain hopes are cropt; all mouthes are stopt,
    sinners have nought to say,
But that 'tis just, and equal most
    they should be damn'd for ay.

"Behold," adds the author in a marginal note in a later edition, "the formidable estate of all the ungodly as they stand hopeless and helpless before an impertial Judge, expecting their final Sentence."

"Others Plead for Pardon both from Gods mercy and Justice;" but "Mercy now shines forth in the vessels of Mercy, the wicked [are] all convinced & put to silence, [and] the Judge pronounceth the Sentence of condemnation."

Ye sinfull wights, and cursed sprights,
    that work Iniquity,
Depart together from me for ever,
    to endless Misery.
Your portion take in that sad Lake
    where Fire and Brimstone flameth :
Suffer the smart which your desert
    as it's due wages claimeth.

They wring their hands, their caitiff-hands,
    and gnash their teeth for terrour:
They cry, they rore for anguish sore,
    and gnaw their tongues for horrour.
But get away without delay;
    Christ pitties not your cry:
Depart to Hell; there may you yell
    and roar Eternally.

Perhaps the hardest case of all is that of " Reprobate Infants,"

> who dy'd in Infancy.
> And never had or good or bad
> effected pers'nally;

who are involved in the condemnation of the ungodly, solely by the force of the guilt of Adam. " How could we sin," they cry,

> How could we sin who had not bin?
> or how is his sin our
> Without consent, which to prevent
> we never had a pow'r?

These infant wights plead with an earnestness and force worthy of older sinners; but "Their Arguments [are] taken off" by a reasoning which, though, to us, contradictory in the extreme, is a concise statement of that doctrine of Adam's fall and infant damnation which still, perhaps, holds a place in darkened corners of the Church.

> Then answered the Judge most dread;
>   God doth such doom forbid,
> That men should dy eternally
>   for what they never did.
> But what you call old *Adam's* Fall,
>   and onely his Trespas.
> You call amiss to call it h.s :
>   both his and yours it wzs.
> .   .   .   .
> Had you been made in *Adam's* stead,
>   you would like things have wrought;
> And so into the self-same wo
>   your selves and yours have brought.

In the end, the inexorable Judge cuts short all pleas, declaring

> A crime it is; therefore in blis
>   you may not hope to dwell :
> But unto you I shall allow
>   the easiest room in Hell.
> The glorious King thus answering,
>   they cease, and plead no longer:
> Their Consciences must needs confes
>   his Reasons are the stronger.

It is refreshing to know that the unfortunate babies are able to weigh conscience and reason, despite their tender age, and are satisfied with the judgment rendered against them; although the sight of Adam, the chief offender,

> Whose sinful Fall hath split us all,
> and brought us to this pass,

sitting on a throne of glory before their eyes, might raise some doubts in their infant minds. We of maturer life and a broader religious faith cannot bring our consciences to confess the justice of the final doom.

If the reader, who rejoices in the light of the nineteenth century, seeks yet farther to know the serious and honest belief of an earnest New England Puritan of the seventeenth century, a few verses, contrasting the fate of the "sinfull wights" with the exalted state of the saints, who "rejoyce to see judgment executed upon the wicked World," may suffice.

> As chaff that's dry, and dust doth fly
> before the Northern wind:
> Right so are they chased away,
> and can no Refuge find.
> They hasten to the Pit of Wo,
> guarded by Angels stout:
> Who to fulfill Christ's holy will
> attend this wicked Rout.
>
> Whom having brought, as they are taught,
> unto the brink of Hell
> (That dismal place far from Christ's face,
> where Death and Darkness dwell:
> Where God's fierce Ire kindleth the fire,
> and Vengeance feeds the flame
> With piles of wood and brimstone flood,
> so none can quench the same.)
>
> With Iron bands they bind their hands
> and cursed feet together,
> And cast them all, both great and small,
> into that Lake for ever.
> Where day and night, without respite,
> they wail, and cry and howl
> For tort'ring pain which they sustain
> in Body and in Soul.
>
> For day and night, in their despight,
> their torment's smoak ascendeth:
> Their pain and grief have no relief,
> their anguish never endeth.
> There must they lye, and never dye;
> though dying every day:
> There must they dying ever ly;
> and not consume away.

Dye fain they would, if dye they could:
  but death will not be had.
God's direful wrath their bodies hath
  For ev'r Immortal made.
They live to lie in miserie,
  and bear eternal wo:
And live they must whil'st God is just,
  that he may plague them so.

. . . .

The Saints behold with courage bold,
  and thankful wonderment,
To see all those that were their foes
  thus sent to punishment:
Then do they sing unto their King
  a Song of endless Praise:
They praise his Name, and do proclaime,
  that just are all his wayes.

Of such material and of such a form was the great New England epic of the seventeenth century. From a subject more vast and terrible than that of the great poem of Milton, which it preceded, the Malden bard evolved a work which shook the religious heart of the Puritan world. Its sulphuric and sombre measures were caught at once upon the lips and sank deep into the minds of a whole people; and its cruel influences, even now, have barely disappeared below the horizon of time to return no more.

"Frightful and blasphemous"[15] though it may seem in the light of a later century, as a recent writer has intimated, we cannot afford to neglect it or to undervalue the part which it bore in the days of the elder New England. It is a part of the history of the past and we may shudder before it or ridicule it; but we must consider it and examine it, if we would become familiar with the religious hopes and fears of our fathers.[16] Happily, it

---

[15] Tyler, *History of American Literature*, ii. 34.

[16] Samuel Kettell, in an article, the historical portion of which is rather of imagination than of fact, says: — "Let not the modern reader turn with disgust from the perusal of his moral sentiments. Repugnant as they may be to our tastes, and grotesque as they appear in an age of refinement, they contributed nevertheless mainly to the formation of that character for unbending integrity, and firmness of resolve, for which we almost venerate the old men who laid the foundation of our republic. Neither let the lover of the sacred nine despise the muse of our author. Homely and coarse of speech as she is, her voice probably sunk into the *hearts* of those who listened to her rude melody, leaving there an impression deeper than any which the numbers of a Byron, a Southey, or a Moore may ever produce." — *Specimens of American Poetry*, i. 36.

is no longer a living thing, having power over the hearts of men. It is now dry bones — a literary curiosity, which has passed so far beyond the range of human interest that, as a literary work, it is a subject neither for criticism nor praise.

Mr. Dean prints a catalogue of the library of Wigglesworth, taken from the inventory in the Middlesex Probate files; and elsewhere he draws attention to its character.[17] The preacher and the physician were consulted in its selection, but the tastes of the poet were set aside. A single volume, that of the sportive and polished Horace — a strange companion for the austere Puritan — relieved the sombre array of theology and mediæval science.

I cannot agree with those who have written of Wigglesworth that he borrowed nothing and that his verses show no indications of an acquaintance with those who had sung before him. In one of his most melodious flights he cries: —

> O Heaven, most holy place
> Which art our country dear !
> What cause have I to long for thee,
> And Beg with many a tear.
> Earth is to me a Prison;
> This Body an useless weight :
> And all things else vile, vain, and nought,
> To one in such ill plight.[18]

He has a dull ear and a duller perception who does not find here, both in spirit and form, an echo of that fine old hymn of the ages, that product of the piety and love of Hildebert, of Peter Damian, and of Davie Dickson — the New Jerusalem.

> O Mother dear, Jerusalem !
> When shall I come to thee ?
> When shall my sorrows have an end —
> Thy joys when shall I see ?
> O happy harbour of God's saints !
> O sweet and pleasant soil !
> In thee no sorrows can be found,
> No grief, no care, no toil.

Similar indications may be found in other parts of the same volume, especially in the second part, entitled, *Riddles Unriddled.*

---

[17] Dean, *Wigglesworth*, 129, 151-152. [18] *Meat Out of the Eater*, Meditation V., v. 9.

Donald G. Mitchell, in his *English Lands, Letters, and Kings,* has drawn my attention to the possible indebtedness of Wigglesworth to Thomas Dekker (1568–1640) whose *Dreame of the Last Judgement* may have suggested the *Day of Doom.* It is, as Mr. Mitchell remarks, " as if this New England poet of fifty years later may have dipped his brush into the same paint-pot." Compare this passage of Dekker with similar passages in the work of Wigglesworth.

> Their cries, nor yelling did the Judge regard,
> For all the doores of Mercy up were bar'd :
> Justice and Wrath in wrinkles knit his forhead,
> And thus he spake : You cursed and abhorred,
> You brood of Sathan, sonnes of death and hell,
> In fires that still shall burne, you still shall dwell ;
> In hoopes of Iron : then were they bound up strong,
> (Shrikes being the Burden of their dolefull song.)

While the *Day of Doom* was passing through the press, Mr. Wigglesworth wrote another " Composure " entitled, *God's Controversy with New-England, written in the time of the great drought Anno* 1662, *by a Lover of New-England's Prosperity.* This poem remained unpublished and unknown until 1850, when it came into the hands of the Rev. Alexander W. McClure, who was then preparing his portion of the *Bi-Centennial Book of Malden,* in the pages of which parts of it were printed. It then disappeared from sight, and eager inquiries and a wide search failed to discover its hiding place until 1871, when, with other papers, it came into the possession of the Rev. Thomas J. Greenwood, formerly of the First Parish, who presented it to the Massachusetts Historical Society, in whose *Proceedings* it was printed in full.

It was written in a year of discouragements and troubles and its author found full scope for his peculiar powers. In England the Puritan cause had failed and the Stuarts had returned; and the cruel Act of Uniformity was driving faithful and pious men, like Marmaduke Matthews, into exile abroad or want at home. Political ruin to the colonies was imminent, and the day of their liberties seemed almost at an end. Besides these, canker worms, that ancient as well as modern pest, had devoured the foliage of the trees and destroyed their fruits, and a great drought, threat-

ening pestilence and famine, pervaded New England and much
sickness prevailed.   Then first appeared that dread disease, the
croup, which has never since been absent from the land.   All
these woes are characteristically referred to the wickedness and
unthankfulness of the people; and the poet, after drawing a
lively picture of the prosperity and decline of New England,
introduces the Almighty, who rates and threatens the ungodly
generation in good set terms, concluding with a menace of physical annihilation.

> Now therefore hearken and encline yor ear,
> In judgement I will henceforth with you plead;
> And if by that you will not learn to fear,
> But still go on a sensuall life to lead:
> I'le strike at once an All-Consuming stroke;
> Nor cries nor tears shall then my fierce intent revoke.

Then begins the punishment — the pleading judgment, in the
vivid description of which we may see the burnt fields of New
England and the afflicted households of " last Autumn and this
spring."

> Thus ceast his Dreadful-threatning voice
>   The High & lofty-One.
> The Heavens stood still Appal'd thereat;
>   The Earth beneath did groane:
> Soon after I beheld and saw
>   A mortall dart come flying:
> I lookt again, & quickly saw
>   Some fainting, others dying.
>
> The Heavens more began to lowre,
>   The welkin Blacker grew:
> And all things seemed to forebode
>   Sad changes to ensew.
> From that day forward hath the Lord
>   Apparently contended
> With us in Anger, and in Wrath:
>   But we have not amended.
>
> Our healthfull dayes are at an end,
>   And sicknesses come on
> From yeer to yeer, becaus o^r hearts
>   Away from God are gone.
> New-England, where for many yeers
>   You scarcely heard a cough,
> And where Physicians had no work,
>   Now finds them work enough.
>
> Now colds and coughs, Rhewms, and sore-throats,
>   Do more & more abound:
> Now Agues sore & Feavers strong
>   In every place are found.

How many houses have we seen
  Last Autumn, and this spring,
Wherein the healthful were too few
  To help the languishing.

One wave another followeth,
  And one disease begins
Before another cease, becaus
  We turn not from our sins.
We stopp our ear against reproof,
  And hearken not to God:
God stops his ear against o' prayer,
  And takes not off his rod.

Our fruitful seasons have been turnd
  Of late to barrenness,
Sometimes through great and parching drought,
  Sometimes through rain's excess.
Yea now the pastures & corn fields
  For want of rain do languish:
The cattell mourn, & hearts of men
  Are fill'd with fear & anguish.

The clouds are often gathered,
  As if we should have rain:
But for o' great unworthiness
  Are scattered again.
We pray & fast, & make fair shewes,
  As if we meant to turn:
But whilst we turn not, God goes on
  Our field, & fruits to burn.

And burnt are all things in such sort,
  That nothing now appears,
But what may wound our hearts with grief,
  And draw foorth floods of teares.
All things a famine do presage
  In that extremity,
As if both men, and also beasts,
  Should soon be done to dy.

This O New-England hast thou got
  By riot, & excess:
This hast thou brought upon thy self
  By pride & wantonness.
Thus must thy worldlyness be whipt.
  They, that too much do crave,
Provoke the Lord to take away
  Such blessings as they have.

We have been also threatened
  With worser things then these:
And God can bring them on us still,
  To morrow if he please.
For if his mercy be abus'd,
  Which holpe us at our need
And mov'd his heart to pitty us,
  We shall be plagu'd indeed.

Beware, O sinful Land, beware;
    And do not think it strange
That sorer judgements are at hand,
    Unless thou quickly change.
Or God, or thou, must quickly change;
    Or else thou art undon:
Wrath cannot cease, if sin remain,
    Where judgement is begun.

Ah dear New England! dearest land to me;
    Which unto God hast hitherto been dear,
And mayst be still more dear than formerlie,
    If to his voice thou wilt incline thine ear.

Consider wel & wisely what the rod,
    Wherewith thou art from yeer to yeer chastized,
Instructeth thee. Repent, & turn to God,
    Who wil not have his nurture be despized.

Thou still hast in thee many praying saints,
    Of great account, and precious with fhe Lord,
Who dayly powre out unto him their plaints,
    And strive to please him both in deed & word.

Cheer on, sweet souls, my heart is with you all,
    And shall be with you, maugre Sathan's might:
And whereso'ere this body be a Thrall,
    Still in New-England shall be my delight.[19]

His bodily weaknesses continuing, if not increasing, "After y[e] first impression of my books was sold," Mr. Wigglesworth writes, "I had a great mind to go to Bermuda, and found many incouragers and incouragements thereto." He records that he got together "a pretty compet. estate" to take with him, and that physicians, with the exception of John Winthrop,[20] encouraged him; and "so we set sayl about the 23 of Sept. 1663."

[19] *Mass. Hist. So. Proc.* May, 1871, 83–93.

[20] This was John Winthrop, Jr., son of the Governor of Massachusetts, whom Wigglesworth frequently consulted. He was graduated at Dublin University; and after performing some public service in England, he followed his father to Massachusetts Bay, but soon returned. Coming again in 1635 to New England, under a commission from Lord Say and Sele and others, holding under the patent of Robert Rich, Earl of Warwick, he built a fort, which he called Saybrook, at the mouth of the Connecticut River. He was instrumental in obtaining the charter which united the colonies of Connecticut and New Haven, and was prominent in the affairs of New England for many years. His practice as a physician seems to have followed from his scientific attainments, which were large and which led him to become one of the founders of the Royal Society of London. "Physicians incouraged," wrote Mr. Wigglesworth, "except M Winthrope, whose counsel came too late, nor did his reasons seem sufficient." Several years later he writes: "M[r] Winthrope being consulted, dares not meddle at such a distance."

The voyage was long and tedious, so that he "received much hurt, & got so much cold as took away much of ye benefit of that sweet & temperate air." A sojourn of about seven months and a half did not result in any great improvement of his health; and this, with other unfavorable conditions, was made the ground of a speedy return. After a "short and comfortable" voyage, the Lord brought him home, "in some compet: measure of Health, blessed be his name."

In a season of characteristic moralizing, Mr. Wigglesworth leads us to believe that his removal, if only for a season, was not wholly unwelcome to his discontented flock. He says: —

> Peradventure the Lord removed me for a season, that he might set a better watchman over this his flock, & a more painful labourer in his vineyard. This was one thing that I aimed at in removing (to help the peoples modesty in this case) & I do beleeve that the Lord aimed at it in removing me for a season.

Cotton Mather smooths the matter in another way. "The Kindness of his Tender Flock unto him," he says, "was answered in his Kind concern to have them Served by other Hands."[21] I do not consider this testimony to be of much weight, opposed to the apparent meaning of Mr. Wigglesworth's own words. The younger Mather was sometimes as unreliable as he was bombastic, and his flowers of rhetoric may be found as false as the deceitful vanities of the world, which he habitually bewailed.

The absence of Mr. Wigglesworth may have softened whatever feelings of dislike the people had towards him; or a better state of health, bringing a more cheerful mind, may have caused him to see them and their actions in a clearer light. That some change had taken place is evident, for he writes: —

> I have found more love from the people g^{n}rally (both Church & Town) since my return then I did before, and they have done more for me of their own accord w^n left to their liberty then they had done for some yeers before I went away. And the Lord hath also made me more serviceable to them, at least in a private way, & given more incouragement & success in ye conversion of souls then ever before.

[21] *A Faithful Man,* 23.

What shall I render to y[e] Lord for all his benefits ! How mysterious are his dealings, & his ways unsearchable ! He brings meat out of the Eater. O blessed be thy graci[s] & holy name, most dear Fath !

While Mr. Wigglesworth was in Bermuda, the church and town called a *pastor* to the field which had become for a season without a *teacher*. This was Benjamin Bunker, the second son of George and Judith Bunker of Charlestown, who was born in September, 1635,[22] and was graduated at Harvard College in 1658. Having become a member in full communion of the church at Charlestown, April 29, 1660,[23] he was, according to an entry of the Rev. Samuel Danforth in the records of the First Church of Roxbury, ordained "to y[e] office of a Pastor in Maldon," December 9, 1663.[24] His elder brother, John, had married Hannah Mellows, a stepdaughter of Joseph Hills, who, as has been seen, was the leading supporter of Mr. Matthews; and it is not unlikely that the influence of Mr. Hills may have brought him to Malden, in opposition to Mr. Wigglesworth.

Little is known of Mr. Bunker, either in relation to his character or his attainments. Mr. Savage, falling into error, in one respect at least, remarks : —

That he well filled his post of duty, though never married (as seems to be essential to the character of a New England minister,) we may be confident, for the long and lamentable verses of his senior colleague reveal no tendency to fiction.[25]

---

[22] "[1635] 7 : mo : day 20. Beniamine Buncker the son of George Buncker and of Judith his wife was Babtised." *Records of First Church, Charlestown.*

[23] He was called to the church at Bridgewater; and it is not improbable that he may have preached there between the time of his becoming a church member and his coming to Malden.

"It is *ordered* and Agreed upon by the towne of Bridgewater freely and willingly to give unto Mr. Buncker, if he shall come hether to supply our wants in the way of the ministrey, the sum of thirty pounds, or twenty pounds and his Diet.

"It is Inacted by the Towne the 22d of february, 1660, that a leve should be made for the sume of five and twenty pounds upon every mans estate, which is what they promised to Mr. Bunker for the carriing Along of the Lords days Exercise and his diet before his time or his year is fully expyred." *Bridgewater Records; Mass. Hist. So. Proc.*, July, 1873, 68.

[24] *Report of the [Boston] Record Commissioners,* vi. 201.

[25] *Genealogical Dict.*, i. 298.

That he *was* married is very evident; for his widow, Mary, resided in Malden after his death and afterwards removed to Roxbury, where she was living, January 12, 167⁶⁄₇.

That he occupied the parsonage, I am not sure — it seems likely that he did; for it is supposed that Mr. Wigglesworth had not returned to his former home, but had built himself a small house on the six and a half acres which he owned east of the ministry lands.[26] In 1666 Mr. Bunker bought the house and

[26] Mr. Wigglesworth purchased of Paul Wilson, December 31, 1657, for thirteen pounds, six and one-half acres of land "lying in Mauldon aforesaid, being lately the land of Jno. Lewis now deceased, & was Sometime part of the propper lott of mr Jno. Allen of Charlstowne." *Midd. Co. Deeds*, ii. 161. This land was bounded easterly by James Green; westerly by the ministry land; southerly by the highway to Winnisimmet; and northerly by the common land. Its prior history is related in the conveyance, and its passage from hand to hand had been rapid. Its acquirement by John Allen in the allotment of the two hundred acres of reserved land in 1640 has already been mentioned. Allen sold to Lewis, March 16, 165⁴⁄₇, his twenty acres of land, "more or less," lying south of the common field and east of the land of William Brackenbury and that which the town had purchased of James Green for the use of the ministry. *Midd. Co. Deeds*, ii. 42. John Lewis died in the following September, having, as was afterwards deposed, executed a writing, or deed, by which he conveyed to Paul Wilson his dwelling house, with the five-acre lot upon which it stood, and "his 20 acre lot of land without the common-field, yt was sometimes Mr. John Allens lot." *Deposition of Mary Cutler*, "sometime the wife of John Lewis, late of Mauldon, deceased." *Midd. Co. Deeds*, iii. 204. The land which Mr. Wigglesworth purchased was the northern portion of the twenty acres.

That the title of Wilson to the Lewis property was early considered to be somewhat doubtful is evident. No record of the transfer was ever made, and its documentary evidence could not be produced a few years later, although several witnesses testified, in 1662–63, to its previous existence. As has just been mentioned, Mary Lewis, herself, was a witness in its favor, although, as administratrix, she had sold to James Green a portion of the twenty acres soon after the death of her husband. If any adverse claim was then made, it was allowed to rest for more than thirty years, and was revived in 1695, when Mr. Wigglesworth, by a payment of ten pounds, obtained a quitclaim from the Lewis heirs. *Midd. Co. Deeds*, x. 419.

Here Mr. Wigglesworth built his house, which appears to have been one of no great pretensions or capacity, although it was, somewhat grandiloquently, called a mansion in a release given by Samuel Wigglesworth in 17⁰⁹⁄₁₀. It stood far back from the road to Mystic Side, which then ran in a south-easterly direction from the meeting house and crossed the line of the present Cross Street, near the corner of Hancock Street. On the land at the north-easterly corner of High and Ashland Streets, near the wall which formerly divided the land of David Hutchins from the old ministry lands, traces of the chimney and cellar of the house, and the location of its well could be discerned a few years ago.

For a more convenient way between it and the meeting house, it was voted, March 1, 168⁴⁄₅, "at a publick Town Meeting that mister wigelsworth have a hy way Granted to his house throw the townes land." In 1710, when the way over the town's land became no longer necessary, by reason of the stoppage of the "Stoney Lane," and its removal

land of Ralph Shepard, comprising about fourteen acres lying
north of the parsonage and meeting house lots on both sides of
"the road to Penny Ferry." The house was upon the westerly
side of the road; and the whole property, in some unrecorded
way, afterwards came into the possession of the Rev. Benjamin
Blakeman, by whom eight acres adjoining the house were sold,
February 20, 167⅞, to John Green. The land lying east of the
road was sold to the town soon after and became an addition to
the ministry lands, as has been related. Blakeman's title was
imperfect; and when John Bunker claimed the estate of his uncle,
in 1695, the westerly lot of eight acres was released on the
payment of ten pounds and twelve shillings, and afterwards
remained in the hands of the Green family until their possessions
were invaded and divided in the ruthless march of modern improvement. It was the well-known Bell Rock pasture; but it
did not, however, include the site of the meeting house below
the rock, which was still a portion of the old parsonage estate
in 1898.

northerly to form what has since been
known as Hutchinson's Lane, Peter
Tufts's Lane, and Cross Street, and
when the house had passed into other
hands, it was voted: "That yᵗ vote yᵗ
past formerly and entred upon yᵉ book
Refering to a way ouer The Towns land
To mʳ wigglesworths hous Js Resumed
and made voide."

After the death of Mr. Wigglesworth,
his widow, by virtue of his will, sold his
real estate, comprising seven parcels,
with the house and barn standing upon
the home lot, to John Hutchinson of
Lynn, for eighty-seven pounds. February 28, 170⅚, *Midd. Co. Deeds*, xiv.
151. Hutchinson moved into the house,
where he appears to have lived until
about 1710, when, it proving too small,
and having, perhaps, become out of
repair, he built a new house further to
the southeast and upon the highest part
of the land, by the side of the way
which had just been laid out along the
southerly line of his field. The tragedy
connected with this house and its destruction by fire in 1730 are related elsewhere. The new house of 1730 was

built around the chimney of the old
house, which attracted much attention,
when it was demolished in 1883, by
its size and the peculiarly shaped and
somewhat rudely burned bricks of which
it was composed.

Early in this century, Wigglesworth's
barn was still standing on its original
site. It was then removed to the land
on the east side of the Hutchinson house,
where it withstood the great September
gale of 1815, although a recent addition
was blown down. It was demolished
about the year 1840.

John Hutchinson was a blacksmith
and had his shop near the house. At
his death, August 21, 1762, he left the
shop with his smith's tools and one half
of his real estate to John Tufts, the
son of his deceased daughter, Mary,
who by the death of his spinster aunt
Mehitable, February 13, 1780, came into
the possession of the improvement of
the other moiety. Hutchinson and the
Tuftses added neighboring lands to the
Wigglesworth lot, portions of which
are still in the possession of their
descendants.

As Mr. Wigglesworth's colleague — or neighbor, if the former term be incorrect — whatever may have been the aims of the dissatisfied members of the church, Mr. Bunker appears to have gained the teacher's love and esteem; and the friendship which a companionship of six years had cemented was celebrated by the poet in an elegy, which rebuked the sins of "Maldon," while it praised the departed saint. He died, February 3, 1669/70, and the record styles him "Pastour of the Church of Christ at Mauldon."[27] He must have been buried at Sandy Bank, but no stone marks the spot where his dust returned unto the earth; and his only memorial is the "Composure" of his friend, Michael Wigglesworth.

Upon the much lamented Death of that Precious
servant of Christ, M^r. Benjamin Buncker, pasto^r
of the Church at Maldon, who deceased
on the 3 of ye 12th moneth 1669.

Mr Buncker's Character.

He was another Timothie
  That from his very youth
With holy writt, acquainted was
  And vers't ith' word of truth.
Who as he grew to riper yeers
  He also grew in Grace ;
And as he drew more neer his End,
  He mended still his Pace.

He was a true Nathaniel,
  Plain-hearted Israelite,
In whom appear'd sincerity
  And not a guilefull sp'rite,
Serious in all he went about
  Doing it with his Heart,
And not content to put off Christ
  With the eternall part.

He was most sound and Orthodox,
  A down-right honest Teacher,
And of soul-searching needfull Truths
  A zealous, painfull Preacher.
And God his pious Labours hath
  To many hearers blest,
As by themselves hath publiquely
  Been owned & confest.

He hath in few yeers learned more,
  And greater progress made
In Christianity, then some
  That thrice the time have had.
A humble, broken-hearted man
  Still vile in his own eyes
That from the feeling of his wants
  Christ's Grace did highly prize.

---

[27] His estate, the inventory of which was taken by John Wayte, Thomas Lynde, and John Sprague, amounted to £421 4s. 6d. in personal and real estate, including books to the amount of £17 16s. 6d., which were appraised by Mr. Wigglesworth. *Midd. Probate Files.* The latter portion of the inventory is interesting, as being a list of books, which were selected by one who seems to have been a scholar as well as a preacher. As a private library of the present day it might be considered as being rather heavy, although it contained a goodly share of mental nutriment both in the classics and divinity.

Still thirsting to obtain more full ;
    Assurance of God's Love :
And striving to be liker Christ
    And to the Saints above.
Although he was endu'ed with Gifts
    And Graces more then many's ;
Yet he himself esteemed still
    More poor & vile then any.

In fruitless, empty, vain discourse,
    He took no good content :
But when he talk't of Heav'nly things,
    That seem'd his element.
There you might see his heart, & know
    What was his greatest Pleasure,
To speak & hear concerning Christ
    Who was his onely Treasure ;

His constant self-denying frame,
    To all true saints his love,
His meekness, sweetness, Innocence
    And spirit of a Dove,
Let there be graven on our hearts
    And never be forgot.
The name of precious saints shall live,
    When wicked mens shall rot.

==========

O Maldon, Maldon thou hast long
    Enjoy'd a day of Grace ;
Thou hast a precious man of God
    Possessed in this place :
But for thy sin, thou art bereft
    Of what thou did'st possess ;
Oh let thy sins afflict thee more
    Then do thy wants thee press.

Great strokes, Great Anger do proclaime,
    Great Anger, Greater sins.
We first provoke, before the Lord
    To punish us begins.
Good Lord awaken all our hearts
    By this most solemn stroke
To search for, find oute, and forsake
    Our sins that thee provoke

Awake, awake, secure hard hearts ;
    Do you not hear the Bell
That for your Pastours Funerall
    Soundeth a dolefull Knell ?
You that would never hear nor heed
    Th' instructions that he gave,
Me-thinks you should awake & learn
    One lesson at his Grave.

Repent, Repent, It 's more then time
    The Harvest's well nigh past,
And Summer ended : but thy soul
    Not saved, first nor last.
The Belows they are burnt with fire,
    The Instruments are gone,
But still thy Lusts are unconsumed :
    Read then thy Portion ;

If that the ffounder melts in vain
    (Thy lusts do not decay)
God will account thee worthless Dross
    Fit to be cast away.
Since words could not awaken us,
    God tries what blowes can do :
He strikes us on the head, & makes
    Us stagger to and fro.

Much more I might have said, but
    Time
Will not the same permit.
Come let us put our mouths in Dust
    And down in Ashes sit.
The Lord hath giv'n us Gall to drink,
    And laid us in the Dust :
What shall we say ? Behold we're vile,.
    But thou, O Lord, art just.

If this, and such like awfull strokes
    Do not our hearts awaken,
Doubtless the Gospel will ere long
    Be wholly from us taken.
If we repent, return to God,
    Esteem his Gospel more
Improve it better : then the Lord
    Hath mercies yet in store [28]

---

[28] This elegy, copied from the autograph original in the library of the New England Historic Genealogical Society, *Ewer MSS.* i. 8, has been printed in the *Puritan Recorder*, Oct. 11, 1855 ; in the *Malden Messenger*, April 4, 1857 ; and in the *N. E. Hist. and Geneal. Register*, xxvi. 11. In the latter publication was printed, at the same time, an earlier poem of Mr. Wigglesworth, which apparently alludes to the condition of the New England churches at that time. The halfway covenant, which was sharply assailed and advocated in Massachusetts from 1659 until long after its adoption by the celebrated synod of 1662, was evidently in the mind of the author when he wrote the first two verses.

We must infer, from several indications, that when Mr. Wigglesworth returned from Bermuda his physical condition prevented him from taking any very active part in the ministry. Several years after he wrote: —

My bodily weaknesses evidently increase & grow upon me; especially that old Malady that annoys me most by night. And what fear & distress it often (yea ever & anon) puts me into, Lord thou knowest, For my sighs & groanings (with my tears) are not hid from thee. By thine immediate hand it hath hitherto been quelled and restrained, when all ye means y^t I can think off are of no force. But still it continueth, & my bondage is greatly increased by reason of it, having no means nor medicine that yields any releef.

Cotton Mather speaks of him as one "that had been for near Twenty years almost *Buried Alive.*" [29] It was about this time that, medicines having failed him, he "spent much time & Labor in studying & seeking after what might be helpful." He adds: —

But yet, I find no releefe in any thing, but am forced to look immediately to the Lord for help, & blessed be his name he hath many & many a time wonderfully and graciously answered me : & rebuked it for me. [30]

"When as the wayes of Jesus Christ
  Are counted too precise,
Not onely by some Babes or ffooles,
  But also by the wise :
When men grow weary of the yoke
  Of godly discipline,
And seek to burst those golden barres
  Which doe their lusts confine.

"When some within, and some without,
  Kick down the Churches wall
Because the doore is found to be
  Too strait to let in all :
The best can then nought else expect
  But to be turned out,
Or to be trampled under foot
  By the unruly rout."

[29] *A Faithful Man,* 24.
[30] He had at this time to bemoan the loss of Dr. John Alcock, H. C., 1646, who practised at Boston, where he died March 27, 1667. He writes in his diary: "Mr. Alcock is gone, whose plaister was heretofore of great efficacy for ye repressing it [his disease], w^n more troublesome then ordinary. Mr. Winthrope [of New London] being consulted, dares not meddle at such a distance." Later he received an unexpected remedy in relation to which he writes : —

"After much exercise this way & many secret sighs unto ye Lord under the pressure of this & many other infirmities, the Providence of ye Lord hath presented to me & provided for me an unexpected & unknown medicine, a box of Mr. Lockier's pills, (whose booke with some pills my Cosen Reyner met with at his Landlords at Mendham, & signifying to me the high commendations given them by their author, & ye experience of sundry there of good by them, at my request he p^{r}cured me a sight of ye book & a box of the pills for 5^s.) And these pills I am now beginning to take this 19 of March, 1669. Lord, be pleased even beyond expectation to bless them, as thou hast by an unexpected & a strange Providence presented them to me, & provided them for me."

Lockyer died in 1672 and was buried in St. Mary Overies, London, where Judge Sewall saw his monument with this couplet : —

"His virtues and his pills are so well known
  That envy can't confine them under stone."

Out of his experiences with his own infirmities, based, perhaps, on the knowledge which he may have acquired at college
while he intended to follow "y* study & Practise of Physick,"
he came to be often called upon, by his own sympathy and
charity or the importunities of his neighbors, to prescribe for
the bodily ills of others.　Cotton Mather says: —

His long Weakness and Illness, made him an *Able Physician.*　He
studied *Physic;* and was a *Faithful Physician* for the *Body* as well as
the *Soul.*　God made him a *Successful Physician,* & a *Beloved* one.[81]

He continued the practice of medicine, even after he became
himself restored to health and had assumed the full discharge
of all the duties of the pastoral office.　Increase Mather, who
appears to have held him in especial friendship, addressing " the
Church and Congregation at Maldon in New England," after
the death of Mr. Wigglesworth, says: —

Although in some of the Reformed Churches, they do not permit a
Minister of the Gospel to practise as a *Physician,* lest he should thereby
be too much diverted from his Sacred Employments, one of these Call-
ings being ordinarily as much as one man can duly attend ; nevertheless
the Lord enabled *him* to manage both with good Success: so that in
being bereaved of him you have lost an able Physician both for Soul
and Body.　Nor are the People in *Maldon* the only Persons who have
sustained a loss by his Death.[82]

It is said that his visits extended far into the adjoining towns,
which is very probable ; as practitioners were not many in those
days, and the sick were obliged to seek help, beyond the homely
practices of old housewives, at long distances.　Mr. Wigglesworth, himself, sought relief from at least two physicians in Connecticut.　Of his abilities as a leech we have the testimony of
the Mathers, just quoted, and the general reputation in which
he was held.　Samuel Sewall says he was "very useful as a
Physician."[83]　The Balsam of Fennel, a favorite medicine of the

[81] *A Faithful Man,* 25.

[82] Dedication to *A Faithful Man.*

[83] *Mass. Hist.Coll.,* xlvi. 133.　Sewall
gives other testimony as to the appreciation of Mr. Wigglesworth's ability
as a physician by himself and others.
"[June 18, 1703,] I sent for Mr. Wigglesworth and his Wife from Deacon
Barnard's in the Coach; to discourse
with my Wife about her and Judith's
Maladies." *Ibid.* 80.　"Aug*. 4, [1703],
I carried Mary to Mr. Wigglesworth's
and left her there; to see if he could
help her against her Sickness and In-

celebrated Dr. Holyoke of Salem, is said to have been prepared from a recipe of Mr. Wigglesworth.[84]

It may be that he received some compensation for the practice of physic and that this, combined with what income he may have received from his books, supported him during the long period of his sickness.[85]　His relationship to the Malden church

firmity. Augt. 6. I visited Mary as I promis'd her. Mr. Wigglesworth thinks her distemper is of a Convulsive nature." ' *Ibid.* 83. "Octob' 14th. 1704. visited Col. Savage. He has kept house 7 weeks. Mr. Wigglesworth came to Town the 9th Inst' and administers to him." *Ibid.* 117.

[84] Mr. Dean, *Wigglesworth*, 128, supposes that "Dr. Holyoke obtained the recipe from Rev. Samuel Wigglesworth, probably while he was studying medicine with Dr. Berry of the neighboring parish of Ipswich." Edward-Stephen, a great-grandson of Mr. Wigglesworth, studied with Dr. Holyoke about the year 1790, and the recipe may have come from him; and, to state another possible means of transmission, it may be mentioned that Dr. Berry, himself, one of the most distinguished practitioners of his time, was a student, after his graduation in 1712, with Dr. Thomas Graves of Charlestown, with whom Samuel Wigglesworth had studied in 1709.

Of the medicine itself it is said: "The article so well known in this place, [Salem], by the name of the 'white balsam drops' or 'fennel balsam,' is a strong solution of sub-carbonate of potass with the addition of a little of the essential oil of sweet fennel, and is a valuable diaphoretic and carminative, especially to children. This was a favorite medicine during his whole practice. He obtained his first knowledge of it from a Mr. Wigglesworth of Malden." *Memoir of Edward A. Holyoke, M.D., LL.D.* (Boston, 1829). 20-21.

The recipe is as follows:—

"*Balsam of Fennel.* Take equal parts of Cream Tartar (or, which will answer as well, of White Tartar, if it be very good,) and common Nitre, let them be reduced in a mortar to a fine powder and thoroughly mixed together; put them into a flat vessel and place it in a chimney, set it on fire by putting into it a small live coal or a red hot iron, when the deflagration is finished and the cake of salt is cool enough to handle, take it out and with a knife scrape off all the black part, and powder it in a mortar; it will be found reduced in weight one full half. Put the powdered salt into a glass vessel capable of containing three times its quantity, add pure water to it by an ounce or two at a time, stirring it after every addition of water very briskly with an iron or strong wooden spatula, and adding gradually about ʒiss or ʒij of the chemical Oil of Fennel to each pound weight of the salt. This stirring or violent agitation of the mixture, ought to be frequently repeated for a day or two, after a sufficient quantity of water has been added, which will be when a quantity nearly equal to the salt is added.

"This Balsam, as it is very improperly called, is a very useful remedy where an alkaline medicine is wanted, particularly for infants, or in those cases in which acidity is predominant in the stomach, and is diaphoretic and diuretic." *Ibid.*, 68-69.

[85] Mr. Dean thinks it not unlikely that "he may also have gained something, as ministers frequently did, by teaching young men who were preparing for college or the ministry;" and he cites a letter written in 1677, by the Rev. Samuel Hooker, of Farmington, to the Rev. Increase Mather, in relation to the education of his son, in which occur these words: "I hear Mr. Wigglesworth, being at greater leisure than som others (becaus of his rare preaching) is thought a man very Idoneous for such instruction as he needs." Mr. Dean adds: "From this it seems that his health was supposed to be strong enough to enable

is very vague.　Although the constant use of later writers has led us to consider him as the teacher and the second and third pastors as his colleagues, it is not altogether clear that the relationship was not suspended; and the title, if used at all, may have been one of courtesy and not of actual right.　I am altogether persuaded that he was not treated as one who had a continuous claim upon the town and church.　Often have I cause to regret the loss of the early town records, never more than while striving to unravel the confused tangle of ecclesiastical affairs.　What were the original terms of Mr. Wigglesworth's settlement? and who performed the ministerial functions during the four years succeeding Mr. Bunker's death?　Were services held occasionally, as Mr. Wigglesworth's health allowed? or, was another pastor settled here?　The fact of Mr. Bunker's pastorate is only known to us by accidental entries in the Roxbury Church records, by the return of his death to the County Court, and the fortunate preservation of the elegy; otherwise it had been wholly unknown to us, as the settlement of another pastor or assistant may be.

During the pastorate of Mr. Bunker, the pen of Mr. Wigglesworth had not been idle.　In September, 1669, he wrote: —

> I have been long imployed in a great work composing Poems about ye cross.　I have already found exceeding much help & assistance from Heaven, even to admiration, so y^t in 3 weeks time I have transcribed 3 sheets fair, & made between whiles above 100 staves of verses besides.　Some dayes ye Lord hath so asisted me y^t I have made neer or above 20 staves.　For wch his great m'cy I bless his name from my soul, desiring stil to make him my a & ω in This great work.　Lord assist me now this day.　Tu mihi Princ.[*ipium*] tu mihi finis eris. à deo et ad deu^m τα παντα.

To this work, which he completed on his thirty-ninth birthday, October 18, 1669, he gave the following title: *Meat out of*

---

him to teach."　Cf. Dean, *Wigglesworth*, 97; *Mass. Hist. Coll.*, xxxviii. 338.

It is certain that he received some assistance from the contributions of churches other than his own, partly, perhaps, because his condition was necessitous, and partly as a deserved compliment to the author of the *Day of*

Doom.　Mr. Danforth writes: "21. 1^m 6⅝. There was a publick Fast throughout ye Jurisdictson.　This day o^r church made a Collection for m^r Wigglesworth, 4^{lb} 17^s."　*Roxbury Church Records*, in *Report of the* [*Boston*] *Record Commissioners*, vi. 205.

the Eater Or Meditations Concerning The Necessity, End, and Usefulness of Afflictions Unto Gods Children. All tending to Prepare them For, and Comfort them Under the Cross.

MEAT
Out of the
EATER:
O R,
Meditations
Concerning the Neceffity, End, and Ufefulnefs of

𝕬𝖋𝖋𝖑𝖎𝖈𝖙𝖎𝖔𝖓𝖘
U N T O
God's Children.

All tending to Prepare them *For,* and Comfort them *Under* the
C R O S S.

By *Michael Wigglefworth.*
Corrected and Amended by the Author, in the Year 1703.

The Fifth Edition.

Boston, Printed by *J. Allen,* for *Robert Starke,* near the New North Meeting-Houfe. 1717.

It was published soon after. Although it did not attain the great popularity of the *Day of Doom*, it was very successful; and six editions have been published, the last having appeared in 1770. Mr. Dean says: —

Except the *Day of Doom* and the *Bay Psalm Book*, I know of no poetical volume published in New England previous to the Revolution, that has passed through so many editions as *Meat out of the Eater.*[86]

[86] *Wigglesworth,* 84.

It treats of afflictions, trials, and temptations; and "truly," says Dr. McClure, " affliction, which had devoured so many of the good man's dearest joys, was made to disgorge far richer treasures than it took away." [87] Professor Tyler esteems it less. He says : —

Here we have simply the Christian doctrine of comfort in sorrow, translated into metrical jingles.   With nearly all sensitiveness to literary form torpid in New England, and with devout feeling warm and alert, it is not strange that this clumsy but sympathetic poem should have found there a multitude of admirers.   It was first published, probably, in 1669 ; ten years afterward, it had passed through at least four editions ; and during the entire colonial age, it was a much-read manual of solace in affliction.   And indeed, it is such poetry as might still serve that purpose, at least by plucking from the memory, for a moment, a rooted sorrow, and substituting a literary anguish in place of it. [88]

The larger part of the volume has a sub-title — *Riddles Un-riddled, Or Christian Paradoxes Broke open smelling like sweet Spice New taken out of Boxes.*   The paradoxes are enumerated in the following verse, which forms a poetical table of contents or a guide to the " songs and meditations " which follow.

> *Light in Darkness, Sick mens Health,*
> *Strength in Weakness, Poor mens Wealth,*
> *In Confinement, Liberty,*
> *In Solitude, Good Company,*
> *Joy in sorrow, Life in Deaths,*
> *Heavenly Crowns for Thorny Wreaths.*
>
> Are presented to thy view
> In the Poems that ensue.
>
> *If my Trials had been thine*
> *These would cheer thee more than Wine.*

Of the several poems which follow, the fourth song of *Heavenly Crowns for Thorny Wreaths* is perhaps one of the best.   It is a good specimen of Mr. Wigglesworth's versification ; although it lacks the action and realism of the *Day of Doom* which, so far as his genius was able to rise above its limitations, were his strongest points.

---

[87] *Bi-Centennial Book of Malden,* 148.   [88] *Hist. of American Literature,* ii. 27.

(1)

Behold what matchless love
The God of Heaven shows
To those on whom Eternal Life
And Glory he bestows !
If now God calls them Sons ;
How Glorious shall they be,
When being made like Christ they shall
Him in his Glory see ?

(2)

Their Body frail and vile
That's in Corruption sown,
Shall then be raised up again
In Incorruption.
This mortal must be cloath'd
With Immortality :
And then shall Death be swallow'd up
In perfect Victory.

(3)

It is at present sown
A Body Natural :
But shall arise again e're long
A Body Spiritual.
We now need many helps
Our vigor to maintain.
As Meat Drink Sleep : but shall need none
After we rise again.

(4)

It's now in weakness sown ;
But shall be rais'd in power :
Sown in Dishonour : but shall rise
In Glory at that hour.
It shall be wholly freed
From all Infirmities,
And be most active, hale and strong,
When once it doth arise.

(5)

Though subject to reproach
Whilst living ; and when dead
Must needs be carried out of sight,
And quickly buried :
Yet Christ shall raise it up
With beauty shining bright,
More lovely than the morning fair,
With Heavenly Glory dight.

(6)

And if the Body shew
So beautiful and fair :
How shall the Soul be beautify'd
And shine beyond compare ?

Adorn'd with costly Robes,
More precious far than Gold,
Of Christ's unspotted Righteousness
Most lovely to behold.

(7)

When as God's blessed Image
That was defac'd by Sin
Is perfectly restor'd again,
And ever dwells therein
When as it shall behold
God's Glory shining bright,
And be transform'd, and glorious made
By that most glorious sight.

(8)

When like a Glass it shall
Receive those Glorious Rayes,
And back again reflect the same
To God's Eternal Praise.
When in the Sea of Bliss
It constantly shall move :
And be for ever ravish'd with
The sweetness of his Love.

(9)

If *Moses* face did shine
By being forty dayes
I'th mount : How shall their faces shine
That dwell with God always ?
Moses his Back-parts saw,
But they shall see his face ;
And to their joy unspeakable
Enjoy the God of Grace.

(10)

Oh happy, happy Souls,
That in God's Bosome rest !
That of the Fountain of all Bliss
Already are possest !
Your Labour's at an end
Your seed in tears was sown,
But now you reap a joyful Crop,
And wear a Glorious Crown.

(11)

We that are still below
Have much work yet undone.
A War to wage, sharp Thorns to wear,
A painful Race to run.
Lord help us so to run,
As that we may obtain :
That when this Life is at an end
We may in Glory reign.

It does not appear that Mr. Wigglesworth resumed the labors of the pen to any great extent after the publication of *Meat out of the Eater.* The only poem known to have been written by him after this time is that which follows, the author's autograph copy of which is in the possession of Mr. John Ward Dean, his biographer and descendant. The evident allusions to his own case give it an interest which it would not otherwise possess.

Upon ye return of my dear friend Mr Foster
wth his son out of captivity
unde^r ye Moors.[29]

A Song of Praise to keep in remembrance
the loving kindness of ye Lord.

1

Come hither, hearken unto me,
  All ye that God do fear,
And what he hath done for my soul
  I will to you declare.
I to ye Lord fro my distress
  Did cry & he gave ear,
Out of Hell's belly I did cry,
  And he my prayer did hear.

2

I shall not die, but live, and shall
  The works of Jah declare:
The Lord did sorely chasten mee
  Yet mee from death did spare.
O set wide open unto mee
  The gates of righteousness.
I will go into them, & will
  The praise of Jah confess.

---

[29] Captain William Foster of Charlestown, who had married Anne, daughter of William Brackenbury, and sister of the husband of Mercy Wigglesworth, was captured by corsairs, while on a voyage in the "small ship" Dolphin to Bilbao with fish, in the summer or early fall of 1671. His son Isaac, who was probably the one who was taken with him, had just been graduated at Cambridge, at the head of the class of 1671; and he afterwards became the minister of Hartford. He died at the early age of thirty years, August 20, 1682. The captives were redeemed and returned home in November, 1673. Cotton Mather, with his usual love for the marvellous, ascribes their liberation to a miraculous interposition of Providence, caused by a prayer of the Apostle Eliot. He says:—

"There was a godly Gentleman of *Charlestown,* one Mr. *Foster,* who, with his Son was taken Captive by *Turkish* Enemies. Much prayer was employed, both privately and publickly by the good people here, for the Redemption of that Gentleman; but we were at last informed, that the bloody Prince in whose Dominions he was now a Slave, was resolved that in his Life-time *no* Prisoner should be released; and so the Distressed Friends of *this* Prisoner, now concluded, *Our Hope is Lost!* Well upon this, Mr. *Eliot* in some of his next prayers, before a very solemn Congregation, very broadly beg'd, *Heavenly Father, work for the Redemption of thy poor Servant Foster; and if the Prince which detains him will not, as they say, dismiss him as long as himself lives, Lord we pray thee to kill that cruel Prince; kill him, and glorify thyself upon him.* And now behold the answer. The poor Captived Gentleman quickly Returns to us that had been mourning for him as a lost man, and brings us News, that the Prince which had hitherto held him, was come to an *untimely Death,* by which means he was now set at Liberty. Thus we now know, *That a Prophet has been among us.*" Mather, *Life of John Eliot* (1691), 445; Mather, *Magnalia,* iii. Cf. *N. E. Hist. and Geneal. Reg.,* xxv. 67; *American Historical Record,* i. 392–393; *Archæologia Americana,* iii. 231–232; Sibley, *Harvard Graduates,* ii. 336–341.

3

Bless thou the Lord, my soul, & all
  In me, his holy name
Bless thou yᵉ Lord, my soul, & all
  His boundless minde the same.
With me together o do yee
  Jehovah magnify !
And let us all herein agree
  To lift his name on high.

4

The God hee of Salvation is
  That is our God most strong
And to yᵉ Lord Jehovah doth
  Issues of Death belong.
The Right-hand of Jehovah is
  Exalted upon high :
The Right-hand of Jehovah is
  A working valiantly.

5

On Princes poure comtempt doth Hee
  Lays Tyrants in yᵗ dust
Who proudly crush the innocent
  To satisfy their lust.
He breaks yᵉ teeth of cruel Beasts
  That raven for yᵉ prey
Out of yᵉ Lion's bloody jawes
  Hee plucks yᵉ sheep away.

6

Thou broken hast yᵉ iron Barrs
  And loos'd yᵉ fetters strong,
Thou rescu'd hast yᵉ poor-opprest
  From all that did them wrong.
Out of yᵉ Dungeon dark & deep
  Thou hast my soul set free
So long as I a being have
  My praise shall be of thee.

7

How beautiful Jehovah is
  Oh taste, & see likewise
Oh great is that man's blessedness
  Whose trust on him relies !
Upon yᵉ Lord for evermore
  See that yoᵣselves you stay
For there is with Jehovah store
  Of strength yᵗ lasts for ay.

8

Oh love yᵉ Lord all yee his saints
  The faithful he doth guard
But he unto proud doers grants
  A plentyfull reward.
Because yᵉ Lord yᵉ poor doth hear
  Nor's prisoners doth despise
Let Heav'n, earth, sea, him praise, and all
  That moves therein likewise.

Of the second colleague of Mr. Wigglesworth, the Rev. Benjamin Blakeman,[40] we know but little as concerning his connection with the Malden church. He was the youngest son of the Rev. Adam Blakeman of Stratford in the Colony of New Haven, who had been a clergyman of the established church in Leicestershire and Derbyshire. Mather relates that,

Coming to *New-England*, from the Storm that began to look black upon him, he was attended with a desirable Company of the *Faithful*, who said unto him, "*Entreat us not to leave you, or to return from*

---

[40] I style him Reverend, as I call him the colleague of Mr. Wigglesworth, the former in deference to his apparent office, and the latter in deference to what has been the general belief. I cannot perceive that he had a complete right to either title ; for there are indications that he was never ordained ; and, as will be seen, he repeatedly styled himself — not Reverend, or Clerk, as was the custom, but — Gentleman. His name is not italicized, as that of a minister, in the early college catalogues.

He always wrote his name as in the text, as did his father. It is written Blakman in the Malden records, except in one instance, nine years after he had left the town, when it is spelled Blackman, a form which the college catalogues and the persistency of later writers have almost made to supersede the elder and correct orthography.

following after you : For whither you go, we will go ; and your God shall be our God." [41]

Benjamin Blakeman was born at Stratford about the year 1643, and was graduated at Harvard College in 1663.[42] Two years after his graduation we learn that, "his thoughts . . . be

not to attend the work of Christ in the ministry," evidently to the disappointment of his father, who diverted from his use a legacy of books in consequence, saying in his will : —

Concerning my books, which I intended for-my son Benjamin, . . . my wish is that my son Atwater [43] make his son Joshua a scholler and to fit him for that work I give unto him my Lattin books ; but if not, they shall be put into my estate and disposed of as my wife and my overseers shall think fit.

Mr. Sibley sententiously adds : "Young Atwater did not become a minister and take the 'Lattin books.' Benjamin Blakeman studied divinity." In 1670 he was at Stratford and was sought to keep the town school.[44]

In 1674 he was still in Stratford ; but the next year he had become settled in Malden. Mr. Savage, with his usual felicity in guessing, says he was ordained here in 1674 ; but there are no indications that he was ever ordained ; and I see reasons for accepting as a fact that which another has intimated — that he was "only statedly employed to preach there for a considerable length of time, without ordination." [45] In June, 1675, he styled

[41] Mather, *Magnalia*, Book iii. (2), chap. 7.

[42] He appears to have been not altogether blameless in his college life, which may have caused the beginning of the disappointment which his father subsequently felt. The following extracts relate to this period of his life. [December 9, 1661.] The constable of Cambridge is ordered "to warne Benjamin Blackman yt he appeare at ye sd Court to Answer for abuse offered to Abram Smith of Charlstown." *Midd. Court Files, in loco.*

"[December 17, 1661.] Benjamin Blackman appearing in Court. & being convicted of abusive disturbance to Abram Smith & his family, the Court sentenced him to be admonished, & to pay the costs of the Court. six shill." *Midd. Court Records*, i. 241.

[43] Joshua Atwater of New Haven, who had married his daughter Mary.

[44] Cf. Sibley, *Harvard Graduates*, ii. 140-141 ; Goodwin, *Genealogical Notes*, 1-2.

[45] *American Quarterly Register*, xi. 193.

himself, "gentleman, inhabitant of Maldon in the colony of the Massachusetts," which he would hardly have done had he become an ordained minister.

He was married, April 1, 1675, to Rebecca, daughter of Joshua Scottow of Boston.[46] That he lived in the "ministry house" is certain; and, as has been mentioned, he appears as the owner of the neighboring lands which had been in the possession of his predecessor. Of his ministry nothing is known, and ás little of his character. If he may be judged by his after life, he was an active and energetic man of business — a buyer and seller and a getter of gain, rather than a self-denying minister of Christ. Some discontent appears to have preceded his departure from Malden.[47] The town record, which now, for the first time, gives its aid to the perplexed antiquary, opens with a memorandum upon its fly-leaf of a settlement with him, by which it appears that he had preached four years and that " of these 4 years m^r Blakm^n was absent 6 m°." At a " Gen^{r}all meeting," in February, 167$\frac{8}{9}$, it was

Voted that Serg^t Haward and Phin^s Sprague be added to y^e Selectmen who with them are impowr^d a comitte for y^e Towne to treat compound & agre with m^r Blakma^n for w^t he hath done about y^e house & land thereto adjoyning according to w^t y^e Town^e is ingaged or to reffer y^e same to men chosen between them

Voted that ye said Comittee Purchase for the Towne all m^r Blakmans Land on ye East side of ye Highway, And that ye said House with all ye land belonging thereto shall Henceforth be & remaine to ye vse of ye ministry for ever.

Voted That ye said Comitte have liberty & power to sell the commo^n

---

[46] Scottow is well known to antiquaries as an author, a Boston merchant, and an early operator in eastern lands. His eastern speculations failed, and his mercantile transactions apparently came to naught. His family did not survive the second generation, and his name has disappeared from New England. He was author of *Old Men's Tears for their own Declensions* [1691], and *A Narrative of the Planting of the Massachusetts Colony* [1694]. A memoir of him is in *Mass. Hist. Coll.* xiv. 100-104.

[47] That there were difficulties in the church, which called for a synod in 1679, appears by a paper printed with the Confession of Faith in 1823. A " Publick Day of Humiliation " was kept by the church April 15, 1680, by the advice of the synod, when a renewal of covenant was made by the adoption of an "Instrument" composed by Mr. Wigglesworth. This instrument appears to have furnished the material from whence was drawn the renewal of covenant of 1727, on a day of fasting and prayer occasioned by the great earthquake of that year, which is noticed in its proper place.

Land at Sandy Banke & some remote land on ye common for mony to pay towards ye purchase of m^r Blakmans land.

In accordance with these votes, the committee " treated, compounded, and agreed " with Mr. Blakeman, who executed a deed, March 4, 167⅞, in which he styles himself "Benjamin Blakeman of Maldon Gent^m," by which he conveyed to the town a portion of the Bunker land as has been stated, and also

My right title & interest to or in the dwelling house for the ministry in the s^d Towne or any the lands thereto adjoyning by vertue of any former gift or grant to me by the s^d Towne or by vertue of or for any disbursements costs or charges by me expended or done either about or upon the s^d House or land thereto adjoyning whatsoever [except & reserving to my selfe the barne built by m^r Bunker & the nursery fenced in by the Kitchin.][48]

The consideration named in this deed of sale and quit claim was one hundred and twenty-five pounds, or according to the report of the committee, made soon after,

The Towne is to pay Mr Blakm^n or his ordr at y^e s^d House in this Town^e the sume of 125$^£$ Wherof 65$^£$ is to be in mony & to be p^d in Man^r. followg : Namly. 30$^£$ in Neat Catle not exceeding 8 yeares old y^e beging of June next : And 32$^£$ 10. mony by y^e midle of July next. And 32$^£$ 10. mony and 30$^£$ in Indian corne the 25th day of March 1680. And the said Committe are bound in 200$^£$ bond in behalf of the Towne for the paym^t thereof.[49]

As an illustration of the business habits of the men of that time, it may be mentioned that this deed was not recorded until May 25, 1686,[50] about which time, perhaps, Mr. Blakeman be-

---

[48] *Midd. Co. Deeds*, x. 574.

[49] *Malden Town Records, in loco.*

[50] Although the General Court had early passed a law in relation to the public records, and provided that all unrecorded land conveyances might be considered void after a certain time, a strict attention to its regulations was by no means universal. The system of land records was unknown in England, where the preservation of original grants or a long occupancy of land gave a suffi-

cient title; and many of the colonists came slowly, or not at all, to observe its wise provisions. Many deeds were not recorded until some emergency arose, like that in the text, and others, not at all. Several instances of either kind may be found in the present volume. From these causes came much of the obscurity which rests upon the early land titles of this and other Massachusetts towns.

gan to push the town for the dues which appear to have been unpaid. At a meeting, May 21, 1688, it was

voted that in case mʳ Blackman should mak any farthr demand of pay from the Towne the inhabitance of the Towne haue chosen a committy John Sprague Seʳ ensine linds left Samuell Sprague Phinias Sprague Deacon green left william green Henery green Joses Bucknam to defend the case if need be

voted and farther the Towne doe Jngage to defray all charges in defending of the Towne in this case depending betweene the Towne and mʳ Blackman.

Soon after leaving Malden, he went to Black Point, on the Saco River, where his father-in-law, Joshua Scottow, had conveyed to him a small tract of land. It appears that he preached in the neighboring town of Scarborough, although he declined a settlement; and he represented that town, in 1682, in the General Assembly of the Province, under the administration of President Danforth. The next year he removed to Saco, and continued a Member of the General Assembly at York as representative from that town. Savage says that " during the great French and Indian war being driven to Boston, he served, 1683, as representative for Saco, but continued to live at Boston; " and he cites the fact that his son Benjamin was baptized, September 13, 1685, at the Third Church.[61] As no other writer has knowledge of an Indian war in Maine from 1678 to 1688, some doubt must be thrown upon this statement; and although his wife may have been with her father in Boston, and Mr. Blakeman, himself, may have come to Massachusetts Bay on "matters of affairs," it seems certain that he continued to live at Saco, where he was a magistrate, being commissioned by Sir Edmund Andros, until his final removal about the year 1689.

He made several purchases of land upon the Saco River; and built a saw-mill upon the falls still known as Blakeman's Falls, where the Pepperell Mills now stand. He added a large tract of land to the purchases already made, with the supposed intention of forming a new settlement of Massachusetts men.[62]

[61] *Genealogical Dict.,* i. 194.　　[62] Folsom, *Hist. Saco and Biddeford,* 168-169.

In the summer of 1688 he was still upon the Saco, when the Indians, incited by the Baron de St. Castine, having commenced depredations in the neighborhood, he seized eighteen or twenty of them, and sent them "with a good Guard to *Falmouth* in *Casco-Bay.*" Mather styles him "Captain *Blackman*" at this time.[53] The Indians immediately began to make reprisals; and the consequent uncertainty of affairs apparently preventing the intended settlement of his lands, he soon after removed to Boston, and never returned as a resident to Saco. No farther trace of him has been found; and as he is starred in the Harvard Triennial of 1700, it is supposed that he died before that year.[54] His wife, Rebecca, died March 29, 1715, aged about sixty-three years; and his daughter, Rebecca,[55] was living in that year, the wife of "Thomas Goodwill of Boston, shipwright." The son was dead.

[53] Cf. Hutchinson, *History of Massachusetts Bay*, i. 364; Mather, *Magnalia*, Book vii. art. 1. Mr. Blakeman's intrepid promptness did not gain him the thanks of Governor Andros, who, after the Indians had been sent from Falmouth to Boston, imprudently "set them all at liberty; not so much as taking care to redeem those of our English for them that were in their hands."

[54] The will of Joshua Scottow was made June 3, 1696, and proved March 3, 169⅞. It devised his property to his children, Thomas Scottow, Elizabeth Savage, Rebecca Blakeman, and Mary Checkley. The manner of the bequest to Rebecca Blakeman may indicate that Mr. Blakeman was then dead, or that the testator had no great confidence in his son-in-law. He says: "And as for my Legacy to my Daughter Rebecca Blackman, I do will it to be left in the hands of my Son Samuel Checkley and my Daughter Elizabeth Savage to be paid to her as she shall need it." *Suffolk Co. Wills*, viii. 110. It may be that Mr. Blakeman was in Malden in 1700, and died in that year. One Benjamin "Blackman" witnessed a deed of John Greenland, August 1, 1700, and another four days later. It may have been the son, who was then fifteen years old.

[55] Baptized at the Third (Old South) Church in Boston, April 14, 1689. Sibley, *Harvard Graduates*, ii. 143.

CHAPTER IX.

CHEEVER AND WIGGLESWORTH.

WITHIN a year after the withdrawal or dismission of Mr. Blakeman, the Rev. Thomas Cheever began to preach at Malden. He was a son of Mr. Wigglesworth's old schoolmaster, the famous Ezekiel Cheever, the author of the long-lived *Latin Accidence*, who had himself been asked to settle in Malden before the coming of Mr. Matthews. His mother was Ellen Lathrop, sister of the unfortunate Captain Thomas Lathrop of Beverly, who with most of his company, "the flower of Essex," was slain by the Indians at Bloody Brook, near Deerfield, September 18, 1675. He was born at Ipswich, August 23, 1658, and was graduated at Harvard College, at the head of his class, like Mr. Wigglesworth, in 1677.

The *Bi-Centennial Book*, copying a writer in the *American Quarterly Review*,[1] says he "began to preach at Malden, February 14, 1679;" but the town record states that "mister cheevers began the worke of the ministry the 14 day feberary 1679 [1679/80]," which, that day falling upon Saturday in that year, indicates the time when he entered upon his contracted work, and not that he then preached his first sermon. As a considerable interval of time had elapsed since the departure of Mr. Blakeman, he had probably preached as a candidate and had become known to the people. His preaching apparently proving acceptable, the church ceased negotiations with another; and at a general meeting of the town, March 8, 1679/80,

It being declared to yᵉ Inhabitants that yᵉ church had sent a letter to Mʳ ffletchʳ to forbear coming hither & the reasons thereof — [2] And allso

---

[1] *Bi-Centennial Book of Malden*, 157; *American Quarterly Review*, xi. 193.

[2] The members of the Malden church might have repeated their experience in the Matthews case had they not "sent a letter to Mʳ. ffletchʳ to forbear coming

17

their motion to Mr Tho Chevis for his helpe & continance in ye worke of the minstry here. The Inhabitants manifested their consent & desyr of Mr Chevis continance amongst them in ye work of ye Ministy.

Voted That Mr Chevis shall have fifftie pounds in mony p^d him for this yeare he continuing in ye worke of ye ministy here.

[December 27, 1680,] Att a meeting of all ye Jnhabitants warned by ye Const^le to Consider about m^r Chevis the year being neer vpp And to renew their former motion to him for Setlem^t Among^t vs in ye work of the min'try

voted The Inhabitants vnanimously manifested their consent and desyre of m^r Tho Chevis continuance & settlem^t Amongst them in ye worke of ye minstry.

voted That m^r Chevis shall haue 60^£ p^r ann. ye one halfe in mony & the other halfe in comon pay. or fifty pounds all in mony which he pleas to Accept: And allso the vse of ye Towns Howse & land therto belonging. And his fyre wood free.[8]

Allso Agreed that in Case s^d m^r Chevis shall dye here & leave his Widdow here that then his s^d widdow shall haue Eighty pounds paid

hither;" for I take Mr. Fletcher to have been the Rev. Seth Fletcher who left Southampton, Long Island, about that time, and who had been that "inconvenient" preacher at Wells who was silenced by the General Court in 1660.

He had gone to Wells in 1655 without ordination, at a time when that place was in that graceless condition which seemed in that day of small things to characterize most of the settlements on the coast of Maine. Bourne says of him, that he "stirred up strifes and contentions wherever he undertook to minister the Word." He remained at Wells until 1660, when the General Court of Massachusetts, taking cognizance of complaints "as touching his unfittnes for the place of the ministrje," passed the following order:—

"[October 16, 1660,] The Court, hauing pervsed the severall evidences presented to this Court refering to Mr Fletcher & the toune of Wells, doe judge meete to declare to the sajd inhabitants that they haue not only liberty, but are hereby enjoyned, to procure some godly able minister to be helpfull to them, and that the sajd Fletcher is hereby enjoyned to forbeare any more to preach amongst them." *Mass. Colony Records*, iv. (1), 434.

Although silenced in Wells, he preached at Saco the next year and thereafter at other places. Bourne remarks that he "was continually exciting dissensions," but allows that "there was something in his ministrations which captivated the attention of many good men." He was a friend of the Rev. John Wheelwright and may have followed him in his Antinomian doctrines, which would account for the dislike of the General Court. He returned to Saco in 1668 and was regularly settled there, the people showing much attachment to him. Here, marrying Mary, daughter of Bryan Pendleton, a prominent settler, he remained until driven away by the Indian troubles of 1675. He then preached at Southampton for two or three years; and, leaving there in 1679, he soon after removed to Elizabethtown, N. J., where he preached until his death in 1682. Cf. Folsom, *Saco and Biddeford*, 130-136; Bourne, *Wells and Kennebunk*, 96-101.

[8] As an addition, the town voted soon after, "[March. 10, 1689/,] That ye Select men Hyre thre or fowr acres of salt marsh annally of m^r Wades or else where for ye vse of ye Ministey: to be p^d for by ye Town."

her within two Yeares next after his decease. the one half part therof in mony & the other halfe part therof in common pay.

Mr. Cheever was not ordained until July 27, 1681, when he became the third pastor of the church. Mr. Wigglesworth apparently still remained in retirement, and no compensation was voted to him by the town. There can be no doubt that he was still looked upon by the people as one who had no claim upon them; and the only instance of a payment or gift to him during a period of thirteen years after the settlement of Mr. Cheever appears in the following record: —

[4. 10. 82]. *voted.* that the cutters & carts in ye Town cutt & cart one load of fire Wood for Mr Wigglesworth : on ye next second day.

voted. Corp^n Jo. Green & serg^t Skin^r overseers to se ye wood cutt & carted.

The salary of Mr. Cheever was regularly paid, in accordance with the vote, at the rate of fifty pounds in money, "which he pleas to Accept; " and the agreement in respect to "fyre wood" seems to have been faithfully kept, although it appears that at one time, at least, there were some " carts behinde."

4. 9mo 81   Att a Meeting of the Selectmen at J. W.[4] Appointed the 9th of novemb^r being ye next 4th day to cutt & cart wood for m^r Chevis Cutters ye 4th day

Symo^n Grouer	Will Teale
Sam Lewis	Sam Haward
Ben^a Whittamor	John winsleed
Will East	Jacob winslead
Robt: Cally	Jsack green

Carts y^t carryed wood each one load

2^d day	Jos Bucknam	Hen. Swnaway
4th day	John Green	Jos wayte
	Hen Green	Jo. Green. hill
	Sam Green	Sam. Sprague
	Jo. Sprague jn^r	Laz Grouer
	Jo Lynde	Phin Vppam
	Ens Lynds	corn^t Green
	John wayt Senr	Jonath knoher
	leu^t Sprague	Jo. Greenland
	nath Haward	most of them Cutt

their wood.

[4] Captain John Wayte.

Carts behinde

Phin Sprague	Will Bordman
Jo. Chadwike	Joel Jenkins
lem Jenkins	Jo. Paull
Jonath. Spragu	Jo. Sargent
Tho Birditt	Jo Chamb'la[n]
Jo. Scholly	Jacob Park[r]
Lewis	Will Buckn[m]
Sam. wayt	Phill Atwood.

Mr. Cheever continued to live in the town's house, although he followed the example of his predecessors and purchased a house and land of his own.[5] Incidental entries in relation to his occupancy of the parsonage and its lands may be found in the records.

Paid to M[r] Cheevers two pound in silver in part of pay for the bulding of a leanto aioyning to his barne and he promising to keep it in repaire the twentieth six of May, 1685.

After Mr. Cheever had been in Malden four or five years, the health of Mr. Wigglesworth was very much changed, and he began to "enter into the ways of men." If we may believe Cotton Mather, the troubles in the church had not only continued, but had largely increased. He says: —

It pleased God, when the Distresses of the church in *Maldon*, did extremely call for it, wondrously to Restore His *Faithful Servant.* He that had been for near Twenty years almost *Buried Alive*, comes abroad again; and for as many years more, must in a *Publick Usefulness*, receive the Answer and Harvest of the Thousands of Supplications, with which the *God of his Health*, had been addressed by him & for him.[6]

Of the nature of the troubles which preceded, and were in existence at the time of Mr. Wigglesworth's recovery, we have no precise information: perhaps the later trouble with Mr. Cheever had already begun to show itself. It is evident that the old dissatisfaction with Mr. Wigglesworth, having its root,

[5] This farm was in the south-east portion of the town, apparently near Turkey Hill. It passed to Mr. Cheever by an unrecorded conveyance from Lieutenant John Smith of Winnisimmet, who had purchased it of Roger Kenicott in 1678. Besides the home land and house, it embraced meadow and marshlands at Moulton's Island and Pemberton's Pond near the South River, within Charlestown bounds.

[6] *A Faithful Man*, 24.

perhaps, in the Matthews troubles of more than thirty years before, and increased by the apparent neglect of the teacher in performing his duties, had never ceased. And to this cause had been added another, in producing which Mr. Wigglesworth himself had been directly instrumental.

For nearly twenty years after the death of his first wife, Mary Reyner, he remained unmarried, preferring, perhaps, to bear alone the ills to which an untimely fate had made him heir. Perhaps the marriage of his only child, Mercy, and her removal to Boston in 1673,[7] may have left him alone and the forlorn experiences of the next few years have turned his thoughts towards a change. That he continued to live in his little house, on the land that "was sometime part of the proper lot of M.r John Allen," is not unlikely. That he had a youthful housekeeper is very certain, and the result was not unnatural. He was in his forty-eighth year when he resolved to change his manner of living; and the means by which he proposed to make that change was then about eighteen years of age. When the news came to

---

[7] Mercy Wigglesworth married Samuel Brackenbury. He was the only son of William and Alice Brackenbury of Charlestown and Malden, and was born, February 10, 164⅚; was graduated, H. C. 16⁵4; and preached as assistant to the Rev. Samuel Phillips at Rowley about two years. He was made a freeman, May 7, 1673, and in the same year removed to Boston, where he settled as a physician and was admitted to the Second Church, November 4, 1677. He died of small-pox, January 16, 167⅞. His widow married the Rev. Samuel Belcher, who preached at the Isles of Shoals and Newbury; and, outliving him, she died, November 14, 1723.

The children of Samuel and Mercy (Wigglesworth) Brackenbury were : —

Samuel, born at Malden, February 167⅔; was a physician in Boston : married, October 22, 1694, Ann Chickering, who died, January 22, 170½; and dying, November 26, 1702, was buried at Malden.

Mary, born in Boston, March 12, 167¾.

William, born in Boston; lived at Ipswich.

Of Dr. Brackenbury's short professional life little is known. He appears to have been the family physician of John Hull, the celebrated mint-master of the Colony; and Samuel Sewall, who married Hull's only surviving daughter, relates that he was called to "Mother Hull" in September, 1676, and the next day dissected one of three Indians who were executed at Boston. The diarist, in a confused account of the sickness of "Mother Hull" and "Han Sewall," his wife, soon after says that "Dr. Brackenbury advises Diacodium to move Rest, and approves Peppar boyled in Milk and Water, alike of each," in cases of dysentery and diarrhœa; but subsequent events caused the observant Sewall to "mistrust Diacodion."

him, Increase Mather, in a letter of alarm and counsel, wrote to Mr. Wigglesworth : —

These for the Rev. *my respected friend M*. *W. Pastor of the Church in M.*

Revd Sr, — Since I saw you the last in B. one that doth vnfeignedly desire your welfare hath bin with mee, expressing grief of hn with reference vnto a mattr wherein yourselfe is concerned. I owe you that respect (& much more) as to informe you what I have bin told. The Report is, that you are designing to marry with your servant mayd, & that she is one of obscure parentage, & not 20 years old, & of no Chrch, nor so much as Baptised. If it be as is related, I wld humly entreat you (before it be too late) to considr of these argts in oposition. 1. For you to doe this, which will be a grief of heart to your dear Relations, if it be not a mattr which God doth command to be done, (for no man will deny but one ought rather to grieve his friends, than to p voke the Lord) is not advisable. Now I hear that they are much troubled at your intended prceedings, & I suppose there is no divine precept requiring your marrying with such an one. Is it not then better to desist? 2. I doubt that considering her youth, & your age, & great bodily infirmities, such a change of your condition, if that which is intimated by the Holy Apsle, 1 Cor. 7, 3, sd be attended, your days would be shortned, & consequently the 5th Comndmnt broken. 3. Such general Rules as those, Phil. 4, 8, doe concern as all chrns, so most eminently Ministers of Ch. And doubtless it will *male audire* for you to doe this thing, yea, I fear it will leave a blott vpon your Name aftr you shall cease to be in this world. 4. The ministry will be blamed, which wee should be very carefull to prvent. 2 Cor. 6. 3. The mouths of carnal ones will be opened, not onely to censure you, but your brethren in the ministry will be condemned also. The world will say, theres such an one, Hee was as justified a man as any of them, & yet wee see vnto what his affections have carried him. 5. I am afraid that if you sd prceed, that Rule, 2 Cor. 6. 14. will be transgressed. It vseth to be said *nube pari*, but to marry with one so much your Inferior on all accounts, is not *nubere pari*. And to take one that was never baptised into such nearness of Relation, seemeth contrary to the Gospell ; espclly for a Ministr of Ct to doe it. The like never was in N. E. Nay, I question whethr the like hath bin known in the chrn world. 6. Doth not that Script. 1 Tim. 3. 11, with others of the like importance, prhibit such p ceedings?

Thus have I made bold to suggest my thoughts unto you. And if I had not respected the interest of Religion, & your credit & comfort, I should have bin wholly silent in a mattr that concerns another & not me, furthr than as I am bound to seeke your welfare, & doe what I may to prevent trouble from coming vpoⁿ my neighbo^r, & broth^r esp^clly such an one, whose Name hath bin, & I hope may still be of precious esteem with the L^{ds} people.

Though your affections s^d be too far gone in this matter, I doubt not but if you put the object out of your sight, & looke vp to the Lord Jesus for supplies of grace, you will be enabled to ov come these Temptations. The Lord be with you,　　I am
3^m 8^d 1679.　　　　Yours vnfeignedly,　I. M.[8]

Hardly had this admonitory and exhortatory epistle been written, when, before it had left the writer's hands, came Mr. Blakeman, who it would appear had not yet removed from Malden, bringing, as Mr. Mather wrote, " your papers, which state the case & mention the Reasons inducing you to marry your servant." Mr. Wigglesworth's case and reasons were communicated to the reverend pastors of the First and Third (Old South) churches of Boston, to the apostle Eliot of Roxbury, and to Mather's friend, Samuel Nowell; but these pious and learned men were " not very forward to give advice." Mr. Mather comforted himself and attempted to confound the Malden lover by writing that they supposed " it is now too late. It is not good after vows to make enquiry. Had you advised with them before your treating with the party concerned, you may be sure they would earnestly have disswaded. Nor is there any of them that dare encourage your proceedings as things are now circumstanced." His letter indicates that the people of Malden were not disposed to look with complacency upon the intended marriage and that some scandal was abroad. He says: —

I have heard such uncomfortable Reflections since I wrote the enclosed as that I see no cause to alter my mind as to what is therein expressed. Indeed if the good people in Malden did approve of your proceedings, & if there were an eminency of the fear of God discerneable in your Damosel, notwithstanding her obscurity upon other accounts, there would be less of scandal in proceedings. But I do not hear any one but yourself speak much concerning that matter. And it is thought that your Affection doth biass your Judgment, & that therefore in this case you are not so competent a Judge. The Lord in mercy be with you, & direct you to do that which shal be pleasing in His sight, & for the honour of His name, yea, & of your own name, & the comfort of those that are concerned in you.[9]

⁸ *Mass. Hist. Coll.*, xxxviii. 94–95.　　⁹ Ibid., 95–96.

The latter letter was written May 12, 1679, and the two were sent together to Malden. If Mr. Wigglesworth had not changed since his college days, the reading of those " composures " must have been the cause of much self-examination and abasement. But the stubborn singer of the *Day of Doom* was not disposed to " put the object out of sight," nor to " ov come these Tempta-tions ; " and in spite of Increase Mather and his " not very for-ward friends," and the displeasure of his relations and the Malden people, he let affection " bias his judgment " and married Martha Mudge, without regard to her " obscure parentage, her youth, and her being no church member."

She was the youngest child of a Malden farmer, Thomas Mudge, and was about six years younger than Mercy Wiggles-worth ; but she made the teacher a good wife and bore him five daughters and one son,[10] among whose descendants have been and are honored clergymen, lawyers, professors, and scholars, who need not hold otherwise than in honor the day when Michael Wigglesworth married his youthful " servant mayd." Her husband testified to her worth in after years ; for in writing to Mrs. Sybil Avery of Dedham, seeking her as his third wife, he said : " My Late wife was a means under God of my recover-ing a better state of Health." [11]   It is worthy of note that the marriage of Mr. Wigglesworth does not appear upon the returns

---

[10] Samuel, the son, was born, February 4, 168⅞, and was graduated at Harvard College, 1707. Harris says he pursued his studies two years longer at Cambridge and began the study of physic in June, 1709, with Dr. Graves of Charlestown. Dr. Thomas Graves of Charlestown had died in 1697 ; but whoever was his master, Wigglesworth entered upon the practice of medicine at Ipswich Hamlet, now Hamilton, in March, 1710, where he remained until the following December, when he returned to Malden. Here he taught school, studied theology, and followed his former profession of medicine. In 1712, his account book shows charges for attendance on people in Dracut and Chelmsford, where he may, perhaps, have been for a time. January 29,

1711¾, he writes: "came to Live att ye Southwest precinct of Ipswich being in-vited to ye ministry There." He was ordained at Ipswich Hamlet, October 27, 1714, being the first minister of that parish. Harris says of him : — " Besides attending to the public and private duties of the sacred office, he still culti-vated his first profession, and like his father, was often useful in prescribing for the ills of the body as well as of the soul." He died, September 3, 1768. Harris, *Genealogical Sketch of the Wig-glesworth Family*, in manuscript. *Ac-count Book* of S. Wigglesworth, in the library of the N. E. Historic Genealogi-cal So.

[11] *N. E. Hist. and Geneal. Reg.* xvii. 141.

of the town clerk of Malden nor has its record been found elsewhere.

That the people of Malden did not look upon this marriage with favor may be readily understood. Added to the dissatisfaction which already existed, it did not lessen the difficulties which were between the members of the church and its teacher. The testimony of Cotton Mather in relation to "the Distresses of the Church in *Maldon*" has already been mentioned; and further indications of hostility or lukewarmness towards Mr. Wigglesworth will appear in the course of our story.

But if the Malden church and people continued to look upon him with disfavor, the displeasure of Mr. Mather and the brethren of other churches passed away; and the author of the *Day of Doom* came to be esteemed and held in "good opinion." Among the *Mather Papers* was found the following letter of Mr. Wigglesworth.

These for the Rev[d] *and hon*[rd] *Mr. Increase Mather Pasto*[r] *of the North-Church in Boston. At his house. With care*

Rev[D] Sir, — I received your loving lines, and having seriously considered the contents thereof, as I find great cause to thank you and other worthy friends, for your & their good will & good opinion of me, yet as to myself, I cannot think my bodily health and strength competent to undertake or manage such a weighty work as you mention, if it were desired, nor have I reason to judge myself in any measure fit upon other accounts. Wherefore I hope the Colledge & Overseers will think of and apply themselves to a fitter person, and that they may speed well in so doing, is and shall be my prayer, who am, Sir, ever

Yours heartily to hono[r] and serve you,

MICHAEL WIGGLESWORTH.[12]

Maldon, Octob. 27, 1684.

Mr. Mather was acting at that time as temporary President of Harvard College, the Rev. John Rogers, the former President, having died, July 2, 1684; and it is very likely that the "weighty work" was that office which had been offered him by the college authorities.[13]

---

[12] *Mass. Hist. Coll.*, xxxviii. 645.
[13] Cf. Quincy, *Hist. Harvard Univ.*, i. 38; Peirce, *Hist. Harvard Univ.*, 49, 56; Dean, *Wigglesworth*, 88–89; Sibley, *Harvard Graduates*, i. 275.

September 14, 1685, he preached at Cambridge, before the Artillery Company of Middlesex, from the text, *Fight the good fight of faith, lay hold on eternal life.* Judge Sewall says he preached excellently.[14] He delivered the annual Election sermon, May 12, 1686. Sewall says: —

Mr. Wigglesworth preaches from Rev. 2. 4 and part of 5.th v. and do thy first works, end of the text. Shew'd the want of Love, or abating in it, was ground enough of Controversy, whatsoever outward performances a people might have. In 's prayer said, That may know the things of our peace in this our day, and it may be the last of our days. Acknowledged God as to the Election, and bringing forth him as 'twere a dead Man, — had been reckoned among the dead, — to preach.[15]

This sermon was ordered to be prepared for the press, "the Court judging that the printing of it will be for publick benefitt;"[16] but as no copy has been found and its title is unknown, it is probable that the early advent of the Andros government prevented its publication.

It was now that the difficulties of the Malden church were to assume a different form; and there can be but little doubt that the animosities and jealousies which the pastorate of Mr. Matthews had introduced, and which the petty quarrels of thirty-five years had not allowed to cease, bore no small part in shaping the charges which in the end were to leave the church without a pastor.

---

[14] *Mass. Hist. Coll.*, xlv. 95. This is the first notice of his public appearance after his recovery and has before been unnoticed. The Middlesex Artillery Co. had always, since their organization, met at Cambridge and had never gone out of the county for a preacher; but the next year their election was held at Charlestown and a minister was brought from Suffolk to address them. Cotton Mather says : —

"[1686.] The Artillery-Company of *Middlesex* this year did a New Thing, in Ordering their Anniversary solemnities to bee at *Charlestown*, and *not* at *Cambridge*; and they did another New Thing, in choosing, as they never did before or since, a Minister not belonging to their own County to be their preacher; and this was my poor *self.* So, on 13.d

7.m I preached at Charlstown, unto a very great Assembly, a Sermon, which was afterwards printed, under y.e Title of *Military Duties.*" Mather, MS. *Diary.*

Sewall says : — "The Artillery Company had like to have been broken up; the animosity so high between Charlestown and Cambridge Men about the Place of Training." *Mass. Hist. Coll.*, xlv. 151.

[15] *Mass. Hist. Coll.*, xlv. 136. There was in his prayer an evident allusion to the evil days which were about to come upon the colonies. Randolph came two days later with the official copy of the judgment against the charter; and in December, Sir Edmund Andros arrived with a commission as Governor of all New England.

[16] *Mass. Colony Records*, v. 515.

It appears that Mr. Cheever had been accused "as Guilty of great Scandals, by more than 2 or 3 witnesses;" of "speaking such words as are scandalous breaches of the Third Commandment, as appears by the Testimony of Mrs. Eliza. Wade and Abigail Russell;" and of using "light and obscene expressions (not fit to be named) in an Ordinary at Salem, as by the Testimony of Samuel Sprague, Jacob Parker, Isaac Hill: Also as he was travailing on the Rode, as p. the Testimony of Thomas, Ester and Eliza. Newhall." [17] That the majority of the church members considered these accusations as of little weight is evident; for they persistently "declin'd all Testimonies against him as to Scandals committed before his Ordination; as also some other Testimonies respecting matters very criminal since that; because they judged the Witnesses on account of Prejudices and otherwise, incompetent." How easily they could forgive the little guilt which they found in him appeared, August 9, 1685, when, "Mr. Chiever made an Acknowledgement of some Evils to the Brethren of that Church, whereto he stands related; and the most part of them were willing to take up with a slender satisfaction." It is added "that on the next Lord's-day, he manifested so little sense and sorrow for his great sins, as that the generality of the Brethren were more dissatisfied than formerly."

That the church as a whole was not inclined to act upon charges preferred by prejudiced witnesses is very evident; while it seems clear that there were a few who were not disposed to lose their hold upon so formidable a weapon as that which seemed to be ready to their hands. There is an indication that Mr. Wigglesworth, himself, was in opposition to Mr. Cheever, and that he thought that his settlement had been made with undue haste. The soil was fertile and all the conditions were favorable for a plentiful crop: that the affairs of the pastor grew worse may be readily imagined.

Sewall wrote in his diary: --

[March 15, 168⅚.]   Mr. Wigglesworth here, speaks about a Council respecting Mr. Thomas Chiever. [18]

---

[17] *Mass. Hist. Coll.*, xlvi. 21⁰.   [18] Ibid., xlv. 127.

[Sunday, March 28, 1686.]   The Lord give me a holy godly Life without End.   Letter read from Maldon directed to the three Churches in Boston, desiring Council respecting their Pastor Mr. Tho. Chiever, who is charg'd with scandalous immoralities, for which hath not given satisfaction.   Mr. Eliot and my Self to accompany Mr. Willard thither next Wednesday come Sennight, 7ᵗʰ April.[19]

On the appointed day, the diarist " Got up about 4 *mane* to go and accompany Mr. Willard to Maldon, went most by Water, some by Land."   Those who went by land, doubtless, crossed the Charlestown ferry, and passing up the neck, came about by the way of Medford; while " Those that went by Water were landed at Switzer's Point, then went about 2 miles on foot." [20]   To realize the simple manners of that age, imagine for a moment a party of divines and laymen sailing up the Mystic to Van Voorhis's Point, and then trudging two miles or more to attend an ecclesiastical council in Malden to-day.   Inward repinings might neutralize their outward prayers, or bodily weariness confuse their sense of justice.

There were fifteen members of the Council at Malden, and among them were five famous ministers from the Boston churches, Increase Mather with his son and colleague, Cotton Mather, James Allen and Joshua Moody from the First Church, and Samuel Willard of the Third or South Church, all bright and shining lights and " painful workers in the vineyard."   With them, though not acting as members of the Council, were Ezekiel Cheever, father of the offending clergyman, with long and pointed white beard,[21] and Samuel Parris of Salem Village, who was soon to become notorious and forever infamous by his connection with the sad tale of Witchcraft.

The Council met at the house of " Father Green," probably James Green, a part of whose house is still in existence, hidden within the walls of the Perkins house now standing on Appleton

---

[19] *Mass. Hist. Coll.*, xlv. 130.

[20] Ibid., 131.

[21] President Stiles of Yale College, in his Diary, quoted by Barnard, *Biographical Sketch of Ezekiel Cheever*, 21, mentions the aged Rev. Samuel Maxwell, of Warren, R. I., who told him, "he well knew the famous Grammar schoolmaster, Mr. E. Cheever of Boston, author of the *Accidence*; that he wore a long white beard, terminating in a point; that when he stroked his beard to the point, it was a sign for the boys to stand clear."

Street. After a prayer by Mr. Allen, it was debated whether they should have two moderators; it was decided to have but one, and Increase Mather was chosen. After some discourse, they apparently went to the meeting house, where Mr. Mather prayed and "some Debates" were heard. They returned again to their "Quarters" and "had the witnesses and Mr. Tho. Chiever face to face." The Council rejected most of the testimony, as had the church, and upon the same considerations; but testimony was admitted and accepted in regard to spoken words upon which all the subsequent action appears to have been based.

Mr. Cheever "absolutely denyed" these words and did not show to the members of the Council "that humble penitential frame that would have become him," so that they saw "cause to fear that he had been too much accustomed to an evil course of Levity and Profaneness."[22] Sewall says : —

> In the evening Mr. Chiever the Pastor was sent for, Mr. Moodey and others acquainted him how grievous his carriage had been and that day not so humble and in such a frame as ought ; told him expected not an Answer, but that should sleep on't. Debated considerably what to do till about 10 at night. Mr. Moderator pray'd, went to Bed. Mr. Moderator and his son to Mr. Wigglesworth's, some to Mr. Chiever, Major Richards and self Kept the House. In the Morn. Thorsday, Ap. 8, Mr. Moderator went to prayer : read over what was drawn up, then discours'd about it. Sent for Mr. Chiever, to see what [he] had to say.[23]

The Council, not finding satisfaction, unanimously agreed upon a "Declaration and Advice." That Mr. Cheever had used

---

[22] A "humble penitential frame" does not seem to have been natural to Mr. Cheever; indeed, there are indications that he was possessed of great self-reliance and some temper to back it. His father owned like traits, as was shown in his troubles with the church at New Haven, which ended in his seclusion. In the language of a contemporary MS., being charged "with a stiff, proud, contradictory frame of spirit," he was "cast out of the body till the proud flesh [should] be destroyed, and he be brought into a more memberlike frame." Cf. *Trial of Ezekiel Cheever before the Church at New Haven,* in *Conn. Hist. Coll.,* i. 22-51.

Of the pastor of Malden, Edward Randolph, the infamous agent of the British Crown in its tyrannical dealings with New England, speaks in his "*Narrative of the Delivery of his Majesty's writ of quo warranto,*" presented to the Privy Council, February 14, 168¾, cited by Palfrey, *Hist. of New England,* iii. 387 : — "Seven or eight days before the Assembly broke up, a libellous paper was dispersed in Boston. . . . It was verily believed that one Cheevers, a hotheaded minister was the author of that paper."

[23] *Mass. Hist. Coll.,* xlvi. 21*.

language not becoming a minister seems likely: that he was not
guilty of worse practices, as has been intimated, appears clearly
in the sequel. That the Council rejected the testimony of prejudiced witnesses has been seen; and only a present suspension
of his office as a pastor and his privileges as a church member
was the immediate result of the session at Malden. The report
recites the facts, which have been given, and closes with the
following advice: —

We conceive it to be Duty and accordingly advise the Church of
Maldon, to Suspend Mr. Tho. Chiever from the Exercise of his ministerial Function; and also to debar him from partaking with them at
the Lord's Table, for the space of Six Weeks, untill which time the
Council will adjourn themselves, to meet at Boston. And that in case
he shall in the mean while manifest that Repentance which the Rule
requires, they should confirm their Love to him, and (if possible)
improve him again in the Lord's Work among them.

And this, our Advice, is grounded on these Scriptures and Reasons.
(1). Among the Lord's People in the dayes of the O. Testament, no
man might be permitted to execute the Priest's office that had a blemish :
He might not come nigh to offer the offerings of the Lord. Levit. 21,
17, 21, which teaches that Men under moral blemishes, are unfit for
holy ministrations, untill they be, in a way of Repentance, healed.
(2) It is in the New Testament required, that an Elder should be
sober and of good behaviour, and moreover he must have a good Report of them that are without, 1 Tim. 3, 2, 7. (3) Christ's Discipline
ought to be exercised impartially, without respect to Persons. 1 Tim.
5, 21. Nor does Mr. Chiever's standing in a Sacred Office-Relation
any way lessen, but greatly aggravate his sin. (4) There is no probability that Mr. Chiever's Ministry will be blessed for good to Souls,
untill such time as his Conversation shall declare him to be a true
penitent. Mat. 5, 13.

Finally, we exhort and advise our beloved Brethren of the Church of
Maldon to set a day apart, solemnly to humble themselves by Fasting
and Prayer before the Lord under this awfull dispensation, and for
whatever failings have attended them, as to the management of their
Differences, in this hour of Temptation which they have been subject
unto. Particularly, for not observing the Rules of Christ, in endeavouring to prevent Evils by giving seasonable notice to Mr. Chiever of their
Dissatisfactions. And for that want of Love, and for that bitterness of
Spirit, which appears in sundry of them. So we pray the God of Love
and Peace and Truth to dwell among you.[24]

[24] *Mass. Hist. Coll.*, xlvi. 22[*], 23[*]

The closing scenes of the Council in Malden are thus related by Sewall : —

Thorsday, Ap. 8. the Bell was rung ; went in publick. Mr. Moderator pray'd, read the Council's Report. Mr. Wigglesworth spake, thank'd him and the Council ; said had cause to condemn themselves, as for other sins, so their sudden laying Hands on Mr. Chiever ; and now God was whipping them with a Rod of their own making. Mr. Chiever the Father, stood up and pathetically desir'd his son might speak, but Mr. Moderator and others judg'd it not convenient, he not having by what he said given the Council encouragement. Mr. Allin pray'd ; went to Dinner ; Council adjourned to that day 6 weeks. Came Home well.[25]

That Mr. Cheever repented, so that the Malden church could improve him again, does not appear ; but it is said that he, at last, confessed to words " more than were charged upon him," and that " with shame and sorrow." The Council held three sessions in Boston and finally adopted the following report : —

The Elders & Messengers of y⁰ churches assembled in council April 7. 1686 at y⁰ desire of the church in Maldon, having upon adjournment mett at Boston May 20 & 27 & June 10, and there taken the state of that church into further consideration, do declare & advise as followeth :

I. Inasmuch as wee understand that Mʳ Thom⁰ cheever has now declared, that as to y⁰ scandalous words which have been Testified and proved against him, he doth know and with shame and sorrow confess that he has spoken words of y⁰ same nature more then is charged upon him, and doth not deny but he might use those very expressions which are by y⁰ witnesses mentioned, and that he doth judge himself before God and man as one that has exposed Religion and y⁰ ministry to Reproach, opened y⁰ mouthes of y⁰ wicked, sadned y⁰ hearts of y⁰ Lords servants, for which he beggs pardon of God & his people. And considering that some of y⁰ Brethren testify, that they have observed his Late conversation to be humble & penitent : Wee conceive that y⁰ church in Maldon may without breach of y⁰ Rule so far confirm their Love to him, as to Restore him to their communion, & to grant him a Loving Dismission to some church according as himself shall desire. We therefore commend to their consideration these scriptures following. 2 Cor. 2, 7, 8. 1 Cor. 13, 4, 7. Deut. 29, 29.

[25] *Mass. Hist. Coll.,* xlvi. 23⁰.

II. Since it is not probable that M' Cheever's continuence in Maldon, nor yet the present exercise of his ministry there, will tend to y' peace of that place, or to y' edification of y' church, nor to his own comfort : wee advise him the said M' Cheever to request his dismission, and we advise y' church to comply with his desires therein. This counsel we conceive to be grounded on such scriptures as these, 2 Cor. 10, 8 and 12, 19. 2 Thess. 3, 16. 1 Tim. 3, 7. 2 Cor. 6.

III. Wee advise the Church & Congregation of Maldon duely to incourage and to hold in Reputation their Rever⁴ & faithful Teacher M' Wigglesworth, according as God in his word does require them to do. 1 Thess. 5, 12, 13. And that they conscientiously endeavour to live and Love as Bretheren, forbearing one another, and forgiving one another, if any man have a quarrel against any, even as christ forgave you, so also do yee.

Thus do we commend you to y' grace of o' Lord Jesus Christ.

> JNCREASE MATHER *Moderato'*
> *Jn y' name & with y'*
> *unanimous consent of y' council.*²⁶

Mr. Cheever probably removed at once; it is certain that he was living at Rumney Marsh in the winter of 168⅚. He sold his house and lands in Malden to Thomas Oakes, April 9, 1689,²⁷ and is found soon after in the occupancy of the farm of one hundred and twenty-seven acres, which had formerly been a part of the possessions of the unfortunate Sir Henry Vane, and which he bought of his wife's father and brothers, James, Jonathan, and Joshua Bill, of Pullen Point, for three hundred and fifty-seven pounds, October 22, 1689.²⁸ Here he remained

---

²⁶ Original in the possession of Artemas Barrett, of Melrose, 1866.

²⁷ *Midd. Co. Deeds,* xi. 87 a.

²⁸ *Suffolk Co. Deeds,* xv. 2. This land, overlooking the sea and the green marshes and meadows of Rumney Marsh, lies upon the southern and eastern slopes of Cheever's Hill, in Revere. It was for many years known as the Fenno farm, from its later possessors. In 1894 it was laid out for building purposes, and has now lost much of its original character.

The allotment of Sir Henry Vane, being the first of " The great Allottments at Rumley Marsh and Pullen Point," comprised two hundred acres, lying north of the creek, which now divides Chelsea and Revere, and extending from the Charlestown (Mystic Side) line to the highway on the east, now known as School Street, in Revere. As early as 1640, if not a little earlier, it had become, in an unrecorded way, a portion of the possessions of Nicholas Parker, when it is described as consisting of two hundred and sixty acres. *Boston Book of Possessions,* 72. Parker sold the western portion, called eight score acres, to George Burden, the ancestor of the Burditts of Malden, who had built a house upon it when he sold it with lands at Mystic Side to Aaron Way and William Ireland, in February, 165½. *Suffolk Co. Deeds,* i. 206. It was from Way's house that Increase Mather escaped, by the

during the remainder of his long life. He continued to be styled "Cleric;" and for a few years he taught school — perhaps as early as 1700, as in that year the town of Boston established in Rumney Marsh "a free School to Teach them to Read, Write & Cypher."[29] A report is extant which shows that he taught thirty-three scholars in the winter of 170⁹/₁₀, some of them coming from a long distance.[30]

It is not improbable that he varied his occupation by preaching to the sparse population which occupied the farms of Rumney Marsh, Winnisimmet, Pullen Point, and Hog Island.[31]

way of Newgate's landing, to the ship in which he sailed to England in 1688.

The eastern portion of the Vane allotment was retained by Parker, and was sold by his heirs to Thomas Savage, whose son, Ebenezer, sold it to Samuel Sewall in 1683, at which time it was in the occupancy of Thomas Townsend. Sewall, whose gossiping diary has often been of service in the preparation of these pages, sold the farm, in April, 1685, to the Bills, who transferred it to Mr. Cheever, as stated in the text.

It is stated that Mr. Cheever occupied the Newgate house, which is still standing in Mill Street, in Revere; but he was living upon the Parker farm before the time of his purchase. The Newgate land bounded his own on two sides and the Newgate house was not far away from that of Mr. Cheever. It is possible that the houses have become confused in the uncertain processes of the village traditions which have preserved the memory of his residence. The house in which Mr. Cheever lived stood within the line of the present street north of Fenno's Corner and came into the possession of his son, Nathan, with the farm. The latter built another house a little to the westward of it, which stood at the present northerly corner of Broadway and Fenno Street until 1893, when it was demolished. At the death of Nathan Cheever, the older house descended to his son, Nathan (H. C., 1741), who died in 1787, and who was the father of the revolutionary officer, Joseph Cheever, afterwards of Malden.

The late Benjamin H. Dewing of

Revere was informed by the aged Mrs. Anna Stowers, a great-granddaughter of Thomas Cheever, that she was present at a party in the old house. When going home they turned and saw that it was in flames; and it was destroyed. It was supposed that some of the guests caused the fire in getting clothes from a closet. Traces of the fire have been found while excavating in the street.

[29] *Boston Town Records*, March 11, 170⁹/₁₀.

[30] *N. E. Hist. and Geneal. Reg.*, xviii. 109. A report, made in February, 171¾, by Mr. Cheever, is given in *facsimile*, *Memorial History of Boston*, ii. 380.

[31] Although it seems certain that no regular preaching had been continued in that remote district of Boston, an early attempt had been made to establish it. In March, 169⁵/₆, Sergeant John Oliver, then about twenty-four years of age, was sent there by the Boston church on a motion "made by such as have farms at Rumney Marsh, that our brother Oliver may be sent to instruct their servants, and to be a help to them, because they cannot many times come hither, nor sometimes to Lynn, and sometimes nowhere at all." *Keayne's MS.* quoted by Savage, *Winthrop's History of New England*, i. 328. Oliver appears to have continued his ministrations at Rumney Marsh, although he entered H. C. and was graduated in 1645. He died of a malignant fever in the spring of 1646, leaving a widow and five children. Winthrop characterizes him as "a gracious young man, not full thirty years of age, an expert soldier, an excellent surveyor

For several years the people there, among whom appear to have been several members of neighboring churches, had been moving towards the erection of a place of worship, when the town of Boston, April 29, 1709, voted "A Grant of One hundred pounds to be raised and Laid out in building a meeting House at Rumny Marsh." Under the date of July 10, 1710, Sewall says: —

Mr. Jn° Marion and I went to Rumney-Marsh to the Raising of their Meetinghouse.   I drove a Pin, gave a 5ˢ Bill, had a very good Treat at Mr. Chiever's; went and came by Winnisimet; *and six days later:* Extream hot wether.   Mr. Cook, Bromfield and I goe to Rumney-Marsh in a Boat, to agree with Workmen to finish the Meetinghouse.   Stowers is to make the windows.   Got home well; *Laus Deo.*   Several died of the Heat at Salem.[82]

Although no church was immediately gathered, it is very probable that religious services were held and that Mr. Cheever preached there.   That the people had become acquainted with his "gifts" is proved by their choice of him as their pastor.   A church covenant was formed and signed by Mr. Cheever and eight brethren; and, October 19, 1715, a Council, composed of delegates from the Second and New North churches of Boston and the churches of Lynn and Reading, received them as a sister church.   Though both Cotton Mather and Samuel Sewall,

of land, and one who, for the sweetness of his disposition and usefulness through a public spirit, was generally beloved, and greatly lamented." He adds: "For some few years past he had given up himself to the ministry of the gospel, and was become very hopeful that way, (being a good scholar and of able gifts otherwise, and had exercised publicly for two years)." Winthrop, *New England,* ii. 257.

After the death of Mr. Oliver, there is no record of any attempt being made to hold public worship at Rumney Marsh until the time of Mr. Cheever; and the inhabitants became connected, if at all, with the neighboring churches of Boston, Malden, and Lynn. Chamberlain has brought out the fact, however, that a meeting house existed earlier than the one erected in 1710; and tradition attempts to fix its location and asserts that it was built of logs. *Chelsea Telegraph,* March 11, 1882. Samuel Maverick, writing of Rumney Marsh in 1660, says: — "There are many good farmes belonging to Bostone, which have a Metting House, as it were a Chapel of Ease," *N. E. Hist. and Geneal. Register,*. xxxix. 38.

[82] *Mass. Hist. Coll.,* xlvi. 283. The window-maker was probably Samuel Stowers, a carpenter, of Mystic Side. The meeting house then built is still standing in Revere, on the road from Fenno's Corner to the beach. It formerly faced towards the north, and its appearance has been greatly changed by modern alterations. A view as it appeared some years since is given by Chamberlain, *Memorial Hist. of Boston,*. ii. 378.

who had been members of the Council at Malden, were present, the former being chosen "to manage and Moderate the whole affair," [33] no objection was made to Mr. Cheever, and he appears to have outlived the "sorrow and shame" of the Malden affair, even if his character had ever been tarnished in the minds and by the report of those who were conversant with the whole matter. Dr. Tuckerman says: —

Whatever were the circumstances which occasioned his separation from that church, they do not appear to have come before the council which ordained him here.[34]

Sewall records the "Church Gathering and Ordination" in his Diary as follows: —

8! 19. Went to Rumney Marsh in Comp* of Dr. C. Mather, Mr. Stobo, Squire Webb, Dr. Oakes, &c. Mr. Brown of Reading pray'd, Mr. Tho. Chiever preach'd. Neither he that planteth. 1 Cor. 3. 7. Dr. C. Mather gave them a Covenant which they made. They chose Mr. Chiever their Pastor. Dr. M! gave him the Charge, he, Mr. Shepard of Lin, Mr. Brown of Reading, laying on Hands, with Mr. Webb, and praying. Mr. Shepard gave the right Hand of Fellowship. Sung the 3 last Staves of the 132ᵈ Psalm, which Deacon Marion read and set the Tune. Mr. Chiever gave the Blessing.[35]

If ever there had been a real cloud over the reputation of Mr. Cheever, it had now passed away; and thenceforth he became the beloved pastor and father of his little flock. Dr. Tuckerman, his successor in the pastoral office, writing in 1821, when some who had sat under his ministry were still alive, says: —

I am told that he was much respected at home; and his records bear ample testimony to the regard that was felt for him by neighbouring churches. There was at that time more of ostensible discipline in the church, than there is at this day; and the minute detail which he has left of complaints and investigations, of publick censures, acknowledgments and pardons, at once indicate the strong feeling which the church then had of its power and its duty, and shew that he was not behind those of his cotemporaries, who were most zealous for ministerial fidelity, in this department of the sacred office.[36]

---

[33] Cheever in *Rumney-Marish Church Book* (MS).

[34] Tuckerman, *Sermon Preached on the Twentieth Anniversary of his Ordination* (1821), 5.

[35] *Mass. Hist. Coll.*, xlvii. 63.

[36] Tuckerman, *Sermon*, 5.

The historian of Chelsea, in his preparatory sketches, writes : —

His services were constantly sought in ecclesiastical councils ; and he most assiduously entered the letters-missive, the proceedings and the results, in his records, which constitute a mine that has often been worked by those curious in such matters.[87]

Perhaps some of his constitutional stubbornness and fire came out in the memorable installation of the Rev. Peter Thacher as colleague of the Rev. John Webb of the New North Church in Boston in 1720, when, after "a long and shameful Tumultuous disturbance in the Meeting-house," he alone stood out in opposition to the Boston ministers, and, asking the necessary questions, declared the candidate "to be the Pastor of that church." Judge Sewall adds : — "No Psalm was sung."[88] By one of those strange coincidences by which time sometimes works a double justice, the man whom the Malden church had rejected in his prime, stood fearlessly in his old age and helped to win a first victory of those principles for which she had suffered nearly seventy years before. Out of this conflict was born again the full right of churches and congregations to choose their own officers – a right which had lain in abeyance since the Malden brethren bowed before the secular power. Five years later, Cotton Mather and the Convention of Ministers, "sorrowing over the mournful decadence of what they esteemed to be good order in the churches,"[89] endeavored to procure the intervention of the General Court and the ordering of a Synod to consider "what may be the most Evangelical and Effectual Expedients to put a Stop unto those, or the like, Miscarriages."[40] History repeated itself. As in the days of the Matthews troubles, the aristocratic Council would have acted as of yore ; but the democratic deputies, full of the nerve and sense of the people, stamped upon the measure ; and the day of synods, supported by the power of the state, passed away forever. It is pleasant to read that, when the Rumney Marsh

[87] Hon. Mellen Chamberlain in *Chelsea Telegraph*, March 4, 1882.

[88] *Mass. Hist. Coll.*, xlvii. 242.

[89] Dexter, *Congregationalism of the Last Three Hundred Years*, 500.

[40] Hutchinson, *History of Massachusetts-Bay*, ii. 323.

pastor returned to his church and recited the affair of the Council, they " declared their approbation of the same." [41]

Of the religious views of Mr. Cheever little may now be gathered. Three sermons preached by him were published during his lifetime. Of one, *The Churches Duty and Safety,* [*Boston. 1715.*] the title only is known. The others, bearing the running-titles of *Constancy in Use of Means : A Duty ;* and *Because there is Wrath, Beware,* were published together in 1726, under the title of *Two Sermons Preached at Maldon.* He appears to have been a puritan of the old stock in principles and faith, tempered, perhaps, by the varied experiences of a long life. Dr. Tuckerman says : —

It is not improbable, that when he grew old, Mr. Cheever became more liberal in his feelings, than he was in the early part of his life. It is the natural tendency of a strong mind, profiting by its own observation and experience. [42]

He remained in the pulpit, serving God and respected by men, until he had passed the full age of ninety years, when in consequence of his age and infirmities, a colleague was ordained *Thomas Cheever:* and he was released from the cares of his pastorate. A little longer he waited until his change should come, and passed from this life, December 27, 1749, [43] " retaining the unabated affection of those to whom he had dispensed the word and ordinances of the gospel." [44] In the little retired and neglected burying ground at Rumney Marsh, which his son Joshua gave to the town of Chelsea, [45] stand, side by side, two rude stones, mossy and weather-worn. They are the crumbling memorials of two who bore together the burden of

[41] *Rumney-Marish Church Book.*

[42] Tuckerman, *Sermon,* 6.

[43] " He lived to be the oldest surviving graduate of the College; Samuel Andrew, of the Class of 1675, the next oldest before him, having died in 1738." Sibley, *Harvard Graduates,* ii. 503.

[44] Tuckerman, *Sermon,* 6.

[45] " Item the Burying Ground in my Land at Chelsea I give the same to the said Town forever, for that use only, with so much more land contiguous as shall be necessary for that use, wᵗʰ a convenient way to Carry their Dead to said Burying Ground, reserving to my Heirs, Executors, admˢ & assignees forever the Herbage." Will of Joshua Cheever, dated October 17, 1750; proved December 18, 1751, *Suffolk Co. Wills,* xlv. 601.

the cross which was laid upon them in the Malden church — Thomas Cheever and his wife, Sarah Bill.

Memento Mori

Here Lies y⁰ Body of	Here Lyes Buried
Mⁿ Sarah Cheeuer	y⁰ Body of y⁰ Revᵈ
Wife To Muster	Mʳ Thomas Cheever
Thomas Cheeuer	Who Departed This Life
Aged 47 Years	Decemᵇʳ 27ᵗʰ Anno Dom
Died January	1749 Aged 92 Years.
the 30ᵗʰ 170⅘.	

Much division and many troubles appear to have occurred after Mr. Cheever left Malden. Whatever reasons the Council may have had in advising the encouragement of Mr. Wigglesworth, they do not appear to have had any great weight with " the Church and Congregation of Maldon ; " nor do the people appear to have held their teacher in greater " Reputation." An attempt was made to have the town " com to a loueing agreement," at a meeting on the first day of the succeeding October. The summons by which this meeting was called is worthy of preservation, not only as illustrative of the condition of ecclesiastical affairs but as being the earliest Malden warrant known to be in existence.

To constable John Sprague you are in his majestyes name required to warne the inhabitance of the Towne to consider what is the best course to take for the providing for goodman felt : and that we may com to a loueing agreement for the vp holding and maintaineing of the worke of the minnistry amongst vs : the time of meeting is the first of october which is friday next at eaight of the clock in the morning.

By order and in the name of the selectmen

September : 25 : 86 :　　　　　　　　JOHN SPRAGUE.[46]

At the meeting, which was duly held, measures were taken for the relief of " ould felt ; " but, whatever discussion may have taken place, and doubtless the debate was earnest — angry, perhaps, there is no indication that any agreement, loving or otherwise, was proposed. The records are silent upon that matter. In the following December, the spirit of dissension was still alive

[46] Original in the possession of Artemas Barrett of Melrose, 1866.

in the Malden church, and the Government again interposed in its affairs.

At a Councill held in Boston New England December 8, 1686.

Upon reading the Petition of severall Inhabitants of Malden relateing to their Ministry

Ordered: That M.ʳ Stoughton, Cap.ᵗ Winthrop and Mʳ Wharton (with such other of the Members of the Councill as can be present) with M.ʳ Mather and M.ʳ Willard be impoured a Com.ᵗᵉᵉ to repair to Malden on Tuesday next the 14ᵗʰ inst: and to call before them the Petitioners and other Inhabitants of Malden, and to hear and finally determine and settle the maintainance of the Ministry there, and that the Clerk of the Councill do give forth Warrant to the Constables of Malden to warn a generall meeting at time & place accordingly.⁴⁷

The committee "repayred" to Malden at the appointed time; and its report shows that a minority of the people, at least, desired the restoration of Mr. Cheever.

In observance of an Order of the President and Council &c. Wee underwritten on the 14ᵗʰ Inst: repayred to Malden and upon a full hearing of all partyes do find that the former usage of that Towne hath been for many years to raise sixty pound per annum by a Rate upon the Inhabitants of the Towne for the maintainance of the Ministry, which of late by a Town vote & agreement hath been converted and altered to fifty pound in mony.

That M.ʳ Wigglesworth was many years since by choice and agreement universall ordained Teacher to the Church there, and though by sickness and indisposition he was for some years uncapiable to perform his worke, yet for many months last past he hath constantly attended the service of the Ministry and administration of the Sacraments amongst them, and declares his willingness so to do untill the people can upon a good agreement invite and obtaine some other Assistant to him and them therein.

That tho' there hath been for some years past an other person (viz.ᵗ M.ʳ Cheevers) ordained to the Service of the Ministry there, yet the said Cheevers haveing been convicted of severall grievous faults and debaucheries very Scandelous to his Ministry, whereby he is made uncapiable of his Office there ;

WEE. do therefore *Order.* That the select Men of Malden for the time being, do according to former usage lay the Rate of Sixty pounds half mony upon the Inhabitants of the said Towne equally, and attend the usuall method for collecting the same, and pay it unto M.ʳ Wiggles-

worth for his service, he continueing there in the supply & support of
the publick Worship and ordinances of God, and that no further disturbance or offer be made by any of the Inhabitants againe to restore
the said Cheevers to the service of the Ministry in that place which
will so apparently attend to the disturbance of the peace, and dishonour of God.

W.^M STOUGHTON
R.^D WHARTON.

The foregoing are true copyes.　Attested this 20th day of December
1686.

ED: RANDOLPH *Sec?* [48]

On the day when Randolph signed the record, Sir Edmund
Andros landed at Boston.　He cared as little for the ecclesiastical affairs of the colonists as the Malden people appeared to
care for the report and order of the committee; and the
Government made no attempt to enforce that which the people
seemed in no haste to obey.　The selectmen laid no ministerial
rates, and nothing favorable to Mr. Wigglesworth came out of
the matter.

Not only is there no evidence that the town did anything
towards the support of Mr. Wigglesworth; but for more than
five years after the meeting of the committee of the Council, he
is not so much as mentioned upon the records.　The people
still appear to have looked upon him as one who had no claims
upon them beyond what they might voluntarily choose to give;
and it is probable that by contributions and gifts made irregularly, joined with what meagre harvest his six and one-half
acres might yield, and the sale of his books and his precarious
gatherings as a physician, and, perhaps, as a teacher of youth
preparing for the college or the ministry, he lived during this
period of his life.　That he considered himself as settled by the
town and possessed of a claim upon it is evident from this
tantalizing passage in the *Bi-Centennial Book:* —

It appears by an old letter still extant, addressed to Mr. Wigglesworth by Samuel Sprague, of date July 22, 1687, that Mr. W. never
resigned his pastoral charge.[49]

[48] *Council Records*, ii. 101–102.　　　[49] *Bi-Centennial Book of Malden*, 156.

That which was extant in 1849 has since disappeared with other papers, the loss of which I must frequently bewail. There is no indication that Mr. Wigglesworth ever attempted to enforce the recognition of his supposed or real rights. He preferred, perhaps, to rely upon the sense of justice in the people, which he may have thought would awaken when he, himself, could properly discharge his pastoral duties.

It was during this period that he met with a serious loss in the death of his young wife, who had been a blessing and help to him. She died September 4, 1690, at the age of about twenty-eight years.[50] Mr. Wigglesworth was now near his sixtieth year; and the happy experiences of his second marriage and the care of six young children, of whom the eldest was not yet ten years old, were the probable inducements which led him soon to cast about for another helpmeet. That the second reason was, however, subordinate to the first must appear, however unwelcome, in the fact that when the candidate objected to the number of children he replied: "The Number may be lessened if there be need of it."

Sybil Sparhawk, the daughter of Nathaniel and Patience Sparhawk of Cambridge, was born about 1655. Her maternal grandfather, the Rev. Samuel Newman, in the wilderness of Rehoboth, by the light of blazing knots, wrote the first Concordance in the English language, which became the basis of the work of Cruden and all later compilers.[51] She married, July 22, 1679, Dr. Jonathan Avery, who died not long before Mrs. Wigglesworth; and she was living a widow at her house in Dedham when Mr. Wigglesworth was there in October, 1690. That she made an instant impression upon the heart of the bereaved and lonely poet may readily be gathered from a letter which he wrote in the following February.

[50] Mr. Wigglesworth took part in the formation of an association of the ministers of Boston and vicinity, October 13, 1690, and was the third signer of its articles. The objects of this association were "the promoting of the Gospel, and our mutual assistance and furtherance in that great work;" and its members agreed to "meet constantly, at the College in Cambridge, on a Monday at nine or ten of the clock in the morning, once in six weeks, or oftener if need be." Cf. Mather, *Magnalia*, Bk. v. (2); Dean, *Wigglesworth*, 106.

[51] Newman, *Rehoboth in the Past*, 52–53.

These for his esteemed friend, Mrs. Avery, widdow at her house, Dedham.

Mrs. Avery —

I heartily salute you in the Lord, giving you many thankes for yo[r] courtesies when I was at yo[r] house last October; since which time I have had many thoughts of you, and desires to speak with you: But not judging it seasonable, I have been still thus long. And now I make bold to visit you with a line or two, desiring to know how it fareth with yourself & children this sickly time, 2ly whither you still continue in yo[r] widdowhood, & be at Liberty or free from any Engagement, that a man may visit you without offence, 3ly And if you be free, whither a visit from me in order unto some further acquaintance would be welcome to you. To which queries if you please to return me a brief Answer by this bearer, I shall take it for a kindness, & shall better understand what God calls me to do, being ready to wait upon you by a visit y[e] first opportunity, if you incourage me so to doe. Not else at present, but with my hearty Prayers for yourself & yours I rest,

yo[r] loving Friend

Maldon, Feb[r] 11, 1690.   MICHA[L] WIGGLESWORTH.

If you cannot conveniently return an answer in writing so speedily, you may trust the Messenger to bring it by word of mouth, who is grave & faithful, and knows upon what errant he is sent. . . .

farewell. [62]

This was so well received that a second visit followed on " y[e] first opportunity; " and that a serious matter was proposed and met with some objections is evident from the long and somewhat curious document which follows: —

Mrs. Avery }
& my very kind friend. }

I heartily salute you in y[e] Lord with many thanks for yo[r] kind entertainment when I was with you March 2d. I have made bold once more to visit you by a few lines in y[e] inclosed paper, not to prevent a personal visit, but rather to make way for it, which I fully intend the beginning of y[e] next week if weather and health Prevent not, craving the favor that you will not be from home at that Time, yet if yo[r] occasions cannot comply with that Time, I shall endeavor to wait upon you at any other Time that may suit you better. Not further to trouble you at this Time, but only to present y[e] inclosed to yo[r] serious thoughts, I commend both it. & you to y[e] Lord & wait for

---

[62] *Christian Register*, June 1, 1850; *N. E. Hist. and Geneal. Reg.* xvii. 139.

an Answer from Heaven in due season, meanwhile I am & shall remain, Yo^r True Friend
& wel-wisher,

Maldon March 23, 1691. MICHAEL WIGGLESWORTH.

I make bold to spread before you these following considerations which Possibly may help to clear up yor way before y^u return an answer unto ye Motion wch I have made to you, I hope you will take them in good Part and Ponder them seriously.

1st. I have a great perswasion that ye motion is of God, for diverse Reasons.

As first that I should get a little acquaintance with you by a short & transient visit having been altogether a stranger to you before, and that so little acquaintance should leave such impressions behind it, as neither length of Time, distance of Place, nor any other objects could wear off, but that my thoughts & heart have been toward you ever since.

2^{ly}. That upon serious, earnest and frequent seeking of God for guidance & Direction in so weighty a matter, my thoughts have still been determined unto and fixed upon yo^{r}self as the most suitable Person for me.

3^{ly}. In that I have not been led hereunto by fancy (as too many are in like cases) but by sound Reason & judgment, Principally Loving and desiring you for those gifts & graces God had bestowed upon you, and Propounding ye Glory of God, the adorning and furtherance of ye Gospel. The spiritual as wel as outward good of myself and family, together wth ye good of yo^{r}self & children, as my Ends inducing me hereunto.

2^{ly}. Be Pleased to Consider, that although you may Peradventure have offers made you by Persons more Eligible, yet you can hardly meet with one that can love you better, or whose love is built upon a surer foundation, or that may be capable of doing more for you in some respects than myself. But let this be spoken with all humility, & without ostentation. I can never think meanly enough of myself.

3^{ly}. Whither there be not a great sutableness in it for one that hath been a Physician's wife to match with a Physician, By this means you may in some things & at some Times afford more help than another, & in like manner receive help, get an increase of skill, and become capable of doing more that way hereafter if need should be.

4^{ly}. Whither God doth not now invite you to ye doing of some more Eminent Service for him, than you are capable of doing in yor Present Private capacity? and whither those many Emptyings from vessel to vessel & great afflictions that have befaln you might not be sent with a design to fit you for further service, & to losen you from ye Place & way you have been in?

5^{ly}. Whither ye enjoyment of Christ in all his ordinances (which at present cannot be had where you are) be not a thing of that weight that may render this motion at this time somewhat more considerable?

6^{ly}. Consider, if you should continue where you are whither ye looking after & managing of yor outward Business & affairs may not be too hard for you, and hazzard your health again?

7^{ly}. If God should exercise you with sickness again whither it were not more comfortable and safe to have a neer and dear friend to take care of you and yours at such a Time, especially now when yor dear mother is gone to Heaven.

8^{ly}. This following summer is Likely to be full of Troubles (unless God prevent them beyond the expectation of man) by reason of our Indian and French Enemyes: now whither it may not be more comfortable and safe to get neerer ye heart of the Country, than to continue where you are & to live as you do?

9^{ly}. The consideration of ye many afflictions, losses & Bereavements which have befallen you, as it hath affected my heart with deep sympathy, so it hath been no small inducement to me to make this motion, hopeing that if God should give it acceptance with you I might be a friend & a Comforter to you instead of yor many lost relations; and I hope upon trial you would find it so.

10^{ly}. As my Late wife was a means under God of my recovering a better state of Health; so who knows but God may make you instrumental to Preserve & Prolong my health & life to do him service.

Obj. As to that main objection in respect to my Age, I can say nothing to that, But my Times are in the hands of God, who as he hath restored my health beyond expectation, can also if he Please Prolong it while he hath any service for me to do for his Name. And in ye mean time, if God shall Please and yourself be willing to Put me in that Capacity, I hope I shall do you as much Good in a little time as it is Possible for me to do, & use some endeavours also to Provide for yor future, as wel as Present, welfare, as God's Bounty shall enable me; for true love cannot be idle.

Ob. And for ye other objection from ye number of my children & difficulty of guiding such a family. 1st. the Number may be lessened if there be need of it.

2^{ly}. I shall gladly improve my authority to strengthen yours (if God shall so Perswade your heart) to do what lieth in me to make the burden as light & comfortable as may be. And I am perswaded there would be a great suitableness in our tempers, spirits, Principles, & consequently a sweet and harmonious agreement in those matters (& in all other matters) betwixt us, and indeed this Perswasion is a Principle thing wch hath induced me to make this motion to yo^{r}self & to no other.

Finally that I be not over tedious, I have great hope, that if God shall Perswade you to close with this motion, the Consequents will be for yᵉ furthurance of yᵉ Gospel, for yᵉ Comfort of us both, & of both our familyes & that yᵉ Lord will make us mutual helpers & Blessings to each other, & that we shall enjoy much of God together in such a Relation, without which no relation can be truly sweet.[53]

That Mr. Wigglesworth went to Dedham very soon, if not as early as "the beginning of yᵉ next week," as proposed, and that the objections of his "very kind friend" were overcome is very evident; for they were married by the Rev. Moses Fiske of Braintree, June 23, 1691.[54] "She was beloved for her kind and charitable disposition," says Mr. Dean; "and her character and standing in society may have aided her husband in allaying the troubles in his parish."[55]

---

[53] *Christian Register*, June 1, 1850; *N. E. Hist. and Geneal. Reg.* xvii. 140–142.

[54] "In the course of his wooing, at what period there is no record, a silver locket in the form of a heart was presented to the lady by her lover. This locket, not larger than a fourpence, is curiously wrought. On the front is a heart with wings on each side. It rests against an anchor; as if it hath flown to her, and there found its resting place. On the back, the words 'thine forever' are marked. After the death of Mrs. Wigglesworth it became the property of one of her daughters by her first marriage, Dorothy Avery; and descended to the great-grandson of the original owner, Rev. Thomas Cary, pastor of the first religious society in Newburyport. Mr. Cary's colleague, Rev. Dr. Andrews, married a descendant of Michael Wigglesworth, a granddaughter of the first Professor of Divinity in Harvard College, who was the only child born to Mr. Wigglesworth, after his marriage with Mrs. Avery. Soon after the death of Mr. Cary's only daughter, the family of his colleague were passing a day at his house. After dinner Mr. Cary told the story of the locket and produced it. A lilac ribbon had suspended it from the neck of a former owner. Mr. Cary placed it on that of his colleague's daughter, saying, that it had remained in his family long enough, and now ought to go to another branch. There seemed indeed a propriety in its belonging to a descendant of both parties. The mother of the child to whom it was given, had, after her father's death, received among other things a small silver box, the cover made of an English shilling, and on the bottom the letters S. W. were marked — the initials of Mrs. Avery's name after her second marriage. For what purpose the silver box was made had never been discovered or conjectured. A finger ring, unless smaller than the usual size, could not lie in it; but the little silver heart fitted in exactly. It was agreed by all who saw them that the box must have been made to keep the locket from harm; but that the latter having been worn round the neck, for a length of time, the box was forgotten; and on the death of Mrs. Wigglesworth, and the division of her effects among her children — her son had taken the box, and one of her daughters the locket, and so they had descended in different branches of the family; and after being separated three generations were re-united in the fourth " The Rev. Andrew P. Peabody, D.D., in the *Christian Register*, June 1, 1850.

[55] Dean, *Wigglesworth*, 105. There was one child by this marriage. Edward Wigglesworth was born in or soon after the year 1692, and was graduated

Under the date of March 14, 169½, appears the first recorded mention of Mr. Wigglesworth as one to whom the town owed aught; and there is an air of constraint about the record which makes the grant appear to have been grudgingly given.

uoted at the same time that the towne will find m͏ʳ wegelsworth with wood in a general way at sartaine dayes a pointed for this present yeare if any refuse or nelect after the time apointed more than 6 days for a teme of 4 oxen to pay : 6 Shillings and for 2 oxen to pay : 4 Shillings and for a man : 2 Shillings and this to be taken by destres by a constabel : by warrent from the selectmen.

The next year, " The 21 of this Instant : March Is apointed to cut and cart wood for m͏ʳ Wigglesworth ;" and a year later, the selectmen passed an order with more directness and force.

At a Meeting of y͏ᵉ select men at Isaac Hills y͏ᵉ 19 of Ianuary 169¾ : Jt is ordered y͏ᵗ one Wensday next which is y͏ᵉ 24 of this Jnstant Janeuary shall be a day for all y͏ᵉ Jnhabitants of this Town to cut an carry firewood for m͏ʳ Wigglesworth.

The tide of public opinion had now turned in Mr. Wigglesworth's favor; and during the remainder of his life he met with the support and respect which his position and his natural good qualities as a man and a Christian deserved. It is probable that his trials and experience in life had chastened and refined his mind and modified or, perhaps, eradicated its morbid ten-

---

at Harvard College, 1710. He was for a while usher of a grammar school in Boston "and left it with the design of settling in the ministry. He took a chamber at college, lived there and preached occasionally 'till June 28, 1721, when he was elected the first Hollis Professor of Divinity, at the age of thirty years. He was inaugurated to this office, October 21, 1722, and held it, with high repute for his piety and learning, upwards of forty years. He was a Fellow of the Corporation of this University, and received the degree of Doctor of Divinity from Edinburgh in 1730." Thaddeus William Harris, *MS. Genealogical Sketch of the Wigglesworth Family.*

Professor Wigglesworth died at Cambridge, January 16, 1765, at the age of seventy-two years, and was succeeded in his chair by his only son, Edward, who was born at Cambridge, Feb. 7, 173⅓ and died June 17, 1794. The latter was father of Thomas Wigglesworth, a well known and successful merchant of Boston during the first half of this century.

The third Hollis Professor was the Rev. David Tappan, a grandson of Mr. Wigglesworth's second daughter, Abigail, the eldest child of the youthful Martha Mudge. " It is a very remarkable circumstance," says Dr. McClure, "that of the four Hollis Professors, the first three, who held the chair for eighty successive years, with high reputation, should have been respectively the son, grandson, and great-grandson of that good man." *Bi-Centennial Book of Malden, 156.*

dencies, which in his earlier days, and while suffering with his many bodily troubles, had not been an especially pleasant quality in his character. His physical weaknesses had passed away; and he was, as Increase Mather says, "restored to such a measure of Health, as to be able to Preach for many years twice every Lords Day, after he had been for a long time in a Languishing condition." [56]

Another generation of men and women had succeeded to the places of those who had formed the church and congregation in earlier days; and most of those who had favored Mr. Matthews, and who had undoubtedly exercised a disturbing influence and formed an opposition to Mr. Wigglesworth, had passed away. Of the nine who withstood the General Court, not one was living in March, 169¾; and it is significant that one of the most prominent, Captain John Wayte, who, after the removal of Joseph Hills to Newbury, had been the most influential man of the town and church, had died but a few months before.[57] If any unjust prejudices and opposition had existed in regard to the teacher they were now forgotten; and thenceforth Mr. Wigglesworth became the faithful counsellor and friend of his flock — "Mauldens Physician for Soul and Body two."

His position and claims were first distinctly and fully recognized, March 12, 169¾, when it was voted: —

That yᵉ town will alow mʳ Wigglesworth fifty five pounds a yeer yeerly Jn money: And yᵉ use of the passonag. and a suficant suply of fierwood. so Long as He carrieth one yᵉ work of yᵉ minestrey: yᵉ yeere begineth yᵉ 12 of March 1694; . . . voted that mʳ Wigglesworth shall haue Thirty Cord of Cordwood Laid a his dore for this present yeer.

At a meeting held, May 18, 1694, it was voted: —

That yᵉ Select men hath liberty granted to order and lay a penalty upon those yᵗ shall neglect to carry their proportion of wood for mʳ

---

[56] I. Mather in dedication prefixed to C. Mather, *A Faithful Man.*

[57] Abraham Hill, February 13, 16⁶⁹/₇₀; Thomas Call, May, 1676, ae. 79; John Upham, February 25, 168½, ae. 84; Edward Carrington, 1684; James Green, March 29, 1687;

Joseph Hills, at Newbury, February 5, 168⅞, ae. 85; Captain John Sprague, June 25, 1692, ae. 68; Ralph Shepard, September 11, 1693, ae. 90; Captain John Wayte, September 26, 1693, ae. 75.

Wigglesworth for This present yeere : and that y⁰ Select men are hereby
Jmpowered to grant warranty to The constables to take y⁰ forfiturs by
destress.

The salary was somewhat changed, perhaps increased, March
18, 1695/6, when it was voted : —

That mʳ wigglesworth shall Haue fifty pounds jn money for this present yeere : to be Raised one this form : by taking a new Jnvoice of all
Reatable Estate : And all y⁰ Straingers money yᵗ coms Jnto y⁰ contri-
butien box mʳ wigglesworth shall haue ouer and aboue.

The method of gathering the contributions and the distinction
of " Straingers money " are explained in a vote passed a short
time previous.

All the inhabitance of this Town that contrabute to the minestry doe
pute thare mony in papers with thare names and some of mony in it
and all those that doue not contrabute shall pay in thare mony quarterly to the deakens and if any man pute in his mony in to the box
naked it shall be luked at as Strangers mony and so lowset.

At a meeting, May 8, 1696, it was voted,

That all male parsons of one and twenty yeers and upwards shall be
Reated three shillings pʳ head to y⁰ minestars sallerey for this presant
yeer Excepting such parsons as y⁰ select men hes Just cause to omit by
Reson of pouerty or other wise.

Mr. Wigglesworth received three lots in the division of common lands in 1695 ; and, in addition, it was voted that

mʳ wigglesworth shall haue all the land betwene his lote in the sec-
cand diuision on the weste side the Riuer and Charlestowne line which
is aboute ane accer and a halfe.

Mr. Dean suggests that,

The delay of the town in recognizing him as their minister, by vot-
ing him a salary, may have been partly owing to an apprehension that
by so doing they would render themselves liable to him for past
services.[58]

There is some color to this supposition. A full settlement of
all arrears appears to have been made at the end of the first
year; and a receipt was entered and signed upon the town
book, which, although no sum was named, was broad enough to

[58] Dean, *Wigglesworth*, 105.

cover any claim which Mr. Wigglesworth may have been able to make.

These lines are to let all men understand That I, Michael Wigglesworth of Malden, doe Herby discharg And acquit the Town of Malden from all claimes that may be made heerafter by my self my haires executors Administrators or a signes upon the acount of aney Salary debt or dues to me for the work of yᵉ ministery from the begining of The world untill the 12 of March 1694⁵⁄₅. In witness of yᵉ primeses, I have hereunto set my hand and seall this 28 of March, 169⁵⁄₆.

MICHAEL WIGGLESWORTH [*seal.*].

June 1, 1696, while his parishioner, Colonel Nicholas Paige, was captain of the " Ancient and Honorable Artillery Company," he preached the annual sermon before that body. It was never printed. Sewall writes: —

Mr. Wigglesworth preaches the Artillery sermon from Ephes. 6, 11, Put on the whole Armour of God, that ye may be able to stand against the wiles of the Devil. In the Applications, said 't was necessary we should doe so by reason of the evil of the Times or else of Popery, or something as bad as Popery should come to be set up. What should we doe? Mentioned Rev. 16, 15, said the Garments there and Armour in the Text were the same. About Dinner Time the Guns were fired at the Castle and Battery for joy that the Plot was discovered.[59]

That Mr. Wigglesworth in taking up the duties of a pastor assumed the title as well is uncertain. There is no indication that he styled himself otherwise than Teacher; and he is so called in the later editions of the *Day of Doom*, issued during his lifetime. But the Mathers, who, surely, fully understood the difference between the terms, called him Pastor; and as such he appears in the inventory of his estate and upon his gravestone.

The few remaining years of his life passed quietly, in the gentle ministrations of his dual office of pastor and physician, and were free from the anxieties and cares, as well as the extreme bodily weaknesses, which had formerly been his portion; but although he was in a measure restored to health, he

[59] *Mass. Hist. Coll*, xlv. 427. The rejoicing was on account of the discovery of the Popish Plot, the news of which had recently been received. Cf. Macaulay, *Hist. of England*, chap. xxi.

never became entirely well. Some time about 169⅞ he passed through a dangerous sickness — perhaps a return of his old malady. Of this and its effect upon the people Cotton Mather says, addressing "the Church and Congregation at Maldon": —

Your *Love*, show'd it self, when a Dangerous Fit of *Sickness* was upon him. You came together with Agony; you *Prayed*, and *Fasted* and *Wept* before the Lord, with Public Supplications for his *Life*. God heard you; God Loves to hear such Prayers. God Spared him yet unto you, *Another Life*. For *Seven years* more, you had him among you.[60]

Sewall adds his testimony to the health of Mr. Wigglesworth at this time.

Feby' 21. [169⅞]. I rid over to Charlestown on the Ice, then over to Stoweri's,[61] go to Mr. Wigglesworth : The snow was so deep that I had a hard Journey, could go but a foot pace upon Mystick River, the snow was so deep. Mr. Wigglesworth preach'd Jan' 23. from those words, who can stand before his Cold? Then by reason of his own and peoples sickness, Three Sabbaths pass'd without publick worship. Feb. 20. a very cold day, He preached from those words; He sends forth his word and thaws them; which began 21 and especially 22, and has thaw'd much and yet moderately.[62]

It was doubtless this sickness which caused the town to vote, March 31, 1698, " y^t ye town will aford m^r wigglesworth sum help 4 or 5 sabath days in ye work of ye minestry." Perhaps he never recovered from this illness; for he was no longer young, and years of sickness had not tended to strengthen his powers of endurance. He speaks of himself in 1704 as one "with a weak body and trembling hands." [63]

Cotton Mather says of him: —

[60] Mather, *A Faithful Man*, 25.

[61] The "house of entertainment" kept by Richard Stowers and his wife Joanna was next to Penny Ferry on Mystic Side. Both host and hostess were dead at the time of Sewall's visit; but the house may still have been kept open by their heirs. It finally came into the possession of John Sprague, who married Elizabeth Stowers. The ancient house, which stood until 1894 at the southerly junction of Broadway and Bow Street in Everett, and was known as the Flagg house, may have been that which was visited by Sewall. It was certainly on or near the site of the Stowers house and it was in the possession of descendants of John Sprague within this century.

[62] *Mass. Hist. Coll.*, xlv. 471.

[63] Ibid., xxxviii. 647.

It was a surprize unto us to see a Little Feeble *Shadow of a Man,*[64] beyond *Seventy, Preaching* usually Twice or Thrice in a Week; Visiting and Comforting the *Afflicted;* Encouraging the *Private Meetings; Catechizing* the Children of the Flock; and managing the *Government* of the Church; and attending the *Sick,* not only as a *Pastor,* but as a *Physician* too; and this not only in his own Town, but also in all those of the Vicinity. Thus he did, *unto the last;* and was but one *Lords-Day* taken off, before his *Last.*[65]

Of his character his descendant and biographer writes: —

He was neither a cynic nor a misanthrope, though sickness, which nourishes and brings to light such dispositions where they exist, had long been his companion. His attenuated frame and feeble health were joined to genial manners; and, though subject to fits of despondency, he seems generally to have maintained a cheerful temper.[66]

Of his characteristics as a poet I have already spoken. As a preacher, his sermons were marked by a modest though energetic clearness of thought, which, joined to the natural polish and grace of his manners, made him when he came to be known without the influence of prejudice and the memory of past troubles to be respected and beloved by his people. His memory long remained fragrant in the church and town and outlived the generation of those who had known him.[67]

---

[64] From a passage in Sewall's Diary, *Mass. Hist. Coll.,* xlvi. 37, it is inferred that Mr. Wigglesworth, contrary to the prevailing fashion of men at that time, wore his own hair, and, like the elder Cheever, "He abominated Perriwigs."

The wearing of wigs was a fruitful source of trouble to the simple-minded Chief Justice. In another place he relates how Mr. Wadsworth appeared in one of the abominations, and he adds: "Mr. Chiever is griev'd at it." Sewall was not alone in his opposition to the new fashion; for, while many other worthies discountenanced it by their example, Mr. Higginson wrote an essay against it, which Sewall wished to have printed, and Mr. Symmes strove against it, although he was "repulsed." The sorrow and surprise of the diarist were great when in a Thursday lecture Cotton Mather vindicated the custom and deprecated hypocrisy. Sewall was not a great friend of the Mathers. Later in life, when he had lost his hair by sickness, he wore a plain black cap as his protest against the vain periwigs which had so troubled him.

[65] Mather, *A Faithful Man,* 26.

[66] Dean, *Wigglesworth,* 9–10.

[67] Within the memory of the living his name has been a sacred one in many families. The late Rev. Samuel Sewall says: — "According to a current tradition in Malden, the venerable Deacon [John] Ramsdell, who died there about 1825 [February 7, 1825, ae. 85.], at a very advanced age and had doubtless heard in his youth from his parents or others of Mr. Wigglesworth's '*good report,*' was accustomed as long as he lived, to make an annual visit to the Grave Yard in which the mortal remains of that good man were deposited, and

At length, after a life of more than usual bodily trials and worldly crosses, while enjoying the full fruitage of a mind

A Faithful Man,
Defcribed and Rewarded.

SOME

Obfervable & Serviceable
Paffages in the

LIFE and DEATH
OF

Mr. Michael Wigglefworth,

Late Paftor of *MALDON*;
Who Refted from his Labours, on the
Lords-Day, June 10th. 1705. In the
Seventy Fourth year of his Age.
AND
MEMORIALS of PIETY,
Left behind him among his Written
EXPERIENCES.

With a **Funeral-Sermon** Preached
(for him) at *Maldon ; June* 24. 1705.

By **Cotton Mather.**

*Factitium Vobis Sermonem in Omni forma
Sanctitatis Dei Servus Exhibuit.*
Bern. in obit. Humb.

Bofton : Printed by **B. Green,** for
Benj. Eliot, at his Shop under the Weft-
End of the Town-Houfe. 1705.

carefully *to rub off the moss*, which had gathered, in each interval, on the Inscription, which told where he lay. The moss which had collected thickly upon it in 1834, bore melancholy witness that no Deacon Ramsdell was then left to keep it plain and legible. Still

' The sweet remembrance of the just
Shall flourish, when he sleeps in dust.' "

American Quarterly Register, xiv. 400.

tempered and chastened by bitter experiences, subdued and rendered gentle and cheerful by Christian sympathy and divine trust, in the midst of a people who had outgrown opposition and indifference and had learned to love him as "a dear friend, a wise counsellor, and a strong helper," the end came.[68] He lived, as he had hoped, to serve God to the last, having preached on the Sunday before he was attacked by fever. He lingered about ten days and "Finnished his Work and Entre^d apon an Eternal Sabbath of Rest on ye Lords Day Iune ye 10 1705 in ye 74 Year of his Age."[69] While dying he said to one who spoke to him: — "For more than Fifty years together, I have been Labouring to uphold a Life of Communion with God; and I thank the Lord, I now find the Comfort of it."[70]

Among his manuscripts was found this verse which to him who reads it aright is as a cloud of gloomy thoughts, born of bitter experiences, illumined by the almost heavenly grace and faith of the dying teacher: —

DEATH *Expected and Welcomed.*

Welcome, Sweet REST, by me so long Desired,
Who have with Sins and Griefs, so long been tired.
And Welcome, DEATH, my Fathers Messenger;
Of my Felicity the Hastener.
Welcome, Good ANGELS, who, for me Distrest,
Are come to Guard me to Eternal Rest.
Welcome, O CHRIST, who hast my Soul Redeemed;
Whose Favour I have more than Life Esteemed.[71]

---

[68] *Mors, Separavit a Nobis, Dulcem Amicum, Prudentem Consiliarium, Fortem Auxiliarium.* Bern. de Humberto. Mather, *A Faithful Man*, 27.

[69] Gravestone at Sandy Bank (Bell Rock). Sewall thus notices his death : — "Lord's Day, June 10, 1705. The Learned and pious Mr. Michael Wigglesworth died at Malden about 9. m. Had been sick about 10. days of a Fever; 73 years and 8 moneths old. He was the Author of the Poem entituled The Day of Doom, which has been so often printed: and was very useful as a Physician." *Mass. Hist. Coll.*, xlvi. 132. At the following Commencement, Edward Holyoke, afterwards President of the College, "began that part of his oration relating to Mr. Wigglesworth with,

Maldonatus Orthodoxus," a double allusion to his dwelling-place and the pious and learned Jesuit Johannes Maldonatus. Cf. Pierce, *Hist. of Harvard University*; 251; *Mass. Hist. Coll.* xlvi. 134; Dean, *Wigglesworth*, 115.

Edward Wigglesworth wrote in the commonplace book of his father: "It Pleased ye Almighty disposer of all things, in his wise providence to exercise me with such an afflicting dispensation y^rof, as ye bereaving me of him who should have been ye Guide of my Youth by causing my Father to rest from his labours on ye Lords day, June ye 10th 1705, In ye Seventy fourth year of his Age."

[70] Mather, *A Faithful Man*, 27.

[71] Ibid., 45.

On Sunday, June 24, 1705, in the little meeting house by the side of Bell Rock, Cotton Mather preached a sermon on "a faithful man," in memory of "that Faithful and Aged Servant of God,"[72] who a little earlier had been laid to rest in the burying ground at Sandy Bank, near by, in the midst of the dead, who when living had been the cause of both joy and sorrow in his heart.[73]

The preacher "remembered" him afterwards in an epitaph, which he appended to the funeral sermon.

> His Pen did once *Meat from the Eater* fetch;
> And now he's gone beyond the *Eaters* reach.
> His *Body*, once so *Thin*, was next to *None ;*
> From Thence, he's to *Unbodied Spirits flown.*
> Once his rare skill did all *Diseases* heal;
> And he does nothing now *uneasy* feel.
> He to his *Paradise* is Joyful come;
> And waits with Joy to see his *Day of Doom.*

Full of quaint and characteristic conceits is the composure of the punning pastor of the Old North Church; but better known

[72] This sermon was preached from the following text: Be thou faithful unto death, and I will give thee a crown of life. *Rev.* ii. 10. It was soon after printed. A modernized edition, in which the authorship was carelessly ascribed to Increase Mather, was issued in 1849, "at the instance, and chiefly at the expense" of the late Mrs. Dolly (Blanchard) Upham, and distributed among the inhabitants of Malden, "in hopes of their sharing in the blessings she has received from its perusal." The reprint contains a short introduction by the Rev. Alexander W. McClure.

[73] The following vote was passed by the town, March 8, 170⁵⁄₆; "*voted y*ᵗ Mʳˢ Wigglesworth shall haue alowed her 4 shiling pʳ weeke for her entertaining yᵉ ministars sinc Mʳ Wigglesworth deces̊ᵈ: which is 30 weeks. *vote* yᵗ Mʳˢ Wigglesworth shall haue 12. 10. 0. money paid her for mʳ Wigglesworth Labour jn yᵉ ministrey yᵉ last quarter of a yeer he lived."

Mrs. Wigglesworth remained a short time in Malden, and then removed to Cambridge among her relatives, where Judge Sewall visited her, July 4, 1707, and found her suffering with the jaundice. She died, August 6, 1708, at the age of fifty-two years. Sewall writes · "Monday, Augᵗ 9. 1708. Went to the Funeral of Mrs. Wigglesworth. Bearers of Mrs. Wigglesworth, The President and Mr. Hobart; Mr. Thacher, Mr. Danforth Dorchʳ; Mr. Brattle, Mr. Walter. Only Col. Phillips and I of the Council were there: Mr. Speaker was there." *Mass. Hist. Coll.*, xlvi. 229. Her son, Edward Wigglesworth, writes of her as "an affectionate, charitable, praying saint, one who desired the good of everybody, and likewise to be herself ever doing in good." He adds that she "endured many sorrows and underwent great afflictions, in all which she was a mirrour of patience and constancy, bearing all with true Christian fortitude, till at length God took her from a sinful and weary world to joy unspeakable and full of glory." MS. of E. Wigglesworth, cited by Dean, *Wigglesworth*, 123.

and more often quoted is the terse and homely couplet on the mossy stone at the dead teacher's head.

HERE LIES INTERD IN SILENT GRAU^E
BELOW   MAULDENS PHYSICIAN
FOR SOUL AND BODY TWO.

CHAPTER X.

WHATEVER the superficial observer may pretend to see in the past which is now two centuries agone, there was very little of romance in the lives of the foredwellers of New England. The land which, when weary leagues away beyond the sea, seemed to flow with milk and honey and to stand forth a later Canaan amid the virgin forests of the new world, became to their nearer vision a reality of bleak and rocky shores, a stubborn land of dark woods and rocky soil wherein Israel might rest; but where existence was to be had at the price of privations not unmixed with suffering, and where a livelihood was only to be gained by the literal sweat of the brow.

Out of such surroundings and from such conditions arose a generation not unlike the country which had given them birth and in which their early youth had been passed. While the first generation of settlers, English born and bred as they were, were English in their ways, the second generation, to whom England was a far-off land — the land indeed of their fathers and mothers, but as unreal to them as a land of dreams, were a step removed from English manners and perhaps from English habits of thought. There was then a beginning of those characteristics of body and mind which had widely diverged from the English standards before the close of the provincial period, and which at the present day distinguish the men of New England from their insular kinsmen.

Much though there may have been of spiritual grace in these men and women of the seventeenth century, there was little of that outward grace which tempers the manners of men and beautifies, if it does not elevate, the lives which fall within the circle of its influence. Out of the hard and simple lives which they led perforce came a race of hard and simple men and women, who were almost without a sense of the beautiful, thinking little of those arts which had borne a rich fruitage in the land of their fathers, and who were as careless of the beautiful in nature as in art. Hardly within the pale of civilization could a people be found, even in the seventeenth century, so destitute of the æsthetic sense. In music, their knowledge was bounded by the few tunes which they painfully sung in a high and unnatural key in the dreary meeting houses, which matched the tunes they sung. Of painting and sculpture they knew comparatively nothing; and poetry of a range above the Bay Psalms or the Day of Doom, and philosophy, except it came within the narrow limits of a prescribed theology, were forbidden fruits.

What little of elegance they might possess was not of that kind which elevates and refines; but rather that which appealed to the lower senses. Something of affectation in dress, some little approach to luxury at table in the direction of richer food or costly wines, some little extravagances in house or lands there were now and then, but nothing more. Articles of silver there were here and there, sometimes, furniture of English make and superior fashion; but they were mostly articles of necessity or things which the love of father or mother had consecrated and which had come to New England in the moving of the household gods. Otherwise, the furniture and service of the people in general were rude and unhandy, save where pride had gathered something better or more costly for ostentatious purposes alone.

Nor was the inner life of the people of a more pleasing cast. Over the souls of men there seemed to rest a sombre cloud, which obscured or wholly hid what might have been open and bright. As were the actions of men, so were their thoughts. They seemed to have been set in a minor key. There was darkness wherever they turned. Man, born in pain, passed through a life of trouble and died. Even the hopes or certainties of a blessed immortality were transmuted in the alembic of their gloomy minds into denunciations of wrath to the children of men; and the brightest hopes and the deepest consolations that they could gather from the grave bore fruit in lugubrious wails and warnings, which at a later day looked out at the passer-by from beneath grinning or painful cherubs carved in all the rudeness of the gravestone cutter's art.

> you that pass by this place may think on me,
> For as you are so once you dide me see;
> what I am now will quickly be your doom;
> Prepare for death before the summonds come.

While such was the prevailing condition of society, if that can be called society where so much is wanting, there was yet a lower depth; and where the influences which held men to a strict and rigid line of morality were relaxed there was a falling away, at times, into debasing crimes, some of which are rare or altogether unknown in New England at the present day. It must not be forgotten, in extenuation, that the seventeenth century was within the limits of the great age of brutality, which outlasted the middle ages and penetrated even into the years of our later civilization. It was an age of excess in all things, even in religion; and if religion, or the moral power which it exerts, were wanting and men indulged their more earthy passions, they ran to wild extremes and horrid depravities.

Yet there was much of promise in the strait and formal habits of life and thought of the fathers of New England. Underlying all was a sound and uncompromising enmity to injustice and wrong, and an unflinching devotion to the right, as they understood it; and more than all, there was a sturdy assertion of the independence of the individual and, through him, of the masses. There was an ever-present democracy, latent sometimes and sometimes militant, but always ready to spring into life and action. They were not always law-abiding; but it was a wicked or an unjust law which they resisted; and their resistance was usually fortified by good and sufficient legal principles. These were English characteristics — or rather, Puritanic-English characteristics, tempered and changed in time by circumstances; for the first comers possessed them at the beginning, although they were not inclined to act as readily and freely as their children of the next and succeeding generations, to whom was given to fill the measure of wrath against oppression. Out of these qualities came all that has endured of the old Puritanic fabric which the fathers reared; and, while the mistakes and weaknesses of the past have disappeared one by one, these enduring qualities have remained with us as a people and are the corner-stones of a great nation.

Of similar characteristics were the settlers and early inhabitants of Malden; and while they may not have reached the higher limits of those qualities, they, happily, did not descend to the lower depths of ignorance and crime. They were the common people of a common New England settlement of the lesser kind — farmers, woodsmen, and craftsmen, who cleared their lands and built their humble homes, jealously guarding their privileges as well against ecclesiastical as against civil encroachments. I have already repeated some part of the story of their opposition to injustice and their independent assertion and defence of their invaded rights. Otherwise, they were a simple folk, as poor in worldly goods as they were in the outward graces; but inwardly as rich in the Puritanic qualities of pluck and patience as they were outwardly poor. I cannot say for them that they were of the better class of settlers in the extraneous matters of birth and rank. There is only a faint indication that William Brackenbury was of an aristocratic family; and William Sargeant was a son of a mayor of an English city. Joseph Hills and John Wayte divided with them the education and honors of the community.[1] Yet what were rank and family,

[1] Happy am I if I have not aroused the ire of my fellow townsmen in asserting the humble origin of our forebears. If I have read aright, the aim of many writers of local history has been to "glorify" the fathers in the face of reason and reality. The founders of New England were humble men, mechanics and farmers — delvers for the most part; and their honors were not

or even education, except so far as it strengthened the man who
owned it, in the woods of Mystic Side? There were fields to
clear, houses, roads, and mills to build, and above all, in God's
providence, the foundations of a nation to lay deep, though they
in their weakness knew it not, happily building better than they
knew.

These were the conditions of the people of Malden during
the period which intervened between their settlement and the
war of the Indian Philip. Their work was that of subduing the
forests and wild lands, and bringing them into forms fit for the
uses of civilization. Then were laid out farms, whose boundary
lines may still be traced, and roads, which from mere winding
paths have become our principal streets.

Although the bounds of Malden have in the course of years
become circumscribed, and its territory divided, it has room for
a present population greater than the men of 1650 could have
ever dreamed would occupy their lands; yet the town was early
found too strait for the handful of settlers who occupied it; and
in 1662 they addressed the following petition to the General
Court: —

Maldens Petition for Pen"ycooke.

*To the honoured Court now Assembled at Boston the 7ᵗʰ of th 4ᵗʰ Mᵒ.
1662:*

the petition of the inhabitants of Maldon humbly Shewing.

That the Bounds of our Town are Exceeding streight; the most of our
Jmproued lands & Meadow being limited About two Miles in length
and one in Breadth; And that Allso the most part of it by purchase
from Charlstᵒ. wherof wee were A small Branch; from whom Allso wee
had all the Comᵐonꞩ wee haue; which is verie small & Rockie.

That hitherto, we haue had no Jnlargement from the Countrie; nor
can wee haue Any neere Adioyning, being Surrounded by sundry
Townshipps.

That our Charges to the Countrie & Ministry much Exceedeth sundry
others, who haue many times our Accomᵐodations And as many here

such as spring from titles and rank.
If, here and there, one exceeded the
others in attainments and birth, it was
an exception to the general rule. Nor
were they always the heroes and saints
which amateur writers affect to believe.
Their weaknesses and faults were those
of humanity, intensified perhaps by the
conditions in which they were placed;
and their virtues were tempered by them.
Local historians have falsified and obscured the truth, thereby gratifying a
false pride. They have their reward.

do know Our Teacher Allso hath been long visited with verie great weaknesses; from which it is much feared he will not be recouered. For this and other weightie Considerations Our most humble Petition to this much honoured Court is; That A Tract of lands of About fowre Miles Square at A place Called Penⁿycooke may be Granted As an Addition to vs, for our better Support And Jncouragement; in the Seruice of Christ & the Countrie; to be layd out by m^r Jonathan Danforth or some other Artist And Capt Ed: Jonson or John Parker.

So with our heartie prayers to God for your vtmost peace & prosperitie; wee Craue leaue to Subscribe ourselues

ye verie humble Seruants

JOSEPH HILLS:	WILL: BRAKENBURY
JOHN WAYTE	JOHN SPRAGUE
ABRA^m: HILL	THO: CALL
JOB LANE	PETER TUFTS.
ROBERT BURDIN	

Jn the name of the rest.[2]

But although the Court recognized the justice of the claim of the Malden people, "the Deputyes [did] think not meete to graunt this petⁿ," as the lands at Pennacook seemed more desirable for other uses — for that of actual settlement, which the petitioners did not contemplate. Other towns asked for grants at the same place; and the Deputies, foreseeing that an early settlement might be made there, passed the following order: —

Upon Jnformation that Penⁿiecocke is An Apt place for A Townshipp; And in consideration of the lords great blessing upon the countrie in multiplying the inhabitants & plantations here; And that Allmost All such places are Allreadie taken up Jt is Ordered by this Court that the lands at Penⁿiecook be reserued for A plantation till so many of such as have petitioned for lands there or at others shall present to settle A plantation there.

The Deputies have past this desiring the consent of o^r Honord magist^s thereto. WILLIAM TORREY, *Cleric.*[3] ·

A few days after, the Deputies, considering the Malden petition, declared: —

This Courte Consideringe the Town of Maldon is very much straightened in regard of Lands, & having p^rsented theire desires to this Court

---

[2] *Mass. Archives*, cxii. 147. Pennacook, the Crooked Place, was the name of the land at the bend in the Merrimac, where now stands Concord, N. H.

[3] Ibid.

for some Enlargment in Answer where vnto this Court thinkes meete
to graunt to the Church & Towne cf Maldon one thousand Acoⁿ of
Land, where they can find a free place neere vnto some plantation
where there is a settled ministery, to be & remayn to them & their
successors for ever, towards the yearely Defraying of their Church
Charges   the Depuᵗˢ haue past this Desireinge the Consent of oʳ
honoʳᵈ magisᵗˢ hereto

21 (3ᵈ) 16ƒ2   WILLIAM TORREY *Cleric.*[4]

The " honoʳᵈ magisᵗˢ " found this order a little too free in its
requirements, and substituted the following, which was " Consented to by yᵉ Depuᵗˢ " on the same day.

21. (3) 1662. Jn Answʳ to the petition of maulden the Court do
graunt to yᵉ ministry there 1000 accⁿ of land in any place not legally
Disposed of. to be forevʳ appropriated to the vse & benefit of the ministry of the sᵈ place & not to be alienated or otherwise disposed off : &
this on condition that they cause it to be bounded out, & put on im-
pʳvemᵗ for the ends pʳposed within 3 : years next ensueing :
voted on yᵉ affirmative by yᵉ magᵗˢ.

                                     T. DANFORTH pʳ E. R. S.[5]

This grant was laid out within the term allowed, and the Court
accepted the surveyor's return at its session, May 3, 1665.

Att the request of the inhabitants of Maulden, as also in obedience
vnto the grant of the honored Generall Court of the Massachusets vnto
the toune of Maulden for the benefit of the ministry of Maulden, layd
out & exactly measured, according to rules of art, by me vnderwritten,
one thousand acres of vpland & meadow, about two miles distant southwesterly from the southwest angle of Lancaster bounds, as also about
a mile distant southwesterly from the lands formerly granted & layd out
vnto Capᵗ Richard Dauenport, beginning at the south end of a high,
rockey, pine hill, at a litle red oake marked wᵗʰ the letter M ; & from
thence a ljne vpon an east southeast point, two hundred & twelue rods,
vnto a pine marked M ; & from the pine marked as aforesajd, a line
vpon a south point, sixe hundred & forty rods ; & from thence, a line
vpon a west northwest point, three hundred & seventy rods ; & from
thence, on line vpon a north & by east point, sixe degrees easterly, six
hundred & twenty rods ; & these fower ljnes, so runne, making vp the
full complement of the abouesajd one thousand acres, as is more plainly
described by a plot ; humbly entreating of this honored Court that they

---

[4] *Mass. Archives,* x. 206.   (2), 45. F. R. S. for E[dward] R[awson],
[5] Ibid. Cf. *Mass. Colony Records,* iv. S[ecretary].

will be pleased to confirme their grant, & that this returne may be recorded.   Tho: Noyes, *Surveyo*.⁶

This tract as then located was in the northern part of that portion of Worcester which afterwards became the town of Holden, where a committee of the General Court found the ancient bound marks in 1742.⁷ But in the year 1701, the town having chosen Thomas Newhall, John Dexter, and John Lynde, Jr. "to go to woster & run yᵉ bounds of malden farm," they found land "which bare some resemblance of Malden grant." This tract, of which nine hundred acres were in the northern part of the present town of Shrewsbury and one hundred acres in that portion of Worcester which was afterwards Holden and West Boylston, was surveyed and "bounded out as belonging to Malden," and was accepted as such by the General Court. It was reserved to Malden in the grant which was made in 1717 to the proprietors of Shrewsbury.⁸ This error of location caused considerable trouble in the course of time, and resulted in several law suits and much protracted business on the part of the General Court; but Malden was finally confirmed in its title to the Shrewsbury land.

Although this grant was made "to the vse & benefit of the ministry," the town endeavored to divert it from its original purpose, but failed to obtain the consent of the Court.

[May 27, 1668]   In ansʳ to the petition of Jnᵒ Vpham, Wᵐ Bracken-bury, Jnᵒ Wayte, Jnᵒ Sprague, in behalf of yᵉ toune of Maulden, the Court sees no reason to grant their request, but judge that the land mentioned in the petition shall remayne for the vse of the ministry wᵗʰout alteration, vnless they shall present that to the Court wᶜʰ they may judge better.⁹

Under this order the land remained for the use of the ministry until it was sold by the First, or North Parish, in 1754. It was the fruitful source of troubles and lawsuits for many years, not only with encroaching settlers and the towns in which it was located, but also between the precincts into which Malden was afterwards divided. It may be questioned whether

---

⁶ *Mass. Colony Records*, iv. (2), 148.   ⁸ Ibid., xvii. (3), 592.
⁷ *General Court Records*, xvii. (3), 593.   ⁹ *Mass. Colony Records*, iv. (2), 377.

the scanty income which the ministry received was worth the years of litigation and anxiety which it cost the officers and voters of the simple little town.

If the people of Malden barely located their grant within the time allowed, they were still more dilatory in improving it " for the ends proposed," although the order required that it should be "put on imp'vem' within 3 : years." A committee of the Court complained, in 1669, that "it is now aboue sixe yeares since, & no improovement made," and that " if it be continued & confirmed in this place it will vtterly hinder the setling a plantation," which had been ordered to be established at that place. "This farme," say they, "conteines a chojce tract of land in the center of this village, & swallowes vp about one hundred acres " of the scant three hundred acres of meadow which the place affords; and they hoped that if this and other obstructions should be removed " it will not be long before this place be setled in a good way, for the honour of God & the publick good."[10] The Court, however, excepted the " Maulden farme," and a smaller grant near by, from the lands which were " reserved for publicke vse ; " and allo+ments were soon after made there to persons contemplating actual settlement.

This " new plantation " at Quansigamug, which was the first attempt to settle the town of Worcester, is described as being " vpon the roade to Sprinkfeild about 12 miles westward from Marlborough." A petition, dated May 27, 1674, contains the names of twenty-nine persons to whom lots had then been granted and laid out. Of these the following are the names of Malden or Mystic Side men, who may have been led thither by the circumstance of the Malden grant : —

Philip Atwood,	Thomas Pratt,
Lazarus Grover,	John Provender,
Simon Grover,	Thomas Skinner,
Stephen Grover,	John Starkey,
Thomas Grover,	Henry Swillaway,
Samuel Lee,	Phineas Upham,
Simon Meylin,	Daniel Whittemore,

Pelatiah Whittemore.[11]

[10] *Mass. Colony Records*, iv. (2), 436.　　　[11] *Mass. Archives*, cxii. 237.

Besides these, Joel Jenkins, Tryal Newberry, John Paul, John Shaw, and Benjamin Webb were in the early part of the following year owners of grants which had been confirmed and registered. Joel Jenkins had a lot of one hundred acres; others had lots of twenty-five or fifty acres. Philip Atwood, Thomas Grover, Simon Meylin, John Provender, and Phineas Upham were actual settlers in the month of April, 1675, when the work was commenced with vigor and several houses were built.[12] That they contemplated a permanent settlement is evident, and other Malden proprietors would probably have followed them, but the enterprise was of a short duration. On the fourteenth of July following, Matoonas, the Nipmuck chief who was afterwards executed on Boston Common for his exploits, attacked the little settlement at Mendon in supposed revenge for the death of his son, who had been hanged for the murder of a man in Dedham in 1671.[13]

In the alarm which followed, induced by the insecurity which prevailed among the frontier towns, the pioneers withdrew into the security of the older towns, or took the field against the enemy. The deserted houses at Quansigamug were burned by the Indians, December 2, 1675,[14] and the land was not again occupied until 1684. A meeting of a committee of the General Court and those who were interested in the plantation was held at Cambridge, March 3, 167⅞, at which Philip Atwood, Thomas Grover, Joel Jenkins, Simon Meylin, John Paul, Thomas Skinner, John Upham, and Benjamin Webb were present as proprietors; but it does not appear that they took personal parts in the resettlement.[15]

In the meantime, although, perhaps, impeded a little by the local causes of strife and the troubles of the church and Mr. Wigglesworth, — impeded somewhat, perhaps, by sickness and privations, by lack of labor and tools, the building of the little town above Mystic Side went on. Forests were felled and fertile fields were opened to the sun, and a school was estab-

---

[12] Cf. Lincoln, *History of Worcester*, 18-20.

[13] Mather, *Brief History of the War*, 5, 43.

[14] Ibid., 19.

[15] Lincoln, *History of Worcester*, 33.

lished. By-laws and regulations were made for the general
good, as simple as the manners of the people, sometimes as
ludicrous as their makers were uncouth. Yet while we smile at
their simplicity, we may remember that in those rules and in
those manners were hid the germs, at least, of manliness and
independence which burst forth after many years into a ripening
harvest; and that the prosperity of the present was born out of
the rudeness of that age, and the apparent sterility of that
unpromising soil.

In the midst of their labor and already heavy burdens, other
troubles and heavier trials seemed about to burst upon them —
did burst at last in blood and a great cost out of the little
worldly treasure which they and their fellows in the Colony
possessed. Rumors of fast couriers flitting from tribe to tribe,
of secret meetings in remote and lonely fastnesses of nature, of
combinations and threatened uprisings, were frequent. However much they may have despised the Indian, they now began
to fear him, and portents were not wanting to add to the general
alarm. The disquietude and fears which as mental spectres
had oppressed their thoughts stalked forth as visible spectres
upon the earth and in the air. Increase Mather tells the
story.

Anno 1667. There were fears on the spirits of many of the *English*,
concerning *Philip* and his *Indians*, and that year, Novemb. 30, about
9, or 10 *ho.* A. M. being a very clear, still Sun-shine morning, there
were diverse Persons in *Maldon*, who heard in the air on the Southeast
of them, a great Gun go off, and as soon as that was past, they heard
the report of small Guns like musket shott, discharging very thick, as if
it had been at a general Training; but that which did most of all
amaze them, was the flying of the Bullets which came singing over their
heads, and seemed to be very near them, after this they heard drums
passing by them and going Westward. The same day, at *Scituate*, (and
in other places) in *Plimouth* Colony, they heard as it were the running
of troops of horses. I would not have mentioned this relation, had I
not received it from serious, faithfull, and Judicious hands, even of
those who were ear witnesses of these things.[16]

---

[16] Mather, *Brief History of the War,*   Niles, *History of the Indian and French*
34. This prodigy is also mentioned by   *Wars,* in *Mass. Hist. Coll.,* xxvi. 255.

" Now, Reader," adds his wonder-loving son, " prepare for the Event of these *Prodigies*, but count me not struck with a Livian Superstition in Reporting *Prodigies*, for which I have such Incontestible Assurance." [17]

At this juncture the military power of the Colony, which had not seen service since the Pequot war in 1637, began to receive more earnest attention. Privileges were granted to troopers, laws were recast or more urgently enforced to accustom the arms-bearing citizens to military duty, and regulations were made to perfect their organization and increase their efficiency.

In common with the other towns, as required by law, Malden had early attended to its military duties. Edward Johnson informs us at the time of the incorporation of the town, that " the Band of *Malden*, being as yet a young Town, who have not chosen their Officers, are led by Mr. *Joseph Hill*." [18] Mr. Hills continued to lead this company until his removal to Newbury in 1665. It will be remembered that in 1655 the place of muster was at Ipswich and Mr. Wigglesworth took advantage of the presence of Mr. Hills at that place to settle some of the disquiet which he felt in relation to his settlement at Malden. Joseph Hills was seldom called Captain, the military title being overshadowed by the more honorable affix of Mr.[19]

No mention is made of the inferior officers until October 7, 1651, when " John Waite is chosen and allowed ensign by this Court for the company at Maldon." [20] The name of the second officer at this time has not been found; but at a County Court, April 4, 1654, " John Waite being Chosen by the Jnhabitants of Mauldon, the Leiftennant of their Military Company is alowed by this Court. and John Sprague in Like man[r] for their En-

---

[17] Mather, *Magnalia*, B. 7, ch. 6, sect. 5.

[18] *Wonder-working Providence*, 192.

[19] The title of Mr. was applied to clergymen, college graduates, and to those who by their position merited a special distinction; and the exactness with which it was used is in strong contrast with 'the present use of the much abused titles of Honorable and Esquire. The somewhat whimsical punishment of Josias Plastow in 1631 is evidence of the importance which was attached to it: " It is *ordered*, that Josias Plastow shall (for stealeing 4 basketts of corne from the Indians) returne them 8 basketts againe, be ffined v[l], & hereafter to be called by the name of Josias, & not M[r], as form'ly hee vsed to be." *Mass. Colony Records*, i. 92.

[20] *Middlesex Court Records*, i. 21.

signe." [21]   Sergeant Thomas Lynde is mentioned in 1658, and William Brackenbury was clerk of the company in 1665. In the fall of the latter year, Joseph Hills having removed from the town, John Wayte and John Sprague were advanced by election to the offices of captain and lieutenant.[22]   Ensign Thomas Lynde was an officer of the company in 1675; and the names of Corporal John Green and Sergeant Samuel Haward appear in 1678.

The Middlesex Regiment, consisting of sixteen companies, had been under the command of Major Daniel Gookin of Cambridge, who was commissioned May 5, 1676; but in 1680 it was divided, and Malden with the neighboring towns formed the First Regiment under Major Gookin, while the western towns of the county were transferred to a new regiment under Major Peter Bulkley of Concord. In the latter year we hear of Sergeant Thomas Skinner in the Malden company, and of Sergeant Samuel Sprague in 1684. John Wayte and John Sprague were continued in their commissions from their election in 1665, through Philip's war and until 1685, when Captain Wayte was dismissed by the General Court in answer to the following petition.

To y° Honoured General Court now sitting at Boston this 18ᵗʰ March instant.

The Petition of John Wayt, senior of Maldin humbly sheweth.

That whereas J have been putt into yᵉ place of a Captain by Commission from the honoured General Court for many years past; but being now by the holy providence of yᵉ All-wise God deprived of my sight, whereby I am incapacitated for any farther attending that service, my humble request to this Honoured Court is that they would be pleased to dismiss me therefrom, & your petitioner shall continue to pray for yᵉ guidance & blessing of God upon you in all your concerns.

J° WAYTE

The Deputys Judge meete to graunt this petition. yᵉ honoʳᵈ magists hereto consenting.

WILLIAM TORREY *Cleric*
March: 19ᵗʰ 1684⅘

Consented to by yᵉ magists.
21 March 84⅘

EDWARD RAWSON *Secreʸ* [23]

---

[21] *Middlesex Court Records*, i. 53.
[22] *Middlesex Court Files, in loco.*

[23] *Mass. Archives*, lxx. 131.

Captain Wayte had been Speaker of the House of Deputies in the preceding year. Soon after Ensign Thomas Lynde, another old officer of the Malden company, presented the following petition.

To the Honored generall Court: now siting in Boston The petision of Thomas Lynde of malden Humbly Showeth : whereas you haue bin pleased to Commission your Suplyant to y⁰ ofise of An Ensigne in y⁰ foot Comp': millitary of malden An through the Jnfirmytyes of age J find my Selfe altogether in capasytated to doe you any further Servis in Said ofise J beg therefore your dismission from yᵗ servis : and shall pray for yoʳ prosperyty and Remaine youʳ Humble Servᵗ.
May 6ᵗʰ, 1685 :   THOMAS LYNDE.[24]

At the General Court in June the following order was passed : —

In ansʳ to the foot company of Mauldens petition, the Court doe hereby appoint Leift Jn⁰ Sprague to be captaine, & grants liberty to Sarjᵗ Samuel Sprague to officiate as leiftenᵗt, & Joseph Wilson to officiat as ensigne vnder him, sajd capᵗ, in order to their establishment & being comᵐissioned.[25]

These officers appear to have been commissioned in that or the succeeding year; but their commissions were voided by the administration of Sir Edmund Andros. After the revolution of 1689 the company was reorganized. There appears to have been some dissatisfaction with Lieutenant Samuel Sprague. With the following paper we may leave, for the present, the " Malden Band," which had now become permanently established.

To The HonᵒᵘʳⁱGenʳall Coᵤrt Now assembled at Boston in The Collony off the Massachusetts Jn ᵢJew-England.
These are to Certifie That at a meeting of the Millitary company Jn Maldon on the first Day of y⁰ Jnstant July: Being Legally Warned Therevnto. The Company Then, & There agreeing To choose Theire Millitary officers. —

       John Sprague Senʳ was chosen Capᵗ :
       Joseph Wilson Senʳ was chosen Leuitⁿᵗ :
       Phinehas Sprague Senʳ was chosen Ensigⁿ :

---

[24] *Mass. Archives,* lxx. 132.

[25] *Mass. Colony Records,* v. 483; also *Mass. Archives,* lxx. 136.

Whom Wee Humbly p'sent To this Hon'ed Courtt for their Acceptance —

Attest BENJAMIN WEBB *Cleark*

That all officers Comissionated in the town of maldin in may 1686
stand in Commission except they se cause to laydown, or Just Exception be brought in against them.

Past by the Representatives in the affirmative.

July 6 : 1689   Attests EBENEZER PROUT *Clerk*

Consented to by y* Governo' and Councill

Js^A ADDINGTON *Sec'*.

Understanding the L¹ Comissionated in 1686 : having layd down his
place the Representatives do allow of the above nomination of L¹ : &
ensign : in there Respective offices and Cap¹ Jn° Sprague

July : 11th : 1689 :   Attests

EBENEZER PROUT : *Clerk.*

Consented to by the Councill

Js^A ADDINGTON *Sec'*.[26]

Not all the available military force of the town was enrolled
in the foot company; for a portion of the men, probably those
of the better class, were members of a cavalry company, which
was in some degree a more aristocratic organization and pretended to some little elegance in its trappings. This company,
which was composed of " The Troopers Belonging to the Towns
of Malden Redding Rumley marsh and Linn," was known as the
Three County Troop and preserved its existence for more than
forty years. It had its origin in the following order of the
General Court: —

[May 26, 1658] In ans' to the petition of some of the inhabitants
of Ljnne & Reading & Rumly Marsh, the Court judgeth it meete to
graunt them liberty to rajse a troope of horse, & choose theire officers,
provided they be not fferry free, nor haue fiue shillings yeerly allowed
them from the country, as other troop's haue.[27]

By a former order of the Court, they were entitled to especial
privileges " as is exprest in this order": —

---

[26] *Mass. Archives*, cvii. 187. Ensign
Phineas Sprague died Jan. 23, 169⁰/₁; and
in April John Greenland was presented
and confirmed by the General Court as
his successor. *General Court Records*,
April 14, 1691.

[27] *Mass. Colony Records*, iv. (1), 341.

First. Exempt^n from all traynings in all foote companies & cunstables watches; 2^{ly}. Freedome from rates for his p^{r}son & horse; 3^{ly}. Free com^{m}onage for his horse in any of the towne com^{m}ons where he inhabits, & in any com^{m}ons where they are exercised during the time of theire exercise; . . . . . 5^{ly}. Lib^{r}tie to chose a leiutenant & other inferio^r officers; 6^{ly}. His horse shall not be prest to any other service.[28]

By a later order it was provided that,

such souldjers listed, amounting to the nomber of thirty, shallbe accompted a troope, and have libertje of chojce and nomination of cap^t, lef^t, and cornet, and quartermaster, who, being allowed by the authoritje of the Courte, shall stand by com^{m}ission, and all other inferior officers to be chosen by the company, and established by the cheife com^{m}ander of the troope, and that all such troopers shall keepe a good horse, and well fitted with sadle, bridle, holsters, and pistolls, or a carbjne and sword, and having listed his horse, shall not alter nor put him of without licence from the com^{m}ander in cheife, and the sajd troope shallbe exercised according to lawe.[29]

Edward Hutchinson was chosen captain of the new troop and confirmed by the Court, May 28, 1659.[30] At the session of June 12, 1663, the troopers of Essex having been divided into two bodies, "In ans^r to the petition of Capt Edward Hutchinson, cap^t of the three county troope, the Court judgeth it meete to declare, — That the troopers of the Three County Troope residing in Ljnne are not taken of from that troope whereof they were," and "That Capt Hutchinsons com^{m}ission doeth bind him to com^{m}and the troopers residing in Lynne, that are listed wth him as formerly."[31] But at the next session it was ordered : —

that henceforth the troopers inhabitting in Lynne shall appertejne vnto & joyne wth Salem troope, any former order of this Court otherwise disposing of them notwithstanding, excepting only such as shall rather choose to continue wth the Three County Troope, & shall certify theire desire so to doe vnder theire hands at the next meeting of Salem troope.[32]

Two years later, " [May 3, 1665.] John Tutle being chosen leiften^t, & Wm Haisy cornet, to the Three County Troope, the

[28] *Mass. Colony Records*, iii. 128.　　[30] Ibid., 369.　　[32] Ibid., 95.

[29] Ibid., iv. (1), 80.　　[31] Ibid., iv. (2), 82.

Court allowes & approoues of their ellection, & ordʳs that the secretary give them their comᵐissions."³³   These officers were inhabitants of Rumney Marsh; and Lieutenant Tuttle held his position until May 7, 1673, when it is recorded: "Vpon the request of Leiftennant John Tutle, leftᵗ to the Three County Troope, he is dismist from yᵗ service, & Mʳ Eliakim Hutchinson is to suply yᵗ place."³⁴   Hutchinson was "chosen & appointed" lieutenant in the following October; but for some reason he laid down his office at an early day.   May 27, 1674, it is recorded that "Cornet Wᵐ Hajsy is appointed to be leftennant, & Jonathan Poole to be cornet to the Three County Troope, vnder the conduct of Edward Hutchinson, their captaine."³⁵

Captain Hutchinson ³⁶ having petitioned "that he might lay doune his captains place of the Three County Troope," it is recorded under the date of October 7, 1674, that "the Court grants his request, and doe order & appoint Mʳ Humphry Davy to be capᵗ of the Three County Troope, & that he haue comᵐission accordingly."   At the same session, however, it is

³³ *Mass. Colony Records*, iv. (2), 149. The commissions of these officers had been withheld more than two years. At a session of the Court, October 8, 1662, it was ordered : —

"In ansʳ to the petition of Jonathan Poole & William Greene, in behalf of the Three Countys Troope, present Mʳ Jnᵒ Tutle as leftᵗ, & Wᵐ Haysy as cornet, the Court orders, that, on certificat to this Court or the Court of Asistants, that iff the sajd persons nominated for officers to yᵉ sᵈ troope be circumstanced as the lawe provides, that they be allowed." *Mass.Colony Records*, iv. (2), 66.

³⁴ *Mass. Colony Records*, iv. (2), 558. Eliakim Hutchinson was a cousin of Captain Edward Hutchinson. He married, in 1668, Sarah, daughter of Henry Shrimpton of Noddle's Island. He appears to have lived at Noddle's Island or Rumney Marsh, and his name is found with Rumney Marsh men in service in 1676.

³⁵ Ibid., v. 6. Jonathan Poole was of Reading. He had an earlier connection with the troop when the Court, May 31, 1671, appointed "Jnᵒᵗʰȧn Poole quᵘter

mʳ to yᵉ tripartit trajne." *Mass. Colony Records*, iv. (2), 488.

³⁶ Edward Hutchinson, eldest son of William and the celebrated Antinomian, Anne (Marbury) Hutchinson, was an inhabitant of Boston. He was experienced in military and Indian affairs, and was well known among the savages, by whom he was trusted. He appears to have resigned his command of the Three County Troop from business reasons; but circumstances caused him to become more deeply engaged in military matters. He was early in the field in the following summer; and his extensive acquaintance in the Nipmuck country caused him to be sent there, with Captain Thomas Wheeler's troop, for the purpose of endeavoring to disengage that tribe from the Narragansett alliance. While seeking a body of Nipmucks who had failed to keep an appointment at a plain in Quabauge, now Brookfield, August 2, 1675, the troop fell into an ambuscade and Captain Hutchinson received a mortal wound, while eight men were killed upon the field. Mather, *Brief History of the War*, 6.

found that "Mr Humphry Davy hauing declared his non-acceptance of the office of cap^t of the Three County Troope, the Court judgeth it meete to respitt any supply for that place till the Court of Election." [37]

It does not appear that a captain was presently appointed; for Lieutenant Hasey commanded the company, and was in active service during Philip's war with the several quotas which the troop furnished. At least eight men from Malden were out with him in 1675, with troopers from the adjacent towns; and ten men were ordered to be raised from the company by impressment, February 21, 1675⁄6, for an expedition towards the frontier.[38] A few weeks later the troop was called upon for its proportion of " eighty troopers, compleatly armed," who were to " repaire to Concord," by the last of May.[39]

It was not until June 1, 1677, that a captain appears to have been confirmed by the Court. " Jonathan Wade is appointed cap^t of the Three County Troope, & Corporall Wm Green cornet, Isaak Brooks quarter master of that troope." [40] Captain Wade continued in command during the remainder of the colonial period; and at the advent of Joseph Dudley in 1686, the company was annexed to one of the Middlesex regiments and so continued during the short administration of Andros. After the Revolution the troopers preferred the following petition, which was granted by the passage of a general order which established the militia upon the former basis: —

[37] *Mass. Colony Records*, v. 17.

[38] Ibid., 73.

[39] Ibid., 85. A list of "Capt Prentises 73 Troopers," who were engaged in the campaign of 1675⁄6, enumerates twenty "Troopers belonging to Capt Hutchinson," of whom Eliakim Hutchinson, Benjamin Muzzey, Samuel Weeden, and Joseph Weeden were of Noddle's Island or Rumney Marsh, and John Guppie, Daniel Greenland, and John Barret of Mystic Side or Malden. *Mass. Archives*, lxviii. 73.

[40] *Mass. Colony Records*, v. 151. Jonathan Wade was son of Jonathan Wade of Ipswich. He married Deborah, the youngest daughter of Governor Thomas Dudley, and lived at Mystic, or Medford, where, with his brother Nathaniel, who married Mercy, the youngest daughter of Governor Simon Bradstreet, he occupied a portion of the Cradock farm which his father had bought of Edward Collins. They were men of considerable local importance. Captain, or Major Wade, as he was sometimes called, died November 24, 1689. William Green was of Malden, and afterwards became captain of the troop. The other appears to have been that Isaac Brooks who was of Woburn, where he died September 8, 1686.

To the Honnourable Simon Bradstreet Esq. *Governour of the Mathashewsetts Collony, etc.*

The Humble petition of The Troopers or the major part Belonging to the Townes of Malden, Redding Rumley marsh and Linn.   Belonging to yᵉ Three Countey Troop. *Humbly Sheweth*

That in the Charter Gouernment formerly there was a Grant and Privilege for a three County Troope, which by the Records will Appeare which Continued accordingly vntill yᵉ Alteration of the Gouernment in the time that Esqʳ Dudly Took and Assumed The Same. and then the Said troope was much Jmpaired by its being brought to a Second Troop in the Western Redgiment in the countey of middle Sex Which After wards was Continued in the Same Posture when Sʳ Edmond Andross was Gouernour : and Stands to this present Time, By which wee find itt very Jngerouse and Troblesome to vs Conserned, To What our former Priviledges was : And much Jmpaireing to the Said Troope.

The Premisses being Considered by your honnours your Petitioⁿˢ Being Willing and Ready to bee at Command for Servise As formerly, Since, and for futor, They humbly Crave, that the Said Troope might bee as formerly, And the Priviledge of Chooseing there officers and Commanders As formerly, and that they might haue the Priviledge to yᵉ same belonging as formerly

And Wee as in Duty bound Shall Euer pray

Jsaack Hill	} for malding	Benjamine Mussey, *Sein*ʳ	} for
Jonathan Sprague		William Hassey	
William Arnald	} for Redding	Rumley march	
Joseph Browne		John Poole — for Linn [41]	

Not only was this petition favorably met by a general order, but a special order for the reorganization of the troop was passed August 22, 1689.

Ordered that the Troop under the Command of Majʳ Jon. Wade do forthwᵗʰ Compleat their Commission Officers, that it may be Setled for the Service of the Country and to that End Major Wade the present Captain do without delay call the Troop together, and Cause them to nominate such Officers as are wanting to be presented to this Convention, or Council for Confirmation ; But if the said Major Wade refuse to Call the Troop together as abovesaid, then William Green is hereby required to Call the Troop together, and Proceed to nominations as well of Captain as of other Commission Officers as are Wanting forthwith to be Presented for Confirmation.[42]

[41] *Mass. Archives,* xxxv. 9.   [42] *General Court Records, in loco.*

That internal dissensions existed in the troop at this time is evident, and the undated paper which follows appears to contain a relation of the causes which led to its early dissolution.

Reasons Given To the Honnourable Gouerno, Counsell & Representatives* by vs Of The three Countey Troope for Not Complying with y* Choise of William Greene Captaine.

Imp. By an order Issued out by the Honnourable Counsell That a Setlement of Malletia Should bee as in y* yeare 1686 Except a vacancy by death or persons otherwayes Disinabled which order your petition's had Reguard vnto and Alsoe to our Cap* Jonathan Wade Being Still in Place & Office — And there being a Sqvadron of Wobern men, the major part haueing beene but of Late taken into the Three Countey Troope Who Being of Such Principalls and Reguarding Neither yo* honnours Order nor Reason, They went and Chose another Captaine by Name William Greene, and Drawd vp Sundry Reasons against the Said Cap* Wade Contrary to our knowledge. Being the Major part of the Three Countey Troope aforesaid

BENJAMINE MUSSEY *Sein*'	JONA^THAN SPRAGG
JOSEPH HASSEY	JOSHUA EATON
ISAACK HILL	JOHN POOLE
JOSEPH BROWNE	

In Behalfe of the Major part of the three Countey Troope.[43]

There appears to have been a petition preceding this paper, which is not now in its place in the Massachusetts Archives, to which the Court returned a peremptory answer, which apparently ended the controversy and struck a blow at the prosperity of the troop.

Upon Reading the Petition of Jsaac Hill, Jon*. Sprague Benjamin Mussey Sen'. &c. in behalf of themselves, and Others late belonging to the Three County Troops, manifesting their Unwillingness to Serve Under the Command of Capt Will Green, And upon Hearing of Both Parties: Jt is *Ordered* that the Said Petitioners, and Others, who are disatisfied with the Said Captain Return to Serve in the foot Company's of the Several Towns, and Places, whereto they do belong.[44]

The process of disintegration now began anew, and the company soon lost its Suffolk men, as it had lost those of Essex in the time of Captain Hutchinson. The Court passed the follow-

---

[43] *Mass. Archives,* xxxv. 10.   [44] *General Court Records,* October 8 1689. Cf. *Mass. Archives,* xxxv. 48.

ing order March 18, 168%0, and only the men of Middlesex were left to the Three County Troop: —

> The train Soldiers inhabiting the Lands belonging to the Town of Boston lying to the eastward of Winnisimet Ferry, Together with Noddles Jsland and Hogg island, are henceforth to be a distinct Foot Company, And are hereby Ordered forthwith to Nominate meet Persons for their Commission Officers, and present them to this Court for their Allowance and Confirmation, And the three County Troops is hereby dismist.[45]

Once more the troop is mentioned, when, June 10, 1690, eighty troopers were ordered to be detached from the several regiments to rendezvous at Andover and Concord for the protection of the frontier, which was threatened by wandering parties of French and Indians. Seven men of this detachment were to be from Captain Green's command.[46]

Thenceforth the Three County Troop disappears from the scene and the records are silent as to its further continuance. If it remained longer, it was but for a few years of feeble life, and its crimson banner and its men and horses mouldered together.[47] Traditions of its existence and of its participation in the gloomy strife of Philip's war may have lingered long in the homes of the three counties; but they, as well as more material things, have utterly passed away. The few disconnected records which are now brought together are all that

---

[45] *General Court Records, in loco.*

[46] Ibid.

[47] In a Herald-painter's book of the time of Charles II., now in the British Museum, is a tricking of a flag "don for New England," and an entry giving its description and cost. It was on crimson damask with a silver fringe and bore a bare arm and hand issuing from a cloud and holding a sword. In the tricking the words "Thre County Trom" are inscribed upon a ribbon on the face of the flag. For a drawing of the tricking and relevant matter, *vide N. E. Hist. and Geneal. Register*, xxv. 138.

A provincial flag of a similar design was carried by the Bedford men on the day of the Lexington Alarm, and is preserved in the Bedford Free Public Library. On slight grounds, this has been claimed to be the flag of the Three County Troop; but it bears the legend, *Vince aut morire*, and the arm is mailclad, which distinguishes it from the elder prototype. It is most likely to have been the standard of a company in that portion of the Province at a later date and not that of the troopers of Malden and the adjoining towns. Cf. *Mass. Hist. So. Proc.*, December, 1885, 166; January, 1886, 199; also Brown, *History of Bedford*, 23. In the latter it is made to appear, by a misquotation, that there were more than one three county troop in Massachusetts.

The arm and sword of the flag of the Three County Troop has been preserved as the crest of the State of Massachusetts.

remain of the band of stalwart Puritans who rode in the name of the Great and General Court, as valiant troopers and as worthy Christians, I doubt not, as their elder brethren who rode at Edgehill or Marston Moor.

In the bloody war which preceded the death of Pometacom of Pokanoket, he who has passed into history under the grandiloquent title of King Philip, the men of Malden performed their duty, whether as soldiers and troopers in the field or as tax payers at home, both in active service and the contribution of their substance. The war, for which busy preparation had been made on both sides, was opened by a desultory attack on the little settlement of Swansea in Plymouth Colony during several days in the latter part of June, 1675. When the news reached Massachusetts Bay the Council convened and resolved " to rayse one hundred foote and 50 horse that shall be speedily upon their march towards Swansey," and issued the following order: —

[June 24, 1675.] To the Militia of the town of Boston, Cha. Camb. Watertown, Roxbury, Dorchester, Dedham, Brantrey, Weymouth, Hingham, Maulden — You are hereby required in his Majesty's name to take notice that the Govr & Council have ordered 100 able souldjers forthwith impressed out of the severall Towns according to the proportions hereunder written for the aid and assistance of our confederate Plymouth in the designe afoote agst the Indians, and accordingly you are to warne af^a proportions to be ready at an hours warning from Capt Daniel Henchman who is appointed Captain and Commander of the Foote Company that each souldjer shal have his armes compleat and Snapsack ready to march and not faile to be at the randevous.[46]

The proportion assigned to the several towns does not appear upon the order. Captain Daniel Henchman, of Boston and the Quansigamug plantation, commanded the footmen, as above stated, while Captain Thomas Prentice of Cambridge led the troopers. Besides the impressed men, about one hundred volunteers took the field under the old Jamaica privateer, Samuel Mosely of Dorchester. Roger Kenicott and John Pemberton of Malden were with Captain Mosely; and, soon after, their townsmen, Thomas Mudge, Simon Grover, and John Larrabee were in garrison at Wading River in the present town of Norton.

[46] *Mass. Archives,* lxvii. 207.

In August the constable of Malden was ordered to " Jmpress ten able horses well shod wth bridles & sadles well shod fitt for the Countreys seruice." The constable's return giving the names of the owners of the horses taken is preserved.

I haue im prest ten horses for the us of the contre a cordin to the tener of the warent.

EDMOND CHAMBERLIN

Captin John wayt	Leftinant John Sprag
Insine Thomas lind	
Samewill Sprag	Samewel lues
Benjemen whitemore	
Joel jenkins	thomas grouer
Steuen grouer	Symon grouer [49]

In September Captain John Wayte was ordered to lead a party of recruits, in which were probably some Malden men, to the rendezvous at the frontier.

The Council do order & Apoint Capt John Wayte to Conduct the 120 men appointed to rendevouse at Marlborough the 28th day of this instant September & to deliuer them vnto the order of maio^r john pincheon comander in Cheefe in the county of Hampshire & it is further ordered y^t in case Capt Samuell Appleton should bee com away from those parts, then the said Capt wait is ordered to take the conduct & charge ot A company of 100 men under maio^r John pincheon, but in case capt Appleton doe abide there then capt wait is forthwith to returne Backe unles maio^r Pincheon see cause to detyne him upon ye service of the Country.

24 Sept. 1675. [50]

At the session of July 9 the Court laid three country rates; [51] and in consideration of "the great & dayly grouing charge of the present warr against the Indians, & the absolute necessity that there is of a further supply & recruite of armes & amunition for the seruice of the country," seven single country rates were ordered October 13. [52] Of this levy the proportion of Malden

[49] *Mass. Archives*, lxvii. 234.
[50] Ibid., 265.
[51] *Mass. Colony Records*, v. 45.
[52] Ibid., 55. The proportion of Medford for a single rate, was £5; and that of Reading, £16 9s. 11d. If the rates were paid in kind, values were fixed

per bushel for wheat, six shillings; rye, four shillings and sixpence; pease, four shillings; indian corn, three shillings and sixpence; barley, four shillings; and for oats, two shillings. *Mass. Archives,* lxviii. 29.

A country rate was a tax on property

was £15. 10. 5. for a single rate; and this was no small burden to the farmers of that day, whose currency was mostly the products of the soil. During the summer and fall of that year soldiers of the town were in active service; several as troopers under Lieutenant William Hasey of Rumney Marsh, the commander of the Three County Troop. Men frequently appear as serving under different captains in the same year, a condition which was caused by short terms of service and the necessity of allowing planters to return to the settlements to secure their crops or to attend to the needs of their families, while others took their places in the field. Some were scouts and were rapidly transferred from command to command as their services were required.

In November a levy was made for an expedition designed to penetrate the Narragansett country, into which Philip had retired. Eight men were impressed at Malden, as follows: —

The names of ye Soûldyers Jmpress^d at maldon for the p^{r}sent Expedition & p vdd According to ye warr^t are

Tho. May :	Jam^s Chadwick
	John Chamberlain:
Jam^s Welch	John Mudge
John Winslade	John Ross
	John prouender
Maldo^n	Jn ye name of y^e . . . .
30. 9. 75	Jo WAYT *capt*.[88]

---

and the profits of mechanics and traders of one penny on a pound; besides which a poll-tax of one shilling and eightpence at first and afterwards of two shillings and sixpence, was levied upon all males above sixteen years of age. A single rate produced about two thousand pounds in 1663, and was usually sufficient for the expenses of a year; although at times the tax was increased by the additional levy of a fractional rate. In 1664, " It is *ordered*, that halfe a single rate be levyed vpon the inhabitants, as an addition to the rate in course, towards the defraying the publicke charges, that haue binn extraordinary this yeare;" but in 1672, no rate was laid, the revenue arising " from incombes due for wines, licquors, peltry, &c." being found sufficient " to answer the occasions of the country." *Mass. Colony Records*, iv. (2), 135, 534.

Besides the ten rates laid in 1675, sixteen were imposed in 1676, which was equal to an assessment on the valuation of over four *per cent.* in the former, and nearly seven *per cent.* in the latter year. A rate of seventy dollars on a thousand would make the tax-payers of the city of Malden unhappy, at least. The proportion of Malden for a single rate in 1675 gives the total valuation of the town as £2525 for that year.

[88] *Mass. Archives*, lxviii. 70.

Edmund Chamberlain took the place of his kinsman, John; and the party reported at the rendezvous at Dedham, with the exception of James Welch, against whose name was written, " not apeard." They were included in " A list of Cap^tn Samuell Mosselys Compa^ny taken att Dedham the 9th Day of Xber 1675;"[54] and the little army of seven companies, under Major Samuel Appleton of Ipswich, marched for the Narragansett country the next day. In the battle known as the Narragansett or Swamp Fight, which took place, Sunday, December 19, 1675, when nearly seven hundred Indians are said to have perished,[55] the company of Captain Mosely was the first to enter the fort of the enemy; and two of the nineteen men which it lost in slain and wounded were of Malden, — Edmund Chamberlain among the former, and James Chadwick among the latter. At the same time Lieutenant Phineas Upham, of Captain Isaac Johnson's company, received a wound from the effects of which he died in October, 1676.[56]

---

[54] *Mass. Archives*, lxvii. 294.

[55] " Two and twenty Indian Captains slain all of them and brought down to Hell in one Day," says Increase Mather, *Prevalency of Prayer*, 10. The loss of the Indians is variously stated. Hubbard, on the authority of Potock, an Indian who was put to death at Boston, makes the statement mentioned in the text, and adds, " Besides three hundred that died of their Wounds the most of them; the Number of old Men, Women and Children, that perished either by Fire, or that were starved with Hunger and Cold, None of them could tell." *Present State of New-England*, 54.

This battle swept away the savage power of the Narragansetts, and they were broken forever. " Without shelter and without food," says Bancroft, "they hid themselves in a cedar swamp, with no defence against the cold but boughs of evergreen trees. They prowled the forests and pawed up the snow, to gather nuts and acorns; they dug the earth for ground-nuts ; they ate remnants of horse-flesh as a luxury; they sunk down from feebleness and want of food. Winter and famine, and disease consequent on vile diet, were the allies of the English ; while the English troops after much severe suffering, found their way to firesides." *History of the United States*, ii. 105.

Original and contemporary narratives of the Narragansett Fight may be found in Mather, *Brief History of the War*, 20 ; Hubbard, *Present State of New-England*, 50–56; Hutchinson, *History of Massachusetts-Bay*, i. 299–303; Church, *Entertaining Passages relating to Philip's War*, 14–17 ; *Continuation of the State of New-England*, 5–8; and *News from New-England*, 1–2. The two rare tracts last named are reprinted in Drake, *Old Indian Chronicle*. The best modern summaries are Palfrey, *History of New England*, iii. 175–180; Drake, *Indians of North America* (1857), 217–220 ; and Arnold, *History of Rhode Island*, i. 403–406

[56] Phineas Upham, son of Deacon John and Elizabeth (Slade) Upham, was

In the early part of January, 167⅚, another levy of Massachusetts men was made and sent into the Narragansett country. They suffered severely from the intense cold. A writer of the time says: " They lost Eleven of their Men on their March, that were frozen to Death and brought many others sick and disheartened with the extreme Coldness of the Season." [57]   In connection with this expedition, which was known as "the long march," the following papers are extant.   They show an evident reluctance against campaigning in the winter season on the part of three of our ancient townsmen.

To the Constables of maulden
These require yoᵘ in his majᵗʸ name forthwith to sumon require & secure John Linde Jnᵒ Cole & James welsh so as they may personally

probably born soon after the arrival of his parents in New England in 1636, and was brought to Malden from Weymouth, where they first settled.   He married Ruth Wood, April 14, 1658, and was living here soon after.   His seven children were probably born here, although the birth of but one is recorded. He was one of the grantees of Quansigamug, in 1674, and an actual settler there in the following April.   The sudden breaking out of the Indian War and his presence upon the frontier brought him into active military service; and some traits of character and habits may have insured his promotion.   After the defeat of Captain Hutchinson at Wickabaug Pond, he was sent, as a lieutenant, with a force under Captain John Gorham, into the Nipmuck country; but finding none of the enemy, he returned to Mendon, where, October 1, 1675, he wrote a report of the expedition, which is preserved in *Mass. Archives*, lxvii. 276.

Soon after he proceeded towards Springfield with a company of recruits, with orders to serve under Captain John Wayte.   A reorganization of the forces upon the Connecticut having taken place, he was assigned to the company of Captain Jonathan Poole and was probably at Springfield or Hadley at the time of the attack upon Hatfield.   Returning to the eastward after the cessation of hostilities upon the western frontier, he joined the little army which was marching into

the Narragansett country and was attached to the company of Captain Isaac Johnson of Roxbury.

Captain Johnson was killed during the first assault; and as the attacking party fell back, it is not unlikely that Lieutenant Upham was wounded before the fort was entered, or he may have rallied his men and led them in the final attack.   During the night, in the face of a driving snow storm, the army marched eighteen miles with its dead and dying. Lieutenant Upham was taken to Rhode Island and, after a while, removed to Boston.   His death is recorded upon the Malden records, and it is probable that he died here.   Drake says he was buried here; but Hubbard says he died in Boston.   He died before October 12, as on that day the General Court passed a bill for the relief of his family.   As to the place of his burial, the graves of his wife (169%) and his little daughter Ruth (1676) are marked by stones in the Bell Rock Cemetery.   A search made, June 17, 1891, showed that a person of good height had been buried by the side of the wife, and that a long period had elapsed since the interment, as nothing was found in the grave but a little dark mould, in which a few pins were imbedded, and a slight discoloration caused by the decay of the wood of the coffin.

[57] *Continuation of the State of New-England*, 14, in Drake, *Old Indian Chronicle*, 195.

Appeare before the Council sitting in Boston on the 11th Jnstant at one of the clock then & there to Answer theire neglect of Duty in not appearing at the randevous at Dedham on the 5th Jnst thereby much disappointing the service of the Country y[ou] are also in like manner to sumon & require some one or more of the comittee of militia of the Toune then & there to Appeare that Jmpressed them to make it out that they were duly Jmpressed making your return at or before the time hereof not to faile at your perrill Dated in Boston the 7[h] of January 1675

By order of the Council
EDW[D] RAWSON SECR[T]Y [58]

[*Acts of Council.*]   January 11, 1675
of Woburn John lynd — returned deserted : hyres pemberton in his
    Stead who went.
    John Cole : absconded & order for. Attachment to Jsue for
    James : Welch cleard by the Councel [59]

On the return of the expedition to the settlements another call for men was made; and a warrant was issued for the drafting of twenty men from the Middlesex regiment. On this warrant, which is dated February 5, 1676, [167⅚,] is endorsed, " there is a failure of almost one halfe in apperance & no return from one towne . . . Malden: no Returne but a man Appeared." [60]

In the early part of April, 1676, John Upham, Simon Grover, Stephen Grover, John Pratt, and Tryal Newberry of Malden, with others from the neighboring towns, were in the company of Captain William Turner, at Hadley, on the Connecticut River; and they participated in the unfortunate action at the Falls, May 19, which resulted in the disastrous flight of the English and the death of their gallant captain in the Greenfield meadows. Sixty years later, when the General Court granted the township of Fall Town, now Bernardston, to the survivors of those who had been present and the heirs of those who were dead, Thomas Pratt, Simon Grover, and Tryal Newberry received shares in the right of their fathers.

During the summer of 1676 Malden soldiers served under

---

[58] *Mass. Archives*, lxviii. 112.
[59] Ibid., lxviii. 120. " Woburn " for " Malden " is a clerical error in the original.   [60] Ibid., 130.

various captains; and in a settlement which was made in August, the town was credited with twenty-nine assignments. The only officer from Malden who served this year was Lieutenant John Floyd,[61] who was under Captain Henchman, with others of his townsmen. He was then of Malden; but he afterwards removed to Rumney Marsh and became celebrated as an officer and a wary and hardy Indian fighter in the later French and Indian wars at the eastward.

From the original journal and ledger of Captain John Hull, treasurer for the war, which are preserved in the library of the New England Historic Genealogical Society, and from other sources, I have compiled the following list of

Malden and Mystic Side Men in Philip's War.

BACHELER, JOHN, may have been of Reading but is among the Malden men in the list of grantees of Narragansett No. 2, in 1732, when William Willis was agent for his heirs.[62]

BARRETT, JAMES, with Capt. Hutchinson in 1675; and with Lieut. Hasey of the Three County Troop in 1675.

BARRETT, JOHN, with Maj. Willard in 1675; with Capt. Prentice in 1675⅚; and with Lieut. Hasey of the Three County Troop in 1676.

BARRON, ELLIS, with Capt. Sill in 1676; had lived at Groton or Lancaster before the war, but was credited to Malden in the settlement of August 24, 1676.

---

[61] John Floyd was of Malden in 1672, having been earlier at Lynn or Rumney Marsh. In 1674, being at that time about thirty-six years of age, he was presented, with others, to the County Court, by John Wayte, constable, to take the oath of fidelity. Before 1682, he removed to Rumney Marsh, where he is supposed to have built the well-known house which stood until recently on the northerly road to the beach in Revere, a view of which is given in *Memorial History of Boston*, i. 450. He was captain of a troop in May, 1690, when he was ordered to march toward Piscataqua. Soon after a levy of four hundred men was made, a portion of which was to be posted at Portsmouth under his command. His active service was at the eastward. His arrest in 1692, on a charge of witchcraft, is elsewhere mentioned. He died at Rumney Marsh sometime in 1701. His children sold to their brother Daniel, in 1702, the farm of ninety acres, near Black Ann's corner, in Malden, with a house on the north side of the Lynn road, west of the rocks. Negroes, Dick, Harry, Lydia, and five others were divided with his personal property.

[62] Narragansett No. 2, now Westminster, was one of the seven townships granted to the soldiers of the Narragansett expedition.

BLANCHARD, SAMUEL, of Wilson's Point, with Capt. Cutler in 1676.

BUCKNAM, JOHN, with Capt. Henchman in 1675; and with Capt. Mosely in 1675.

BUCKNAM, JOSES, with Capt. Wheeler in 1676; and, perhaps, with Capt. Henchman in 1676.

CALL, JOHN, with Capt. Cutler in 1676.

CARTER, ROBERT, with Capt. Cutler in 1676; credited to Malden in settlement of August, 1676.

CHADWICK, JAMES, was with Capt. Mosely and was wounded at the Swamp Fjght, December 19, 1675. He was the James Cheak whose heirs were among the Malden grantees of Narragansett No. 2.

CHADWICK, JOHN, with Capt. Sill in 1675.

CHAMBERLAIN, EDMUND, with Capt. Mosely, and was killed at the Swamp Fight, 1675.

CHAMBERLAIN, JOHN, impressed November 30, 1675, but Edmund went in his place; was in garrison at Hadley with Capt. Turner in 1676.

COLE, JOHN, impressed, but did not appear at Dedham, January 5, 1675/6.

DEXTER, JOHN, with Maj. Willard in 1676.

DUNNELL, THOMAS, in garrison at Groton in 1675.

FAULKNER, DAVID, JR., was in garrison at Dedham in July, 1676, with his father, David, Sen. They had, probably, gone from Boston, but they were credited to Dedham in the settlement of August, 1676. The younger man afterwards came to that part of Malden or Boston near Black Ann's Corner, and was the ancestor of the Faulkner family here.

FLOYD, JOHN, lieutenant under Capt. Henchman in 1667; was credited to Malden in the settlement of August, 1676. See note 61.

GREEN, HENRY, was with Lieut. Hasey of the Three County Troop in 1675; with Capt. Wheeler in 1676; was lieutenant later in life.

GREEN, JOHN, brother of Henry, was a corporal with Lieut. Hasey in 1675, and 1676; was with Maj. Willard in 1676, and with Capt. Oakes in the same year. He was captain of a company later in life.

GREEN, SAMUEL, youngest brother of the foregoing, was with Maj. Willard in 1676.

GREEN, WILLIAM, brother of the foregoing, was a corporal with Lieut. Hasey in 1675 and 1676; was, perhaps, with Capt. Mosely in 1675; and was with Maj. Willard in 1676. Opposition to him as captain of the Three County Troop is noted elsewhere.

GREENLAND, DANIEL, was with Lieut. Hasey in 1675; with Capt. Prentice in 1675/6; and with Capt. Henchman in 1676.

GREENLAND, JOHN, brother of Daniel, was with Lieut. Hasey in 1675; with Capt. Henchman in 1676.

GROVER, SIMON, was in garrison at Wading River in 1675; was with Capt. Turner at Hadley in April, 1676, and was at the Falls Fight, May 19, 1676; was with Capt. Henchman in 1676.

GROVER, STEPHEN, was at Hadley with Capt. Turner in 1676.

GUPPY, JOHN, was with Capt. Prentice in 1675/6.

HAYWARD (*Haward, Howard*), SAMUEL, was with Capt. Cutler in 1676; with Capt. Oakes in 1676.

KENICOTT, ROGER, was with Capt. Mosely in 1675. He removed from Malden to Swansea in 1678.

LAMSON, JOSEPH, of Mystic Side, was with Capt. Turner on the Connecticut River in March, 1675/6, then aged eighteen years.

LAROBY (*Larrabee*), WILLIAM, was with Capt. Cutler in 1676.

LEROBY (*Larrabee*), JOHN, was in garrison at Wading River in 1675.

LYNDE, JOHN, was impressed, January, 1675/6; "hyres pemberton in his Stead;" was with Maj. Willard in 1676.

MARTIN, JOHN, with Capt. Cutler in 1676.

MAY, THOMAS, with Capt. Mosely in December, 1675.

MUDGE, JAMES, son of Thomas, was a teamster in the train, convoyed by the "Flower of Essex" under Capt. Lathrop, marching from Deerfield to Hadley, September 18, 1675, on which day he was killed at Bloody Brook.

MUDGE, JOHN, brother of the foregoing, was with Capt. Sill

in 1675 ; with Capt. Mosely in December, 1675 ; and was the only Malden survivor of the Swamp Fight among the grantees of Narragansett No. 2 in 1732.

MUDGE, GEORGE, brother of the foregoing, was impressed in 1675. His heirs were among the grantees of Narragansett No. 2.

MUDGE, THOMAS, brother of the foregoing, was in garrison at Wading River in 1675 ; was with Capt. Mosely in 1675 ; and with Maj. Willard in 1676. He is supposed to have died in the service or soon after the war.

MUZZEY, BENJAMIN, was with Capt. Prentice in 167⅚; with Capt. Henchman in 1676. He lived at Rumney Marsh, near Black Ann's Corner.

NEWBERRY, TRYAL, was at Hadley with Capt. Turner in 1676; was at the Falls Fight, May 19, 1676.

NEWHALL, THOMAS, was with Maj. Willard in 1676. He was a lieutenant later in life.

NICHOLS, JAMES, was with Capt. Cutler in 1676.

PAINE, STEPHEN. One of this name was with Capt. Prentice in 1675; and the same, or another, was with Capt. Oakes in 1675 and 1676. The Mystic Side man bore this name in common with several then living in New England.

PEARCH, BERNARD. This otherwise unknown man was credited to Malden in the settlement of August 24, 1676.[63]

PEMBERTON, JAMES, was with Capt. Brattle in 1676.

PEMBERTON, JOHN, was with Capt. Henchman in 1675 ; with Capt. Poole in 1675 ; and with Capt. Mosely in 1675 and 1676.

PRATT, JOHN, was at Hadley ; and was at the Falls Fight, May 19, 1676.

PROVENDER, JOHN, was with Capt. Mosely in December, 1675.[64]

ROSS, JOHN, was with Capt. Mosely in 1675 and 1676 ; with Lieut. Sweet in 1676.

---

[63] Bernard Peache was a witness at the trial of the unfortunate Susanna Martin of Amesbury at Salem in 1692. There was a family of the name in the county of Essex.

[64] John Provender removed to Framingham, where he died in or about 1712, leaving descendants.

SARGEANT, JOHN, was at Quabauge and with Maj. Savage in 1676.

STANLEY, JOHN, was impressed in 1676.

SKINNER, ABRAHAM, was with Capt. Prentice in 1675. His son Abraham was his representative among the grantees of Narragansett No. 2 in 1732.

SMITH, PELETIAH, was in garrison at Groton in 1675.

SPRAGUE, JOHN, was with Maj. Willard in 1676.

SPRAGUE, JONATHAN, was in garrison at Groton in 1675; was with Capt. Mosely in 1675 and 1676; and with Capt. Henchman in 1676. His son John, in his father's right, was one of the grantees of Narragansett No. 2.

SPRAGUE, PHINEAS, was with Lieut. Hasey of the Three County Troop in 1675 and 1676; was with Maj. Willard in 1676; and with Capt. Wheeler in 1676.

TUFTS, JAMES, son of Peter; removed from Malden to Deerfield, and is accounted as among the first settlers there; was in Capt. Lathrop's company, and was killed at Bloody Brook, September 18, 1675.

UPHAM, JOHN, was the "fatherless and friendless" lad from Barbadoes, who was brought up by Deacon John Upham. He was at Hadley with Capt. Turner in 1676. He died at Charlestown, November 27, 1677, aged thirty years, leaving his property to his betrothed wife, Elizabeth Mousal, except a musket to Phineas, the eldest son of Lieut. Phineas Upham.

UPHAM, PHINEAS. See his life and services in note 56.

WAYTE. ALEXANDER, with Lieut. Cutler in 1676. He died at Malden in 1681.

WAYTE, *Capt.* JOHN, led a party of recruits to Marlborough in September, 1675, with orders to take command of a foot company under Maj. Pynchon on the Connecticut, in case of the absence of Capt. Appleton.

WAYTE, JOHN, son of the foregoing, was with Lieut. Hasey of the Three County Troop in 1676.

WELCH, JAMES, was impressed in December, 1675, but did not appear.

WHEELER, THOMAS, was with Lieut. Hasey in 1675 and 1676.

WILSON, JOSEPH, was with Capt. Henchman in 1675 ; with Maj. Willard in 1676.   He was a captain later in life.

WILSON, PAUL, elsewhere named as the lover of Priscilla Upham, was with Capt. Sill in 1675 and 1676.   He had married and become an inhabitant of Charlestown.

WINSLAD (*Winslow*), JACOB, was in garrison at Groton in 1675.

WINSLAD (*Winslow*), JAMES, was credited to Malden in the settlement of August 24, 1676.

WINSLAD (*Winslow*), JOHN, was with Capt. Mosely in 1675 and 1676; was with Capt. Cutler in 1676.   His son John received his right in the grant of Narragansett No. 2.

This war, which was closed by the death of Philip, at Pokanoket, August 12, 1676, was productive of much suffering in all parts of New England; but not to such an extent in Malden as in towns nearer the frontiers.[65]   There are extant petitions which portray cases of individual hardships here; and fourteen families, comprising fifty-two persons, received aid in this town from the Irish Charity,[66] a contribution sent from Ireland for

---

[65] Original and recent authorities on the subject of Philip's War are those named in the note on the Narragansett Fight.   In addition, Drake, *Origin of Indian Wars*, prefixed, as an introduction, to his second edition of the *Old Indian Chronicle*, should be consulted; and several town histories contain matter of a local nature in relation to Indian hostilities.

[66] In August, 1676, "the Good ship call'd the Katherine of Dublin" sailed from that port laden with "releife sent to the distressed persons in New England."   She arrived in the harbor of Boston, Sunday, November 26.   Her cargo, which was known as the Irish Charity, was a "Contribution made by divers Christians in Ireland for the releiffe of such as are Impoverished Destressed and in Nessesitie by the late Indian Warr."   At the head of the subscribers was an elder brother of the Rev. Increase Mather of the Second, or North, Church in Boston, the Rev. Nathaniel Mather, H. C. 1647, who was then the pastor of a church in Dublin.

The Rev. John Eliot wrote, in the *Roxbury Church Records:* —

"month 9, day 26. [1676.] the x^a b^m in Dublin in Ireland sent a gracious gift of charity to relive such as suffered in o^r late warr, the ship arrived y^t day at night the master was at Boston on the Sabboth.

"day 27. next morning a dreadfull fire broke forth in Boston, wch consumed many dwelling houses & many rich shops & warehouses, & the north meeting house, in 2 hou's time, by reason of a v^y feirce wind, the history w^{r}off I leave to oth^{r}s to describe, but this is observable y^t so much p'visions was consumed, & so many pore aded to such as were made pore by the war, y$^:$ (though the gift was only dispenced according as it was given to such as w^r made pore by the warr) yet the seasonablenesse of their charity was very much magnifyed, and a crowne of beauty was set upon the head of their charity thereby." *Report of the [Boston] Record Commissioners*, vi. 195.

In a spirit of true charity, the conthe relief of those who had suffered. The following papers are characteristic of the times.

To the Hon'ed Councill now sitting in Boston. the Humble petition of Hannah Stanly in behalf of her Husband Jn° Stanly of Maldon Humbly sheweth

Whereas your poor petitioners husband hath been lately impressed for y⁰ service of the country, and by reason of a lameness in his joints is utterly incapacitated to do any service for the country or any way to endure hardship and also haveing hired a farm none to manage his buisness his corn lying on spoil: for want of tending. his four children ill & weak his brother haveing been out in the service nineteen weeks already at Narraganset and at Hadly and other places and now at home not able to carry things . . . end for o' selves and family's maintenance, and so o' whole family exposed to want in his absence if not ruined with other reasons move yo' petitioner to supplicate yo' hon's for relief by haveing my husband released from the service, and yo' petition' shall as in duty bound ever pray for yo' hon's prosperity

HANNAH STANLY.[67]

tributors desired " that an equall respect bee had to all godly p'sons agreeing in fundamentals of faith & order though differing about the subject of some or dinances, & p'ticularly that godly Anti-peodobaptists bee not excluded : wch wee the rather thus perticularly insert because sundry reports have come hither suggesting that godly p'sons of that p'swasion have been severely dealt withall in New England, & also because divers of that p'swasion in this Citty have freely & very Considerably concurred in advanceing this releife." They further add : "If any of y⁰ Indians in New England who have adhered to the English in the present Warr bee brought to distress by their barbarous country men we desyre that they may by no means bee forgotten, but share, respect being had to their condition in this present releife: Especially those of them that are of y⁰ houshold of faith wee desyre may be singularly regarded."

The value of this "releife" and its distribution, exclusive of what may have been sent to Connecticut was as follows : —

	£	s.	d.
Amount paid for freight	450	0	0
To towns in Massachusetts Colony .	363	3	0
" " " Plymouth Colony . .	124	10	0
	£937	13	0

The amount paid 'o the Malden families was £7 16s. Cf. *N. E. Hist. and Geneal. Reg.*, ii. 245-250.

The bread thrown upon the waters was returned one hundred and seventy-one years later, when the U. S. sloop of war Jamestown sailed from Boston harbor freighted with provisions for the starving people of Ireland.

[67] *Mass. Archives*, lxix. 80. John Stanley is otherwise unknown to me. It appears that he had recently hired a farm in Malden ; and it may be that he was one who had come in from the frontier with his family for security. Onesiphorus Stanley was with Mosely in the Narragansett campaign and with Captain William Turner on the Connecticut River in April, 1676. Savage says he was of Roxbury, and he may have been the brother who is mentioned in the petition.

To the Hon'ed council sitting in Boston the Humble Petishon of Mary Ross of Maldon in behalf of her Husband Humbly sheweth

Whereas your petitioners Husband hath now for a long time bin out in the countrys service against the barbarous heathen under the comand of captain Samuell Mosely at y⁰ Narraganset, & being antient, sick & crasey neer threescore yeares of age, none to manage his buisenese at Home, my self and family being in a suffering condition, our land lying untild at Home and some other considerashons moveth yoʳ petitioner Humbly to beg that favor of yoʳ Honⁿ that my Husband may be freed from the present service, and may return to his family again who are in great want through his absence and yoʳ petitishoner shall dayly pray for yoʳ Honⁿ & the countrys prosperity

MARY ROSS [68]

About this time Malden had not only her portion of the troubles caused by the war to bear, but a contagious disease, the nature of which I cannot discover, pervaded the town. In the year 1674 I have the record of thirteen deaths, and in 1676 of nine deaths, while during the remaining eight years of that decade I find but eighteen. Beyond the fact of an excessive mortality in the two years mentioned, I find but little to indicate the existence of this disease. Mr. Lewis on the authority of a leaf of a Bible says, " [1676.] there was a great sickness this year; " [69] and the following extract from a letter written by the Rev. John Russell to the Rev. Increase Mather, dated at Hadley, April 18, 1677, indicates that it was carried to the frontier.

My poor family hath thro the Lord's goodnesse escaped the contagion and frequently deadly disease among us; the same I thinke that hath beene some yeers at Maldon, & as I judge brought hither by some souldiers of that town, who were first taken ill here, and then it went furthest in these & the neighbo ing families; having beene almost wholly in one end of our Town; the other end almost quite free. [70]

It was not war and disease alone which afflicted the men and women of Massachusetts Bay in the closing years of the seventeenth century. In the gloom and terror of the days of 1692, when the delusion and insanity which reached its strongest development in Salem threatened to spread over New England,

---

[68] *Mass. Archives,* lxviii. 205. The petitioner was wife of John Ross and daughter of James Barrett.

[69] Lewis, *History of Lynn,* 265.
[70] *Mass. Hist. Coll.,* xxxviii. 79.

Malden, in the persons of its inhabitants, did not wholly escape. Elizabeth Fosdick of Malden and Elizabeth Paine of Mystic Side were arrested and placed in Salem jail on a charge of witchcrafts said to have been practised on the bodies of those much-bewitched young reprobates, Mercy Lewis and Mary Warren of Salem Village. Peter Tufts of Mystic Side, who many times during a long life appears in the court records and files, and not always as a desirable neighbor, also complained of them.

Complaint v. Elis^e Fosdick & Elis^e Paine.

Salem May the 30th 1692.

Lt Nathaniell putnam and Joseph Whipple both of Salem Village made Complaint in behalfe of theire majes^{ts} against Elizabeth ffosdick of Maulden the wife of John ffosdick afores^d Carpenter & Elizabeth paine off Charlstown the wife of Stephen paine of s^d place husbandman for sundry acts of Witchcraft by them Committed Lately on the bodys of Marcy Lewis and Mary Warren of Salem Uillage or farmes to theire great hurt therefore craues Justice.

> NATHANELL PUTNAM.
> JOSEPH WHIPPLE.

The abouesayd Complaint was Exhibited before vs Salem May the 30th 1692.

> JOHN HATHORNE } *Assist.*
> JONATHAN CORWIN }

peter Tuft of Charlstown also appeared before vs Salem June 2^d 1692 and also Complained against both ye aboues^d for acts of Witchcraft by them Committed on his negro Woman.

> The mark of
> PETER + TUFTS

Warrant v. Elizabeth Fosdick & Elizabeth Paine.

To the Marshall or Sheriff of the County of Middlesex or dep^t

You are in theire Majest^s names hereby required to apprehend and bring before vs at Salem forthwith or as soon as may be Elizabeth ffosdick the wife of John ffosdick of Maulden Carpenter and Elizabeth paine the wife of Stephen paine of Charlestowne husbandman, for sundry acts of Witchcraft by them Committed Lately on ye Bodys of Marcy Lewis Mary Warren &^c of Salem Village or farmes to theire great hurt and Jnjury accord^g to Complaint Exhibited before vs appears, fail not, Dated Salem June the 2^d 1692:

> JOHN HATHORNE } *Assists.*
> JONATHAN CORWIN }

I doe Appoint Sam¹ Gibson of Cambridge To Serue this warrant To Effect.   June 2ᵈ 1692.

SAMᴸᴸ GOOKIN *Marshᵘ for Mddx.*

June 2ᵈ 1692. J haue Apprehended the aboue named Elizebeth paine and delivered her unto the Sheriff of the County of Essex att Salem in yᵉ County afores in order to her examination and waite in expectation of the above sᵈ Elizabeth Fosdick by mee.

June 3, 92 J haue all so apprehended the body of Elizabeth ffosdick of mauldin and delivered her to the above said Sheriff of Essex,

SAMᴸᴸ GIBSON yᵉ marᵗʰ dep.[71]

A warrant was issued at the same time against Captain John Floyd, who had removed from Malden to Rumney Marsh. During the examination of Abigail Faulkner of Andover, at Salem, August 11,

Phelpses daughter complayned her afflicting her : but she denyed that she had any thing to doe with witchcraft : she sᵈ ffalknʳ had a cloth in her hand, that when she squeezed in her hand yᵉ afflicted fell into grevous fits as was observed : yᵉ afflicted sayd Danⁿ Eames and Capt ffloyd was upon that cloth when it was upon yᵉ table.[72]

By such whimsicalities were judges and jurors overwhelmed. The cases of Fosdick and Paine brought the question of the reality of diabolical possessions to the homes of Malden ; and it was not strange that some one was soon found who was able to impose upon the credulity of the public, as the children and girls of Salem Village had shown the way. This ready instrument was found in the person of Mary Marshall, whose husband, Edward, had recently died. It may have been the weakness of age or sickness and grief which put the cruel fantasies into her head.

Lydia Dustin, the widow of Josiah Dustin of Reading, a woman of eighty years, had been arrested in May for " Witchcraft done or Comitted by her upon yᵉ Bodys " of the afflicted persons at Salem Village. Mary Marshall had lived in Reading and, apparently, had been intimate with Lydia Dustin and the others whom she afterwards accused. Her afflictions began upon the day when Dustin was taken to Salem and continued for several months. It does not appear that she accused all her

---

[71] *Witchcraft Papers* in Clerk's Office at Salem, *in loco.*   [72] Ibid.

tormentors at once; but the list of her victims, at the end, included Lydia Dustin and her daughter, Mary, the widow of Adam Colson, a former schoolmaster of Reading, Mary, the wife of Seabred Taylor, and Jane, the widow of George Lilley, also a former schoolmaster, all of Reading.[78] Colson, Lilley, and Taylor were brought before the magistrates at Salem, September 5, 1692. The minutes of the examination of Mary Colson are as follows: —

Mary Coullson you are here accused for afflicting m^{rs} mary marshall by witchcraft m^{rs} marshal with divers fell down at her coming into ye court s^d Couleson helped m^n marshall up by a touch of her hand : but s^d Coullson s^d she never hurt s^d marshall in her life : m^n marshal was asked how long coulson had afflicted her : she s^d: at times : she had afflicted her ever since her mother Dastin had been in prison & that she did it in vindication of her mother these 3 : Taylor : Lilly & Coullson came to me & s^d though m^r pearpont sang that Psalm : god will be a husband to ye widdow : but he would be none to me they said : they told me also : if J had served their god my husband had been alive yett : but s^d Coullson was bid to look on ye afflicted persons : and some of the afflicted was bid to look on her : and Eliz Booth : & George Boothes wife & Allice Booth : with others : was struck down with her look & afflicted : & helped up : & was well by a touch of Coullsons hand : they were asked when they were well agayn who hurt : them & s^d it was Coullson it was told Coullson : it was evident that she acted witchcraft now before them : & it was like to apear that she had a hand in w^m Hoopers Death & in Ed marshals death : but she s^d if she should confes she should be ly her selfe : [74]

At the examination of Jane Lilley several of the afflicted persons were stricken down as she came into the room, as they had been in the presence of Colson.

Mary Warin Allice Booth & Susanna Post & m^{rs} mary marshall was asked who struck them down : they answered y^t it was s^d Lilly Jt was s^d to her : Jane Lilly you are accused for afflicting m^n mary Marshall by witchcraft : & now you have hurt many others : now you have oppertunity to tell ye truth : in this matter : but she answered the truth was she knew nothing of it nor was she sensible y^t she was in ye Devills snare.[75]

Lydia Dustin was indicted and brought before the Superior Court of Judicature at Charlestown, January 31, 169⅔. The record of her indictment and trial is as follows: —

---

[78] *Suffolk Court Files*, xxxii. 2710, 2714.   [74] Ibid., 2714.   [75] Ibid.

LIDIAH DASTIN of Reding in the County of Midlesex widow being
Indicted by the Iurors ffor our Soveraigne Lord and Lady the King &
Queen upon their oaths upon one Indictment. That is to say.

For that shee the said Lydia Dastin of Reding in the County of
Midlesex widow on or about the second day of May in the year 1692
and divers other days and times as well before as after Certaine destest-
able Arts called Witchrafts and sorceries wickedly mallitiousely and
ffeloneously hath used practised and exercised at and in the Towne of
Malden in the County of Midlesex aforesaid upon an against one Mary
Marshall   by which wicked Arts the said Mary Marshall the day and
year aforesaid & divers other dayes and times as well before as after
was afflicted Tortured Tormented Consumed pined & Wasted Contrary
to the peace of Our Sovereigne Lord and Lady the King and Queen
their Crowne and dignity and the Lawes in that case made and
provided

UPON the aforesaid Indictment the said Lidia Dastin was then and
there before the Iustices of our Lord and Lady the King and Queen
aforesaid arraigned and upon her Arraigem! did then and there the
day and year aforesaid Plead Not Guilty and put her selfe upon tryall
by God and the Country.

A Iury being called Samuel Green foreman and accordingly sworne no
exception being made by the prisoner the said Indictment being read,
together with the Evidences and Examinations and the prisoners
defence being heard The Iury went out to agree on their verdict, who
returning did then and there in open Court deliver their verdict. That
the said Lidia Dastin was Not Guilty of the ffelony by Witchcraft for
wich she stood Indicted in and by the s^d Jndictm!

> The Court Orderd the said
> Lydia Dastin to be dis-
> charged paying her ffees [76]

Phineas Sprague, who died at Malden, January 23, 1699/1, left
a widow, Sarah (Hasey), and a daughter, Martha, and other
children. The widow soon married Moses Tyler, and those of
her children who were unmarried appear to have removed with
her to a new home in Andover or Boxford. The daughter,
Martha, became prominent as an accuser and witness in the
witchcraft cases and with Rose Foster, Abigail Martin, and
others formed a band of afflicted ones, whose work was quite as
busily and persistently performed as that of the Salem circle.

[76] *Records of Superior Court of Judi-*
cature (Charlestown, January 31, 1693⅘.),
i. 35. Had she been tried at the Special
Court of Oyer and Terminer she would
have been hung.

Among their earliest victims were Mary Barker and William Barker, both of Andover, who each confessed. The latter was a boy of fourteen years and a precious rascal. At his examination he said he hated the devil and that there "was such aload upon his stomach that he could not speak;" but he told a wonderful story and managed to implicate six persons, whose names were endorsed upon the back of the examination as accused persons by the ready magistrates. One of these was Samuel Wardwell, who was hanged at Salem, September 22, 1692; and another was Mary Parker, who suffered at the same time. Both of these persons were indicted for their "detestable arts" against Martha Sprague. Of the others who were accused by her, Abigail Faulkner and Sarah, the widow of Samuel Wardwell, were condemned but not executed; and a number were tried and discharged. The examination of Rebecca Johnson, who was accused by Sprague, is worthy of attention for a bit of folk-lore which it preserves.

Sept   *The Examination of Rebecca Johnson, widow, Taken before*
1692   *Ino. Hauthorn Esq' & other their majest" Iustices*

She denyed what she was accused of, But she acknowledged the turning of the Sieve, in her house by her daughter, whom she desyred to try if her brother moses Haggat was alive or dead — and that if the Sieve turned he was dead and so the Sieve did turn, And my daughter said that m' Bernards maid told her the way. The words used were, By Saint Peter & Saint Paul if Haggat be dead Let this Sieve turn round ; & so it did —

Elizabeth the wife of George Booth was struck down by the said widow Johnsons looking upon her, and martha Sprague s^d she saw the s^d widow Iohnson afflict her and Rose foster saw the same and further that said Johnsons apparition told them she Intended to spoyle George Booths wifes child

The s^d widow Johnson upon her examination as was Iudged afflicted Sprague & foster into fitts and by her touch recovered them againe martha Sprague and Rose foster said they saw s^d Rebeck Johnson afflict Abigail martin & alice Booth —

alice Booth said she saw s^d Johnson afflict her sister booth and that she saw her at our house partake of the sacram!

— Rose foster, alice booth & martha Sprague said they saw the devill stand before her and also before her daught! [77]

[77] *Suffolk Court Files,* xxxii. 2707.

Martha Sprague was sixteen years of age when she began the wanton accusations which brought suffering and death to her innocent victims. She was afterwards married to Richard Friend, a seaman, of Salem, and it may be hoped that her after life was more free from sin than her youth had been.

A Malden woman is mentioned in the following paper as one who consorted with witches; but how far she was implicated is not now known.

The Examination of Sarah Coles of Lynne   Octob^r — 3 — 1692

She saith y^t ye same night Capt Osgoods wife was examined — she saw Eliz: Colston & Abrah. Coles wife come into her house personally to her apprehension and Jno. Wilkinsons wife of malden & one of her sisters & a little Girle she did not know, about 10 years old one of them had a piece of board wth nails in it thro the board at the end about 2 foot long as broad as her hand. That one of her children was sorely afflicted at y^t time, and s^d one of them did strike her in ye head w^h s^d board — They seemed to turn side ways and so were gone, wch was about midnight — The child was afflicted till Abr Coles wife was taken up — The beginning of ye affliction in our family was upon a fast day about a month ago Abrah Coles wife was at my house she Commended my children much for pretty children & they w^r both taken sick my boy & girle, ye Girle s^d she saw A. Coles wife afflict her seuerall times, had pins thrust into her was bit & scratched had a blow on her nose wch caused her nose to run down wth blood ye last fit my child had and Complained of her aunt Cole was when s^d A. Coles wife was brought to Salem One night being in bed J was sorely afflicted, & saw a ball of fire J arose to see w^t was the matter before J got a light it went away — the last thing J saw was a dog wch J went to strike wth aspade and was beat down my selfe this was about a week ago, The dog went out at a crack in ye side of the house.[78]

The witchcraft delusion or imposture was productive of no serious results in Malden, save that the inhabitants must have experienced their part of the fear and sorrow which pervaded New England. The action of the Superior Court of Judicature that superseded the Special Court of Oyer and Terminer, which owed its bloody, though brief, existence to the witchcraft cases, and the returning sense of the people, working upward from the body of the commonalty and acting upon juries and judges, happily put an end to the excitement; and a general jail de-

[78] *Suffolk Court Files,* xxxii. 2712.

livery released those who survived. This burning flame of superstition and deception returned no more to plague the people
of Massachusetts Bay; and the futile efforts of Cotton Mather
and others to revive its dying embers were met with ridicule
and scorn. But a terrible weight rested on the consciences of
the accusers and judges and jurors, which caused many a bitter
cry for mercy and humble plea for forgiveness.

It is not known what part, if any, Mr. Wigglesworth took in
the affair of 1692; but what he thought of it a few months before his death, when, "with a weak body, and trembling hand,"
he wrote his testimony, may be gathered from his letter to the
Rev. Increase Mather.

Rev^d & Dear S^r — I am right well assured that both your self, your
son & the rest of our Bretheren with you in Boston have a deep sence
upon your spirits of the awfull symptoms of divine displeasure that we
lie under at this Day, both in respect of this long and so oft renewed
warr, that hath been so chargeable & distructive to us, and also now in
this sore drought which hath already brought a famine upon our Catle,
and is like to bring a greater upon our selves, unless God appear
spedily for us : I doubt not but you are all endeavouring to find out
and discover to the people the causes of Gods Controversy, and how
they are to be removed, to help forward this difficult and necessary
work, give me leave to impart some of my serious & solemn thoughts.
I fear (amongst our many other provocations) that God hath a Controversy with us about what was done in the time of the Witchcraft. I
fear that innocent blood hath been shed ; & that many have had their
hands defiled therwith. I believe our Godly Judges did act Conscientiously, according to what they did apprehend then to be sufficient
Proof : But since that, have not the Devils impostures appeared ? &
that most of the Complainers & Acusers were acted by him in giving
their testimonies. Be it then that it was done ignorantly. Paul, a
Pharisee, persecuted the chu[r]ch of God, shed the blood of Gods
saints, & yet obtained mercy, because he did it in ignorance ; but how
doth he bewaill it, and shame him self for it before God and men afterwards. 1. Tim : 1 : 13. 16. I think and am verily perswaded God ex-
pects that we do the like, in order to our obtaining his pardon : I mean
by a Publick and solemn acknowledgment of it, and humiliation for it, &
the more particularly & personaly it is done by all that have been actors ;
the more pleasing it will be to God, and more effectual to turn away his
Judgments from the Land, and to prevent his Wrath from falling upon
the persons and families of such as have been most Concerned.

I know this is a *Noli Me tangere,* but what shall we do? must we pine away in our iniquities, rather than boldly declare the Counsel of God, who tells us, Isaia : 1 : 15, when you make many prayers I will not hear you, your hands are full of blood? Therefore God Commands you and me & all our fellow Labourers in the Ministry, Cry aloud, spare not, lift up thy voice like a trumpet. Isai. 58, 1.

Moreover, if it be true as I have been often informed, that the families of such as were Condemned for supposed witchcraft, have been ruined by taking away and making havoke of their estates, & Leaving them nothing for their releiff, I believe the whole Country lies under a Curse to this day, and will do, till some effectual course be taken by our honored Governour & Generall Court to make them some amends and reparations. If it be objected, our charges are exceding great and heavy already, and we cannot add to them. But what if this verry thing be none of the least of those evill things that have brought us under these sorrowfull circumstances; and that they cannot be removed till we have put away this evill? If the thing were agreed upon, time might be taken for the performance of it Gradualy, as God shall enable us : and I am perswaded God would soon make us able, if we were but willing. Sir, I desire you would Communicate these my thoughts to the Rev^d Mr. Willard and the rest of our Bretheren in the ministry, as you shall have oportunity, and if they do Concurr in their apprehensions, that then it might be humbly spread before his Excellency ; and, if he see Cause, before the Generall Assembly at their next sessions. I have, with a weak body, and trembling hand, endeavored to leave my testimony before I leave the world ; and having left it with you (my Rev^d bretheren) I hope I shall leave this life with more peace, when God seeth meet to call me hence.

I remain your Faithful friend & fellow Watchman in the Lord,

MICHAEL WIGGLESWORTH.

Maldon, 5 month, 22 day, 1704.[79]

---

[79] *Mass. Hist. Coll.,* xxxviii. 645.

CHAPTER XI.

TOWN OFFICERS AND COMMON LANDS.

AS has been stated, the loss of the early records of the town deprives the antiquary of much which would illustrate the beginning and early growth of Malden. It is not until after the close of Philip's War that the records, as they now exist, assist in rehabilitating the dry bones of the past. The first entry is that of a regular annual meeting of election, wherein is found all the machinery of an early New England town as it had developed out of the germ of church organization. There are the five townsmen, or chosen men, who came to be called selectmen; the constables; and last, though not least, perhaps, in the body-politic, those whose office it was "to see to swine order,"— the hog-constables, or hog-reeves of a later day.

30. 10. 78 Att a generall meeting of y* all y* Jnhabitants : Deacon John vppham was chosen moderato*

voted Allexand* Waite & Willm. Leraby : chosen Const.

John Wayte. L*. John Sprague
Corpo*ll John Green : Co*n*. will. Green } sele* men.
and Ensigne Thomas Lynds.

John Paull : John Sprague jn^r \
John Scholly. Jonathan Knoher } s^rveio^rs. \
James Chadwick & John Sargen^t : — veiw^rs of fences. \
Joseph Wayte & Tho. Newhall — to see to swine ord^r.

A little more than two months later a change was made in the time of holding the annual meeting for the election of town officers, which had formerly been on the last Monday in December, it being voted : —

[2^d 2^d day 1st mo. 1678 9] That y^e Generall Towne Meeting for ye Choyce of ye Publiq office^rs in the Towne. viz: Sel'men constabls s^rveio^rs &c. form'ly stated on ye last second day in the 10th m^o : Shall Henceforth be on the second second day of ye first month from year to year. Any form^r order or Custom to ye contrary notwithstanding. And all & any p^rson concernd therin is to take notice therof without any p^rticular warning on penalty : as formerly : namly 18. pence. to be paid by euery p^rson y^t shall neglect to appeare at the affors^d time to be leuied by ye constabl for the vse of ye towne.

On the day thus fixed, the second Monday in March, the meetings were held for about twenty years, when it was changed to the first Monday in March, which remained the annual town meeting day until 1857, when by a previous vote of the town it was changed to the third Monday of the same month. The time-honored date was resumed in 1874, and was followed, in 1879, by the first Tuesday. The latter day remained during the brief continuance of the town government.

The records are now full of quaint entries that indicate a general advance in the prosperity which the sturdy yeomanry were shaping out of the wilderness. Roads were laid out or made more definite, commons were surveyed and divided, provision was made for the support of the ministry, and regulations for the preservation and advancement of morals and property were considered and fixed.

Outside of the church troubles, which have been sketched, the lives of the Malden settlers in the latter part of the seventeenth century were as those of their fellow settlers in other parts of the Colony. Though the great danger which had threatened the life of New England had passed away with the death of Philip, and the dispersion of the Narragansetts and the tribes of the Nipmuck country, the echoes of savage warfare came at times from the more distant frontiers; and troopers or footmen were drafted out of the town to ride or march by weary stages to the relief of their more exposed brethren.

In the gradual encroachments of the jealous and hostile government of the mother country the people found enough to watch and fear; for in the threatened extinction of the Charter lay the dissolution of all their hopes; the end of their close religious liberty, if liberty that may be called which recognized no rights beyond the narrow limits of a prevailing creed; the abrogation of their political rights; and the loss of lands, which were held, as has been seen, in free and common socage for fealty only, and whose ownership depended upon the Charter for its warrant, and might die with it.

It has been related how the foremost man of Malden, Captain John Wayte, stood among those who upheld the Charter against its enemies, and how he incurred the wrath of Randolph and gained the honor of being denounced in the "Articles of High Misdemeanour." After a prolonged struggle, the Charter fell, and the Court of England triumphed over the Puritans of Massachusetts Bay. Yet the immediate triumph was not prolonged; for after the brief Presidency of Joseph Dudley and an administration of little more than two years, the king's governor, Andros, and his council were in prison, and the streets of Boston were alive with the throngs which poured in from the surrounding country to the threatened conflict.

We may not doubt that the men of Malden and Mystic Side were represented in the uprising which overthrew the authority of the Stuarts in New England. The old soldiers of Philip's War, and the troopers of Lieutenant Hasey were there; and returning, they met in town meeting, and called upon the Charter officers, who had been displaced in 1686, to resume their powers.

May 6ᵗ 1689   At a Town meeting of yᵉ Jnhabitants of Maldon
Voted, agreed, and declared by the Freeholders & Jnhabitants of the Town of Maldon, that Wee do desire & expect that our Honoᵉᵈ Gov-

erno', Deputy Governo' and Assistants, elected, & sworn by the Free-men of this Colony in May 1686 together with y⁰ Deputies then sent down by the Respective Towns to the Court then holden, & which was never legally dissolved, Shall convene, resume and exercise the Gov-ernment as General Court according to our Charter, on y⁰ ninth day of this Jnstant May; and in so doing we do hereby Promise and engage to aid and assist them to the utmost of our Power with our Persons and estates

Ensigne Jos. Wilson & Henry Green are chosen by y⁰ Town to carry this writing to y⁰ Council

As attest   JOHN SPRAGUE
JOHN GREEN.[1]

But the days of the Charter were never to return; and the provisional government, which acted by its authority and the will of the people, soon gave place to a governor appointed by the King and a provincial establishment, that remained until the revolution which severed the dependence of the colonies upon the mother country. The days of Puritanism were past, though their traditions lingered, as they still linger in church and state. Many old errors passed away with them giving place to newer errors, which in their turn have disappeared. It may not be denied that a weaker generation had succeeded the strong men of the colonial days. The treacherous Dudleys, the easy and simple Sewalls, and the intriguing Mathers were sorry representatives of the just Winthrops, the austere Endi-cotts, and the pious Cottons of the early time. It was an age of transition, moreover, — a time when men in their weakness reached forward, gropingly, for better things than they had known, and with many a let and hindrance grasped them with imperfect knowledge at the end. And so the weary years rolled on, while out of their doubts came, slowly, earnest con-viction, and out of their weaknesses came tardy strength; and from those twin elements was born the independence of a new nation.

[1] *Mass. Archives*, cvii. 17. This docu-ment is not to be found in the town rec-ords. A leaf is missing or the clerk neglected to do his duty. There is a striking resemblance in spirit between this vote and the Jnstructions of May 27, 1776. "The utmost of our Power with our Persons and estates" becomes in the latter "the last Drop of their Blood & the last farthing of their Treasure."

All this is a part of the general history of Massachusetts Bay — of New England, in the making of which the farmers of Malden played their parts; and although no great leader or hero may have come out of them, they were as the rest of the commonalty — men of nerve and muscle, in spite of their many imperfections, ready to fight and die, if need be, in the common cause. Out of the records which they left may be spun threads for a fabric in which may be discerned some outlines of their quaint and circumscribed lives — some glimpses, perhaps, of a striving for, and an advancement towards, the better things of the future, which they could not forecast. There may be little of continuity or unity in the story; the colors may be faded and the fabric rudely patched; idle curiosity may find little to interest or excite: but the loving patience of one who feels a sympathy with the endeavors and struggles of mankind may not be unrewarded.

As a political body, the town was, as has been seen, under the immediate oversight of five townsmen, or selectmen, godly Christians and upright men, chosen at first, and for many years, by the freemen of the town, who were also members of good standing in the church. They were overseers of the poor and assessors by virtue of their office at a time when overseers of the poor and assessors were otherwise unknown. They met sometimes at the house of one of their number, oftener at the ordinary, or public house, where they partook of some little refreshment at the expense of the town,[2] reckoned with the constables, who were the tax-gatherers, and passed such minor orders as were urgently needed or were not of sufficient importance to bring before the body of the freemen, who usually met, when warned, at the meeting house. One of the earliest meetings of the selectmen of which we have knowledge was held at the house of Lieutenant John Sprague and had reference to the duties of an office of much importance. The record is as follows: —

[2] The "Expences at Isak Hills," February 18, 169½, amounted to the sum of three shillings and sixpence. Eight days later the bill for the expense of another meeting was four shillings and twopence; and eleven days later still a debt of two shillings and fourpence was incurred.

[11. 3ᵐᵒ 80.] Att a meeting of yᵉ Select men. at Lᵗ Spr.

Appointed to yᵉ seuerall Tithing men the p'ticular familyes they are to take the care & Charge of

Allso gaue them the Summs belonging to each p'son in their precincts of there p'ticular rate to yᵉ minstry namly of yᵉ whole year due from mʳ Blakmans ending to mʳ cheurs begining : And if any pay all their said rate in mony, then to be abated one third part therof : else one q'ter part in mony & yᵉ rest in corne

And allso each p'sons part in mony to this p'snt years rate, beginᵍ last febr. which rate is all mony desyring sᵈ Tithingm to Jnforme each p'son in their precincts of their p'porcons & to sturr yᵉᵐ vpp to their duties & to take their accounts. & what remains vnpaid to order them forthwith to pay in to Deacon [John] Sprague.

These officers had been chosen by the town at the annual meeting in the preceding month and were seven in number : —

Ensign Thomas Lynde,	Corpˡ John Green,
Joel Jenkins,	James Green,
Sergᵗ Thomas Skinner,	James Nichols,
	John Sargeant.

The tithingmen, so called from being originally set over divisions of ten families, in addition to their primitive duty of watching over the moral welfare of their special charges, preserved order in the meeting house and enforced the general observance of the Lord's Day.[3] A regulation made by the selectmen in 1684 would seem to have interfered somewhat with the duties of the regularly constituted tithingmen.

27. 8. 84. At a meeting of the select men for the regulating of Disorder in the meeting house one the Lords Day by boys and youth playing it is agreed and ordered by the Selectmen that all house holders or masters of familyes in this Towne shall take there turns sucsessiuely euery Lords day both below and in yᵉ galires ensine [Thomas] Lind to begin below and Sargent Samuell Sprague in the gallire

in reference to the law little Children and youths it is agreed and ordered by the Select men that ensine [Thomas] Lind and henery green on the north side of the riuer and deacon John Sprague and deacon John Green on the south side of the riuer.[4]

---

[3] The office and duties of the tithingmen are discussed by Herbert B. Adams in *Johns Hopkins University Studies*, first series, iv.

[4] An old colonial law, which was several times reaffirmed, required the selectmen to see "that all children & youth, vnder family government, be

At the annual meeting, March 8, 169⅚, the selectmen were authorized to appoint the tithingmen; and they accordingly met at the house of John Greenland and chose,

Samuel Green, Sr.,   Edward Sprague,
Jonathan Sprague,   Simon Grover,
Obadiah Jenkins,   Joseph Lamson,
Samuel Wayte,   Nathaniel Nichols.

This would indicate that about eighty families were then living in the town, if the original significance of the office were still observed; but the next year only four were chosen, and in 1699 John Lynde and Jacob Winslad[b] divided the duties and honors which were formerly shared by eight. The number was limited to two for more than a century, until 1806, when three were chosen. In 1810 several refused to serve and none were

---

taught to reade perfectly the English tongue, haue knouledge in the capitall lawes, & be taught some othodoxe chattechisme, & that they be brought vp to some honest imployment, proffitable to themselues & the Com^monwealth." *Mass. Colony Records*, iv. (2), 395.

[b] This uncommon name appears in the records under the various forms of Winslad, Winslead, and Winslow, and has suffered some strange perversions at the hands of modern copyists. Although the only gravestone bearing the name at Sandy Bank makes it Winslead, the standard seems to have been the spelling of the text, if a standard there may be for a name which is both Winslad and Winslow in a single paper. To illustrate the curious changes which have occurred in some family names this case is valuable.

John Winslow married Sarah Moulton, daughter of Thomas and Jane Moulton of Malden or Mystic Side, May 5, 1652; and their children when born were recorded under the names of Winslade and Winsled. Their son John died January 10, 168¾, aged twenty-eight years, and his gravestone is that of John Winslead; but Jacob Winslow

was soon after granted letters of administration upon the estate of his brother John Winslow "of Mauldon deceased." In the following April guardians were appointed for Jonathan and Thomas Winslead, and Jacob Winslead is mentioned as administrator of the estate of John Winslead "late of Malden." *Midd. Court Records*, iv. 93, 100.

Over the date of April 13, 1690, Thomas Winslow, in consideration of "being bound out against the ffrench, and not knowing how it may fall out, and whether I shall return again or no," made a deed of gift to his brother, Jacob Winslow, mentioning also his sister, Sarah Knower, his brother Joseph, and his mother, to each of whom he gave a cow. *Midd. Co Deeds*, xi. 23; also the original in *Midd. Probate Files, in loco.* He died within a year and his estate was appraised, April 6, 1691, as that of Thomas Winslade of Malden, deceased. Administration was granted to Jacob Winslow, who gave a bond which he signed as Jacob Winslad, although both he and his deceased brother bore the name of Winslow in the body of the paper. Nine years later Jacob Winslad of Malden, blacksmith, gave a bond as administrator of

elected for that year; but the next year Captain Unite Cox and
John Townsend accepted the office and thereafter, until 1837,
from two to six tithingmen were chosen annually. From the
latter date the office ceased to be continuous; and in 1843
Henry H. Hyde, Thomas J. Whittridge, and Isaac Cowdrey
bore the honors if they did not perform the duties of the last
tithingmen in Malden. They had gradually lost their early importance; and in time they filled the measure of their existence
by pulling the ears of uneasy boys or rapping the heads of unwary sleepers, when the weather was close or the preacher dull.
Latterly, they served to answer the unrepealed statute, which
required their election, rather than any definite purpose.

The first constable of the town was Richard Adams, who has
been mentioned as holding that office in 1651. Those who were
chosen at the first recorded meeting, in 1678, refused to serve;
and at the next meeting the town chose " Sarg^t Tho. Skin^r.," and
it was voted : —

y^t ye selec^t men agree with him & to be paid by ye whole Towne
voted. — y^t the select men levie ye fines According to law of Allexand^r
waite & willm Leraby that were chosen Constab^ls & refused to serue :
vnless they clear themselues by law.[6]

An unwillingness to accept this office was not uncommon.
Thomas Waite was chosen, March 2, 170½, but hired Samuel
Bucknam to take his place; and it was recorded at the next
meeting that " this town has exepted of ye s^d Sam^ll bucknam."
At the meeting of March 1, 1713¾,

Samuel Green^Ju : at ye farms js chose constable. Petar Tufts js chose
constable : and ye said Tufts has hired Thomas burdit jun^r To sarue jn

---

the estate of his brother, Jonathan Winslad of Malden. *Midd. Probate Files, in
loco.* A deed was executed, July 1, 1701,
purporting to be by Jacob Winslad,
blacksmith, of Malden, and his wife
Elizabeth, to Thomas Mitchell, of land
on the west side of Moulton's Island;
but although the husband had signed
his name as Winslad in the preceding
December and the writer of the deed
had used the same form, the grantors
signed as Jacob and Elizabeth Winslow.

This change of the name may be
attributed to the peculiar pronunciation
of the original word, Winslad, in which
the final letter became silent and a sound
was given to *a* as in *far.*

[6] Thomas Skinner was again chosen
the next year and his compensation
fixed.

" [March 8, 167%0] *voted* S^rg^t. Skin^r
Constable for this yeare ensueing And
the Towne to pay him three Pounds."

his stead — And yᵉ said Thomas burdit js excepted as a constable by a vote jn yᵉ Roome and stead of yᵉ sᵈ peetar Tufts for yᵉ yeer ensuing :[7]

Sometimes a fine was incurred and paid in lieu of service, as in March, 173%, when "Samuell Tufts being chosen constable at this meeting paid five pounds & so answered yᵉ Law in that affair, and yᵉ Town voted again and chose Isacc Green constable." Ensign Joseph Lynde paid a like fine a year or two later.[8]

During the colonial period, one constable appears to have answered the requirements of the town; and although two were chosen in 1678, Thomas Skinner served alone in 1679 and 1680. At the annual meeting in 168%, it was voted to choose two, one from each side of Pemberton's Brook; and Joses Bucknam was chosen from the south, and Henry Green, from the north side. This vote was reaffirmed, March 1, 170⅔, when it was

voted that Jt shall be A standing order for the furtur that ther shall be Two Constables Yeerly chose jn this Town. one constable on yᵉ north side of yᵉ Riuer : and one constable on yᵉ south side of yᵉ Riuer.

The constable was potential. He could "speede away all hues & crys, effect & signe them, where no magistrate is neere at hand, agᵗ theeves, robbers, murderers, manslajers, peacebreakers, & other capitoll offendors." He could "appʳhend wᵗʰout warrant such as be overtaken wᵗʰ drincke, swearing, Saboath breaking, lying, vagrant persons, [and] night walkers." He was obliged "to take notice of comᵐon coasters, vnprofitable fowlers, & other idle pʳsons, & tobacco takers ; " to secure "any inhabitant or strainger after tenne of the clocke at night, behaving themselves deboist, or that giveth not a reasonable ground to yᵉ connstable or watchman, or shallbe in drincke ; " to give warning "vnto any inhabitants of theire toune, wᵗʰer men or

[7] Each end of the town was well served in this instance ; for both Tufts and Burditt were inhabitants of the south-eastern portion, near the Boston line, while Green lived "at yᵉ farms " at the northern extremity. The more central parts of the town may have been very orderly or have taken care of themselves.

[8] The twenty-fourth article of "The office & power of a counstable [May 19, 1658,] " is : —
"Not to refuse the office of a connstable, being orderly chosen thereto, on pœnalty of five pounds, & if in Boston, tenn pounds pœnalty." *Mass. Colony Records*, iv. (1), 326.

weomen, that live from theire husbands or wives, to appeare at
the next Court of y^t county to ans^r for theire so doing." [9]   That
he might be known, the Colony law provided " y^t ev^{r}y cunstable
shall have a staffe, wth some remarkable distinction, p^{r}vided by
ye towne, wch may be as a signe or badge of his office, & this
staffe to take along wth him, when he shall go fourth to discharge
any p^{r}t of his office, wch staffe shalbe black, & about five foote,
or five & a halfe foote long, tiped at ye upper end, about five
or sixe inches, with brasse." If any person " wilfully, obstinately,
or contemptuously" refused assistance to any constable " in
ye execution of his office," he was liable to a fine of " fortye
shillings to ye use of ye country, upon ye iust complaint of
ye cunstable." [10]

Besides his duties in taking a general cognizance of offences
and offenders, the constable was the executioner of the law.
The whipping post and the stocks were under his charge; and
he was " to whip or punish any to bee punished where there is
not another officer appointed to do it wthin his owne towne, unlesse hee can get another to do it." [11]   He was also a server of
writs, collector of taxes, and coroner; and his time was well
taken if he were faithful in fulfilling all the duties prescribed in
the twenty-six articles which the General Court caused to be
printed for his guidance. [12]

A town clerk and a treasurer are not mentioned in the record
of the meeting held in 1678; nor was a clerk chosen by the

---

[9] *Mass. Colony Records*, iv. (1), 324–327.

[10] Ibid., ii. 151.

[11] Ibid., i. 339. The whipping post and stocks had their places under an ancient Balm of Gilead tree which stood before Hill's Tavern. Those thrifty trees which now stand south of the City Hall are seedlings of the same stock. Mary Degresha, otherwise Moll Grush, is said to have been the last sufferer by the lash. The soft-hearted officer who inflicted the punishment is reported to have said: — " Hold still, Molly, and I won't hurt you." The stocks, of heavy oak, after a long service, were preserved in the attic of the First Parish meeting house; but, be-ing removed about 1857, they have now disappeared.

[12] *The office & power of a counstable, collected out of the seueral lawes of this collony.* " [May 19, 1658.] Itt is ordered by this Court & ye authority thereof, that the office & power of a connstable, expressed in these twenty sixe articles, be forthwith printed, that so each connsta-ble may vnderstand his duty." *Mass. Colony Records*, iv. (1), 324–327. An essay on the genesis and growth of the office of Constables by Herbert B. Adams is in *N. E. Hist. and Geneal. Register*, xxxvi. 174–187, 255–276, and in *Johns Hopkins University Studies*, first series, viii.

voters until the annual meeting, March 9, 1684/5, when Samuel Sprague [13] appears as " clark of the writs." This must be considered as a nomination rather than as an election; for the County Court held the power of appointment, and at its session, October 6, 1685, " Samuel Sprague of Maldon is allowed Clarke of the writts for that Towne." [14]

The office of Clerk of the Writs was an old one, dating from 1641, when the General Court ordered " that in every towne one shalbee appointed to grant summons & attachments in all civill actions . . . . . These are chosen for a yeare, & till new be chosen in their roames." [15] The appointments were made, at first, by the General Court, afterwards, by the County Courts, acting upon the nomination of the towns, as in the instance just cited. The duties of the office were gradually abridged, and finally merged in those of the town clerk, a change which began to be apparent in 1686, when the Court appointed Lieutenant Samuel Sprague of Malden among other " Clerks in the several Townes of this County to take account of all Births and Deaths in their respective Towns and to act in said office according to the order of the President & Council." [16] Samuel Sprague apparently held the office several years, although no other appointment is mentioned. His name appears several times in the records, even after he had been superseded, as " Clark Samuel Sprague " to distinguish him from others of the same name.

At length, for the first time, the town proceeded to the election of a town clerk; and at the annual meeting, March 6, 169⅔, John Greenland was chosen " Clark of the Town." As has been stated, John Wayte, being a selectman,

john Greenland Town clerk

was the first in Malden to perform the common duties of the town clerk and he appears to have continued in office by the choice of his associates nearly thirty-five years, until he was incapacitated by blindness in 1684.

---

[13] John Sprague in the town records, which may be an error; or, perhaps, John was chosen by the town but not confirmed by the Court.

[14] *Midd. Court Records,* iv. 189.
[15] *Mass. Colony Records,* i. 345, 346.
[16] *Midd. Court Records. — General Sessions, Anno.* 1686.

Even after the clerk began to be elected by the town meetings, he was chosen from the selectmen until 1699, when the selectmen, of whom the clerk, John Greenland, was one, for some unrecorded reason, refused to serve and another board and another clerk, John Sprague, who was not a selectman, were chosen. At the same time, the new town clerk was chosen "scool-master." His fitness for the former office it is to be hoped was superior to that for the latter, which was not of a high order, if we may judge from the records which he has left. However, he appears to have been more appreciated in the latter office, for he taught several years later, while the old town clerk was restored at the next election.

The duties of a treasurer appear to have been performed by the selectmen in common, although one among them may have been, by consent of the others, the special custodian of the funds. No record appears in relation to the office until March 9, 1695/6, when Edward Sprague was chosen town treasurer. His services were considered in a grant of common land in 1697; but at the next annual meeting he was chosen constable and Phineas Upham, treasurer. A commissioner of assessments, Benjamin Webb, was chosen in March, 1693/3, who was succeeded by Samuel Green, Sen., in March, 1693/4, and by John Greenland, in June, 1695.[17] Edward Sprague was chosen to the same place by the meeting which made him treasurer. Nothing more is heard of the former office; and circumstances indicate that the two were practically one and that the former commissioners of assessments performed the functions of treasurer. If the responsibilities of the treasurer in those days of small things were comparatively light, his emoluments were not excessive. Phineas Upham received ten shillings, by a vote of the town, for his services in 1700. At first, the selectmen made settlements with the treasurer, as they had with the constables in former years, but later, a committee — the financial committee of more recent times, was annually chosen by the town for that purpose.

[17] "[August, 1687] Left Samuell Sprague was chosen commissioner to joyne with the Townes men to make the country rate." Joseph Wilson was commissioner in 1688. After this I have seen no notice of a similar office until that mentioned in the text.

It has been noticed that the selectmen at first performed the duties of assessors; but, July 20, 1694, John Sargeant, Sen., Phineas Upham, and Jonathan Sprague, who were not select-men, were chosen at a general town meeting. At the annual meeting in March, 169⁶⁄₇, three assessors were chosen, of whom one was not a selectman. No assessors were chosen in 1700; but at a meeting of the selectmen in April the whole board of five members was sworn to perform that duty. In 170⅔ the selectmen were assessors with a joint daily compensation of six shillings and " John Greenland [was] Chose Commissioner To Join with yᵉ Assessers." [18] The next year the selectmen were again designated as assessors and so continued until March, 170⁹⁄₁₀,[19] when Phineas Upham, Thomas Newhall, Sen., and Samuel Sprague, who were not of that board, were chosen. At the next annual meeting the selectmen were again made asses-sors, "And to haue wages but for three men;" but a change was made the next year, when John Greenland and Phineas Upham, Jr. were chosen in company with the selectman, Samuel Sprague. In 1713 the selectmen again performed the duties; and at the meeting in March, 171¾, "The Selectmen are chosen to be assessors and To sarue for Three mens wages." This system continued, subject, perhaps, to some changes in the rate of compensation, until March 14, 1780, when five assessors were chosen and special instructions given them by a committee. This change, which was apparently made for the purpose of cor-recting some real or fancied abuses in the valuation, was not of long duration. A return was made to the old order in 1784, and the selectmen continued to be the assessors for many years.

Among the minor officers chosen at the town meetings were several whose duties referred to the care of cattle and other domestic animals, as the hog-constables, who were chosen in the earlier years and whose duties were afterwards performed by

[18] He was already a selectman and town clerk.

[19] During some of these years three of the board were specially designated to the office. A valuation of the town was ordered and a special committee was chosen for that purpose, January 26, 170¾, when it was, "*uoted* deacon John Greenland Commissinor and John Green and Let Henry Green and Sam-uell Sprague iun Chosen Trustees to take and make a ualuation of all the Ratabell Estates of this town Both Real and personal acording to the acte of the Generall Cort."

the common drivers and the field drivers or haywards. The hog-constables were elected in 1678 and during a few years later. In 169¾ Joseph Lamson and John Pemberton were chosen " To looke after the yoaking and ringing of swine." In 169¾ Joseph Floyd and Jonathan Sprague were chosen common drivers and Nathaniel Upham and Obadiah Jenkins, " field drivers or howards; " and the next year the common drivers disappeared, but Lazarus Grover and James Nichols were " howards." March 4, 170⅗, " willium Teele [was] chosen to se to the swine that thay [be] yoked and Ringed that thay may not do damige in the medowes." At the annual meeting in March, 171¾, William Teele, John Lynde, and Ebenezer Sargeant were appointed " to se yᵗ yᵉ swine be yoked and Ringᵈ according to law; " and the next year Benjamin Hill and John Sprague were chosen " To se to yᵉ due obsaruation of yᵉ laws Relating to swine." The swine officers were called " hawerds " in 1717. Swine were permitted to go at large, at certain seasons, properly yoked and ringed, according to law, by the annual vote of the town until April 5, 1802, when it was voted " Not to liberate the Swine." At the same meeting it was voted " Not to let the Cattle Go at large." The latter had been allowed to feed on the highways and were prevented from straying, in the early part of the last century, by frequent gates across the roads. Young cattle and sheep were, earlier, turned into the town commons, sometimes in charge of a common shepherd. It was voted, May 8, 1704, " yᵗ there shall [be] a Shepard chose to keep yᵉ town flock of sheep for this yeer; " and Richard Sprague, a youth of eighteen, having been chosen, his father, Jonathan Sprague, engaged that the duty should be " cearfully and faithfuly don." Orders relating to rams are frequent upon the records. In the case of estrays, it was ordered, March 8, 170¾: " yᵉ finder shall forthwith set up a papar on capt Wilsons Shop: and also a papar on jacob winsleds Shop both fairly written." [20] Cattle were known by owners'-marks,

[20] Joseph Wilson's blacksmith shop, which stood near his house at the present corner of Main and Salem Streets, was a favorite place for posting notices. Jacob Winslad, also a blacksmith, had his shop in the south-eastern part of the town.

which were often recorded upon the town-book. An entry made March 12, 1704/5, is as follows: — "Nath¹ Waite yᵉ markes of his creatures. The top of yᵉ neere eare cut of. A slit jn yᵉ top of yᵉ far ear. And a half peney cut out of yᵉ underside of yᵉ same." Upon the same page are entered the marks of John Sargeant, Phineas Upham, Samuel Sweetser, Samuel Sprague, Jr., Samuel Sprague, 3rd, and John Lynde, and others are recorded elsewhere. As cattle and other domestic animals became confined to the premises of their owners and ceased to go at large the importance of the haywards, or hog-reeves, decreased, and their duties descended to the field drivers, an office which still exists and to which it was formerly, for many years, the facetious custom to elect newly-married men.

John Sargeant, Sen., was elected "Clark of yᵉ market" at the annual meeting in 169¾ and several years after. In 170½ John Sargeant, his son, was chosen "sealer of waits & clerk of yᵉ market," and he appears to have been annually re-elected until 171⅔, when he was succeeded by his son, Jonathan Sargeant. This officer apparently took cognizance of the prices of produce and other commodities, which were frequently subject to fixed rates, and considered and settled questions arising from their exchange. No election was recorded in 171¾, nor until March, 173¾, when Jonathan Sargeant was again chosen. Three years later Moses Hill was chosen "sealer of waits and measures," an office which still exists, and no more is heard of the "clark of markets." The office probably fell into desuetude with the cessation of the necessity of making payments of taxes and other debts in kind and the more general use of money in business transactions.

At a meeting held, December 31, 1739, it was

vot. that James Green and Giles Goddard are chose to see that the violators of a late act made for the better preservation of dear within the province be presecuted and punished : sworn.

At the annual meeting in the ensuing March, Samuel Green, 3rd, and John Sprague, Jr. were chosen for the same purpose; and in 174⁰/₁ James Green and Timothy Upham were appointed

" to put the new law in execution refering to the better preservation of the dear within this province." Others were chosen
yearly until March 5, 174¼, when the office assumed a name
and Ensign John Dexter and Nathaniel Jenkins were chosen
"Dear reves." No other elections are recorded until 174⅝,
when Isaac Hill was chosen. He was succeeded the next year
by Israel Cook, and the office became a permanent one for
nearly fifty years. The deer-reeve was called "Informer of
Deer" in 1778, but received his original name in 1782; and so
continued until 1792, when the office ceased. The last deer-
reeve was Samuel Green; but the last deer had disappeared
from the Malden woods nineteen years before.

There was another office that the freemen of Malden filled at
the annual town meeting which has long ceased to be elective,
or even a town matter. It was that of bellman, sexton, and
grave-digger. The latter function of this triple office concerns
more nearly the burying place at Sandy Bank. They had no
need of bellman or sexton who came under the official hands of
the grave-digger. The others concerned the living men of the
town and were of importance to them.

Who rang out the call from the little frame on Bell Rock
under the summer sun and in the cold storms of winter for more
than forty years, I know not. No record has preserved the
early bellman's name; and Thomas Dunnell has the honor of
being the first recorded choice of the town for that office.

[1690.] Thomas Dunnell is made choyse of by the Towne to ring
the bell and sweep the Meeting house the 1 of March 90 for which he
is to have one pound fifteen shillings in pay by the yeare.

A few days later the selectmen settled with Philip Atwood
for the like service, which had probably been performed in the
preceding year; and for some reason they made an agreement
with Samuel Lewis, in the following August, for the same compensation that had been voted to Dunnell. However, Dunnell
distanced his competitors, if competitions there were; for in
March, 169⅔, it was agreed to transfer the bell from the rock
to the meeting house and it was

voted Thomas dunnell Is chose to Ring y⁰ bell and sweep and look after y⁰ meting hous for this year: and the Town doth agree to give him Thirty five shillings by a Reate: y⁰ said dunnell Is also to dig the graues.

Thereafter, for twenty-seven years, he was as regularly elected as the selectmen or the constables, with varying fortune as to the amount of his compensation, which increased from thirty shillings in 1696 to three pounds in 1717. In 1710 a love of office, or its emoluments, appears to have taken possession of him; for while he was chosen " Belman " with the provision that " he js also to sweep y⁰ meting hous," it is added to the record that " he also desiers to dig y⁰ graues." It is to be hoped that the privilege was accorded to him that year as it was in 1713, when to the record of his election is added " he is to dig y⁰ graues." His duties were again specified in 1714, when it is recorded: —

[March 1, 171¾.] Thomas dunell js chose To Ring y⁰ bell and to clens and look aftar y⁰ meting hous for y⁰ yeer ensuing and js to haue for his saruic 02–10–00 for y⁰ yeer ensuing.

Thomas Dunnell was re-elected, March 7, 17¹⁹⁄₂₀, and appears no more.[21] I suspect that he performed his duties until the next winter, and that Sandy Bank took to itself all that it could claim of the bellman and grave-digger; for Ambrose Hines was chosen, December 2, 1720, bellman until March. At the next annual meeting, he was chosen for the year and allowed three pounds for his services. His term was not a long one. At the meeting in March, 172½, the selectmen were instructed to find a bellman; and a year later, Jeremiah Howard, who had, per-haps, been employed by the selectmen was chosen by the town. There is no record of an election for several years after 1724, until March 2, 17²⁹⁄₃₀, when Thomas Degresha was chosen and the compensation raised to four pounds. The next year occurs the first mention of a sexton under that name, it being " *Voted* — that y⁰ selectmen provide a sexton for y⁰ year Ensueing."

---

[21] Thomas Dunnell lived north of Forest Street on the old road to Read-ing. The cellar of his house remained in the land now occupied by the Wyom-ing Cemetery in Melrose until filled by Charles Pratt many years ago.

Thomas Degresha was still the sexton in 1733; but Thomas Manser was elected by the town in March, 173⅘, and continued until March 5, 173⅘, when Degresha again appeared and the following vote was recorded: —

vot That Thomas Degresha Shall be belman to ring the bel for town meetings and that the s^d bellman shall have eight shillings for diging a grave for any person above ten years old in the winter season and six in the sumer and six shillings a grave att any time of the year for those persons that are under ten years of age.

By a later vote he was allowed forty shillings for ringing the bell for town meetings. Manser may have continued to "clens" the meeting house, which was now under the charge of the parish, although the town continued to choose sextons for more than seventy years. Every voter of the town, whether of the north or of the south, had a voice in the election of the town sexton; and their choice was usually adopted by the voters of the North Parish or by their committee. Meanwhile, the voters of the South Precinct, in their separate capacity, had chosen Joseph Burditt and were paying him forty shillings "for Sweeping and taking Care" of their meeting house on Sargeant's Hill.[22] Thomas Manser was again chosen by the town in March, 173⁹⁄₄₀; and, although he was numbered among the paupers in 1763, a bellman and sexton he continued to be until 1775. His compensation varied from year to year as it was paid in debased currency or lawful money. In 1755 he received twenty-five shillings from the town and twelve pounds, old tenor, from the parish; but the latter was made thirty-two shillings, lawful money, the next year. At the annual meeting, March 5, 1770, it was voted "To give three Pistarenes per grave for grown Persons, & two for children the Year round." Manser was re-chosen by the town and parish in March, 1775, receiving from the latter the sum of thirty-two shillings; and his name appears no more. He probably soon went the way of his predecessor, Thomas Dunnell. Whatever was the cause of his retirement from his long term of service, it was not long after his re-election; for as early as June 21 of that year it was

---

[22] *South Precinct Records*, Dec. 19, 1738; March 7, 173⅘.

Voted, That M: Martin be forbidden, for the present to ring the bell on any account what ever, except that it may be rung for an alarm, and tolled for funerals.[23]

At the next annual meeting it was " *Voted* That [the] Select-men be Impowered to agree with a Saxton for the Insuing year on such terms as they shall think Proper; " and a vote giving their committee the same authority was passed by the North Parish soon after. John Martin, an Englishman and an old sol-dier of the French wars, appears to have been the person selected; and he was chosen by the town in 1778 and 1780, and by the parish in 1779 and 1780. The parish voted him five hundred dollars in the currency of the day for his services in those two years. He continued to be the town and parish sexton, receiving for his labors in 1786 the sum of thirty-six shillings from the town. The purchase of a pair of shoes for his use by the town in 1788 marks him as a pauper; and he died, May 28, 1793, being recorded as " states-poor." No other sexton was mentioned meanwhile except Jacob Pratt, who was chosen by the town in March, 1792. The life of the new sexton is very well summarized in the following extract : —

Jacob, second son of Thomas [*and Sarah*] Pratt (*born February 15, 1754,*) never had any trade. He worked some on his small place & went out to work some by the day. He was sexton for many years, until the new meeting house was built, viz. the brick meeting house which is the Universalist's meeting house. It was built in 1802, at which time Charles Hill became sexton. . . . The latter part of his days he followed fishing with John Jenkins, much of the time. The landing from which they started is about a quarter of a mile from Black Ann's Corner.[24]

[23] This was four days after the Battle of Bunker Hill, when the country was in a state of intense excitement; and the vote was passed not only to prevent an unnecessary alarm, but to emphasize one when it should become necessary. Such an alarm was doubt-less given on Sunday, August 6, 1775, when a party of the British landed at Penny Ferry and sent the provincials flying up the road.

[24] MS. of the late John Pratt. The town record says Jacob Pratt was born February 19, 1754. He lived in a house

With him the old succession of bellmen and sextons came to an end. They were an humble race, generally with a tendency to indigence. Neither Lewis nor Dunnell was a freeholder, and Degresha, Manser, and Martin became paupers.

near Reedy Pond, which, changed in appearance, and removed a little from its former position, is still standing, in 1898, on the northerly side of Forest Street, and is owned by O. W. Ennis. It was probably built during the first quarter of the eighteenth century, and was sold to John Pratt in 1777 by Anna Howard, "Seemster." This house, a view of which is given, in its original condition was an interesting example of arrested development. It was a common practice to build a portion of the house, the chimney and front door being at one end. As the family increased, other rooms would be built around the chimney and the house would be extended to twice, or more, of its original capacity. This house, as will be seen in the sketch, never passed the first period.

With the completion of the new meeting house a young man was inducted into the office of sexton, who for the greater part of a lifetime enjoyed as well as fulfilled its duties. Charles Hill was a son of Charles Hill, the landlord of Hill's Tavern, and was a man of much natural shrewdness and wit. He became prominent in the parish, being its clerk, as well as sexton, for many years. He was active as well in town affairs, holding several offices, and serving on important committees. Above all, he was the well-known constable of Malden, and as such he was a terror to the evil-doers of two generations. His voice, no less than his cane, was potential in the quelling of disorder. He was the last sexton chosen by the town or by its authority; and his term of service exceeded even that of his veteran predecessor, Thomas Manser. As sexton of the First Parish he was active and careful, not ceasing from the performance of his duties until about 1844; and for many years he enjoyed the monopoly of grave digging and burying in the town. His son, Charles Hill, Jr., succeeded him, and continued the office in the name for twelve years longer.

The old-time sextons have passed away, nor have they left a legitimate successor; for the janitors and undertakers of to-day have neither the importance nor the individuality which formerly attached to the office. They have passed into literature as a gossiping, easy race of men, who were not unphilosophical nor unwise in their degree. Nor does the reputation which they have acquired appear to have been undeserved. All the passing events of the town came under their ken; and they knew its people as they knew its traditions, from the first to the last. They were as familiar with the parson and the doctor as with their equals. If their emoluments were light, their position had many advantages, which were not to be measured by the standards of lawful money or old tenor; and by the force of their surroundings they assumed a dignity which was far above that which was warranted by their station or the humble duties of their office.

John Lynde and Joseph Wayte, "Overseers of the ministers wood," were among the town officers chosen in 1686; and jurymen were frequently chosen by the town at the early annual meetings. A " Sealar of lethar " was chosen in March, 1709/10, and afterwards. The first to hold that office was James Moulton, who was followed by his neighbors, Joseph Lamson and James Upham. These were inhabitants of the southeastern part of the town, where the business of tanning hides appears to have been begun at an early day and continued until near, if not after, the period of the Revolution.[25]

Highway surveyors and viewers of fences were among the early and later officers of the town. Surveyors of hemp and flax, and measurers of " Timber, boards Clabords & Shingles," and other special officers were chosen at times, and committees

---

[25] A tan-yard was established at the South Spring and was in active operation until about 1815. The ancient house, still standing west of the Everett Spring house, was for the most of the time the property and the residence of the proprietors. It has been seen that the easterly five acres of lot eleven were sold by Thomas Moulton to Richard Dexter in 1646. Here Dexter built a house which, by equal proportions of gift and sale, he transferred to James Mellens, who had married his daughter, Elizabeth. At the same time he conveyed one acre " on the South Side the high way over ag^t the said house." *Midd. Co. Deeds*, iii. 285. John Brintnall, who married Deborah, a granddaughter of James Mellens, became by inheritance and purchase the owner of this part of the " Millinses " land, having previously established a tan-yard on the southerly one acre on which he was seated in 1713. Here he had a tan house, a bark mill, and the necessary tan and water pits. Thomas Campbell of Marblehead, a cordwainer, purchased the property of Brintnall in 1721 and sold the tan-yard to Benjamin Blaney of Lynn in 1724. Blaney, although a cordwainer, began the business of a tanner, and soon after bought the house and land on the other side of the road. He became captain of the Malden company and a justice, and was a prominent and useful citizen. His violent death in 1752/; will be noticed elsewhere. His son, Benjamin, the Revolutionary captain, continued the business of his father until late in life, when in 1815 he sold both the house and tan-yard to Jabez Sargent of Boston, who, the next year, transferred his purchase to Nathan Nichols. Nichols in his turn sold it in 1817 to Miss Joanna Tileston Oliver, a niece of Mrs. Sarah (Sigourney) Waters, the wife of Captain Daniel Waters. who lived on the adjoining land. Here " Aunt Joey," as she was familiarly called by the townspeople, lived until her death, October 19, 1865.

The old house, with its two noble horse-chestnut trees, which were brought from the garden of Gardiner Greene in Boston, probably in 1835 when Pemberton's Hill was taken down, is one of the landmarks of Everett. Although in its present form it is apparently of the first quarter of the eighteenth century, it probably contains in its construction the earlier house of Richard Dexter.

" Blaner's tan-yard," a triangular piece of ground on the south side of Chelsea Street, could easily be recognized until 1894, when the building of a large tenement house caused all the evidences of the old-time industry to disappear. It was sometimes known as " Joey Oliver's Close," a rare survival of an old English term. Blaney added to this part of his original purchase a parcel of common land on its easterly side, which included the Spring Gutter within its bounds.

were often appointed for various purposes. School committees and overseers of the poor, as independent officers, did not exist in the colonial and provincial periods. They were of a later day and will be noticed in their places.

The country rates have been mentioned in a former chapter, and there were those which at various times, with some irregularity, were laid for highways, for schools, and for the poor. Besides these and the ministerial tax, there was another for town charges, which the voters sometimes allowed with promptness, and at others refused to authorize. With these various claims

Blaney House.

upon them, the men of the seventeenth and eighteenth centuries bore a burden of taxation which was no light load in those days of small things; and the public rooms of Hill's and Newhall's taverns echoed on town meeting days, no doubt, with many an honest growl from discontented and impecunious taxpayers. Sometimes the load was lightened, as in 1686, when it was "Voted at a publick Town meeting that the mony that was given towards the redemption of Mr Gold he being dead in captivity showld return vnto the Towne for the Townes Vse and not vnto his Widdow." The next year the "Towns Meadow at Woster [was] let to Mr Dauson of Boston for this year 87–20 shill silver."

At a meeting, May 18, 1694, a rate of twenty-five pounds was ordered for town charges. The town rates committed to the constables for collection in July of the same year amounted to

£34 7s. 8d. which included other items besides that of town charges. Of this amount John Mudge was to collect £20 14s. 4d. and Samuel Green, £13 13s. 4d. May 8, 1696, thirty-four or thirty-five pounds were voted for "nesesary" charges, and ten pounds to pay an amount due Charlestown. The next year about twenty-four pounds were considered sufficient to meet the town charges; and a few days later the selectmen met at Isaac Hill's tavern, and made a town and country rate amounting to £27 3s. 9d. This was probably only a portion of the amount to be raised, as it was the custom to make two or more rates each year — a wise provision where much was paid in kind and but little in money. The three shillings and ninepence may have been swallowed up by a "bill for charges at Isak Hills," an item which is by no means infrequent in the records. This refreshment of the inner man must not be confounded with the modern junketing; for to a man who had ridden from the north end or Scadan through the woods on a cold day much might be forgiven in that early time, when little harm was thought to be in "something warm."

It was somewhat easier to lay rates than to collect them. In a settlement with the treasurer, Phineas Upham, in March, 1699/1700, it appeared that four shillings and tenpence were still due, which, adds the record, "js jn yᵉ wido Marshall and wido greens hands and Cant be had." A "Town Reate" was made April 9, 1700, which, covering other items besides town charges, amounted to £52 3s. 11d., and was committed to constables John Green and Jacob Winslad, to be returned by the last day of July. In October of the same year it was "*uoted* yᵗ ther shall be between eleuen and twelue pounds Raised to defray Town charges;" and a second rate of £20 11s. was laid soon after. Twenty-two pounds were raised, May 16, 1701, of which three pounds were "for ammonition for yᵉ towns stock." By a vote of the town, May 19, 1712, "Collectors [were] to haue 20 shillings for their Saruis for yᵉ Town."

The amounts raised for town charges varied from year to year, being twenty pounds in 1706, and forty pounds in 1716.

Some allowance must be made for the difference in values, which resulted from the issue of paper currency.[26]

In the spring of 1729, perhaps by the influence of those of Mystic Side who had recently been annexed from Charlestown and were not in good humor over the meeting house question, the town twice refused to raise money for general expenses. Perhaps it was those of the northern section who at the same time refused to pay Jonathan Sargeant, a south end man, for his services as representative in 1728. However, a more accommodating spirit pervaded the meeting in August of the same year, when seventy pounds, money, were raised for expenses, and a temporary compromise was made in relation to the location of the new meeting house. An addition to the town charges was made for more "ammonition" in March, 173$\frac{3}{4}$, when a committee was instructed to buy forty-three and a quarter pounds of powder at a cost of twelve pounds, money. The value of money had so decreased that one hundred and fifty pounds were raised for town charges in October, 1736, and the same sum in 1741. School and other charges appear now to have been included in the amounts raised for general expenses.

The following table shows the sums raised for town charges at intervals of five years until the Revolution. Appropriations for special purposes were also made from time to time.[27]

[26] Bills of credit were worth, in 1710, at the rate of eight shillings for an ounce of silver; in 1716, ten shillings; and in 1725 they had fallen to seventeen shillings. In 1749 the evil had reached its highest point and the currency had fallen to sixty shillings.

The blessings of a paper currency were experienced by the people of Massachusetts to the utmost. The reign of paper extended over a period of sixty years. From the first issue in 1690 until the close of this fateful period, emission after emission was put forth until the outstanding bills of the Province exceeded two million pounds; and every fresh expedient worked additional loss and financial suffering. The people were entangled in a mesh of "Old Tenor, Middle Tenor, and New Tenor," which choked enterprise and impeded, if it did not destroy, every branch of legitimate trade. Nor were the loss and deprivation borne by widows and orphans and salaried men exceeded by the troubles of mercantile business. The resumption of specie payments by the Province in 1750 was the beginning of a period of prosperity which continued until the opening of the Revolution. Cf. Felt, *Historical Account of Massachusetts Currency;* and Derby, *History of Paper Money in the Province of Massachusetts.*

[27] March 25, 1742, the selectmen made a rate "of forty pounds old tenor to answer the payments that may be demanded upon the town for Black birds Crows Squirrels and wharf rats together with other charges of the town."

July 26, 1742, ... £150 00 00, old tenor.
May 14, 1747, ... 200 00 00, ,,   ,,
May 13, 1752, ... 66 13 4, lawful money.
May 16, 1757, ... 80 00 00, ,,   ,,
May 17, 1762, ... 150 00 00, ,,   ,,
May 18, 1767, ... 120 00 00, ,,   ,,
May 18, 1772, ... 150 00 00, ,,   ,,
May 19, 1777, ... 130 00 00, ,,   ,,

When the several allotments of land were made on Mystic Side the large tract covered by the hills, which stretch easterly from Wayte's Mount to the old Boston line, and the larger part of the present town of Melrose remained common land covered with wood; and in a large part of its extent, being extremely rugged and rocky, it was of little worth save for the timber which it bore or as affording a scanty pasturage, for which purpose the better portions appear to have been used. Within the limits of this territory were a few natural fields and some remote meadows, which had been taken either by unrecorded allotments or otherwise, and two or three houses had been built thereon. Thomas Dickerman had settled towards the Boston line, where Dickerman's Hill in the easterly portion of Salem Street still preserves his memory; and the town confirmed his heirs in the possession of the house which he built with land around it. The Greens had cleared their farm and built in the northerly portion upon the westerly side of the road to Reading; and the town voted,

[May 18, 1694] that Samuel Green shall Injoy his hous and yͤ land Jt stands on and so much land about It as yͤ commite shall se cause to lay to Jt: and jt js Jntend for him and his asigns foreuer.

The commons were the occasion of many votes and orders relating to the felling of trees and pasturage; and the encroachments of the Charlestown neighbors were frequent. In 1681 Stephen Barrett, Joseph Lamson, and Thomas Barlow, of whom the former and latter, at least, were Mystic Side men, were warned against taking wood from "our common;" and a vote was passed in March, 168¾ : —

That no fyrwood shall be feld or cutt vppon the common this yeare ensueing but what is or shalbe lying on the ground on penalty of fiue shillings p' tree. Excepting on the south syde of the rocks from Joseph Wayts house to Lem¹¹ Jenkins & from thence on the South'ly side the swamp to the Town lyne.³⁸

Similar votes were passed from time to time; and in 1684, was entered

Thomas newhalls complaint to the Townes men against Jose Buck-nam for selling seventeen green trees for fire wood vpon the common oute of the bounds set contrary to the towne order:

Such offences were common. It was

[March 9, 1686/7] *voted* at a publike Towne meeting that nathaniell potter [Parker?] for carriing and cutting timber of the common con-trary to a Towne order paid three pound and ten shillings in siluer J say receued by mee John Sprague senior in the behalfe and for the vse of the towne   8. 1. 86.

In November, 1689, it was voted that no young trees under a foot over should be felled for firewood under a penalty of five shillings for each tree. This order was to remain in force until March 22; and it was farther voted " That Charlsetowne men one this side of the riuer shall be forwarned for cutting and carting any wood of the Common that belongs to Maulden."

The Mystic Side men continued their offences and frequent orders and warnings were issued in consequence, until, in 1691,

the inhabitance of maldon voted at a publik Towne meeting that the in habitance of charlsTown one mistak side are not to cut nor carry of any wood or timber of maulden commen after warning giuen to them to forbeare:

Allso voted at the same time as followeth John green Jnʳ Joses Buck-nam Seʳ Thomas newhall Jsak Hill Jacob parker thay were chosen as a committy to prosecute in a course of law any that shall offend by cutting and carring wood of malden common.

Previous to the passing of this vote, the "townsmen" had been empowered to sue Richard Stowers, the innkeeper of Mystic Side, for his offences; and this energetic action seems

---

³⁸ This exception covered that por-tion of the common which lay below the Scadan hills, between the present Lebanon Street and the Boston line.

to have stopped the encroachments. The rights of commonage began to be abused; and a vote was passed,

[March 14, 169½] that no malden man shall take any sheep out of any other towne to keepe upon malden common directly or indirectly he shall forfeit: 1 : shilling in siluer for euery sheepe so taken and kept upon the common to the use of the Towne.

At the next annual meeting, it was

[March 6, 169⅔] *voted.* That all y⁰ inhabitenc one y⁰ south sid of y⁰ River that puts ther sheep one y⁰ common they shall be put under the care of one shepard.

A committee was chosen, July 12, 1693, to run the line between the lands of the proprietors and the common, and its action is recorded as follows: — [29]

nouember
y⁰ 6 : 1693.

deken Green Henery
Green Joses Bucknam

Jsaac Hill and John Greenland being y⁰ maigor part of y⁰ comite chosen to Run y⁰ line betwen the common and proprietors land : Run y⁰ line between Joseph floyds land and y⁰ common neer y⁰ spring and marsh a white oke tree with leter C a litle within Joseph floyds wall neer y⁰ marsh :

The same day Run y⁰ bounds Round Joseph floyds hous and barn one y⁰ east cornr : of his garding bounded by a stake. from thence upon a line to a stake set a litell below y⁰ dore of his hous. from thenc upon a straight line y⁰ foreside of his barn to a hape of stons by a Rock one y⁰ South cornr. y⁰ backside bounded by Seuerall Rocks or great stons y⁰ Rang upon a line one y⁰ side of y⁰ hill

The same day john floyd was warned to Remove his fenc from of the cuntrey Rhod And all y⁰ land aboue the Rhod Is Juged to be common y⁰ Js against John floyds land : Lemuell Jinkens warned to Remove y⁰ hous y⁰ was dikermans from of y⁰ common : and Ezekell Jinkens warned to Remove his fenc from of y⁰ common.[30] The same day In y⁰ pres-

<hr>

[29] The lands whose bounds were questioned, November 6–March 7, were in Scadan and near Black Ann's Corner. The farm of Joseph Floyd, which had formerly been that of John Doolittle, with a new house in 1667, was bounded by the Boston line and was apparently upon the southerly side of the Salem Road. That of Captain John Floyd was mostly south of the road; but the house stood upon one acre of land on the northerly side, which was bounded north and west by the common, and east "upon vacant Land commonly called the Rockes." This location may still be identified. The town soon after voted, "That John floyd hath Liberty granted him to erect an end to his dwelling hous one y⁰ common."

[30] The town had confirmed the Dickerman land, as before stated. John Dickerman sold Lemuel Jenkins, November 21, 1690, a piece of meadow land and upland, with a dwelling house,

ents of Seuerall witnesses — Jonathan Sprague Sam¹ Sprague Joseph floyd and James Chadwick Henery Green : John Green Isaac Hill.

nouember   phines Upham and John Greenland as a comitte chose by
y⁰ 20: 1693. y⁰ Town puld up a peece of fenc y¹ stood one y⁰ common neere dickermans hous : and also Run y⁰ line between y⁰ common and Jonathan Spragues land and did drive a stake at y⁰ corner betwen y⁰ lot formerly caled Mathew Smiths lot : and Jonathan Spragues land : and y⁰ common.⁸¹ And marked y⁰ stake next y⁰ common with letter C. and likewise did driue a stake neer Hawards barn between John Sargants Jun' his land and y⁰ common : and marked y⁰ stake next y⁰ common and next the highway with leter C.

The same day y⁰ select-men warned Samuel Green Jun.' To Remoue his fenc of y⁰ common y¹ stands neer His hous : and all y⁰ land aboue y⁰ Rhod y¹ is against y⁰ said Greens land Js lookt at to be comon land.

December   The same Committe : Run y⁰ line between y⁰ common and y⁰ 5: 1693 Lemuell Jinkins land   It was agreed between both parties y¹ y⁰ land Without y⁰ said Jinkens fenc before his hous Js and doth Remain common : and we markt a maple tree That stands neere y⁰ said Jinkens hous by y⁰ fenc with letter C.

ffrom thenc westwardly to three small buttenwood trees y¹ does Raing one a line all markt next y⁰ common with letter C : from thenc to a heap of stons at y⁰ corner. so that ther Js a convenent passag way for cattell between Jinkenses land and y⁰ Rocks.

on y⁰ sam day y⁰ line was Run Round y⁰ land y¹ was Sargant hawards and erected seuerall heaps of stons upon y⁰ line and markt seuerall trees with letter C next y⁰ common.

[March 7, 169¾.] deken Green Henery Green Iohn Green Isaac Hill Phines upham And John Greenland : who are y⁰ maigor part of y⁰ commite formarly Chosen To Run y⁰ Line between propriotary Land and y⁰ common Run y⁰ Line from a heape of stons erected for a mark at y⁰ head of Lemuell Jinkens land next y⁰ common : ouer a thurt by y⁰ head of Leutanant Samuel Spragues land upone a straight line about Twelve foot below a greate singl Rock to a heap of stons erected one y⁰ other sid of y⁰ said Spragues land next y⁰ common from thenc as y⁰ fenc now stands to y⁰ said Spragues hous and markt a walnut tree In y⁰ fenc next y⁰ common with Leter C.

in Malden — 4¼ acres, E., James Chadwick; w., Ezekiel Jenkins and John Bunker; N., the town commons; s., John Dickerman; "only excepting and reserving the Dwelling House aforesaid for the free use and Improvement of anna Dickerman widow and Relict of Thomas Dickerman deceased during the Term of her life." *Midd. Co. Deeds,* xxxviii. 47.

⁸¹ The lot of Matthew Smith was the most westerly lot in the fifth range of the allotment of 1638, and was numbered ninety-two.

[March 26, 1694.]   The former Comitie met and Run yᵉ bounds Round Reedy pond yᵉ bounds Are first a great buttenwood tree before Joseph Lines dore.[82] and so bounded Round with seuerall trees marked with letter C next common.

And erected seuerall heapes of stons

The same day Run yᵉ line about Joseph waits plain : and markt seuerell trees with letter C next yᵉ common.

yᵉ same day Run yᵉ line Round Swains pond meddow and marked seuerall trees with letter C next yᵉ common :

yᵉ same day yᵉ bounds was Run about wilkesons land and marked seuerall trees next yᵉ common with letter C.[83]

The same day yᵉ bounds was Run about Squiers meddo and marked seuerall trees next yᵉ common with letter C :

This action was preliminary to a final division of the commons, which at first was intended to be " only yᵉ deuiding of yᵉ wood And timber; " but came at last to include both " bottom and top yᵗ is land And wood."   This allotment was the occasion of many town meetings and meetings of committees, as will be seen by the extracts which follow.

[April 23, 1694.]   *voted:* by yᵉ maigor part of yᵉ proprioters present That the Town common shall be deuided That all those Jnhabitants

[82] The house of Joseph Lynde was that which was built by his father, Thomas Lynde, above Mount Prospect or Wayte's Mount. It passed from the Lynde family to the Pratts, and is described as being bounded on the " Townway that leads from Reading Road to Dexter's Rocks." It was demolished, about 1828, by John Pratt, who built in its place the house now standing at the entrance of Forest Dale Cemetery.

Reedy Pond was near the Lynde house, on the southerly side of the road, and until 1894 its place was marked by a hollow and a small brook that drained a swamp or meadow on the easterly side of Mount Vernon Street. It was "sometimes in the occupation of Thomas Green," before his death, February 13, 167½. Joseph Hills, father of Widow Rebecca Green who had died a few months before, deeded it in 1674 to Thomas Newhall, who had married his granddaughter,

Rebecca, daughter of Trumpeter Thomas Green. It was then described as two acres of meadow called Reedy Pond, bounded by the rocks and the land of Thomas Lynde. *Midd. Co. Deeds,* viii. 543. The land around, except upon the north, was common land, a portion of which was allotted to Thomas Newhall in the general division. As Reedy Pond Pasture it remained in the possession of his descendants about a hundred years. A view in this chapter shows the farm buildings of John Pratt, as they remained in 1883.

[83] Isaac Wilkinson's land was towards Long Pond, near the Boston line. Squire's Meadow, which was a portion of the estate of William Boardman in 1705 [*Suffolk Co. Deeds,* xxiv. 142], was still farther north in the vicinity of the Boardman house, which is still standing, an interesting relic of the seventeenth century, in Saugus, near the Melrose line. See the view in this chapter.

that haue a huus and Land of freehold Jn this Town shall haue theire due proportion In y* common

voted : That Joseph Hasey hes common priveledges granted him to the house and land that was william bucknams [34]

voted : That consarning y* deuiding of y* common : It Is ment only y* deuiding of y* wood And timber

[November 20, 1694.] *Voted* That y* town doe leue It To a commite of 3 men that are Resedent jn sum other town or towns for To prescribe a Rule how to deuide y* town common

voted : That y* common shall be deuided : bottom and top y' is land And wood

voted : That maigor Johnson Cap' John Smith Cap' John brown are Chosen to be y* men abouesaid

voted : That no Green wood nor Timbar shall be feld one y* common eney time between this and next tuesday night after y* date heerof vpon penalty of five shillings fine for each tree

[November 26, 1694.] Wharas we Subscribers are Requested or Impowed : by y* jnhabitants of maldon To prescribe a way for y* deuiding of their common both Land and wood : — we considering the seuerall methods and way of Their Raising of Town Charges for time past :

[34] William Bucknam, son of William Bucknam, who married Hannah, daughter of Captain John Wayte, died September 17, 1693, leaving land described as "lands which my father left me," to his widow with reversion to his brothers and sisters. The widow married Lieutenant Joseph Hasey of Rumney Marsh, who soon after purchased the right of the Bucknams to the reversion. *Midd. Co. Deeds,* x. 294.

first we doe adjug their be a commite chose of Jndeferant men To set out so much land for perpatuall common as they shall see meete

2ᵗʸ· that there be a true Invoice taken of every true propriotors estate And twenty pounds aded for the heads of euery freeholder acording To town vote whather male or fafale

3ᵗʸ : then for yᵉ Rest of yᵉ common draw lots for equall proportions Acording to the Inuoice beginning your lots at yᵉ uper end of your common next Reding : at yᵉ southwest corner and so Run dowards in two deuisions or more if you see cause

Majᵒʳ WILLIAM JOHNSON
Capt JOHN SMITH
Capt JOHN BROWN.[34]

A committee was appointed, December 17, to prepare a list of the inhabitants; and at a meeting held by adjournment, December 25, Deacon John Green, John Greenland, Tryal Newberry, Phineas Upham, Thomas Newhall, Lieutenant Joseph Wilson,[36] and Henry Green were chosen to proceed in dividing the common " according to the direction of yᵉ formar committe namly those gentillmen That ware chosen out of this town : jn order to yᵉ drawing of lots to proportion Two thousand accres."

At a meeting of yᵉ commitie at Thomas newhals yᵉ 31 of desembar 1694 Then and Their agreead how and whare to begin to deuide yᵉ common   To begin first : at The Southwest corner of nathaniell eueneses land next to Charlestown Line : And Run lots Eighty pool in length next To Charlestown line : and so take yᵉ breadth of yᵉ common :

And when lots but : and fall short jn leangth : against propriotors land or ponds yᵉ said lots shall be meade up jn breadth.

And where lots doe bound by properioters lands and not hauing a nuf to make up Their mesure : jf yᵉ owner of said lot be their present he shall haue his liberty whether to haue yᵉ Remaining part of his lot made up jn yᵉ next Rainge butting against his own or to Remoue to yᵉ other side of The said properiotters land and haue jt Theire.

And euery properioter haue one lot jn one Thousand accres acording to his proportion And Then euery properioter haue one lot more jn anothar Thousand accres begining whare The leaue of Rainging The same way as aforesaid

---

[34] Major Johnson was of Woburn. Captain Smith was an innholder in Reading, and Captain Brown was of the same place. The latter married, June 24, 1697, Rebecca (Crawford), widow of Samuel Sprague of Malden.

[36] Lieutenant Wilson is called Captain in the record of this appointment and in several other places in the town records. This is sufficiently proved to be an error.

Also agreead upon by yᵉ commitie yᵗ for yᵉ deuiding of yᵉ common euery properioters name shall be writ distintly : and yᵗ yᵉ lots be well shufled together : And one man chose by yᵉ town : To draw yᵐ out of a bag : and yᵉ first man yᵗ js drawen shall haue yᵉ first lot jn yᵉ common begining as aforsaid And so sucksesiuely as yᵉ are all drawen To the proportion of 1000 accres and then to proseed jn yᵉ same way and method for anothar 1000 accres

Jt js also agreead upon by yᵉ commitie That there shall be 2 pols jn breadth between euery Raing of lots for high wais : [87] and that euery mans lot shall Run Eighty two pool jn leangth for yᵗ end

At a town meeting, held a few days later, it was voted that " this comitee hes pouer to jmproue An artis to lay out yᵉ lots : " and at a later meeting provision was made for the payment of the " artis " and his assistants.

Janeuary yᵉ 28 : 1694/5 A generall town meting Leutanant Sprague moderator : *uoted* Henery Green js chosen to carry one end of yᵉ chain jn order to laying out of yᵉ lots jn yᵉ common for 2000 accres

Jonathan Sprague Jsaac Hill Thomas newhall Thomas Okes doe jn-gage To assist yᵉ suruayer jn carrying yᵉ chaine jn order to finish yᵉ deuiding of The first Thousand accres

John Greenland Clark Samuell Sprague John dexter Samuell Green junʳ : Lazrus Grouer and John upham doe jngage to carry yᵉ chaine jn order to deuid yᵉ second thousand accres

uoted That euery man that carrieth yᵉ chaine shall haue alowed him Two and twenty penc pʳ day untill 2000 accres js layd out :

uoted That mʳ fisk yᵉ suruayer shall haue fiue shilings pʳ day for euery day he worketh jn deuiding the common.

At the annual meeting, March 11, it was voted " That Long pond medow lye to the minestry ; " and at an adjourned meeting, a few days later, it was agreed " That the commone lying A Boue the uper Range of Lotes shall be for the use of the min-estry." [88] This meeting was still farther adjourned, until March

---

[87] Some of these range-ways still remain, having developed into town highways, as will be noticed hereafter. Others may remain as rights of way which are still enjoyed, although their origin has been forgotten ; while others have lapsed altogether and become a part of the adjoining lands.

[88] Long Pond Meadow lies near the pond of that name, near the old Boston line. In 1704 liberty was given to flow it, probably for mill purposes, for the term of three years.

The land at the head of the town was in the present village of Greenwood and was, with other lands, set off to Reading in 1729. Being " minestry land," it came into the possession of the First Parish. A portion was sold in 1784 ; but the remainder was retained by the

20, when arrangements were made for the division of the remainder of the common; and it would appear that John Sargeant, Jr., who had been chosen at a previous meeting for that purpose, proceeded "To draw y^m out of a bag" in accordance with the recommendation of the committee. The record is as follows: —

uoted — That all the woode land on both sides the Riuer be loted in two diuisons

uoted — That thay will drawe for lots At this time

uoted — That all the Common that wase intended for shepe paster one the Este side the Riuer shall bee all loted.

At a meeting, April 8, 1695, a highway was ordered to be laid out on the west side of the Three Milé Brook Meadows and others in the commons above Scadan and beyond Wayte's Mount. A committee was chosen, consisting of Lieutenant Joseph Wilson, Isaac Hill, Lemuel Jenkins, and Nathaniel Upham, which made an early report.

[May 8, 1695.] Wee subscribers have done acording to the town vote at our understanding in staking of highwayes in the sheep paster and the three hundred accres namly two poles wide with stakes blazed one the inside and pillers of stones at the bottom of them

1. as one the neck side from the Spragues Land up through the neck unto John Greenlands lote in Charlestown bounds

2ly. A Roade from Joseph Linds house through the sheep paster to dexters Rockes then through the lots to the second diuision and from the foote of Dexters Rokes northeste up Squiers hill through to the seckend diuision

3ly. A Roade from Joseph floyds through the sheepe paster and three hundred accres to Swaines ponde into the seckend diuision.

4ly. A Roade from Ezekell Jankens a longe in the sheep paster and crosing the Roade that comes up from Joseph floydes . and pasing on

---

parish many years. A portion of the expense of a tower built upon the meeting house, in 1824, was met by money "obtained from the sales of Wood taken from the Parish lot."

Lieutenant Henry Green and Lieutenant Thomas Newhall were appointed, March 4, 170⁹⁄₀. "To Rune the Lines Betwext Reden and our common and the propreriators of our Town and S^d common;" and Thomas Upham and Thomas Green were chosen at the same meeting "to Se that no Boody cuts aney wood of The Towns Land next Reding."

towerds the ☉ then winding to the left through lots in to the seckend diuision [39]

5ly. A Roade from Leftent Spragues land up through to the Road that comes from Joseph floyds.

6ly. A Roade from haywards land and branching out to dexters Rockes likewise branching up to Swaines pond brooke and through the lots to the Roade that comes from Joseph floyds:

JOSEPH WILLSON   LAMUELL JANKENS

NATHANELL UPHAM   ISACC HILL [40]

The allotment was finally completed; and the record begins as follows: —

Recorded May y 30 : 1695:* An a Greement of the Town of malden Jn deuiding of The common The first deuision begining at the upar end next to nathaniell eueness land by Charlstown line : Jn mannar As followeth: y* lots Runing 82 pool jn length.

This division, which contained nine hundred and thirty-one acres and fifty-one poles, was laid out in seven ranges and seventy-four lots. It comprised the northern portion of the town between the bounds of Boston and Charlestown. The Evans farm of sixty acres, on the westerly side of the road,[41]

---

[39] The Round World is probably indicated here. *Vide* note 66, chap. iii. If the clerk did not make an error, the turning of the road to the left is puzzling.

[40] The course of these ancient roads may be recognized with more or less distinctness. The first mentioned is that portion of the later Stoneham Road, now Washington Street, which lies north of the bridge over the Boston and Maine Railroad. The second is not less certain. The site of the house of Joseph Lynde, near Reedy Pond, has been shown. This report was a confirmation of the old way running eastward to the "Roade from haywards land." Dexter's Rocks were the great ledges which lie in the woods southwest of Swain's Pond, the ancient road to which may be found north of Lebanon Street, near its junction with Forest Street in Melrose.

The sixth road may also be recognized with some certainty as that portion of Lebanon Street which is south of the Melrose line. Hayward's land was in the Round World, which is now traversed by Cherry Street. Now, as then, the way branches "out to dexters Rockes" and "up to Swaines pond brooke," the latter branch being a portion of the present Swain's Pond Road.

Several old ways may be found in the Scadan woods, among which we may look for the other roads of 1695. One running easterly from the Swain's Pond Road, a short distance above Lebanon Street, after being nearly lost in the undergrowth, leads into the old Salem Road in the vicinity of the land formerly owned by Ezekiel Jenkins. Three of these old ways diverge from the easterly end of Swain's Pond. Two of them, which are still used to some extent, although not recognized as town ways, lead towards the old road which formerly ran from the Salem Road to the iron works at Hammersmith on the Abousett, or Saugus, River.

[41] Joseph Hills sold Henry Evans of Malden, January 8, 166¾, a sixty-acre

and the woodland, which had been reserved for the ministry, on the easterly side, alone parted it from the Reading line at Smith's Pond.   This tract of common was broken by the Green farm, by a piece of land north of Ell Pond which belonged to the estate of Thomas Coytmore as early as 1653,[42] by ten acres of meadow "aboue the old cow pen in Mauldon" which Joseph Hills had sold to Henry Evans in 1660, and, perhaps, by smaller lots of appropriated land.

The second division of the two thousand acres, containing nine hundred and forty-two acres and twenty-eight poles, was laid out in six ranges and seventy-five lots.   Beginning "by elle ponde," it stretched over the highlands towards the Boston line, covering the country east of the Reading Road and north of Swain's Pond.   Some of the ways reserved for passage between the ranges in this division became highways in time and still exist.   It will be noticed that there were seventy-five lots in this division.   The odd and last lot, containing seven acres, had been previously granted by a vote of the town to Sergeant Thomas Skinner, then an old man, who having, according to an old custom, made a deed of gift of his estate for future maintenance to his son Abraham, had no part in the general allotment.[43]   These

lot in Malden bounded as follows: N., "a great pond parting Mauldon and Redding bounds;" E., the highway leading through the Malden common to Reading; S., Malden common; W., the dividing line between Charlestown and Malden common. In this deed were also conveyed a house frame, which was lying on the ground, and the ten-acre lot of meadow, mentioned in the text, which was bounded on all sides by the common. *Midd. Co. Deeds*, ii. 131. This land, which is in the present village of Greenwood in Wakefield, remained in the possession of the Evans family until within the present century; and the cellars of their respective habitations may still be traced, or have recently disappeared. Cf. Eaton, *History of Reading*, 69 *et seq.*

When the northern part of Malden was annexed to Reading, in 1727, the line between the fourth and fifth ranges of the first division was made the south-

ern limit of Reading. This line was confirmed in 1744/5 and with perhaps a slight change west of Main Street, still remains.

[42] *Mass. Colony Records*, iv. (1), 176.

[43] "[March 15, 1694/5,] *uoted* That Sargent Skiner shall haue seuen akers of land in the common for his life time next to Joseph fflids lote after the 2000 ackes is lade out and after his death to Return to the towne"

"[March: 28: 1695,] *uoted* That Sargent Skiners seuen accars of common wood land formerly granted him for his life time is now giuen to him and his wife and then to Return to his children."

The house and land which Thomas Skinner and his wife Lydia gave their son Abraham in February 1694/5, *Midd. Co. Deeds*, x. 534, had been the estate of her former husband, Thomas Call. The house stood near the southeasterly corner of Cross and Walnut Streets.

two divisions comprised the territory known as the two thousand acres and contained, together, eighteen hundred and seventy-three acres and seventy-nine poles, as measured by Mr. Fisk the " artis."

The third division is described as " The third diuision for the Remander of the wood Land one the este sid the mill brook called the three hundred ackrs Begining at sargent Skiners Lote and are to rune 40 poles in length." Its seventy-four lots embraced three hundred and eleven acres and fifty-eight poles of the woodland between Swain's Pond and Scadan.

" The fourth deuision of lots: which js The first deuision one y⁰ west side of The mill brook begining one that peece of common next to y⁰ old dam: Runing forty pools Jn length," and the fifth division, which is described as " The second deuision one y⁰ west side," comprised the woodlands around and above Tyot and the south-easterly portion of the Middlesex Fells.⁴⁴ Each division was laid out in seventy-four lots and, together, they contained four hundred and twenty-six acres and nine poles.

The sixth division — the " Lotes in the laste diuision which was called the sheep paster," contained five hundred and eighty-one acres and fifty-four poles of rugged land lying among the hills east of Wayte's Mount and in Scadan, and apparently on the western and southern borders of the three hundred acres. It came as far west as Sprague's Ledge or the present Mount Vernon Street, and perhaps included the former. Reedy Pond, lying " before Joseph Lines dore" on Forest Street near the northerly end of Mount Vernon Street, was certainly within its limits. The following vote, preceding the division, throws some light upon its western borders.

Vide chap. xii. note 11. Abraham Skinner died soon after, leaving a widow, Hannah, to whom his father deeded the lot numbered seventy-five in the second division, in consideration of maintenance " with meat drink and clothes for my life." May 27, 1698. *Midd. Co. Deeds*, xii. 749. Thomas Skinner died March 2, 170¾, and his widow lived until December 17, 1723, when she died at the age of about eighty-seven years.

⁴⁴ Tyot was a local name which was formerly applied to the territory between Oak Grove and the cascades near the Fells Station. It was in use as late as 1850, and may still be used by some old residents.

[March 20 : 169⅘]. Jn ansewar to the Request of thomas Newhall *uoted* — That Thomas Newhall shall haue his preportion of that part of the Common that was intended for a Shipe paster : next to his one land ; he bindeing himselfe his Eares and Exetuers to finde the town with a suficent traineing place both for horse and fote.[45]

Under this vote it appears that Thomas Newhall, who then owned the land north of the Salem Road from the present westerly line of Sprague Street to the hills at Faulkner, received lot sixteen in the division of "the sheep paster," to which he added by subsequent purchase of the adjoining lands. From these acquisitions his son, Lieutenant Samuel Newhall, came into possession of the easterly side of "the Captains Mount," and the hill since called Sprague's Ledge, including the land on its north-easterly side, then known as the Reedy Pond pasture.

The seven proprietors who failed to receive their shares in the sixty-seven lots of the great sheep pasture, found their proportions in the seventy-six acres and sixty-eight poles of a tract called "The sheep : parstor one The west side of y⁰ mill brook."

The lands thus allotted amounted to thirty-two hundred and sixty-eight acres and one hundred and eight poles, according to the footings of the several divisions. If the usual overrun of old surveys and the allowance for waste land be considered, it will be found that a territory of more than thirty-five hundred acres, or nearly one-half of the town, as it was then constituted, became for the first time proprietary land.

The seventy-four proprietors and freeholders who shared in the allotment were as follows : —

Atwood, Philip	Fosdick, John
Bucknam, Judith, widow of Joses	Green, Henry
Bunker, John	Capt. John
Burditt [*Burden*], Thomas	John
Calley, Robert	Samuel, Jr.
Chadwick, James	Samuel, Sen.
Dexter, John, and the estate of John	Thomas, estate of, deceased
Dexter, deceased	Capt. William
Evans, Nathaniel	Greenland, John
Floyd, Capt. John	Grover, Lazarus
Joseph	Simon

[45] Newhall's training place was on the plain which Mountain Avenue now crosses, east of Main Street.

Hasey, Joseph
Hill, Abraham
 Isaac
Hills, Ebenezer
 Gershom
Howard [*Haward*], Jonathan
 Samuel, estate of, deceased
Jenkins, Ezekiel
 Lemuel
 Obadiah
Knower, Jonathan
Lamson, Joseph
Lane, Job
Lynde, Elizabeth
 John
 Joseph
Marshall, Widow, and the estate of Edward Marshall, deceased [46]
Mudge, John
Newberry, Tryal
Newhall, Thomas
Nichols, James, Jr., and the estate of James Nichols, deceased
 Nathaniel
Oakes, Thomas
Paige, Col. Nicholas [47]
Parker, Jacob, estate of, deceased
Pemberton, John, house of, deceased

Pratt, Richard, estate of, deceased
Sargeant, John, Jr.
 John, Sen.
Sayes, Dorcas [48]
Shute, Richard
Skinner, Abraham, estate of, deceased
Sprague, Edward
 John
 Jonathan
 Phineas, estate of, deceased
 Phineas
 Samuel
 "Clark" Samuel
 Lieut. Samuel
Swillaway, Henry
Tufts, Peter
Upham, John
 Nathaniel
 Phineas
Wayte, Joseph, estate of, deceased
 Capt. John, estate of, deceased
Whittemore, Benjamin
Wigglesworth, Rev. Michael
Wilkinson, Isaac
 John
Wilson, Lieut. Joseph
Winslad [*Winslow*], Jacob

---

[45] Edward Marshall of Reading married Mary Swain in 1665. He removed to Malden and was admitted as a freeman in 1690. He died before the summer of 1692, when his widow committed those freaks in connection with the witchcraft cases which are elsewhere related.

[47] Colonel Paige, as has been related, was a resident of Rumney Marsh and not of Malden; but he possessed real estate in the town to an amount which gave him a freehold and entitled him to a share in the allotments.

[48] Dorcas Sayes was, perhaps, the sister of Christopher Sayes, who, having a wife, Hannah, was possessed of twenty-eight acres of land in Charlestown, near the Dexter and Mellens lands on Mystic Side, which he mortgaged to Elias Row of Charlestown, in 1678, and never redeemed. *Midd. Co. Deeds*, vi. 424; *Midd. Court Files*, April, 1680. In 1684 he lived in the house which belonged to the estate of James Mellens. *Midd. Court Records*, iv. 93. His widow, Hannah, in 1704, was the owner of a house

and six acres of land on the west side of the road from Black Ann's Corner to Sagamore Hill. This piece of land, which was a triangle, appears to have been that six acres of woodland which was the property of Francis Norton in 1638. How it was conveyed or transmitted does not appear. Widow Sayes was living in 1710, being then in the list of those who did not pay "publique charges Jn malden;" and she died soon after.

Dorcas Sayes, spinster, sold to Jonathan Barrett, January, 15, 171⅔, her lot in the fifth range of the first division, which was bounded east by Boston line, and was that which was allotted to her in 1695, *Midd. Co. Deeds*, xx. 653. July 5, 1715, calling herself a single woman, she deeded to James Millinor the house and land which had been the property of Hannah, "in Consideration of the Love good will and affection which she hath and beareth unto the said James Millinor as also for his Love and Kindness to her in providing and supporting of her In a long time of Lameness and also In

Besides that which was specially granted to Thomas Skinner, six lots of six acres each were "laid out on ye land at ye end of ye 300 accres — The first lot begining next Obadiah Jenkins: lott:" which was the last lot in the third division. The grantees were John Chamberlin, Thomas Grover, Samuel Lewis, Thomas Dunnell, Benjamin Webb, and William Teele.[49] Soon after [June 3, 1695] it was "*uoted* That John dexter shall haue the hill that lieth betwene his land and the Spragues land in satisfaction for the want he had in his formor lotes."[50]

Charlestown still claimed the right to timber and wood from the woodlands above the Spragues' land on the west side of the Three Mile Brook, which had been reserved for the Charlestown men on Mystic Side in the agreement of 1649. The title to the lot of five acres at Sandy Bank, which Malden had conveyed to Henry Swillaway in 1674 and which Charlestown claimed as a portion of her common landing place there, was also in question. At a meeting held September 23, 1695, Henry Green, Joseph Hasey, Joseph Lamson, Phineas Upham, and Jonathan Sprague were chosen to attend the town's interest "consarning the wood one the weste side of the mill Brook: and Swillaways land at Sandybanke: against Charlstown men thare laying claime to

---

her sickness." This land was bounded: E., the country road; s., Thomas Waite; w., Simon Grover; N., it runs to a point. *Midd. Co. Deeds*, xxxv. 198. The land of Thomas Waite is now owned by the proprietors of Woodlawn Cemetery.

There is no record of the death of Dorcas Sayes. Hannah, the wife of James Millinor, who may have been her niece and the daughter of Christopher and Hannah Sayes, died in February 17^{39}/$_{40}$. James Millinor removed soon after to Mansfield, where he was a resident in 1744, when he married Ruth Pierce of Malden. Previous to his removal he sold the Sayes house and land to Hugh Floyd. *Midd. Co. Deeds*, xliii. 708. Eighty years ago, the house, which is still standing near the Revere line a short distance northeast of Woodlawn Cemetery, was occupied by a negro known as old Samson.

[49] This grant appears to have been made under peculiar circumstances. The grantees were not among the proprietors and freeholders and were not entitled to a share in the division. If they were not paupers, they were apparently such as needed assistance. Dunnell was the town sexton and Lewis had acted in the same capacity. Three of the six, at least, Grover, Dunnell, and Teele, were not taxpayers in 1710, although living in the town. Teele sold his six acres in 1706 to Philip Atwood of Bradford. *Midd. Co. Deeds*, xiv. 147.

[50] This was, apparently, that rocky hill on which now stands the house of the Kernwood Club on Alpine Street. The land of John Dexter is described in chap. iii. note 33. That of the Spragues, extending from the rocks at Tyot (Oak Grove) to the Malden River, comprised nearly one-half of the territory now covered by Ward IV and that portion of Ward III which is east of Cedar Street.

it." At a later meeting they were given full power to settle or to protect the town in law. The Charlestown people pushed their claims and the matter was finally settled by arbitration. In a deed, dated December 30, 1695, John Cutler, acting as agent for Charlestown, conveyed to the committee all the rights of that town in the Swillaway land and " to all the wood and

Bedmaman House

timber standing or being on y⁰ Lands in maldon to the West-ward of Spot pond Brooke." [51] Although this deed was dated in December, 1695, it was not recorded until May 20, 1699. Some delay apparently occurred in its delivery after its pro-visions were settled. The following entries are found in the town records : —

[January 6, 169⅚.] *uoted* That Chap^t John Green and Deaken John Greenland are Chosen and in poured to treeat and demand of charls-town men what land is due : to us from them.

March 9, 169⅚.] *uoted* That Capt John Green and Lett Joseph willson and Thomas newhall are fully impoured to agree with Charls-town men in all diferances Betwene Charlestown and molden.

The rights which had been reserved in the common landing place at Sandy Bank continued to be enjoyed by the inhabitants of Charlestown on Mystic Side, although it appears that the Malden people were inclined, at times, to encroach upon the privileges of their " Charlestown neighbors." An order which was made by the selectmen of Charlestown in 1710 was intended

[51] *Midd. Co. Deeds*, xii. 329.

to correct that evil; but I find no evidence that it was recognized by Malden, or that it was ever enforced.

At A Meeting of the Selectmen of Charlstowne June the 26ᵗ 1710. Wheras Complaint is made to us by Severall, of the Inhabitants of our town that thos parts of the upper and Lower Sandy banks which belongeth to Charlstowne is generally so Cumbred with Wood &c. Laid thereon by the Inhabitants of Maldon and others not Inhabitants of Charlstowne that our Inhabitants Can not find room to Lay any Wood, Timber &c. for transportation for Remiding of which and that the Town may [have] some benifit of their parts of the said banks or Landing places. The Selectmen have orderᵈ and impowred Mʳ Henry Green and Mˢ Thᵒ Gary both Inhabitants of Charlstowne. To demand and Receive of Every person that Shall Lay any Cord on either part of Said bank that belongeth to Charlstowne Excepting the Inhabitants of Charlstowne the sum of three pence pʳ Cord·for every Cord shall be Laid on our parts of the bank as aforesaid and if it Lye above one month three pence pʳ month and the persons appointed to put this order into Execution are ordered to acquaint the Selectmen of Maldon of this order that they (if they se Cause) may acquaint their Inhabitants herof.

pʳ ordʳ of the Selectmen   Nathˡˡ Dows *Town Clerk.*[52]

Landing and loading at Sandy Bank continued to be practised by the Mystic Side men as they brought timber and wood from their distant commons in the Middlesex Fells, west of the Malden line; and it was productive of strife until the union of "Charls: Town on the North Side of Mistick River" with Malden, in 1726, merged the conflicting rights and transferred contention to a wider field.

Some parcels of common land remained after the division, but nothing of considerable extent. It was

uotted [May 27, 1697,] That Edward Sprague shall haue : that peece of common yᵗ lieth nere wilkensons to him and his haires foreuer : and yᵉ town doth giue jt him jn consideration of what does fall short of his proportion jn one of his lots latly layd out to him one yᵉ west side of yᵉ mill Riuer : And for that saruic : he hes don for yᵉ town jn yᵉ yeer 1696 : and jn yᵉ yeer 1697 : as a town tresurar : yᵉ abouesaid peece of common containeth by estemation three accres more or les bounded one yᵉ southestardly cornnar by a spring of watar : northwestardly by long pond meddo so caled northestardly by wilkensons land southardly by mʳ lains lot :

[52] *Charlestown Records,* vi. 78.

Corporal John Green, Phineas Upham, and Joseph Floyd were chosen, April 17, 1699, to run "ye bounds and renew ye marks between proprioters land: and ye small peece of common land: adjoining to L pond: which was left for convenence for wattering."

Seven or eight acres were reserved in the small plain on the southerly side of Wayte's Mount and Sprague's Ledge, in reference to which the following entry appears in the records: —

[iune: 3: 1695.] *uoted* The propositions propounded to Edward Sprague Consarninge A peece of Land for A training felde he hath untell wensday night next after the date heareof to Consider of and then to give an ansear

The Remaining part of the Common one the weste side next to John prats lote allso the peece of Common that is be hinde Thomas newhalles land shall be deuided betwten sixe men namely Joseph Sargent John uinton Thomas upham Joseph Balldin Jsacc Green and James Huffy jf the Said Sprague Exepts then the said Green and Houey is to haue that peece by the said newhals land if not then Green and houey must agree or draw which shall go: ouer to Charlestown side for his Equall parte with them thare and fore accres one the beste side of this last mencined land to be at the townes disposing

uoted That Thomas newhall and Ebenezer Hills are Chosen to make choise of foure accres out of the peece of common be hinde Thomas newhales land for the use of the towne jf there be ocasion

The propositions to Edward Sprague were evidently not accepted; and the "sixe men," who do not appear among the proprietors and freeholders, being young men or new comers, may have received lots "one the weste side," but the training field lot was not divided. Ten years later James Hovey's case was considered and it was voted,

March ye 12: 170⅚ That peece of land behind Tho newhals land That lieth between ye towns 4 accres And John waits part of ye mount: Js Giuen to James Houey Jt beeing by estamation between 3 and 4 accres.

The remaining four acres probably continued to be used as a "traineing place both for horse and fote," for which purpose it was admirably adapted. It was still common land in May, 1720, when a committee was appointed to renew its bounds;

and it was voted to sell it soon after. It became a part of the adjoining Newhall land.

Other parcels remained, and in time were absorbed by the highways, sold, or quietly taken in by the neighboring proprietors. Such were the landing place at Sandy Bank, a strip of land by the highway near Hill's tavern, the way to the North Spring, and other rights of way. The annexation of Mystic Side brought others — the landing places at Wormwood Point and Moulton's Island, the watering place at the South Spring, and other small lots which have disappeared as common lands. Land on the northerly side of the First Parish meeting house was mentioned as common land within the present century; and other land on its southerly side was given for public uses or acquired in some unrecorded manner in the early half of the last century. It was in reference to the latter lot that the following vote was passed: —

[March 1, 174½.] *vot.* that the town will build a new pound and that it shall stand at the southwest corner of the towns land that is adgoyning to the land wher on the meeting hous now standeth.[68]

[68] The original location of the pound was on the west side of the present Main Street and apparently south of the bridge by which the Medford Road crossed Three Mile Brook. Its site may be very nearly represented by that of the present engine house, opposite Irving Street. It is incidentally mentioned in March, 170⅘, as being near the house of Isaac Hill, which stood on the site of the City Hall. The first mention of a pound in the town records is under the date of September 2, 1701, when it was "*uoted* That yᵉ select men shall se yᵗ yᵉ pound be Repaired speedily. Isaac Hill js uoted pound keepar."

The old pound had become dilapidated in 1740 and it was voted not to rebuild but to repair it; but at the annual meeting, March 1, 174½, the vote recorded in the text was passed. At an adjourned meeting the new pound was voted to be thirty feet square and "built with sels and cap peces and that it shall be six foot and a half high." The work appears to have been performed with the tardiness which was common with our fathers in such matters; and at the meeting in March, 174⅘, it was "*vot* that the old pound shall be improved to repair the personage fence." The new pound was placed on the southerly side of the meeting house, as indicated by the vote; and near it a school house was built about twenty years later.

In 1771 it was voted to raise fourteen pounds in lawful money "to build a Stone Pound," which appears to have been placed in the same location. That the school house was contiguous is ascertained by a vote, which was passed in 1778 at a meeting that had been adjourned to the tavern of Charles Hill near by.

"*voted* that the Serveyors put the Stones by the pound in a wall Between the said pound and the School house."

The rebuilding of the meeting house in 1802 necessitated the removal of the pound; and it was voted to use the stones of which it was composed about the new house. The record adds, "this Voted was protested against by Missrs Thoˢ. Hills & John Waitt." The next

Some common rights of pasturage in the sheep pasture and the Scadan hills may have survived the division; for it was voted, May 28, 1703,

That Joseph floyd hath Liberty to hang two Gates upon ye town highway between ye Country Rhoad : and ye Rocks : on ye east side of his House : And ye Gats to stand : so Long as ye town-cattle may haue free passag from aboue ye Rocks down to ye s^d country Rhode : between ye s^d Jo floyds hous and his brothar daniels hous.

year it was voted "To Build a wooden pound," which was to be "as near the old spott [as] may be convenient;" and it was placed near the northerly corner of the Reading and Medford Roads on a spot now covered by Central Square. It was so placed that the brook flowed in upon its westerly side, making a convenient watering place for impounded cattle. It was removed in 1833, when the town for thirty dollars bought of William Barrett a piece of land, two rods square, lying west of the brick school house on the hill. *Midd. Co. Deeds*, cccxxiii. 366. Here it remained, a "wooden pound," which the boys of "the old brick" will well remember,

until the burning of the school house in 1848. The four square rods of the old pound became a part of the adjoining lands and the site is now covered by the easterly portion of the Cox block. A new pound, which has now disappeared, was built on the north side of Salem Street on land which is now the westerly corner of Bowers Avenue, which was bought of John B. Faulkner, in 1849, for fifty dollars.

Charles Hill was chosen pound keeper in March, 1804, succeeding his father, Charles, the innholder, who died the next month. He held the office for many years in connection with those of constable and sexton.

CHAPTER XII.

POVERTY AND SLAVERY.

THE people of Malden, while struggling with their poverty of worldly goods, were forced to recognize a lower depth to which some, more unfortunate than others, descended, to give assistance to whom became no less a matter of charity than of Christian duty. Truth compels me to admit that charity and Christian duty were sometimes overcast by considerations of a worldly economy or a calculating expediency, which shows that our foregoers were possessors of a portion, at least, of the ordinary weaknesses of humanity.

I am not aware that the record of the poor and unfortunate has received much attention from the local historian, who is usually more at home in eulogizing the men of the past and their deeds or magnifying the little greatness of some man of the present, whose success in the minor things of life has given him a local reputation, which the perspective of time will soon reduce to its proper proportions. If we pause for a while to consider the poor of the past, we may violate some fancied rule of historical propriety; but if we are wise, we may take to ourselves a lesson of humility, which may not be amiss. Lazarus at the gate is not always a pleasing object; but he is very obtrusive in the life around us, and his condition is a sharp and, perhaps, needful contrast to the many follies which we cherish.

Doubtless poverty came to Mystic Side with the earliest, or sickness and adverse circumstances may have soon invited its presence. Pity or importunity may have induced neighborly hands to lighten its woes; but neighborly hands were tied by their own necessities, for the conditions of life were hard, and the poor soon became a public charge.

The first pauper case, which can with certainty be connected with Malden, is that of Richard Smith, a brother-in-law of

Thomas Dickerman, who as the apparent cause of his misfortune "did hyre" a house of one John Ripton, a Scotchman — "Ripton y⁺ liues at the house where yᵉ Scotchmen once were in Boston Bounds" — beyond the Written Trees or Black Ann's Corner,¹ and entered into a " bargaine " with Benjamin Muzzey, who was then, or soon after, a tenant on the Keayne farm at Rumney Marsh. In this case the General Court passed the following order.

[1658, 19 October.] In ansʳ to the petition of Richard Smith humbly desiring this Courts favoʳ so to order it that he may not be exposed to misery, wᵗʰ his wife, being denjed to haue his bargaine wᵗʰ Benja. Muzzey, & by that meanes is harborlesse, &c, the Court judgeth it meete to referre the petitioners for releife to next Court in Midlesex.²

The County Court, hearing the matter, did "order that the select men of mauldon take care for the disposall & Pʳvission for Richard Smith & his wife, vntill the next Court of this Coun; " and at the session in April, " not finding just reason to impose him as an Jnhabitant, on any towne wᵗʰ in this County," referred the case back to the General Court, "for further settlemᵗ . . . as also for the sattisfactᵑ of Mauldon for wᵗ they already have expended for his pʳsent supply." ⁸ The General Court finally disposed of the matter by the following order: —

[1659, 28 May.] The Court on hearing the case comend to this Court by the County Court of Cambridge for the setlement of Richard Smith & his wife, on a full hearing of the case, *order*, that Maulden beare the chardg of Richard Smith & his wife for the tjme past, and that the sajd Smith and his wife belong to Boston.⁴

George Felt, or Felch, who was destined after some prosperity and many trials to trouble the people of Malden not a little,

¹ *Midd. Court Files*, viii. 2. John Ripton and the Scotchmen, whoever they may have been, have escaped the notice of local historians and I am unable to give aught concerning them. They may have been workmen at the neighboring iron works with their countrymen, Archibald Anderson and MacCallum More Downing, who lived near by; or they may have been some of the Scotch prisoners whom Cromwell took at Dun-
bar in 1650 and sent to New England. Ripton was living in 1665. "The Scotch house " is mentioned in 1671, and by a correction in the line was found to be about four rods within the bounds of Lynn. It is noticed again in 1678. *Boston Town Records*, ii. 92, 114.

² *Mass. Colony Records*, iv. (1), 355.
⁸ *Midd. Court Records*, i. 168, 178.
⁴ *Mass. Colony Records*, iv. (1), 375.

appears as an inhabitant of Charlestown in 1633. In the first division of lands at Mystic Side he received the five-acre lot numbered seventeen ; and in the later great allotment he had his proportion of land in five acres in Scadan, on the northern edge of the Great Swamp, and twenty acres "above y° Ponds." These lands appear in the Book of Possessions in 1638, with other lands which he had purchased from the allotments at Mystic Side and elsewhere within the bounds of Charlestown.

At this time he lived in his house on the Charlestown side ; but he soon crossed the river and built upon land which he had acquired near the South Spring, where, as has been seen, his house is mentioned in 1640. He brought with him his wife Elizabeth, a daughter of Widow Prudence Wilkinson, who also became a settler upon her five-acre allotment not far away. With them came their children, George, Elizabeth, and Mary. The wife had been admitted to the Charlestown church, January 19, 1639/40, and these children were baptized in her right a week later, as was also her younger child, Moses, December 10, 1641.[5] The husband was therefore not a church member at that time ; and as he does not appear to have ever attained the condition of a freeman, it is not probable that he ever joined the Malden church, whose records for that early period are not extant.

About this time Felt became a landholder at Wescustogo, or Broad Cove, now North Yarmouth, in Casco Bay, purchasing of the Welshman, John Phillips, three hundred acres within the Gorges patent. Phillips had probably squatted upon the land or gained an Indian title, which Felt strengthened in 1643 by a repurchase of Richard Vines, the agent of Sir Ferdinando Gorges. He or Phillips, before him, had built a stone trading-house or garrison thereon.[6] Although his arrival there is said to have marked "the birth day of North Yarmouth,"[7] I see no reason for assuming that he became an immediate settler. I rather suppose that he was a trader along the eastern coast, as were Thomas Mitchell, the Moultons, and perhaps other Mystic Side

⁵ *Charlestown Church Records, in loco.*   ⁷ *Old Times in North Yarmouth,*
⁶ *N. E. Hist. and Geneal. Register,* 442.
xix. 128.

and Malden men then and in later years. His storehouse, in a convenient location, was the headquarters of himself and his men during the season of traffic, and a safe place of deposit for his goods. From it he extended his enterprises along the coast and, perhaps, into the country for short distances; and around it the savages gathered, trading their skins and fish for his powder, his beads, his blankets, and strong waters. I receive this opinion of Felt rather than that which makes of him a quiet settler in those stormy days.

While he was engaged at the eastward, his wife and young family remained at Mystic Side. In 1648 he is styled " Georg Felch, Inhabitant in Charltown, on mistike syde; " [8] and after the incorporation of the new town he continued an inhabitant of Mystic Side, but not of Malden, his house lot " butting on the High way leading from the said house towards the Spring and on the line which runeth between charlstowne and Maulden." [9] This was that land which was afterwards the home of the Revolutionary captain, Daniel Waters, and is now occupied by the Everett Crystal Spring Water Company, at the westerly corner of Ferry and Chelsea Streets in Everett.

Elizabeth Felt does not appear among the women who petitioned, in 1651, in favor of Mr. Matthews; but she was presented for not attending public worship, in 1653,[10] which may

[8] *Charlestown Archives*, xxxiv. 121.

[9] *Midd. Co. Deeds*, iii. 154. The easterly five acres of lot number eleven were assigned to Ezekiel Richardson in the first allotment and were acquired by Felt in some unrecorded way. It was upon this lot that he had built in 1640, as is elsewhere stated. He had sold his original five-acre lot to Gaudy James, perhaps as early as 1638, the record of 1649 in *Charlestown Archives*, xxxiv. 121, being, apparently, a confirmation of an earlier transaction. The lot, with the house that he had built, was a part of his possessions in Charlestown and Malden, which he sold to John Phillips in 1664; but I cannot explain how its five acres had grown to nine while its bounds and abutters evidently ran upon the old lines. From Phillips

it passed to Joseph Stower, in 1668, and was occupied by Samuel Stower in 1721. In 1771, with an approach to its original extent, it was sold as six acres, with the house and barn, to Daniel Waters, by Nathan Sargeant, acting as administrator of the estate of Mary, his late wife. The house, which appears to have been the early structure of Felt, enlarged and improved by later owners, was demolished about the year 1850.

[10] At the same Court, Flora Lahorne was presented for Sabbath breaking. " Maulden Rowland Layhernes wyfe of Charlstowne [Mystic Side] for making Disturbance in the tyme of the publick ordinances on the Lords Daye att Maulden Meeting howse witnes Thomas he:t Edwd Carington Charletowne Rowland Lahernes wyfe for washing or rensing

indicate that her interest in spiritual matters was not intense. It has been said that Felt removed to Casco about 1660, but as his house at Mystic Side was "claborded" by William Bucknam in 1662 and in the same year he was accused of defaming the character of Bridget, the wife of his neighbor Richard Dexter, "saying she was a lyar,"[11] the inference that he remained at Mystic Side is not strained. He certainly appears as one of the inhabitants of Charlestown in November, 1664, although he had signed a declaration as an inhabitant at Casco in the previous year.[12] In a deed made to John Phillips of Boston, November 1, 1664, conveying his lands "in the bounds of the Townships of Charlestown and Maldon," to the amount of ninety-four acres, he is called "of Casco in N. E. mason."[18] Two years later he was at Casco Bay serving upon a jury in a murder case. There he remained, adding to his possessions a further purchase of two thousand acres of John Phillips, and continuing, perhaps, the trading enterprises which had first taken him to Broad Cove, until the Indian war of 1675–6, when, with other settlers of the main land, he took refuge upon some of the neighboring islands.

During the troubles which followed, the eastern coast was swept of its inhabitants and the improvements which the thrifty settlers had made were destroyed. In September, 1676, George Felt, the eldest son of our subject, was slain with others at Peak's Island. He was the head of a family and a man of enterprise and courage, and his death was greatly lamented.[14]

After the Indian troubles had closed in 1678, Felt is supposed to have returned to his possessions at Broad Cove, where he remained but a short time, parting with a portion of his land to Walter Gendall in 1680, and losing the Phillips purchase of two thousand acres, which appears to have possessed only an Indian

cloathes vppon the Sabb Daye witnes John Gobe william Ayers."

Upon trial " shee freely acknowledged and confessed her sin and fault in the Court, and her husband Rowland Layhorne consented to alow the 4 witnesses 4ˢ pʳ diem." *Midd. Court Files,* iii.; *Midd. Court Records,* i. 51.

[11] *Midd. Court Files,* xi. 10.

[12] Cf. *Charlestown Records,* iii. Nov. 5, 1664; *N. E. Hist. and Geneal. Register,* v. 264. There is a possibility that it was the son, and not the father, who signed the declaration.

[18] *Midd. Co. Deeds,* iii. 154.

[14] Hubbard, *Indian Wars,* ii. 45; Williamson, *History of Maine,* i. 540.

title that was set aside by the courts at a later period. The little right which he retained under the Gorges title at Casco Bay he finally conveyed to his son and grandson, Moses and George, in 1684.

Although in his settlement in Massachusetts Bay he had never been of Malden he came here, where his son-in-law, James Nichols, who had married Mary Felt, was an inhabitant. If he received any compensation from Gendall, it soon disappeared; for an entry in the Malden records, which may have been made in 1681, or a few years later, shows that the town paid " To Goodm. Cully [Scollay] for Howsroome for George ffelt & his wife 0. 10. 0." A little later the town

paide to Robert Calle [Calley] by constable Jacob parker ten shillings for ould felts dwelling in his house for the yeare 85.

In 1686 the case was of more moment, and the town appears to have refused to support the Felts, perhaps, because they had been inhabitants of Charlestown and had not come to Malden until they were in a condition to become public charges. Under this condition, the matter, in some way now unknown, was brought to the attention of the County Court; and at a town meeting, October 1, 1686, it was

voted. that the Selectmen are to take care of ould felt till the county courte

voted that the select men are impoured to mannag the case at the county courte next at cambridg conserning ould felt in the behalfe of the Towne and the towne to Beare the charges :

Soon after, the Council of the Colony

[November 9, 1686.] *Ordered:* That George Felt and his Wife (poor persons at Malden in the County of Middlesex) be maintained by an assessment to be made in the said County of Middlesex next County Court [16]

The records of the County Court and the Court files for the period to which the order was referred are not extant. Felt and his wife remained in Malden ; and the next notice of them is found in 1688, when it is recorded in the town book that

---

[16] *Council Records, in loco.*

The Select men haue receved of reading constable foure pound ten shillings and three pence for the vse of gorge felt and his wife the seventh of aprill : 1688 :

About the same time a petition was made, which presents the condition of the petitioner as one of great extremity, but nothing came from the application. Indeed, I am forced to believe that while his case was one to excite sympathy, it was not one which was entitled to a legal consideration. The purchase of an invalid title was a misfortune for which the law then, as now, afforded no remedy.

To His Excellency Sr Edmund Andros Kn^t. &c.
The Humble Petition of George Felt Senr. of Maulden

Sheweth : That it is my grief that I am compelled to trouble yor Excellency at this time But having about eighteen yeares since purchased of one In° Phillips of Boston Gen^t late Deceased a farme or Plaintation at a place called the Great Cove (in Caskoe Bay) containing about two thousand acres of upland and marsh as by a firm Deed under s^d Phillips hand and seale &c. for which I then paid him Sixty pounds money, and improved s^d Farme or Plaintation severall year's before I bought it so that the whole time of my occupying of it was about one and twenty years But some time after the late Indian warr it was withheld from me by some of the inhabitants of s^d Town of Caskoe Bay and being by s warr much impoverished I could not recover it out of their hands. I also am now forced to suffer for want of convenient care taken of me in my present distresse being about Eighty Seaven year's old and very crasy and weak

Therefore yor Petitio^r recomendeth his case to yor Excellencies prudent consideration humbly beceaching and earnestly begging that if it seem meet and convenient yor Excellency would be pleased to favo^r yor petitio^r that he may have a confirmation of his s^d land und^r such moderate quit rent &c. as well as an ord^r to ye Townsmen of Maulden aboves^d for something at present to releave yor petition^r in this his extreem poverty &c. The which shall farther oblige yor petitio^r as in duty bound daily to pray for y^r Excellency &c.[16]

After the failure of this petition, James Nichols, the son-in-law, apparently had the burden of the maintenance of the Felts thrown upon him; and in 1691 he asked the General Court for relief in a petition which is not now in its place in the archives. Its answer is, however, preserved.

[16] *Mass. Archives,* cxxviii. 282. This petition is undated and unsigned.

[May 29, 1691.] Upon Hearing the Petition of James Nichols Senr: of Malden *Ordered* that George Felt, and his Wife be Accounted Inhabitants of the Town of Malden, and Accordingly the Select Men of the Town to take the care of them.[17]

This order, which settled the Felts upon Malden and made them "town's poor," was promptly obeyed.

maldon June 8th 1691, *voted* at a publik Towne meeting that there be raised 4 or 5 pounds for the present supply of gorge felt and his wife to be paide in provision in or as mony:

The next provision made for the unfortunate Felts by the town combined an admirable forethought with the performance of present and, probably, pressing duties.

[March 14 169½] *voted* at a publick towne meeting that the towne doe alow goodman nicols aleuen pound in or of mony for this present yeare ensuing for the maintanance of his father and mother felt if ether of them dy with in the year after funirall charges what is left to return to the select men or there order

I think that "ould felt" outlived the year and that no part of the "aleuen pound" returned to the selectmen. It is probable that he died sometime in May, 1693, being then about ninety-two years of age. It is very certain that his name does not again appear and the following agreement from the town records shows that he was no longer a burden upon the town.

An agreement made the 26 of June 1693 between the selectmen of This town and James nickels sen^r for ye keeping of old goodwif felt: his motherinlaw: ye said nickels doth Jngage himself to keep her one yeere: begining the second: second: day of may last past for fiue and forty shilings: to be paid him by ye selectmen within ye said yeer: also he is to haue her cow: and likewise the forty shilings ye Justises ordered that her granchildren should pay for her use:

Goodwife Felt did not long survive to enjoy the "keeping" which this contract secured to her, although the time of her death is not known. It is to be hoped that the cow remained as a heritage and a consolation to her son-in-law.

The names of other "town's poor" of the later colonial time, if any there were, have not come down to the present day; and one Mary Floyd is distinguished as having been, after the Felts,

[17] *General Court Records*, vi. 190.

the first who is known to have become a town charge in the provincial period.

[March 16, 169½,] Recned with Joseph Lamson conserning his charges with mary floud: The town indepted to Joseph lamson two pound in or as mony.

A contribution for the relief of the poor, which probably was not altogether cheerfully paid, was made by the town in 1693, when the selectmen, being presented at the County Court

to answer for theire neglect of the payment of forty-three shillings and four pence to y⁰ County Treasurer being theire arrears of y⁰ County Rate in y⁰ year 1688 : Are ordered to pay the Same toward y⁰ releife of y⁰ poor in Maldon.[18]

The next to claim the protection of the town was Hannah Howard, whose case is intimately connected with that of the watch house.

[October 9, 1694.] The Select men of maldon appearing in Court to answer to theire p'sentment by y Grand jury of Jnquest for said County, for not Releiving Hannah Haward and for want of a Watch house, and Informing the Court that they have a watch house partly built and that they haue not been Jnformed of any such want that y⁰ said Howard is in : And y⁰ there is an Estate left by her husband in her hands, The Court order that they proceed to Erect their watch house, and that They Releive y⁰ woman according as the Law directs.

[December 11, 1694.] The Return of Maldon Select men as to theire being prouided wᵗʰ a wach house and as to theire provision of Sufficient apparrell for Hannah Howard for wᶜʰ they stand p'sented is accepted and allowed and is on file.[19]

John Bucknam was the only son of William Bucknam, the progenitor of that family in New England, by his first wife, who was a daughter of Prudence Wilkinson, "widdow & inhabitant on mistick Side." After his mother's early death, his father married Sarah Knower and there was apparently no room in the growing family for the "firstborne," who was taken by his grandmother Wilkinson. By the will of the latter, he received five acres of land "without the fence on Mistick Side."[20] A

---

[18] *Midd. Court Records — General Sessions,* Oct. 6, 1693.
[19] Ibid , *in loco.*

[20] *Midd. Probate Files.* This will was dated, 11, 9, 1647, and proved in July, 1655.

portion of the will of his father, which was written in 1667, presents a quaint bit of family history and appears like a somewhat labored attempt to stifle parental conscience.

Least J shold be supposed by Any, to be vnnatural or iniurious vnto my Son John as being my firstborne ; J hereby declare the true grounds and iust Reasons of the Seueral gifts and Legacies, disposed vnto my wife and Children as hereafter Stated, And why no more, is Setled, or otherwise Stated, on my Son John though my firstborne. First because the Estate, whereby J purchased All my lands (And for that Allso by the improuement therof through the blessing of God on my Labours, J haue built my housing and brought vp my Children hithervnto, And haue in my measure been helpfull in Church, Town And Cuntry Affayres) Came vnto mee by my wife Sara, that now is, And from her Kinred, who in a Special Manner, intended it, for the benefit of her Children. 2^{d}ly. by means of much weaknes of his mother my first wife, And Expences for him in his infancie, J was much run in debt, to sundry persons : the which were Allso payed out of this woomans portion. 3^{d}ly this my Son John was After by his Grandmother taken from mee before he came to Abilitie, to doe Any thing for mee, And on her desire bound As Apprentice to her till he shold be 21 years old, So that J had no Seruice or help of his ; to the raysing of my Estate. 4thly he Allso with my Consent, Enioyeth A portion, from his Grandmother, in stead of the portion due to mee, in the right of his Mother, to About twentie pounds value.[21]

Prudence Wilkinson's five-acre lot of " About twentie pounds value " was a poor substitute for his birthright in the possessions of his father; but the lands of William Bucknam descended by will to the widow Sarah and her children, and John Bucknam was left with that alone. He was out with Henchman and Mosely in Philip's War. Soon after he lost the use of speech and apparently became of unsound mind. About this time he probably became dependent upon the town or the bounty of his brothers and sisters. In 1694 he was unable to join in a deed of the estate of his deceased brother William, " by reason of present distraction."[22] Two years later his faculties were wonderfully restored. Sewall says of him at this time : —

Octr 30. [1696.] Mr. Wigglesworth tells me that one John Bucknam of Malden, above 50 years old, has been perfectly dumb near 18

---

[21] *Midd. Probate Files.*   [22] *Midd. Co. Deeds,* x. 294.

years, and now within about 3 weeks has his understanding and speech restored. He is much affected with the Goodness of God to him herein.[22]

It was probably to recover any right which he may have had in the estate of his brother that the following vote was passed.

[July 29, 1698] Ebenezar Hils and Joseph floyd are uoted and chosen to be y⁰ men to agree with Samuell Bucknam or aney other consarning John bucknam:

Likewise y⁰ said Ebenezar hils and joseph floyd are fully jmpoured to sue for and Recouer aney Estate: jn behalf of y⁰ town y⁰ may be suposed to be y⁰ said John bucknams: and y⁰ town will be at y⁰ charges ther of:

A suit was brought; and in September, 1699, Jonathan Sprague, Joseph Lamson, and Edward Sprague were chosen

to stand sute or sutes jn law with john Linde and jude his wife jn y⁰ case now jn hand: depending between the selectmen and y⁰ said john Linde and his wife: or to make a finall agreement in all contreuarcies in refranc to john bucknam for time past.[24]

It appears, however, that "a finall agreement in all contreuarcies" was not made; for at the next annual meeting, Jonathan Sprague, Joseph Floyd, and Joseph Lamson were appointed "to prosecut y⁰ apeall: jn y⁰ case depending betwen Sam¹¹ bucknam and y⁰ town. and y⁰ town will defray y⁰ charg:" Two months later the selectmen made the following agreement: —

At a meeting of y⁰ selectmen at J G: sumtime jn y⁰ month of may jn y⁰ yeer 1700: Then agreead with Samuell bucknam Jn behalf of y⁰ town: for y⁰ said Samuel bucknam to keep entertain and maintain his unckle john bucknam from y⁰ first of march last past: To y⁰ last of march next aftar this date: and for his so doing the select men of this town shall alow him out of y⁰ town-Tresuary: 2–15–0 jn money.

Samuel Bucknam's care was not of long continuance. At a meeting of the town, May 28, 1703, it was

voted That y⁰ select men are apointed to agree with Cap⁰ william Green Consarning y⁰ trouble he was at Consarning John bucknams beeing sick at his hous last winter:

---

[22] *Mass. Hist. Coll.*, xlv. 436.

[24] John Lynde married, between February and September, 1699, Judith (Worth) Bucknam, widow of Joses Bucknam who died Aug. 24, 1694, and became a party to the suit in behalf of his wife.

In the meantime Samuel Bucknam had got into trouble through the misdeeds of his "negro peeter" and Sarah Howard,[25] who became a town charge; and Joseph Floyd and Nathaniel Upham were chosen to attend to the town's interest in the matter at the Cambridge Court. The case was continued to the Charlestown Court and finally the town recovered two pounds and twelve shillings of Samuel Bucknam. Nearly one-half of this amount disappeared in expenses; but twenty-six shillings and sixpence remained, which the selectmen very properly expended in purchasing clothing for the unfortunate John Bucknam. He died June 14, 1705.

There may have been other poor besides those which have been mentioned. Whether they were few or many in comparison, their condition appealed to the sympathy of their fellows and was not unrecognized. On the town record is the following entry: —

On a Thanks-giuing day: was 4–3–8 money Gathared by a free contrebution And Committed jnto ye hands of ye Town Tresurer Edward Sprague or his Sucksesor: and to be disposed of by order from ye select men for ye use of The poore of This town: date ye 12 of feburary 1696/7.

At a town meeting held January 6, 169⅞, the following vote was passed: —

If Bethiah Wilkenson doe com or be sent from Salam to this town The select men of this town atend ye law jn sending her back again.

This vote was annulled, April 17, 1699, and the wants of its subject were probably supplied by her brother, in reference to whom the following entry was made many years after: —

---

[25] The character of Sarah Howard was not good. The following paper relating to her contains the first notice of a house provided in Malden for a small-pox patient.

"To Jacob Wilson Town Tresurer you are desired to pay unto Joseph Green Two shillings and sixpenc money out of ye Town Stock jn your hand for his presing a hous for to entertain Sarah howard when she had ye foull deseas: malden date ye 10: of feb 17⁰⁹/₁₁, by order of ye Selectmen

JOHN GREENLAND *Town clark*

to william Sprague constabl you ar desired to pay the contents of this to iosep green and in so much you will oblidg your frend:

JACOB WILLSON *town tresurer.*"

Green Family Papers.

[June 2, 1727] A vote was called for to see if ye Town would consider m^r Isac wilkenson anything for his keeping his sister bethiah, and it past in ye negetive.

Six years later the selectmen were obliged to minister to her necessities; and the following quaint entry appears: —

An acount of sundery nesecaries provided for Bethiah wilkison by The select men of malden aprill The 9th day 1733

to one pair of tow sheats £1 – 10^s – 0 to one pair of Shoos £00 – 12^s – 0 to one Apron and handarcheif £00 – 9^s 6 To a Pettycoat and makeing £00 – 15^s – 00 To two caps and makeing £00 – 6 – 0 To two cotten and lining shifts £1 – 10 – 3 The aforesaid cloathing purchesed by the five pounds money which insign Joseph lynds paid for the yous of the town of malden when chosen constable excepting 2 shilings and 9 penc worth of said things entered by order of the select men.

The long procession of the poor had now begun. The next to claim the care of the town was Hannah Fensum, a daughter of Thomas Dickerman of Scadan. The town, while the commons were being divided, had refused to acknowledge her husband as an inhabitant, by the following vote: —

[March 20, 1694/5.] *voted* whether the town would receve Isack fensum as inhabitant of this town and the vote passed in the negitife.

She had lived before her marriage in the family of Thomas Shepard at Wilson's Point, within the limits of Charlestown; and in a suit between Malden and Reading she had been settled by the Court upon the latter town.[26] The next year Malden was willing to take her and passed the following vote: —

[April 14, 1702.] *voted* That ye select-men are apointed to Treet with ye select-men of Reding And make an exchaing Abigaill Lille for hannah fensum jf ye can.

As nothing more is heard of Abigail Lillie in Malden, it is probable that the exchange was effected. Hannah Fensum was drowned in Mystic River, July 18, 1706.

William Teele was in Malden as early as 1685. In the division of commons, among those who apparently had no claim to

[26] *Midd. Court Records — General Sessions,* March 18, 1709/:. Eaton, *History of Reading,* 41, calling her Hannah Ferson, says she was warned out of that town in 1700; and, she refusing to go, a warrant was issued for her forcible removal. Her husband appears to have survived her, and married Sarah Saunders of Reading, October 14, 1713.

recognition, save for charity or some kindred reason, he received six acres in the "Lots laid out on y* land at y* end of y* 300 accres," which he sold to Philip Atwood of Bradford in 1706.[27] He seems to have been one who needed occasional assistance rather than absolute support, although he may have finally succumbed and become entirely dependent upon the town. At a meeting, April 1, 1702, it was "*vot* y* y* money y* william Teel was to pay to y* minestar jn y* yeer 1699 shall be forgiuen him: and the town must loos jt:" In August, 1713, a small piece of the town's land "on y* northwardly side neer y* end of john wilsons land aboue y* clay-pits" — at the southerly corner of the Burying Ground Lane and the Great Road — was granted to him and his wife for their use during their lives. Here, being himself a carpenter, he built a small house, where he lived until his death, enjoying the privilege of closing the road and pasturing between the gates. Other favors were granted him. At the annual meeting in March, 171¾, his rate of ten shillings was "forgiuen him;" and it was voted: —

Also y* s^d Teel has libarty to fenc jn a litle cornar of land joining part to m^r parsons land and part by Samuel Greens land neer to Sandy bank: so much land as shall be set out to him by: [*blank.*]

William Teele died before May 21, 1719; and his widow was continued in his privileges of gates and pasturage.[28] She was living as late as January 16, 173⅚, when it was

voted that the town will do somthing towards the repairing the widow teals hous: and that the select men shall repare said hous as they shall see necessary.

At last she, too, went down the grassy length of the Sandy Bank highway to the grave yard, and others enjoyed the benefits of the house which William Teele had built. It was voted, March 3, 174⅚: —

[27] *Midd. Co. Deeds,* xiv. 147.
[28] William Teele and Mary, his wife, had five children, the last of whom, Rachel, was born August 1, 1703. Although he remained in Malden and died as stated in the text, the careful Wyman, *Genealogies and Estates of Charlestown,* 934–935, removes him to Charlestown, gives him a second wife and seven more children, and continues him in life until after 1723. The second William, who really enjoyed these blessings, was probably the son, and William Teele, the ferryman, mentioned by Wyman, the grandson of the indigent carpenter of Malden.

That Edward Hollowell shall have liberty to live in the house that was the teels and pasture a cow at the burying place and that for one year.

The Hallowells appear to have been poor from the first. "Goodwife Holloway" is mentioned, in 1710, as one apparently with a family but contributing nothing to the treasury of the town. Edward Hallowell, who may have been her son, was here, December 25, 1730, when he married Huldah Farrington of Lynn; and the town was anxious before many years to be rid of him. In the record of a meeting, held December 7, 1738, the following entry appears : —

vot. that the town doth alow to Edward Hollwell 10 pounds money out of the towns stock provided he removes with his family from this town to the town of Killinsly to support them in there removal.

If he went to Connecticut, he returned in season to enter upon the occupancy of the Teele house, the possession of which he retained during the remainder of his life, enjoying the privileges which his predecessors had received.[29] After he had lived in the house a year, it was confirmed to him at the annual meeting, when the following entries were made : —

[March 2, 1746/7.] *vot* that the town dos quit their right to the house that Edward Hollowell now lives in on the towns land at the corner of John Willsons pasture to said Hollowell and his Wife and that said Hollowell And his Wife shall have liberty to improve said house on said land duering their natural life and that then the town shall have liberty to purchas the house of the heirs of the said Hollowell if standing on said land but if the town refuse to by said house then said heirs shall have liberty to remove said house from of said land.

vot That Thomas Manser and Edward Hollowel Shall have liberty to keep a cow a pece upon the towns land at Sandy bank this year and that they shall have liberty to hang a gate a cross the road near said Hollowells house.

Thomas Manser occupied the important position of sexton and grave-digger and was a neighbor of the Hallowells. It will be seen, by and by, that he, also, became one of the "town's poor." Edward Hollowell was a soldier at Fort Edward

---

[29] Mary Hollomon, perhaps the sister of Edward Hallowell, was warned out of town in May, 1749.

in 1756, and died soon after, perhaps in service; for his wife, " Huldeth," was a widow in the following May. She was living, July 6, 1786, when the death of Hannah Bodge, daughter of the " widow Hollowell," is recorded; and she died before September 2, 1795, when the selectmen, for twelve pounds, lawful money, sold to Samuel Wheeler one-eighth of an acre of land which is described as

a certain Lot of Land lying in Malden aforesaid lately occupied by the widow Hollowell late a pauper of Malden deceased bounded as follows (viz) Eastwardly on the great road Southerly on land of James Kettell dec^d & northerly on a lane leading to the poor house.[20]

[20] *Midd. Co. Deeds*, cxxvi. 174. This piece of land, the history of which has been followed from its grant by the town to William Teele to its sale and transfer by the same grantor to Samuel Wheeler, now forms the southerly corner of Main and Madison Streets. It was a part of the lands of John Lewis, and was, perhaps, left in its peculiar shape and condition by the undefined line of the way from Lewis's Bridge to the meeting house, which appears to have gradually grown into use across the intervening land. In 1661 Ralph Shepard, who had come into possession of that portion of the Lewis land since known as the Bell Rock pasture, entered a claim to its ownership, in which it was described as a triangle containing about sixty rods, "bounded easterly by a Highway leading to ye meeting house, nor westerly by a Highway leading to Sandy bank, & southerly by some lands of Thomas Lindes of mauldon aforesaid, Sometime ye lands of Jno Lewis deceased, & [he] desires his claime may be Recorded according to ye law for possession pag. 65." *Midd. Co. Deeds*, ii. 384.

This claim does not appear to have been recognized, as the adjoining land was described in 1696, when it was conveyed by John and Joseph Lynde, sons of Thomas Lynde, to Lieutenant Joseph Wilson, as bounded north and west " by the highway leading to Sandy Bank and a high way from Lewis bridge leading . . . to the meeting house going through the said Land." Ibid., xii. 569. Nor did Shepard mention his claim in 1666, when he sold his house and land in the Bell Rock pasture to the Rev. Benjamin Bunker. Ibid., iii. 235. Until its appropriation to the uses of the Teeles, the land appears to have lain as one of those isolated pieces of common lying open at the corners of roads or by watering places which remained after the division of 1695. It is not improbable, however, that the Lyndes, who also held their lands under the Lewis title, had a claim upon it, as the description of the land conveyed to Wilson may indicate. This opinion is strengthened by the fact that when John Kettell, as the administrator of the estate of his father, James Kettell, who had held the Lynde land through his wife Elizabeth Wilson, a granddaughter of Lieutenant Joseph Wilson, sold, in 1797, four acres to Bernard Green, it was bounded as follows : N., by the road to the burying-ground; E., by the road to Malden Bridge ; and S., by land of Bernard Green. Ibid., cxxvi. 52. Wheeler's land was not mentioned, although he had purchased it two years before. Two months later, Bernard Green sold Wheeler forty-six rods, bounded N. and N. W., by the road to the burying ground; E., by the great road ; S., by land of Bernard Green. Ibid., cxxvi. 175. This, if any adverse claim existed, put the latter in full possession of the sixty rods which had been claimed by Ralph Shepard.

No house is mentioned in the deed given by the town; but it is said that Wheeler enlarged the Hallowell house,

In the margin of " A list of y⁰ families y¹ bares publique charges Jn malden," which is given in full in another place, appear the names of seven who are separated from their fellows. Two of them, at least, were small landholders, but they were apparently in a condition which prevented them from becoming taxpayers. Besides William Teele and " Goodwife Holloway," who have been already mentioned, they were " Tho dunell, Tho Grouer Tho degrce, wido Sayes, and Zachriah Hill."

Claimants of other races now appear in the persons of Jack Welcome and his wife, Black Ann. Tradition says that he was a negro, or at least a mulatto, while she was an Indian. It was voted, March 2, 171⁸⁄₉,

That y⁰ Town will Giue unto Jack welcom a small pece of Land about a quarter of an acre nere to boston line on y⁰ upar side of the Greate Rhoad.

Here they lived with a family springing up about them until the death of the husband and father, November 8, 1744. He had previously deeded to his wife — " For and in Consideration of the Love and affection which I have towards my wife Ann," the improvement of the land " as also my dwelling house stand-ing on said Land." After her death it was to become the prop-erty of their son William on condition that he paid ten pounds in bills of credit, old tenor, to his sister Thankful. In 1755 a mulatto child was laid at the door of this house, which was given to Joseph Barrett, with fifty-two pounds and ten shillings, old tenor, he agreeing to clear the town

which he sold to Elias Currell in 1797, conveying therewith about fifty rods of land with the bounds already given. Ibid., cxxxiv. 35. Currell sold the same to Edward Newhall in 1799, who in turn sold it to Benjamin Burditt, baker, in 1810. Ibid., cxxxiv. 34; cxci. 74. Burditt mortgaged the property, then described as containing about one-half of an acre with a dwelling house and other buildings, to Field and Bradshaw, merchants, of Boston, in 1817, and re-leased his right of redemption the next year. Ibid., ccxix. 187 ; ccxxiv. 510. The latter parties sold it in 1819 to Timothy

Bailey of Roxbury. Ibid., ccxxviii. 523. Mr. Bailey came to Malden and estab-lished the business of tinplate working in the buildings attached to the house, which he occupied. The business was very successful and was continued by Mr. Bailey until his death, in 1852, and for several years after by his sons. Mr. Bailey was a well-known and influential citizen and was prominent in local finan-cial affairs. The old house, which was removed a few years after his death, now stands on Madison Street a short distance southwest of its original loca-tion.

from any charge that may arise upon the account of said child so long as it may be made a slave to me my heirs or to them that I or my heirs shall assign said child too.

[May 16, 1757,] *Voted,* That the town dos alow to An Wellcom ten pounds old tenor to be laid out in repairing her Shatterd habitation and that on the account of her nursing a child eight weaks that was laid at the dore of her house.

[June 6, 1757,] *Voted,* that the selectmen shall take care that said money be laid out for that purpose.

Ann Welcome died November 4, 1764; and Black Ann's Corner still bears her name, marking the site of her little cabin under the side of the hill on the northerly side of the road.

After the death of his mother, William Welcome, who was called Black Will, succeeded to the ownership of the house. That he was a shoemaker is shown by an order entered in 1766, on which he received three shillings, fivepence, and two farthings for making a pair of shoes for Agnes Nichols, a pauper. He died, unmarried, in 1793, being called upon the record " a negro — town's poor." He may have become an inmate of "the house for the poor;" as the selectmen, having been authorized by a vote of the town, sold John Waite, Jr., July 5, 1792, for fifteen pounds and twelve shillings, lawful money,

a certain peice of Land lying in Malden aforesaid (containing about a quarter of an Acre more or less with a small Building thereon standing) on the upper side of the great Road leading from Malden to Lynn near to Chelsea line, and has for a number of Years past been improved by William Welcome and was given by the Town aforesaid to Jack Welcome in the Year 1718/9 and was afterwards conveyed by the said Jack by a Deed of Gift to the said William Welcome.[81]

The number of the poor increased during the second and third quarters of the eighteenth century; and their individual cases are not as prominent on the records as those of their earlier kindred. In 1727 Jacob Wilson agreed for thirty pounds to keep the town from any future charge for his wife's sister, Hannah Ross.[82] Cases of a similar kind were not infrequent. Joseph Ramsdell married Rachel, a daughter of William and

---

[81] *Midd. Co. Deeds,* cvii. 504.

[82] Jacob, son of Lieutenant Joseph

Wilson, married Susanna Ross, May 20, 1696.

Mary Teele, and after having four children, they disappear from the records.[83]   That they both died during the year 1745 seems probable.   The following entries appear in relation to their two youngest children: —

[January 14, 1745⅚,]   *Voted*, That Edward Wayte shall have John Ramsdell who is about five years old till he comes of age and said Wayte shall have thirty pounds old tenor with him in case said Waitt will be obliged to learn said child to read wright and cypher and also to learn him the Shoemakers trade.

[May 14, 1747,]   *Voted* That the Select men shall have liberty to put out the youngest child of Joseph Ramsdell deceast til it comes of age if they think it shall be for the benefitt of the town.

Lynn august the 31ˢᵗ 1748   Then received of Stephen Paine one of the ouer seeres of the poor forty pounds old tenor in full for taking and bringing up of Joseph Ramsdels child as my own J say received by me

RUTH

her + *mark*   *Wife of*

PITMON   *John Pitmon.*[84]

The indenture by which John Ramsdell was bound to Edward Waite is a good specimen of a class of papers which were formerly common but are seldom, if ever, executed in Massachusetts at the present day.   The following copy is from the duplicate signed by Edward Waite, which is preserved among the *Green Family Papers.*[85]

---

[83] Rachel, daughter of William and Mary Teele, born August 1, 1703, married to Joseph Ramsdell, of Malden, April 29, 1730.   Children — Joseph, July 1, 1730; Mary, December 29, 1736; John, April 5, 1741; and Nathan, March 18 174⅚.

[84] It is elsewhere stated that overseers of the poor did not exist as a separate board in the colonial and provincial periods.   Their duties were performed by the selectmen, who sometimes received the name, as in the case in the text and in the indenture by which John Ramsdell was bound to Edward Waite.   The name itself first appears, May 14, 1744, when it was "*vot* That the select men shall be over seers of the poor this year."   In 1780 five men were chosen

as selectmen and overseers of the poor, and again in 1805.   Although not always stated in the record, this appears to have been the custom until the annual meeting in 1822, when the first distinct board of overseers was chosen.   It was composed of Henry Gardner, Esq., Captain Isaac Stiles, and Major Nathan Upham.   At the next meeting, an appropriation of fifteen hundred dollars was made for the poor.

[85] This collection, comprising papers of much interest concerning public and family affairs during two centuries, was formed by the late James Diman Green, and is now preserved in the library of the New England Historic Genealogical Society.

This Indenture witnesseth, That Joseph Lynde Thos Wait John Dexter Stephen Pain and Joseph Wilson Select-men, Overseers of the Poor of the Town of Maldon in the County of Middlesex in New-England by and with the Consent of two of his Majesties Justices of the Peace for said County have plac'd and by these presents do place and bind out John Ramsdell a poor Child belonging to Maldon afores^d unto Edward Wait of Maldon in the County of Middlesex yeoman, and to his Wife and Heirs, and with them after the manner of an Apprentice to dwell and Serve, from the Day of the Date of these Presents until the fifth Day of April, which will be in the Year of our Lord one Thousand Seven Hundred and Sixty two at which time the said Apprentice if living will arrive at the Age of twenty one Years, during all which said Time or Term the said Apprentice his said Master and Mistress well and faithfully shall Serve, their Secrets he shall keep close, their Commandments lawful and honest every where he shall gladly obey, he shall do no Damage to his s^d Master &c nor Suffer it to be done by others without letting or giving Seasonable notice thereof to his s^d Master &c he shall not waste the Goods of his said Master &c nor lend them unlawfully to any : At Cards Dice or any other unlawful Game or Games he shall not play : Fornication he shall not commit : Matrimony he shall not contract : Taverns, Ale Houses or places of Gaming he shall not haunt or frequent : From the Service of his s^d Master &c by Day nor Night he shall not absent himself; but in all things and at all times he shall carry and behave himself towards his s^d Master &c and all theirs, as a good and faithful Apprentice ought to do to his utmost Ability during all the Time or term afores^d — And the Said Master doth hereby covenant and agree for himself his Wife and Heirs to teach or cause the s^d Apprentice to be taught the Art and Mystery of a Cordwainer and also to read write and cypher. and also shall and will well and truly find allow unto, and provide for the s^d Apprentice Sufficient and wholesome meat and Drink, with Washing, Lodging and apparrel, and other Necessaries meet and convenient for Such an Apprentice during all the time or term afores^d : And at the End and Expiration thereof shall dismiss the s^d Apprentice with two good Suits of Apparrel for all parts of his Body one for Lords-Days, the other for working Days, Suitable to his Quality — In Testimony whereof the s^d Parties have to these Indentures interchangeably Set their Hands and Seals the thirtieth Day of April, in the twenty first year of the Reign of our Sovereign Lord George the Second King of Great Britain &c. Annoq: Domini one Thousand Seven Hundred and forty eight

Signed Sealed and Delivered
in presence of,   EDWARD WAIT ⟨L.S.⟩
JOHN SHUTE
JOHN WILLSON

Edward Waite was a prominent citizen and a selectman for fourteen years. He had no son; and if the future life of his apprentice be considered, it appears that he faithfully performed his obligations and that John Ramsdell profited by his precepts and example. The latter married soon after he attained his freedom, had children, and became a landowner and a respected and useful citizen. As a Christian he was a shining light in the church. His character was beyond reproach, and his influence was always exercised for good. He was chosen one of the deacons of the First Church in 1776 and continued in that office for nearly fifty years, until his death in 1825, when Dr. Ephraim Buck was chosen to fill his place.[86] His care for the gravestone of Michael Wigglesworth has been noticed. It was a happy thought, perhaps his own, which gave him for an epitaph two couplets of the Malden singer's rhymes, which may be read upon the stone at Sandy Bank.

> Welcome, sweet rest, by me so long desir'd,
> Who have with sins & griefs so long been tir'd,
> Welcome, O Christ, who hast my soul redeem'd ;
> Whose favour I have more than life esteem'd.

Abigail Pratt appears as a pauper in 1755; and the next year Dr. Simon Tufts of Medford[87] was allowed two pounds, thirteen shillings, and fourpence for " what he has don for Martha Mansur in the time of her sickness." In 1762 the town refused to pay Dr. Isaac Rand of Charlestown for doctoring Amos Stower in his last sickness, and Dr. Tufts for attendance on Germain Tibodo, one of the unfortunate French neutrals who had been sent to Malden by the provincial authorities. The next year the selectmen of Medford acknowledged Widow Abigail Waite,[88] who was then boarding in Malden, to be one of their poor ; but to offset this advantage, the town was indebted in another direction, as appears by the following order.

The following a true account of bill granted to Docter Porter.

To Cap! Ebenezer Harnden town treasurer or his Sucsessor in said office you are to pay unto Doctor Porter five pounds eight shillings

[86] *First Church Records*, April 13,1825.

[87] Dr. Simon Tufts, H. C. 1744, was a great-grandson of Peter Tufts of Malden.

[88] Widow of Peter Waite, son of Joseph of Malden, who died in Medford, December 8, 1721.

thre pence and three farthings out of the town stock in your hands which is in full for visits and medicines for the poor of the town (viz) to mr Cowens family to the widow Jemima Burditt to Thomas Manser to mr. Simms to Jeremiah Tabodo and to the widow Mary Whitemore.

Dated in Maldon the 22 day of June 1763 By order of the select men.

5–8–3–3   JOHN SHUTE *town Clerk.*

The Cowen family lived at the north end. Israel Cook, who kept the only store there, received the following order in 1769: — [39]

Granted to Jsrael Cook an order on the town treasurer of £0–7 – 8^d–3^f for sundery things out of his shop to Cowen [40] in the time of his sickness. Dated in malden the 7th of march 1769.

By order of the select men :

                            JOHN SHUTE *town Clerk.*

Others who are mentioned soon after, as receiving aid from the town, are Widow Elizabeth Berry, Mary Paine, Thomas Degresha, who boarded with the Widow Pratt, Abigail Howard, Widow Zibiah Sherman, Agnes Nichols, [41] and Daniel Floyd.

---

[39] Israel Cook, of Boston, married, January 11, 1744/5, Hannah (Waite), widow of Phineas Upham. He inhabited the house of his predecessor, which stood at the present corner of Green and Howard Streets in Melrose. Here he "kept the first store in this town [Melrose], and was granted a license to sell rum, by the General Court, as early as 1759; and that article was continued to be sold here up to, and beyond, the time of the Revolution, if we judge from the story of the two Lynn minute men, — Hadley and Wellman, — who, filled with the spirit of patriotism, were on their way to Lexington, stopped here and became filled with another kind of spirit ; then went on their way and were both killed. In this house was used the first stove in our town, and as a whole the old house had an interesting history, but it is now a thing of the past." Goss, *Historical Address*, July 4, 1876, 16. This writer incorrectly says that the house stood on "a part of lot No. 37 of the division of 1695," which Phineas Upham, the father, bought of

Joseph Wilson in 1703. The four acres sold by Joseph Wilson were a part of lot 37 in the third range of the second division, which was near the Boston line. It was probably upon this lot that Phineas Upham built the house which was still standing near Upham Street in Melrose in 1898, and of which a description and a view are given in Upham, *Descendants of John Upham*, 79.

[40] James Cowen had been an inhabitant of Malden since his marriage with Jean Crawford, of Lynn, February 22, 173⅔. Patrick he was called in the record of Intentions of Marriage at Lynn and in the record of marriage at Malden; but as James he appears in all other instances. He had a large family of children. His wife died in or after 1751; and he married, March 17, 1763, Ruhamah Parker, of Reading. By reason of sickness or some other misfortune, he soon after became dependent upon the town. He died, December 2, 1769.

[41] Agnes Leveston, or Livingston, married John Nichols, son of Deacon

In February, 1767, the selectmen entered "an order on the Treasurer to m^{rs} Reb^a Emerson for two pounds twelve shillings seven pence & one farthing for Supplyes of Cloathing for the Poor."

In 1767 John Mudge, who had been a worthy citizen and a deacon of the South Church, appears in the following order as one who had become dependent upon the town.

an order on the Treasurer to m^r James Kittle for one pound ten Shillings & ten pence for Supplies of Rum & Sugar for Dea^a Mudge Eight month (viz) from march 10th to Octr 27th 1766. Dated in malden Feby 18th 1767

By order of the Select men   Ezra Green *Town Clerk*

He had been living with Joseph Pratt, who was paid for his board in March, 1767, and died before October 1, of that year.[42]

Nathaniel Nichols, December 11, 1740. He was a soldier in the Louisburg expedition in 1745, and died in the service in that year. She died in April, 1793, — one of the "towns-poor." Widow Zibiah Sherman, who is mentioned in the text, died December 28, 1772. I think she was the daughter of Robert Levenston and perhaps a niece of Agnes Nichols.

[42] Mudge, *Mudge Memorials*, 196, says, with great apparent exactness, that he died, November 26, 1762, aged seventy-one years, one month, and eleven days, making him to have died on the same day as did his son John at Lynnfield, and estimating his age by the birth of John Mudge who was born October 15, 1685, and died December 21 in the same year. Deacon John Mudge was born November 21, 1636. He was acting as a deacon of the South Church in June, 1761, but there was a vacancy in that office, February 23, 1763. when "the C^{hh} meet to chuse a Deacon." *South Church Records.* That he was living in October, 1766, is evident from the order in the text, and he may have died about the time when the "Supplies of Rum & Sugar" ceased. That he died before October 1, 1767, appears from an entry in the town records.

John Mudge, the father of the deacon, bought of the heirs of Job Lane, in 170$^{4/}$, for two hundred pounds, a tenement and farm of sixty-five acres, at Turkey Hill. *Midd. Co. Deeds,* xiv. 186. Part of this land was a portion of lot 34 of the allotment of 1638, which had been set-off to the Rev. John Harvard, the benefactor of Harvard College, and was sold in 1649 by Ralph Hall to Richard Cooke. *Suffolk Co. Deeds,* i. 103. Deacon John Mudge, by inheritance and the quitclaim of his sister Martha and her husband, Peter Edes, of Needham, came into possession of the farm in 1738, which he occupied but a few years, until 1745, when he sold it to Peter Edes, his brother-in-law. Edes removed to Malden and lived on the farm until 1762, when he sold it to Isaac Chittenden, of Boston. The Chittendens owned and occupied the land until 1813, when it was conveyed by Samuel Chittenden to William Hurd, of Charlestown. From Joseph Hurd, of Portsmouth, who had purchased it in 1816, it passed in 1831, for forty-five hundred dollars, to Leavitt Corbett, of Charlestown, who resided there until his death, August 9. 1855. The farm is now in the possession of the proprietors of Woodlawn Cemetery: and the Chittenden-Corbett house, which probably contained a portion of the Mudge house, was still standing, in 1895, on the west side of Turkey Hill, near Elm Street in Everett. It was torn down soon after.

The poverty of the South Church at that time, perhaps, prevented the assistance which its deacon should have received from its funds or its contributions; for it was the custom then, as now, for churches to help their members so far as possible. Contributions for the unfortunate were sometimes made at the close of the weekly lecture service, and especially on days of public fasts and thanksgivings. An early instance has already been given, and the lost diary of the Rev. Joseph Emerson mentioned, at least, two contributions which were made for "Nat Nycholes."[43] Sometimes the neighboring churches were helpful in the work of charity. The *Rumny-marish Church Book* contains the following entry, made by the former pastor of Malden, Thomas Cheever: —

November 10 [1726]. Public Thanksgiving. The Contribution was appointed for Ebenezer Hill of Maldon, who, having a sore leg for several years which the Doctours at last judged incurable unless his leg was cutt off (which was done the 7ᵗʰ of this month,) petitioned our Church and Congregation for our Charity, there was gathered about five pounds ten shillings — £5.10.11.

A distinction must be made between the workhouse, where the poor gathered daily to perform light tasks, and the almshouse, where they dwelt; although the former was finally merged in the latter where they both lived and worked. The workhouse preceded the almshouse, having been at first some house temporarily hired for the purpose, while the poor dwelt in their own dilapidated houses or were "boarded out" at the expense of the town. It was refused in March, 174½, to "build a house to imploy the poor in;" and in 1753, it was proposed to join with Cambridge, Medford, Woburn, and Reading in building a workhouse; but the town declined to entertain so extravagant a proposition. Some effort to bring the poor together was made in 1765 or 1766, but it does not appear to have been of long duration. In February of that year, the selectmen issued an order in favor of John Paine for two pounds and four shillings

⁴³ *Bi-Centennial Book of Malden*, 202.

for work don on the school house by the meeting house upon the account of rent due from the town to the propriators of said house for the poors living therein.

Finally, at the annual meeting March 2, 1772, it was voted "To hire a Work House for the poor of the Town;" and soon after, "That some Part of the Work House, to be hired for the poor, be also an Alms House if need be." The house which was hired was that which stood near the present easterly corner of Salem and Sprague Streets and which had formerly belonged to Thomas Burditt, Jr. The west end of the house, which had been set off to Widow Sarah Burditt, was that which was apparently used; and it may be that the keeper, John Gould, lived in the other part, which had recently been sold to Samuel Merritt. However this may be, it is certain that John Gould was master of the workhouse in 1773, when Zaccheus Banks, cordwainer, was apprehended and committed to his care; and here he dwelt in the latter years of the century.[44] It was voted, March 1, 1773, "To support the poor at a Work House the ensuing Year, according to the Rules & orders of the last Year." A committee was chosen the next year "to lay a Plan for building a work-house;" but the town refused to accept its report at a subsequent meeting, and continued to hire until March 6, 1786, when it was recorded that Widow Burditt refused "to lett her house for the use of the poor."

In the meantime, the town had come into the possession of an almshouse and it had been voted, March 6, 1780,

that the Ouerseers of the poor shall moue the poor to the Towns house which lately Thomas Mancer lived in as soon as thay Conveniently can.

Thomas Manser had been sexton of the town and North Parish many years and in 1769 had become old and feeble,

---

[44] John Gould has been remembered in tradition as an extremely honest man. It is said that when he found himself in danger of becoming angry he would go into the woods at the foot of Wayte's Mount and pray until the temptation had passed away. He died June 2, 1800. Samuel Merritt, the town clerk, was his adopted son.

though he performed the duties of his office several years
longer. His house on the north side of the Sandy Bank highway was getting old like himself; and, considering the circumstances, the town passed the following vote: —

[November 17, 1769,] *Voted* To repair yᵉ House of mʳ Thomas
Manser, & provide for his comfortable Subsistance, during his natural
Life, together with his Endeavours to Support himself, upon Condition
that he will give a legal Conveyance of said House, with his other Real
Estate to the Town.

Voted, That Capt John Dexter, Capt. Harnden & Mʳ James Kettell be
a Committee to acquaint Mʳ Thomas Manser with the preceeding Vote ;
which Vote he complied with and gave a Deed of yᵉ Premises to the Town.

At the annual meeting in 1783, it was voted that the surveyors of highways " Shall make a Stone wall on the towns land by
the Road to the Buring place that the poor may have a garden."
The almshouse probably absorbed the workhouse after the
refusal of the Widow Burditt to let her house longer for the
town's use, and no more is heard of the latter. An enlargement
of the former became needful in 1791, and a committee reported
in April of that year that it was

Necessary that an addition of eighteen feet be added on the West
part of sᵈ House to have a Gambrel Roof the Smoke to be carried into
the Chimney of the Old house.

No action was taken on this report until May 7, 1792, when a
committee was chosen " to employ workmen & furnish materials
for enlarging the house for the poor." The little house of
Thomas Manser, with a sun-dial — " the economical town time-
piece of Malden," standing before its door,[45] continued to be the
almshouse until 1822, when the town having purchased a portion of the Blanchard farm and adjoining lands on the Medford
Road, sold for one hundred and forty-nine dollars and fifty cents
the house and land on the " road leading to the Bank so called
commonly called the old poor house." [46] The old house,
enlarged and kept in good repair, yet stands on the northerly
side of Madison Street, showing on its exterior few marks of age
to distinguish it from its neighbors.[47]

---

[45] *Bi-Centennial Book of Malden*, 224.
[46] *Midd. Co. Deeds*, ccxlvi. 289.

[47] It had been built on a lot of about
a quarter of an acre, which Jonathan

At a Generall Town meeting the 13th of July 1696 Cap william Green: moderator.　This town taking jnto consideration ye jnconuenences and damig: Acurring To them: by Jnmates. And Jll efected parsons setling themselves amongst them Ahaue *uoted:* and ordered: that Jf aney par son whatsoeuer: that shall Resaiue any Jnmate: Jnto their hous more then fourteen days before they Giue notis Thereof to the select men: or that shall Lett out their hous to hier; to aney parson: but such as the select-men shall aproue of from time to time shall forfit fiue shillings p^r weeck: so long as they continue defecttiue: heer jn: and pay all such damiges as shall com to the town thereby And that the Constable shall take the forfit: of those y^t transgres herin by destres: by a warrant from ye select men: for ye use of the town:

This vote, which was based on a Province law, continued, with various modifications in force nearly a century, and simplified the settlement of paupers.　Upon receiving notice, or within a reasonable time thereafter, the selectmen issued their warrant and the constable proceeded to warn the new comers to depart. Apparently the first to experience the operation of this vote was Thomas Degresha, in reference to whom it is recorded: —

Thomas degreuch⁴⁷ entred as a parson Resedant jn malden ye 14 of decembar 1699: wharupon the select men of this town gaue ordar by a warrant to Thomas okes constable to warn ye said Thomas degruche^r and his wife to depart ye town of malden and be Resident no longar ther jn baring date ye 21 of decembar 1699.[48]

Rich or poor, those who came to remain or those who came for a season — all were treated alike.　It was not always neces- sary to obey, as the legal effect was usually produced by serving the warrant, which cleared the town from future liability. Sometimes, however, the constable was ordered to take a party

Howard, Jr. had deeded December 16, 1730, "for and in Consideration of love good will and affection which J have and dou Bear towards my freind and towns man Thomas Mansser." This land was bounded easterly "on a High way that goes to ye Burring Place in s^d Town and Near s^d Burring place." *Unrecorded deed* in the writer's posses- sion. This property was afterwards purchased by Timothy Bailey and was for many years occupied by the late Samuel Shute.　It is now known as 53 Madison Street.

[48] Thomas Degresha was married to Agnes Cracker by the Rev. Thomas Cheever at Rumney Marsh, March 16, 169⅞. They did not "depart ye town" but continued therein.　They were the parents of Thomas and the grandparents of Mary, the well known "Moll Grush" of later days. Grushy Pasture, on Forest Street, preserved the name in Malden until recent years.

by force and deposit him outside of the town limits. Sometimes the law required that notices of such warnings should be given to the County Court and approved by that authority. Thus, at the Court of General Sessions, March, 1734, the following entry was made: —

The Selectmen of malden are allowed to enter their caution against Richard Perkins and Judith his wife, mary Perkins their daughter and James Connon their servant, who have been warned to depart out of the s⁴ Town of malden, as appears by a warrant with a return endorsed thereon on file.

The notices given by heads of families and landlords under this vote sometimes contain valuable information in relation to the origin and movements of families. The following is one of many which may be found in the town records: —

Maldon June the 5ᵗʰ 1756
To mr John Shute town Clerk of Maldon   These agreable to a law of this Province in such case provided are to acquaint you that mr John Rumbly & his Wife and children ware by me the subscriber admitted into my house in Maldon as tennants upon Rent on the twenty eighth day of may last and they were then first received and admitted into the possession of my said house and the said John and his family came last from medford he is a Brickmaker, J belive he is an industrious man and that he will maintain himself and family and pay his rent and nothing more of his or his familys Curcumstances are known by your Humble Servant   EBENEZER PRATT *Juʳ:*

Uriah Oakes, in January, 1758, took Mary Saunders and her children, Mary and Margaret, into his family as boarders. Her husband was a seafaring man with " nothing els to trust to but his prosperity." In the same year, Rose Clough, a widow from Boston, was reported as one " who is under good sircumstances; " and John and Abigail Cades, who came from Stoneham, were said to be " young and industrious." Soon after Susanna Downing, "a garl from Boston . . . under poor surcumstances," was taken in by Isaac Wheeler; while Joseph Lynde sheltered Mary Welch, a young woman from Charlestown, who was reported to be "not compos mentis; " and John Shute took Isaac Doubt of Boston — " he has been welthy but now very much reduced."

A few years later Timothy Sprague certified to Mary Hendly "a poor garl from Marblehead;" and Isaac Wayte had two children, Richard and Elizabeth Sanders, from Boston, whose father is recorded as being "a strong laborious man but has no great matter in the world." In 1764 Thomas Shute received Joseph Grant from Boston — "much disordered in mind and has but little worldly substance." Timothy Waite gave the following notice in 1772: —

Sarah Parsons of Leicester, a single Woman, came to live with me one year. She came the 29ᵗʰ Day of May last 1771, in Order to learn to be a Taylor.

Negroes are mentioned at times, coming probably as servants or farm laborers. Rebecca, "a melatto woman," was warned in 1745; and Jonas Green had "a molatto woman" named Mary Fair, from Lincoln, in 1768. Worster and Jupiter with their wives, Phyllis and Mary, from Medford,[49] were warned in 1780; and in 1786 appears the following entry in relation to one whose name and appearance, in her latter years, are still remembered by a few old inhabitants: —

To Ebenezer Waitt Constable of the Town of Malden Greeting, in the Name of the Commonwealth of Massachusets. you are Required forthwith to warn Deborah Sawco a Negro woman (Daughter to Cuffe Sawco of Medford) who Came into town from Salem in Janʳ. 1786 — that she forthwith Departe out of this town to Salem and that she be nolonger Resident herein — And Make Returne of this warrant with your Doings here on to me the Subscriber. Dated Malden July 18. 1786 — By Order of the Selectmen JOSEPH PERKINS *Town Cleʳ*

Agreabl to the within writtin warrant I have warned the within mentioned Person to Departe out of this Town to Salem from whence she Came — Malden, Augᵗ. 1786 — EBENEZER WAITT *Constable*

Deb Saco, who was thus warned to "Departe," died at the almshouse in Malden, June 17, 1839, aged about eighty years. Whether she was a negro or an Indian, I cannot say. Those who remember her are divided as to that matter. The name of her father is that of a negro, and the record of her death calls

---

[49] Worster had been a slave of the Rev. Ebenezer Turell, of Medford; his wife Phyllis, of the Rev. Eliakim Willis, of Malden; and Jupiter of Timothy Fitch, of the former town. A daughter, Rebecca, accompanied the latter.

her " a colored person." The late Augustus D. Rogers, of Salem, in a note to me, says that she was an old colored servant of Collector De Witt of that town, and that she was popularly supposed to be one hundred years old. He says, " I often gazed on her with awe, when, as I rode to Malden, she might be seen bending on her staff, with ' arbs' to sell." A representation of her as a fortune-teller was formerly in the East India Museum in Salem, and she has often appeared by proxy at ladies' fairs. I suspect that she was of two races, having an Indian mother. This was a not uncommon mixture during the continuance of slavery; and it was popular with the negroes, as the children of an Indian mother were free. She was a tramp, or, in the speech of that day, a " walk-about," ranging the country from Salem to Cambridge. She would disappear for months, returning suddenly, as eager to tell fortunes, as dirty, and as fond of rum as ever.

Of a similar character was Hannah Shiner, known also as Squa Shiner, an older woman, in whose veins the Indian blood predominated, if it were not wholly pure. She was a small woman with a thin face, and she usually travelled, with a small dog, selling baskets and herbs. She, too, was known in all the neighboring towns; but her home was near a spring on the borders of Turkey Swamp in Middlesex Fells, where she lived with a kindred spirit known as Old Toney. She is said to have been " kind-hearted, a faithful friend, a sharp enemy, a judge of herbs, a weaver of baskets, and a lover of rum." She was drowned in the Abajona River in Woburn, having been blown off a bridge by a high wind, on a cold winter day [December 22, 1820].[60] She was eighty-two years old at the time of her death.

Mary Degresha, otherwise Moll Grush, was another individual of the " walk-about" class. She was a daughter of Thomas Degresha and first appears as a town charge in 1786, when at a town meeting it was

[October 16, 1786.] *Voted* to put up Mary Degrusha to a vandue to see who will take her at the next Parish Meeting of this North Parrish.

[60] Cf. Brooks, *History of Medford*, 81 ; *Winchester Record*, i. 274.

[October 25, 1786.]   Charles Hills west Room then meet accordingly and Lieu! Francis Phillips bid her of for one year and the Town was to Cloath her Deacently and by him to keep her Deacently Cloathed and the Town to Give Lieu⋅ Phillips Six Dollers for his taking her and taking Proper Care of her and he is to keep her from being any farther a Town Charge for one year from the time that the Selectmen Delivers her to him the said Lieu! Phillips.

Mary Degresha is said to have been an active and spirited woman and to have been offended when called Moll Grush. The story of her being the last sufferer at the whipping post in Malden is related elsewhere. In her old age she is described as having a thin body and a dark yellow complexion, from which she was popularly supposed to be of Indian blood.   She lived a short time in a hut near Bear's Den, and died at the almshouse about 1838.

Whatever deals with poverty in its many forms has little to relieve it.   Grotesque it may be, or a trace even of the comic may at times pass through it as a gleaming thread; but its grotesqueness becomes hideous, and the gleaming thread is tarnished when for a moment is seen beneath it stolid despair, starvation, sickness, lingering death — all the many woes which have attended the poor in all ages.   What they suffered who are gone, what they are suffering who are living none may know save those who may live as they.   Yet there is a deeper depth to which men and women in Massachusetts have descended without hope; for SLAVERY was here from the beginning and remained under the protection of the law until after the Revolutionary period.

It matters not that it existed in a mild and patriarchal form; for it was still a real slavery, wherein human beings had a money value and were sold like cattle or the ground on which they trod.   The names of a few of these servitors have come down to us; but the names of Brahma Bucknam and Cato Lynde, of Phyllis Willis and Violet Hills, belong to a day and a condition which have passed away.   So far removed are they from us — so remote from the thoughts and customs of the present is the condition in which they lived that the record of their existence has no living interest, and we look upon it only as a curiosity of the past. As such, with much care and no slight labor, I have brought together from scattered sources the little that remains to illustrate the story of slavery in Malden. Its existence spans the time from the incorporation of the town to a day almost within the memory of man. Indeed, within sixty years I have taken the hand of the last survivor of enforced servitude here.

That slavery was almost coeval with the Colony cannot be doubted. Antiquaries know the story of the negro who was lost in the woods in 1633, and who, after frightening some Indians, who thought he was Abamacho — the Devil — was conducted to his *master*.[61] The ninety-first article of the Body of Liberties, established by the General Court in 1641, concerns the

Liberties of Forreiners and Strangers.

91. There shall never be any bond slaverie, villinage or Captivitie amongst us unles it be lawfull Captives taken in just warres, and such strangers as willingly selle themselves or are sold to us. And these shall have all the liberties and Christian usages which the law of god established in Israell concerning such persons doeth morally require. This exempts none from servitude who shall be Judged thereto by Authoritie.[62]

This article has been cited to prove that the spirit of the early Massachusetts laws was against slavery; and yet it recognized the right of property in human flesh and provided for its transfer as clearly as any law of the later slave-holding colonies or states. By its authority captives taken in the Indian wars were sold into domestic servitude, or sent to the West Indies in exchange for negroes; and Africans were subjects of sale for nearly a century and a half. Nor was it ever expressly repealed; nor can the closest student of the subject point to the exact date when slavery in Massachusetts became legally extinct.[63]

[61] Wood, *New-Englands Prospect*, 77. (Ed. 1634.)

[62] *Mass. Hist. Coll.* xxviii. 231.

[63] The history of slavery in New England is unwritten. Moore, *Notes of the History of Slavery in Massachusetts*, and Williams, *History of the Negro Race in America*, have entered upon the field; but the one is written in a controversial spirit, and the author of the other is influenced by sympathy with his race. On the other hand, the historical writers of New England have ignored or misrepresented the subject, or have at-

The first notice of slavery in Malden is implied in an order of the General Court in relation to the servant of Job Lane, who had been found guilty of "runing from his s^d master."

[May 18, 1653.] *Ebedmelecks ye negros censure.* In ans^r to the petetion of Job Lane, in the behalfe of Ebedmeleck, his servant, for the remittment of the rigor of the lawe, &c, the Court judgeth it meete, that the sajd Ebedmelecke, for his stealing victualls and breaking open a window on the Lords day, shall, the next lecture day, be whipt with five stripes.[54]

The next is in a bond of Job Lane to John Leverett, afterwards Governor of the Colony.

Know al men by these p'sents that I Jobe Lane, of Malden in the Covnty of midelsex in New Engld., Carpenter, acknowleg my selfe to be indebted vnto John Leverett, of Boston in the Covnty of Svffolke, in the Massachvsets Collony in New Engld, for a negro boy called mercvry the svm of thirty povnds of Cvrrant monney of new Engld., the which svm, I, the sayd Jobe Lane p'mise to pay vnto the sayde Leverett at his Now dwelling hovse in boston, or in other pay to his Content, as for monney, or to his heyres execcvto's or assignes, for the trve performance of the same, I doe hereby fyrmely bynd myselfe my heyres, execcvto's & assignes in the penalty of sixty povnds of like Cvrrant monney. In witnes whereof, I have herevnto set my hand & seale this 12th day of Jvne 1667.

Witnes,   JOB LAINE.   [55]
WILLIAM SEDGWICKE
ISAAC + GROSS.

The close of Philip's War was fruitful in "servants" of another race — of heathen, who for their souls' everlasting good were doomed to temporal servitude. There is extant a paper written by Daniel Gookin in 1676, the endorsement and one item of which are as follows: —

tempted to excuse that which they could neither ignore nor misrepresent. The simple truth is that slavery was just and its purposes were righteous in the eyes of those who saw their profit therein, and there were few who could see its enormity under the influence of a present advantage. It was not until a spirit of liberty and resistance to oppression began to pervade the land that a general public opinion against slavery was aroused. When the truth of history is sought before the undue exaltation of the fathers, the history of slavery in Massachusetts may be fairly told.

[54] *Mass. Colony Records,* iv. (1), 137.

[55] *N. E. Hist. and Geneal. Register,* xiii. 204.

A List of the Indian Children put to seruice that came in with John of Packachooge. . . . 1 *Boy*. To Goodman Greenland a carpenter of Charles towne on Misticke side, a boy name Tom aged twelue yeares, his father named Santisho of Packachooge.[56]

Besides this I have found no case of Indian servitude on Mystic Side or in Malden, and slavery here, with this exception, seems to have been confined to the negro race.

"Turan Negro Serv' to Edw Carrington, & a negro wench serv' to old m'rs Lines" are mentioned in 1677; and their acquaintance, resulting in a presentment at the Court, brought fifteen stripes to the former and ten to the latter.[57]

In the will of William Bucknam (1693) a negro is mentioned; and others are found, as property, in wills and inventories made prior to the Revolution. Samuel Bucknam's "negro peeter," and his troubles in 1703, have been mentioned. Jonathan Knower (1722) was possessed of a "Negro woman named Jenne," who was to serve his wife during her life and to be free at her decease; and Deacon John Greenland (1728⁸⁄₉) left to his grandson, John Shute, "one negro woman," who was valued at fifty pounds. The comparative value of human flesh in Malden during the early half of the eighteenth century may be known by the inventory of Deacon John Pratt, which was made in 1742, when an "oald negroman" and a cow were alike valued at ten pounds each.[58]

During this period, the condition of the slave was hardly as tolerable as it afterwards became. He was a barbarian — a heathen whose conversion was hardly worth the cost, and whose soul, if any he had, was of little moment in the scheme of salvation. Rarely did his children receive the rite of baptism; nor were his brothers and sisters often admitted to the privileges of church membership before the middle of the century. The reason was obvious. If he became a church member he became eligible to the privileges of a freeman, which might by some favoring circumstances be brought within his reach; and no freeman could remain or become a servitor, save after a legal

---

[56] *N. E. Hist. and Geneal. Register,* viii. 272. There are twenty-one boys and eleven "mayds" in this list.

[57] *Midd. Court Records,* iii. 176.

[58] *Midd. Probate Files, in loco.*

judgment of the court for some sufficient reason. His life and limbs were protected by the letter of the law; but the slayer of a negro was hardly to be set by the side of one who killed a white man. In the former case the law might interpose with a show of authority and a faint zeal; but public sympathy was usually with the murderer. In the following extract, pity for " the poor man" who lost his temper chokes any appearance of regret for the death of his victim.

[December 2, 1728] On Thursday last an Irishman hapning to quarrel with a Negro man belonging to *Sweetser* of Malden, proceeded to strike the said Negro, and thereby wounded him to that degree that he dy'd on Saturday last, and the poor Man was the same day committed to Goal in order to be try'd for the said Crime.[59]

Yet, to the slave the attainment of freedom was not impossible. Faithful servants were sometimes freed by will, after the deaths of their masters; and sometimes an earlier manumission was given. Nor was the release of aged or unhealthy dependants, from considerations of economy, uncommon; and the unfortunate freedman became a charge to the town or turned the mill of his poverty and distress alone. So frequent did such cases become that the General Court passed an act in 1703–4, which prohibited the freeing of servants, except upon giving bonds to save the public from future charges.[60]

[59] *New - England Weekly Journal.* There is a tradition, which can hardly be connected with this story, that a negro was killed in the house of Thomas Hills, which stood on the easterly side of Harvell's Brook Lane, near the present corner of Cross and Lyme Streets. In the course of time, the old house became not only dilapidated but haunted, so that no tenant, save the unearthly one who was supposed to have returned, could be found to remain in it. A *black cat* was seen there, and people said that spirits could take a great many forms. The house became more uncanny and ruinous, and was demolished about seventy years ago. Perhaps this story may have been connected with Jack, "a negro who lived at Mr Thos Hills," who died, May 25, 1800, aged fourteen years.

[60] *Province Laws*, chap. 1, 1703–4.

"There is a tradition that one of the old Esquires of this town had a slave who had been in his family until he was about seventy years of age. Perceiving that there was not much more work left in the old man, the Esquire took him one day, and made him a somewhat pompous address to the following effect: ' You have been a faithful servant to me and my father before me. I have long been thinking what I should do to reward you for your services. I give you your freedom ! You are your own master; you are your own man.' Upon this the old negro shook his grisly head, and with a sly glance, showing that he saw through his master's intentions, quietly replied: ' No, no, Massa, you eat de meat, and now you must pick de bone.' " *Bi-Centennial Book of Malden,* 131.

By the middle of the century, a feeling antagonistic to slavery began to work a change in public opinion and the condition of the slave began to improve. The laws for his protection became more direct or were better observed; and he was more freely admitted to the enjoyment of Christian rites and privileges. ·His children might be baptized and he might become a member of the church. " Ginne negro servant to M! Thomas Pratt of Chelsea" was baptized in 1750, by the Rev. Aaron Cleaveland of the South Church; and there were at least two negroes who were members of the same church, in full communion, before the Revolution — Tower, " servant to Mrs. Blany," who was admitted, April 3, 1763, and Peter, "servant to M' Darius Green," who was admitted March 17, 1765. The children of the latter, Margaret, Simon, and Phebe were baptized at the South Church.[61] He was familiarly known as Old Peter, and he afterwards became the slave, or servant, of Ezra or Bernard Green.

The Green family had several slaves, as had also the Lyndes, the Dexters, and the Bucknams.[62] The inventory of Ezra Green, taken July 5, 1768, contains the following items: —

To the Servents

To a Negro man Named Jeferre	£20.00.00
To a Negro Boy Named Simon	33.06.08
To a Negro Garl Named Vilot	10.13.04 [63]

Some of the papers by which Ezra Green obtained ownership of his slaves are extant and are worthy of preservation, not only

---

[61] *South Church Records, in loco.*

[62] There were several slaves attached to the farm of William Bucknam and his descendants, a portion of which is now occupied by Joseph Swan, whose house on Bucknam Street in Everett is upon the site of that of the Bucknams. " The two last woolly-haired residents upon the place rejoiced in the decidedly euphonious names of Pomp and Samp." *Malden Mirror*, August 14, 1875. " Pomp and seser," are mentioned as fiddlers at a country frolic in 1777, in a piece of doggerel which is said to have been written by one of the slaves

of this estate. This rhyme, which, with other curious or interesting papers, is in the possession of Mr. Swan, is hardly to be compared with the work of Phyllis Wheatley, the slave poet of Boston. It was to be sung " In the tune of the black swan;" and two couplets of the seven of which it is composed will fairly present its merits.

" theare was five cobbelers made a frolick
an one was taken with the collick.

" the fidlers name was pomp or seser
and dauid danced with a mop squeeser."

[63] *Midd. Probate Files, in loco.*

as showing how a legal right and title to the bodies and life
service of men could be transferred and preserved, but as
undeniable proofs of the reality of African slavery in New
England.

Know all Men By These Presents That I Peter Hayes Iun' of Stoneham in the County of Middlesix in his Majesties Province of the
Masachusetts Bay in New England Yeoman Have Sold a Negro man
Servant Named Tom : to Ezra Green of Malden in the County aforesaid Gen! and in Consideration of the Sum of Fifty Five pounds which
I Do By These Presents Acknowledge I have Received of the above S.ᵈ
Ezra Green for the above S.ᵈ Negro man Servant and am there with
fully Satisfyed and contented, and I the Said Peter Hayes Iun! have in
my Self Good right full power and Lawfull Authority to Sell and Dispose of S.ᵈ Seruant as above Expressed and I do hereby Covenant and
promise to warrant and Defend the above S.ᵈ Ezra Green in the quiet
and peasable possion of the above S.ᵈ Negro man Seruant to his own
proper Use and Disposal as he Shall think fitt In Wittness whereof I
have hereunto Sett my hand and Seal the Twenty Sevnth Day of Oct.º
Anno Dom: one Thousand Seven Hundred & Sixty And in the Thirty
Forth year of the Reign of our Sovereign Lord George the Second
King &c ———

Signed Sealed and Delivered   PETER HAY JUNᴿ.   ◇ ⁶⁶
in Presents of
    JAMES HAY
    MARY BROWN

Know all men By These Presents that we Tho.º Burditt Iabez Burditt
Sam.ᵘ Sweetser & Ioseph Burditt all of Malden & Iacob Burditt of
Charlstown Being All of the County of Middlesix & province of the
Massachusets Bay in New England Have Sold a Negro man Servant
Named Ieffrey to Ezra Green of Malden & County aforesaid Gentle-
man for and in Consideration of Thirty Seven pounds Six Shillings &
Eight pence which we Do By These Presents Acknowledge we have
Received of the above s.ᵈ Ezar Green For the Above S.ᵈ Negro Man
Servant & am therewith Fully Satisfyed & contented, and we the above
S.ᵈ Thomas, Iacob, Iabez, and Ioseph Burditt and Samuel Sweetsar
Have in our Selves good Right full Power & lawful Authority to sell and
dispose of s.ᵈ Servant as above Express.ᵈ & we do hereby Covenant and
Promise to warrant and defend the above s.ᵈ Ezra Green In the Quiet
And Peasable Possesion of the above S.ᵈ Negro Man, to his own Proper
Use & Disposal as he Shall Think fit In witness whereof we have Here-

⁶⁶ *Green Family Papers.*

unto Set our Hands And Seals this eighth Day of February Anni Dom; one Thousand Seven Hundred & Sixty two In the Second Year of the Reign of our Soverein Lord George the third King; &c.

Signed Sealed & Delivered

in Presents of

    JAMES HOUEY

    JOHN NICKOLS.

              THOMAS BURDITT ◊

              JACOB BURDIT ◊

              SAM^LL SWEETSERER ◊

              JABEZ BURDITT ◊

              JOSEPH BURDITT.[65] ◊

Boston June ye 7th 1762

Rec^d of Joseph Bryant of Stoneham Twenty Six Pounds thirteen Shillings & four pence in part of pay for a Negro Man for pay of Whom I have s^d Bryants Note of hand.

Witness my hand   EZRA GREEN.[66]

The town records contain an entry relating to "a Malatto child" who was "made a slave" to Solomon Townsend, who afterwards occupied the house and land on Ferry Street since known as the Haskins estate.

Maldon february the 4th day 1761 be it known that whereas the select men of said town have put a Malatto child to me The subscriber alowing me thirteen pounds six shillings and eight pence for my trouble in bringing up of said child and having received an order for said money J the subscriber do promis for me and my heirs to endemnify and clear the said town from any charge that may arise upon the account of said child so long as it may be made a slave to me or my heirs or to them that J or my heirs shall asign said child to Jn witness wherof J have hereunto put my hand the day and date above said.

SOLOMON TOWNSEND.

There were forty-eight negroes in Malden in 1764–65, many of whom were slaves; and thirteen "servants for life" formed an item in the valuation of 1767.[67] There were a few free blacks whose situation was not superior to that of the servants, even if it were not more pitiable, for they were suspected and despised.

---

[65] *Green Family Papers.* The sellers of Jeffrey were sons and heirs of Lieutenant Thomas Burditt, an elder of the South Church, who died October 15, 1758, aged 75, whose estate had not been settled at this time. Samuel Sweetser married Mary Burditt, July 8, 1736.

[66] Ibid. Perhaps this "Negro Man" was Tom, who does not appear in the inventory of the estate of Ezra Green in 1768.

[67] *Columbian Centinel*, August 17, 1822. The negroes were about five per cent of the population, which was then nine hundred and eighty-three persons.

They were usually of a shiftless or roving disposition — vaga-bonds and wanderers; while their enslaved brothers were, at least, housed, clothed, and fed.

It is probable that at this time slavery in Massachusetts was at its height and that it soon began to decline.[68] Property in slaves became precarious when the sense of the community awoke to its enormity; and instances began to appear in which servants asserted their freedom and invoked the protection of the law. So gradually did it pass away that, as I have before stated, its final extinction cannot be marked. In 1780 negroes were openly advertised as merchandise in the Boston papers. The next year Nathaniel Jennison of Barre, in the county of Worcester, was indicted " for assaulting, beating, and imprison-ing" his slave, Quork Walker. At his trial, before the Supreme Judicial Court in 1783, he was found guilty and fined forty shillings.[69] A note, which had been given for the price of a slave in 1787, was sued, when "the Court ruled that the maker had received no consideration, as man could not be sold."[70] These cases denote the ebb of slavery. It might linger a few years longer under the plea of indentures of service or appren-ticeship and be no less the slavery that it had been; but in its latest form it was of short duration. The following notice is a relic of its later days.

Ran away from the Subscriber, on the 3ᵈ inst. an indented negro Servant, named EPHRAIM POMP, 18 years old, about 5 feet 3 inches high; walked lame; speaks broken by reason of a hair-lip which has been cut and sewed up; wore or carried away a blue cloth coat, a white do. waistcoat, dark colored cloth pantaloons, and a straw hat.

[66] That the importation of fresh vic-tims had not wholly ceased a few years earlier is shown by the following adver-tisement : —

"JUST imported from Africa, and to be Sold on board the Brig *Jenney*, Wil-liam *Ellery* Commander, now lying at New-Boston, A Number of likely NEGRO BOYS and GIRLS, from 12 to 24 Years of Age; Inquire of said *Ellery* on board said Brig, where constant Attendance is given.

Note, The above Slaves have all had the Small-Pox. — Treasurer's Notes, and New-England Rum will be as Pay." *Boston Gazette*, July 17, 1758.

[69] *Mass. Hist. Coll.*, iv. 203. The several cases in which Quork Walker was the real party concerned are treated by Washburn, *Extinction of Slavery in Massachusetts*, in *Mass. Hist. Coll.*, xxxiv. 333–346. This writer declares that the decisions of the Court in these cases gave the death-blow to slavery in this state.

[70] Nell, *Colored Patriots*, 59.

All persons are forbid trusting or harboring said Lad, as they would avoid the penalty of the law; and any person that will take up and return said Lad, shall receive a reward of ONE CENT for their trouble. Malden, Sept. 13, [1804].   BERNARD GREEN.[71]

Several individuals who had been slaves were living in Malden within the last sixty years, among whom may be mentioned Katie Lynde and Simon Knights. The latter and his worthy and industrious wife are well remembered by many. He was the son of Old Peter, who has been noticed as the slave of Darius Green and as a member of the South Church. He was baptized by the Rev. Eliakim Willis, October 28, 1770, and was brought up by Bernard Green, with whom he lived some years after the extinction of slavery. Afterwards he earned his living as a laborer at whatever offered. He had the unstable and improvident ways of his race and it is said that his energetic wife would sometimes rebel at his thriftless proceedings and clear the house, either of him or herself. These separations were never of excessive length, as both were inclined to forgive and forget, and a few words from a neighbor would usually settle the matter. This was not an uncommon occurrence and sometimes several would join in the work of reconciliation, which was popularly called "marrying Simon Knights." They lived in a small black house of one story and two rooms, which after serving the children of Scadan as a school house for thirty years, was removed to Haskins's Lane, where it stood a little east of the site of the Unitarian Church, and made a comfortable, though humble, home for the worthy couple.

Lydia Knights was younger than her husband by a number of years; and while he was an unmixed African, there was white

[71] *Columbian Centinel*, September 15, 1804. Ephraim Pomp, "a poor negro boy under our care," was bound to Bernard Green by the selectmen of Charlestown, January 20, 1802. He was to serve until January 21, 1807, when he would arrive at the age of twenty-one. His master was to teach him the calling of a husbandman, besides giving him the rudiments of an education and keeping him well-fed, sheltered, and clothed. He was to receive at the expiration of his time one hundred and ten dollars in money and two suits of apparel — one being "suitable for the Lords Day." *Green Family Papers*. He was a graceless dog to run away from so many benefits and so great a reward, unless there was an inside view of the system under which he served which was not indicated in the indenture.

blood in her veins.   As has been intimated, she was industrious and energetic to an unusual degree, and her character entitled her to the respect of all.   She was *the* "Miss Knights" of the town, while her husband was simply "Simon"; and neither wedding nor funeral was complete had she not borne a part in its preparation.   She was the adjunct of the minister at the former, nor was the sexton more indispensable at the latter. Her presence at either insured skilful preparation and good service after the simple manner of the times.   She was an autocrat in her department on such occasions, and it was said that parties had been postponed at her behest.   Indeed, it was facetiously asserted that no one dared to die in Malden until it suited the convenience of "Miss" Knights.   She left Malden to visit a son or a daughter, by her first marriage, in Tennessee, contrary to the wishes of Simon, who said she would never return.   It is said that she died there very suddenly; but there were those who feared that she had been abducted and thrown into slavery.   The latter, although not probable, was not impossible, as she was active and her skill as a cook would have made her a desirable servant.

After the departure of his wife, Simon, being infirm and beyond the performance of any considerable labor, became an inmate of the almshouse, where he lived several years.   He was an early member of the Baptist Church, having been baptized in 1804-1806; and although he was once set aside and at other times became the subject of visitations and discipline for neglect of duty, he was on the whole a consistent and sincere Christian. He died in July, 1847; and his funeral service, which was held in the Baptist Church, was attended by the townspeople as that of a neighbor and friend.[72]

[72] Simon Knights was not the only person born in slavery who has been a member of the First Baptist Church. Peter Nassau, or Nassus, was baptized, April 8, 1803. He was born a slave in Martinique and was brought to Medford by his master, Joseph Domier, a French merchant. Having some difficulty with his master, he fled to Malden and was sheltered by Charles Hill of Hill's Tavern, who defended him when it was sought to take him back to Medford. He remained in Malden several years, and was afterwards in the service of John Coffin Jones of Boston and others as coachman. When an old man, he went to Woodstock, Vermont, and became in time a town pauper.

Peter Nassau was popularly supposed to be an extremely old man. A portrait

Although the subject be lowly and the names humble, the record of these servitors may not be wholly useless, even though it may serve only to give another proof of the reality of slavery. The names in the following lists are in addition to those already mentioned.[73]

MARRIAGES.

James and *Margrett*, negroes. Nov. 20, 1727.

Tobia, negro of Malden, and *Ziporah*, negro of Lynn. Dec. 18, 1729.

Sambo of Stoneham and *Mercar* of Malden. By Rev. James Osgood. Jan. 11, 173⅚.

John, a negro belonging to Joseph Lynde of Malden, and *Vilot*, a negro belonging to Thomas Hills of Malden. Jan. 26, 174⁹⁄₅₀.

Cesar, a negro belonging to Benjamin Thwing of Boston and *Phyllis*, a negro belonging to Joseph Wilson of Malden. By Rev. Joseph Emerson. Dec. 6, 1751.

Peter Perkins, a negro of Lynn, and *Jenney*, a negro of Malden. By Rev. Joseph Emerson. Nov. 19, 1755.

Bramer,[74] a negro belonging to Benjamin Bucknam of Malden, and *Dinah*, a mulatto belonging to Mr. Toler of Stoneham. By Rev. Joseph Emerson. Jan. 24, 1760.

---

of him, which is said to have been a good one, was given in *Ballou's Pictorial Drawing-Room Companion*, December 13, 1856, with an article in which he was called the oldest man in America and said to have "reached the extraordinary age of one hundred and twenty-six years." His age, however, was exaggerated. I was informed by the late Benjamin Goodwin Hill, a son of the landlord, Charles Hill, that he was merely a large boy when he fled to Malden, which was apparently about the year 1790. He was accustomed to make lengthy visits to his Malden friends — at first with considerable regularity but less frequently as his years increased. His last visit was in March, 1857, at which time he was probably about eighty-five years of age. He disclaimed any knowledge of his real age and said

he felt about two hundred years old. He died soon after his return to Vermont.

He retained a lively interest in the sons and daughters of his old protector, Charles Hill; and in their honor two of his daughters are said to have been named Sally John Sprague Nassau and Mary James Crane Nassau, coupling the names of husband and wife in each instance.

[73] Not all the names in this list are those of slaves. Some are undoubtedly those of free negroes or persons of negro and Indian blood; but it is not possible to separate them.

[74] Brahma. Brammer or Grammer, "a Negro man Slave to Benjᵃ Bucknam," was accused of stealing "a Cow Calf Spotted red and white and with a white face" from the close of Ezra Green in May, 1763. *Green Family Papers.*

Dover, a servant to Mr. Stoddard of Boston, and *Vilot*, a servant to Mr. Ebenezer Pratt of Malden. By Rev. Eliakim Willis. Oct. 7, 1764.

Prince, servant to Thomas Hills, and *Tarmar*, servant to Ezra Green, Esq., of this town. By Rev. Joseph Emerson. Nov. 9, 1764.

Cato, a servant to Nathan Lynde, and *Mareri*, servant to Capt. Dexter. By Rev. Joseph Emerson. April 5, 1765.

Jupiter, servant to Jonathan Waite of Lynn, and *Vilot*, servant to Thomas Hills of Malden. By Rev. Joseph Emerson. Dec. 26, 1765.

Bristol, servant to Zachariah Pool of Medford, and *Violet*, servant to Mr. Ebenezer Pratt of Malden. By Rev. Peter Thacher. Feb. 7, 1771.

Worster, negro servant of Rev. Mr. Turell of Medford, and *Phyllis*, negro servant of Rev. Mr. Willis of Malden. By Rev. Eliakim Willis. Nov. 25, 1771.

Samuel, servant of Joseph Lynde, and *Phyllis*, servant of Nathan Lynde, both of Malden. By Rev. Peter Thacher. April 16, 1772.

Prince, servant of Thomas Hills of Malden, and *Hannah*, servant of Francis Brown of Medford. By Rev. Peter Thacher. Oct. 7, 1773.

Sampson Bassett and *Bilhah Emerson* of Maldon, negroes. By Rev. John Treadwell [of Lynn]. Aug. 8, 1776.

Pompey Magos of Malden and *Zipporah Barjina*[76] of Stoneham. By Rev. Peter Thacher. May 26, 1778.

INTENTIONS OF MARRIAGE.

Fortune, servant to Nathan Sargeant of Malden, and *Violet*, servant to William Oliver of Chelsea. Oct. 3, 1770.

---

[76] These were free persons of mixed negro and Indian blood, if the woman was not purely of the latter race. They were parents of Sal Magos another peripatetic fortune-teller and vendor of herbs who was well known here sixty years ago. As a "walk-about" she divided the honors with Deb Saco and Hannah Shiner. Pompey Magos was a soldier of the Revolution and is mentioned elsewhere.

BIRTHS AND DEATHS.

Seasorr, son of *Roger* and *Margaret*, negroes, born[76] Aug. 27, 1730.

Cesar, a negro boy, son to *Peg*, died Sept. 30, 1741.

Sippeo, servant to Capt. Jonathan Green of Stoneham, "Came to his Death by Accident By Slipping of a Raft of Seag & was Drowned [in Malden River]."[77]   Sept. 22, 1762.

Dinah, negro, servant to John and Mary Shute, died July 22, 1768.

Titus, a negro man, servant to Capt. John Dexter, died July 3, 1782.

Flora, a negro woman, servant to Lydia Holmes, died July 17, 1782.

Samson, a negro man belonging to Benjamin Bucknam, died, Jan. 5, 1786.

Cato, a negro, aged 70, died of dropsy, Oct. 23, 1797.

Jack, a negro who lived at Mr. Thomas Hills', aged 14, died, May 25, 1800.

SOLDIERS.

Titus, negro, served with his master, Jacob Lynde, in the army in 1760.

Samuel Harden, in service, 1777, and said to have deserted.

Prince Hills, in service, 1775.

Aaron Oliver, in service, 1775.

Pomp Magos, in service, 1779.

---

[76] This is the only birth of a negro child which can be found recorded in Malden prior to 1840. Married slaves and their young children were not looked upon with favor. Dr. Belknap wrote that "Negro children were reckoned an incumbrance in a family; and when weaned were given away like puppies. They have been publickly advertised in the news-papers 'to be given away.'" *Mass. Hist. Coll.*, iv. 200. The "Seasorr" who is mentioned in this entry was probably the "Cesar" of the next.

[77] Original inquest, signed by Jonathan Porter, coroner, in *Green Family Papers.*

CHAPTER XIII.

HIGHWAYS AND BRIDGES.

THE roads existing on Mystic Side and in Malden during
the colonial period have been described; and the record
relating to the ways laid out in the commons has been given in
full.

On Mystic Side, the way from Penny Ferry to Malden; the
Winnisimmet Road running from Malden by the Bucknam land,
Nichols's Hill, and Powder Horn; the highway from the house
of James Barrett along by the head of the five-acre lots into the
Winnisimmet Road; and perhaps a way leading into Malden
bounds over Sargeant's Hill to the point of rocks [Black Ann's
Corner] in the Salem Road, were the principal ways, as they
are to-day.

Although the way from Mystic River to Malden had existed
since the settlement of Mystic Fields, it seems to have been
vaguely defined and partially unsettled. At a meeting of the
selectmen of Charlestown it was ordered,

[May 2, 1670.] Thomas Lynde, Will Dade and Richard Kittle
Are to laie out A highway from the Gate Standing in the countrie highway from the peny ferrie and vp along that way so farr as Stephen paines
land runs in that way towards maulden.[1]

This committee reported during the next month, when it
appeared that they had required Stephen Paine to make "that
wet place on this side his house to be a sufficient high way for
horse & cart."[2] This was apparently merely a survey or confirmation of the way already existing through the Carrington
land, which Stephen Paine appears to have occupied in the
lifetime of his father-in-law, Edward Carrington. The "wet

---

[1] *Charlestown Records*, lii. *in loco.*   [2] Ibid.

place" may be readily identified in the low ground formerly known as "the swamp," lying south of the Carrington house.[3]

The portion of the road nearer Mystic River ran through the land of the innholder, Richard Stowers, whose house of entertainment stood near by. He requested "[February 4, 167⅝,] allowance for a highway y^t has bin frequently thorow his land to penny ferry;" and a lot of two and a half acres was granted him "on ye North side of North Spring at Mistick Side . . . with a highway thorow it."[4] Three years later, March 19, 168%, a highway was laid out and settled "at Misticke side from ye Meadows belonging to ye north River through Ric. Stower^s his grovnd and so downe to ye watter side," and also a way from Thomas Rand's marsh "downe upon a line to a whitte thorne bush & so downe to ye watter side right over against ye whitte Iland."[5] These ways, which were practically one, were for the convenience of the owners of the marsh lots. Indications of the old way upon the shore opposite White Island were apparent twenty years ago, and some traces may perhaps still be found in other portions of its course. The thorn bush has disappeared; but the name of Thomas Rand is preserved in Rand's Creek, which runs through the marshes from Everett to North River and formed the northerly boundary of his land. In the record of this way, the former settlement of the country road through the land of Richard Stowers is mentioned and it is added: "he owned to vs yt he hath had satisfaction for it."

The way to Wormwood Point, although it has lost its former importance, is one of the oldest on Mystic Side. It gave access to the common landing place at the point, which was freely used by the inhabitants of the easterly bank of the Mystic many years, and was called "an antient high way" in 1681, when the following report was made: —

The Return of an order that was Jshued out aug^t ye 1st 1681 for the laying out of an antient high way of malden Side leading to peney ferry and from thence down to wormores point the committee chosen ware

---

[3] Henderson Street, in Everett, east of Main Street, is laid out through the centre of the old swamp.

[4] *Charlestown Records*, iii. *in loco.*
[5] Ibid., iv. *in loco.*

Edwd: Carrington Willm: daudy Richard Stowers: which made this there return feb^r: y_e 13th 1681 the high way that was appointed to be laid out from Bengamin Sweetsers gate that stands upon the high way that goeth to penney ferry & so along upon the ground that was formerly William Daudyes & goeth upon the ferm ground to the upper side of a great Rock & so goeth streight a little above bengamin Sweetsers hous and so goeth streight till we come down against Sarg^t: Lawrances Dowces Meadow then goeth along by said Dowces meadow with an elbow upon ferm land in the old way till we come to Barnibus Davises ground and on the upper side of a Couchple of trees at one corner of said Dowces meadow and so goeth through the lower side of barnibus davises ground on the upland to the water side and this foresaid high way is to be one pole wide till we come to Barnibus Davises ground and through Barnibus Davises ground to be two pole till we come to Cap^n Thomas Brattles meadow and then four poles wide till we come through his meadow to the water side:

Atest   the mark WD of: ᴹ: DAUDY
J^no: NEWEL *Record^r*.   RICHARD STOWERS
                             EDWARD CARRINGTON

A true Copy Book 4th page 23 Exam^d: p^r:

                            NATHANIEL DOWS *town Clerk*

the above said is a true Copy of what was taken out of Charlestown Book of records and recorded here by order of the select men of Malden in the year 1738

         Atest   JOHN SHUTE *town Clerk* *

The condition of the Mystic Side ways in 1714 may be understood by the following extract from a report made in that year by a committee chosen by Charlestown " to prevent incroachments."

MISTICK SIDE. — The Way at mistick side as followeth:
there is a Small peice of land belonging to the town left for a pound or any other use: lying between m^r James Barrets Land & m^r Tuffs land formerly Stoweres.

* This extract from the *Charlestown Records* was apparently entered in the *Malden Records* in consideration of the evidence which it afforded respecting the public rights which were thought to be threatened in the controversy with Joseph Wilson in relation to his gates, to which reference is made in another place. The way then laid out or confirmed is represented, so far as it is now a public way, by the present Beacham Street in Everett. There was formerly a large rock on its westerly side, which was probably the "great Rock" of the report. It is now under the sidewalk, the road having been widened about twenty-five feet since 1827.

The high way or contry road leading down from Malden to peney ferery is wholly inclosed & improved by m^r Stowers Sprague & Accknoledged by him & he paid one shilling:

There is a highway of one pole wide bordering on the head of the lotts within Stowers Spragues land from the contry road or high way by a ditch between the lotts formerly Thos. Rand & s^d. Spraages land North west ward & so along till it comes to Phinneas Uphams land: and the said high way runs from the said Thomas Rands marsh down till it comes over against the White Island: the s^d high way was for the Accommodation of the marsh lotts on the North & North westerly Side of the said Stowers Spragues Upland, And is all inclosed & improved by said Stowers Sprague:

Att the lower end of the said high-way by the river there being formerly an old thorn bush, & that being demollished & gone, wee have driven down a stake on each side the high way near where the said thorn bush stood: over Against the White Island:

There is a highway belonging to the town of one pole wide leading out of the contry road by Samuel Switsers through the said Switsers land, & so through m^r Benj^a Swittsers land by his house to wormwood point: the said high-way is one pole wide till it comes to the head of the marsh formerly Dowses & then turns on the said Benj^a Swittsers Upland: att the head of the marsh till it comes to the gate between m^r Swittsers land & m^r Odleins land formerly mitchells, now in the possession of James Nicholls: & then the said high way is two poles wide down to wormwoods point untill it comes to the Southerly corner of Brattells marsh & there measures two poles.

from the Old Stump against the barn & then the way & towns land is four poles wide for a landing place by the Watter side round the point till it comes to the cove or harbour against the door of the now dwelling house:

There is incroached and inclosed 7 or 8 foot of the towns land by James Nicholls within his garden fence att wormwoods point.[7]

After the annexation of Mystic Side to Malden, some controversy existed in relation to gates across the way to Wormwood Point; but the way, itself, seems to have been neglected. At the annual meeting, March 5, 174¾,

Jt was put to vot whether the town would do any thing respecting the way to wormores point as well for the accommodation of mr Joseph Willson as the persons that have occasion to pas over his land to the salt marsh and water side and it past in the negetive.

[7] *Charlestown Archives*, xxxiv. 265–266.

At the same meeting liberty was given to Thomas Richard ·
son "to build a wharf upon Wormores point down from high
water mark to half tide sixteen foot wide upon the high way
where it is four poles wide for the benefit of the town or any
perticular person thereof." This landing place continued, as it
had been from the earliest settlement, to be much used by the
general public. Men like Ebenezer Pratt of Moulton's Island,
and others, who made boating a means of livelihood, lived in
the vicinity; and their boats were used to transport produce,
timber, wood, and supplies to and from this and the neighboring landing at Moulton's Island. Both landings continued to
be used until the building of Malden Bridge, and even after,
when the wharves gradually disappeared. A boat, that tradition
says was from the landing at Wormwood Point, met with a mis-
hap which is thus recorded in the Malden record of *births:* —

John Rudge, James Sargeant and Nathan Burditt on the 5 day of
May 1759 by the overseting of a small boat in a high gail of wind were
drowned between boston and winesimmit Providence ordered it so that
an aged woman mother to the said burditt who was over with him was
saved alive by taking hold of an oar and a bag of bred.

In 1768 the road to Wormwood Point was again called in
question; and at the annual meeting in that year, the selectmen
were authorized to join with John Beacham, who had purchased a large portion of the Sweetser land, " in settelling And
in haveing a town road confirmed to the town that leads from
the said Beachams house to wormores point so called." Two
years later [March 5, 1770] it was " *Voted*, to accept ye Report
of ye Committee chosen to lay out the Way to Worm-wood's
Point;" but the report was not recorded. It apparently did
not settle the question; for at a meeting, November 3, 1800, it
was " *Voted* to hear the Report of a Committee which is that
M^r. Lewis Acknowledges their is a Town Roade from the
County roade to Beachams point so Call^d but Mr Beacham does
not." The matter was delayed until November 11, 1801, when
" the Selectmen with the Town^s Committe for the purpose
of finding out the Old Roade leading to Beachams point so
Cal^d, after obtaining a Coppy of the Record of s^d Roade: pro-

ceeded & staked out s⁴ Roade agreable to the s⁴ Record." The record used was the Charlestown report of 1714, a copy of which forms a part of the committee's return.

The earliest entries in the town records in relation to high-ways, after the division of the commons, are as follows: —

[March 13, 169⅞.] *Voted* That yᵉ Select-men are Chose a Com-mitie to set yᵉ bound between yᵉ peece of land that Capt Wilsons shop and Coal-hous stands on: and yᵉ highway And to signe and Acknowleg a deed of it.

[August 24, 1699] The Select-men are jmpoured to set yᵉ bounds of yᵉ high way by yᵉ clay-pits neer Lewisis bridg: and punish transgres-sors yᵗ shall intrench on yᵉ high ways jn diging of clay: by laying a fine on yᵐ.ᵇ

[May 16, 1701.] *voted* yᵗ john Sargeant Senʳ john Greenland, jona-than Sprague joseph Lamson and nathaniell upham are a commitie to bound yᵉ country Rhoads jn this town and also to see whare jt may be most conuenant to Stop: or stake town highwaise: and make Report therof to yᵉ next town meting:

The committee mentioned in the last entry made the follow-ing report, which the town approved: —

[September 3, 1701,] We find Recorded jn yᵉ first Town book a highway laid out from The Cuntry Rhoad between Mʳ Hils & Mʳ Bun-kars farmes to thomas calles hous 4 pols broad from thomas calls to john wilkensons & by Thomas Moltens Richard prats & peetar Tuffts to Charlestown Line towards yᵉ South Spring.⁹

ᵇ Joseph Wilson's house and land have already been mentioned as being at the corner of the Salem and Reading Roads. He was a blacksmith, and his shop was one of the public places of the town. Whether it was on the former or latter road does not appear; but it may have been on the westerly side of Main Street, as tradition says the rubbish of a forge was found there while excavating many years ago.

Of the clay-pits near the bridge, some were at the corner of the present Main and Madison Streets, and others were in the land on which the First Parish meet-ing house was afterwards built. Bricks were made near by for many years after; and the Frog Pond, well remembered by Malden boys of the writer's generation, was a relic of the clay-digging days.

From it were made the bricks which form the walls of the First Parish Church. Clay-pits were also opened near Shute's Meadow, in the vicinity of the present Holyoke and Wyeth Streets; on Hutchinson's Lane (Cross Street) near the Skinner house; and on Harvell's Brook Lane (Cross Street), south of the present Willow Avenue. In the southern part of Mystic Side, from the marshes of the North River to Rumney Marsh, an extensive deposit of clay early attracted an industry which still remains; and the kilns which to-day are burning on the line of the Eastern Railroad in Everett are the successors of those which were lighted more than two centuries ago.

⁹ This was Harvell's Brook Lane, or that part of the present Cross Street

Also a way from Thomas Cals hous to ye meting hous 2 polls broad.
furthar this commitie doe think : whare ye formar commitee laid out
The abou s^d wais js most conuenant for ye east end of ye town.
And also y^t Row of ye naighbour-hood do pas from pembartons brook
to ye meting hous other waies ye jnhabitants on both these parts of y^e
town haue no alowed way to ye meting hous.
Also we doe jug jt nesesary y^t ther be a way laid out for ye east &
south end of ye town to pas to ye buring place.

At the meeting at which this report was presented, the Reading Road was considered; and it was

uoted y^t Henery Green Joseph Linde, Phines upham Thomas okes
And john Greenland are apointed a commitie to bound out ye highway
of 2 pols broad from Capt william Greens to ye meting hous whare y^e
formar commitie yt was chose between malden & charlestown Laid it
and to Giue notic y^t ye incumbrances now upon it be remoued by the
first of nouember next jnsuing this date.

The selectmen, in answer to the request of Thomas Burditt
of Malden and John Marble of Mystic Side,

Layd out a highway on ye 10 of June 1702 between ye s^d thomas
burdit and John Marbls land from Joseph Sargeants land : of one pool
broad to ye northeast cornar of John Rigways land : also ye same way
js laid a pool wide along by ye head of the s^d Rigways land jnto ye Great
Rhoad.

This way was laid out for the use of the persons whose lands
are mentioned; and for some consideration connected therewith Joseph Sargeant paid John Marble eight shillings in
money. This was upon the easterly side of the present Ferry

which runs from Salem Street to Ferry
Street. The farm of Joseph Hills, as
has been stated, comprehended most of
the land between Salem, Ferry, and
Cross Streets, north of Harvell's Brook,
as well as other lands north of Salem
Street and south of the brook.

Bunker's farm was a parcel of upland
and swamp lying south of Salem Street
and east of Cross Street. It was that
seventy acres of woodland, "scituate in
misticke fielde," which was owned by
George Bunker in 1638. *Charlestown
Archives*, xxxiv. 36. To this he added,
by unrecorded purchases, a large tract
of other lands in Scadan, out of which,

in 1661, he deeded to his son John two
hundred acres in Malden, bounded w.
by Joseph Hills and others; s. by the
great swamp; and N. by the common
and three small lots. *Midd. Co. Deeds,*
ii. 181. Most of the Bunker land in
Malden finally came into the possession of John Bunker, the saddler of
Cambridge, grandson of George, whose
claims so troubled the town and individual landholders in 1695.

The house of Thomas Call, near the
present corner of Cross and Walnut
Streets, is noticed in note 11 of the present chapter. The others were between
Call's house and the South Spring.

Street; and it was that lane which, having been extended to Washington Avenue in Chelsea, has become Nichols Street in Everett.[10]

A committee was appointed, June 11, 1706, " to lay out a conuenant highway for the jnhabitants of y⁰ East end of y⁰ town to goe to y⁰ meting hous : or to say whare y⁰ highway js jf alredy layd out." A way from Scadan already existed ; but it was circuitous, and in a portion of its course the right to pass appears to have been somewhat doubtful. It was over that way which has been mentioned as leaving the Salem Road and rùn-ning " between M⁰ Hils & M⁰ Bunkars farmes to thomas calles hous " — the later Harvell's Brook Lane and a part of the pres-ent Cross Street. From Thomas Call's house, which stood near the present southeasterly corner of Cross and Walnut Streets,[11] a narrow way called the Stony Lane ran southwestwardly over the hill towards the ancient Green house, which is still standing on Appleton Street, near the Everett line, and entered the Win-nisimmet road of 1653. A longer way was open then, as now, over the Salem and Reading Roads by Wilson's Corner, Hill's Tavern, and Lewis's Bridge. The report of the committee, if made, was not recorded ; but the following vote may have been its result : —

[10] It ran easterly no farther than the house of Joseph Sargeant, which, after his death in 1717, appears in the records as that of Widow Mary Sargeant. All the land around it ultimately fell into the hands of the Nichols family. There were but two houses upon it as late as 1856 — those of Andrew D. Nichols and Ebenezer Nichols. The latter house, which stood at the head of the lane, was probably the old house of Joseph Sargeant.

[11] Thomas Call died in November, 1678. His widow, Lydia (Shepherdson), married Thomas Skinner, and carried the house of her former husband into the Skinner family. The process by which it came into the possession of Abraham Skinner, and finally of his widow, Hannah, has been described. *Vide* chap. xi. note 43. After the death of Hannah Skinner, January 14, 172⅚, it was in the occupancy of Abraham Skinner, perhaps her son ; and it after-wards passed into the hands of the Parkers in some way of which I have found no record. This estate, when deeded to Abraham Skinner in 169⅚, comprised three acres of land, with the house and barn, on the *northerly* side of the road, running to a point at the easterly end, and twelve acres on the southerly side of the road. The re-moval of the highway in 1729 left the house on the southerly side of the new way. The old house was not standing in 1798 ; and it had been demolished, it is supposed, many years before. Its cellar remained until within sixty years past ; and a large rock, which stood in the field near the southeast corner of the present Cross and Walnut Streets, bore the name of Skinner's Rock, and preserved the name of its former owners long after they had passed away. It was removed in 1887.

[May 28, 1708,] *uoted* ensin phinas upham sam⁰ wayt sen john prat john mudge and Thomas okes To Be acomity to uewe the lain throw john Greens paster commonly called the stonny lain in order unto the stoping of it and Remoueing of it down to john hutchinson land that now is and to maike a Return of your dowings heare in at the next Town meting

The Return Wee the Subscribers Being chosen and Apointed By the *of the com* Town to uewe the Ground from the highway aGainest john *mity* Greens house alonge By the Towns fence and so to john hutchinsons fence and so to the litel Gate By widow Skiners and Likewise to uewe the highway commony called the Stoney Lain and whare it may Be Beste to Stope it in order to the Remouel of it if the Town See case douen to that Sid of John Greens land next to john hutchinson fence and so to the litel Gate By widow Skiners

Which Saruis wee dide some time in june lâst past and doe judge that it may Be most for the Towns Benifet to Remoue it And that the Best placeses to Stope the Stony laine is Belowe widow Skiners hous at end And aGainst the fence that is Between nathanell uphames land and obeds jankens land on the South Sid of nathanell uphams land

SAMUEL WAYT SENER
PHINAS UPHAM
THOMAS OAKES

The report of the committee was made to the town, March 4, 170⁸⁄₉; and it was voted "that the Stoney laine Be Stoped as the commity has mad thar Return and the Sad john Green to hange Gats at each end of Sad way." The committee was also authorized to "stake out the highway Through john Greens land from the Contery Roode A Gainest John Greens To the Contery Rode By widow Skinners."

This way, which was now opened by John Hutchinson's fence, was that portion of the present Cross Street which was known as Hutchinson's Lane and more recently as Peter Tufts's Lane. It began at the Winnisimmet road, which crossed the line of the present street near the corner of High Street as it now exists. There is some uncertainty as to its course after it reached the highway over the hill. The present Walnut Street, which it joined, is a portion of the old way from Lewis's Bridge, which ran along the easterly side of the Hutchinson land in its present course. It is clear that the way did not run straight from Hutchinson's Corner to the house of Thomas Parker, which stood on the hill at the present corner of Ferry and Cross Streets, where was lately the house of James H. Whitaker;[12] but it proceeded more directly by the *southerly* side of the Call, or Skinner, house to the old way from the Salem Road to the South Spring. This left a V-shaped piece of road, around which the weary Scadanites had to trudge on their way to the meeting house. To overcome this difficulty, it was voted, May 15, 1710, " That ye Town doe think jt needfull That ther be a highway of 2 pols broad from Thomas parkars house To ye meting hous." In accordance with this vote, the select-men met May 25,

and layd out a high-way for ye use of ye Town of Two pols broad on ye norwest side of Abraham Skinars stonwall from ye high way neer Thomas parkers house to ye highway at ye end of s^d Skinars Garding.

This was not satisfactory and, in fact, there seems to have been some opposition to the whole way. The matter was carried by somebody to the Court of General Sessions of the Peace, which performed among its other duties those of the later County Commissioners. At a town meeting April 20, 1711, Lieutenant Henry Green, Deacon Phineas Upham, Isaac Hill, and Benjamin Whittemore were chosen " to apere at ye Sesions of ye peece to be held at charlestown on Tusday ye 24 jnstant to answer jn Referanc to ye high way jn contreuarcy." After hearing the case, the Court passed the following order : —

[April 24, 1711]. Upon hearing the Petition or motion of Phineas Upham & Henry Green & others of ye Town of maldon refering to a p'tended high way thro the p'sonage Land in maldon from Thos Calls house to the meeting house, which seeming contrary to ye primitiue Return of the comitte of maldon for ye laying out of high wayes in sd Town in ye year 49 : And that the Town of Maldon haueing appointed a Comittee of late to stake out the high way of Two Rod wide through

---

[12] The house of Thomas Parker, which was originally of one or two rooms, is supposed to have been built in the latter part of the seventeenth century. When it was enlarged is not known ; but its former appearance indicated a date not later than the early half of the last century. It was removed about 1860 to the vicinity of Ashland Street. Ferry Street from Parker's Corner at Cross Street to the easterly spur of Powder House, or Liberty Hill, did not exist until 1835. The land over which it passes was a meadow, around which the old way passed on the firmer land by the present Walnut Street.

Jnᵒ Greens Land from the Country Road against John Greens to the Country Road by the Widow Skinners along by the outside of John Hutchinsons fence & the Towns fence which is the pʳsonage Land, which sᵈ comittee on or about the year 1709 did lay out or stake out sd way as pʳ theire Return under their hands of theire Doings therein Exhibited in Court fully appears   This Court (Sundry of the members wʳof haveing been upon the place and viewing the same) upon hearing of all parties Referring to yᵉ same, Conclude and order that the sᵈ Report of the late Comittee now Exhibited to yᵉ Court as aforesaid Js to be accepted and Jmproved as the Settled high way from sᵈ Thomas Calls house lot that way upon a straight Line to yᵉ Road leading to the meeting house of Two rods wide, and for pʳventing of Charge, That there may be hanged a gate at Each End for the Conveniancy of those that haue occasion of yᵉ said Way Till further order of this Court and that all parties Concerned bear theire own cost.¹⁸

This closed the way between the Parker and Skinner houses; and the east end people had to "go 'round" for more than eighteen years, unless, as may have been, they were allowed to "cut acrost."   At length it was voted: —

[November 26, 1729.]   That yᵉ selectmen shall move yᵉ Highway that is by Abraham Skinners barn, to yᵉ north sid of His Land, & lay it out so as shall be most Conveiant for yᵉ Town

Five days later the selectmen finished the work and Hutchinson's Lane, or Peter Tufts's Lane, as it was afterwards called, was completed and so remained, tolerably straight but very narrow, until it was straightened, widened, and otherwise improved, and became the westerly portion of Cross Street.   That section of the street beyond Ferry Street, equally narrow, and crooked to excess, was long known as Harvell's Brook Lane, from the brook which it crosses a short distance below Salem Street.¹⁴

¹⁸ *Midd. Court Records, — General Sessions, in loco.* The "primitiue Return" of the committee of 1649 is a record or paper which has disappeared.

¹⁴ A mill was established at an early date on the easterly side of Cross Street on the brook by the Eastern Railroad. The dam, crossing the meadow from bank to bank, was very distinct and perfect until the ground was graded for building purposes in 1887. The mill appears to have been owned and operated, prior to 1706, by William Mathews,

who had been brought up by Job Lane, and who in that year, a few months prior to his marriage with Mary, daughter of Robert Calley of Sandy Bank, sold to James Harvell of Lynn a dwelling house with half an acre of land, bounded west on the highway and north on the brook then called Stone Brook. *Midd. Co. Deeds,* xxiv. 697.

William Mathews, apparently, afterwards occupied a house and fourteen acres of land in the division lots, which he sold to John Lynde, Jr., in 1714. He

Memorandum, Malden December yᵉ : 1 : 1729 : yᵉ Select men Did then move yᵉ High way that was laid out behind Abraham Skinners Barn, & laid it out on yᵉ north side of His land, two pole wide yᵉ sd way is laid out part in Skinners & part in Thomas parkers land yᵉ North side of yᵉ sd way is laid from apost standing in yᵉ fence at yᵉ south End of yᵉ sd parkers primmhedg, & so to a post south of yᵉ Claypitt, & near yᵉ same, & from thence on a Straight line to yᵉ corner of John Hutch‧ ensons stone wall, & yᵉ south side of yᵉ sd way is bounded by aheep of stones lying on an old Dichwall by yᵉ side of yᵉ highway leeding toward Nathanell nickoles,[15] & so to a stake, and from yᵉ sd stake, on aline to

had then removed to Lynn, and was still called a miller. *Midd. Co. Deeds*, xvii. 50.

James Harvell and his wife, Mary (Waite), had three children born in Malden. Another James, probably their son, had a wife, Sarah, and two sons, one of whom died in infancy.

No other traces of the Harvells in Malden are known to me. They may have lived and died here or removed; but their name, although changed in time to Harvey, became firmly attached to the road and brook on which they lived, and has remained unto the present day. The mill is supposed to have been used as late as the close of the Revolution.

In 1813 the town gave Aaron Waite of Salem, who then owned the farm which John Bunker had sold to Samuel Waite, " Liberty to dig a ditch through Harvey's Brook so Called in Malden for the purpose of taking the water of his Meadow," and " to tak up & new lay the Bridge over sᵈ brook." A convenient watering place was made at the side of the road, where the women were accustomed to wash their yarn in the earlier days of this century, when spinning was a female accomplishment.

[15] The house of Deacon Nathaniel Nichols was that which stood upon a lane which formerly ran from Ferry Street a little south of the present Harvard Street. The farm upon which it was situated became the property of Nathaniel and Samuel Nichols after the death of their father, May 10, 1725. The former sold the western half of the house with adjoining land, bounded s. e. upon the lane, to Jacob Parker in 1742. *Midd. Co. Deeds*, xlviii. 396. Samuel Nichols, the owner of the other half, went in the expedition to Cape Breton in 1745, and died, with his younger brother John, during the siege of Louisburg. His widow, Jemima, married, July 18, 1746, John Polly of Medford, and joined with her son, Samuel Nichols of Medford, in 1761, in conveying the moiety to Jacob Parker, who thus became sole owner of the house and surrounding lands. *Midd. Co. Deeds*, lix. 278.

Jacob Parker married Rebecca, a daughter of the Rev. Joseph Emerson; and died January 17, 1779, of small-pox, which was brought into the town by his wife, and of which seven others died. After his death his widow enjoyed the customary widow's third of his estate and occupied a portion of the old house, where she kept a school at the expense of the town until her marriage with Deacon Benjamin Brintnall of Chelsea, August 3, 1780. In 1800 Asa Tufts, who had married Elizabeth Parker, and had come into possession of two-thirds of the house and homestead land, conveyed his portion to David Faulkner, and with his brother-in-law, Joshua Parker, quitclaimed the remaining third to the same grantee. *Midd. Co. Deeds*, cxxxv. 385, 387. At the demise of the widow, who died insane, July 21, 1816, being then the relict of Deacon Samuel Waite, the estate came wholly into the hands of David Faulkner. His son, the late David Faulkner, razed the old house in 1849, and built that at the corner of Ferry and Harvard Streets in which his widow resided until her death in 1892.

The kitchen of the old house extended the whole length of the building at its rear; and its chimney and oven

yᵉ north corner of yᵉ sd Thomas parkers pastuer & so yᵉ way comes fluch with yᵉ way from faulkners, to Hutchenes (with a little winding) yᵉ East End of yᵉ sd way is all in Skinners land as far as to yᵉ post by yᵉ clay-pitt.

In consequence of the closing of the Stony Lane and the moving of the road to Hutchinson's fence, the way formerly granted to Mr. Wigglesworth through the parsonage land was discontinued. Soon after the inhabitants of the easterly portion of the town, for whose convenience the new way had been laid out, prayed the County Court to remove the gates which had been hung across it. Their petition was as follows: —

To the honored Justices of yᵉ Cort of Sessions now siting jn Charlestown The 10 of march: 1712/3 The Humbl peticion of sundrey of yᵉ Jnhabitants of the East and north-east side of yᵉ Town of malden Humbly Sheweth: that whar as your honours were pleasᵈ to Take the pains to com to malden sum time jn yᵉ yeer 1710 And did then setle a high way Then jn contreuercy: And did say yᵉ way should ly on yᵉ out side of yᵉ Towns land: — that js jn yᵉ possesion of our Reuerand ministar: — And whar as there was At yᵗ time 3 Gates did hang a thwart yᵉ said way: — you honourᵉ were then pleasd to say Those Gates should Remaine there untill furder ordar: — And whar as yᵉ peec of way js a bout: 100: pols jn length and yᵉ one half almost fencᵈ alredy the othar half ther js fencing stuff lyeth neer:

Therefore we humbly jntreat your honours yᵗ Those Gats may be Remoued and Remain no longar there: — That we and our families may haue the same priueleg: as all our frends and naighbours haue jn our Town — To haue our way cleer from Aney jncumbranc — To yᵉ publique worship of God

And your peticionars shall as duty binds Euer pray

malden date yᵉ

3 of dec 1712

JOHN GREENLAND	JONATHAN KNOWER ᔆᴺᴿ
SIMAN GROUER	JOHN MUDG ᔆᴺᴱᴿ
PETER TUFTS	JEAMES WHITTEMORE
JONATHAN KNOWER ᴵᴺᴿ	WILLIAM SARGEANT
JOHN MUDG ᴵᴺᴱᴿ	JEAMES HOUEY
JACOB HASEY	BENIAMIN HILLS

JOSEPH: LAMSON [16]

were famous for their size even in the days when large chimneys and capacious ovens were common. A smaller house, which stood in the lane near by, was supposed to be of an early date, and may have been the "old shop" which is mentioned in the deed of Asa Tufts.

[16] *Midd. Court Files, in loco.*

This petition was considered at the Court in April and its prayer allowed to the inconvenience of Samuel Green, the then owner of the Green farm and the son of John Green, who had died March 22, 170⁹/₁₀. He carried the matter back to the Court of Sessions with his complaint.

[July 7, 1713] upon hearing the petition of Samuel Green for satisfaction for Land of his Jmproved in maldon for a high way, on which the gates that hang thereupon were ordered to be taken down some time Since. The Court *order* that yᵉ gates be made convenient for Travellers, and continued so till the next Quarter Sessions and there to make Report of theire Doings therein.[17]

At a town meeting soon after [July 20, 1713,] the case was considered and

It was put to vote whether yᵉ Town will mak Samuell Green Resonabl allowanc for yᵉ land called yᵉ way from yᵉ litle Gate by widdo Skinars to yᵉ Gate by The contrey Road and jt past on yᵉ negitiue : The jnhabitants of yᵉ town said yᵗ Samuell Greens fathar took yᵗ way jn yᵉ stoney lane jn lew of yᵉ way by huchensons fenc.

That the "jnhabitants" were determined to stand by their opinion is evident; for at the same meeting a committee was appointed to defend the " cause in law with Samˡˡ. Green: in Refrence To yᵉ high way from yᵉ Litle Gate neer yᵉ widdo Skinars To yᵉ Gate by yᵉ countrey Road neer yᵉ sᵈ Greens hous." The Court sustained the inhabitants and recorded an order which settled the case.

[December 8, 1713.] The Court are of opinion upon view of the euidence before them, that the Complanants Father hath had satisfaction for the same And do order that the high way be where it lyeth and so continued.[18]

In the meantime other roads were being considered and laid out. Nathaniel Upham, Jonathan Sprague, Sen., and John Green, Sen., were chosen, May 24, 1710, to run the line between "Eueness farm and yᵉ Countrey Rhoad " at the northern extremity of the town. At the same time, a committee was appointed to view the land "between James houe's and boston

---

[17] *Midd. Court Records, — General Sessions, in loco.*   [18] Ibid.

Rhoad : [19] And se whar jts most conuenant to lay a high-way out for yᵉ use of yᵉ Town." [20] This committee made the following return, which was accepted at a meeting three days later : —

[June 2, 1710,] first we Turn out of yᵉ highway jnto Jonathan Knowars land by yᵉ cornar of James houes orchard and so by sᵈ orchard To yᵉ north east cornar and from thenc on a line to a black oke Jn sᵈ houeys feeld neer yᵉ fenc on yᵉ southwardly side of sᵈ Tree And so through said houes feeld : on yᵉ southwardly side of two white oke trees standing neer to gethar jn Thomas waits land neer to yᵉ sd houes feeld on yᵉ eastwardly side and so jn yᵉ old way As jt Runs along to Steuen Lerebes cornar of his cornfield and so along jn yᵉ Raing Line to boston Rhoad. [21]

At a meeting held July 20, 1713, "It was putt to vote whethar yᵉ Town will mend yᵉ way yᵗ Runs from yᵉ country Road neere Samˡˡ Grouars To John Wilkinsons between yᵉ Raig of lots. And jt past on yᵉ negitiue." In consequence of this vote, John Upham, Jonathan Barrett, and other inhabitants of the northern portion of the town petitioned the Court for convenient highways from their houses to the meeting house ; and the Court ordered the selectmen " to look to such matters." [22] Soon after it is recorded

[September 29, 1713.] yᵗ yᵉ select-men doe lay out a conuenant high way for Them . . . 2 pols broad on yᵉ northwardly side of That Raing of lots yᵗ Runs from John Wilkinsons Land neer his hous down to yᵉ cuntrey Road yᵗ leads to Reding. — beginning at yᵉ sᵈ wilkinsons land.

---

[19] Boston Road, the road from the point of rocks, or Black Ann's Corner, to Winnisimmet, so called because it was near the line and partly within the limits of Boston.

[20] The duties which were here imposed upon a committee were sometimes performed by the selectmen, as appears in the following vote, relating to a highway or lane in the southeastern part of the town.

"[May 8, 1704] *voted* That yᵉ selectmen hath liberty to lay out a conuenant high-way of Two pools broad from leut

Josep haseys : land so yᵗ he may pass from his one land jnto sum Cuntrey highway."

[21] This was evidently a confirmation in part of an old way, the location of which I cannot closely determine. It is, however, certain that it was north of the tract now occupied by Woodlawn Cemetery, and east of the old highway which ran from Sargeant's Hill to Black Ann's Corner.

[22] *Midd. Court Records,* — *General Sessions,* August 25, 1713.

This was a confirmation to public uses of one of the rights of way which were laid out between the ranges of common land in 1695. From the fact that John Wilkinson's house and lands were on the highlands towards Long Pond, and other indications, it is evident that the way now laid out was that long known as Upham's Lane and now as Upham Street in Melrose.

[March 1, 171¾,] *vote:* That Jose Line has libarty Granted to him and his haires To Raise the causeway y^t Lyeth betweene ye medo formarly cap^t waits : and ye sd Lines medo so high as to flow ye s^d lines meddo : and ye s^d Lins doe oblige him self and his haires To maintain ye s^d causway jn good Repair suficant for both Town and countrey to pass : — so long as they se cause to flow ye s^d medo Also ye said line hes libarty to take earth and grauill on ye high way on ye Top of ye hill near ye s^d caseway for ye ends aboue s^d

The proximity of Captain John Wayte's meadow proves this causeway to have been across the meadow near Island Hill,[23] and so marks the origin of the present Main Street in that direction. It afforded " a short cut " to the meeting house to a portion of the north end people who may have passed across the Lynde land by a private way on the westerly side of Boston Rock.[24] Another private way ran along the southern side of Boston Rock to the old Reading Road near the present Wyoming Cemetery, which, widened and made a public way, has become Sylvan Street in Melrose. An entry made in the records in 1717 may have reference to a connection made between the Reading Road and the way over the causeway at its southern end, or it was in the near vicinity.

sum time in ye mounth of June or July in ye years 1717 ye select men Laid out away by ye side of Joseph Lynds Land estly in to ye old Road Sam^{ll} wait giveing up his Right in s^d Land.

---

[23] Island Hill, north of Wayte's Mount, which sometimes has been confounded with Island End on the South River, was formerly a picturesque object in the landscape. It is situated on the westerly side of Main Street, a little north of Forest Street. At the present time the ledge of which it is composed is being removed, and it will soon become a thing of the past.

[24] Soon after an attempt was made to close a way which had, perhaps, fallen into disuse or become of doubtful public benefit. Its location is uncertain.

"[May 10, 1714,] Jt was putt To vote whether ye way shall be stopt neer to Iames Moltons hous ouer To obadia Jenkins land — and jt past on ye negitive."

The select men of malden mett y⁰ 17. of feb 1721/₂ And doe alow of yᵉ Two pools jn bredth yᵗ lieth Att yᵉ south end of the first Raing of yᵉ second Thousand acrs — from boston line to Reding Road To be a Town high-way :

The select men on the 15ᵗʰ day of nov! 1754 opened A town road from mʳ James Barrets orchard to Chelsea line between the first and second range of lots in the second devision.

Although the latter entries are nearly thirty-three years apart in time, they refer to a single way in North Malden which had existed as one of the rights of way between the ranges, and now became a settled town road. It was formerly known as Barrett's Lane, and is now Porter Street in Melrose.

The roads which had now been laid out answered the needs of the people for many years; and no new ways were granted until several years after the close of the Revolution. The few notices which appear in the meantime relate to repairs or confirmations of old ways, or to regulations and agreements respecting private ways which had become of public use. In 1751 Phineas Sprague, Nathaniel Howard, Samuel Sprague, Thomas Vinton, Benoni Vinton, and Phineas Sprague, Jr., inhabitants of the north end, were allowed to work out their highway rates for three years on a private way from Jonathan Howard's house to that of Phineas Sprague. The few houses which then existed at the north end west of the Reading Road appear to have had no allowed town ways by which they could be reached. Their owners passed by private ways over the neighbouring lands; and as these ways came to be of more than local convenience they were adopted as town ways. Thus, over the way from Jonathan Howard's house and its extensions running in all directions but a straight one, as it passed from house to house,²⁶ was laid out in time the road to Stoneham. This road in its eccentric course is now represented by Vinton Street, and by

---

²⁶ How it ran in changing courses from house to house, as it grew up to suit the convenience of the neighboring farmers, may be seen in the report of the selectmen, who laid it out as a town way in 1789, and in the plan of the North District in 1830, which will be given in a succeeding volume. On the plan it is that road which runs from the house of Joseph Howard to that of Aaron Vinton and the Stoneham line.

portions of Foster, Cottage, and Hurd Streets, and that section of Wyoming Avenue which ends at Main Street.

In 1755 it is recorded that Timothy Sprague had given the town a deed of land " near the place called the water falls which accommodates said town for a road."[26] At the same time he asked for a portion of the town's land at Sandy Bank, and was refused. It is mentioned in 1761 that "Timothy Sprague by moveing his fence has incroached on the high way or towns land near to the house of Elizabeth and Tabitha willson; "[27] but the town refused to act upon the matter at the annual meeting in that year.

In 1769 the ancient way and public landing place at Moulton's Island were laid out anew. The report of the committee, and the records relating to the neighboring landing place at Wormwood Point, which have been freely quoted, are interesting as defining the ways and town rights at the earliest settled portions of Mystic Side.

Malden May ye 2nd 1769

We the Subscribers being chosen a Committee to Stake out the Way leading to the Jsland End, have laid out Said Way, from ye Country Road to the Landing Place, about one Rod and an half wide, as ye Road now runs; and have Stak'd out the Landing Place; beginning at ye Head of ye East Dock, & from thence across ye Well, on a straight Line to ye Westerly Stake, which is about 16 Rod, & from thence to the Southeast Corner of Mr Blaney's Wharffe, & from Sd Bounds to low Water Mark

The above Way and Landing Place, Mr Ebenezer Pratt gives to ye Town, to be kept free and clear of all Jncumbrances, except Liberty to hang & maintain a good Gate across Sd Way, where it now Stands, wide enough for Carts to pass and repass; Said Liberty to be reserved to him & his heirs for ever

EBENr HARNDEN
JOHN DEXTER
JOHN BUCKNAM } *Committee*
JONAS GREEN
EBENr PRATT

---

[26] Near his mill at Black Rock, since known as Odiorne's Mill. This was some part of the lane that became Mill Street, and afterwards Mountain Avenue, which had been an allowed public way for many years.

[27] At the corner of the Salem and Reading Roads.

[May 18, 1769.]   *Voted*, To accept the Report of the Committee respecting the Way leading to the Jsland End.[28]

It was voted, May 18, 1772, " To exchange yᵉ Road, formerly laid out on the East Side of Swain's Pond, for the Road now improved."   A committee was appointed to agree with the owners of the land; and the new way was confirmed " where the Road is now improved on the East Side of Swain's Pond." The discontinued way was one of those which were opened in the sheep pasture and three hundred acres; and the new way was probably only a slight removal to easier or firmer ground. It was that which, with perhaps a few slight changes, is now known as Swain's Pond Avenue.   It is described as running from John Grover's field and by his mill on Swain's Pond

[28] The road from the South Spring to the end of Moulton's Island was one of the earliest on Mystic Side. It is mentioned as a highway in 1650. Closed by gates and vaguely defined, it remained more for the use of the owners of the land over which it ran than as a public road. The few who passed to the common landing place at its end alone raised it to the dignity of a travelled way. Both the landing place and the highway are mentioned in 1717 — the former as the Charlestown landing place. Thomas Mitchell, who married Mary Moulton, and died in 1709, built a house on the east side of the highway, near the landing place, which he passed by a deed of gift to his only son, Captain John Mitchell, in 1703. After the death of Elizabeth, widow of John Mitchell, in 1749, Ebenezer Pratt bought the rights of the several heirs, which, added to the lands which he inherited from his father, Ebenezer, a few years later, gave him the possession of most of the island and the adjacent marshes. The old house was standing within the second quarter of the present century; and its cellar remained until the ground was levelled for the improvements made in its vicinity. The station of the Eastern Railroad now stands on or near its site.

The landing place was improved in 1750, when Captain Benjamin Blaney, whose tan-yard was at the South Spring, was allowed by the town

" To build a wharf upon the beach at the Island end thirty foot front Said wharf to be about forty foot from mʳ Thomas pratts marsh and not so nigh the bank but that there may be room for a cart way between said wharf and said bank said blany to improve said wharf for the term of thirty years and then to have liberty to remove said wharf."

This wharf was known for many years as Blaner's Wharf, and later as Clapp's Wharf, from Timothy Clapp, who manufactured bricks at the clay-pits near the South Spring early in the present century. In 1890 some remains of the wharf and its easterly dock were to be seen.

The town way has disappeared with the hill over which it formerly passed. It left the main road near the South Spring at the present corner of Everett Avenue and Vine Street in Everett, taking a course a little west of the latter street. In 1890 a slight inequality in the ground where it passed over the meadow alone remained to reveal it.

Moulton's, or Mitchell's Island was an extensive mound of glacial waste of the same character as Powder Horn and other hills in its neighborhood. In 1898 but slight indications of its former existence remained, and the little that was left was rapidly disappearing. As large quantities of the material of which it was composed has been deposited upon the surrounding marshes, its original character as an island exists no longer.

Brook[29] to "ye road formerly laid out to Chelsea, as ye cart way now goes." On the northerly side of the pond it existed for many years as a vaguely defined and partially discontinued way leading up to Upham's Lane. Relocated and changed in many portions of its course, it is now a settled street.

There is upon the town record an agreement between Nathaniel Paine and John Grover, dated July 2, 1772, in relation to a way beginning at the road from Black Ann's Corner to Winnisimmet, near Grover's house, and running to Paine's house through the fields. This way, which was accepted by the town at its next annual meeting, was that which old inhabitants will remember as formerly leading to the house of Benjamin Nichols, which was built upon the site of the house of Nathaniel Paine. It may be readily recognized on the plan of Malden South School District, which will appear in a future volume.

The Spragues, who passed from Naumkeag to Mishawum in 1629, must have crossed the Mystic at a ford a few rods above the location of the present bridge at Medford. A few years later Nicholas Davison, the agent of Governor Cradock, whose farm stretched along the easterly bank of the Mystic, built a bridge near by. On the Charlestown side it was reached by a long causeway over the low land; and it is described as having been "exceedingly rude and dangerously frail."[30] It seems to have been built primarily for the use of Cradock's men; but it soon became a public convenience and as such was recognized by the General Court, when it ordered "[(10) 10: 41.] that Leift Sprague & Edwd Converse should repair the bridg at Meadfoard, over Mistick River, & the same to bee paid for out of the treasury."[31] It was apparently of the most simple construction and required frequent attention. It soon again became unfit for travel, and the Court appointed Ralph Sprague and Edward Converse again

---

[29] The site of the mill of John Grover could be found in 1894 in the meadow on the easterly side of Swain's Pond Avenue, near its junction with Lebanon Street. The dam was then as distinct as in the days of its builder; and on the west side of the brook the shape and size of the little mill could be traced.

[30] Brooks, *History of Medford*, 59. This writer says it was built in 1638.

[31] *Mass. Colony Records*, i. 343.

to veiw y[e] bridge at Mistick, & what charge they conceive meete, to be p'sently expended for y[e] making it sufficient & p'vent y[e] ruine thereof, or by furth[r] delay to endang[r] it, by agreeing wth workmen for y[e] compleate repairing thereof, & to make their returne to M[r] Willowghby & M[r] Russell, & w[t] they shall do herein to be satisfied out of y[e] treasury.[82]

Two years later the Court again took it into consideration, and fearful, perhaps, of the expense which seemed to attend its proper maintenance, ordered

[October 27, 1648,] that the said Mistick bridge henceforth shall not, by the country, any way be repaired, & that the passage for travellers shall be over the foarde w[ch] is above the bridg[e]; & further, for the p'venting future charges about bridges & high wayes, it is ordered, that all bridges & highwayes, in the limitts of the severall towneships, that now are or hereafter shalbe made by the severall townes, in whose limits such bridges and highwayes are, be by them repaired, made, & maintained.[83]

This was the origin of the law, now so well established, by which towns are made responsible for the maintenance of public ways within their borders. The order appears to have become a dead letter at once, and the bridge fell into a worse condition. It was, however, of value to the Cradock tenants and to the country above the Mystic, and if its users could be made to contribute to its support it might be properly maintained; so Davison, for his principal, petitioned the General Court and obtained the passage of the following order, which established the first toll bridge in New England, if not in the British Colonies : —

[June 2, 1653,] Itt is by this Court ordered and declared, that if any person or persons shall appeare that will engage sufficyently to builde, repaier, and maintajne the bridge at Misticke at his or theire propper costs and charges, it shall be lawfull, and all and euery such p'son or p'sons so engaging are heereby authorized, and haue full power, to aske, requier, and recouer of euery single p'son passing ouer the sajd bridge 1[d]; and for euery horse and man, 6[d]; for euery beast, 2[d]; for euery cart, 1[s]; and this to continew so long as the bridge shall be sufficyently majntajned as aforesajd.[84]

<hr/>

[82] May 6, 1646. *Mass. Colony Records,* ii. 149.

[83] Ibid., ii. 263.

[84] Ibid., iv. (1), 148.

Still, neither Davison the agent, nor Edward Collins, who had recently purchased the Cradock lands, undertook to rebuild the bridge, nor did any others appear to assume the responsibility; and the passage across the ford became the common highway. The need of a better passage, however, appears to have been obvious; and the following petition was presented to the County Court: —

To the honoured Court now holden at Cambridge octo: 2ᵈ 1655 Samuel Hough: Edw: Convers and Joseph: Hills, on behalf of the Countrie humby shew

That, the Countrie (as is well known to this Cort) haue Sustained great loss and damage for some yeares past by the decay and want of the Bridg Called mistick Bridge notwithstanding the Severall Complaintes petitions and presentments made to Several Courts concerning the same ; our humble request Therefore to this honnoured Cort is that Deacon Mousal of charlstowne Deacon child of wattertowne mᵣ Tho: Danforth. of Cambridge mᵣ Edw: Collins of medford Will: Coudre of Redding Sam: Richardson of Wobuⁿ and Litᵗ John Waight of moldon, or any 3 : or 4 of them or Such others as the Corte Se good may be appointed and Authorized forthwith to make vp a sufficient Cart Bridge over the Sayd river in Such Convenient place as may be most comodious for the Cuntrie in generall. And that the same may be Effectually carried on wee further humblie desire that there be by this Court An Assesment made on the Severall Townes within this Countie for raysing the Sum of one hundred and twenty poundes and warrants Jsued forth to the Severall Townshipps for levying and collecting the Same by due Course of lawe According to the Assesment for Countrie rates. And to pay it in vnto mᵣ Collins at his howse at meadford or as he shall appoint. And that the Comitte be ordred to giue Account of the said som at the next Countie Courte to be holden at Cambridg or the Court following at Charlstowne So shall wee with many others be bound to blesse God for your furtheranc of Soe needfull A Service.[86]

[At a County Court, April 1, 1656,] Capᵗ Norton, mᵣ Edward Collines, mᵣ Joseph Hills & mᵣ Brattle, are appointed by this Court a Committee to errect misticke Bridge, and to levy the charges there of vpon the County, according to Law.[86]

---

[86] *Midd. Court Files, in loco.* Rev. Samuel Hough was the pastor of Reading; Edward Convers, a leading inhabitant of Woburn ; and Joseph Hills, the well-known deputy of Malden. The inhabitants of Reading preferred a similar petition at the same time.

[86] *Midd. Court Records,* i. 97.

The rebuilding of the bridge was performed in accordance with the order, and during its progress the County Court was drawn by its cost to the consideration of its future maintenance. A committee reported to the Court at Charlestown, April 7, 1657, as follows: —

> Wee quæstion the countjes abilitje to mainteine & beare the charge thereof, and having some experimentall knowledge that tounes will be more cautious in laying out theire oune costs then the countjes, both in building & repayring, doe therefore conclude, according to our weake ap'hentions, that as few bridges should be built at the countjes charge as possibly maybe, only those two bridges, i. e., at Billirrikey & Misticke, to be finished at the countys charge, and for tjme to come majnteined in repajre by the tounes & precincts in which they are.

This report, which was accepted by the County Court and confirmed by the General Court soon after,[87] led to the taxation of the several towns which were benefited by the bridge and caused many disputes and lawsuits.

During the next thirty years little appears in relation to the bridge and the connection of the several towns with its maintenance; but its later history was probably a continuance in spirit and form of that which preceded it. Mr. Brooks remarks that "The bridge seemed to have a wonderful aptitude in getting out of repair; and, as Medford was liable to be indicted for the fact the bridge became the standing vexation of the town."[88] An entry in the Malden records, November 29, 1689, shows that "maulden workt a mistak bridge with cart and 4 oxen and 3 hands to gravell the bridg." In less than two years the town was delinquent and, with Woburn and Reading, neglected or refused to pay her dues. The selectmen of Medford petitioned the General Court and were referred to the County Court for "a finall Jsue of that matter referring to the Settlement of Said Bridge."[89] The latter favored the petitioners, although the opposing towns made a concerted defence. It was, perhaps, in connection with this case that Malden at a meeting, November 20, 1694, allowed Henry Green his charges "with Lawers and expenses consarning mistick bridg."

[87] *Mass. Colony Records,* iv. (1), 306–308.

[88] Brooks, *History of Medford,* 64.
[89] *General Court Records,* vi. 189.

The towns were again unsuccessful before the Court in 1698; and Deacon John Green was chosen, on the part of Malden, to carry out the following vote: —

[May 6, 1698,] *Voted* — That this town will joyn with oborn and Reding jn tryall of law vpon apeall: from yᵉ jugment of yᵉ justices of yᵉ peacē: at yᵉ Court Last held at Charlestown: To yᵉ next Superior Court or Courts Consarning mistick bridg.

Several ineffectual attempts were made to cast off the burden. At a meeting, April 1, 1702, it was

voted yᵗ Leuᵗ Henery Green and Thomas newhall are apointed to Join with oborn and Reding: and yᵗ they haue full power to agree with medford: as they can Jn Refranc to mistick brig: not Exceeding our proportion to eighteen Shillings pʳ yeer: prouided Jn so doing: yᵉ town shall haue an aquitance for euer: for euer hauing aney furthar charg consarning sᵈ brig:

The proposed agreement with Medford came to naught; and in the following December Isaac Hill and John Greenland were chosen to meet with " oborn And Reding men to consider what to doe in Referanc to mistick brig." " Sargᵗ upham & sargᵗ dextar " were appointed to the same service in 1714; and at a meeting, held November 29 of that year, it was voted not to raise " 15 pounds to pay Towards yᵉ Rebuilding of mistick bridg." [40] However, in spite of the opposition of the neighboring towns, the rebuilding was completed and Medford applied to the Court of Sessions for redress. The Court apportioned the charges upon the five towns of Charlestown, Medford, Reading, Woburn, and Malden to the amount of one hundred and thirty-five pounds and three shillings — the proportion of the former town being sixty-four pounds and fourteen shillings, and those of the others seventeen pounds, twelve shillings, and three-

[40] This was in consequence of the following order of the Court of Sessions:

" [Concord, August 31, 1714.] Pʳsuant to yᵉ Return & Motion of the undertakers of yᵉ Building of Mistick Bridge referring to their provision of Timber Plank and Labour already provided . . . *order* that there be forthwith raised the sum of Sixty pounds by the Town of Charlestowne, and paid in p suant to yᵉ Courts order, and Sixty pounds more to be raised forthwith by the Towns of Woburn Reading Maldon & Medford in equall proportion To say ffifteen pounds to be raised by Each of sᵈ Towns and to be paid in to yᵉ Respective Town Treasuⁿ hands, etc." *Midd. Court Records — General Sessions, in loco.*

pence each.[41]   At a meeting, August 8, 1715, Malden voted to
raise twenty-four pounds, twelve shillings, and sevenpence " to
defrey yᵉ charg of mistick bridg; " for which the selectmen
soon after laid a town rate of twenty-five pounds and sevenpence.

Disputes with Medford and presentments at the Court were
not unfrequent during the succeeding years until the early part
of 1760, when the town refused to join with the other towns in
repairing or rebuilding the bridge; and a committee was chosen
to carry the matter before the General Court.   At the April
session of the Court the following entry was made: —

[April 24, 1760,] A Petition of Joseph Lynde and others, a Commit-
tee of the Town of Malden, Setting forth That, in the Year 1671. the
Great and General Court ordered That Medford, Woburn, Reading and
Malden, should Build and maintain the one half of a Bridge, lying on
Medford River, and Charlestown the other half.[42]   That the circum-
stances of said Towns are since greatly alter'd.   And Praying that the
Town of Malden may be freed from that charge for the future.[43]

Consideration of the petition was referred to a future time;
and notice was given to the other towns, who answered according to their several interests.   The reply of Woburn gives in
review some of the reasons adduced in the Malden petition.   It
says: —

1. they say a Considerable part of the Town [Malden] that Jmproued
said Bridg in that Day are since anexed to the Towns of Reading and
Stoneham and those are the Persons that mostly vse said bridg: to
which by Jnformation their is but two families that is set to Reading
from said malden that go ouer said bridg more than one apeace in
three year and we are sencable that one half of the Town of malden must
of Necessity go the same way to boston that woburn Doth so that if the

----

[41] Brooks, *History of Medford*, 65.

[42] This must be an error. There is
no notice in the *Mass. Colony Records*
of the passage of such an order in 1671.
The Council, whose records from 1656
to 1686 are not known to be in existence,
may have acted in the matter; but the
following extract from the petition of
Woburn indicates that a settlement by
the General Court followed the order
of 1657 which is given in the text, and

appears to correct the error of the
Malden committee.

"about the year 1657 The Towns of
Charlstown Medford Woburn Reading
and Malden were ordered by yᵉ Court
Relateing to the Bridge at Medford as
followeth (viz) Charlstown to maintain
the Southerly half of sᵈ Bridge & Medford woburn Reading and Malden the
northerly half Equally between them."
Mass. Archives, cxxi. 366.

[43] *General Court Records*, xxiii. 322.

said bridge be not an advantage to the Town of malden it is No benefit to the Town of woburn : and as to woburns being so much Larger then the Town of malden it Needeth no answer the Tax bill will set that in a True Light

2 The Town of malden say that the Line being Run between Chelsy and their Town that they haue a Considerable bridg to maintain which bridge as we apprihend is Not So Chargeable to the Town of malden as a Number of bridges in woburn.[44]

The reply of Medford was an answer not only to the Malden petition but to those, as well, of the towns of Woburn and Reading, which had also prayed for relief.

To his Excellency Thomas Pownall Esq. Captain General & Commander in Chief in and over his Majesty's Province of the Massachusetts Bay aforesaid, the Honble his Majesty's Council and House of Representatives in General Court Assembled June 2^d 1760 ———

Whereas the Towns of Wobourn, Reading & Malden lately Exhibited to this Honble Court by their respective Committees their Several Petitions, requesting your Excellency and Honours, that the said Towns may for the future be freed from any Charge relating to the Maintaining the northerly Half of a Bridge in Medford for Reasons therein mentioned,

In Answer to which Petitions we in behalf of the Town of Medford beg Leave to offer what follows, That is to Say

That by the Acknowledgment of the Petitioners their Predecessors and they have been at the Charge of Repairing & Keeping in good Order Three Quarters of the northerly Half of said Bridge, for more than an Hundred Years past, notwithstanding their frequent applications to the Court of General Sessions, his Majesty's Superior Court of Judicature and this Hon^d Court, to be freed from the said Charge, Yet they at this Time of Day pray to be excus'd from the Charge and Trouble of Maintaining their usual Proportion, Because Say they, the Town of Medford is Enlarg'd and grown much more able than heretofore and also that there was Land Assign'd for the Maintenance and Convenience of each Half of said Bridge also that they are straitned for Room on the northerly Side of the Bridge for Landing Materials for the Repair of the Same, Also that they are at a great Charge in maintaining Bridges, Highways &c ; Now granting the Town of Medford is Larger than heretofore, yet our Charges as to other Bridges (excepting the Two over Medford River) are more in Proportion to our Bigness

---

[44] *Mass. Archives,* cxxi. 373. The bridge mentioned was that over Pines River below Black Ann's Corner.

we Apprehend than any of the before mentioned Towns — and as to any Lands assigned to the Building or Repairing said Bridge, we know not of any, neither have heard of any on the Northerly Side, neither have we Receivd any more directly or Indirectly than about the Sum of Seventeen Pounds towards supporting the Southerly Half of said Bridge & Causey adjoyning, Since a part of Charlestown has been Annexed to Medford, Tho' the Charge we are now Obliged to be at in Order to Rebuild said Southerly Half of the Bridge & Causey will amount to more than an Hundred Pounds as near as we can think — As to Room the said Towns have the same that the Town of Medford has for Landing Materials for Rebuilding & Repairing said Bridge. Moreover, The aforesaid Towns make a much greater Use of said Bridge for Carting &c than the Town of Medford aforesaid does, Who maintain Five Eighths of the Same. Besides we are at the Charge of one Half of the Bridge over the Same River at a Place called the Wears, where it is considerably wider than where the first mentioned Bridge is, the Repairing of which this Year we Apprehend will amount to Twenty Pounds at least to us.

Upon the whole we Humbly Conceive that there is not so much as the Shadow of Reason for the said Towns being Excused from bearing the Same Proportion of Rebuilding and Keeping in good Order the said Half of said Bridge which their Grandfathers readily agreed to do — And therefore Entreat your Excellency and Honours wou'd not Excuse said Towns from bearing the Same Proportion of the Charge of Rebuilding & Keeping in good Order said Half of the aforementioned Bridge but Dismiss their Petitions which Apprehend are vexations —

Your Excellency's & Honours most Obedient Hum! Servants

SAM BROOKS	FRANCIS WHITMORE	Committee
B POOL	SIMON TUFTS	for Medford.[44]

At the General Court in June a committee was appointed to " take the same under consideration ; " but they made no report until April 17, 1761, when the matter was recommitted, perhaps in consideration of a prospect of an early settlement being made between the towns.

At a town meeting, June 30, 1761, Timothy Sprague, Edward Waite, and Stephen Paine were appointed " to act what they think may be most for the towns benefit refering to medford bridge which said towns are in controversy about." The recent annexation to Medford of a portion of Charlestown on the south-

[44] *Mass. Archives,* cxxi. 371.

erly bank of the Mystic had thrown the bridge and its approaches entirely within the territory of the former town; and it seems to have been considered desirable for several reasons that that town should assume its complete control. Arrangements were made with the neighboring towns; and August 18, 1761, a committee acting for the town of Medford, for sixteen pounds, thirteen shillings, and fourpence, lawful money, paid by the Malden committee, gave a release of "all the said town of Maldons part of supporting said Bridge forever," [46] and the controversy of more than a hundred years was at an end.

Mystic Bridge was not the only bridge out of its limits which the town was called upon to assist in maintaining. At a meeting of the selectmen, December 20, 1699, a county rate amounting to four pounds, nine shillings, and threepence was made "for cambridg great bridg and othar County Charges." At the annual meeting in March, 1746/7, no action was taken on a question referring to a charge with Chelsea in repairing the bridge between Benjamin Waite's and David Parker's, and the county bridge over Pines River on the road from Black Ann's Corner to Winnisimmet, sometimes called the Boston Road. The latter bridge, although within the Malden line, was considered of more advantage to the inhabitants of Chelsea and the county of Essex than to those of Malden, and it was sometimes a charge to the former town. A committee was appointed by the Court of Sessions, December 8, 1747, to "view the Bridge in Maldon between Oliver's Farm, and Black Anne's (which m[r]. Benj[a]: Kent inform'd the Court is defective & dangerous)." This committee reported in the following May that they "find the same to lye within the Township of Malden, and to be much decayed, and are of opinion that it be thoroughly repaired as soon as conveniently may be." [47]

Early mention is made of Lewis's Bridge, through which the

---

[46] *Malden Town Records, in loco.* The Mystic Bridge was of great importance to all the country above the river. Although it was within the territory of another town, I have considered it of consequence in a history of Malden, more especially as the annalists of Medford have treated it with slight attention.

[47] *Midd. Court Records — General Sessions, in loco.*

tide flowed into the meadow of Joseph Hills lying between the Reading Road and Cedar Hill. Pemberton's Creek, or Harvell's Brook, which it spanned, has ceased to be the pleasant stream of yore and has become a dirty ditch by the side of the Eastern Railroad track, and Lewis's Bridge a mere culvert under Main Street. At a County Court, December 27, 1659,

> Mauldon being p'sented for a defective Bridge neere to the ordnary are fined two Shill: 6^d & are injoyned to repayre the same before next Court on Penalty of 40^s & to pay Costs of Court 2^s & 6^d.[48]

The City Hall now stands on or near the site of Abraham Hill's ordinary and the bridge may have been that just mentioned or that which crossed the Three Mile Brook at the junction of the Medford and Reading Roads. Both these bridges are frequently mentioned. They were probably rudely built of logs and so continued many years. John Wilson and Joseph Green, " in behalf of themselves & the rest of the Selectmen of Malden," appeared before the Court, April 13, 1725,

> to answer to ye p'sentment of the Grand Jurors for want of a Bridge. They declare that there is a new sufficient Bridge Erected over the way that is presented. are dismissed paying fees and costs.[49]

The selectmen of Malden had a frequent acquaintance with the Court through the vigilance of the Grand Jury. Two years later they were presented " for not keeping in good repear a Bridge in malden aforesaid commonly called Lewis's Bridge." They failed to appear when cited and a warrant was issued to secure their appearance " to answer their contempt." At the next session they appeared and " do say that the said Bridge is now & has been for sometime in good repair." How they were purged of their contempt does not appear; but it is to be supposed that the Court was satisfied, as they were dismissed after paying fees.[50]

In however " good repair " Lewis's Bridge may have been in 1727, it soon required rebuilding. At a meeting held, December 7, 1738, the town refused to raise money "to defrey the

[48] *Midd. Court Records*, i. 194.
[49] Ibid., *General Sessions, in loco.*
[50] Ibid., *General Sessions*, April 4, June 13, 1727.

charge that the surveyors have been at in building the new bridge near the meeting hous;" but the next month a more liberal spirit prevailed, and fifty-one pounds, one shilling, and one penny were raised for "building the new bridge near the north meeting house in this town." It was voted, May 19, 1760, to "build anew the bridge called Lewis's and the bridge by mr Jsaac Hills with stones when they need to be rebuilt." Our fathers were not given to haste. Six years elapsed before it was voted, "[May 19, 1766] To Build anew the Bridge at Lewises creek with Stone this Year;" and another year passed before it was decided "That the town will rebuild the bridg by mr Kettles this year and that with stone."[61] That the work in the latter instance was done is evident, as James Kettell was paid in October, 1768, for "a cart to carry stons to build the bridge near his house." When the bridges were rebuilt it was voted, after the usual delay, "[May 18, 1772,] To erect Rails on each Side the two Bridges, near the North Meeting House, for the greater Safety of Travellers."

Other bridges are mentioned. At a Court of Sessions, March 13, 171⅚, the selectmen were called to answer "for not repairing a bridge over a Brook neer Capt Dexters."[62] The building of Malden Bridge at Penny Ferry belongs to a later period.

The charges for roads and bridges appear to have been met at times with liberality and at other times grudgingly, although for the most part convenient ways adapted to the prevailing methods of travel were well maintained. In 1705 the selectmen made a highway rate of twenty pounds, one shilling, and sixpence.[63] This was hardly adequate to the purpose; for the next year the selectmen appeared before the Court to answer "for the Defect of yᵉ high way neer Lewisses Bridge, Jnforming

---

[61] James Kettell, who added to the calling of a tavern keeper, the office of a deputy sheriff and the trade of a baker, now kept the Rising Eagle, or Hill's Tavern, to which he had recently succeeded by his marriage with Sarah (Haven), the widow of Isaac Hill, the former landlord. The bridge by Hill's, or Kettell's, was near the present southern corner of Main and Pleasant Streets,
the course of the brook having been materially changed within the last forty years.

[62] *Midd. Court Records — General Sessions, in loco.*

[63] This was proportioned to the inhabitants of the north and south sides of Harvell's Brook as follows: to the north side, £12 11s. 7d.; to the south side, £7 9s. 11d.

the Court they are mended." [64]   In 1707 the appropriation was
twenty pounds in money, and the same sum was voted in 1709;
but at the annual meeting, in March, 171⅔, it was raised to
thirty pounds, "to mend yᵉ high wais." During the distress
occasioned by the issue of paper money in the earlier half of
the eighteenth century, the appropriations varied from time to
time as the amounts were fixed in money or the depreciated
currency of the several issues. Reduced to twenty pounds in
1715, the amount was raised to one hundred pounds in 1734
and was the same in 1741. For many years, during the scarcity
of ready money, much of the highway rate was "worked out"
at fixed rates, as in 1750, when the work of a man with a cart and
two pairs of oxen, or with one pair of oxen and a horse, was
rated at six shillings and fourpence a day. With one pair of
oxen and a cart a man could decrease his highway tax at the
rate of five shillings and fourpence a day; while the poorer man,
who brought his hands alone to the task, received a daily quit-
tance of two shillings and eightpence. The custom of working
out taxes was not wholly abandoned until within fifty years.
Many an old inhabitant now living has wielded the shovel and
the hoe upon the town highways in his earlier years.

The closing of even the most important roads by gates was
common in the early part of the eighteenth century and in some
instances survived to a time within the memory of persons now
living. This was necessary to prevent the straying of cattle
from the fenced farms into the open roads, whence they might
wander into the woods or uninclosed meadows. At first this
was done at the convenience of landowners without the intervention of the authorities or the town; but as travel increased
and the great inconvenience of frequent gates appeared, it
became a question to be acted upon at town meetings and
sometimes, even, considered by the County Court. A committee of the Court made a report in 1701 concerning "Gates
in Maldon," by which it appears that they were ordered "to
open both wayes Easie for Travailers;" and the petition of
the selectmen of Malden, "for the hanging of a Gate neer the

[64] *Midd. Court Records — General Sessions,* July 9, 1706.

pound by Jsaac Hills," was allowed in 1705.[55] This gate, not far from the site of the City Hall, may have crossed the Reading Road or closed the way to Medford. The roads at that point were narrow and no indication as yet existed of the present square, which gradually grew by the appropriation of a watering place at the northwesterly corner of the roads.

At the annual town meeting in March, 170⅚, Leonard Drown and William Teele were allowed to set a gate and fence across the highway "Betwene John willsons and Samuell wayts fence nere the apelltree." They were to pay for "the fede within the sad Gate." The next year this privilege was given to William Teele alone upon the same terms, it being voted that he "may haue yᵉ feed on yᵉ Towns land between yᵉ gate and The landing places [at Sandy Bank.]" In March, 171⁰/₁, he had liberty

To feed or pastor yᵉ Towns land at Sandy bank: between yᵉ Gate neer Lewiss bridg and Lannard drowns land this presant yeer prouided yᵉ sᵈ Teel. doe maintain a gate That Shall hang well a Thwart yᵉ way whare yᵉ Gate now Stands.

[March 1, 171¾,] *vote:* yᵗ william Teel hes libarty Granted for yᵉ presant yeer: To jmproue yᵉ land that lyeth between yᵉ clay pits and goody drowns fenc for pastoring — and also he may hang agate jn yᵉ usuall place neer The clay-pits:[56]

---

[55] *Midd. Court Records — General Sessions,* March 18, 170⁰/₁; March 13, 170⁴/₅.

[56] John Wilson's land was on the south side and Samuel Waite's land and "the apelltree" on the north side of the way to Sandy Bank at the corner of the great road. The clay-pits were near by. The house of William Teele on the small piece of town land, at the southerly corner of the roads, is the subject of a note elsewhere.

The land and house of Leonard Drown, on the way below the burying ground, were those of Robert Calley, who died February 15, 170⅔. Leonard Drown married Widow Mary Calley and entered upon the estate of his predecessor; but his occupancy was not of long duration. There is a story of a child put to nurse with the wife of Leonard Drown by Jonathan Sprague, who refused to inform the Court of the names of its father and mother, and was obliged to give bonds to save the town from charges concerning it. Wyman, *Genealogies and Estates of Charlestown,* makes an ugly intimation in respect to its parentage. Drown appears to have left his wife and lived in Charlestown with John Johnson, who married his sister or, perhaps, his daughter by a former marriage. The land was mentioned in 1714 as "goody drowns" and as Calley's soon after. In 1737 widow Drown and Robert Calley, the son, sold seven acres on the south side of the burying ground to John Waite of Lynn. This land afterwards became a part of the Green farm and was known as the John Waite pasture until recent years. While excavations were being made on Converse Avenue, a few years since, indications of a cellar were found, which probably belonged to the Calley house.

This privilege was granted yearly to William Teele, during his life; and after his death it was voted to his widow, Mary Teele, in 1719, when she had liberty " To hang a gate a thort sandy-bank high-way neer her hous, and to haue yᵉ benefit of yᵉ feed or paster in yᵉ buring place."

In 1709 it is recorded that " Seuerall parsons haue desired to hang a gate a cross yᵉ Town high-way between william waits and dextars Rox: and jt js granted by a vote." The report relating to a road " between James Houes and boston Rhoad," in 1710, was accepted by the town,

> prouided yᵉ propriotors of yᵉ land shall not be compeld To fenc on each side of sᵈ way but haue libarty to hang and maintain Gates between each propriotars land upon sd way.

The County Court, in 1713, allowed the petition of the inhabitants of Malden

> for the Removeing of Three gates standing athwart the highway settled by the Justices of sᵈ County Anno: Dom. 1710 that lyes on yᵉ outside of the Towns Land in yᵉ possession of the minister.[87]

Liberty was given Joseph Waite, in 1714, to hang three gates on the town highways in Scadan: —

> one acros The way neer To dextars Rocks, one on yᵉ way yᵗ leads Towards Samuel greens, and one on yᵉ way yᵗ leads Towards Zachre hills for this presant yeer.

Seven years later Nathaniel Jenkins entered his "decent" against the following vote: —

> [March yᵉ 13: 17²⁰/₂₁] Samᵘ wayte—daniel newhall—nath: upham — samᵘ newhall — eben upham — eben hils — samᵘ Green — And Abraham skiner desireth liberty of The Town To hang foure Gates a thurt yᵉ Towns high-way: one neer To nath Jenkins — one a thurt yᵉ way leading to swains pond one upon The line of The sheepastor: and one a thurt The way neer To william prats — The Town hes Granted there desier by A vote att yᵉ abousᵈ Meting:

The obstruction of highways by gates was now beginning to be met with disfavor, as appears in the following votes: —

[87] *Midd. Court Records — General Sessions*, April 14, 1713. The difficulties which attended the removal of these gates from the way between Thomas Skinner's and the meeting house have been noticed.

[May 12. 1738] it was put to vote to see if the town will grant liberty to Joseph Willson to hang a gate for one year near his hous upon the town road that leads to wormwood point upon this consideration that said Willson alows the town ten shillings for said liberty and it past in the affirmative

it was put to vote to se if the town will grant any other person or persons liberty to hang and keep up a gate or gates on any other road or roads belonging to the town : and it past in the negetive

At the annual meeting in March, 1738⁄9, the privilege of Joseph Wilson was not renewed, and the town refused to allow Ebenezer Pratt to close the way to the landing place at Moulton's Island. Wilson either disregarded or disputed the vote of the town; and at a later meeting the interposition of the Court was asked.

[July 5. 1739] *vot* That mr Timothy Sprague shall request in behalf of said town. of his Magesty's Justices of the sessions of the peace to be holden at Cambridge the tenth day of this instant July that there may not be any gate hang acros any town road in said town conterary to a vote of the town and to the damage of any of the inhabitants thereof

Timothy Sprague presented his petition and motion to the Court at Cambridge, and the case was referred to the December term. · The landowners at Wormwood Point may have had some prescriptive rights which were considered valid. The following petition, which was preferred to the selectmen, indicates fears of " a needless contention: " —

To the Select men of The Town of maldin.

Gentlemen — Whereas at a General meeting of the Inhabitants of said Town, on the fifth Day of July Last Timothy Sprague was Chosen as Agant for said Town To prefer amotion on the Towns behalf To the Court of General Sessions of the peace To be held at Cambridge on the tenth of July last by adjourn' Desiering that the Gate which Joseph Willson Set up On the way Leading To wormwood point might be removed and fearing the Consequence of Involving the Town in a needless Contention, we the Subscribers, Inhabitants of said Town Desier that in your next warrant for a General meeting in said Town you would insert such words as these viz' that they Give their vote whether they will recall the power Given To Timothy Sprague as agent for the Town of maldin Respecting the removal of Joseph Willsons Gate Standing on

the way Leading To wormwood point, and also whether they will with-
draw the motion made by the said Timothy Sprague on the Towns
behalf Be fore the Court of General Sessions of the peace held at
Cambridge in July Last by adjournment for the removing the said Gate,
(which Is Continued Till December Court next.) in Doing which you
will we humbly conceive Serve the Interest of the said Town as well
as Gratify Gentlemen your Humble Serv[ts]

Maldin Sept. 25. 1739.

JAMES BARRIT	SAMUEL STOWER
STOWER SPRAGUE	JOSEPH CASWELL
SAM[LL] GREEN	JABEZ SARGEANT
SAMUEL BLANCHARD	JONATHAN SARGEANT
JOSES BUCKNAM IUN	JOHN GREEN JUN[R].[66]

This petition received no favorable attention. The case was
continued from Court to Court until May 20, 1740, when the
petition was dismissed.

While travelling was entirely on foot or on horseback, the
inconvenience of gates was not great; but the gradual introduction of chaises and other vehicles rendered unobstructed roads
desirable. Little thereafter appears concerning gates across
county and town roads, save on the less travelled ways, where
some rights were still granted. At the annual meeting,

[March 4, 1765] Jt was put to vote to see if the town will give
liberty to mr Samuel Green and others to run a fence between ell
pond and the high way. provided they leve a convenient way open for
watering of cattle at the pond And keep convenient draw bars or
a gate for people to pass and repass with their teams in the usual place
of their going to and from said pond with their flax. And it past in
the affermative.

Some old gates, doubtless, remained for a while. The way
to Wormwood Point was so stopped for many years, and the
portion towards the river and landing place gradually merged
in the adjoining lands. The road to the burying ground and
landing place at Sandy Bank was closed by a gate until nearly
the middle of the present century.

[66] Original MS. in the possession of Artemas Barrett of Melrose, 1866.

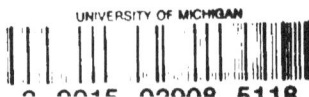

CPSIA information can be obtained
at www.ICGtesting.com
Printed in the USA
BVHW040529231218
536261BV00007B/430/P

9 781297 856754